# Charles XII
## Warrior King

*A coronation portrait of Charles XII, made
after he ascended to the throne at the age of 15.*

*Painting by David Ehrenstrahl (1628-98), 1697.
Nationalmuseum, Stockholm, Sweden.*

Protagonists of History in International Perspective – 4

# Charles XII
## WARRIOR KING

EDITED BY

**John B. Hattendorf, Åsa Karlsson,**

**Margriet Lacy-Bruijn, Augustus J. Veenendaal, Jr.,**

**and Rolof van Hövell tot Westerflier**

KARWANSARAY PUBLISHERS

2018

Published in 2018 by
Karwansaray bv

www.karwansaraypublishers.com

With assistance from Karolinska Förbundet (The Caroline Society, Sweden), Kungliga
Patriotiska Sällskapet (The Royal Patriotic Society, Sweden), M.A.O.C. Gravin van
Bylandt Stichting (the Netherlands), and the J.E. Jurriaanse Stichting (the Netherlands).

ISBN 978-94-90258-19-1

Copy-editing by Margriet Lacy-Bruijn
Image research and coordination by Christianne C. Beall
Layout by Christianne C. Beall, original design by Jan van Waarden
Maps © Karwansaray bv, designed by Tina Ross
Lithography and printing by High Trade bv, Zwolle, the Netherlands
Printed in the EU

# Contents

# Introduction

by John B. Hattendorf

In the series on '*Protagonists of History in International Perspective*' this fourth volume, *Charles XII: Warrior King*, is directly complementary to the second volume in the same series, *Marlborough: Soldier and Diplomat*.[1] Each volume focuses on one of the two wars that nearly simultaneously engaged Europe: Marlborough with the War of the Spanish Succession in western Europe between 1701 and 1714 and Charles XII with the Great Northern War in northern and eastern Europe between 1700 and 1721. Both volumes outline the momentous changes that these two long wars produced in the structure of Europe's internal relations through shifting balances of power within Europe, each with internal consequences for many nations. The two wars were not entirely separate from one another, although historians usually deal with them individually due to their complexity and aims. Nevertheless, the personal meeting between Marlborough and Charles XII at Altranstädt in Saxony in April 1707 symbolises the contemporary fears of the two wars' merging and the ultimate success in keeping them apart.

King Charles XII of Sweden has remained one of the most fascinating and enigmatic of the protagonists who crossed the stage of European history in the early modern era. In facing his antagonists—King Frederik IV of Denmark, Augustus II of Saxony and Poland, and above all, Tsar Peter I of Russia—Charles became much more than just another warring prince in the tumultuous annals of European history. Views of Charles XII have changed over time. Voltaire, who wrote a biography of him in 1731, saw him as the embodiment of the warrior king *par excellence*. At the same time, he saw Charles's story as a cautionary tale. 'Where is the sovereign who can say: "I have more courage, more virtues, a stronger mind, a robuster body, a better understanding of warfare, and better troops than Charles XII?,"' Voltaire asked. 'And if, with all these advantages, this king was so unfortunate, what can other princes, who have the same ambitions, with less talents and resources, hope for?'[2]

As Ragnhild Hatton noted in 1976, Voltaire's *Charles XII* is a classic work of French literature, and because of this, the author's views have become deeply etched in the historical consciousness of Europeans.[3] Voltaire was certainly the leading exemplar of the 'Old School' in his interpretation of Charles XII, while Dr. Samuel Johnson expressed similar sentiments in English in his volume of poetry entitled *The Vanity of Human Wishes: The Tenth Satire on Juvenal Imitated* (1749). Among the 32 lines on Charles within that work, Johnson wrote:

> *No joys to him pacific sceptres yield;*
> *War sounds the trump, he rushes to the field;*
> *Behold surrounding kings their power to combine,*
> *And one capitulate, and one resign;*

*Charles XII of Sweden, on horseback. Made after a print by Georg Philipp Rugendas (see page 353).*

*Sculpture by Guillielmus de Groff (1676-1742), 1742. Nationalmuseum, Stockholm, Sweden.*

*Peace courts his hand, but spreads her charms in vain;*
*'Think nothing gained,' he cries, 'till nought remain.'[4]*

At the same time, as the story of Charles XII and his wars became better known in popular culture, it was used to illustrate a broad range of political viewpoints. This practice has continued well into the twentieth and twenty-first centuries with militarists and others evoking a largely unhistorical view, at times seeing Charles as some mystic military martyr.[5]

Beginning just a century ago, in 1918, academic historians started to make serious efforts to see Charles within a historically accurate and documented context, basing their work on both deeper and wider archival research. For the following half century, though, most historians wrote about Charles only within a Swedish context. In a most significant contribution to the field, Ragnhild Hatton's biography of Charles XII, published in English in 1968-69, was based on deep research into Swedish, Dutch, French, and German archival sources. This work has been the most influential in defining Charles XII within the context of Swedish history and in showing how international affairs shaped his reign.[6] Amidst the enormous amount of writing over the past three hundred years on Charles's life in Swedish, Hatton's work created a scholarly neutral, middle view. It lies between what became known in the early twentieth century as the 'Old School' and what she saw as the overreaction and narrow approach of the 'New School' to the Swedish historiography on the topic.

The purpose of the present volume is to build further on the academically robust foundations laid by Ragnhild Hatton and to broaden international perspectives on Charles XII through the contributions of a wide range of scholars—from Austria, Denmark, Finland, France, Germany, the Netherlands, Poland, Russia, Turkey, the United Kingdom, and the United States as well as from Sweden—who have been working in different countries and in the contexts of their native languages and national archival resources. In addition to the international scholarly insights, the six contributors from Sweden, through their research, provide significant new domestic perspectives on the subject.

Each contributor has faced a variety of different intellectual and scholarly challenges in dealing with Charles XII. In several national scholarly traditions, it is now uncommon to focus on individual leaders and heroes as this series does. This situation is particularly the case in modern Sweden, where a biographical approach to kings, queens, and generals seems outdated. In the Anglophone world, the situation appears quite the opposite. Charles XII presents a particular challenge to all. In his case, it is hard to understand his personality among the numerous written and graphic images of him that exist both from his lifetime and afterwards. Charles XII wrote very little. Historians are limited in their sources to the contemporary opinions and observations of others. These sources present many difficulties of interpretation, but they were the traditional way of trying to understand Charles. They are also the basis for the debates in the past, in which the king's personality and actions became the foundation upon which to understand the course of Swedish history.

Modern historians in Sweden have deliberately taken a very different approach, as shown in the contributions that Swedish scholars have made to this volume.

Scholars now consider broad thematic approaches to the period in placing Charles XII in historical context. Key historical studies now examine the nature and character of the absolute monarchy and dynasty that kings Charles X Gustav and Charles XI built and analyse how Charles XII understood and developed further this heritage of absolutist monarchical power. In this, Charles XII's grandmother, Hedvig Eleonora of Holstein-Gottorp, queen consort of Charles X Gustav and later regent during Charles XII's minority, was very important to Sweden's dynastic politics. Thus, Sweden provides an example and case study of the manner in which dynasties were politically and culturally relevant throughout Europe.

Another major theme in European history that is illustrated by Sweden in the late seventeenth and early eighteenth century, is the development of increasing absolutist power among monarchs. This theme links to that of dynastic politics. In Sweden's case, Carl X Gustav had expanded the nation's borders, while his son, Charles XI, developed an absolutist state with greater control over the population. The expansion of the state carried with it both an increased vulnerability to attack and the need to organise and to strengthen the military and naval power of the Swedish state to defend its enlarged geographic area. This development, in turn, required greater control over the nation, bringing the king into internal political conflict with the aristocracy on one side and with the wider population, on the other. The defence of the realm required increased internal coordination, central control, and organisation as well as funding, supplies, administrative support, and labour.

In Sweden's modern-day political context Charles is sometimes linked, without any historically accurate foundation, to extreme nationalist or racist viewpoints, which tends to narrow the scope of discussions and makes unbiased evaluations difficult. Our objective is to present a different image of Charles XII. This volume utilises the best historical scholarship that is available to place the events of 1697-1723 within a European-wide context. As a counterpoint, several of the Swedish scholarly contributions to the volume show a different image of Charles XII from that of the usual warring king. In contrast to the traditional views, modern Swedish historians tend to emphasise the situation at home, the problems of ruling from faraway places, and the king's policies during his five years in the Ottoman Empire, when he had more time for domestic issues and launched several new policies.[7] The wider international perspective that this volume has produced demonstrates the significance of Charles XII's reign in coinciding with a turning point in European history. This period involves fundamental shifts in the structure of European politics with the rise of both Great Britain and Russia, the relative decline of Denmark, Sweden, and the Dutch Republic, as well as the formative development of a military monarchy in Brandenburg-Prussia during the four decades between 1688 and 1725.

The focus on Charles XII in this volume also highlights a change in perception for western Europeans that the cartography of the time documents. At the outset of the Great Northern War, western European observers vaguely lumped eastern Europe with northern Europe as shown in Nicolas Sanson's map published in Amsterdam in 1700 of the *Téatre de la Guerre des Couronnes du Nord* (see map on

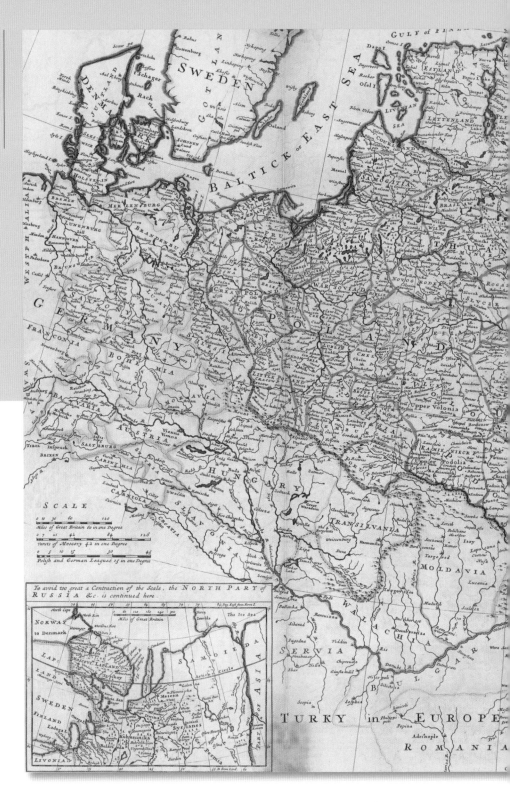

pages 12-13). Within six years, Charles XII's activities had led western Europeans to a different, much more complete, and defined view of eastern Europe, as shown in Herman Moll's *Map of Muscovy, Poland, Little Tartary and ye Black Sea*, published in London in 1706 (see above).[8] Even more broadly, the defeat of Charles XII's efforts to defend the Swedish Empire in the Great Northern War of 1700-21 combined with the earlier results of the War of the Spanish Succession of 1702-14

to create a major turning point in European history. Previously Europe had been divided into distinctive and isolated regions in the west, east, north, and south. The results of these two wars jointly produced the recognition that all regions of Europe had a political as well as a geographical interrelationship, leading to the establishment of closer relations among European states and integration into a single continental international diplomatic system.

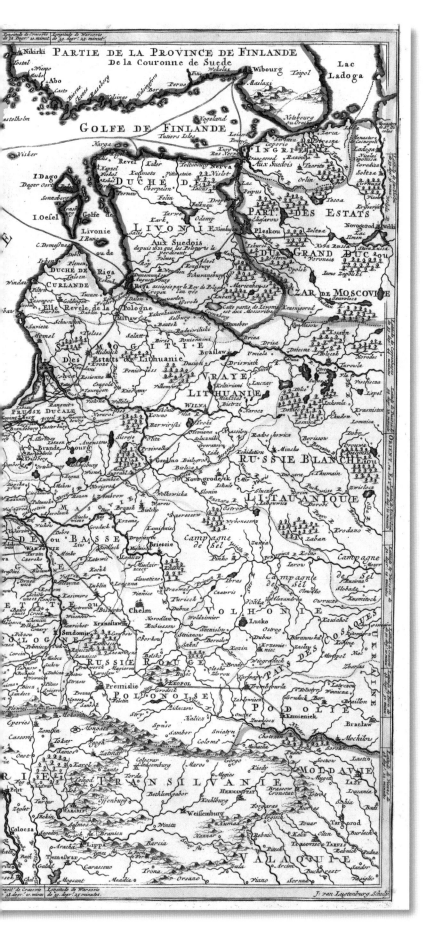

CHAPTER 1

# The Great Northern War (1700–21) and the Integration of the European States System

by Hamish Scott

*Téatre de la guerre des Couronnes du Nord.*

*Engraving by Nicolas Sanson (1600-67), Alexis Hubert Jaillot (1632-1712), and Pierre Mortier (1661-1711), 1708. The David Rumsey Map Center at Stanford University Library, Stanford, USA.*

*© 2000 by Cartography Associates.*

## ■ The Road to Altranstädt

During the early months of 1707, two rival diplomats travelled to the headquarters of the Swedish King Charles XII at Altranstädt, a small castle a few miles outside Leipzig in the electorate of Saxony.[1] The first was a French emissary, Baron Jean-Victor de Besenval.[2] His ostensible mission was to offer Sweden's ruler the role of mediator in the War of the Spanish Succession (1702-14), in which France, assisted primarily by Bavaria and the Spanish supporters of the Bourbon candidate to the throne, fought against an imposing coalition headed by Britain, the Dutch Republic, and the Austrian Habsburgs. Though the war had had a promising start for Louis XIV's monarchy, it appeared that the allies had gradually gained the upper hand and forced France's ally, Bavaria, to withdraw from the conflict in 1704, when the electorate had been occupied. France's mediation had already been rejected in that same year, and its renewal by Besenval was part of a wider diplomatic initiative.

By the end of 1706, the French monarchy was on the defensive and, in addition to disrupting the military effort of its enemies, optimistically hoping to draw Sweden—a traditional ally of France, though more recently inclining towards its enemies—into the war on its side. Mediation was offered disingenuously, in the clear hope that it might eventually lead Charles XII to intervene directly, but this was quickly acknowledged to be unrealistic.[3] Though Sweden had indeed mediated the peace settlement at the end of the previous conflict—the Nine Years' War (1688-97)— it had become concerned at both the extent of France's newfound preponderance and at the threat posed by the Anglo-Dutch dynastic union after 1688, and now aimed to avoid entanglement in western European rivalries. The Swedish king soon rejected any thought of mediation, and made clear he intended to concentrate on the struggle in which his state was engaged, the Great Northern War (1700-21).[4] Besenval's overtures were bluntly rejected and in a particularly humiliating way. Initially the French diplomat was denied an interview with the Swedish king and had to insist before he was granted one. When it took place, Charles listened to Besenval's initial compliment—the formulaic opening to any diplomatic audience—and then walked out without saying a word.[5]

By early April 1707, France's King Louis XIV and his experienced foreign minister, Jean-Baptiste Colbert, Marquis de Torcy, had acknowledged that they would be unable to draw Sweden into France's struggle with the allied coalition.[6] Their wider aim was to uphold the status quo within the Holy Roman Empire, threatened by Charles XII's victories and the appearance of his troops in Saxony.[7] France—like Sweden—was a guarantor of its territorial and constitutional settlement embodied in the Peace of Westphalia (1648) and took its role seriously, particularly since it provided the opportunity for initiatives directed against its traditional enemy, the Habsburg emperor.

The second mission is far better known and was more important at the time.[8] In late April 1707, the leading allied commander and statesman, John Churchill, Duke of Marlborough, travelled to Altranstädt, where he remained for only four days, during which he had a celebrated meeting with the Swedish king. Despite the importance of preparations for the new campaign, in which he played a central role, and a delay of over two weeks due to travel problems, the planned mission to Saxony went ahead.[9] This in itself underlines Sweden's important place in allied strategy, and in European politics more generally. Two months earlier, Marlborough had declared to Anthonie Heinsius, the veteran Grand Pensionary of Holland and de facto leader of the Republic, that 'we would leave no stone unturned to satisfy the king of Sweden.'[10] During the first six years of the Great Northern War, Charles had refused to permit anyone, including diplomats, to travel in his entourage and with his army. Political negotiations instead had to be conducted in Stockholm, ensuring that diplomacy effectively came to a standstill, in view of its distance from the Swedish monarch's headquarters and the difficulties of communication with the field chancery. This prohibition was relaxed after Charles based himself at Altranstädt, and Marlborough and Besenval were only two among a tribe of emissaries who descended on the Saxon castle from late 1706 onwards.

During a whirlwind journey of eighteen days, the duke first visited Hanover, whose elector was the son of the aging heir apparent to the British thrones, travelled on to Altranstädt, diverted to nearby Leipzig for an audience with the deposed Polish king, Augustus II, who remained elector of Saxony, and then went to Berlin in order to inform another member of the coalition, the elector of Brandenburg and king in Prussia, Friedrich, about his discussions. That the duke considered a personal mission necessary highlights the importance of the situation faced by the allies.

The explanation was the contrasting progress of the two wars by 1706-07. Though the coalition's forces commanded by Marlborough had won impressive victories at Blenheim (1704) and Ramillies (1706), there was an increasing allied awareness of a military stalemate. In western Europe the allies might be gaining the upper hand, but in the Iberian Peninsula the new Bourbon king, Philip V, was establishing an impregnable political and territorial position. During the previous generation, France's northern and eastern frontiers had been formidably strengthened by the foremost fortifications expert of the age, Marshal Vauban, and the resilience exhibited by this network of fortresses was delaying the allied advance, making the duke's dreams of an invasion and a dictated peace more unrealistic than ever.[11] War weariness was increasing in the Dutch Republic and in England too, while the third major ally, the Austrian Habsburgs, faced a serious secessionist war in Hungary, where a rebellion led by Prince Ferenc II Rákóczi was achieving remarkable successes.[12]

In this perspective, Charles XII's military and political triumphs during the first phase of the Great Northern War appeared even more impressive to contemporaries, and both sides looked expectantly towards Sweden. While French observers hoped for its intervention, British statesmen would always have been satisfied by its continuing neutrality. They were alarmed that his support for the cause of Habsburg Lower Silesia's Protestants and his efforts to ensure that they were permitted to benefit from the favourable terms of the Peace of Westphalia (which the emperor had hitherto refused to implement, but was obliged to comply with in autumn 1707 under Swedish pressure) might inflame the religious situation, and they were even fearful that he could support Rákóczi's struggle. Britain and its allies were also concerned that direct Swedish intervention in the Empire would lead states such as Brandenburg-Prussia, Hesse-Kassel, and Denmark to withdraw their substantial contingents from the allied army, because of their existing treaty commitments to Augustus II and fear of a German civil war.[13] The situation which seemed to exist by spring 1707 exemplified the extent to which the Empire once again had the potential to act as a lightning conductor for continental rivalries.[14] It also underlined Charles XII's wide-ranging campaigning, which ensured that the Great Northern War—unlike earlier conflicts—extended across the wide expanses of Poland-Lithuania, the Empire, and Russia, and would soon involve the Ottoman Empire as well, enhancing its political implications for all Europe.[15]

In 1700, Sweden's young king, on the throne for a mere three years, had been attacked by a coalition assembled by Augustus II of Saxony-Poland (fighting as elector and not king) and including Denmark and Russia. The military struggle which followed, however, had not led to the rapid Swedish defeat widely anticipated. During the first year of the conflict, Charles XII had forced Denmark to withdraw from the war by a swift campaign against its capital, Copenhagen, leading to the Peace of Travendal (18 August 1700)—guaranteed by Anglo-Dutch force and diplomacy—and then transferred his army across the Baltic to Sweden's eastern possessions, Livonia and Ingria, where a Russian force three times its size was routed in a snowstorm outside Narva (30 November 1700).

Thereafter, the Swedish king turned against his main opponent in the initial phase of the Great Northern War, Augustus II, winning significant victories at Kliszów (1702), Pułtusk (1703), and Gemäuerthof (1705). Though his success was delayed by Poland-Lithuania's unique constitutional structure and entrenched aristocratic rivalries, particularly in Lithuania, it could not be prevented. In 1704, Charles XII had formally deposed Augustus II (February) and then elected a rival king, the Polish magnate Stanisław Leszczyński (July); two years later, after Carl Gustav Rehnskiöld's impressive victory over a Russo-Saxon army at Fraustadt (February 1706), he finally appeared on the point of replacing Augustus with Leszczyński. He still needed the Saxon elector, however, to acknowledge publicly his deposition as king. In the interim Augustus II had become Russia's political dependant, signing an alliance in August 1704. More concerning for the allies, Sweden's ruler appeared to be on the point of invading Saxony, the deposed king's homeland, which hitherto he had refrained from undertaking in accordance with his promise to the coalition not to campaign within the Empire. This posed a particular threat to Austria, already at war with France and in Hungary, and now confronted by a challenge to its Imperial authority.

Anglo-Dutch policy had traditionally been that of supporting Sweden as a way of neutralising the Baltic region and thereby securing the all-important trade in naval stores, especially important during a period when the English fleet expanded significantly. It was axiomatic that Copenhagen should not control both shores of the Sound. In 1700, Sweden's victory had been facilitated by an Anglo-Dutch naval squadron, which conveyed its expeditionary force across the Baltic to Zealand and discouraged Denmark's navy from any attack. In the next year Sweden had promised to abstain from the imminent conflict over the Spanish succession, in return for an allied subsidy of 200,000 thalers and a guaranteed loan of 300,000 thalers, and over the next six years Charles XII had observed this commitment, facilitating the separation between the wars.[16] The king valued the Anglo-Dutch guarantee of the Travendal agreement, which conferred protection against any Danish attack and freedom to operate in central and eastern Europe. Two years later he had gone even further, promising in an alliance with the Maritime Powers to provide 10,000 soldiers for the allied army when the Great Northern War ended.[17] Charles XII's favourable attitude

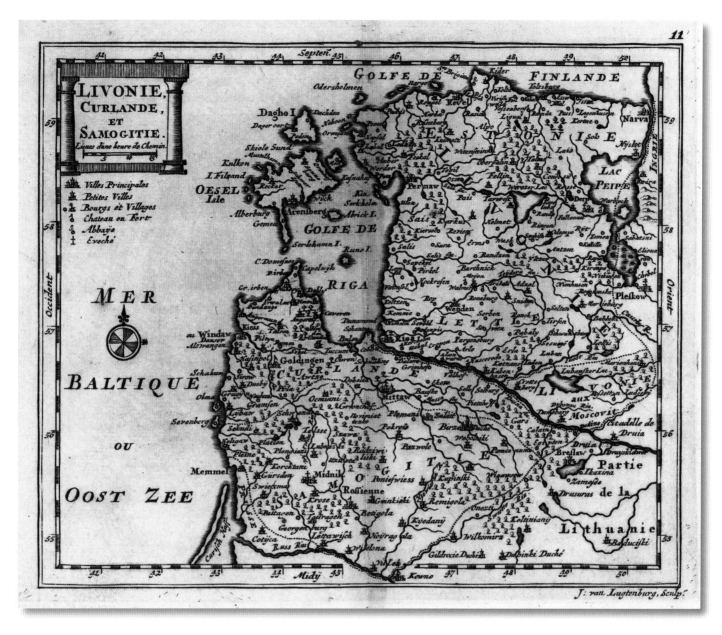

*Map of Livonia and Courland from* **Théatre complet et particularisé de la guerre du nort.**

*Engraving by Guillaume Delisle (1675-1726) and Johannes van Luchtenburg, 1711. University of Amsterdam, Amsterdam, the Netherlands. Bijzondere Collecties, Universiteit van Amsterdam, plaatsnummer (OTM: HB-KZL XII G 74).*

was welcomed by the allies, who wanted to keep the two conflicts from intersecting, fearing that any such development might be exploited by France. They were also very happy to have potential French allies, above all Saxony, tied up against Sweden.

By the winter of 1706-07, however, this appeared to have broken down. Sweden's invasion of Saxony in autumn 1706 was calculated to force Augustus II to abdicate formally as Polish king, and this was rapidly achieved (Peace of Altranstädt, September). The political leaders of the allied cause—Marlborough himself, Sidney Earl Godolphin (head of the British government), Heinsius, the Habsburg Emperor Joseph I—were all concerned that Charles's initiative might create the kind of diversion France could exploit or even, more fancifully, that Sweden's king might march to Rákóczi's aid. That such notions could be contemplated underlined the strength of the political position created by Charles XII's military victories, which suggested there was no limit to what he might attempt.

Marlborough's journey to Altranstädt ostensibly aimed to reassure the king of allied friendship, to discourage him from damaging actions in the Empire, and if possible to discover his future political and military strategy. Though, in order to match the French offer of mediation, a similar allied offer was made for the future, it was rightly anticipated it would be declined. In a series of audiences, the duke skilfully flattered the king's vanity and sought to divine his intentions when the campaigning season began. Marlborough's conclusions were reassuring. Charles intended to advance into eastern Europe and attack his remaining enemy, the Russian ruler Peter the Great. The map of Russia which lay on a table in the Swedish king's quarters, seemingly confirmed the allied leader in his view that this was the king's intention. He returned to The Hague visibly relieved about Sweden's future policy, which he believed posed no real threat to allied strategy against France.[18] The journey, however, had a second purpose which only became evident subsequently and has not been generally appreciated by historians. Marlborough verbally promised that the allies would guarantee to defend Sweden's territories in Germany in return for a renewed undertaking of neutrality in the Spanish succession conflict, which Charles XII willingly provided.[19] The full implications of these commitments, and their importance for the allied cause, would only become evident three years later.

The episode possesses a wider importance which provides the *Leitmotiv* for the present chapter: the way in which military and, to a lesser extent, political events were drawing the two parallel wars together, in spite of determined efforts to prevent any such fusion. With hindsight, the Great Northern War can be seen to be an important—and probably the decisive—stage in the political integration of the European states system and of Russia's emergence as a more important factor within this. Evident in spring 1707 when Marlborough made his celebrated journey across Germany, it was to be reinforced by the outcome of the military struggle around the Baltic after the conclusion of peace in the west in 1713-14. By the 1720s Europe's political system was becoming far more unified than a generation before, due primarily to the Great Northern War.

## ■ Parallel Conflicts, 1707-14

In autumn 1707 Charles XII, confident that his rear was now secure, left Altranstädt to join his army which was already advancing to attack Russia, the only member of the original anti-Swedish coalition still campaigning. The events which followed are very well known. The invasion posed enormous logistical challenges and even more difficult strategic choices. By July 1709, when Sweden suffered an overwhelming defeat at Poltava, Charles XII was heading down what was—at best—a strategic one-way street and may have been a dead end. The king fled the battlefield, becoming a political exile in the Ottoman Empire, in the frontier town of Bender in Moldavia. He appeared unable to continue the war or even return to his homeland: before long, his enemies controlled all possible land routes back to Swedish territory. The remnants of his army surrendered later in the same month at Perevolochna and, while the Regency in Stockholm attempted to keep the war going, Sweden's enemies now held the initiative.

The scale and importance of Charles XII's defeat was immediately evident to allied leaders, and also the danger which the fighting now posed to the coalition.[20] Britain's representative in Russia, Charles Whitworth, commented when he first heard of Poltava that 'This victory will in all probability give a great change to the affairs of all Europe.'[21] Shortly after news arrived in western Europe, Marlborough confided to the Grand Pensionary that the new situation could be 'troublesome' for the allies.[22] The neutrality upon which the coalition had depended, now appeared threatened and with it the all-important trade in naval stores from the Baltic.

The anti-Swedish coalition, disrupted by Charles XII's military successes, began to re-form as soon as news of Poltava arrived. Denmark was already preparing to re-enter the war. Augustus, too, had been making preparations, signing treaties with Denmark and Brandenburg-Prussia and assembling troops in Saxony. In July—the same month as the Swedish defeat—he revived his alliance with Peter the Great and by October he had driven Leszczyński into exile, enabling the Saxon elector to reclaim the Polish crown. He now ruled as a Russian puppet: the Treaty of Thorn (Toruń) which Augustus II was forced to sign later in 1709 made clear that, henceforth, he had to accept Russian dictation of his policy. The huge strengthening of Saint Petersburg's control over its vast western neighbour was to be the principal strategic consequence of the Great Northern War. The prospect of a partition of Sweden's Baltic empire encouraged established members of the coalition and new states alike. A Danish army crossed over to Scania in southern Sweden and its troops mobilised in Norway; by October Russia had concluded new treaties with Denmark and Brandenburg-Prussia. This boosted the established allied concern that contingents from all these states might be withdrawn from the coalition army, depriving it of as many as 40,000 soldiers.

The imperative of preventing the two wars merging was stronger than ever.[23] Extended negotiations in 1709-10 had failed to produce a peace settlement with France. Yet war-weariness was increasing in all allied capitals, particularly after the fall of Britain's Whig government in 1710 and its replacement by a Tory ministry intent on peace. That year also saw the beginning of a French military recovery in the Low Countries. Though it was not yet decisive, a shift in the balance of the armed struggle was becoming evident. Increasingly, real fears that the Northern War would spread and engulf the allies, together with the exigencies of the search for peace, pointed in the same direction.

The fear that the German members of the coalition might withdraw their contingents was a particular anxiety by early 1710, as the failure of the peace negotiations with France slowly became evident.[24] The established objective of keeping the Empire at peace and denying France any opportunity to intervene in a German civil war, now assumed a new guise: a determination to prevent the revived anti-Swedish coalition from launching hostilities in northern Germany. This produced one of the most important diplomatic agreements of the earlier eighteenth century, and also one of the most neglected: the Neutrality Convention for the Empire concluded in 1710.[25]

Its specific origin was a wish to neutralise a Swedish military force now based in Swedish (Western) Pomerania. Commanded by Major-General Ernst Detlov von Krassow, this had been left in Poland-Lithuania by Charles when he marched east to attack Russia. Its original purpose had been to support King Stanislaw Leszczyński, but it had been forced back into Swedish Pomerania by a Russian advance. In December 1709 Krassow had been replaced by Field-Marshal Nils Gyllenstierna af Björkesund, who gave way in turn to Carl Gustav Dücker in October 1710.[26] Originally some 8,000 strong, this force had been covertly strengthened until, by spring 1710, it may have been twice that size.[27] Its very presence epitomised the threat which a revived war in northern Germany posed to the allies. This was apparent to the Swedish Regency which, immediately after word arrived of Poltava, requested the Maritime Powers and Hanover to cooperate with Vienna to provide for the 'security' of Swedish possessions in Germany. This was in accordance with Marlborough's secret commitment at Altranstädt two years earlier, which had been communicated to the Regency in Stockholm.[28]

The Neutrality Convention formally concluded in The Hague in late March 1710 was the product of these various concerns. Marlborough had promised to protect Sweden's German possessions during his discussions with Charles XII, in return for its continuing neutrality. The agreement at The Hague was the logical and perhaps inevitable consequence of his secret undertaking three years before. The duke was becoming aware of the threat from his domestic political enemies, particularly after the bloody, though indecisive, victory at Malplaquet (September 1709)—in the War of the Spanish Succession—highlighted the costs of a war which appeared to be a strategic draw, at least in the western theatre of operations, and he was anxious to avoid an even wider conflict. By the following month Britain had decided to neutralise Krassow's corps.[29]

Heinsius strongly supported the initiative, and may have been the real originator of the detailed scheme; he certainly pushed very hard for it to be adopted during the winter of 1709-10.[30] In the second half of December, against the background of a Danish attack on mainland Sweden from Norway and Scania in the previous month, the Dutch Republic convened an informal conference of diplomats from the eventual signatories, which led to a decision on the 23rd to establish a neutrality zone. It then took the lead in seeking a further reassurance from Stockholm of its neutrality. This was soon forthcoming, opening the way for a formal agreement.[31] The Emperor Joseph I, engaged in wars with France and in Hungary, was also anxious to neutralise northern Germany and pressed this upon the Imperial Diet at Regensburg during the winter of 1709-10.[32] This was important since the projected agreement primarily concerned the Empire, and therefore had to be negotiated at the Imperial Diet. Within the Empire there was a long-established tradition of regional collective security agreements, while a precise precedent also existed: in 1658, during the First Northern War (1655-60), the integrity of Sweden's possessions of Bremen and Verden had been guaranteed by the Rhenish Alliance, a French-backed league of German princes.

These various interests all pointed in a similar direction, and in the winter of 1709-10 they coalesced, producing a single agreement to neutralise the southern shore of the Baltic. Informally discussed in Regensburg (where the Diet met) and agreed in January 1710, it was formalised at The Hague two months later, on 31 March.[33] Though the Empire was its focal point, the agreement's geographical remit was wider still, extending to neighbouring Schleswig and Holstein, Jutland, and the kingdom of Poland-Lithuania.[34] This effectively neutralised all the regions where fighting seemed possible between Sweden and its enemies. The principal signatories were Britain, the Dutch Republic, Prussia, Russia, Denmark, Hanover, and Saxony, together with some minor German principalities. Later in the same year (4 August 1710), a second convention was signed, establishing a 15-16,000-strong army of neutrality: Britain and the Dutch Republic were to provide 8,400 infantry (which would be detached from the main field army in the Low Countries) and the emperor 2,000 cavalry, with smaller contingents from the other signatories.[35]

This was a striking agreement, in its intentions and political significance though not in its military impact: the proposed army of observation was never formed. Its purpose was clear: in effect, the states fighting France united with Charles XII's enemies in order to protect Sweden's German possessions and in this way prevent the two wars merging.[36] The Swedish Regency confronted not merely a continuing military conflict, but was receiving strident demands from Bender (where the king was still marooned) for more troops and more money, to be supplied by an exhausted realm. The harvests in both 1708 and 1709 had been poor, and a serious plague epidemic reached the capital, Stockholm, in mid-1710 and devastated the provinces. Between 100,000 and 150,000 people died, in a country whose total population was less than three million.[37] Swedish foreign trade was periodically reduced and even interrupted by the presence of Danish troops in Scania, enabling Copenhagen to control both sides of the Sound, and this deprived the Swedish exchequer of much needed income. The Regency, aware of the allied commitment at Altranstädt three years earlier, therefore quickly embraced the Neutrality Convention, which promised protection for its important Pomeranian salient and a limit upon further hostilities.[38] But Charles obdurately refused to ratify the agreement, dreaming that the Pomeranian contingents might be the foundation of a dramatic Swedish recovery which he intended to lead.

British diplomacy now pressed for the king's agreement. Captain James Jefferyes, who had served as a volunteer with the Swedish army after 1707, been captured at Poltava and then repatriated back to Britain, was sent to Bender with instructions to secure Charles XII's acceptance of the Convention, but his mission proved unsuccessful.[39] The king's advisers in Bender seem to have favoured acceptance, but he remained intransigent, apparently because of a conviction that the allies had exploited his predicament at Bender, rather than providing support.[40] Behind Jefferyes' mission, and the Neutrality Convention itself, can be glimpsed an important shift in Britain's approach: maintaining Sweden as a barrier to Russian control of the Baltic region was becoming more and more important in the aftermath of Poltava. In autumn 1711, Marlborough would emphasise the importance of taking 'the best care that Sweden be not overrun, so as to preserve in some measure the balance in the North.'[41] Yet when, in 1711, Sweden's enemies advanced in Pomerania, the signatories of the Convention hesitated and then stood aside, because Charles XII had refused to accept it, though there were to be no serious military consequences.[42]

Russia by contrast signed and supported the Hague agreement. Victory at Poltava had opened the way for a succession of striking Russian gains in 1709-10 in the eastern Baltic, where first Ingria was re-occupied and then the key fortresses of Riga, Reval, and Vyborg were captured. In 1710 Peter had arranged the marriage of his niece, Anna Ivanovna, to the ruling duke of Courland. The duke's opportune death in the following year made his wife regent and transformed this strategically important duchy into a Russian protectorate. These gains had been made possible by continuing good relations with the Ottoman Empire, enabling Peter to concentrate on northern Europe, but during the second half of 1710 these broke down and in November Constantinople declared war; Russia did likewise four months later, in March 1711.[43]

The campaign which followed, with the humiliating surrender of an outnumbered and surrounded Russian army at the Pruth (19 July 1711), only partly redeemed by the lenient provisional peace settlement negotiated with the Ottoman Empire a few days later, ensured that Peter became a firm supporter of the proposed neutrality. Russia's ruler always believed that his strategic position was weaker than it seemed to his enemies (as it also has appeared to historians with the benefit of hindsight), and this suggested a period of caution and consolidation. The sharp deterioration in Russo-Ottoman relations during the second half of 1710 was accompanied by a clear signal that Russia would not merely support the Neutrality Convention but would do nothing to disrupt the allied war effort.[44] When, during the first half of 1711, news of the Ottoman declaration of war led to the delay and then the suspension of plans for the agreed contingents of troops to be assembled and march into northern Germany, the Russian representative at The Hague protested vigorously.[45]

In the event peace was preserved without the creation of the planned neutrality corps. This is partly to be explained by Russia's continuing preoccupation with the Ottoman Empire. A provisional settlement had been negotiated by summer 1711, but it was two more years—during which Constantinople declared war on two further occasions and relations remained tense—before this could be transformed into a formal agreement (Treaty of Adrianople, June 1713). The allied political leadership, for its part, remained concerned at any potential weakening of its army in the face of France's continuing military recovery. The repercussions of Joseph I's unexpected death in April 1711 were even more important, however. During any interregnum authority was placed in the hands of two Imperial vicars: the Palatinate in southern Germany and Saxony in the north. The Saxon elector, of course, was none other than Augustus II of Poland-Lithuania, and he promptly exploited his temporary authority to allow anti-Swedish forces to enter the eastern half of the intended neutrality zone, forcing Sweden's corps to take refuge in a handful of fortresses. Further west, the zone was compromised by Denmark's renewed aggression, though its effective collapse proved to be unimportant.

By this point, the peace conference at Utrecht was about to assemble, and the fighting in western Europe was reduced in scale. Though concern periodically arose at the repercussions of Charles XII's potential return from his exile, the two wars re-

mained separate until the conclusion of peace at Utrecht (1713) and Rastatt (1714).[46] The purpose behind the Neutrality Convention had thus been achieved, though not in the way that its signatories anticipated.

## ■ The Emergence of a Russian Baltic, 1714-21

The conclusion of the fighting in western Europe produced an intensification of the war in the north, caused primarily by the enhanced freedom of action now enjoyed by the leading belligerents.[47] Though mediation was periodically attempted, particularly by the emperor, most states were avid for territory when the trans-Baltic possessions were partitioned after Sweden's defeat, and believed this was now inevitable. This was particularly true of Hanover, whose elector was now also Britain's George I. His hopes of securing territorial gains and enhanced political status in northern Germany were as great as ever. The elector-king was able to deploy the resources of his island kingdom and especially its navy, to further them. Brandenburg-Prussia, now under the more ambitious leadership of Friedrich Wilhelm I, was equally eager to share in any partition. He declared war formally in May 1715, and forged a close alliance—personal as much as political—with Peter the Great. Russia, too, enjoyed significantly greater freedom of action after the signature of a definitive peace settlement with the Ottoman Empire in June 1713.

Charles XII's return from exile to Stralsund in Swedish Pomerania in November 1714, after a whirlwind six-week ride across Europe, also contributed to this. During the final four years of his life—he would be killed besieging the Norwegian fortress of Fredrikshald on 11 December 1718—the king continued to believe that only military

*Silver medal commemorating Charles XII's crossing of the Dvina River on 19 July 1701.*

*The obverse of the medal shows the king's profile without a wig. It bears the inscription 'Charles XII, by the grace of God, king of Sweden. The new century's ornament.'*

*The reverse shows an image of Mother Svea, the female personification of Sweden, flying over the smoke of battle and the Dvina River with the defeated Saxons on the left and the attacking Swedish army on the right. The inscription at the top reads 'Neither rivers nor enemies hinder him' and, at the bottom, 'The Saxons were slaughtered on the opposite shore of the Dvina River.'*

*Silver medal by Bengt Richter (1670-1735), 1702. Skoklosters Slott, Sweden.*

PLAN DER BELAGERUNG ... VON FRI...

anmungen von CARL dem XII (glorwürd Andenckens) der Schweden Goth und ...
edirt von IOHANN BAPTIST HOMANN Der R...

Wenden König mit 10000 Ma...
Kais: May.t Geographo...

Danische Postirung
so sich retirirret

Königl: Schwedisch Lag...
den 20. December Anno ...

Schwedische
Batterien von
18. Canonen

EIN THEIL DES KÖNIGR... EA... HS...

Weg nach Christiania

Weg nach Fridrichstat

Kaggi

Königl: Danische
Postirung so sich ab...
zurück gezogen

Klanne

Roo

Das Fort Güldenloo
erobert d.4 Dec...

Nort-Seite

Eosbrychen

Die offene Stadt und Hafen
FRIDRICHSHALL

Sep:

Occ. Or.

Mer:

IDEFIORD

In dieser Gegend ist die Schwedische
und Dänische Flottille offt aneinander
gewesen

FRIDRICHSTEIN

Stor Tornet

Knardahl

Schwedische
Postirung

Saves

Bartoe Insula

SWINE SUND

TISTEDALENS ELBE

victory could enable Sweden to retain part at least of its empire. Yet he also pursued bilateral peace negotiations with his enemies and launched diplomatic initiatives designed to disrupt the opposing coalition, which had some effect. The central issue increasingly became the struggle to limit Russian gains. It was a particular concern of the new emperor, Charles VI. By the time of Charles XII's return from exile, Sweden's former territories in the eastern Baltic were completely controlled by Russia. It soon became clear, however, that Peter the Great's ambitions extended to northern Germany, where some Russian troops had been stationed since 1711, and this brought him more and more into conflict with Britain-Hanover, which came to be supported by France (its ally after 1716) and by Vienna.[48]

The duchy of Mecklenburg came to occupy the central role in this confrontation.[49] Its duke, Karl Leopold, was involved in a bitter and long-standing dispute with his Estates which also concerned the emperor and the Imperial authorities. This had begun in the 1660s and was the product of intermittent efforts by successive dukes to levy direct taxation without the consent of the powerful, noble-dominated Estates, to pay for an ambitious military build-up. In 1716 Karl Leopold turned to Peter for support, concluding an alliance and marrying his niece, Ekaterina Ivanovna. Russian backing and, crucially, Russian soldiers were provided, enabling the duke to rout his domestic enemies and establish a more absolutist regime.

Peter's intention was clear: to turn Mecklenburg into a political satellite and a commercial *entrepôt* for the export of Russian produce to western Europe. Simultaneously, Russia's military build-up in northern Germany was vastly increased to facilitate an ambitious plan to invade southern Sweden from Denmark and so end the war. As many as 40,000 troops, together with a powerful fleet, were stationed there. In autumn 1716, Russia's ruler—aware of the logistical and strategic difficulties of any such expedition and belatedly recognising its political drawbacks—fi-

*Plan for the 1718 Swedish Siege of Fredrikshald.*

*Hand-coloured engraving by Reinier Ottens (1698-1750), ca. 1719-25. University of Amsterdam, Amsterdam, the Netherlands. Bijzondere Collecties, Universiteit van Amsterdam, plaatsnummer (OTM: HB KZL XX G 74 of OTM: HB KZL 1808 A 6).*

nally abandoned the plan, but it would be another twelve months before this power-ful corps would be withdrawn from the region. Two years later, troops from Hanover and Wolfenbüttel, enforcing an Imperial decision, invaded the duchy, expelled Karl Leopold, and restored the Estates under a temporary Hanoverian regime.

The presence of substantial Russian forces in Mecklenburg in 1716-17—the furthest west they would reach until the final stages of the Napoleonic Wars almost a hundred years later—was even more important than Poltava in alerting contem-poraries to the new power and ambitions of the Petrine state, no longer a politically negligible outsider. It ensured that efforts to limit Russia's gains in the eventu-al peace settlement would dominate the final years of the Great Northern War. Britain-Hanover, backed by its ally France, took the lead in these initiatives, which were aided by Charles XII's death late in 1718 but enjoyed incomplete success. All the members of the anti-Swedish coalition secured significant gains in the treaties which ended the conflict in 1719-21, with the single exception of Saxony-Poland, the architect of the initial onslaught against Charles XII's monarchy two decades before. It suffered more than any other belligerent, apart from Sweden itself, effec-tively being reduced to the status of a Russian satellite: in 1716-17 Russia became the guarantor of a constitutional settlement between Augustus and his subjects which kept Poland-Lithuania weak and divided for the rest of the eighteenth centu-ry and would facilitate its partition between 1772 and 1795.

Denmark annexed the Holstein-Gottorp lands in Schleswig, and prevented Sweden securing exemption from payment of the Sound dues, the tolls which all ships had to pay to the Danish government on entering or leaving the Baltic. With-in a decade it was forced to face Russian influence in Holstein-Gottorp, its imme-diate neighbour to the south, after another dynastic marriage: in 1725 Peter's own daughter, Anna, married the reigning duke, creating a potential Russian salient in northern Germany. Denmark was now a satellite of Saint Petersburg. Copenhagen's hopes of securing Bremen were thwarted; that territory, together with Verden, passed to Hanover, greatly enhancing its standing within the Empire. Branden-burg-Prussia secured Stettin and the greater part of Western Pomerania, though Sweden retained Stralsund, Wismar, and the district of Greifswald.

The final treaty was the most important: the Russo-Swedish Peace of Nystad signed in 1721, after extended negotiations. Its terms set out the huge Russian gains and recorded Sweden's almost complete defeat. Stockholm had to hand over most of its former possessions in the eastern Baltic: Livonia, Estonia, Ingria, together with Kexholm and part of Karelia all passed to Russia; the rest of Finland was returned to Swedish rule. The Russian protectorate over Courland since 1710-11 gave Peter a long strip of coastline, stretching from the southern shore of the Gulf of Finland west and south for several hundred miles, and so controlled the important trade of the hinterland. Within a single generation Russia had emerged as the leading power in northern and eastern Europe, and a state which the western monarchies had to include in their political calculations as never before.

This advance had been facilitated by a near simultaneous *détente* on the distant Siberian-Manchu border, a traditional area of strategic concern to Russian rulers.[50]

Between the 1680s and the 1720s the political and commercial rivalry, which had intensified since the mid-seventeenth century, was resolved and relations between Russia and China stabilised. A series of agreements, the product of negotiations which began during Peter's final years and culminated in the Treaty of Kyakhta (1727), helped to free Russia to adopt an enhanced European role. One source of its powerful strategic position during the rest of the eighteenth century was to be a relatively stable eastern frontier with China. In contrast to continental rivals, it had to concern itself with only one border, albeit a frontier that ran for over a thousand miles from the Baltic to the Black Sea. The period of confusion and, at times, weakness which followed Peter's death in 1725 ensured that this increased status was not immediately exploited by the leadership in the new capital of Saint Petersburg, itself built on territory seized from Sweden. It would be another generation before Russia advanced into the ranks of the European great powers, through its major military contribution to the anti-Prussian coalition during the continental Seven Years' War (1756-63). But that breakthrough rested upon the advance made during the earlier struggle with Sweden.

## ■ Sweden, Russia, and Europe's Political Integration

Sweden's seventeenth-century rise had been accomplished at a period when there was a political vacuum in northern Europe and, specifically, when Russia was cut off from access to the Baltic and initially preoccupied with internal consolidation. The Swedish 'Age of Empire' always rested upon exiguous economic and demographic foundations, and these were exposed by the dynamism of the Petrine state during the Great Northern War. Charles XII's military leadership could do no more, faced with the Russian Behemoth, than delay the inevitable. The Peace of Nystad recognised that Russia had eclipsed Sweden as the leading Baltic state and, in the process, secured novel importance within European international relations.

By the 1720s there was a wholly new awareness of Russian power and disruptive potential within the international system. Viewed a generation earlier as on the continent's periphery and primarily interested in Eurasia and in relations with the Ottoman Empire, it now appeared Europe's most dynamic state.[51] Britain was particularly concerned because of Russia's naval power. During the Great Northern War it had, for the first time, acquired a Baltic navy. In 1714 the first ship of the line had been launched from the shipyard at Kronstadt, the new naval base located outside Saint Petersburg. Its potential remained limited: construction was on a relatively small scale, and depended upon foreign shipwrights, first from the Dutch Republic and then mainly from Britain itself, while during the rapid expansion in the 1710s many warships were purchased abroad. A maritime tradition on which a fighting navy could be based was lacking. Russia had been cut off from the Baltic by Swedish territory since the earlier seventeenth century, when its commerce either went through Archangel in the extreme north or was in foreign hands. Officers in the protean navy were usually foreigners, while manning was a permanent problem which the recourse to conscripted peasants could not solve. But its naval potential was evident, and the victory at Hanko (August 1714) over the Swedish fleet a portent of the transformation to come. Russia's newfound control over northern European sources of naval stores, crucial for the expanding British fleet, was even more important from London's perspective. Efforts to develop an alternative source in the North American colonies had enjoyed limited success: in 1727, only 219 masts came from there, but no fewer than 2,842 were imported from Russia.[52] This symbolised its clearly established importance for Britain and the other maritime states, though it was still believed its political influence could be contained.

The attitude of the other leading western state, France, was more complex, but it too was deeply concerned. French diplomacy had long maintained an 'eastern barrier' directed against its traditional rival, the Austrian Habsburgs, and comprising Sweden, Poland-Lithuania, and the Ottoman Empire, but all three were now in decline and located within the enlarged Russian orbit. A year after Peter's death, French problems were compounded by the conclusion of a Russo-Austrian alliance which would endure until 1762. This axis, French diplomacy soon concluded, had brought Russia and its formidable army into central Europe, strengthening the Habsburgs there, and undermining France's traditional policy.[53] Russia's importance was clear. Yet there were significant limitations, as Peter himself found when he turned up at the French court in spring 1717 hoping to conclude a dynastic marriage and even an alliance, only to be bluntly refused both.[54] Assumptions of political superiority took a long time to be eroded by the new realities of power.

France, as a continental state, nevertheless was well aware of Europe's growing political integration, the result primarily of Russian victories and highlighted by the presence of Russian soldiers in Mecklenburg and Denmark.[55] Peter's two celebrated journeys to western Europe, the 'Great Embassy' in 1697-98 and its successor in 1716-17, contributed to this. It had become unusual for reigning monarchs to travel abroad and to negotiate in person, and his travels increased the attention which was paid to his state. But military victories and territorial gains, together with the expedition to Mecklenburg and the acquisition of an invisible empire over Poland-Lithuania, did far more to boost Russian prestige. These were also central to the creation of a more unified European political system, which began to emerge after 1700.

Until the later seventeenth century, Europe had contained three distinct subsystems, which were only periodically and then imperfectly unified. In southern and eastern Europe, the Ottoman Empire's dynamic advance had been central to a system in which the Spanish Habsburg monarchy, Venice, the Papacy, the Austrian Habsburgs, Poland-Lithuania, and Muscovy/Russia were involved in trying to check and contain the progress of Islamic power. In northern and northeastern Europe, around the Baltic, Sweden, Denmark, Poland-Lithuania, and Muscovy/Russia—and latterly Brandenburg-Prussia too—were engaged in a shifting but essentially regionalised struggle for supremacy. The Great Northern War had been the latest and, as it proved, decisive round. Finally, in the western sector the hegemonic aspirations of first the Spanish monarchy and, from the mid-seventeenth century, of the French Bourbon kingdom provided the central issue within a regionalised states system extending as far east as the Empire and involving the rising powers of the Dutch Republic and the British state.

Europe's leading states were all involved in more than one of these subsystems: as Spain was in the Mediterranean against the Ottomans and in western Europe as the principal rival of France, or Poland-Lithuania—until the later seventeenth century a major military power—around the Baltic and in the struggle with the Ottoman Empire. The frequent conflicts which resulted, had also been essentially regional. The lengthy and wide-ranging series of conflicts known as the Thirty Years' War (1618-48) had come closest to extending over the entire continent, but even that had not directly involved Europe's northern-eastern and southeastern sectors. The simultaneous but separate conflicts after 1700 over the Spanish succession and around the Baltic thus corresponded to the established pattern: wars in Europe, even the most wide-ranging, remained essentially regional struggles. This was threatened and eventually undermined by a combination of the stalemate in the west and the decisive victories first of Charles XII and then Russia.

These regional rivalries had their counterpart in the pattern of diplomatic representation, which around 1700 remained equally fractured. Resident diplomacy, originating in the Italian peninsula during the second half of the fifteenth century and spreading across southern and western Europe during the next hundred years, was far less well established in the southeast and north. There, continuous representation was in its infancy even in the later seventeenth century. Instead of permanent embassies and continuous political relations, diplomacy had been conducted by occasional missions sent for a specific purpose—the conclusion of an alliance or a peace treaty, the negotiation of a dynastic marriage—or by quasi-official intermediaries who kept the channels of communication open at other times. This was particularly evident in the Mediterranean, where the Ottoman Empire was unwilling to embrace reciprocal diplomacy.

The development of resident diplomacy in the western half of the continent after the 1660s intensified this contrast. France's political ambitions together with its wealth had driven a significant expansion. Eager to be better informed than its rivals—the provision of reliable information remained a more important part of a diplomat's duties than negotiations—and also willing to employ diplomacy in a more creative way, it led the way in establishing a diplomatic network which, by around 1700, linked the capitals of southern, western, and central Europe. Its political rivals, led by the Dutch stadholder and English king, William III, established permanent embassies of their own and pursued a more ambitious diplomacy as they struggled to contain Louis XIV's seemingly hegemonic aspirations. Even Sweden had maintained an average of over twenty resident diplomats between the 1650s and the 1690s, evidence of the enhanced ambitions and responsibilities created by successful military imperialism.[56]

The Great Northern War provided a direct stimulus to the expansion of the diplomatic network and, in particular, to Russia's incorporation.[57] The demands of wartime cooperation together with the huge increase in Russia's prestige, ambitions, and importance after Poltava provided the main impetus; a secondary purpose was the search for western expertise to advance the Petrine transformation. When the fighting began, Russia had one permanent mission abroad: in Poland-Lithuania, created as recently as 1688. Within a year this had counterparts in Sweden, Denmark, Austria, and the Ottoman Empire. These embassies were followed by the Dutch Republic (1700), Brandenburg-Prussia (1707), Great Britain (1710), Hanover (1711), France (1720), and Spain (1724). By the time of Peter's death, Russia had no fewer than twelve permanent embassies abroad, together with a number of consulates, and there were eleven foreign missions in the Russian capital.[58] Within one generation it had become part of a continent-wide network of reciprocal diplomacy.

Russia's diplomatic emergence was accompanied by a sustained attempt to learn from, and also to translate, many of the writings which provided the theoretical foundation of the wider international system. Initiatives such as these, which began long before 1700, exemplified Russia's determination to master diplomacy's distinctive political culture.[59] Language was to be a major obstacle. By 1689 the so-called Ambassadorial Department (Posol'skii Prikaz) already contained fifteen translators, though many were expert in the languages of Eurasia and of the polities to which Moscow had traditionally sent embassies, and this number increased to twenty-three by 1701. Yet finding diplomats of the requisite social standing able to converse in the languages of central, far less western, Europe was to be a continuing problem. The contemporary emergence of French as the principal language of diplomacy intensified the challenge, since at first relatively few Russian noblemen were able to converse in French. This situation gradually improved, partly due to Peter's initiative in sending noblemen to learn western European languages and to experience foreign countries at first hand, though it resurfaced after his death in 1725 and would long be an obstacle to Russia's full incorporation.[60]

There were other symptoms of Russia's emergence. The traditional framework for conducting diplomacy, the Ambassadorial Department, was replaced as part of the wider Petrine administrative overhaul, first by the Ambassadorial Chancellery (after 1710) and then by the College of Foreign Affairs (1719). This gave the Russian Empire what many European states were acquiring at this time: a larger, more modern and specialised department equipped to handle the vastly expanded volume of negotiations created by its enhanced status and ambitions. In 1712 a western commentator, the Abbé de Saint-Pierre, unequivocally ranked Russia—for the first time—among the continent's leading powers.[61] Four years later the French *Almanach Royal* listed the Romanov family among Europe's ruling dynasties, again for the first time. A generation later, when Jean Rousset de Missy produced his celebrated guide to diplomatic ceremonial at Europe's courts, Russia was prominently included: along with other outlying polities which had only recently been admitted to full membership of the integrated states system such as Sweden, Brandenburg-Prussia, and Poland-Lithuania.[62] This was the clearest possible guide to the extent of Russia's political integration.

The successful efforts made to keep Europe's two parallel wars separate until peace could be restored in the western half of the continent, were symptomatic of a more fundamental political change. Russia's territorial gains at Sweden's expense in 1721 announced the emergence of a new great power, as Europe's leading states would begin to be styled during the third quarter of the eighteenth century.

Contemporary definitions of this status emphasised that such a state should have the resources to pursue an independent foreign policy without external support, whether financial or military. Russia certainly met this test by Peter the Great's death in 1725, and its status would be further enhanced by the vast territorial gains during Catherine the Great's reign (1762-96). Its new power and ambitions, and the political integration of the continent which these fostered, were the most important legacies of the Great Northern War and of Sweden's decisive military defeat.

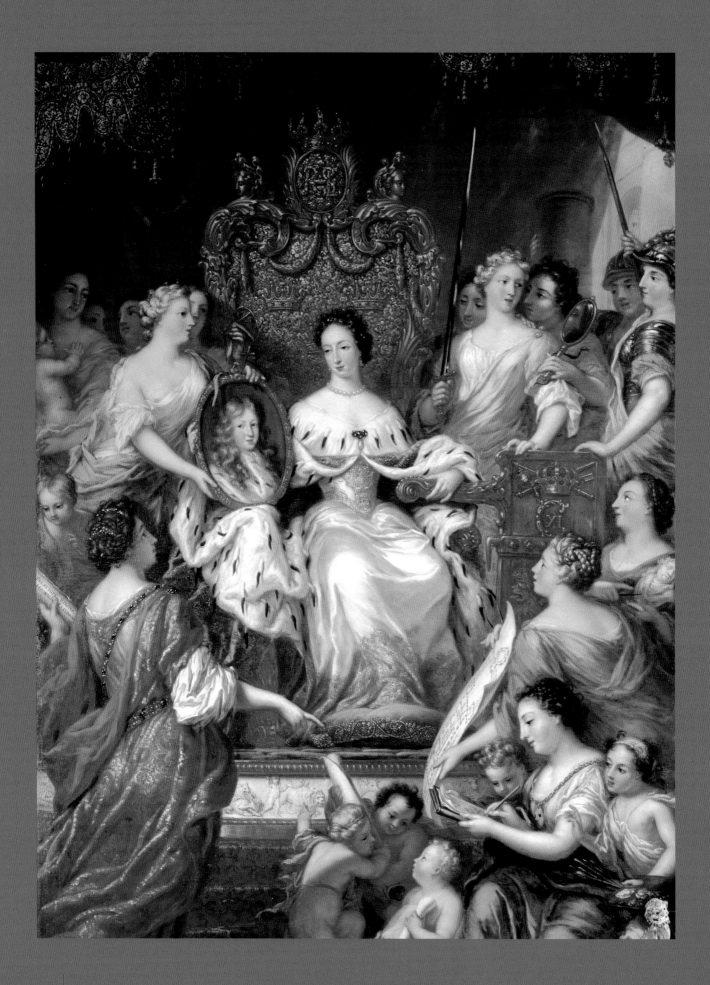

CHAPTER 2

# Charles XII
## *A Biographical Sketch*

by Åsa Karlsson

More than three hundred years after Charles XII acceded to the throne, he continues to be a source of fascination. He was born in 1682, two years after his father, Charles XI, had introduced absolutism to Sweden, gathering all political power into his own hands. Charles XII succeeded his father when he was only 15 years old, and at 18 was forced to go to war when Denmark, Saxony, and Russia launched a combined assault on Sweden. For the rest of his life he was either on campaign or in exile, attempting to maintain Sweden's status as a great power. His death on 11 December 1718 (30 November 1718 according to the Swedish calendar) marked the definitive end to the Swedish Empire and royal absolutism alike.

Charles XII has long been a controversial figure and has excited considerable interest among historians and a wide cross section of the general public. His personality is often found as puzzling as his actions. For historians, some of his decisions are difficult to understand. Why did he choose to embark on a campaign against Russia in 1707? Why did he choose to remain in the Ottoman Empire for five years? Why did he march on Norway? The fading knowledge of history among the general public has meant that such questions no longer receive much attention. Speculation is now mostly limited to how the king died: was he killed by an enemy bullet, or murdered by one of his own side? There is also some interest in the reasons why he never married. Was it a sign that he was a homosexual?

Whether we can understand someone like Charles XII at a remove of several centuries is questionable. It is a good start, at least, to recognise his role as an absolute monarch and as a military commander. In the early modern era it was both important and honourable to play one's part well. Spontaneity or remaining true to oneself were not qualities that were applauded at the time. This makes it difficult for later observers to get to know the king's personality. In the sources available to us, we find contrasting depictions that to varying degrees mirror the impression that Charles XII himself wished to present to those around him. New interpretations that emerged after his death also influence our view of him.

■ **The New Dynasty**

Charles XII was a much longed-for son, but he was not his parents' first child.[1] His sister Hedvig Sofia had been born the previous year, yet a princess was not what Sweden's ruling dynasty needed. On 27 June 1682 a prince was born, in the royal castle of Tre

*Allegory representing Queen Hedvig Eleonora's regency during the minority of her son, Charles XII of Sweden.*

*Painting by David Ehrenstrahl (1628-98), 1692. Nationalmuseum, Stockholm, Sweden.*

Kronor in Stockholm. The event was celebrated in the capital all that day and night, with much wetting of the baby's head. His father noted in his diary that 'On the 17th, on the Saturday morning . . . my wife was delivered of a son, praise and eternal thanks be to God, who aided her, and may He soon return her to her former health.'[2] The son was named Karl (Charles) after his father and grandfather, a name which signalled his membership of the Pfalz-Zweibrücken branch of the House of Vasa. When he was christened just under a month later, one of his godparents was Queen Christina, who by then had been living in Rome for over 25 years—it was on her abdication in 1654 that the throne had passed to Charles X Gustav, the prince's grandfather.

Charles XII's mother was a Danish princess, Ulrika Eleonora, who had become queen of Sweden in 1680. As was normal for royalty at the time, his parents' marriage had been purely one of political convenience. Their betrothal in 1675 was an attempt to prevent the looming war between Sweden and Denmark. As it turned out, the war could not be avoided, but the engagement stood, and marriage ceremonies took place after peace was concluded. Despite the less than auspicious start, there were many who bore witness to the couple's happiness. When the queen died in 1693, only 37 years old, Charles XI was grief-stricken, and he could never bring himself to take a new wife, despite pressure from those around him.

In addition to being a happy family occasion, the birth of the little prince was an important dynastic and political event. The House of Pfalz-Zweibrücken had not occupied the Swedish throne for very long. Charles X Gustav's reign had only lasted six years, but in that time he had conducted several campaigns that expanded the borders of Sweden. Indeed, it was during his reign that the Swedish Empire reached its greatest extent. Sweden was not especially populous. In 1700, it had 2.5 to 3 million people—a very small number compared to that of France, which with its 20 million people had both the largest population and one of the highest population densities in Europe. Geographically, however, Sweden was far larger. It consisted of the landmass which makes up present-day Sweden and Finland, plus the German provinces which it had held since the Peace of Westphalia in 1648— which were essential, as they provided a justification for Sweden to act as a European power, and a base from which to do so—and the Baltic provinces of Estonia, Livonia, and Ingria, plus the county of Kexholm in Karelia.

Charles X Gustav not only enlarged his realm, he also began a process of strengthening royal power. In the mid-seventeenth century, this process was underway in many European states. Large armies and the need for increased public revenue to finance war had contributed to this development. Sweden already had what by contemporary standards was a well-organised bureaucracy, which successfully raised both money and men for the army. Political power lay with the king, the Privy Council, and the Diet. The Diet was a gathering of the four estates—nobles, clerics, burghers, and peasants— but was largely dominated by Sweden's elite, the nobility, who were also in the majority in the Privy Council. Charles X Gustav, however, succeeded in increasing his power at the expense of the Privy Council and the Diet. The military campaigns were contributing factors in this development, for in the field the king ruled with the help of a council of war whose members he appointed himself. While at war, when decisions needed to

be made quickly, it seemed natural that the king and his field chancery would have a stronger position relative to the government in Stockholm. A similar development took place during the Skåne War in the 1670s, when Charles XI concentrated power in his field chancery and ruled with the help of a few trusted advisors.

Charles X Gustav had died in 1660 when his son was only five years old, so the country was ruled by a regency council for the next twelve years. During that time, the high aristocracy was able to regain some of the ground it had lost, but when Charles XI attained his majority and acceded to the throne in 1672, he continued his father's efforts to strengthen royal power.

Two years before the birth of the future Charles XII, Charles XI had taken a decisive step towards seizing all political power in Sweden: at the Diet of 1680 he was declared independent of the Privy Council, and thereafter ruled as an absolute monarch without having to consult the Privy Council before making decisions. On the same occasion, it was decided there was to be a 'Great Reduction' of noble estates, a re-enfeoffment of property that had previously been granted to the high aristocracy,

*Charles XII as a baby, playing on a silver drum.*

*Painting by David Ehrenstrahl (1628-98), 1684. Nationalmuseum, Stockholm, Sweden.*

but which now was returned to the Crown. The Great Reduction strengthened public finances substantially, while weakening the economic basis of aristocratic power.

In 1682, Charles XI also engineered his independence of the Diet. In so doing, he succeeded in attaining his father's political goal: royal absolutism. Yet, this change would be only temporary if he had no heir. In the early modern period, political power was still very much an individual attribute, and this was only further emphasised by the establishment of an absolute monarchy. With the birth of a son, Charles XI could finally hope that his absolutist achievements would not die with him.

An important member of the royal household was Charles XII's paternal grandmother Hedvig Eleonora. She came from the duchy of Holstein-Gottorp and had married Charles X Gustav in 1654. Widowed when only 24 years old, she was queen dowager until her death in 1715 and sat on the regency councils for both her son Charles XI (1660-72) and her grandson Charles XII (April-December 1697). She played another important role, albeit one with less overt political influence, during Charles XII's absence on campaign in 1700-15, when she was the senior resident representative of the royal house. As a widow, she commanded a substantial income from her dower lands (the estates allocated for her maintenance), which she used to strengthen the position of the House of Pfalz-Zweibrücken, amongst other things by building and furnishing several mansions, commissioning art, and supporting Swedish cultural life. The castles, furniture, and paintings all extolled the royal house and its absolute power.[3]

Despite the birth of Charles XII, the future of the royal house was not secure. Many children died of disease in infancy, which was just as true of the Swedish royal family. Of their five sons, only Charles grew to adulthood. His four younger brothers all died before the age of two, to the great grief of their parents. The couple did have another daughter, however, who was christened Ulrika Eleonora after her mother. In 1719 she became queen after her brother was killed in battle. The early deaths of their other sons meant that Charles XII's parents were very concerned about their children's health, and Ulrika Eleonora was an unusually active presence in their lives compared to other contemporary queens. Diaries and letters bear witness to the fact that she nearly always kept the children at her side.

## ■ The Education of a Crown Prince

As a young prince, Charles received a thorough and extensive education to prepare him for his role as king. In his earliest years, it was his mother who was primarily responsible for his upbringing and schooling. His religious education was of paramount importance. Morning and night he said his prayers with his mother, who also taught him biblical stories. Every day he was tutored by Bishop Erik Benzelius, who would go through a chapter of the Bible and explain the sermon for the coming Sunday. Charles XII remained a faithful reader of the Bible his whole life, but we know less about his private prayer as an adult. In Ukraine in the summer of 1709, a young second lieutenant called Petré noted seeing the king on his knees under a cherry tree, sunk deep in prayer, which suggests that religion remained important to Charles XII.

It was characteristic of the times that absolutism had strongly theocratic overtones: it was believed that the king derived his power directly from God and was answerable to him alone. It is important to bear in mind that it was in this spirit that Charles XII was raised. He was the first Swedish sovereign who was born to rule with absolute authority. It is probably impossible to overestimate the significance of this fact in his conception of himself and in his understanding of his role and responsibilities as king.

During Charles's childhood in the 1680s, his father was heavily engaged in refashioning many aspects of Swedish society. One important area was the Church. A series of reforms were introduced that were intended to create a unified Evangelical Lutheran Church, of which all of Charles XI's Swedish subjects would be members. The king wanted to instil confessional unity, and a number of official publications were to further this goal, including a new catechism, psalter, and hymnal. A new translation of the Bible was also begun, although it would not be completed until the reign of Charles XII—indeed, it is still known as the Charles XII Bible.

Charles XII's childhood was officially over at the age of six, and responsibility for his upbringing passed from his mother to his tutors. The change was marked by the prince moving out of the queen's quarters, as Charles XI noted in his diary: 'On the evening of 2 January, Prince Charles slept for the first time in his own room, and came under the care of men.'[4] Besides having his own suite of apartments, the young boy had his own household and a private regiment.

The first surviving plan for his education dates from this period. Charles XI himself listed what his son needed to learn. Naturally, the first item was religious instruction, followed by knowledge of Swedish, German, and arithmetic. The remainder of the list shows that the young prince was expected to study a series of daunting subjects. After familiarising himself with recent parliamentary legislation, he was to learn about military matters. Charles XI also regarded the law and the legal process as important subjects, as well as fortification, artillery, fencing, and riding. All this for a six-year-old child.[5]

When the prince was eight years old, a new curriculum that was more in line with the standard classical models was designed for him. First came the Bible, which he was to read each morning, retelling afterwards what he had learned. Language studies now also included Latin. Initially, though, he was to be spared the worst of the grammar cramming, and instead was to read Latin fables to minimise 'boredom and that dislike of study, which easily could insinuate itself into His Royal Majesty's heart.'[6]

In addition to Latin, the prince was to study classical history in detail, and he was to immerse himself in the history of leading figures who might serve as examples to follow once he was king. It was important to mould his character, and this second plan states that the prince 'must become used to taking pleasure in good advice.'[7] On this point his tutors did not fully achieve their educational targets: the adult Charles XII was deeply reluctant to take advice and preferred to follow his own inclinations.

This was an age when an aristocratic education included learning to ride, fence, and dance. Prince Charles acquired these skills and had his own dancing master. Riding and fencing were especially important accomplishments that he would need as the country's military commander, for according to Swedish tradition the king led the armed forces in practice, and not just in name. He learned to ride early, inspecting his first guard of honour on his fourth birthday, while his ever-present mother watched from a coach.

From the age of nine, Charles was taught the art of fortification, which became his favourite subject. His father's and grandfather's campaigns were used as teaching material, which he learned by heart: as an adult he was still able to give a detailed account of Charles X Gustav's three-day battle in 1655 with the Poles at Warsaw. Both his father and grandfather served as important examples. His father's death at a young age surely strengthened Charles's ambition to follow the path set out for him. His grasp on the reins of power and his desire to reform Swedish society show clear traces of his father's policies, while his long campaigns and conduct of war on several fronts bear similarities to the situation his grandfather had faced in the 1650s. A careful student of history, Charles XII could hardly have been unaware of these parallels.

An important object of Charles XI's reforming zeal had been military affairs. One prime concern had been to create a standing army—the backbone of any absolutist regime. Charles XI's military reforms constituted the basis of the Caroline army that was to become so famous throughout Europe under the leadership of his son. The soldiers were drilled regularly, and Charles XI often took part in regimental manoeuvres and troop inspections. Sometimes Prince Charles was allowed to accompany his father, as is recorded in Charles XI's diary. When the prince was 12 years old, his father noted: 'On 23 July, His Majesty drilled the Guards in the morning out in Apollohagen, His Royal Highness the Prince accompanying.'[8]

The prince also took part in the hunts that his father loved so much. Charles XI recorded with pleasure that at the age of eight his son had shot three stags in Djurgården, the royal game park in Stockholm, and at twelve shot his first bear.[9] After the queen's death, the bond between father and son became even closer. The prince almost always accompanied the king on his travels; he was also present at court ceremonies and celebrations. In 1692 a banquet was held at Stockholm Castle to celebrate the visit of the royal family's German relatives. Some 40 couples took part, each costumed as instructed by a prepared list. All the members of the royal family were involved: Prince Charles was a 'Muscovite' and Princess Ulrika Eleonora wore Swedish traditional dress from the province of Dalarna. After a procession through the palace, everyone sat down to dinner, served by young men and women from noble families. The guests enjoyed a meal of 125 dishes, rounded off by 28 pyramids of confectionery. After the banquet, the hall was prepared for a ball, which lasted the whole night. Prince Charles was thus given the chance to show what he had learned from his dancing master.[10] After his mother's death, the following year, these kinds of festivities became much less common.

## ■ The Young King

Charles XI died in the spring of 1697, only 41 years old. A couple of days before his death, Prince Charles had been closeted alone with his father. Not much is

*Carolus delineavit. A° 1689*

known about what the king said to him, other than that he should fear God and love his subjects. It is likely that Charles XI also gave his son concrete advice about whom to trust and whom to be wary of. The king surely knew that those opposed to royal absolutism would attempt to capitalise on his death, and also that his son might be manipulated in matters of foreign policy.

When Charles XI died, a regency government was appointed which included the queen dowager, Hedvig Eleonora. It was not to last long, however, because the supporters of absolutism, led by the royal advisors Lars Wallenstedt and Carl Piper, set about having the king declared of age, thereby limiting the opposition's opportunities to act. When the Diet convened in November 1697, the estates called upon Charles XII to take up the reins of government. He agreed, and thus came into his majority as king when he was only 15.

When Charles XII came of age, he had not completed his education: it had been intended to continue until he was 18, but was now broken off early. None of those close to the king thought this was appropriate, but those who supported the declaration of majority were more numerous and more powerful. There is no indication of what the king himself thought, but he had been told his entire life that God had chosen him to rule Sweden, and now the time had come to assume that role.

It was in conjunction with the coronation, and more specifically the ceremony itself, that it became clear to many what absolutism actually entailed.[11]

*A drawing by the young Charles XII, depicting combat near a tent.*

*Pen and ink drawing by Charles XII of Sweden (1682-1718), ca. 1689. National-museum, Stockholm, Sweden.*

Royal coronations were ancient rituals in Sweden, with a ceremonial form of ancient pedigree. On most points Charles XII followed tradition, but afterwards it was the departures from the Swedish norm that observers mostly remembered. The ceremonies were held on 24 and 25 December 1697, only a few weeks after Charles XI's funeral, so the participants were still in mourning. On the first day the king, seated on a podium furnished with a throne and a canopy of state before which were placed two bronze lions, received the homage of his subjects. He had made his entrance onto the podium through a door at the back of the hall, and afterwards left the same way. For the entire ceremony it was as if he were on a stage, quite literally above all the other participants, his superior status duly spelled out. The ceremony itself drove home this message. The four estates demonstrated their loyalty to the king by swearing an oath of fealty, after which everyone came forward in order of precedence to kiss his hand.

The act of homage was not new in itself, but the fact that it happened before the king took the royal oath was a break with tradition. The next day, the actual coronation took place—or, rather, the anointment, as it was termed in official documents. When Charles XII processed to Storkyrkan, Stockholm's cathedral, he was already wearing the crown. It was a statement that he had been born an absolute monarch, and so did not need to be crowned to achieve this position. This was much commented upon by the foreign diplomatic corps, as was an incident which occurred when the king was about to mount his horse: the crown fell off, whereupon the king himself put it back on again. This was interpreted as a bad omen for Charles XII's reign. The procession was the scene of another novelty, for only the king was mounted and everyone else had to walk, which once again ensured that he was shown as being superior to all others. The religious part of the ceremony was held in Storkyrkan. After prayers and a sermon, Charles XII took off the crown and kneeled before the high altar. The archbishop anointed him with holy oil, and Charles replaced the crown on his head.

The unique aspects of Charles XII's coronation have often been emphasised by later commentators, but the changes were not without contemporary precedent, for the ceremony bore similarities to Denmark's first coronation of an absolute monarch in 1671, when Christian V was anointed—but not crowned—in a similar fashion. It is not unlikely that Charles XII and his advisors drew inspiration from this modification to his uncle's anointing.

Equally, Charles XII did not take a royal oath at the coronation, which surprised those who attended. The oath of fealty sworn by the estates therefore received no response. The king was 'anointed by God' and was answerable only to God, not to his subjects, the Diet, or the government. They, on the other hand, were to trust him and obey him.

Modern scholars have increasingly emphasised how rites and ceremonies are not just of symbolic importance, but are political in themselves and send messages to those watching. From this perspective, Charles XII's coronation is telling. It shows how the king and his closest circle regarded royal absolutism. It was made perfectly clear that Charles XII would take autocracy to a new level.

His father had been an absolute monarch, but he had still retained the traditional forms of politics, for example by summoning the Diet. Charles XII did not.

## ■ To Marry or Not?

One pressing question in the first year of Charles XII's reign was the future of the House of Pfalz-Zweibrücken. An appropriate queen had to be found, but this did not prove easy.[12] The king's intended had to be of a suitable age and come from a Lutheran royal house. Thoughts turned to Denmark and the king's cousin, Princess Sophia Hedvig. She was said to be very much like Charles XII's mother in appearance, which appealed to him. He could not inspect his prospective bride himself and, instead, one of his pages was sent to the Danish court in order to report back. The page delivered a highly complimentary description of Princess Sophia's beauty and goodness, which did not lessen the king's interest. However, things had not progressed beyond that stage when war broke out in 1700.

The king's marriage had to wait until after the war, but as this dragged on ever longer, the lack of a queen and an heir became troubling. Queen Dowager Hedvig Eleonora, who was always alert to dynastic matters, wrote in the 1710s to the field chancery in the Ottoman Empire on this matter; she did not wish to write to Charles XII directly and, instead, addressed the letter to the secretary of state, Casten Feif. Because Charles XII read Feif's correspondence—a secretary of state on campaign had little in the way of a private life—he learned of his grandmother's unease. Atypically, he wrote back in person, promising to marry, but not before there was peace.[13]

The fact that the king never married has been the subject of extensive speculation that he might have been homosexual. It is impossible for posterity to learn anything definite about Charles XII's sexuality, for the sources are silent on this point and speculation has been fuelled largely by the simple fact that he remained a bachelor. Charles XII himself believed that he had to remain unmarried while the war lasted, just like his father during the Skåne War of the 1670s. Charles XI had only married Ulrika Eleonora after the end of that war.

## ■ The First Year in Power

Charles XII had been on the throne for barely three years when the Great Northern War began, in 1700. These early years of his reign have rarely been considered by historians, but they constituted an intensive time for the young king.[14] How was he affected by shouldering the heavy responsibility of ruling a country at the age of 15? It seems that he changed greatly as a person after coming of age. From having been open and showing an interest in most things, he became self-contained and silent. He listened to others' opinions, but kept his own views to himself. Perhaps it was a way for the young man to cope with his new role. By adopting a quiet, reserved demeanour, he could mask his insecurity and lack of experience.

He followed his father's example in everything. He applied himself diligently to the business of government and took pains to understand the issues. When faced with conflicting opinions, he asked himself what Charles XI would have done, and followed that line. Yet, he was not a copy of his father. Charles XII seems to have been generous with money and gifts, both to the poor and to his friends, which Charles XI never was. Contemporaries even complained about the way he squandered money. His youth also showed at times, whether in occasional bouts of wild partying or in his superciliousness towards people he did not like. This was particularly true of the old men among the nobility, for example Bengt Oxenstierna, whom he could treat very haughtily.

This period on home turf did not last long. In 1700 the king left Stockholm, never again to return to his capital and the traditional life of the court in which he had grown up; he would spend the rest of his life in the field, commanding his army. Even if conditions on campaign were not quite as spartan as is sometimes made out, they were certainly quite different from life in the palace in Stockholm. The king spent the majority of his waking hours on horseback in personal reconnaissance, inspecting dispositions, defences, and troop conditions and quartering. He himself lived in a rather simple fashion, hence the comparatively plain uniform he chose to wear, and without a wig—which was unusual among the elite.

He combined a modest lifestyle with active participation in combat. That he should fight was not at all self-evident. Most European princes contented themselves with observing their engagements from a nearby vantage point. Swedish kings, however, had a tradition of personally leading their troops into battle. Charles XII followed this tradition and explained why: since his soldiers were ordered to defend their homeland, he believed it was important to show that he, too, was willing to risk his life by fighting alongside them. Naturally, this was not without risks, and Charles XII was wounded on several occasions.

The Great Northern War, its decisive consequences for foreign relations, its battles, and life under canvas dominated Charles XII's life from 1700 until his death. These aspects of the war are covered in other chapters in this volume.[15] The key feature of the war addressed here is Charles XII's role as an absolute monarch, and the way he succeeded in ruling his kingdom from a distance. The impact his policies had on the situation at home is, however, treated elsewhere.[16]

## ■ A Distant King

From the outbreak of war until the autumn of 1715, Charles XII found himself far from his kingdom. This must have appeared wholly unique to his contemporaries: yes, he was an absolute monarch and held all political power, yet he did not wield that power from a base in his own capital, or even in his own kingdom. During the victorious early stages of the war, he handed a great deal of political responsibility to the government at home. Relations between the king and his officials in Stockholm were not particularly good, however. From the very outset there was dissent about how and where the war should be conducted.[17] This continued throughout the war, and the conflict deepened further after the defeat at Poltava. The king was rarely inclined to listen to the Privy Council and, instead, often chose to follow his own counsel. This was especially true in foreign affairs, whereas in matters of domestic politics he accepted help from his various officials more readily.

As long as the Swedish forces continued to be successful, right up to Poltava in 1709, the government at home was left responsible for domestic affairs. The matter of raising new resources to fight the war was of foremost importance. The Privy Council, in an attempt to influence the king, reported regularly on the difficult economic situation caused by the war, but he quickly became immune to the complaints, which he regarded as exaggerated. His rejoinder was that the huge costs kept being met, despite the Privy Council's pessimism, and he therefore did not take their concerns seriously. After the Battle of Poltava the differences between the king and the government at home became more acute. From the reforms instituted during the 1710s it appears that Charles XII was influenced by Stockholm's protestations and thus set about improving the state of the public purse. However, this was not at all the effect desired by the Privy Council, whose members had instead hoped that their laments would prompt the king to sue for peace.

After the Battle of Poltava, Charles XII spent five years in the Ottoman Empire. The Swedes settled in Varnitza, a village outside the town of Bender on the present-day border between Moldova and Transnistria. Here they created a 'city' in miniature which went by many names, being called at various times Carlopolis, New Bender, and New Stockholm. The last of these names indicates what this place really was: the new capital of Sweden.

Charles XII remained at Varnitza until February 1713, despite the Ottoman government's increasingly impatient demands that he go home. The start of 1713 saw an escalation in tension, but despite being placed under siege the king refused to give in. It was not until the brief clash known as 'the Skirmish at Bender' (*Kalabaliken i Bender* in Swedish) that he eventually left Varnitza, and then only because he was captured and taken as a prisoner to Edirne (Adrianople) and then on to Didymoteicho in Greece. There he remained until the autumn of 1714, when he made his famous journey through Europe back to Sweden. Taking only two weeks, he rode incognito with two attendants, using a passport in the name of Captain Peter Frisk and wearing a dark wig. He passed through Siebenbürgen in Transylvania, Hungary, and Austria to Nuremberg in Bavaria, and then north to Stralsund.

## ■ Reform

In Varnitza, the king had had a staff of about ten to help him take care of all official business.[18] The most important members of this field chancery were the secretaries of state Henrik Gustaf von Müllern, who was responsible for foreign affairs, and Casten Feif, who handled domestic matters. Formally, it was Charles XII who took all decisions in the field chancery, but his actual participation in the process varied. It appears from letters and reports that it was the king who determined foreign policy, while in domestic affairs, which became increasingly important, he relied more on his advisors.

The nine years between Poltava and the king's death in Norway were characterised by an increasingly urgent hunt for money. More and more Swedes became sub-

Presidenten i Stats Contoret.
Friherre. CASTEN. FEIF
Född 1661 d.29 Sept. död 1759 d.12. Mars
Gift 1691 med ANNA. CHRISTINA. BARKHUSEN

ject to taxation; more and more resources were dedicated to servicing the war. This extensive mobilisation was initiated during the years in exile in the Ottoman Empire, when a large number of reforms were formulated by the king and his advisors.

These reforms concerned Sweden's economy and public finances, but also its administrative organisation. However, even purely administrative changes had a bearing on government revenue, as was the case with the strengthening of the Board of Trade in 1711. Such issues were mostly handled by Casten Feif, a skilled official from a middle-class family in Stockholm and exceptionally well suited to his post. Fascinated by economics, he was well-read in the contemporary economic writers and had a wide range of ideas about ways to develop commerce and public finances.[19]

In common with the prevailing economic theory of the age, Feif thought in the long term when trying to improve the state of the government's finances. He suggested that trade and commerce be stimulated to increase national wealth and thus the king's opportunities to levy taxes. In a letter he wrote that the king was dispirited by his role as a 'lord of impoverished subjects.'[20] Despite his many ideas about encouraging trade and commerce, few of them were actually implemented. Charles XII simply could not wait a decade until a general increase in prosperity would allow him to increase taxes. Money was needed quickly to continue the campaign, and so tax reform was to be the most important component of the economic policy adopted in the years after Poltava.

The constant complaints from the Privy Council informing the king that many of his subjects were unable to pay their taxes, and the fact that the wealthy were exceedingly unwilling to put their resources at the disposal of the Crown, strengthened Charles XII's conviction that the Swedish tax system needed reforms, and in 1713 a capital tax was introduced.

## ■ Equality before the Taxman

The 1713 reform radically changed the basis of taxation on several points. Tax was to be levied equally on all Swedish subjects, no matter which estate they belonged to. It was set at 2 per cent of a person's total wealth, which included everything one owned, even one's clothes. This principle of equality broke with the attitudes that had prevailed:  instead of connecting taxes and other obligations to a person's standing in society, the new capital tax was innovatively based on a person's wealth.

Another important aspect of the reform was that taxpayers were more clearly seen as individuals, separate from the collective society of the estates. At the same time, their property also acquired greater importance and property rights were strengthened as well. Charles's reforms emphasised that it was an individual's total wealth that was taxed, and not, as previously done, the various activities or distinguishing marks related to a person's social status, be they titles, wigs, or fine carriages. Thus, Caroline absolutism took the first steps in dismantling the estates-based society, a process which culminated 150 years later in the replacement of the Diet of the estates by a bicameral Parliament. Today, this may be regarded as a modern, forward-looking development, but the motivation for it must be understood from the perspective of the ideology of an absolute monarch. Charles XII's purpose was to strengthen Sweden's public finances in order to defend it militarily, but the policies implemented in the 1710s should also be seen as an expression of his view of society, an embodiment of his political will.

One revolutionary aspect of the tax reform was that taxpayers were to declare their wealth themselves—an early forerunner of the Swedish system of general taxation through personal tax returns that was introduced in the twentieth century. Another novelty was that the administration of the tax was placed in the hands of an entirely new bureaucracy, the Kontributionsränteriet (the Exchequer of Imposts), which was to ensure that the money was actually used for military expenditure.

While the state of the government's finances had provided the initial motivation to reform the tax system, more money was needed to continue the military campaigns. For this reason, Charles XII was eager to broaden the tax base and to include forms of property that had not previously been taxable. This change affected the country's landed aristocracy most strongly, and its members protested loudly. However, the reform was more than a significant financial adjustment: it also gave expression to a more absolutist view of society than had previously been found in Sweden. Here the king was in fact enlarging on his father's reforms from the 1680s. Charles XII believed that all inhabitants of Sweden were, first and foremost, his subjects, and that all should therefore contribute to their government's finances in the same way, regardless of privileges they might have enjoyed in the past. Underpinning this was an absolutist view of society as a household in which the king was father to all his subjects.

## ■ The Office of the Principal Secretary

Another of Charles XII's important administrative reforms during his years in the Ottoman Empire was the reorganisation of the civil service, which was carried out in the autumn of 1713.[21] The aim was to make the Chancery's operations more effective by various means, for instance through specialisation: previously, the office had suffered from a lack of expertise in several areas, but this was now remedied, strengthening the Chancery's position vis-à-vis the Privy Council and other government offices in the process. The Chancery was divided into six offices, each one responsible for a different area. One of these was Revisionsexpeditionen (the Audit Office), led by Högsta ombudsmannen (the principal secretary). Among its responsibilities, the Audit Office was tasked with supervising the Chancery as a whole, checking that regulations were observed and that officials carried out their duties. In 1719, the Office of the Principal Secretary became the Office of the Chancellor of Justice, which still exists—the longest-lived of Charles XII's administrative reforms.

The work of the Chancery offices was regulated down to the minutiae. Quite apart from the Chancery ordinances, which ran to sixty-three paragraphs, there were specific terms of reference for the principal secretary. These were almost certainly written by Casten Feif, who had gathered information about other countries' approaches to such matters. That the king himself also had a hand in their formulation is suggested by the fact that one of his favourite subjects appears in the ordinances: the instruction that officials should write in plain, lucid Swedish, and not use foreign words, is very much his.

In common with the other administrative reforms at the time, one important reason for the introduction of the 1713 ordinances was to make government more efficient and to increase the king's control over it. Nominally, an absolute monarch exercised total power over his realm, yet in practice there were many obstacles, some of them considerable. One of them was the fact that government operated at various administrative levels, which made it difficult to control the extent to which reforms were actually implemented. Charles XII was clearly unhappy with the government administration in Sweden, from the Privy Council down to individual departments. He was also mistrustful of the ways in which regional and local officials carried out their functions.

There were various attempts to make the government administration adhere more closely to the king's intentions. Through Casten Feif, Charles XII tried to persuade individual officers in Sweden to support his policies, and he also appointed men from Feif's circle to important posts in government. A more formal method was to alter the organisational structure in various ways. It is in this light that the administrative reforms should be regarded, including the creation of the Kontributionsränteriet and the new Chancery ordinances. Indirectly, the new disposition of 1713 reduced the Privy Council's say and increased the personal influence of the king; however, this consequence did not become fully apparent during Charles XII's reign.

A study of Charles XII's reform policies of the 1710s highlights certain typical characteristics that serve to demonstrate the social attitudes of absolutism.[22] It is significant that in his reform policies and his relationship with the Diet—which he never once summoned—Charles XII showed an evident dislike of the estates and the rank-based thinking that had pervaded seventeenth-century feudal society. Instead, for him it was his subjects who were central. As said before, all Swedes were his subjects, and in that sense, from Charles XII's point of view, all his subjects were equal. To talk of equality can sound paradoxical. However, in the early eighteenth century, equality did not have the connotations of democratic change that it has today; instead, equality meant that the king's subjects would be treated alike, whatever their estate. The purpose behind this focus on the king's subjects rather than the estates was surely to create greater sympathy for absolutist royal power. Absolutism was certainly helped by the fact that the wealthy landowning classes were more heavily taxed, while the peasants' and urban bourgeoisie's burden was lightened.

Plainly, Charles XII lost faith in his government in Stockholm in the 1710s, convinced that its members were not making strenuous enough efforts to find resources to fund the war. During these years, the king attempted to gain better control of the central administration by appointing trusted new members of government; by attempting various administrative reforms; and by allowing his closest associates to use their personal networks to influence members of the government. That said, it was only after his return to Sweden that he once again had a firm grasp on the machinery of government.

## ■ Charles XII and the East

In the years following Poltava, contacts with the Ottoman Empire were not limited to diplomacy.[23] The field chancery also discussed trading opportunities, and a secretary from the Board of Trade, Johan Silfvercrantz, was dispatched on a tour to study trade and commerce. Religious issues were of interest as well. At the Swedish legation in Istanbul were Swedish priests who, in addition to caring for their flock, were expected to minister to any Lutherans in Istanbul.

Swedes at this date demonstrated an interest in Ottoman society and culture that went beyond politics, trade, and religion. It was strongly influenced by the religious orthodoxies of Swedish absolutism, which promoted an interest in the language and topography of the Holy Land. During his stay in the Ottoman Empire, Charles XII sponsored three so-called oriental expeditions to the biblical lands. One of these included the legation priest Michael Eneman, who in 1711 set off with the aforementioned Johan Silfvercrantz. Eneman had studied oriental languages at Uppsala

*Sketch of Charles XII.*

*Drawing in black and red crayon by Johan David Swartz (1678-1740), ca. 1708-10. Kungliga Biblioteket, Stockholm, Sweden. Maps and Pictures PH St.f. Kungl. Karl XII 2.*

University and was extremely eager to visit the Holy Land. Their main destination was the holy sites, but, under the influence of Silfvercrantz, the expedition's remit was broadened to include identifying the potential for trade, and especially Swedish products it might be possible to sell in the Ottoman Empire.

## ■ Back on Swedish Soil

In the autumn of 1714, Charles XII finally returned to Sweden. He made his way first to Swedish Pomerania and the city of Stralsund—then in the fourth year of its siege— where he remained until December 1715. He then handed command to General Dücker and gave the order that the city capitulate once the king had set sail for the Swedish mainland. From Stralsund, he crossed to the southernmost mainland province of Skåne (Scania), where he established his headquarters because he would be better able to resume the reins of power from there. Sweden was in a precarious state both at home and abroad. Danish troops threatened from the south and west; in the east, Finland was ruled by the Russian army; the economy and government finances were in a terrible condition after many years of war. The king's way out of this crisis was yet another war, this time against Norway.

It was at this point that the Holsteiner Georg Heinrich von Görtz became Charles XII's most important advisor, even though he did not hold any formal office in Sweden. He occupied a vital position when he became head of the newly formed Upphandlingsdeputationen (Procurement Commission), which took over leadership of the whole of the central treasury department, causing dissatisfaction among Swedish officials. After the king's death, Görtz was arrested for his extreme financial policies and was executed after a summary trial.

At the siege of Fredriksten, the fortress at the border town of Fredrikshald (Halden), Charles XII was shot and killed on 11 December 1718 (30 November 1718, according to the Swedish calendar). Who fired the shot that killed the king has been a topic of debate ever since. Was he killed by a hired assassin from his own lines, or was it an enemy bullet? Various eyewitness accounts, several post-mortem examinations of the body, most recently in 1917, and ballistics investigations have not been able to settle the question. Most, however, believe that it was an enemy bullet that ended Charles XII's life.[24]

## ■ The End of Absolutism

The bullet that killed the king also spelled the death of Swedish absolutism. Charles XII, who had so admired his father and grandfather and followed dutifully in their tracks, had taken a course of action that ironically reduced to naught what they had achieved: absolute rule ended and Sweden lost its position as a great power. The king's sister, Ulrika Eleonora, and her husband, Friedrich of Hesse-Kassel, acted quickly and decisively in an attempt to uphold royal power. Ulrika Eleonora declared herself to be the absolute monarch as soon as she heard that her brother had been killed, but the political winds were not in her favour. The Swedish estates

had had enough of absolutism and were determined to claw back their powers; government officials were disgruntled by all the new administrative arrangements and years of unpaid salaries; the military were exhausted by the long and increasingly fruitless campaigns; and the Swedish populace had had more than enough of taxes, conscription, billeted soldiers, and military purveyors. Ulrika Eleonora was deposed and absolute sovereign power ended. Ultimately she did become queen, however, albeit as an elective monarch and stripped of most of her powers.[25]

## ■ The Judgment of Posterity

*A man extraordinary rather than a great man, and fitter to be admired than imitated. His life, however, may be a lesson to Kings, and teach them, that a peaceful and happy reign is more to be desired than so much glory.*[26]

This was Voltaire's summation of the life of Charles XII. These words have been read by millions around the world, for few books have run to quite so many editions as this biography of the Swedish king. For many readers in Sweden, it has provided a way into the French language, while at the same time giving them a lasting impression of the Swedish king's life and character.

Voltaire had begun to toy with the idea of writing about Charles XII as early as the 1720s. He had met Görtz personally in 1716, at a time when the latter was the king's closest advisor, and later on he met many others who had known Charles XII. Yet, even though Voltaire was a contemporary with access to sources close to the king, his account is very much his own. Thanks to his skilfully constructed biography, Voltaire has—directly or indirectly—coloured people's understanding of Charles XII ever since.

In the eighteenth and nineteenth centuries, opinion on Charles XII was divided. The gulf between the adulation of his admirers and the jaundiced view of his detractors was enormous. For his supporters, he was a courageous hero-king who fought against overwhelming odds to his last drop of blood. His critics instead saw a man drunk on war, who drove the Swedish Empire to ruin. A stream of publications—poems, novels, plays, and history books—mirrored the opposing viewpoints. However, there was one thing common to both sides: they all acknowledged the king as a decisive figure in Swedish history.

Towards the end of the nineteenth century, the dispute over Charles XII entered a new phase. He now became a political weapon. First up was the minister of war, Axel Rappe, who in 1892 gave a lecture in which he discussed Charles XII's Russian campaign. Rappe emphasised Charles XII's brilliance as a military strategist and leader. The lecture was given just as Parliament was discussing Rappe's proposals for a new defence plan. It might seem strange that a lecture about Charles XII could have contemporary relevance, but in the late nineteenth century it was common in public debate to use historical arguments. Examples were plucked from the arsenal provided by history in support of many arguments. Charles XII was thus used by the military hawks to argue that defence spending should increase. The proposed plan was indeed passed by Parliament.

However, the use of Charles XII as a national figurehead and, in right-wing propaganda, for a stronger defence did not go unopposed. Because he appealed to the general public and because his memory could be a powerful argument when used adroitly, it was important for the more left-minded to lay their own claim. The most skilful among them was August Strindberg. He, too, recognised the connection between the modern defence reforms and Charles XII, whom he regarded as the root cause of all of Sweden's miseries. In a text published in 1910, Strindberg wrote: 'That the founder of the country, Gustav Vasa, with his undoubtedly great qualities, should be celebrated is, of course, also right. But in rallying the nation around this scourge, this notorious destroyer, there is definitely something sick, not to say rotten!'[27]

The debate about Charles XII in the early years of the twentieth century also left its mark on historical research, for despite developing new scholarly approaches, Swedish historians found it difficult to free themselves of these preconceptions. Unfortunately, eagerness to pronounce judgment on the king was so strong that accounts of his actions, and indeed the time in which he lived, were forgotten. It was only in the later twentieth century that it became possible for academics to study the age of Charles XII without being drawn into a political conflict over his legacy.

Charles XII still excites a great deal of interest among the Swedish public, which was probably why the anniversary of his death became a focus for political struggle in the early 1990s. Swedish neo-Nazis and racist groups held demonstrations, which were met by counterdemonstrations by anti-racist groups. For several years, 30 November became a day on which people stood up to be counted for or against Swedish immigration, and the violence which often resulted was firmly in the media spotlight. Exactly why Charles XII was chosen as a symbol of racism has been hard to explain—which is surely why these demonstrations ceased after a few years. The nationalistic veneer imparted to Charles XII by right-wing politicians a hundred years ago was probably the most important reason why the king had again surfaced in Swedish political debate.

*The Battle of Poltava - 8 July 1709.*

*Engraving with watercolour by Charles-Louis Simonneau the Elder (1645-1728), after Pierre-Denis Martin, 1724-28. The State Hermitage Museum, Saint Petersburg, Russia. © The State Hermitage Museum / photo by Svetlana Suetova, Konstantin Sinyavsky.*

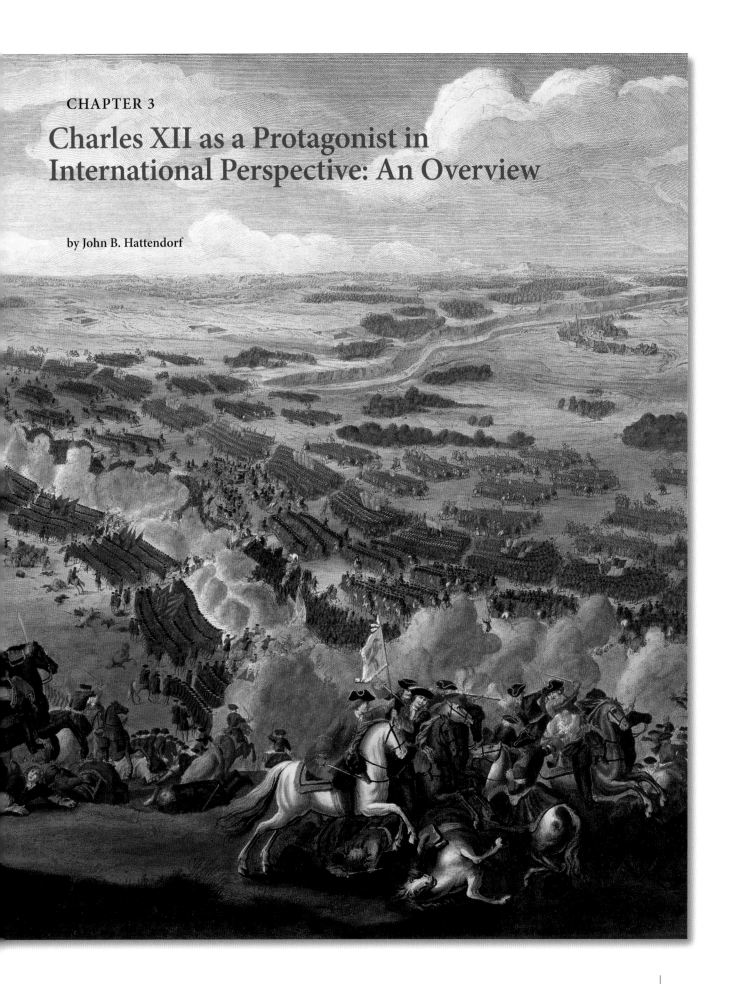

# CHAPTER 3

# Charles XII as a Protagonist in International Perspective: An Overview

by John B. Hattendorf

On King Charles XI's death in 1697, he bequeathed to his 14-year old son, Charles XII, a strong absolutist state with very well-equipped and trained armed forces. Charles XI had built and refined the Swedish absolutist state so to be largely dependent upon the characteristics of his personal rule. As the British historian Anthony F. Upton described Charles XI:

> Here was a king with a proven ability as a warrior, who sought to avoid involvement in war, the universal sport of kings. He was cautious, conservative on most things, but willing to contemplate change, a pious, workaholic administrator, ruled by his conception of how God required him to guide and protect his subjects.[1]

Charles XI's policy of maintaining neutrality in war and serving as a balancing power for the conflicts between other states in the 1680s and 1690s had been a crucial factor in establishing the conditions for effective internal reorganisation within Sweden. At the same time, Charles XI and his advisors harboured fears over the dominance of France under Louis XIV. They also had concerns that the Stadholder-King William III might unite the Dutch Republic and England in a way that would make the Maritime Powers into an overbearing influence in northern affairs. In response, they decided that the best course for Sweden was to stand outside the power struggle in western Europe during the Nine Years' War between 1688 and 1697. Sweden was to be an independent state that could mediate or even intervene in a war at a decisive point to exploit its position. Under Charles XI, this policy had initially been beneficial to Sweden and helped the kingdom become a mediator among other nations. In the end, however, this self-centred independence sowed distrust. By the time of Charles XI's death, Sweden's role as a mediator at the Peace of Rijswijk had become an honorary post with little influence.[2]

## ■ The Origins of the Great Northern War

Shortly after Charles XII's accession to the throne, Duke Friedrich IV of Holstein-Gottorp, married Charles's elder sister, Princess Hedvig Sofia. The marriage was only the latest in a series of dynastic connections that cemented a political and strategic position for both the kings of Sweden and the dukes of Holstein-Gottorp. Earlier, the queens consort of kings Charles IX Gustav and Charles X of Sweden had also come from the House of Holstein-Gottorp. The continuing political and strategic issues centred around the fact that the kings of Denmark and the dukes of Holstein-Gottorp ruled a patchwork of intermingled territories in the provinces of Schleswig and Holstein on Denmark's southern border. They were located not far from the Swedish territories in Germany: Bremen and Verden to the southwest and Swedish Pomerania to the southeast. Swedish leaders calculated that their support to Holstein-Gottorp provided the means to contain Denmark and to prevent a Danish invasion of Sweden.

Facing the new regime in Sweden, King Christian V of Denmark-Norway looked at two main options to try to resolve the situation on his southern border. On the one hand, he offered Charles XII the opportunity to marry his daughter, Sophie Hedvig, as a means to balance the marriage of the duke of Holstein-Gottorp and to continue the dynastic alliance that Charles XI had by his Danish marriage. On the other hand, Chris-

tian opened secret negotiations with Augustus II of Saxony and Poland and Tsar Peter of Russia with the idea of a coordinated triple attack on Sweden before the young Charles XII was securely in charge as king. Following Christian V's death in the summer of 1699, his son and successor, King Frederik IV, pursued these plans energetically after it became apparent that the teenage Charles XII was not interested in marriage to Frederik's sister or any other suitors. The three sovereigns developed a plan that called for Augustus to attack Swedish Livonia, Peter of Russia to attack Sweden's Baltic provinces on the southern shore of the Gulf of Finland (Estland and Ingermanland), while Denmark would attack the south to drive the duke of Holstein-Gottorp out of Schleswig-Holstein. Then, after Sweden was fully engaged in dealing with the two other attacks, Denmark would turn to invade southern Sweden to recover Skåne and the other provinces on the Scandinavian Peninsula (Halland, Blekinge, and Bohuslän) that Denmark had earlier lost to Sweden.

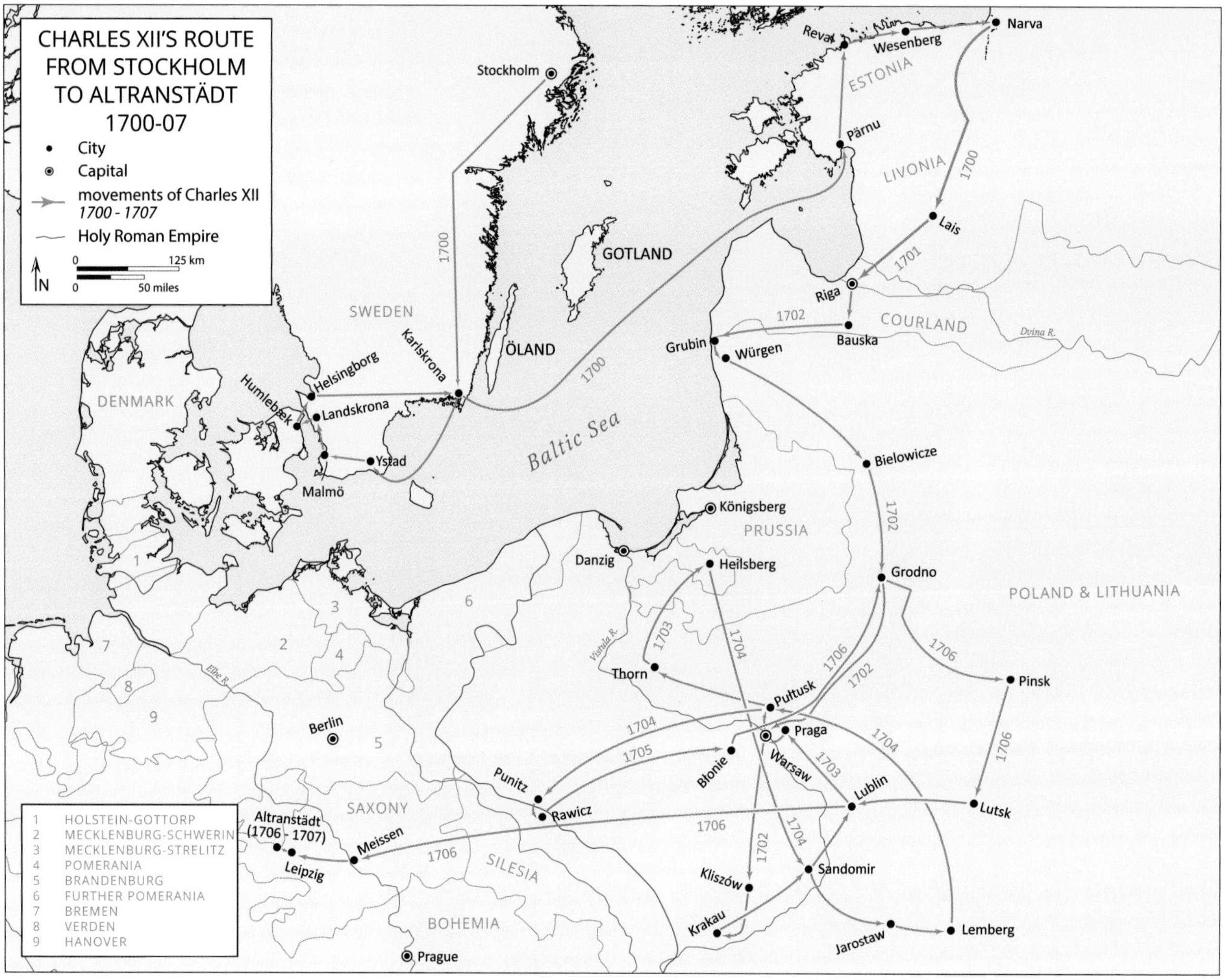
CHARLES XII'S ROUTE FROM STOCKHOLM TO ALTRANSTÄDT 1700-07
City
Capital
movements of Charles XII 1700 - 1707
Holy Roman Empire
0 125 km
0 50 miles
N
Stockholm
Narva
Reval
Wesenberg
ESTONIA
Pärnu
LIVONIA
Lais
Riga
COURLAND
Bauska
Dvina R.
Grubin
Würgen
GOTLAND
ÖLAND
SWEDEN
Karlskrona
Helsingborg
Humlebæk
Landskrona
Ystad
Malmö
DENMARK
Baltic Sea
Bielowicze
Königsberg
PRUSSIA
Danzig
Heilsberg
Grodno
POLAND & LITHUANIA
Vistula R.
Thorn
Pinsk
Pułtusk
Praga
Warsaw
Błonie
Punitz
Rawicz
Lublin
Lutsk
Berlin
SAXONY
Meissen
Altranstädt (1706 - 1707)
Leipzig
SILESIA
Kliszów
Sandomir
Krakau
Jarostaw
Lemberg
BOHEMIA
Prague
Elbe R.
1700
1701
1702
1703
1704
1705
1706
1 HOLSTEIN-GOTTORP
2 MECKLENBURG-SCHWERIN
3 MECKLENBURG-STRELITZ
4 POMERANIA
5 BRANDENBURG
6 FURTHER POMERANIA
7 BREMEN
8 VERDEN
9 HANOVER

Following their agreement, Augustus opened the war in February 1700 when Saxon troops attacked Swedish Livonia from Polish territory. Shortly thereafter, Denmark sent troops against Holstein-Gottorp.

## ■ The War with Denmark, 1700

Charles XI had educated his son to avoid Swedish military aggression against others, but he had also trained him to protect and to maintain the Swedish Empire. Under the circumstances of the Saxon and Danish attacks, with the Russians not far behind, Charles XII and Sweden could not avoid war. Personally, Charles saw the situation as his opportunity to participate in a dynastic tradition in the mould of his father and grandfather—and more distantly, Gustavus II Adolphus—for a Swedish king personally to lead his troops in war. Swedish officials had long thought about the contingency of a simultaneous attack on the Swedish Empire from both east and west and had developed plans for mobilisation and an offensive attack against the closest enemy as the preferred way to defend themselves.

Thus, in 1700, Sweden mobilised her military and naval forces quickly to attack Denmark by land and by sea, with the objective of not only countering the Danish attack on Holstein-Gottorp but also eliminating Danish naval superiority in the Baltic. The Maritime Powers—the Dutch Republic and England—in an effort to maintain peace in the north and to entice Sweden to join them in alliance against France in the looming War of the Spanish Succession, had earlier agreed to assist Sweden if Denmark should threaten Holstein-Gottorp. In the summer of 1700, Admiral Sir George Rooke with an Anglo-Dutch squadron arrived in the Sound and provided local naval superiority as Charles XII personally led Swedish forces across the Sound in making an amphibious assault on Denmark. Landing on the island of Zealand, just north of Copenhagen, Swedish generals Karl Magnus Stuart and Karl Gustaf Rehnskiöld executed, under Charles's supervision, the first phase of the plan to halt Denmark's attacks on Holstein-Gottorp by counter-attacking Copenhagen and destroying the Danish fleet in the harbour. In this, Charles's first experience of war, he showed for the first time his proclivity for taking risks by ordering the Swedish fleet to join the Anglo-Dutch squadron by sailing through the narrow Flintrännen Channel against the advice of his more cautious admiral. In the event, Sweden lost the opportunity to destroy the Danish navy, as Denmark's warships remained in port and King Frederik IV agreed, at Travendal in August 1700, to withdraw from Holstein-Gottorp and to cease his country's alliance with Saxony-Poland. With this defeat, Denmark dropped out of the war for several years.

## ■ The War against Russia, Saxony, and Poland, 1700-07

With Holstein-Gottorp secure and Denmark removed as an immediate threat, the Maritime Powers withdrew their fleet, seemingly unaware of the seriousness of the threat to Sweden on her eastern borders. To counter Augustus's attack on Livonia, Charles XII favoured an immediate and direct attack on his enemy's home territory in Saxony, rather than engaging his forces further north in Swedish Livonia. Only the diplomatic pleas of the Stadholder-King William III in England and Grand Pensionary Anthonie Heinsius in the Dutch Republic persuaded Charles to refrain from this course of action. The Maritime Powers feared that war in Germany would affect Louis XIV's adherence to the Second Partition Treaty of the Spanish Empire. Also, it precluded Swedish and Saxon military support for the Grand Alliance that was beginning to form between the Maritime Powers and Austria if France and Spain chose to create a dynastic union.

With the option closed of attacking Saxony directly, Charles XII moved quickly in October 1700, using his maritime forces to transport the Swedish army from Denmark to cross the Baltic to Swedish Livonia before the sea froze for the winter months. Taken by surprise, Augustus and the Saxon army of 18,000 men had expected that Denmark would have distracted the Swedish army for a much longer time. Not yet ready to face the main Swedish army, the Saxons withdrew and crossed the Dvina River out of Swedish territory and into Courland, south of Riga. Meanwhile, Tsar Peter had declared war and moved Russian forces into Ingermanland and besieged Narva. Making a forced march north, Charles XII with his army under generals Arvid Horn and Rehnskiöld quickly defeated some 23,000 Russians. At Narva, he experienced his first major pitched battle and showed to his generals a fundamental understanding of military movements in the context of the terrain and a clear awareness of the need to act militarily at decisive moments.

When the Battle of Narva pushed the Russians away from the Swedish Baltic provinces, Charles and his generals needed to consider their next step. Stuart developed a plan to follow up with an immediate winter attack on Moscow, but the difficulties of logistics, the need for reinforcements from home, and sickness among the soldiers led to putting the army into winter quarters. When spring came, Charles and his generals decided that a two-front simultaneous war against both Russia and Saxony was too much of a risk and that it was wiser to concentrate their forces to eliminate Saxony first in a decisive battle and then to turn to the larger threat that Russia posed. Swedish forces crossed the Dvina River in July 1701 and surprised the Saxons, who quickly withdrew further to the safety of Poland and then into Saxony itself as Sweden occupied Courland. Charles's earlier pledge to the Dutch and the English that he would not disturb German lands prevented him from pursuing the Saxons.

This situation left Charles and the Swedish army in a strategic dilemma. Unable to attack their most powerful enemy, Russia, until Charles had defeated Augustus, Swedish advisors looked for an alternative means to neutralise Augustus and Saxony. They preferred that their king remain neutral in Polish politics, but despite their advice found an answer through political intrigue among dissident Poles, who disapproved of Augustus's extension of power from Saxony to Poland and of his alliance with Russia. The dissidents' plan was to remove Augustus from the Polish throne and to send him back home to Dresden as only the elector of Saxony. On the military side, Charles and Rehnskiöld defeated Augustus's army at Kliszów in 1702, and Swedish forces captured the Saxon garrison in the siege of Toruń (Thorn) in 1703.

The dissidents, however, had been unable to agree on a candidate to the Polish throne. After a series of false diplomatic and political starts in Poland on the Swedish side and Augustus's counter moves, Austria, England, and the Dutch Republic had become anxious to have Sweden redirect her military support to their war against France. These allies offered to mediate peace between Saxony and Sweden, but Augustus showed no serious interest and any peace proposals—even proposals for a truce between the two states—required Sweden to relinquish some of her own or Polish territory. Peter continued to make gains on his side, founding the new city of Saint Petersburg not far from the old Swedish trading post at Nyen, Ingermanland. As the situation was developing, Charles saw that to defeat Russia, he first needed to have a Polish king who supported Sweden's goals and whose forces could serve to contain Saxony, while Sweden eventually launched attacks on Russia from Poland. As a result, Charles and his advisors concluded that they must continue the war in eastern Europe and renew their attempts to remove Augustus from the Polish throne. Finally, in 1704, with no consensus from the Polish dissidents, Charles made his own choice for king of Poland, Stanislaw Leszczyński, who was duly elected. The Swedish army backed this decision by using intimidation to procure support for Leszczyński as well as to remove Saxon troops and their Russian auxiliaries in their attempts to oppose the election. In 1705, the situation had swung in Charles's favour to the point that enough Poles supported the coronation of Leszczyński that took place in that year. In early 1706, the Russians escaped total defeat at Grodno and retreated from Poland in the aftermath of the battle. At nearly the same time, Rehnskiöld defeated the Saxons at the Battle of Fraustadt, marking the end to Augustus's active resistance to Charles's plans in Poland.

During the successful Polish campaign, Charles matured his skills in both the political and military realms. His religious convictions deepened as he became hardened to the military life and death that surrounded him. At the same time, he became disillusioned with those who swayed in allegiance from one political faction to another as military circumstances changed. A hard-working military leader and sovereign, he found it a necessity to be secretive and taciturn as he engaged increasingly in irregular warfare, sometimes causing confusion among his officers. Realising that his duties forced him to be single-mindedly devoted to the tasks at hand, Charles eschewed close personal relationships and maintained a guarded stance. He sought to instill in his officers and men a stoicism that would allow them to face offensive combat with an emotional control and courage founded in religious belief. In making decisions, Charles was often unwilling to compromise his vision for Sweden and was inclined to reach for risky, radical solutions to achieve his aims.[3]

By 1706, with Charles's military successes in Poland, the only point remaining was to force Augustus to accept his dethronement. The members of the Grand Alliance had previously restrained Charles from entering German territories, but the allied victories at Blenheim in 1704 and Ramillies in 1706 led Charles to think that his continuing restraint was no longer essential to the allied cause. Thus, in the autumn of 1706, he and his army crossed the Polish border into Silesia and moved on into the electorate of Saxony. Saxon emissaries quickly moved to agree with Charles. Among other points in the September 1706 treaty of Altranstädt between Sweden and Saxony, Augustus renounced the Polish throne and recognised Stanislaw. Additionally, Augustus granted permission for the Swedish army to stay in Saxony in winter quarters near Altranstädt to recover their strength after a difficult campaign, await reinforcements from Sweden, resupply, repair, or replace equipment. Before moving on, Charles wisely tried to put in place precautions to prevent Augustus from reneging on his treaty commitments. His efforts met with mixed success. Brandenburg-Prussia refused Charles's request to station auxiliary troops under Swedish command in Poland to prevent the Saxon army from interfering with the Swedish army's future movements. When Charles asked the Maritime Powers for their formal recognition of Stanislaw as king of Poland along with a guarantee of peace, the Dutch were initially ambivalent as Russia seemed to encourage Dutch maritime commerce in the eastern Baltic. Marlborough, however, explicitly agreed to try to obtain the requested guarantee in England. With this promise, Charles confirmed his neutrality in the War of the Spanish Succession. In British eyes, the sooner Charles could defeat the Russians, the sooner the allies could purchase Swedish troops as auxiliaries in the war against France. Britain formally recognised Stanislaw in the spring of 1708, but the Dutch Republic would neither recognise the new king nor guarantee the treaty between Sweden and Saxony.

### ■ The War with Russia, 1707-09

Charles and his officers laid careful plans for their long-awaited campaign against Tsar Peter and Russia. At this point, Charles's clear objectives were to force Peter to relinquish his hold on Sweden's Baltic provinces and to establish a border between the Swedish Empire and Russia and between Poland and Russia. He took care that he had several alternative

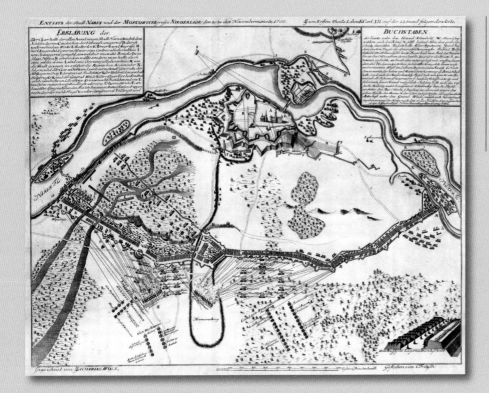

*Map showing the fortifications, troop placements, batteries and movements at the Battle of Narva in November 1700.*

*Engraving by Zacharias Wolf (1667-1726), ca. 1700. Barry Lawrence Ruderman Antique Maps Inc., La Jolla, USA.*

routes and means to achieve these objectives. Thus, he developed contacts through Polish connections with Kahn Devlet II Giray in the Crimea and with Ivan Mazepa, Hetman of the Ukrainian Cossacks, who was looking for independence from Russian domination.

Charles had decided that he had to deal with Russia in the same way that he had successfully dealt with Denmark and with Saxony. The Swedish army needed to march directly into Russia and to threaten the Russian capital at Moscow just as it had threatened Copenhagen in 1700 and Dresden in 1706. Charles had four main strategic routes that he could follow to attack Moscow:

- through the Swedish Baltic provinces by way of Narva and Novgorod; or
- from Poland and Lithuania by way of Vilna, Minsk, and Smolensk; or
- across Severia and the Ukraine by way of Kiev and Kaluga; or
- from Tartary and Turkey through Cossack territory by way of Belgorod, Kursk, and Tula.

To achieve strategic surprise, Charles kept his options open and avoided as long as possible an irretrievable commitment to a single course of action. Starting out towards one of the two northern routes, Charles also left a force in Poland that could threaten to enter the Ukraine and eventually bring in the Cossacks and Tartars through the fourth route. In heading to the northern routes, Charles first had to manoeuvre his army to avoid the Russian forces that had quickly moved into Poland in 1706, when Charles had marched into Saxony. The Swedish army's choice to pass through the woods and marshes of the lake-covered region of Masuria in northern Poland let them avoid battles while at the same time forcing the Russians into leaving

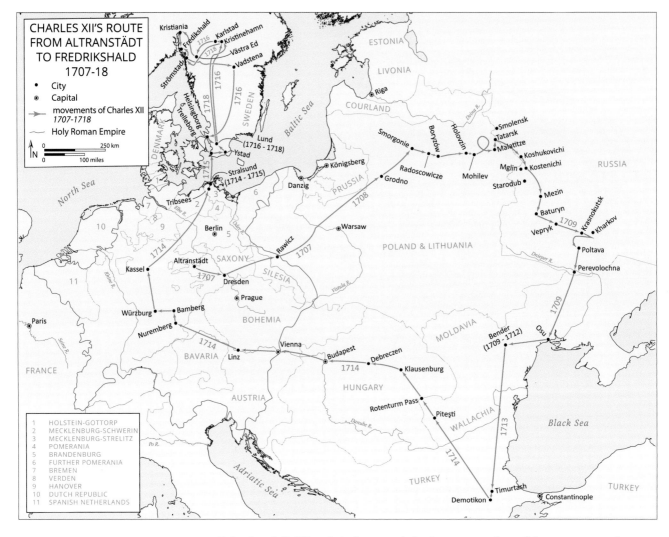

CHARLES XII'S ROUTE
FROM ALTRANSTÄDT
TO FREDRIKSHALD
1707-18
• City
◉ Capital
→ movements of Charles XII
  1707-1718
— Holy Roman Empire

0        250 km
0    100 miles

1  HOLSTEIN-GOTTORP
2  MECKLENBURG-SCHWERIN
3  MECKLENBURG-STRELITZ
4  POMERANIA
5  BRANDENBURG
6  FURTHER POMERANIA
7  BREMEN
8  VERDEN
9  HANOVER
10 DUTCH REPUBLIC
11 SPANISH NETHERLANDS

Poland and dividing their forces to defend one or another of the routes towards Moscow. Overall, the Russians now had a much better-trained and -equipped army, unlike the relative novices that Charles had defeated at Narva in 1700. Yet, when the Russian army made its first attempt to stop Charles in a major battle at Holowczyn on 14 July 1708, the Russian generals proved unable to coordinate their separate units. The Swedes drove the Russians back, but suffered high casualties on their side.

Unable to move forward without reinforcements, Charles occupied the Russians with feints while he awaited the arrival of the Swedish forces under Count Adam Ludwig Lewenhaupt from the Baltic provinces. Eventually, Charles decided to take the alternative southern route through the Ukraine without waiting further for Lewenhaupt. Peter and the Russian army took advantage of the situation and forced Lewenhaupt at the Battle of Lesnaya on 9 October to abandon his supply wagons and to leave his army isolated and out of reach of Charles's assistance. Taking a proactive stance, Peter moved his troops ahead of Charles's army and blocked the passes into Severia, while at the same time endeavouring to destroy every available possibility for the Swedes to live off the land.

These Russian actions forced Charles and his army to take a longer and more difficult route to reach the Ukraine. He had planned on obtaining assistance from the Cossacks, but Mazepa was not ready and resented that Charles had arrived before he was confident that the Swedes could defeat the Russians. In retribution for Mazepa's defection to the Swedish cause, a Russian army under Prince Alexander Menshikov sacked the Cossack capital, Baturyn, in the northern Ukraine in November 1708 and killed thousands of civilians and Cossack soldiers, while destroying the city.

The harsh winter of 1708-09 punished western Europe as well as the Ukraine, where Charles found it difficult to establish winter quarters. Despite continuing Russian raids and strenuous conditions, Charles managed to maintain operations against the Russians, who had effectively cut Charles's lines of communication and supply to Poland and Sweden. But the Swedish army still had the means and finances available to continue, obtaining supplies from the Tartars and Turks. The Swedes' lack of success against the Russians led, however, to a swing in support in Poland against King Stanislaw and to the revival of Augustus's claim to the Polish throne. By the spring of 1709, Charles was looking for a major victory that could impress the sultan in Constantinople to come to his active aid, as Khan Devlet II Giray of the Crimea was recommending on Charles's behalf, as well as to bolster the supporters of Stanislaw in Poland. The Russians, too, were looking for a major victory. As the two opposing armies skirmished across the Vorskla River in advance of the major engagement they both sought, a stray bullet hit Charles in the foot. Although not a life-threatening wound, he was disabled and temporarily unable to command the army in person. Taking advantage of this situation, Tsar Peter moved his entire army across the Vorskla. Peter then set up a well-defended camp near the city of Poltava, deliberately forcing the Swedish army to attack them. Facing a Russian army with improved tactics and morale, the Swedish attack on 8 July 1709 went awry due to the cumulative effect of some operational and coordination issues. Charles's army had lost over 10,000 men in casualties and prisoners taken, including Charles's field chancery officials along with General Rehnskiöld. The Swedish army was still a capable force after its abortive attack on the Russian army's position at Poltava. However, three days later, General Lewenhaupt surrendered with 15,000 exhausted and demoralised men to Menshikov at Perevolochna. Charles and some 3,000 Swedes and Cossacks, including Mazepa, evaded capture and, with the assistance of the Cossack Kost Hordienko, crossed the Dnieper River near Perevolochna and escaped to Bender and Varnitza on the Dniester River in Moldova.

## ■ In the Ottoman Empire, 1709-15

Having taken temporary refuge in the Ottoman Empire, Charles immediately made plans to resume the war against Peter as soon as possible. At first, he expected to stay only as long as it took for his foot to heal and fully expected to be back with his army in Poland by the end of 1709. A wide range of unexpected events prolonged his stay to five years. The Russians did not honour their promise to allow the Swedish officers who surrendered to them at Perevolochna to return home. Then the plague shut the frontiers of the Ottoman Empire and Habsburg lands from 1709 to 1714. France, Great Britain, and the Dutch Republic all offered to bring Charles home by sea, but he refused their offers, reluctant to become a hostage to any of the warring western European powers and the demands they would undoubtedly make on Sweden's military capacity. Left with few options, Charles worked to persuade the Ottomans to attack Russia.

Meanwhile, many of Charles's gains in the first nine years of the war vanished after Poltava and Perevolochna. Augustus returned to Poland and reclaimed the crown. Frederik of Denmark-Norway re-entered the war, and his forces invaded Sweden and seized Holstein-Gottorp. As the guarantors of the Peace of Travendal, the Dutch Republic and Great Britain were no longer in a position to force the Danes out of Holstein-Gottorp. Instead, the Maritime Powers agreed in 1710 to the neutrality of Swedish lands in Germany to maintain peace there and to continue to use auxiliary troops from Saxony and Denmark in their war against France. This agreement eliminated Charles's plan to use Swedish Pomerania as a base for reinforcing the Swedish troops in Poland. As a result, his relations with both the Dutch and British soured, despite the emphasis placed by the King's Council in Stockholm on the vital importance of maintaining good relations with the Maritime Powers.

Frustrated by the Council's attitudes in Stockholm, Charles shifted responsibility for the army to one person, Magnus Stenbock, who implemented Charles's desire to put his army back in Germany. Stenbock drove the Danes out of Skåne in 1710 and within two years organised an army of 16,000 in Swedish Pomerania which was able to defeat Saxon and Danish troops at Gadebusch in December 1712. The Danish navy successfully blocked supplies, ensuring that Stenbock could not exploit his success ashore at Gadebusch. He then turned to invade Jutland, but Danish, Saxon, and Russian forces stopped his army at Tönning in Holstein, forcing him to surrender in May 1713.

Meanwhile, Charles's several efforts to mobilise other powers to oppose Russia came to little. By late 1712 and early 1713, Ottoman officials were becoming tired of Charles's continued presence and conspired to remove him. Unwilling to be forced into the unfriendly hands of Augustus or Peter, Charles organised the *Kalabalik* or tumult at Varnitza[4] to oppose those planning to remove him under unfavourable circumstances.[5]

## ■ The Return to Sweden, 1714-18

Charles understood that he needed to return to Sweden, not only because of the situation in the Ottoman Empire but to resolve issues at home. While in his enforced stay in Ottoman lands, Charles had given both thought and direction to economic and administrative reforms at home that would bear fruit after 1714. Avoiding all entanglements, he travelled incognito in a post-chaise; he then continued on horseback through the Habsburg lands to reach Stralsund within two weeks on 21 November 1714. He left Stralsund, just as that city fell to the enemy, and landed in Sweden on 24 December.

On his return home, Charles continued with renewed energy his economic and administrative reforms. At the same time, he set about developing new military and naval forces. The king's sister, Ulrika Eleonora, had been his close confidant and an unofficial co-regent during his many years away from Sweden. One of the first events after his return was his sister's long-awaited marriage to Prince Friedrich of Hesse-Kassel, who during the War of the Spanish Succession had become a lieutenant-general in Dutch service. About this time, concerns began to appear about the succession to the Swedish throne and with it were sown the seeds of opposition to absolutist rule, even though Charles hinted at the thought of an eventual marriage.

The external international situation had changed in western Europe following the end of the War of the Spanish Succession. Britain, Hanover, Prussia, Denmark, and Russia began to develop new strategic and political objectives. At this point, Charles sought to use diplomacy and negotiations for peace to paralyse his enemies while he continued to strengthen his armed forces. By late 1718, the newly reorganised Swedish army was ready for combined operations. Exactly what Charles's strategic intentions were for his revitalised forces remains in some doubt, but the first operation was in Norway. At the very outset of the campaign, on 11 December 1718, a bullet killed Charles during the opening phase of the siege of Fredriksten fortress.

## ■ The Epilogue

Charles XII's death added a new uncertainty to the international situation by bringing to the fore the immediate question of who would succeed him on the Swedish throne. Observers had already been speculating that Tsar Peter was in poor health and might not live long. At the same time, James Francis Edward Stuart had active Jacobite supporters who were planning to remove George I and restore the House of Stuart in Britain. In Sweden, Charles XII had refused to acknowledge that succession might be a problem, hinting that he would someday marry and produce an heir when the war was over, but there now were two major parties in Sweden with definite ideas about the succession. The highly influential Georg Heinrich von Görtz, Baron of Schlitz, Sweden's ambassador at The Hague, was promoting Duke Karl Friedrich of Holstein-Gottorp, Charles's nephew and second cousin, who had the strongest claim by primogeniture. At the same time, Friedrich of Hesse-Kassel, who had married Charles's sister Ulrika Eleonora, was promoting his wife's claims by developing political ties to Swedish leaders who were opposed to the continuation of the absolutist regime and Charles XII's reforms. In the event, Ulrika Eleonora immediately claimed the throne on learning of her brother's death. She gained the support of the opposition by agreeing to end the absolutist state. In early 1719, after Ulrika Eleonora signed the Instrument of Government that limited royal power and established a parliamentary system, the highest authority of the land—the Riksdag of the Estates that included the nobility, clergy, burghers, and the peasantry—elected her queen. She ruled in this capacity for a little over a year. Unable to obtain her goal of making her husband co-ruler on the model of William III and Mary II of England, she abdicated in favour of her husband, who then became King Fredrik I and ruled from 1720 until 1751.

Charles XII's death and the new political regime in Sweden did not end the Great Northern War nor did it end Sweden's desire to defend her empire. Swedish leaders ended the military campaign in Norway, but still held some hopes of maintaining at least some of the empire. The Russians continued their attacks on Sweden, which even reached the Stockholm area and quickly convinced Swedish leaders to align themselves for their country's protection with King George I of Great Britain, who also was elector of Hanover. The belligerents were keen to divide up Sweden's possessions: Hanover wanted Bremen and Verden; Prussia wanted Stettin; Denmark wanted Holstein-Gottorp as compensation for giving up the Swedish lands it occupied near Wismar. Britain wanted to maintain some semblance of Swedish power to create a balance of power

in the north. She used her naval forces and diplomacy in the Baltic region to ally with Sweden in an arrangement that would both restrain Russia and encourage Tsar Peter to withdraw his army from Poland and Germany. Manoeuvering around the conflicting objectives and mutual suspicions among Austria, Prussia, Denmark-Norway, Sweden, and Hanover, French diplomats lent their assistance to Britain in negotiations that led to the two treaties of Stockholm and the treaty of Frederiksborg.[6]

In the first treaty of Stockholm, Sweden ceded Bremen and Verden to Hanover in 1719. By the second, in 1720, Sweden ceded to Prussia part of Swedish Pomerania. This territory included the islands of Usedom and Wollin on the southern coast of the Baltic Sea, the towns of Stettin (Szczecin), Gollnow (Goleniów), and Damm (Dąbie), and the area south of the Peene River and east of the Peenestrom Strait. In the 1720 Treaty of Frederiksborg between Denmark-Norway and Sweden, the four treaties regarding the former Danish territories in the Scandinavian Peninsula signed between 1660 and 1679 were reconfirmed, preserving these provinces under Swedish control. At the same time, Denmark-Norway acquired the Holstein-Gottorp lands but returned to Sweden the portions of Swedish Pomerania that Denmark-Norway had occupied, for a payment of 600,000 riksdalers from the subsidies that France and Britain provided. Sweden also relinquished her exemption from paying the Sound Dues. On the positive side, Sweden retained Stralsund, Wismar, the island of Rügen, and the nearby coastal area of Pomerania until the Napoleonic wars.

Sweden had continued to defend itself from the continuing Russian attacks along its Baltic coast and in the Gulf of Bothnia. British attempts to bring Russia to the peace table through naval intervention in the Baltic proved to be ineffective. By 1721 Sweden had reached the point of exhaustion. Due to internal and external distractions, France, Britain, and Hanover found it impossible to carry out their intention to use military and naval force to compel Russia into a peace negotiation. Instead, Sweden was left to her own devices to meet Russia's demands. On 10 September 1721, the two states reached a peace agreement at Nystad (now Uusikaupunki, Finland). In this agreement, Sweden formally ceded to Russia most of the lands that Tsar Peter's army had occupied: Ingria—where Peter had founded his new city of Saint Petersburg—Estonia, and Livonia. Russia returned to Sweden most of Finland but retained the fortress at Vyborg, most of Karelia (Karjala), and the southern part of Kexholms län (Käkisalmen lääni). In return, Russia paid Sweden two million riksdalers for these territories and also allowed Sweden to continue to import an annual amount of grain from Livonia, which had long been important to the Swedish economy. Additionally, Sweden and Augustus II of Saxony signed a convention to end hostilities, but there was no peace agreement with the Polish-Lithuanian Commonwealth. The Treaty of Nystad included a provision for Russia to act as a mediator between Sweden and the new client, King Augustus of Saxony-Poland. It would take another decade before the two signed a formal agreement, in 1731.

After twenty-one years of exhausting warfare, Europe welcomed the peace in 1721. For many, it was the golden peace—*Den Gyldene Freden*, as a Stockholm tavern-owner named his establishment in 1722. With the Peace of Nystad, Sweden lost the great-power status that Gustavus II Adolphus had won for his country. After that king's death in 1632, the 1648 Peace of Westphalia that ended the Thirty

Years' War confirmed, with some ambiguity, Sweden's control of German territories under the nominal rule of the emperor in Vienna. King Louis XIV of France with successive emperors—Leopold, Joseph, and Charles VI—created a notable trend in European international relations from the late 1670s onwards as they worked independently of each other to reclaim their losses in the Westphalia settlement. Nearly three-quarters of a century later, the series of treaties that ended the Great Northern War reflected that long-term trend in European history.[7] All of the leading antagonists in the Great Northern War—Denmark-Norway, Saxony-Poland, and Russia—sought either to reclaim earlier losses to Sweden or to improve their position by seizing Swedish-controlled territories.

As the protagonist, Charles XII, together with his leading advisors turned to war, not as the instigator nor as warmonger for the mere sake of fighting wars, but rather as the defender of his inherited ideals and realm. The ultimate failure of Sweden's effort had several causes. The Swedish armed forces proved to be remarkably efficient and resilient during the first nine years of the war. Yet, despite their effectiveness, they had limited strength. Charles's predecessors were aware of those limitations and had established an independent, neutral position for the kingdom, restricting the use of her forces to the defence of her self-interests. This policy proved to be weak as it sowed distrust and prevented participation in alliances with other powers.

This situation made Sweden vulnerable to an old rival, Denmark, and to a rising power, Russia. Additionally, new local rivalries developed as three German electoral princes within the Holy Roman Empire became kings: the elector of Saxony, Augustus, in 1697 became the new king of the Polish-Lithuanian Commonwealth, while the elector of Brandenburg, Friedrich, became king in Prussia in 1701. In 1692, in recognition of his role during the Nine Years' War, the emperor had raised the duke of Braunschweig-Lüneburg (Hanover) to fill the position of the newly formed ninth elector in the Empire, which the Imperial Diet confirmed in 1708. A new Hanoverian prince-elector, Georg Ludwig, came to power in 1698. In 1714, he became King George I of Great Britain in addition to being the elector. The rise of these three new ambitious kings with lands that touched the borders of the Swedish Empire raised further complications by changing the calculus of the power rivalry upon which Sweden had acquired her position within Germany in 1648.

Simultaneously, the rise of Great Britain to great-power status as a result of the War of the Spanish Succession and the newly cemented relationship between Britain and Germany by way of Hanover, led Britain, with French backing, to become the major counterweight to Russia. Britain ensured Sweden's survival to maintain a power balance with the Baltic, while the emperor and Austria were content to have Sweden's independent role in Germany replaced by sovereigns who had ties to the Empire. Among other effects, the costs of sustaining long wars helped fuel the early beginnings of opposition to absolutist rule, not only in Sweden but elsewhere. At the same time that absolutism was reaching peaks in Austria, France, Prussia, and Russia, the Scandinavian monarchies, as well as Great Britain and the Dutch Republic, were subject to established limits under the rule of law through the consensual nature of their governments and political cultures.[8]

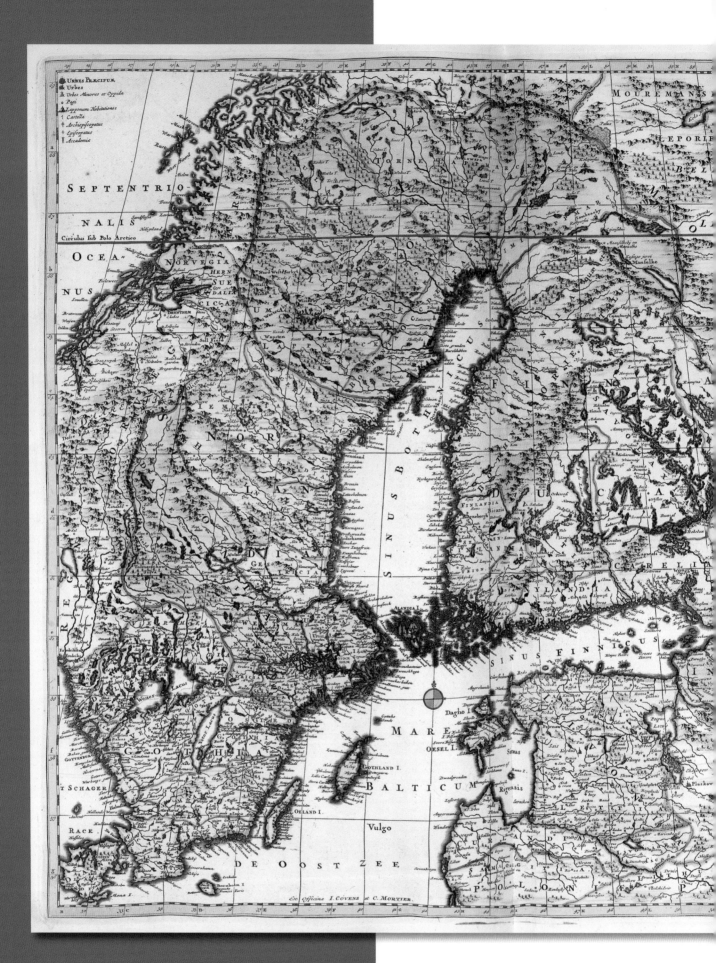

*Map of Sweden and the Baltic.*

*Hand-coloured engraving by Reinier Ottens (1698-1750), ca. 1719-25. University of Amsterdam, Amsterdam, the Netherlands. Bijzondere Collecties, Universiteit van Amsterdam, plaatsnummer (OTM: HB KZL XX G 74 of OTM: HB KZL 1808 A 6).*

## CHAPTER 4

# Swedish Grand Strategy and Foreign Policy, 1697-1721

by Gunnar Åselius*

In a recent book on the Swedish Empire, Charles XII is described as 'the most controversial figure in Swedish history.'[1] Yet in reality the controversies surrounding the king have been more specific, as they centre on his foreign policy and strategic priorities. How much freedom of action did he actually enjoy? To what extent was he responsible for the misfortunes which befell Sweden during a war that raged for much of his reign and beyond, and which is thought to have cost the lives of at least 200,000 Swedish soldiers?[2] Swedish grand strategy and foreign policy in the years 1697-1721 are therefore of central importance to any understanding of Charles XII's role in his country's history.

For nineteenth-century liberal Swedish historians such as Anders Fryxell and Fredrik Ferdinand and Ernst Carlson (*père* and *fils*), the king was a skilled military commander and tactician. They did not doubt that his daring and willingness to endure the dangers and hardships of war alongside his men made him an inspiring figure. Yet he was equally seen as vainglorious, impulsive, and unwilling to listen to advice, with little understanding of strategy and diplomacy, and giving scant thought to the sufferings of those on the home front. Later, this disapproving view of Charles XII coalesced into 'the old school,' as it was labeled by its critics.[3]

An alternative view of Charles XII—the 'new school'—was first advanced by the Swedish chief of the general staff and minister of war, Major-General Baron Axel Rappe, in an address to the Royal Swedish Academy of War Sciences in 1892. Historians such as Harald Hjärne and Arthur Stille developed it further, and it was ultimately taken as established fact in 1918-19 when, in addition to a weighty Festschrift, an official four-volume history of the king's campaigns produced by the military history section of the Swedish general staff marked the bicentenary of the king's death.[4] This new school of thought held that any appraisal of the king ought in the first instance to be informed by the contemporaneous political context and should not be so concerned with the king himself (although, it has to be said, hero worship of Charles XII was not completely alien to Carl Bennedich, the leading general staff historian): the king had not only been an outstanding commander in the field, but the revisionists believed that when the record was set straight using primary sources and adopting a broader, European perspective, his role on the stage of world history as a protector of the west against Russian expansion would also become clear. For the first half of the twentieth century this was the dominant view, although of course it did not go wholly unchallenged. Authors, including some with a military background such as Major-General Carl Otto Nordensvan or the naval officer Arnold Munthe, were critical of Charles XII's poor strategic judgment.[5]

Today, Charles XII is not as lively a topic as he was at the start of the twentieth century, when political struggles over royal power, parliamentary rule, and defence policy made differences of scholarly opinion particularly heated. If nothing else, historians who now study the decline of the Swedish Empire have a much greater tendency to apply a structural perspective than did their predecessors a century ago. How an individual monarch's lifework should be evaluated is no longer seen as a fruitful question from a scholarly perspective. The issues surrounding Sweden's loss of empire are thought to be divorced from any discussion of Charles XII's personal failings or merits.

What follows is an examination of the Swedish Empire's resources in relation to the rest of Europe, Sweden's efforts to manoeuvre between the European power blocs in the run-up to the Great Northern War of 1700-21, and its gradual displacement as the leading power in the Baltic—a role the country had enjoyed since the 1640s—until it was finally overtaken altogether in the peace treaties of 1719-21.

## ■ Sweden's Resources

The strength of the Swedish Empire's position in Europe is an indispensable factor in any discussion of what Charles XII could or should have done. True, it has been suggested that 'geography', not resources, was the most important element in the strategic problems which Sweden faced during the Great Northern War.[6] However, to imagine that the Swedish Empire could have survived a combined assault by Russia, Brandenburg, Hanover, Saxony-Poland, and Denmark if only Charles XII had been of a different mindset is as unrealistic as the notion that Nazi Germany could have defeated the allied forces of the US, the USSR, and the British Empire if only it had been led by a more competent strategist than Adolf Hitler.

What is most striking in comparison with the rest of Europe is Sweden's relative poverty. The power it attained was sustained from the sixteenth century onwards by the state's ability to mobilise society's resources to its chosen ends. By the late seventeenth century, however, the Swedes' advantage was being eroded by the introduction of more effective forms of government administration in neighbouring states such as Russia and Brandenburg—partly along Swedish lines. For Russia in particular, research has highlighted the important role played by Swedish models in that country's modernisation under Peter the Great.[7]

In the heartlands of the Swedish Empire, in what is now Sweden and Finland, the population in 1700 is thought to have been about 1.4 million. When its provinces in Estonia, Livonia, Ingria, and northern Germany are added, the Swedish Crown probably had some 2.5 million subjects—far fewer, in other words, than the estimated populations of France (19 million), Russia (16 million), the British Isles (8 million), or the Habsburg Empire (8 million) in the same period. The Swedish Empire was more populous, though, than Brandenburg-Prussia (2 million), the Dutch Republic (1.7 million), or Denmark (which had barely 1.5 million inhabitants, including Norway and Iceland).[8]

By European standards, Sweden did not have any sizeable cities either. The population of Stockholm in 1700 is thought to have been 57,000: small compared with Europe's largest cities, London (575,000) and Paris (500,000), although about the same size as Copenhagen, the capital of its archrival. The next four largest cities in the Swedish Empire were Riga, Reval (Tallinn), Stralsund, and Stettin (Szczecin) with populations between 10,000 and 12,000. With the exception of Stockholm, there was no city in the area that constitutes present-day Sweden and Finland with more than 6,000 inhabitants, and two towns in three had a population of fewer than 1,000.[9]

Just how sparsely populated subarctic Sweden must have seemed is evident from estimates of population density elsewhere in western Europe. Although the figures reflect the situation a century earlier, they nevertheless give an idea of the relative proportions. Around 1600, there were about 40 people per square kilometre in the Dutch Republic; in France, 34; in Germany, 28 (before the Thirty Years' War); in Spain and Portugal, 17—and on the Scandinavian Peninsula, a mere 1.5.[10] Sweden was heavily wooded, and the proportion of the total land area under cultivation is estimated to have been approximately 2 per cent in 1700, compared with a western European average of around 14 per cent.[11] During the 1690s, Finland was particularly hard hit with crop failures. Nearly a quarter of the population in Sweden's Finnish counties died in the course of just two years.[12] The reports of starvation, hardship, and unrest in the eastern parts of the kingdom convinced the neighbouring powers that Sweden had been weakened, which was why in 1699 they chanced forming an alliance.[13]

At the best of times, Swedish farmers had to turn their hands to iron production, forestry, tar-burning, or fishing in order to survive. They also paid the majority of their taxes to the Crown in kind, which meant that in normal circumstances the Swedish state was chronically short of cash, even though it commanded far greater resources than government budgets seemed to indicate. According to calculations by the historian Eli Heckscher in the 1920s, Sweden's national revenue at the start of the eighteenth century reached 63 barrels of gold (one barrel of gold being worth 100,000 daler silvermynt)—his equivalent figures for Denmark being 43 barrels, for Britain 168 barrels, and for France a staggering 880 barrels—yet he was of the opinion that the figure for Sweden did not give an accurate picture of the Crown's actual resources, because its expenditures were largely met by payments in kind.[14] This was especially true of costs such as salaries for public officials and those in the armed services. As long as Sweden pursued an expansive foreign policy, the burden of maintaining its army could be pushed onto the overseas regions where it was operating. This had worked well during the Thirty Years' War in Germany in the 1630s and 1640s, but less so during the Polish campaigns of Charles XII's grandfather, Charles X Gustav, in the 1650s. When Sweden then began to take a defensive stance in the hopes of preserving the status quo, a reorganisation of the military became necessary.

Military reform was forced through by Charles XII's father, Charles XI, and was implemented in parallel with the Great Reduction (the re-enfeoffment of aristocratic estates by the Crown) and the introduction of royal absolutism. For a relatively small outlay, the Swedish king was assured of a large standing army that was loyal to the Crown. This was achieved partly through *indelningsverket*, the so-called allotment system that saw Crown land allocated to support individual military officers and other officials, and partly through the division of rural communities into *rotar*, or wards, each of them responsible for providing and equipping a soldier, in return for tax reductions or freedom from conscription. At the outbreak of the Great Northern War in 1700, the Swedish army could mobilise about 60,000 men (with another 16,000 in the navy), a figure that should be compared with the forces that the other, far more numerous and wealthy European powers were able to muster at around the same time: France, 400,000; Russia, 170,000; the Dutch Republic, 73,000; Britain, 70,000; and the Habsburg Empire, 50,000.[15] Of course, once the army was in the field, cash was required to pay for extra musters to make up numbers and for materiel, yet a closer study of the Swedish mobilisation in 1700 shows that the government had no great difficulties raising these funds. Amongst other methods, some of the cost of mobilisation could be spread through what was largely an agricultural society by using the framework of the allotment system.[16]

In addition to the well-proven militia-based army provided by the allotment system, Swedish strategy was to rely on fortifications in its Baltic and northern German border provinces. These defences were supposed to be able to hold up an attacking force long enough for the army to be mobilised and transported across the Baltic to reinforce them, but their construction was extremely expensive and it was never possible to make them as extensive as desired. A large naval fleet was required in order to transport the Swedish army to the Baltic provinces and to supply its operations there. Although the manning of the fleet was organised using a militia system similar to the army's, the building and equipping of naval vessels were more difficult to arrange with payments in kind; however, compared with other European powers, Sweden was at a distinct advantage because it had direct access to tar, iron, timber, and masts, and it produced its own high-quality artillery pieces. Thus, despite its lack of cash, the Swedish Crown ever since the sixteenth century had managed to maintain one of Europe's largest navies. In 1700, it amounted to 7 per cent of the total naval tonnage in Europe, with 53,000 tonnes and 39 ships of the line. The only fleets that were larger were the British (with 25.8 per cent of the European total, 196,000 tonnes, 127 ships of the line), the French (25.7 per cent, 195,000 tonnes, 108 ships of the line), and the Dutch (14.9 per cent, 113,000 tonnes, 83 ships of the line), while its main rival, the Danish fleet, was slightly smaller in size (6.1 per cent of the European total, 46,000 tonnes, 32 ships of the line).[17]

## ■ Sweden's Foreign Policy before the Great Northern War

The measures implemented by Charles XI in the 1680s and 1690s, designed to establish Sweden as a defensive, status quo power, went beyond the allotment system and the Great Reduction to include a reorientation of foreign policy. The alliance with France, which dated back to the Thirty Years' War, had drawn Sweden into the catastrophic Franco-Dutch War of the 1670s, so it was now abandoned in favour of an alignment with the two Maritime Powers, Britain and the Dutch Republic. Such a reorientation was only possible because after 1680 the Great Reduction of the nobles' estates had lessened the Swedish Crown's dependence on French subsidies. Denmark remained the most serious threat, and with that in mind the Dutch and British were valuable allies as their fleets could increase pressure on the entrances to the Baltic and on Copenhagen. In the 1680s, Sweden allied with the Dutch Republic, and in 1692 Swedish troops were hired out to the Republic for the allies' summer campaign on the Rhine. In 1697, in recognition of its assistance, the Maritime Powers accorded Sweden a nominal role as a mediator in the peace negotiations in Rijswijk that ended the Nine Years' War, and in 1700 they entered into an alliance with Sweden.

However, despite this closeness to the anti-French bloc in European politics, there were also points on which Sweden disagreed with the Maritime Powers. The blockade of French harbours declared by the Dutch Republic and Britain in 1689 ran contrary to Sweden's commercial interests. The Maritime Powers, in turn, were keen to carry on, without any disturbance, their trade with Russia, importing cordage, hemp, timber, and masts for their navies, and this also brought a potential conflict with Sweden. The Danish historian Knud J.V. Jespersen has compared the Baltic at the close of the seventeenth century with the Persian Gulf at the close of the twentieth—a restricted body of water and a transit point for strategic raw materials, where powers from outside the region jealously guarded access for their shipping.[18]

Since the 1650s, a central tenet of Sweden's defence strategy against Denmark had been to maintain close relations with the duchy of Holstein-Gottorp, which occupied a key position on Denmark's southern border. This relationship was secured dynastically through marriage. Charles XII's grandfather, Charles X Gustav, had married Hedvig Eleonora of Holstein-Gottorp in 1654. Duke Friedrich IV of Holstein-Gottorp subsequently married his cousin, Charles XII's older sister, Princess Hedvig Sofia, in 1698. In the 1690s, Swedish troops were stationed in the duchy, to the great irritation of the Danes, and as late as the summer of 1699 Charles XII sent strong reinforcements there at the request of his brother-in-law.[19]

In 1689, Charles XI had received guarantees from the Maritime Powers that they would help Sweden protect Holstein-Gottorp's sovereignty. The Swedish alliances intended to protect the duchy from Danish expansion also included agreements with the electorate of Brandenburg and the duchies of Brunswick-Lüneburg (Hanover) and Celle. However, these states were not only allies, for given the right opportunity they could also pose a threat to Sweden's territories in northern Germany.

Relations with Saxony-Poland had been relatively good. Augustus II the Strong was Charles XII's cousin on his mother's side. Although there had been reports in Stockholm of a secret alliance between Denmark and Saxony in the summer of 1698, its purpose was unclear, and Augustus II was simultaneously negotiating a similar treaty with Sweden, which he continued as a diversionary tactic up to the outbreak of war.[20] As far as Russia was concerned, the Swedish Privy Council was increasingly uneasy about Russian plans for revenge, and there were rumours of intensive diplomatic contacts between Russia and Denmark. Despite this, after Charles XII's accession in 1697 the tsar was permitted to import large numbers of cannon from Swedish foundries, and a Swedish ambassador was sent to Moscow to confirm 'the eternal peace' between the two countries. These expressions of friendship were not a sign of a naive credulity on Sweden's part, but rather a calculated attempt to break Russia free from the Danish alliance.[21]

The long-running conflict that pitted Louis XIV's France against the Maritime Powers and the Habsburg Empire would soon be reignited in western Europe, this time in the guise of the War of the Spanish Succession (1702-14), and ran parallel with Sweden's war against its Baltic neighbours. The main European power struggle saw both France and its rivals exert every influence over Sweden's foreign policy and strategic priorities to their own best advantage. Criticism of Charles XII's foreign policy has generally focused on his cool reception of the various attempts at conciliation, particularly those made by the Maritime Powers. According to some, the fall of the Swedish Empire would have been delayed if the king had been more positive in his response.

### ■ Picking Enemies, 1700-02

One question raised by historians is where Charles XII's priorities lay in choosing his opponents in the opening phase of the Great Northern War. On 16 March 1700, he received word that Augustus II the Strong of Saxony-Poland had invaded Livonia four weeks previously, and on 30 March came the news that the king of Denmark had attacked Sweden's ally Holstein-Gottorp. In this situation Charles XII chose to prioritise Denmark, despite the fact that his councillors, led by the Chancellor Bengt Oxenstierna, recommended that the bulk of the army be shipped immediately to the province of Livonia, which, unlike Holstein-Gottorp, was actually part of the Swedish realm. The historian Gustaf Jonasson believes that in this instance the king was driven by solidarity with his brother-in-law, but the Maritime Powers and Sweden's ally Lüneburg were probably also a factor. It was only if it went to war against Denmark to protect Holstein-Gottorp that Sweden could expect any help from its allies. The Maritime Powers wanted a quick end to the war, and were reluctant to see the Swedish forces in Germany strengthened, as many states in the area would have regarded this as a threat, making the recruitment of German troops more difficult. The Swedish army was shipped to Zealand under the protection of the Dutch and English navies.

On 21 August, while advancing on Copenhagen, the Swedish army received the news that Denmark and Holstein-Gottorp had signed a peace treaty in Travendal three days before. Immediately, the earlier scheme to deal with Saxony was resumed. The plan not only involved shipping troops to the beleaguered province of Livonia, but also pushing through Brandenburg into the Saxon heartlands from Sweden's possessions in northern Germany. Once again, the western European great powers intervened, as they were highly

*Standard belonging to one of the regiments of Charles XII of Sweden.*

*Painted and embroidered textile by unknown maker, ca 1700-21. Armémuseum, Stockholm, Sweden.*

reluctant to see a war between Sweden and its neighbours spread further into Germany and disturb the impending settlement of the Habsburg Spanish inheritance. French attempts to mediate between Sweden and Saxony were brusquely rejected by Charles XII, however, for he was of the opinion that France, along with the Holy Roman Emperor, Brandenburg, and the Maritime Powers, should all help him punish Augustus II's breach of faith. The king's plans had to change again on 2 October, when he learned that the tsar had declared war a little over a month earlier and had laid siege to Narva. This was compounded by the fact that the Maritime Powers were also bringing pressure to bear: like France, they were reluctant to see Sweden's war spread to Germany, even though they would benefit from Russia's advance on the Baltic being halted. Ultimately, Charles XII's decision to postpone the campaign against Saxony was also influenced by worries about what Denmark might attempt, if the Swedish army were to march south into Germany.[22]

Instead, the king moved the majority of the army to Estonia, where on 30 November he inflicted a crushing defeat on the Russians at Narva, and thereafter retired to winter quarters. According to the plans laid by the Swedish command, the tsar would rank first amongst their enemies once the next campaigning season began. Smaller-scale assaults were to be carried out across the Russian border, while the king moved the main army towards the river Dvina (Daugava) and Riga in order to defeat the Saxons, secure Courland, and then swing eastwards to join up with the rest of the army in Russian territory in order to overwinter.[23]

This plan was never realised. The Swedish army divided in June 1701, duly defeated the Saxon army on the banks of the Dvina on 19 July, and advanced into Courland. Although preparations for an invasion of Russia continued into September, the operational task of driving out the Saxons before marching eastwards imperceptibly mutated in the face of a different strategic aim: to remove Augustus II from the Polish throne. This meant that the war was carried into Polish territory, despite the fact that Poland, at this time a unique aristocratic republic, was formally neutral in the war between its monarch and the Swedish king. In January 1702, the Swedish army crossed the border from Courland, and for the next five years would remain in the Polish-Lithuanian Commonwealth in order to engineer Augustus II's deposition. During this period, Russia forced a way through to the Baltic and in the process conquered Sweden's Ingrian and Baltic territories without meeting any great resistance. Charles XII's critics among later historians have had much to say on this remarkable ranking of priorities. It is known that the king's advisors, the Board of Chancery in Stockholm under Bengt Oxenstierna (who died in 1702), and the field chancery under Carl Piper (which had been attached to Swedish headquarters since the outbreak of the war) were all highly critical of the invasion of Poland and warned Charles of the consequences. They were particularly concerned that Augustus II, as elector of Saxony, had lent troops to the Holy Roman Emperor and had allied himself with the anti-French bloc in European politics. Piper feared that by adopting an uncompromising stance against Augustus II, Sweden risked losing the crucial assistance of the emperor's allies, the Maritime Powers.[24]

Later, historians such as Harald Hjärne who chose to defend Charles XII, believed that an invasion of Poland was inevitable because it had not been possible to win a decisive victory over Augustus II, and he could not be allowed to remain undefeated at the Swedish army's rear during any later invasion of Russia. Moreover, any campaign in the east was predicated on Polish-Swedish cooperation and continued access to Poland for supplies. A modern historian, Robert I. Frost, a specialist in the history of Poland-Lithuania, is of a similar opinion.[25] Yet there is no evidence that there was any long-term strategic reasoning behind the decision in the winter of 1702 to cross the border from Courland into the Polish-Lithuanian Commonwealth. Even if it is certain that Charles XII was determined from an early stage to remove Augustus II from the throne, the choice to invade seems to have been an adaptation to military technicalities, the wider significance of which does not seem to have been appreciated by the king until afterwards. Even though Sweden was not at war with Poland-Lithuania, the king believed he had the right to operate on Polish territory because Augustus II was doing so. Once Swedish cavalry had chased a force of Lithuanian horsemen over the border, he allowed the rest of the army to follow for reasons of logistics.[26]

### ■ 1702-07: Poland or the Baltic?

The Swedes captured Warsaw in May 1702 and defeated the Polish and Saxon forces at Kliszów in July, but the decisive blow seemed to elude them. Like so many other leaders in history, Charles XII discovered that military success does not automatically transform into political gain. Several opposition groups in Poland would have gladly seen Augustus II deposed, but real diplomatic finesse was required to unite them, and the Swedes, in their attempts to find willing adherents for their policies in Poland, risked being used in turn, in their case as tools in the power struggles among Polish noble families. Poland's primate, Bishop Michael Radziejowski—whose place it was to act as chairman of any assembly of Polish nobles and who could lend legitimacy to an attempt to depose Augustus II—vacillated between Charles and Augustus, and finally fled to Danzig (Gdańsk) to avoid having to make a decision. It was only in January 1704 that the Swedes succeeded in persuading an assembly of nobles in Warsaw to depose Augustus II and, five months later, to choose the Swedish candidate, Stanislaw Leszczyński, as the new Polish king. And it would not be until July 1705 that Stanislaw was formally crowned king—under the protection of Swedish troops.  Since Radziejowski chose not to be present, the bishop of Lemberg (Lviv) officiated at the coronation. In November that year a formal peace treaty between Sweden and Poland was concluded. No land was ceded, but Poland promised not to seek to secure any Baltic harbours of its own that might compete with Riga. The countries also entered into an alliance against Russia. Sweden would aid Poland in retaking land lost to Russia and would receive compensation for doing so (Courland and possibly Polish Livonia were the territories in mind).

Augustus II had not yet given up his fight for the Polish crown, and at the start of 1706 was to be found entrenched with the remains of his army and Russian auxiliaries in his Saxon lands to the west. At the same time, a Russian supporting army was operating in the east of Poland in the region of the city of Grodno. While Charles XII and his main army chased the Russians from Grodno and out of Poland, Field Marshal Rehnskiöld crushed the Saxon-Polish-Russian force at the Battle of Fraustadt (Wschowa) in February 1706. When summer came, the Swedish army moved west towards Saxony, looking for a decisive engagement. Charles XII advanced over the border into Germany and received Saxon negotiators at the castle of Altranstädt, outside Leipzig. Here, a peace treaty was signed on 24 September, in which Augustus II recognised Stanislaw as the king of Poland, promised to revoke his alliance with the tsar and to accept the Holy Roman Emperor and the Maritime Powers as the guarantors of the peace treaty, and agreed to pay the billeting costs of the Swedish army in Saxony until all was completed.

Charles XII's stay at Altranstädt, which lasted from September 1706 to August 1707, was in many ways the apogee of his career, as he became the focus of diplomatic attention and not only met his cousin Augustus II in person, but also the duke of Marlborough. During the previous year's campaign in Poland, the Holy Roman Emperor and the Maritime Powers had continued their attempts to effect a reconciliation and permit Saxony the freedom to join them as an active ally in the war against Louis XIV. For its part, France—which was keen that Saxony's forces remain committed elsewhere—encouraged Sweden to continue the war in eastern Europe. Both sides had wanted the Swedish-Saxon theatre of war to be contained outside Germany's borders, so that it would not interrupt their recruitment of soldiers for their own conflict; now, however, the Swedish army had entered German territory. France tried without success to engage the Swedes on its side in the War of the Spanish Succession, and offered to mediate peace with Russia. The Maritime Powers had no such ambitions, but even so wanted to prevent Sweden from joining in on France's side or—as was thought more likely—from frightening their German allies so that they would not commit fully to their cause.

It was Charles XII's concern for the Lutheran community in Silesia that was a source of particular irritation for the Holy Roman Emperor. In September 1707, in an agreement with Sweden, the emperor was forced to guarantee the Silesian Lutherans freedom of religion, as first established by the Peace of Westphalia in 1648, and to allow the free passage of Swedish troops through Silesia on their way to Russia. Quite apart from Charles XII's religious convictions and his concern for Sweden's prestige as a guarantor of the Peace of Westphalia, realpolitik dictated that he adopt this high-profile Lutheran position. Religious identity was of abiding political significance in Europe—not least in Germany. Religion could also be used as a hold over the other electors, including Augustus II, who had converted to Catholicism when elected king of Poland, but whose Saxon subjects, like the Swedes, were Protestants.

According to the historian Jerker Rosén, Sweden's great diplomatic failure at Altranstädt was its inability to persuade the Maritime Powers to give a written guarantee of the peace treaty with Augustus II. The British were anxious not to risk exposing their trade with Russia to reprisals. The absence of guarantees from the Maritime Powers meant that the hard-won result of the war in Poland could never be a part of an officially recognised peace accord. Everything depended on the Swedes' military presence, and '[a]s the armies withdrew, there was a corresponding weakening of the solidity of the negotiated peace.' This would become all too clear when the Swedish army suffered a crushing defeat at Poltava, in Ukraine.[27]

The watchful stance of the Maritime Powers seems understandable. In 1707, Sweden was no longer a self-evident ally in the Baltic region. Its focus on Poland over the preceding five years had led to a thinning out of military resources along the front with Russia. As early as the autumn of 1701, Russian skirmishers had begun to harry the countryside in the Baltic provinces, and soon the Swedish strongholds in Ingria and Estonia began to fall: Nöteborg (Shlisselburg) in 1702, Nyenskans in 1703, and Narva and Dorpat (Tartu) in 1704. At Nyenskans, Peter the Great had promptly founded the city of Saint Petersburg, and he laid out the Kronstadt naval base on the island of Retusaari (Kotlin). For the first time since 1581, Russia was once again a Baltic power—one with whom there were good reasons for the western European states to maintain good relations. In 1701, the Swedes had sent a (failed) naval expedition to Archangel on the White Sea, until then the only port where western Europeans had had direct access to Russian markets. The attempt made The Hague and London uneasy and, of course, was used to the full in Russian propaganda directed at the Maritime Powers. The war in Poland, which had secured political influence for Sweden while Charles XII was resident in Altranstädt in 1706-07, paradoxically undermined Sweden's importance in Europe in the longer run, because it initiated the decline of Swedish dominance in the Baltic.

In this too, Charles XII's advisors had been quick to warn him of the consequences of his Polish policies. As early as the autumn of 1702, both the Council of State in Stockholm and the king's old teacher of fortifications, Quartermaster-General Carl Magnus Stuart, had expressed their concern at the Russian advances in Ingria. In May 1703, the governor-general of Riga, Lieutenant-General Carl Gustaf Frölich, begged Charles XII to make 'peace with Poland and set upon the Russians.'[28] The same month, the Swedish ambassador to The Hague, Nils Eosander, Count Lillieroot, warned of the Russians' advances in Livonia in a letter to Piper: 'Were His Majesty to win the whole of Poland, more would be lost than won, if Russia were thereby to accomplish its aims.'[29]

Those historians critical of the king have seized on this, pointing out that even contemporary observers had difficulty seeing the campaign in Poland as anything other than a sideshow that was allowed to distract from the main conflict with Russia.[30] The counterargument calls attention to the impoverishment of the Baltic provinces during the famine years of the 1690s and the fact that Russian depredations in the first years of the war prevented any recovery, and contends that it would not have been possible for Sweden to maintain the large military force required to defend the Baltic provinces.[31]

## ■ The Russian Gamble, 1707-09

In early September 1707, the Swedish army broke camp in Saxony and marched east. The invasion of Russia—which commenced in July 1708 with victory at Holowczyn, after overwintering in eastern Poland—followed the main highway to Moscow via Smolensk, a route which requires the fewest river crossings and which both Napoleon's Grande Armée and Hitler's Heeresgruppe Mitte would later take. Without doubt, the invasion of Russia was the single most controversial point of the king's career as a field commander. Charles XII's detractors have described the enterprise as an irresponsible gamble, while his supporters see it as the proof of his unparalleled gift for strategy.[32] The king's critics do not explain how Russia was supposed to be defeated without an invasion; the king's admirers hide behind the fact that the Swedish army's archive in the field was burned after Poltava, and we therefore cannot judge the campaign plan on its merits—indeed, we do not even know if any such plan existed. As Robert I. Frost remarks, Charles XII's grand strategy was 'undoubtedly risky,' but that does not necessarily justify describing it as 'the work of a madman or an aggressive psychopath.'[33]

In the event, the Swedes carried out three parallel invasions of Russia. Furthest north, General Lybecker advanced from Finland into Ingria and on towards Saint Petersburg with 11,000 men, tasked with pinning down the Russian forces. Further south, General Lewenhaupt invaded from Riga with 14,000 men and a baggage train of 4,500 wagons, with orders to meet the main army. Lybecker was quickly forced to retreat for reasons of logistics, while Lewenhaupt's supply column was taken by surprise at the Battle of Lesnaya in October 1708. The supplies it was carrying, which in any case would have only been sufficient for a few weeks, were lost. Half of Lewenhaupt's force succeeded in joining up with the main army.[34]

The king now chose to retire south into Ukraine, drawn by the availability of supplies and the ongoing Cossack revolt under Ivan Mazepa, which offered the chance to make common cause. The underlying problem was that it was unlikely in the extreme that an independent Ukraine would acquiesce to Sweden's promise to Stanislaw Leszczyński to help the Poles retake their lost lands in the east. In the event, those responsible for Swedish foreign affairs never had to address this problem because after a hard winter the army suffered a decisive defeat at the hands of the Russians outside the city of Poltava in July 1709. The king fled with about a thousand men into Ottoman territory, while the rest of the army capitulated at Perevolochna.

In a letter from Turkey, Charles XII tersely informed the Privy Council in Stockholm that 'by a fateful and unlucky chance the Swedish troops have suffered loss in

battle' in which 'the majority of the foot soldiers have been lost, and the cavalry too has suffered heavy losses.' Everything now depended on the speed with which Stockholm could raise a new army, so that the enemy could be defeated once and for all: 'It is essential that one should not falter in one's courage and decisiveness of action, but rather one should strive to the utmost to put things once more in good order.'[35]

It was now that the Swedish allotment system demonstrated its unparalleled resilience, as within only a few months it produced a new well-equipped army under the command of Count Magnus Stenbock.[36] Whether to use this army in a new offensive on the continent or to put it in to reinforce the failing front in the east was to be a point of contention between the king and the Privy Council in Stockholm.

## ■ The Collapse of the Swedish Empire, 1709-15

After Poltava, the Swedish Empire around the shores of the Baltic began to unravel. When news of the Swedish defeat reached Augustus II of Saxony, he declared the terms of the Treaty of Altranstädt invalid and was immediately recognised as king by much of Poland. Stanislaw Leszczyński, who had been installed on the throne by the Swedes, was forced to flee to Swedish Pomerania, together with the troops Charles XII had left behind in Poland for his protection. Denmark resumed hostilities, and although the threatened attempt to retake the Swedish province of Skåne was averted at the Battle of Helsingborg in March 1710, both the Danish fleet and the security of the border with Norway to the west were continual headaches for the Privy Council in Stockholm. And of course the victors were free to resume their advance towards the Baltic Sea: Riga, Reval (Tallinn), Pernau (Pärnu), and Vyborg all fell to Russia in short order. Sweden's rule in the Baltic, which had lasted for 150 years, was over for good by September 1710.[37]

Initially, the situation in the German provinces appeared to be different. Sweden's enemies knew that all the combatants in western Europe—the French, the Maritime Powers, and the Holy Roman Emperor—were adamant that they did not want to see a nordic war spill over into German territory and for that reason were willing to recognise Swedish Pomerania, Wismar, and Bremen-Verden as neutral areas in the continuing conflict. A settlement to this effect—which also included Denmark's territories in Germany—was signed in The Hague in March 1710 by the Swedish Privy Council, with the Maritime Powers, the Holy Roman Emperor, Prussia, and Hanover as guarantors, and it was simultaneously recognised by Russia and Saxony-Poland. The Privy Council began negotiations to lease the Swedish troops in Pomerania to the Maritime Powers; however, neutrality and the leasing out of troops ran contrary to the plans Charles XII had laid out in his Turkish exile. His view was that the sultan should be persuaded to revive the Turkish war against Russia—which had reached a hiatus in 1701 after 14 years of hostilities—while he himself would fight his way back through Ukraine to the Baltic with borrowed Turkish troops. In 1710-12, he succeeded in persuading the Ottomans to declare war on Russia on three occasions, which at least in the short term appeared to reduce the pressure on Sweden's tenuous grasp on northern Europe. However, each time hostilities were broken off in exchange for minor Russian concessions—as happened in July 1711, when Peter the Great was himself surrounded at the Pruth with his entire army, yet was able to buy his way free by offering to surrender a small amount of land. An important element in Charles XII's plans was that a Swedish army would march south to meet up with the Turks, but after the loss of the Baltic provinces, northern Germany was the only area where such an army could be based. In March 1711, the Privy Council in Stockholm therefore learned that Charles XII had refused to accept both the treaty of neutrality and the leasing out of troops.[38]

Sweden's German lands thereby became open targets for its enemies. That same summer, Danish, Russian, and Saxon troops laid siege to Wismar and the following year Bremen-Verden was invaded by Danish forces, while Russians and Saxons marched into Pomerania and blockaded Stettin and Stralsund. From Turkey, Charles XII commanded the Privy Council to prepare Stenbock's army for transport to the continent. The idea of dispatching this expeditionary force—which finally disembarked on the island of Rügen in August 1712—met with opposition in the Privy Council, which under the leadership of Arvid Horn may have tried to delay it.[39] Later commentators such as Arnold Munthe have not been uncritical either, and more recently Gunnar Artéus has written of the king's 'wholly stupid decision' to send Stenbock over to the continent.[40]

As the German provinces were under threat, it was not necessarily a bad decision to attempt to relieve them; however, the king's insistence that Stenbock's army be moved to Germany was motivated in the first instance by his desire for revenge against Russia with the support of Ottoman troops, who were to advance northwards through Ukraine towards the Baltic. Given his predicament, it was not irrevocably 'stupid' to attempt to regain the initiative and personally dictate the course of events, but the chances of success were plainly slim. Charles XII's relations with the Ottoman Empire broke down in mutual disillusionment, however; he was interned by his hosts following the incident at Bender (the *Kalabalik*), and his dreams of a Turkish supporting army went up in smoke. True, Stenbock won a victory against the Danes at Gadebusch, but he was unable to proceed any further; his army was encircled at the fortress of Tönning and he was forced to capitulate in May 1713. Sweden's chance to turn the course of the war was lost. It is usually taken for granted by Charles XII's critics that Stenbock's army would have been decisive had it been sent to the eastern front, yet it is not at all certain that the miraculous reversal of fortune in Pomerania hoped for by Charles XII would otherwise have translated to some section of that front. As Christer Kuvaja's studies of the administration of Russian-occupied Finland demonstrate, it would have been impossible to find supplies for Stenbock's army in those areas for any length of time.[41]

When the threat of Ottoman intervention in the war was removed, Peter the Great was able to conquer Sweden's Finnish provinces in a combined land and sea campaign in 1713-14. The Åland Islands were also occupied, and in subsequent summers the Swedish coastline was raided by Russian galleys.[42] Sweden could not hope for any active help from the Maritime Powers, because of its rejection of neutrality for the German provinces. Similarly, Charles XII's efforts to initiate a new

Russian-Turkish war were a source of annoyance to the Holy Roman Emperor and the Maritime Powers, who were in favour of peace and stability around the Black Sea. Relations between Sweden and the Maritime Powers were furthermore complicated by the king's orders to his fleet, in March 1711, to blockade all Russian exports from Sweden's lost Baltic ports, for the result was that Swedish naval vessels began to seize Dutch and British ships in the Baltic. The confrontation escalated in 1714 when, with a breach between Sweden and Hanover looming, the elector of Hanover acceded to the British throne as George I.

At the end of 1713, with no hope remaining for Sweden's German provinces, the Privy Council had accepted the occupation of Stettin in Pomerania by Prussia and of Verden and parts of Bremen by Hanover, rather than see these areas fall into the hands of Sweden's enemies. Formally, this was a matter of a provisional 'sequestration,' but in reality Prussia and Hanover were being allowed to join in the dismemberment of the Swedish Empire. Finally able to leave Turkey, Charles XII arrived at a besieged Stralsund in November 1714, where he refused to acknowledge the sequestration. Prussia and Hanover were therefore driven into an alliance with Sweden's enemies and declared war (in June and October 1715 respectively). Stralsund fell in December 1715, Wismar five months later.[43] Swedish rule on the continent had come to a conclusive end. Soon, the final curtain would fall.

## ■ Finale, 1715-21

During Charles XII's years in Turkey it was obvious to many that there were two different Swedish foreign policies: one formulated by the king in exile, and one by the Privy Council in Stockholm. When Charles XII returned to Sweden in December 1715, leadership became more consistent.

Sweden's relations with Britain had never been worse following the declaration of war by Hanover, and the increased attacks on commercial shipping ordered by Charles XII on his return prompted the British to send an escort fleet to the Baltic to protect their ships from the Swedes.[44] Charles XII refrained from provoking the British fleet, and since George I was worried by growing Russian dominance in the Baltic, conditions were right for a reduction in tension. The War of the Spanish Succession was over, and it was no longer necessary for Sweden to strike a balance between the Maritime Powers and the Holy Roman Emperor on the one hand and France (which in 1715 agreed to provide subsidies to Sweden) on the other. Starting in 1717, the four great powers instead formed an increasingly open alliance in European politics. The bloc-building mirrored a growing mistrust of Russia in western Europe and meant that Sweden's enemies were split into two camps as Hanover and Denmark, under the aegis of Britain, squared off against Prussia and Russia. Naturally, Swedish diplomacy concentrated on playing both sides against the middle, in which a crucial role was played by the Holstein-Gottorp diplomat Georg Heinrich von Görtz, who from 1715 was Charles XII's personal advisor, despite holding no official Swedish post. Görtz's main concern was to keep various negotiating options open and to feed the suspicion between the members of the enemy coalitions, so it is not clear how seriously meant his various initiatives actually were. In 1716-17, he was in the Dutch Republic negotiating with the Jacobites, offering Swedish military assistance for the Stuart claim to the British throne. The British government heard of it, and in February 1717 both Görtz and the Swedish envoy in London were arrested and remained incarcerated for six months. Görtz went on to initiate peace negotiations with Russia on Åland in the summer of 1718: Sweden would accept the Russian conquests of Ingria and the Baltic provinces if the tsar supported a Swedish conquest of Norway. The negotiations failed after opposition from Charles XII, who refused to consider any territorial concessions.[45]

The conquest of Norway was to be Charles XII's next great venture. One theory, which cannot be proved either way, is that he wished to cut off Norway's timber exports in order to damage the Danish war effort. If Denmark was forced out of the war, the pressure on Sweden's sea routes would ease considerably and a reconquest of Estonia would become possible.[46] In any case, since no Swedish bridgeheads remained on the far shore of the Baltic, the land border to the west was the only front on which Sweden could readily attack. Presumably, Görtz was particularly eager to see Sweden strike at Denmark, since his homeland Holstein-Gottorp had been under Danish occupation since 1713. With great effort, a third Swedish army was raised. While the first invasion of Norway in 1716 had to be broken off because of logistical difficulties, the preparations in advance of the second attempt in 1718 were more thorough. However, Charles XII was killed on 11 December at the siege of Fredriksten fortress, in Norway. An immediate retreat followed, during which the main part of the northern invasion army died in a snowstorm.

The death of the king precipitated the long-awaited succession crisis, with the throne contested by the 'Holstein party,' who preferred the duke of Holstein-Gottorp—Charles XII's nephew Karl Friedrich —and the 'Hessian party,' who supported Charles XII's younger sister Ulrika Eleonora and her husband, Prince Friedrich of Hesse-Kassel. The latter emerged triumphant. Görtz, who had close connections with the Holstein party, was arrested, sentenced to death, and executed. In order to win over the Swedish aristocracy to her cause, Ulrika Eleonora had to accept that absolutism would be abolished. In 1720, she abdicated in favour of her husband, who as Fredrik I became the Swedish king. The uncertainty concerning the succession, however, left Fredrik vulnerable in the peace negotiations with Russia which were then underway.

Sweden's power was on the wane, and the end of the war had been hastened by the death of Charles XII and the changes to the political system. Britain, which now regarded Sweden as a useful buffer against further Russian expansion in northern Europe, played an important role in the peace process. In August 1719, as the Russian galley fleet harried the Swedish coast in order to make the Swedish negotiators more accommodating, a Swedish-British alliance was formed, which meant that British naval escorts in the Baltic could protect Sweden against further incursions. In this way, the Swedes gained the hope of continuing support and became far more willing to compromise in the separate peace negotiations with its other adversaries, of which Britain was one. In November 1719, peace was agreed with Hanover, which paid a sum equivalent to one million riksdaler for the right to hold Bremen-Verden; in January 1720, peace was signed with Prussia, which received Stettin and much of Pomerania; in June of the same year, peace was agreed with Denmark, as a result of which Sweden abandoned its support of Holstein-Gottorp and gave up its ancient exemption from the tolls in the Öresund Strait. To its disappointment, however, Britain, weakened by the market crash of the South Sea Bubble swindle, then chose to withdraw, leaving the mediation between Sweden and Russia to the French. To the very last, Fredrik I and the Privy Council hoped to be able to retain the majority of the Baltic provinces. Yet, Sweden lacked the capability to continue the war, and in both 1720 and 1721 the Russian galleys once again raided its coast in order to precipitate an agreement. This was compounded by Fredrik I's fears that the tsar would support Duke Karl Friedrich and the Holstein party in the struggle for the succession if peace negotiations were to drag on. In September 1721, a peace accord was finally signed in Nystad. Sweden conceded Ingria, Estonia, Livonia, Ösel (Saaremaa), Dagö (Hiiumaa), and Vyborg and its environs, but kept the rest of Finland and the right to import large quantities of Baltic grain duty free.[47] With that, the Great Northern War was over. No formal peace treaty was ever concluded between Sweden and Saxony-Poland, but peace was officially proclaimed by mutual declaration in 1729 and 1732 respectively.[48]

Charles XII had been in a better position than any other single individual to determine Swedish grand strategy and foreign policy during the Great Northern War. It has therefore been easy to assign him the blame for the misfortunes that befell Sweden during the conflict. His identity as an autocratic warrior king—and a hero to the ultra-right-wing Swedes—is a source of discomfort in modern Sweden and has naturally contributed to the harsh verdict of many historians. There can be no doubt that the king's refusal to compromise came at a high price, for at critical moments it limited his room for manoeuvre. At the same time, given Sweden's desperate situation, his tendency to take risks and to go on the offensive is understandable. There was no other way to create a turning point in the war. Neither can we be sure that there would have been a better outcome from any of the alternative courses of action identified with the benefit of hindsight. From the very start, Charles XII's rebuffal of the many offers of mediation was founded on an unshakable scepticism about his neighbours' intentions and ability to keep their promises, and in an era of cabinet government such suspicions were perfectly reasonable. The problem was that the Swedish Empire did not command the resources required to carry out the policies which he regarded as necessary. The question is whether he and his contemporaries truly understood this. After all, the reason why modern accounts of the various states' populations, productivity, and public revenue draw so heavily on later approximations is that at the time people lacked the ability to form a coherent view of the situation. When the physical factors are then factored in, it is clear that the Swedish Empire in the Baltic was doomed. There are those who agree with this, but who nevertheless believe that it was no coincidence that the end came in Charles XII's reign, thanks largely to the king himself: his was the decision to wage war in Poland for five years, while Russian troops captured vital areas of the Baltic provinces; his was the choice of focus in the war against Russia; his was the reluctance to heed his advisors' warnings; his was the overfondness for radical solutions.[49]

However, as Carl von Clausewitz was to remark, war is dialectic in nature, for it takes its character from the dynamic interplay between combatants. If blame is to be apportioned for the fall of the Swedish Empire, then one must single out Charles XII's implacable enemy Peter the Great of Russia, who spared nothing to break the Swedish dominance in the Baltic, because it stood in the way of Russia's modernisation. Neither, for that matter, can the battle for dominance in northern Europe around 1700 be described, pace the revisionists, as a 'clash of civilisations' in which Lutheran Sweden self-sacrificingly defended the west from seething hordes of Orthodox Slavs. In reality, the Great Northern War was more of a test of strength between various early modern administrative systems that copied one another to a high degree, and where access to resources that could readily be mobilised would prove decisive. It is barely credible that the struggle could have ended any other way. From that perspective, the question of Charles XII's personal significance for the loss of the Swedish Empire may quite reasonably be dismissed as meaningless.

## CHAPTER 5

# Charles XII's Armies in the Field

by Christer Kuvaja*

The research concerning Charles XII on the battlefield has generally centred on the major battles. Consequently the Swedish army's military tactics and combat methods have been emphasised by historians as the most important reasons for its successes during the first decade of the Great Northern War.[1] Above all, Gunnar Artéus has pointed out that effective combat methods explain Sweden's ability to sustain a successful war against enemies who were superior in numbers, and to win nearly all of its battles up to 1709.[2]

Jan Lindegren has pointed out that the emphasis on the role of battle and the focus on specific Caroline military tactics have resulted in a misinterpretation of Charles XII's method of warfare. The main aim of the king and his commanders was not to seek out enemies in order to confront them in battle, but to conquer as large an area of territory as possible in order to ensure that food and fodder could be obtained for the soldiers and the horses. Good prospects of supplies determined to a large extent the marching route of the Swedish army, according to Lindegren.[3]

Other researchers have also emphasised that logistics—here food and fodder— largely dictated the course of wars and that the availability of provisions often was a decisive factor. An army that had major supply difficulties and suffered from a constant lack of provisions and fodder had small prospects of winning a war.[4] The army that succeeded in forcing its enemy to operate in a small or resource-poor area rapidly gained the advantage because supply shortages led to the exhaustion of the opponent's soldiers and horses.[5]

In early modern times, provisioning was the main logistical problem for an army. It was often a major challenge to obtain food for the soldiers and fodder for the horses during a campaign. Unlike clothing, equipment, weapons, and ammunition, provisions were needed daily and in enormous quantities.[6] The stipulated daily food rations for a private soldier in the European armies was usually 600-700 grammes of bread, 400-500 grammes of meat or fish, and 2.5-3.5 litres of beer. In summer, the horses could graze or, as was more common, be fed green fodder. A horse consumed around 25 kilogrammes of the latter per day. In winter, the horses had to be fed dry fodder. If it was hay, 9-10 kilogrammes were consumed daily per horse, but generally some of the hay was replaced by other fodder such as oats, straw, and chaff.[7] The rations in Charles XII's army were largely equivalent to these figures.[8]

The focus on battles has meant that attention has not always been paid to the fact that sieges and the capture of fortresses and fortified towns were an essential part of warfare.[9] The conquest of fortresses was important because only then an army would be able to secure the occupation of an area. The fortress was also a useful base in en-

*Detail from a plan for the Battle of Gadebusch.*

*Pen and ink with watercolours by Magnus Rommel, 1712. The Swedish Military Archives, Stockholm, Sweden. Sveriges Krig 13:014.*

emy territory. Moreover, the conquerors got hold of the stores inside, if they had not been destroyed, and the inhabitants of the town could be taxed.[10] The Great Northern War began with sieges of fortified towns. In February 1700, Saxon troops surrounded the Swedish fortress in Riga and, one month later, the Danish army besieged the duke of Gottorp's largest fortified town, Tönning. In September, the Russians launched a siege of the fortress at Narva. The war also ended with a siege, namely that of Fredriksten fortress in Norway, in late 1718.[11]

The major part of an army's time was spent marching, in camp, or in quarters. Twenty to thirty kilometres was the normal daily distance. On long marches, rest days had to be scheduled at regular intervals. A camp was a place where troops gathered for a short rest and recovery, while quarters involved a longer stay. Winter quarters were most common, as it was yet unusual in the eighteenth century for armies to fight in that season.

In camp, the troops usually lived in tents, but only if their stay was intended to be short. If an army was encamped for a longer period, barracks might be built by felling trees or demolishing houses from the surrounding area. Winter quarters had to be chosen with great care. It was important that they were located in areas with plenty of supplies and opportunities for lodging. Therefore, they were frequently set up in the vicinity of a town where the officers could be billeted in the homes of the wealthier citizens. Non-commissioned officers and soldiers had to make do with simpler quarters, in poorer homes and farms in the countryside. The high command was often established in manor houses or castles in the vicinity.[12]

In this chapter I shall review the logistics of the Swedish armies and consider their importance for military operations, particularly during Sweden's Polish and Russian campaigns. A major question is the extent to which logistics can explain the Swedes' successes and setbacks. Moreover, the function and importance of winter quarters for Charles XII's army will be discussed, as well as the role of battles and sieges.


## ■ Field Armies: Weapons, Horses, and Civilians

In the early eighteenth century, field armies comprised foot soldiers (infantry), mounted forces (cavalry and dragoons), and artillery. Infantry usually made up two-thirds of the entire force. The musket was the firearm for the infantrymen and dragoons, while the cavalry was equipped with a carbine (a short rifle). The rapier was used as a side arm. It remained in use in most armies even though the bayonet gradually became common from the beginning of the eighteenth century. In this period, the Swedish infantry still had a large number of pikemen, who were armed with long thrusting spears or pikes, but no firearms.[13] The artillery did not play as important a role in Charles XII's army as it did in his main enemies' armies. Although the Swedes generally did not use artillery in battles on open ground, it did play a role in Magnus Stenbock's army, especially in the Battle of Gadebusch in 1712.[14]

Charles XII's army always had a large number of horses. Apart from the cavalry and dragoons having horses, the officers had both riding and draught horses. In addition, they were needed to pull artillery and wagons, although oxen were also used for this purpose. The number of horses and other draught animals usually totalled at least half of the number of men.[15] At the end of 1704, for example, Charles XII's army in Poland had just over 32,000 soldiers and 20,000 horses.[16]

Armies also included civilians. During the seventeenth century there had been considerably more civilians in the Swedish army but their number had declined by the beginning of the eighteenth century, when most civilians were either servants or officers' wives. A number of women were also allowed in every company to launder, sew, and repair clothes.[17] After the Battle of Poltava and the surrender at Perevolochna, the Russians took as prisoners 3,402 civilian servants and workers and 1,657 women and children.[18]

## ■ Supplies: On Foreign Territory

The Swedish army operated in Estonia and Livonia from October 1700 to July 1701, i.e., in territories belonging to the Swedish Empire. However, by crossing the river Dvina (Daugava) in the summer of 1701, it entered enemy country. In enemy land, provisions were either taken from the field of operations or transported from the home country to the war scene. All armies tried to take as many supplies as possible from the enemy's territory. The benefit was twofold: the enemy suffered an extra financial burden and had more trouble finding food and fodder for his own troops and horses. For most armies, it was absolutely necessary to gather provisions this way, as it was seldom possible to arrange long-term transport from the home country. The horses' fodder nearly always had to be taken on location, because the enormous quantities needed made long-distance supply next to impossible.[19]

Communication with the homeland was not only important for food supplies, but also for ammunition, weapons, and personnel, and as a possible line of retreat. For supplies sent overland from Sweden, the distance to the theatre of war could not be overly long, as transport then became too difficult. If sea routes were available, an army could more easily be supplied at a greater distance from the home country.[20]

When a campaign was launched, armies always carried supplies with them in wagons drawn by horses or oxen. In addition, the soldiers carried provisions in their rucksacks. Packsaddles on horses might be used as well. Live cattle were also brought along. Provisions could only be carried for a maximum of one month; otherwise the number of wagons would become too great.[21]

The provision wagons were part of the baggage train, which also included wagons containing money, ammunition, weapons, and tents, plus equipment for blacksmiths, carpenters, and barber surgeons. A large baggage train required many horses or other draught animals, which in turn needed fodder. A slowly moving baggage train of 2,000 wagons was at least 10 kilometres long, if two wagons could be drawn abreast, and was hard to protect from enemy attack. Particularly in autumn and spring, it was difficult to proceed along poor and muddy roads; the wagon wheels often got stuck in the mud. Rivers, streams, and other watercourses caused additional problems. Bridges had often been destroyed by the enemy and the soldiers had to cross with boats or on temporary pontoon bridges.[22]

## ■ Supplies: Procurement

The armies could obtain supplies near the theatre of war in various ways. The most common methods were plundering, forced taxation, contributions, and purchases.

Plundering had been largely rejected as a supply system in the early eighteenth century, as it undermined options for retreat through the area. It did occur, though, in connection with acts of vengeance against a recalcitrant population. Military command might also allow it when an army was suffering a major shortage of supplies or, occasionally, as a reward after a successful siege or victory in a battle. The scorched-earth policy was a strategic type of plundering, intended to strip the enemy's potential supply areas and thus prevent his advance.[23]

Forced taxation was a one-off tax, mainly levied on towns and usually paid in money. To enforce this measure a town was threatened with plundering and fire. It was thus a type of ransom and once the town had paid, it would be protected from pillage.

The contribution was a war tax collected from the population near the theatre of war or in the occupied area, paid in provisions and money and sometimes also in fodder. This tax was levied on both towns and countryside.[24]

During the Polish and Russian campaigns, the Swedish army typically tried to extort provisions and fodder through contributions and forced taxations, but plundering also occurred. The officers received their annual and monthly salaries in cash and had to buy their provisions from the local population or merchants. The soldiers and non-commissioned officers had less to spend because they received smaller sums of money as salary. In some situations, an army could become a huge marketplace and constitute a lucrative source of income for the people of a local community.[25]

During the Swedish army's barely one-month-long summer campaign in Zealand in 1700, supplies were requisitioned through a contribution and the food supply was stable. The population remained on their farms and initiated a lively commerce with the Swedish officers and soldiers, who paid reasonable prices for their goods.[26]

## ■ The Swedish Army Lives on Polish Bread

When the Swedish army crossed the river Dvina and left Swedish territory in the summer of 1701, it was to live mainly on the resources of the land. After the river crossing, the army marched into the duchy of Courland, which was then a vassal state under Poland. The supply issue was the main reason for the occupation of Courland. Collection of money, provisions, and fodder began immediately through contributions, and since payments were not made quickly enough, some plundering occurred. The practical task of levying and collecting contributions was carried out by a special body, the war commissariat (office of the quartermaster-general), under the command of Quartermaster-General Jöran Adlersten, who was assisted by commissioners and quartermasters, including—in Courland—Lieutenant-Colonel Anders Lagercrona. By early 1702 the provisions and fodder collected from Courland were used up and the Swedes therefore left the territory at the end of January and marched to Kovno (present-day Kaunas) in Lithuania, where they were encamped for around a month and replenished their stores.[27]

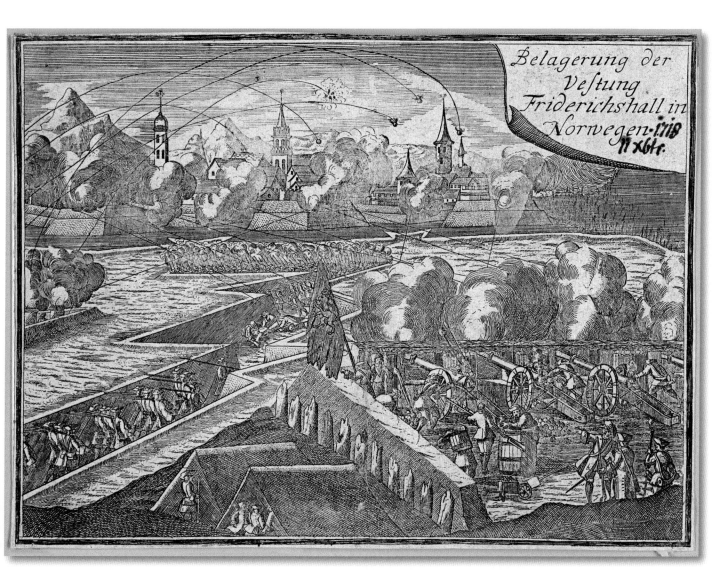

*Siege of Fredrikshald, Norway in 1718.*

*Engraving by unknown artist, eighteenth century. Kungliga Biblioteket, Stockholm, Sweden. Maps and Pictures Sv. HP C XII A. 137.*

The Swedish army's supply system functioned according to the same principles throughout its years in Poland-Lithuania. On marches, food was carried in rucksacks, packsaddles, and wagons. Polish rivers, particularly the Vistula, were used for transport. Commissioners and quartermasters were sent ahead with military forces to collect supplies and fodder, which were laid up in magazines set up along the line of march and particularly in the planned overnight locations. Provisions had to be collected rapidly; it was not unusual that they were taken with some violence from the Polish population. All the towns which were captured, with or without a fight, had to pay a contribution or forced taxes. When the Swedes gained control of larger areas, a contribution was always immediately levied. In connection with a longer encampment, particularly when the army took up winter quarters, it was often necessary to collect provisions from distant areas. Larger military forces under the command of the war commissariat were detached for such duties.[28]

In August 1702, Charles XII appointed Major-General Magnus Stenbock as head of the supply service and he remained in office until the spring of 1707. The staff of the war commissariat, including Adlersten, was placed under Stenbock's command and Lagercrona was removed from office. The reorganisation was part of an attempt to establish

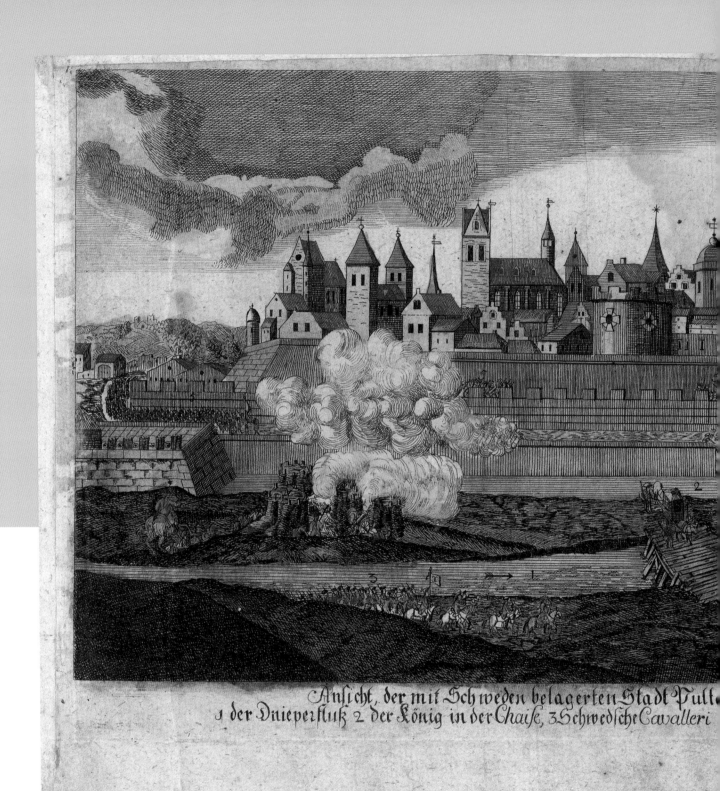

Ansicht, der mit Schweden belagerten Stadt Pult...
1 der Dnieperfluß 2 der König in der Chaise, 3 Schwedsche Cavalleri

a more controlled collection of provisions and orderly bookkeeping. In the summer of 1703, Stenbock drew up regulations for the war commissariat which included the appointment of a quartermaster in every regiment to supervise the implementation of these goals. It was in the interest of the Swedish supreme command that supplies were collected in an orderly manner and that plundering and assaults, which would antagonise the Polish population, were avoided as much as possible. Nevertheless, if someone refused to

dcArtilleri 5.Rußische Belakung.

*The town of Poltava under siege.*

*Coloured engraving by unknown artist, ca. 1709. Kungliga Biblioteket, Stockholm, Sweden. Maps and Pictures Sv. HP C XII A. 83/1.*

pay a contribution, it could be extorted with violence. Houses could also be burnt down to warn others of the consequence of resisting the Swedish army. Estates belonging to noblemen fighting on Augustus's side could likewise be pillaged.[29]

From October 1702 to the end of February 1703, Magnus Stenbock and his corps of 2,000-3,000 men managed to bring large areas east of the Vistula—Red Russia and Volhynia—under taxation. Contributions were levied on both farmers and noblemen, and the towns were forced to pay taxes. Charles XII gave express orders for tougher methods and reprisals against those who were refractory with payments. Villages and towns were plundered and burnt to the ground, and noblemen's estates were pillaged and destroyed. As a consequence, Stenbock's corps became involved in many skirmishes with hostile Polish troops and with noblemen on Augustus's side. The greater the resistance from the population, the more violent Stenbock's methods were. Although his name became synonymous with plundering, acts of violence, and fire, his expeditions were successful in terms of supplies. He managed to collect over 300,000 riksdaler in addition to 70 wagonloads of grain, slaughtered cattle, and other items, as well as large quantities of valuables.[30]

In the autumn of 1703, the Swedes collected forced taxes and contributions from the towns of Thorn (80,000 riksdaler) and Elbing (260,000 riksdaler), and in the spring of 1704 from Danzig. Contributions were also collected from Warmia and Polish Prussia during the winter of 1703-04.[31]

From November 1704 to early August 1705, the Swedish army was billeted in Rawicz in western Poland. The area had not yet been subjected to any major collections of contributions but Stenbock put large areas under taxation during these nine months. In May and June 1706, the Swedes collected significant contributions in the districts around Pinsk and in Volhynia.

After peace was concluded between Sweden and Saxony on 24 September 1706 at Altranstädt, Swedish troops were billeted throughout the electorate. The Swedish army had the right to collect contributions from Saxony and demanded payment of very large sums from all social classes of the population, both rural and urban. Saxony became a goldmine for the Swedish army. Salary arrears could be paid to the officers and the soldiers were allocated generous necessities. Moreover, there was money left to re-equip the army, horses and cannons were bought, and several new regiments were raised. Weapons and ammunition arrived from Sweden and were probably paid for, at least in part, with Saxon money. New wagons were acquired and old ones repaired.[32]

The Swedish army was able to live on the regional resources during the operations in Poland and the year-long sojourn in Saxony because it was not too large in relation to the area from which supplies were collected. At the same time, it was too small to be able to control effectively a large area of Poland. Because of this, Charles XII had to move his army in all directions in Poland in order to secure sufficient supplies for his troops. Moreover, it was necessary to find areas where the Saxon, Russian, and Polish forces had not recently collected supplies. The Swedes became successful in this, particularly when they were in winter quarters.[33]

Although the Swedes could extort nearly all their provisions in Poland, it was important to maintain a line of communication to the homeland in order to bring in men, equipment, weapons, and ammunition, and to send booty back to Sweden. Throughout the Polish war, the Swedes were able to do this, usually by way of the Vistula and via Danzig.[34]

## ■ A Hungry Swedish Army

The logistical situation changed completely during the Russian campaign. While the Swedes were in Saxony, the Russian army exploited the military vacuum left in Poland, invading and pillaging large areas of eastern and southern Poland. At the same time, the Russians took the opportunity to build a strong line of defence, the so-called Narysjki line, which began in Pskov, extended some 20 kilometres west of Smolensk, and continued some way across the river Desna in the direction of Kiev. By the summer of 1708, it was largely finished. A Russian defence plan drawn up in the spring of 1707 amounted to not engaging in major battles with the Swedes in Poland. Instead, the Russian army would retreat to Lithuania and try to delay the enemy's advance through minor attacks at river crossings and in narrow passes. They would also make it difficult for the Swedes to get supplies. The entire plan was intended to facilitate a decisive battle on Russian soil.[35]

Charles XII's army left Saxony in the autumn of 1707 and began marching eastwards. Some 8,000 dragoons were left behind in western Poland under Major-General von Krassow's command. The plan was that these forces, together with King Stanislaw's Polish and Lithuanian army, would later join the main army and take part in the Russian campaign. For several reasons, this never happened.[36]

The Swedish army was to receive additional provisions from western Poland as long as it remained in Polish-Lithuanian territory. From March to June 1708, it was billeted in the districts of Smorgon and Radoszkowicze. At this point, the lines of communication to the rear could no longer be maintained, and both food and fodder had to be taken from the land. Although large, the area was poor in resources. Nevertheless, the Swedes managed to collect key supplies for continuing the campaign. The major supply problems only began in the autumn.[37]

While billeted, Charles XII gave orders to the commander of the Courland army, General Adam Ludwig Lewenhaupt, to join the main army. At the end of June 1708 Lewenhaupt with about 14,300 men began his march eastwards. His corps hauled an enormous baggage train of at least 4,500 wagons, of which 1,300 were loaded with provisions and 200 with ammunition for Charles XII's troops. Furthermore, Lewenhaupt's army had a large number of live cattle in tow. The column moved forwards very slowly on bad roads, which the rainy summer made more difficult than usual. This made the planned junction of the Courland army with the main army in eastern Lithuania impossible.

Lewenhaupt crossed the river Dnieper on 29 September, when Charles XII's troops were already on the march towards the Russian province of Severia. At the village of Lesnaya, just south of the town of Mohilev, Russian forces attacked Lewenhaupt on 9 October. The result was catastrophic for the Swedes: a large number of men were killed or wounded and nearly the whole baggage train was lost. Almost half of the wagons had to be left behind at Lesnaya and the remainder were destroyed or abandoned 20 kilometres away at Propoisk, where the Swedish army reassembled in the dawn after the battle. On 20 October, Lewenhaupt reached the main army, but with only 6,000-7,000 men and without the eagerly awaited provisions.[38]

When Charles XII and his army broke up from their winter quarters in June 1708, they marched in the direction of Smolensk, in order to continue from there towards Moscow. Despite victory in the Battle of Holowczyn in July, the supply situation did not improve. The Russians applied the scorched-earth policy and made constant attacks on the Swedish detachments that had been ordered out to collect provisions and fodder. Grazing horses were also stolen. The population fled to the forests and hence there were no provisions to purchase. It was for supply reasons that Charles XII was forced to march southwards, towards the town of Tjerikov, in order to make his way from there to Smolensk.[39]

When the Swedes reached the town of Starycze on the Lithuanian-Russian border, 80 kilometres from Smolensk, on 21 September, they observed that the Russians were burning the ground even in their own land. Charles XII had no alternative but to turn southwards again and march to Severia to take up winter quarters.[40] The Swedes tried to prevent Russian troops from forcing their way into this province but failed, and the Russians continued their scorched-earth policy. The Swedish army was therefore forced to make its way further south into Ukraine. South of the river Desna there were good opportunities for supplying the army as Ukraine had not been ravaged. Here Charles XII was also to gain an ally in Hetman Ivan Mazepa and his Cossacks, who wanted to liberate Ukraine from Russia.

The Russian troops, however, did everything to make it difficult for the Swedes to get supplies in Ukraine. In the Cossack capital, Baturyn, abundant stores were available, but the Russians reached it first and requisitioned everything before sacking and burning the town. Mazepa suggested that the Swedish army should continue further south to the districts around the town of Romny. The Swedes took up winter quarters there from 18 November and spread out over a wide area. Some Swedish regiments and 2,000 of Mazepa's Cossacks were billeted in the town of Gadjatj, 55 kilometres east of Romny. Winter arrived in November and was the worst in living memory.

The Russians made a feigned attack on Gadjatj to delude the Swedish army into breaking up its quarters in Romny at Christmas time 1708 in order to come to the town's rescue. The Russian troops retreated as soon as the Swedes drew near, while another Russian force captured Romny and the good quarters in the town fell into Russian hands. The march to Gadjatj in the severe cold took a heavy toll on the Swedes, and because it was a challenge to find shelter and warmth for all the soldiers, many were frostbitten and thousands froze to death. Although the weather also affected the Russians, they had the advantage of being constantly able to replenish their ranks and supplies. Obviously, the Swedes lacked this opportunity.

The Swedish army could not stay in the district of Gadjatj without supplies and was forced to move on. Charles XII gave the soldiers the right to plunder. The whole winter, the Swedes advanced pillaging and ravaging both west and east of the river Vorskla. Minor battles between Swedes and Russians occurred, particularly when the Swedes captured a town to get hold of the stores. At the end of February, the Swedish army found good supply areas on the west bank of the Vorskla, some 20 kilometres north of Poltava. The army was billeted there and finally had an opportunity to rest. In early May, the army laid siege to the town of Poltava.[41]

The Russian campaign clearly underscored the importance of logistics in warfare. By making it extremely difficult for the Swedes to get food and fodder, the Russians prevented them from advancing towards Moscow. Charles XII's troops were hungry, freezing, and they died in epidemics. During the winter months of 1708-09, 3,000-4,000 soldiers met their death due to the hardships in the bitterly cold Ukraine.[42] All

this took an extremely heavy toll on the Swedes, both physically and mentally, weakening their self-confidence and morale. It was an exhausted Swedish army that faced the Russians at the Battle of Poltava on 8 July 1709.

*Charles XII leads his army across the Dvina River in 1701.*

*Painting by Johann Philipp Lemke (1631-1711), early eighteenth century. Private collection. © Photograph courtesy of Bukowskis art and design.*

## ■ Battles and Sieges

Battles were fought when an army tried to prevent the enemy from conquering an area or a town, when it wanted to force the enemy to retreat from a certain area, and when a besieged fortress was relieved. Although these battles were rarely decisive for the war, a victory in battle was significant, particularly if the enemy suffered major losses. The defeated army was forced to retreat, often far from the war scene. This meant improved logistical opportunities for the victorious army and problems for the defeated troops. The Battle of Poltava did not mean the end of the war, but it was decisive in so far as the Swedish army no longer constituted a threat to Russia. Similarly, the Swedish victory in the Battle of Helsingborg in 1710 resulted in the Danish army being forced to retreat from Scania and Sweden.[43]

A fortress or fortified town could be captured without a battle, if the defensive forces had already retreated or if they capitulated when the enemy approached. If the garrison was prepared to fight, the capture of the fortress required a regular siege and assault.[44] This often was a difficult task, as a strongly fortified town could

## The Swedish Army's Battles, Major Operations, Sieges, and Quarters, 1700-18[45]

*Charles XII's main army's battles, major combats, sieges and quarters, 1700-09*

| Type | Date and year | Location/region | Forces (approx.) | Outcome |
|------|---------------|-----------------|------------------|---------|
| Battle | 30.11.1700 | Narva, Estonia | Swedish 10,500 Russian 24,000 | Swedish victory |
| Quarters | December 1700-May 1701 | Lais (Laiuse), Estonia | | |
| Battle | 19.7.1701 | Dvina (Daugava), near Riga | Swedish 7,000 Saxon 9,000 | Swedish victory |
| Quarters | July 1701-January 1702 | Courland | | |
| Battle | 19.7.1702 | Kliszów, Poland | Swedish 12,000 Saxon 16,000  Polish 8,000 | Swedish victory |
| Quarters | October 1702-February 1703 | Lublin, Poland | | |
| Major combat | 1.5.1703 | Pułtusk, Poland | Swedish 3,000 Saxon 3,500 | Swedish victory |
| Siege | 25.5-13.10.1703 | Thorn (Toruń), Poland | Swedish 12,000 Saxon 6,000 | Swedish conquest |
| Quarters | December 1703-July 1704 | Elbing (Elbląg), Poland | | |
| Battle | 19.8.1704 | Poznań, western Poland | Swedish 2,600 Saxon 6,000 | Swedish victory |
| Siege | 6.9.1704 | Lemberg (Lviv), southern Poland | Swedish (?) Polish (?) | Swedish conquest |
| Battle | 7.11.1704 | Punitz (Poniec), Poland | Swedish 7,000 Saxon 5,000 | Swedish victory |
| Quarters | November 1704-July 1705 | Rawicz, western Poland | | |
| Battle | 31.7.1705 | outside Warsaw | Swedish 2,000 Polish 6,000 Saxon 3,500 | Swedish victory |
| Siege | 25.1-9.4.1706 | Grodno(Hrodna), Lithuania | Swedish 19,000 Polish 8,000 Russian 34,000 | Russian retreat with major losses |
| Battle | 13.2.1706 | Fraustadt(Wschowa), western Poland | Swedish 10,000 Saxon-Russian 18,000 | Swedish victory |
| Battle | 30.4.1706 | Kletsk, Lithuania | Swedish 1,500 Russian 4,700 | Swedish victory |
| Siege | 25.3-12.5 1706 | Lachowicze, Lithuania | Swedish 2,000 Polish-Lithuanian, Saxon 1,400 | Swedish capture |
| Quarters | April-July 1706 | Pinsk and Volhynia, eastern Poland | | |
| Battle | 29.10.1706 | Kalisz, Poland | Swedish-Polish 14,700 Russian-Saxon 35,000 | Russian-Saxon victory |
| Quarters | 6.9.1706-1.9.1707 | Saxony | | |
| Quarters | February-June 1708 | Radoszkowicze, eastern Lithuania | | |
| Battle | 14.7.1708 | Holowczyn, Lithuania | Swedish 12,500 Russian 40,000 | Swedish victory |
| Battle | 10.9.1708 | Malatitze, Lithuania | Swedish 4,000 Russian 13,000 | Swedish victory |
| Battle | 9.10.1708 | Lesnaya, Lithuania | Swedish 13,000 Russian 18,000 | Russian victory |
| Quarters | 28.11-27.12.1708, (2.1-9.6.1709) | Romny and districts of Gadjatj and Budisjtje, Ukraine | | |
| Siege | 3.1-17.1.1709 | Vepryk, Ukraine | Swedish 3,000 Russian 1,200 | Garrison capitulated |
| Major combat | 21.2.1709 | Krasnokutsk, Ukraine | Swedish 2,500 Russian 5,000 | Swedish victory |
| Siege | 11.5-8.7.1709 | Poltava, Ukraine | Swedish 20,000 Russian 4,000 | Garrison holds out |
| Battle | 8.7.1709 | Poltava, Ukraine | Swedish 16,000 Russian 40,000 | Russian victory |

hold out for a long time against a besieger, particularly if there were large stores in the town or if necessities could be brought in. If there was a major shortage of food, though, a town might have to capitulate even before an assault began. Neither was it unusual that the besiegers faced logistical problems during a prolonged siege and, therefore, had to break it off. Sieges could also be lifted if enemy forces came to the rescue, in some cases only after a battle had been fought. The siege of Tönning ended in May 1700, when the Danes found out that Swedish and Lüneburg troops were on the way to relieve the town. The large and strong fortress in Riga held out against the Saxons, who failed to capture the town in both the spring and the autumn of 1700. Before Narva, the Russians continued their siege despite the approach of Charles XII's main army because they believed they would eventually be victorious. However, the battle in November 1700 was a catastrophic defeat for the Russians and Narva was rescued.[46] Sieges characterised warfare in the Baltic states, Ingria, and Karelia from 1703 to 1710, and in the Swedish provinces in northern Germany from 1710 to 1715. Nearly all Swedish fortresses in these places had to endure shorter or longer sieges, and one after the other fell to the enemy.[47]

Below and to the left are listed the battles, major operations, and sieges in which the Swedish army was involved during the years 1700-18. The lists do not

*Battles and major combats in Estonia, Livonia, Courland, Ingria, and Finland, 1701-09*

| Date and year | Location/region | Forces (approx.) | Outcome |
|---|---|---|---|
| 15.9.1701 | Rauge (Rouge), Livonia | Swedish 2,000 Russian 7,000 | Swedish victory |
| 9.1.1702 | Erastfer (Erastvere), Livonia | Swedish 2,200 Russian 13,000 | Russian victory |
| 29.7.1702 | Hummelshof (Hummuli), Livonia | Swedish 5,000 Russian 30,000 | Russian victory |
| 29.3.1703 | Saladen, northeastern Lithuania | Swedish 1,000 Russian 5,000 | Swedish victory |
| 26.6.1704 | Wesenberg (Rakvere), Estonia | Swedish 2,000 Russian 8,000 | Russian victory |
| 5.8.1704 | Jakobstadt (Jēkabpils), Livonia | Swedish 3,000  Lithuanian 2,000 Lithuanian/Russian 13,500 | Swedish victory |
| 26.7.1705 | Gemäuerthof (Mūrmuiža), Courland | Swedish 7,000 Russian 12,000 | Swedish victory |
| 8.10.1708 | Koporje (Koporye), Ingria | Swedish 2,000 Russian 3,000 | Swedish victory |

*Battles and sieges, 1710-18*

| Type | Date and year | Location/region | Forces (approx.) | Outcome |
|---|---|---|---|---|
| Battle | 10.3.1710 | Helsingborg, Sweden | Swedish 14,000 Danish 14,000 | Swedish victory |
| Battle | 20.12.1712 | Gadebusch, Mecklenburg | Swedish 14,000 Danish 16,000 Saxon 3,500 | Swedish victory |
| Battle | 17.10.1713 | Pälkäne, Finland | Swedish 7,000 Russian 15,000 | Russian victory |
| Battle | 2.3.1714 | Storkyro, Finland | Swedish 4,500 Russian 9,000 | Russian victory |
| Battle | 16.11.1715 | Rügen, Pomerania | Swedish 3,000 Prussian 15,000 | Prussian victory |
| Siege | 20.11-14.12.1718 | Fredriksten, southeastern Norway | Swedish 6,000 Norwegian 1,800 | Fortress holds out |

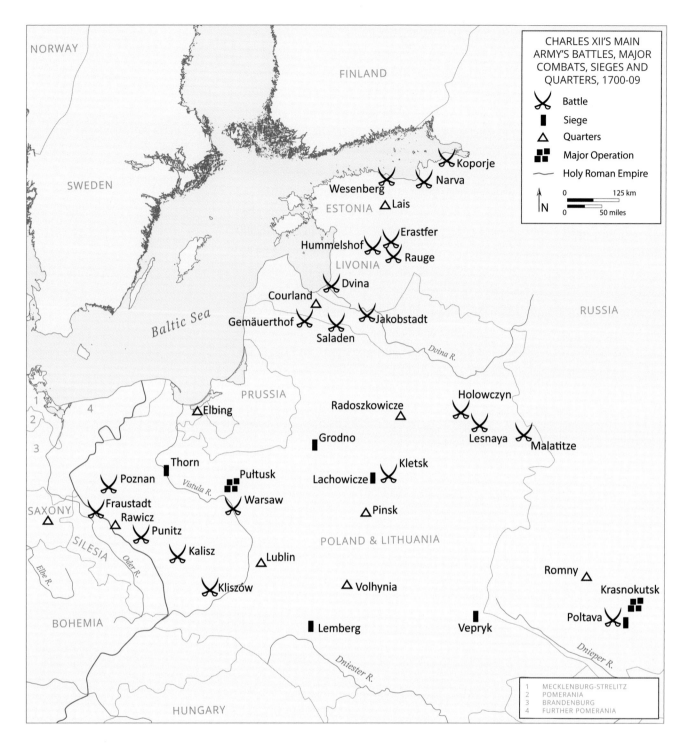

CHARLES XII'S MAIN
ARMY'S BATTLES, MAJOR
COMBATS, SIEGES AND
QUARTERS, 1700-09

⚔ Battle
▮ Siege
△ Quarters
▦ Major Operation
— Holy Roman Empire

N

| 0 | 125 km |
| 0 | 50 miles |

1 MECKLENBURG-STRELITZ
2 POMERANIA
3 BRANDENBURG
4 FURTHER POMERANIA

include the sieges that affected Swedish garrison troops in fortresses. The winter quarters for the Swedish army up to 1709 are also listed.

In the battles in Poland-Lithuania, local nobles with private armies were the Swedes' enemies, their allies, or remained neutral, depending on their interests. Those who sought Swedish support wanted to dethrone Augustus or wanted to fight against noblemen on the Saxons' side. They could and did switch sides depending on the military situation. Russian infantry sent by Tsar Peter to help Augustus often fought together with the Saxons from 1704.[48] The tables clearly show that battles were not an

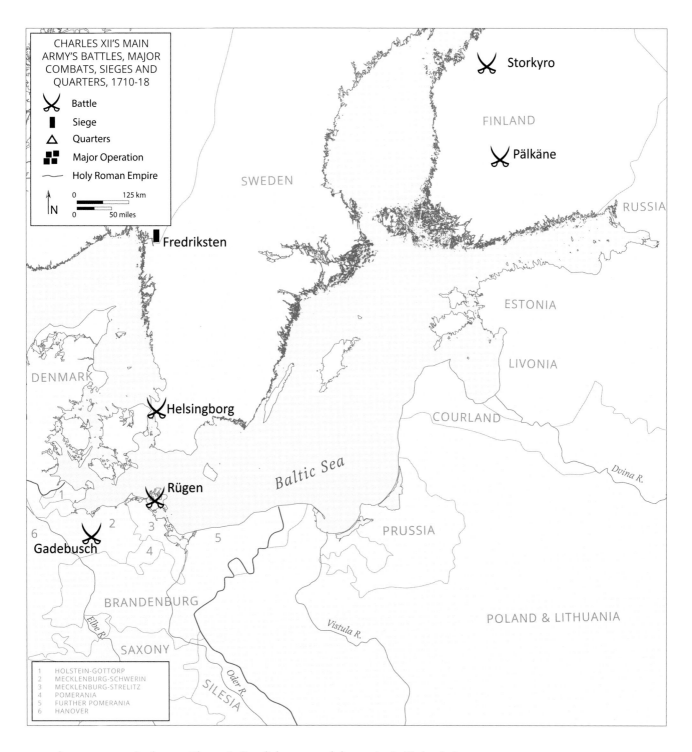

everyday occurrence in the war. The main Swedish army and the armies in Finland, the
Baltic states, Courland, and Germany were involved in no more than a few battles per
year. In the Baltic states and Ingria, only one battle occurred after 1705 and that was, in
fact, a combat in September 1708 between Swedish (Finnish) forces and Russian troops
near the fortress of Koporje in Ingria.[49] During the Norwegian campaigns in 1716 and
1718, no actual battles were fought, only minor skirmishes.

The Swedish field army was not involved in many sieges during the war. This was
partly because many fortified towns opened their gates to the Swedes without appre-

ciable resistance.[50] The largest and longest siege was that of Thorn in 1703. Actually the town was only under blockade until the beginning of September when heavier artillery arrived from Riga and an ordinary siege could be launched.[51] The Swedes wanted to take up winter quarters in this part of Poland and it was therefore important that the strong garrison in Thorn did not constitute a threat.

The most successful siege was that of Grodno in 1706. Russian and Saxon troops of around 34,000 men had forced their way into eastern Lithuania in the autumn of 1705 and had occupied winter quarters in the district around the town of Grodno. After a forced march from Warsaw, 360 kilometres in 18 days, Charles XII's army of approximately 20,000 men and Polish forces of 8,000 turned up at Grodno in late January 1706. The Swedes' arrival came as a surprise to the Russians and Saxons who did not dare to fight, but broke up quickly from their quarters, the Russians withdrawing inside the town walls. The Swedish infantry was stationed in a semi-circle, some 60 kilometres east of the town, while the cavalry with the aid of their Polish counterpart were on patrol closer to the town. The Swedes' aim was to starve the Russians, and although they could not prevent some supplies reaching the town, they caused the confined Russians to suffer a major shortage of provisions after a while. Neither could the Saxon army come to the rescue, as it was defeated by General Carl Gustav Rehnskiöld's army of 12,000 men at Fraustadt in western Poland on 13 February. When Tsar Peter heard of the defeat, he gave orders that the Russian forces should evacuate Grodno and retreat southeast to Ukraine. Several thousand men had by then died of illnesses caused by hunger and the Russian army left the town in early April 1706.

Charles XII and his army took up the pursuit of the retreating Russians. The operation was full of hardship for both sides. When the Russian army reached Ukraine, it had lost 17,000 men since the encircling of Grodno. When Charles XII arrived at the town of Pinsk, not far from the Russian border, on 4 May, he had to confess that a continued pursuit was no longer possible. The Swedes had won by using logistics as a weapon. As a result of the food shortage, the Russians had no choice but to retreat and go back to Russia to obtain food and fodder.[52]

Charles XII's main army did not follow the practice of staying in winterquarters from early autumn to spring. In 1702 (October) and 1704 (November) only, the Swedes took up winterquarters early in the autumn. In 1700, 1703, and 1708 it was not until December, and in winter of 1707-08 they waited until February 1708. In the winter 1705-06, the Swedish army was not in quarters at all. The occupation of Courland in 1701 and of Saxony in 1707 caused the troops to be billeted already in the summer. In 1702 and 1703 the Swedish army broke up from its quarters in the winter. In all other years the Swedes were billeted until the summer, except in 1709. Logistics was often the reason for both the early and late decampments. If there was a shortage of food and fodder, the Swedes had to move on in winter, and if the quarters were good, they wanted to replenish their stores before launching the summer campaign. The reason for the late decampment in 1706 and 1708 was a much-needed rest for the men, after the strenuous winter campaigns.

When the Swedish army was not engaged in battles and sieges or when it was not resting in quarters, it was on the march and had to take a rest in camps at regular intervals. Some years saw much marching and other years less. In 1701 the Swedish army conducted active warfare, with marches, camps, and battles, for approximately six weeks only, from the decampment from Lais at the end of May to the invasion of Courland in mid-July. However, 1702 saw almost constant marching from late January to the end of October. In all other years the Swedish army also marched a great deal, apart from 1703, when it was engaged in the siege of Thorn for many months. When the army was on the march or encamped and billeted, minor fights and skirmishes often occurred between Swedish troops and enemy forces, particularly when military units had been ordered out to collect fodder and provisions. Skirmishes were an everyday occurrence in the war, while major combats and battles were not.[53]

## ■ The Swedish Army's Military Tactics and Combat Methods

Charles XII's main army had won all the battles and sieges up to Poltava. It was not involved in the two battles that were lost in Poland-Lithuania: the first one of these took place in Kalisz in 1706, after peace had already been concluded between Sweden and Saxony (the Swedish army was led by General Mardefelt); the other was at Lesnaya in the autumn of 1708 (where the Swedes were led by General Lewenhaupt).[54]

In the Baltic war scene, Swedish victories exceeded those of the Russians, and Stenbock's army was victorious in the two major battles in which it participated: at Helsingborg (1710) and Gadebusch (1712).[55] Moreover, the Swedish victories were mostly against an enemy superior in numbers, as at Narva in 1700, Kliszów in 1702, Jakobstadt in 1704, Fraustadt in 1706, and Holowczyn in 1708.

Without trying to make comparisons between the Swedish king and his own generals or with the leaders of other armies, it is reasonable to say that Charles was a most competent leader. General Carl Gustav Rehnskiöld, his senior commander, was particularly skilful and the high command was united and successful in strategic and tactical deliberations, as well as in making rapid decisions on the battlefield. The Swedish offensive military tactics and the fighting spirit of the soldiers played a major role in the army's triumphant progress. The king himself set a good example with his courage, mental strength, and concern for the soldiers' welfare. Combined with battlefield successes, this created a powerful fighting spirit in the Swedish army. Well-exercised and well-trained, the soldiers mastered the art of warfare and the many victories made them braver and braver. Hardened and experienced, they led the recruits by example. In particular, the cavalry's effective combat method and strong self-confidence contributed to the battle successes.[56] Furthermore, the Swedish army seldom needed to go into battle hungry and exhausted during the campaign in Poland.

Swedish military tactics emphasised the offensive, considerably more so than their opponents. Charles XII's infantry battalions almost always attacked, and the musketeers would fire only one shot, some 50 metres from the enemy lines, before breaking in. The battle then was to be decided in close combat with cold steel. The

Danish and Saxon infantry devoted all their energy to firing, which was intended to decide the battle. The Danes fired from a stationary position, but the Saxons could also attack and then continue fighting with swords. Russian tactics often included an active defence, followed by an attack and a close combat with the sword.

After 1704 the Swedish horsemen's speed of attack seems mainly to have been a gallop or a full gallop (full speed), in tight combat formations such as knee behind knee. They used only the rapier and did not fire at all. The Danish and Saxon cavalrymen and dragoons, as well as the Russian dragoons, seem to have attacked primarily in trot and knee to knee. The Danes often attacked with only the rapier in their hands, while the carbine was more common in the Russian and Saxon cavalry.[57]

In the Saxon and Russian, and particularly the Polish, armies there was no interaction among the members of the high command, the tactical capability was flawed, and the soldiers were more inclined to flee than fight. Lack of self-confidence and lack of trust in their supreme command, rather than poor training, made the Russian, Saxon, and Polish soldiers less good warriors than the Swedes and made them retreat at the first setback, instead of engaging in a hard fight. Narva, the crossing of the Dvina, and Kliszów haunted the Swedes' enemies right up to the Battle of Poltava.[58]

### ■ Marching Routes and Battles

The presence of good supply areas and quarters often determined the marching route chosen by the Swedish army, but it certainly al so sought out the enemy to force him to retreat from a territory or a town.[59] Towns were often abandoned without resistance, while a battle was usually necessary to expel the enemy from a larger area.

Charles XII's army marched to Narva expressly to help the fortress and force the Russians out of Ingria. He also sought out Augustus's Saxon troops at Kraków and the Battle of Kliszów was fought. He initiated the siege of Thorn in the summer of 1703 to drive out the Saxon garrison stationed in the town. The intention of the campaign to Grodno in 1706 was to throw the Russians out of eastern Lithuania. In 1712 Magnus Stenbock marched against the Danes to challenge them to a battle, which then took place at Gadebusch in Mecklenburg.

Some battles were fought when the enemy tried to stop the Swedes from marching into an area, as at the crossing of the Dvina in 1701 and at Holowczyn in 1708. In Finland and the Baltic, battles broke out when the Swedes, in a defensive position, tried to prevent Russian forces from penetrating Swedish territory. Only in Courland, under Lewenhaupt's command, was the Swedish army more active, and the battles of Jakobstadt in 1704 and Gemäuerthof in 1705 where a consequence of Swedish activity. Some battles were of major importance for the course of the war, while others were insignificant.

### ■ Conclusion

Logistics clearly played a decisive role in the Swedish army's warfare in Poland and Russia during the years 1701-09. In Poland, the often good supply situation for

Charles XII's army was a major factor in its successes. The Swedes did not have to go into battle on an empty stomach, which strengthened their mental and physical well-being and their fighting spirit. During the Russian campaign, however, it was the Russians who used logistics as an effective weapon. By ravaging large areas, they managed to prevent the enemy from marching towards Moscow. The Swedish soldiers were exhausted because of lack of food. It was a morally and physically weakened Swedish army that faced the Russians at Poltava. Well-supplied and well-fed it might have had good prospects of winning the Battle of Poltava.

# CHAPTER 6

# Swedish Naval Power and Naval Operations, 1697-1721

by Lars Ericson Wolke*

*The Battle of Hangö on
7 August 1714.*

*Engraving by Alexei Zubov (1682-1741),
eighteenth century. Regional I. Kramskoi
Art Museum, Voronezh, Russia.*

## ■ The Swedish Maritime Empire

The Swedish-Finnish realm of the early eighteenth century was a maritime empire built around a central axis that ran from the Mälaren Lake Valley, across Stockholm, the Åland Islands, and the Archipelago Sea (in Swedish, Skärgårdshavet—a part of the Baltic Sea between the Gulf of Bothnia, the Gulf of Finland, and the Sea of Åland), and up the Gulf of Finland to Vyborg.[1] Over the centuries, a number of territories had been attached to its growing dominions along this watery axis. The Swedish-Finnish realm was held together by water, and that basic fact was not changed by the addition of its Baltic, Ingrian, and Pomeranian lands; if anything, they merely accentuated Sweden's position as a maritime empire.

It would be best to see this realm not as a unified landmass, which it never was, but as a constellation of different provinces, tied together by its waterways. It would then be far easier to understand how areas that were culturally and linguistically so diverse could be brought together in a way that we easily forget when we consider the Swedish Empire. It was from this whole that the Swedish conglomerate state emerged, as the historian Torbjörn Eng has so eloquently described.[2] This being the approach, it was also quite natural—indeed, relatively straightforward—for the Swedish Empire to absorb various former Norwegian and Danish provinces. It did not change the structure of the realm in any significant way, and even if the attempted conquest of Courland, begun in 1701, had been successful, it would have fitted well into the pattern.

In terms of warfare, the Baltic Sea in the early eighteenth century, as in most ages, was highly unusual compared to most other theatres of naval war. Anyone who waged war in the Baltic had to bear in mind constantly how close he was to land, as the distance to the coast was never great, even by eighteenth-century standards. Equally, anyone campaigning on land had to remember how close he was to the sea. All this meant that most military commanders had to be able to conduct operations on land and at sea, and where at all possible to coordinate them.

There are many examples that show how land and sea came together. Long after its conquest in 1621, Riga was the largest city in the Swedish realm before it was finally overtaken by Stockholm. Even at the outbreak of the Great Northern War in 1700, Riga was still a commercial centre of the first importance. Its harbour saw most of the major imports bound for the grand duchy of Lithuania, which was in union with Poland and thus tied to Sweden's enemy, Saxony, whose king, Augustus II the Strong, sat on both the Saxon and Polish thrones. Viewed from the other direction, Riga's economic hinterland was Lithuania and Belarus (then divided between Poland and Russia), from where the majority of eastern Europe's crucial grain exports to western Europe passed up the Dvina (Daugava) River to be shipped from Riga. Finally, both Swedish and Polish Livonia, along with Courland, were valued sources of naval supplies—the timber, tar, and pitch that the western European sea powers needed constantly. All this trade flowed through Riga, which made the defence of that city and its port a cornerstone of Swedish security policy.

In order to make sense of the Great Northern War (1700-21), one must therefore take into account the prevailing military conditions both on land and at sea.

However, it is at this point that one becomes aware of the profound imbalance in the research. Land warfare has been extensively researched and described; naval warfare has not. One probable explanation is the absence of major naval battles. Apart from the Battle of Køge Bay in 1710 and a couple of engagements off the Pomeranian coast in 1715-16, the campaigns of the Great Northern War were notable for the total absence of major pitched battles at sea of the type that had left their mark on the Swedish-Danish wars in the 1640s, 50s, and 70s. Yet it is precisely this form of low-key naval warfare that can be so revealing when one tries to understand how and why the Great Northern War played out as it did.

## ■ Maritime Operations during the Great Northern War

The standard picture of the Great Northern War almost invariably concentrates on the fighting on land, with battles such as Narva, Fraustadt, Poltava, and Gadebusch brought to the fore: great and dramatic events of the kind that the naval campaign does not have to offer, it is true, but likely to introduce a bias into accounts of the war, with implications for historians' ability to explain what happened. Attempts to understand why the war continued for twelve years after Sweden's catastrophic defeat at Poltava in 1709 would be aided greatly, I would argue, by studying the naval warfare of the 1710s.

The traditional bias persists to this day. Even modern accounts of the Great Northern War, excellent as far as they go and written by knowledgeable historians, exhibit an almost total lack of interest in naval operations, even where they influenced the course of the war in its entirety. Arnold Munthe attempted a general picture of the naval campaign and its importance during the Great Northern War. He was deeply critical of Charles XII's strategic and operational thinking, which he believed manifested itself in indifference to naval warfare. The very fact that the Swedes were unable to stem the Russian advance into the Gulf of Finland in 1701-03 and the subsequent expansion of Russian naval power in the area was to Munthe's mind a biting indictment. The Swedes showed an unconcern about the Russian galley fleet that he considered to have been fatal. For Munthe, this was as much a cause of the collapse of the Swedish Empire as the Battle of Poltava ever was. Gunnar Unger, writing in 1929, for his part firmly placed the blame for Sweden's inability to counter the Russian galley threat in time at the feet of Charles XII and the navy command under Admiral Hans Wachtmeister.

The impression of a mismanaged naval war, and not least the grave error of letting Russian naval power penetrate the Gulf of Finland in the first place and then grow unchecked, is found in all the literature, including the naval historian Gunnar Grandin's short but thought-provoking overview from 1989.[3] He also attempted to establish the reasons for Sweden's behaviour, writing of Saint Petersburg at the mouth of the Neva River that 'It was probably the case that in Sweden it was not believed possible or reasonable to build a city in the marshes. They doubtless imagined that if Tsar Peter wanted a Baltic port, his first choice would be to capture Riga, which was an ancient trading city.' Grandin did note the contemporary warnings, not least from Vice-Admiral de Prous, who in 1704 was commander of Swedish naval forces in the inner Gulf of Finland. He was alarmed that the Russians were building the major naval base of Kronstadt on the island of Retusaari, which they had just seized from Sweden: 'A mightily pressing matter it is, best to be sought out as directly as possible before it is brought to ruin and overthrow, that so by that to be able to forbid him [Russia], that he should not in any time, as is his purpose, bring a naval power into the Baltic Sea, to the detriment and charge of Your Royal Majesty and Your realm.'[4]

It was with Jan Glete's pioneering research, combining an unmatched command of the archives with a broad operational and strategic perspective on Sweden's actions in an international context, that our knowledge of naval warfare in 1700-21 took a major leap forwards.[5] For Glete, Sweden's inability to combine different naval weapon systems was a crucial failing. Sweden needed sailing ships if it were to match the Danish navy, but in the archipelago it was the Russian galley fleet that was the growing threat, and there the heavier Swedish vessels could not operate. Glete was the historian who most clearly demonstrated Sweden's long tradition of naval warfare in the archipelagos, not least with the help of galleys, often in combination with amphibious forces in shallow waters—an approach that worked well throughout the sixteenth and seventeenth centuries. However, towards the end of the seventeenth century, the tradition was lost, and the consequences while attempting to regain it in the 1710s were dire, for in the meantime the Russian navy had managed to establish itself in the Baltic and had already done Sweden irreparable harm.

In 1700, Sweden was attacked by a three-power alliance consisting of Denmark, Saxony-Poland, and Russia, All three were bent on revenge. Denmark was keen to regain the province of Skåne and other Danish-Norwegian areas that had been lost to Sweden under the peace treaties of 1645 and 1658. Russia had been excluded from the Baltic by the Treaty of Stolbovo of 1617, but now, as Peter the Great strove to modernise Russia and make it a superpower on a par with those in western Europe, one of his main goals was to win one or more ports in the Baltic (Russia being limited to Archangel in the far north for its direct trade with the British, Dutch, or French, all its other trade routes running across a third party's territory, not least the Swedes'). King Augustus II of Saxony-Poland was for his part intent on fulfilling the old Polish ambition to reconquer Riga, lost to the Swedes in 1621, and if possible the rest of Swedish Livonia and Estonia.

Sweden had the good luck that its attackers were not organised; on the contrary, they struck without the slightest coordination, which gave the Swedes the opportunity to fight them off one at a time.

### ■ The Invasion of Zealand, 1700

After the Danish attack on Sweden's ally Holstein-Gottorp, the Swedish fleet put out from the naval city of Karlskrona in the summer of 1700: 38 ships of the line and 8 frigates with 2,700 guns and 15,000 crew. Against this largely new fleet, Denmark was able to mobilise 29 ships of the line and 8 frigates with slightly more than 2,000 guns. In addition, however, the Swedes could count on the active support of England and the Dutch Republic: 18 Dutch ships under Admiral Philips van Almonde and 16 English vessels under Admiral Sir George Rooke arrived in the Sound, giving the

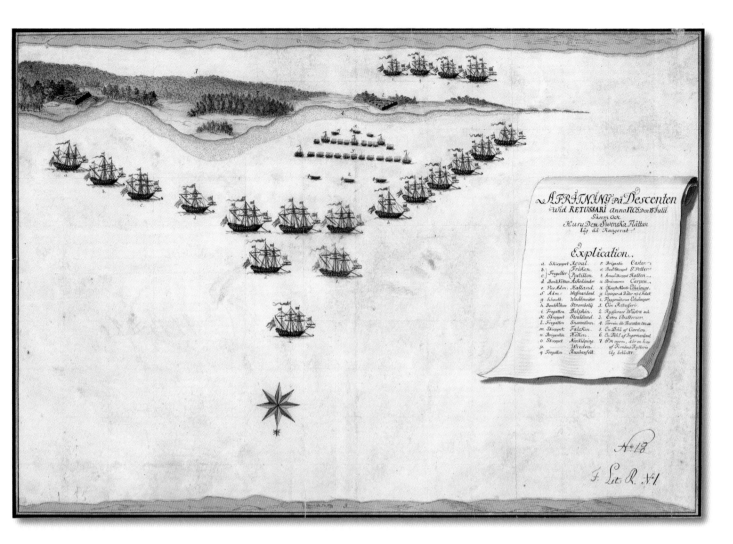

*A battle plan showing the failed Swedish attempt to wipe out the Russian naval base at Kronstadt in 1705.*

*Pen and ink with watercolours by unknown artist, ca. 1705. The Swedish Military Archives, Stockholm, Sweden. Sveriges Krig 11:98.*

allies overwhelming superiority of numbers over the Danes, who did not dare engage this fleet in open battle as it passed through the Sound, but instead waited safely behind Copenhagen's fortifications and in the southern Baltic.

During the night of 3 August 1700, 4,900 men from the Life Guards, Uppland, and Kalmar regiments, and the Malmö garrison (a battalion of the Queen's Life Regiment of Foot) boarded the allied ships in Landskrona on the eastern shore of the Sound. For logistical reasons, the cavalry could not be included in the initial stages of the operation. An unfavourable wind and the sudden appearance of Danish men-of-war caused delays, and the actual landing on Zealand did not begin until three o'clock in the afternoon of 4 August. The fleet anchored approximately 600 metres off the beach and the troops went ashore in boats—22 dugouts, 25 sloops, 3 English pinnaces, 16 Dutch dugouts, longboats, and hoys and fishing boats pressed into service. The allied men-of-war with 7 ships of the line (*Fredrik Amalia, Västmanland, Skåne, Livland, Norrköping, Estland,* and *Wachtmeister*) and 4 frigates (*Fama, Svanen,* the Dutch *Beschutter,* and the British *Queensborough*) formed up in a 900-metre-long line. They proceeded to fire broadsides from about 250 guns at the Danish positions on the beach.

The shallow water forced the landing party to wade the last 200 metres to the beach, which proved the most dangerous stage of the battle. There, some 4,000 Danish soldiers waited in unfinished defences. Even though they were expected, the attackers were able to get ashore and drive off the defenders after two hours of fighting. A second wave of 5,000 men, including some mounted units, then came ashore, at which point a powerful army of nearly 10,000 men was arrayed, ready to march south on Copenhagen.

Before being completely overwhelmed, the Danish king, Frederik IV, and his government decided to give up. On 18 August, Denmark signed a peace treaty with Sweden's ally, the duke of Holstein–Gottorp, in Travendal. The Maritime Powers—Britain and the Dutch Republic—were now satisfied, and pressed a reluctant Charles XII to break off the campaign. On 21 August, the fighting on Zealand ceased. Denmark had been forced out of the war, but Copenhagen was saved from mortal danger and, crucially, the Danish fleet remained intact after the brief summer war.[6]

## ■ The Russian Advance along the Neva

Inland waterways, rivers, and lakes had been an important part of the naval field of operations ever since the dawning of the Swedish Empire in the second half of the sixteenth century. Collaboration between the army and navy was patently a pre-requisite for military operations in that type of environment. What was new about the Great Northern War, compared with the whole seventeenth century, was that the naval engagements came to be dominated by the ocean-going ships of the line and frigates. Naval supplies were long gone and the knowledge of fighting in inland waters forgotten when war broke out in 1700. It was only in 1715-16 that the Swedish naval command—which in practice meant Charles XII personally—began to push to increase the navy's ability to fight in the archipelagos and inland waterways. But it was far too late. Sweden had been left far behind.

For eastern Finland, Karelia, and Ingria, the first years after the outbreak of war were characterised by just this type of warfare. Russian forces took full advantage of their smaller vessels to launch quick raids and amphibious operations behind the Swedes' backs on Lake Ladoga and the Neva River, and before long on Lake Peipus. A common factor in these naval battles in the eastern part of the country was that the Swedish fleet faced demands that were completely different from those in the Baltic proper. Heavy ships of the line were of no use; in the narrow waters in the border areas with Russia fast, shallow-drafted, but well-armed ships were needed, as well as the crews to man them, able to manoeuvre and fight in these types of waters and, crucially, possessing a good knowledge of local rivers and lakes. Much of this was lacking, however, at the outbreak of war in 1700.

The first to fall to the Russians was the fortress of Oreshek at Shlisselburg (Swedish Nöteborg), where the Neva River flows into Lake Ladoga. Pummelled by 10,080 cannon shots and 6,042 mortar bombs, and having repelled three attempted assaults, the commander, Gustaf Vilhelm von Schlippenbach, decided to capitulate. On 23 October 1702 he handed over the fortress to the Russians in return for free passage for himself and his remaining 83 men. Both sides realised the importance of what had happened. Peter the Great immediately changed its name to the German Schlüsselburg—the key to control of Ladoga, yes, but also the key to the way west into the Baltic.

Swedish resources were far too limited, and nothing could stop the Russian advance down the Neva River, supported by the Russian army units that pushed along its Ingrian south bank. May 1703 saw the surrender of the fortress of Nyenskans (Nyenšanc). Without delay the Russians began to put into effect the tsar's orders to demolish the remains of the Swedish settlement and to build what was to be the completely new city of Saint Petersburg, which in 1712 would be made the capital of Russia.[7]

## ■ Swedish Collapse in the Baltic Provinces

In 1704, the year after the fall of Nyenskans, Narva and Tartu (Swedish Dorpat) fell to Russia, which ended the Swedish naval presence on Lake Peipus. The last vessels on the lake were burned to keep them from falling into Russian hands. In the years that followed, the Swedish fleet dispatched annual expeditions to the Gulf of Finland to try to confine the growing Russian fleet, and in 1705 even made a concerted attempt to land at the new Russian naval base of Kronstadt, guarding the approaches to Saint Petersburg, but it was all in vain. The attack on Kronstadt was repelled. In 1710 Reval (present-day Tallinn), Pärnu, and Riga fell, as did Vyborg, and suddenly the Baltic lay open to Russian ships. Its galleys were joined by more and more Russian ships of the line and frigates, yet even so the Swedish navy still outnumbered them. In 1713-14 the Russians conquered Finland, thanks in large part to a masterly joint operation by ground troops and galleys.

The problem for Sweden was that Denmark had re-entered the war in 1709, forcing the Swedish navy to operate on two fronts, which culminated in the indecisive Battle of Køge Bay in 1710 and Swedish defeat off the German coast in 1715. In 1715-16, the Swedish positions in northern Germany also collapsed when Pomerania and Wismar fell to Danish, Prussian, and Russian troops. Of the countries locked in the struggle for power in the Baltic region, three—Sweden, Denmark, and Russia—had the ability to mount land and naval operations, while the fourth, Saxony-Poland, had no naval capability to speak of. Such an imbalance in its armed forces was surmountable in the steppes of Ukraine or Belarus, but not further north. Poland's losses during the Great Northern War underline the importance of naval warfare in the course of the war and the final outcome.

It is not surprising that the eminent British naval historian Andrew Lambert concluded that Sweden's loss of supremacy at sea meant that the country's ground forces could no longer be moved quickly across the Baltic to wherever its borders were threatened, and thus the country's position as a force to be reckoned with in the Baltic region had come to an end.[8] In addition, the fleet's increasing weakness towards the end of the war meant that it could not deploy troops for the defence of all the threatened stretches of coast, which was exactly what happened during the Russian attacks on Sweden's Norrland coast in 1721.

It was not only a question of a two-front war: an additional problem was that war against Denmark called for large sailing ships, while shallow-draft galleys that could manoeuvre in the archipelagos were needed to fight the Russians. Sweden's

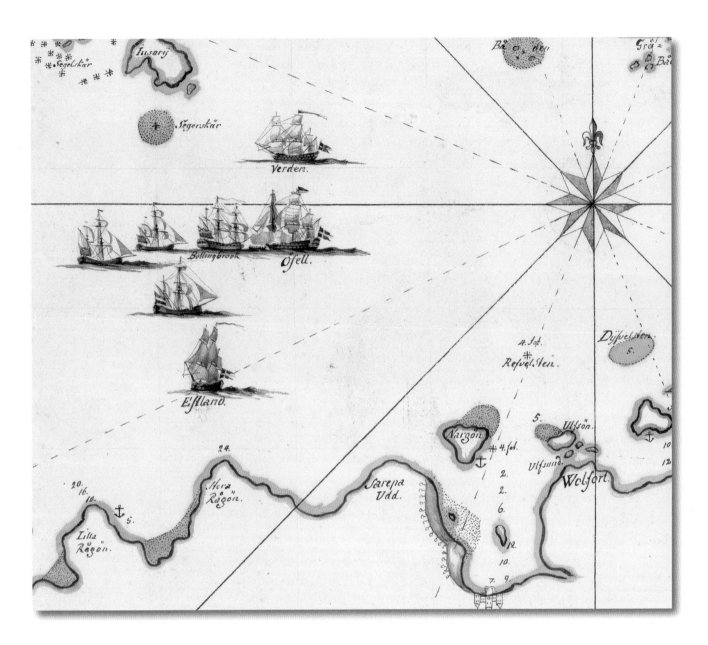

*In this detail from a sea chart, three Swedish privateers attack a group of Dutch and British ships in the Gulf of Finland.*

*Pen and ink with watercolours by unknown artist, ca. 1713. The Swedish Military Archives, Stockholm, Sweden. Sveriges Krig 13:73.*

men-of-war could not operate in the way the Russian galleys could, and Sweden thus lacked the wherewithal to counter the Russian fleet.

Certainly, Sweden began to build galleys in 1715, basing them in Stockholm (which once again became a naval base, after naval headquarters had moved south to the newly founded naval city of Karlskrona in 1680), but it did not have sufficient resources. In 1713-14, the Russian conquest of Finland had seen the clever use of land troops and smaller vessels in the archipelago, with the latter often advancing behind the Swedes' lines, forcing them to abandon their defences against the advancing Russian ground troops.

In 1714 the Russian galleys won a small but significant victory over Swedish ships off the Hanko peninsula in Finland. The symbolism of this victory was so important to the Russians that they marked it in a number of ways. The day of the battle, 7 August, corresponded to 27 July in the Old Style calendar. That was Saint Panteleimon's Day in the Russian Orthodox Church, and Peter the Great ordered that a church dedicated to the saint be built in Saint Petersburg as a memorial to his triumph over the Swedes. It was completed in the 1730s. Moreover, a series of ships in the tsarist and Soviet navies have borne the name Gangut (Russian for Hanko), and as late as 1939, Stalin, keen to invoke the old tsarist Russian military traditions, decided that the last Sunday in July would henceforth be celebrated as navy day—Hanko Day.[9]

## ■ Charles XII and the Privateering War

Back in 1709, Sweden had launched a privateering war against Denmark, especially on the sea routes between Denmark and Norway. When Russian troops captured a series of Baltic ports, the Swedish privateers' activities were extended to attempt to block Russia's trade with western Europe out of those ports. It was in this context that Charles XII felt compelled to make a point of principle about the privateering war.[10]

In 1710-14 alone, privateers brought 110 foreign vessels into Gothenburg, where the Admiralty's prize court found no fewer than 99 to be prize ships, and only 11 to have been seized on illegal grounds and therefore slated for release. Of the prizes, 35 were Danish or Norwegian, while fully 61 came from the Dutch Republic or Lübeck. Over the course of the 1710s, at least 136 British ships were seized by Swedish privateers operating from their west coast—not only from Gothenburg, but also from a number of smaller ports.

The privateers' depredations aroused protests, mainly from the British and Dutch who were dependent on the goods they could buy in the Baltic ports. In London and The Hague there was scant interest in adhering to the Swedes' trade ban on Russia's new Baltic ports. Eventually the British and Dutch navies stepped in, not only convoying their merchant ships and providing men-of-war as escorts as soon as they moved east of the Dogger Bank and the threat became acute, but even attacking Swedish privateers.

The latter did not restrict themselves to coastal waters. In growing numbers they sought prizes further out in the North Sea, the English Channel, and even in the Bay of Biscay or the Irish Sea. They often crossed the fine line between legal capture and outright piracy and sold seized merchant ships, cargo and all, to unscrupulous merchants in Dunkirk and other continental ports. A slew of diplomatic protests from The Hague and London arrived in Stockholm as the privateers' activities hit Dutch and British trade. On several occasions Sweden and the sea powers stood on the brink of open war, but they backed down at the last moment, as neither the British nor the Dutch were interested in a weak Sweden, which would leave room for complete Russian dominance in the Baltic region.

It is impossible to determine the exact effects of the privateering war. Both Britain and the Dutch Republic complained noisily, and probably rightly, about the losses inflicted on their trade and shipping. At times the seaways between Denmark and Norway were severed, while Danish trade with Iceland was attacked periodically. Yet at the same time Russian and Danish privateers were wreaking havoc among Swedish merchants. The latter, who for fear of foreign privateers shipped their goods in neutral bottoms, also ran the risk of seeing their cargo captured by Swedish privateers who did not always understand who it was they were attacking. Many valuable goods were brought into Gothenburg and from there to the rest of Sweden as privateers disposed of their prizes.

As stated above, it was probably only the British and Dutch concern that an unchallenged Russia would be too strong in the Baltic region that kept the two sea powers from inflicting harsher penalties on Sweden. Swedish diplomats in London and The Hague had an uphill task placating their hosts. These diplomatic efforts were not made any easier by Sweden's political leadership. Throughout the 1710s, until his death in 1718, Charles XII persisted in the claim that the Finnish and Baltic ports that had fallen into Russian hands in 1710—Vyborg, Reval, Pärnu, and Riga—along with Saint Petersburg and Narva, as well as Helsinki once it was conquered in 1713, were all in purely legal terms Swedish ports. That was incontrovertible, and so until peace was concluded in 1721, Charles XII's stubborn assertion prevailed. As Sweden's ruler he had the right to decide who could trade with Sweden's Russian-occupied ports, and, not surprisingly, he forbade all trade with them. There was no room for compromise.

The effect was that Swedish privateers could openly attack British and Dutch merchantmen, while Swedish diplomats in Britain and the Dutch Republic found their hands were tied: their host countries had to balance their need for naval supplies and the protection of their merchantmen with their desire for a balance of power in the Baltic and their fears of unchecked Russian expansion in the area. These complex interests, together with Peter the Great's incautious approach, and especially his brusque handling of the city of Danzig and the deployment of Russian troops in Mecklenburg, left London particularly wary. Sweden thus avoided open conflict with the western powers, despite what was at times a very aggressive privateering war. True, Sweden was at war with Hanover (whose elector was also Britain's George I), but London never threw its full forces against Sweden; on the contrary, in 1720-21 the presence of a large British naval strength in Swedish waters saved Sweden from a Russian invasion.

## ■ The Expedition to Pomerania, 1712

On two occasions, Charles XII had a hand in the navy's operative planning and on both occasions it concerned Pomerania, which was hardly surprising since it was a key piece in the king's political ambitions to persuade the Ottoman Empire to join him in a new invasion of Russia.

In 1712 Sweden had managed to assemble a new army under the command of Magnus Stenbock, who then had the thankless task of trying to finance the transport of his men down to Pomerania. Charles XII had given strict orders that his army be there, yet the Admiralty was at pains to explain that it had no money for troop transports because no funds had been allocated to cover the huge expense. Between May and August 1712, Stenbock struggled to solve his financial quandary. Ultimately he succeeded, beyond all expectation, scraping together money, ships, men, horses, and supplies for the expedition.

In early September 1712, a Swedish squadron under the command of Admiral Hans Wachtmeister lay to at the southern entrance to the Sound in order to pin down the Danish fleet under Admiral Gyldenløve. The cordon prevented the Danish ships from reaching the fleet of transports when it was at its most vulnerable, crossing the open water from mainland Sweden to Pomerania. Before leaving on 5 September to take command of the transports, Stenbock joined Wachtmeister on his flagship and reminded him that he had already requested six men-of-war, to serve as escorts and also, if necessary, to block the path of a Danish squadron under Hannibal Sehested, which was patrolling Pomeranian waters.

But on the 8th, Wachtmeister left his position and sailed past the Falsterbo peninsula, the southwesternmost tip of Sweden, en route to Bornholm. At the same time, the transports' departure from Karlshamn, some 200 kilometres to the northeast, was delayed for various reasons, chief among them a severe storm. Stenbock had arrived in Stralsund on the 7th, where he impatiently awaited the fleet of transports. 'Here I lie like a woman in childbed,' he wrote to Charles XII on 23 September, 'and waiting for delivery by the arrival of the transports. May God avert all evil, for Christ's sake.'[11] On the 25th both the Swedish men-of-war and the transports arrived in Rügen, where they anchored. The following day the crew began unloading the transports, which had docked in the Bay of Libben, between the Dornbusch and the narrow Wittow peninsula. They had deliberately put in as close to shore as they possibly could.

By the 27th, unloading had progressed so far that all the soldiers (a total of 9,423 men) had come ashore along with horses, cannons, and the regimental baggage. Remaining on board were all the stores—everything for the expedition's needs. It was at this point that Wachtmeister chose to weigh anchor and sail out to meet Gyldenløve's Danish fleet, which by now had left the Sound bound for Rügen. The two fleets that approached each other were fairly equal in strength: 22 Danish ships and 6 frigates, against 24 Swedish ships of the line and 3 frigates. However, the Danes intentionally turned aside in order to avoid a fight that day.

Meanwhile, the unloading was going more and more slowly. To save time, the grain had been loaded by tipping it straight into the ships' holds, the idea being that on arrival the crews would fill sacks and then bring them ashore. However, it was found that the 3,000 sacks that Stenbock had acquired for the purpose had been left in Karlshamn. First the grain had to be loaded by hand into small boats, rowed ashore, and then—there being no wagons and horses to transport—stored in makeshift warehouses awaiting transport to Stralsund.

The fateful day of 29 September dawned. Through a combination of changes in wind direction and skilful manoeuvring, Gyldenløve managed to put his ships between the Swedish navy and the fleet of transports. Disaster was upon the Swedes. At four o'clock in the afternoon, Gyldenløve sent forwards five frigates and a few smaller vessels that immediately attacked the transports. When the Swedes realised the danger they hoisted the signal to set sail right away and cut their anchor cables hurriedly, but only a couple of ships and a number of small transports managed to reach the safety of the Swedish line, and most of the transport fleet remained, however. By five o'clock the massacre was in full swing. The crews could do nothing but try to escape ashore to save themselves, while Danish guns destroyed the ships and their cargo.

In short order, a huge quantity of supplies, uniforms, ammunition, timber, and, crucially, bridging supplies and equipment went up in smoke. Everything needed for Stenbock's planned campaign was destroyed, and when the Swedish men-of-war finally reached the Bay of Libben, they found the water strewn with debris and floating cargo of all kinds. On the sandy beaches, the wreckage washed ashore along with the surviving Swedish sailors.

A lone Danish frigate was still in evidence and came under Swedish fire, but managed to escape. Of the Swedish transports that had managed to get out of the bay before the trap was sprung, most proceeded rapidly northwards towards the Swedish coast. Once there, they did not always even bother to seek a harbour, and no fewer than six ships were stranded deliberately on sandbanks by their terrified crews, who then tried to save themselves by fleeing ashore.

Gyldenløve had conducted a tremendously skilled operation in which, without losing a single ship of his own, he had been able to do the Swedish army in Pomerania incalculable harm, right under the eyes of the Swedish navy. All Stenbock could do was make the best of the new situation, which was easier said than done because it was almost impossible to feed all the troops in the coming winter, let alone carry out the offensive operations that Charles XII was expecting. Rarely had a naval engagement had so immediate an effect on a land war as the dramatic events at Rügen in September 1712.[12]

### ■ Fighting in the Fehmarn Belt and off Rügen, 1715

Given Charles XII's determination to defend Swedish Pomerania to the bitter end, it is not surprising that it was in German waters that the fighting between Sweden and Denmark culminated in 1715.

Even so, the two fleets' duel began further north, in the usual place around the southern entrance to the Sound. The Swedish fleet could still mobilise 30 ships of the line and a significant number of other vessels, which by any standard was a considerable achievement, but it was forced to divide to meet the threats from various quarters, and thus it could not rally sufficiently to strike a decisive blow against the enemy. Instead of mustering their strength, the Swedes, probably against their better judgment, were forced to fragment it.

As 1715 began, the fleet was in its winter quarters. In Stockholm there were 6 ships of the line, 6 frigates, a floating blockhouse, 2 bomb ketches, and about 10 light galleys—a total of 25; at navy headquarters in Karlskrona there were 18 ships of the line, along with 3 frigates; 6 ships of the line were overwintering in Kalmar; in Gothenburg, 10 frigates and 10 or so galleys; while 5 frigates and 2 bomb ketches were in Stralsund. The fleet thus comprised a total of over 30 ships of the line, 24 frigates, 4 bomb ketches, and 20 galleys, besides some smaller ships. It was, however, a geographically dispersed fleet.

At the beginning of 1715, the Danish fleet numbered 29 ships of the line on paper, but 5 of them were not seaworthy, and 4 more required extensive repairs before they could set sail again. In reality, then, the Danish fleet comprised 20 ships of the line, which roughly corresponded to the Swedish force in Karlskrona, but was significantly inferior to the Swedes if one took into account the ships in Kalmar. On the other side of the Baltic, where Finland and the Åland Islands had fallen into Russian hands in 1713-14, there was not only a large Russian galley fleet, but also 17 ships of the line and 6 frigates in the growing Russian Baltic fleet. It was a force that demanded the attention of the Swedish navy.

Pending detailed orders from Charles XII for the coming year's naval operations, the Admiralty in Karlskrona chose on 22 February 1715 to divide its forces into three squadrons, the first to be used for the defence of the Swedish archipelago, the second to patrol between the island of Gotland and the Finnish coast in order to keep an eye on the Russian navy, the third squadron to find the prime position from which to monitor the Danish fleet. In March, Charles XII ordered the creation of a fourth squadron to intercept any vessels purchased by the Russians from Britain and the Dutch Republic, which were expected to come sailing through the Sound at any moment.

His admirals became increasingly concerned at the splintering of the navy's strength, and on 20 April they appealed to Charles XII to appoint an admiral with overall command of all the squadrons, so that 'according to the time and opportunity they might be able to come together and do the enemy damage and re-separate when that proves timely and useful'. The king was prepared to concede up to a point, and on 29 May he gave permission to the Admiralty that if the opportunity presented itself, they could appoint Admiral Sparre to muster the entire fleet between Rügen and the Danish islands in order to attack the Danish fleet. If the Danes stayed away, Sparre would be allowed to sail north with the entire fleet to lure the Russians into battle.

Charles XII also gave the navy the right to attack any British and Dutch squadrons in the Baltic before they could join forces with the Danes and Russians and create an unmatchable force. The king's reason was simple: 'For they have already attacked us as soon as they come upon us unannounced in men-of-war in our waters, which is the Baltic Sea.'[13] Charles XII's claim that the Baltic was Swedish could not count on the least support from The Hague and London, to put it mildly.

In March, it was decided that 20 (if possible, 21) Danish ships of the line would be refurbished under Admiral Raben. Their task was to prevent the Swedish fleet from providing support for the defence of Pomerania, and then at a later stage of the operation to secure the seaways between Denmark and Norway. In mid-April the ships were divided into two squadrons that duly sailed into the Baltic: 8 ships of the line and a frigate under Schoutbynacht (Rear-Admiral) Gabel; and 8 more ships of the line under Raben, who began patrolling between the Danish island of Møn and the German coast.

On the Swedish side, Schoutbynacht Karl Hans Wachtmeister led 4 ships of the line—*Hedvig Sofia, Nordstjernan, Södermanland,* and *Göteborg*—south from Karlskrona. Off Møn, he was joined by 2 frigates, the *Hvita Örn* and *Falken*. However, on 10 April Wachtmeister received the king's direct orders by courier from Stralsund: he was to seek out and fight the enemy, and to that end should make sail 'for Lübeckian waters.' Wachtmeister obeyed, even though it meant he would end up in narrows where he risked being trapped. On 12 April, he came across the Danish frigate *Örnen* (also known as *Sorte Örn*), which was captured after a brief but sharp battle. She was sent with a Swedish crew to Karlskrona, while Wachtmeister's ship lay off Travemünde. There he seized a number of Danish merchantmen, but at the same time lost valuable time. When Gabel's Danish force of eight ships of the line, soon joined by four frigates, spotted the Swedish ships, they had them trapped in the Fehmarn Belt.

On 24 April, the battle broke out, intense but short. The Danish ships, helped by a following easterly wind, attacked at about half past two, and by nine o'clock in the evening it was over. Most of the Swedish ships were badly damaged and Wachtmeister saw no way of escape. Finally he gave the order to run the Swedish ships aground on the sandbanks at Bülk, close to the mouth of the Kiel Fjord. Even then the ships were not sufficiently damaged, whereupon the crews tried to complete the job so that none could fall into Danish hands. The Danes soon arrived on the scene and interrupted the process. Four Swedish ships were captured and the *Hvita Örn*, which tried to flee, was forced to go about and then also fell into Danish hands.

It was a disaster for the Swedes. The surrender of Wachtmeister's forces at the Fehmarn Belt saw the Swedish navy lose 6 good ships, of which 3 ships of the line and 2 frigates could be used by the Danish navy straight away. Additionally, 2,000 Swedish officers and sailors were lost (353 killed and 1,626 prisoners), whereas Danish losses were much smaller (65 killed and 224 wounded). Wachtmeister himself was taken prisoner and brought aboard Gabel's flagship *Prins Christian*. He later described in a report how his ship received 12 hits at the waterline and how 'I could only hear the water streaming in,' while at least 20 men had been killed and 50 wounded, including Captain Åberg, who had 'lost his leg, of which . . . he died.'[14]

One solitary vessel tried to escape: Wachtmeister's flagship *Princessan Hedvig Sofia*. Launched in Karlskrona in 1692, she had sailed as the *Drottning Ulrika Eleonora* in 1692-94 and then briefly as *Wenden* in 1694. She was equipped with 80 guns, although in practice it may have varied slightly between 70 and 80 pieces. In 1715 she was carrying 26 twenty-four-pounders, 24 twelve-pounders, 22 six-pounders, and 4 three-pounders, or a total of 76 guns. Right up until 14 May the Danes struggled to pump out and salvage the Swedish flagship, but eventually were forced to give up. The written sources note that she was set on fire, but the archaeological excavations of the wreckage show no evidence of it.

The wreck of the flagship still lies at the mouth of the Kiel Fjord, and during the summer of 2010 it was examined by Danish and German marine archaeologists. Their excavation findings, although not yet fully analysed, have proved to be an important contribution to our knowledge of early eighteenth-century men-of-war. Over the years, upwards of 20 guns have been salvaged (several of them having plainly been cast in Swedish foundries), along with a great deal of musket ammunition and 2 cannonballs. Particularly interesting is the as yet incomplete analysis of a shrapnel shell—an artillery shell filled with grapeshot, specifically designed to maim and kill. Its presence on the flagship, like the hand grenades found on other ships, serves to confirm that even in the early eighteenth century naval combat had retained important elements that were primarily directed against the enemy crew and not their ships.

The Swedish disaster off Kiel meant that the Danish fleet could now operate freely in the waters between Møn and the so-called Pomeranian Bank. This situation could not be accepted if the Swedes were to retain control of their increasingly beset positions in Pomerania, and therefore a new and larger squadron was fitted out in Karlskrona. Charles XII also demanded that the navy's various squadrons actively seek out and attack the Danish and Russian navies.

On 28 July 1715, Admiral Sparre was ready to put out from Karlskrona with 20 ships of the line, the backbone of the Swedish navy. However, light winds kept them in port, and it was not until 7 August that they arrived off Rügen. It was here they found the Danish fleet's main force of 22 ships of the line. After some manoeuvring, during which the Danes kept their distance while waiting to be able to prepare properly, Admirals Sparre and Raben decided to allow their fleets to fight.

On 8 August, 21 Danish ships of the line and 4 frigates engaged 20 Swedish ships of the line and 2 frigates in the Battle of Rügen. The battle, which began at two o'clock in the afternoon, evolved into a prolonged artillery duel, but neither side tried to settle the matter conclusively, and instead they simply disengaged at eight o'clock in the evening. However, several ships had suffered significant damage. The worst on the Swedish side was the flagship *Gota Lejon*, which suffered 40 hits on the waterline and 60 killed and wounded crewmen.

This was the last major battle between Swedish and Danish warships during the Great Northern War, and Charles XII watched it in person from a vantage point on the Perd promontory on Rügen. Before the year was over, there was also the first naval battle between the Swedish and Russian fleets off the central Baltic island of Gotska Sandön. It actually was a minor skirmish of a primarily symbolic nature. So ended 1715, which was to be the last of the war with major engagements of the classic type between arrayed ships of the line. After the Swedish invasion of Zealand in 1700 and the Battle of Køge Bay in 1710, events in 1715 marked the zenith of the traditional naval battle during the Great Northern War. The war at sea was certainly not over, but from now on it was largely an asymmetric struggle between the Swedish ships of the line and frigates on the one hand and the Russian galleys on the other.

## ■ Concluding the Great Northern War

After Charles XII's death at Fredrikshald in December 1718 came the desperate summer of 1719, when a fleet of 130 Russian galleys ravaged Sweden's east coast from Norrköping in the south to Gävle in the north. The Swedish army was pulled back to defend Stockholm, deliberately leaving the archipelago open to Russian attacks as the price for the capital's safety. In a purely military sense it was a wise choice, given the limited resources available, but the result was that the civilian population of the archipelago was in effect sacrificed to the Russian invaders. Thousands of people fled inland as the islands were set ablaze before the marauders returned east via the Åland Islands and Reval.[15]

The following year a number of English men-of-war anchored in the Stockholm archipelago to prevent new Russian attacks—for London, it was a question of the

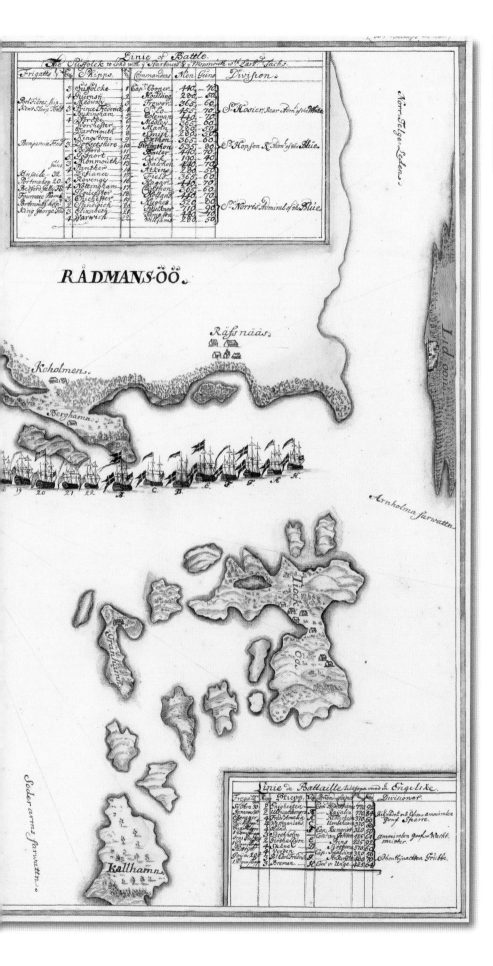

*A sea chart showing Swedish and British ships in Stockholm´s archipelago, 1720.*

*Pen and ink with watercolours by unknown artist, ca. 1720. The Swedish Military Archives, Stockholm, Sweden. Kungsboken 12:2.*

balance of power in the Baltic. Sweden did not quite founder; Russia was not allowed to become too strong. Instead the Russian galleys turned northwards and in 1720 and 1721 descended on Sweden's Norrland coast.[16]

Under the Treaty of Nystad in September 1721, Sweden ceded Estonia, Livonia, Karelia, and Kexholm, giving Russia not just one but a string of ports along the Baltic coast. For more than two decades the Swedish navy had been at war with several enemy fleets, although not always with high intensity. When the navy's sailors were paid off in Stockholm and Karlskrona in September 1721, many of them had never experienced a single peaceful year in their entire lives.

Unlike the history of the land war, Sweden's naval warfare in 1700-21 at first glance gives an episodic impression, without a solid strategic or operational thread. This in part reflects the reality: it was quite true that a coherent vision was often missing when it came to marine defence. Contemporaneous and later scholars alike criticised the decision in 1701 to advance south into Poland, ignoring the defence of the Baltic provinces or the invasion by Russia in 1708; the same was true of the stubborn defence of Pomerania at the cost of Finland's defence. Yet in all these cases there were clear strategic and operational reasons behind the decisions, even if their wisdom and importance can be questioned.

The impression given by the navy's operational thinking is much more disjointed. Charles XII often ignored naval matters altogether in order to concentrate on the land war, of which he had a much better grasp, but sometimes he did issue orders to the Admiralty, as in 1715 when his intervention led to the annihilation of a Swedish squadron off Kiel. Neither was the navy's leadership straightforward in its operational management. The admirals in Karlskrona prioritised the maintenance of the sailing fleet, the principal defence against Denmark. They were painfully slow to understand the importance of organising units for archipelago and amphibious warfare in the eastern part of the realm. When they began to put together such forces in the 1710s, it was too little, too late.

In this essay, Sweden's king and supreme commander Charles XII does not feature much, and with good reason. The king was far more uninformed and (probably as a result) far less interested in naval warfare than he was in his land wars. There is no simple explanation why this was the case, but the roots of this imbalance can almost certainly be traced to his education at the hands of army officers.

At the same time, it must be said that few Swedish monarchs have shown much understanding of naval issues, even though they ventured into naval warfare with varying degrees of success. Gustav Vasa (1521-60), and to some extent Johan III (1568-92) and Gustav II Adolf (1611-32), can be said to have shown some expertise in their handling of the navy, and perhaps even an understanding of the importance of coordinating land and naval forces, mainly in the form of amphibious operations. Far greater insight into naval warfare was demonstrated by Gustav III (1771-92) and especially by Charles XIII (1809-18), when a duke during the Russo-Swedish War of 1788-90. Viewed in this perspective, Charles XII's poor grasp of naval affairs becomes less egregious than typical, the logical consequence of a strong army tradition among Sweden's rulers. The only Swedish monarch with a proven knowledge of both land and naval warfare, and to some extent their operational implementation, was Erik XIV (1560-68), a king grossly slandered by his enemies in a way that often blinds posterity to his military insight.

Ultimately, the naval problems of 1700-21 stemmed from far more than the Admiralty's priorities in Karlskrona or Charles XII's lack of knowledge and interest in naval warfare. The emergence of a series of naval threats during the Great Northern War shows that the overall task eventually became too much for the Swedish fleet—or, if one prefers, the Swedish Empire had outgrown its resources, leaving it unable to defend itself when its enemies became more numerous and their military power ever more diversified.

STOK HOL

STOK HOLM

*Orientem* *versus*

*Templ. S. Francisci*

*Templ. S. Gertrudis*

*M Ä L A R  L A C U S*

CHAPTER 7

# The Absent King and Swedes at Home

by Marie Lennersand

*A view of Stockholm from the east.*

Engraving by Erik Dahlbergh (1625-1703) and Willem Swidde (1660-97), 1693. Kungliga Biblioteket, Stockholm, Sweden. KoB Dahlb. I:13 Ex. I.

In the year 1700, Charles XII left Sweden at the outset of the Great Northern War, never to return to the Swedish capital again. At that time nobody could know that the war would go on for two decades and that the king would remain abroad for so long. Charles XII, being an absolute ruler, intended to continue governing Sweden in the same way as before the war. Consequently, he did not hand over power to some kind of home government; instead, the plan was for him to use his field office to carry out his orders. However, the development of the war made his preferred way of absolute government hard to maintain. What became characteristic of the reign of Charles XII was, apart from absolutism, his absence from the realm.

For the people living in Sweden, the war years in the early eighteenth century meant great sacrifices and very hard times. This is true even in comparison to the seventeenth century, which also to a large extent had been filled with war, poverty, and other misfortunes. The situation became especially difficult for people living in the Baltic provinces and Finland, where many of those who managed to stay alive were forced into exile. Despite these hardships, the king expected his people to contribute to the war by paying extra taxes and sending soldiers to the army. The needs of the Crown were seemingly endless during the war, and no matter how many resources were gathered, there was always a need for more.

## ■ Ruling from a Distance

During the war a small group of members of the Royal Council remained in Stockholm and carried on, albeit with undetermined powers. The Council had no authority to act, except with direct orders from the king or in case an urgent matter could not wait for his decision. Initially, it was even considered unnecessary that the Council would hold regular meetings. Instead, the plan was that the king himself would exercise as much power as possible and that his field office would handle most political matters, especially those that concerned foreign policy. To this office belonged some of the persons whom Charles XII seems to have trusted most, like the secretary Casten Feif.[1]

The policy of ruling through the field office proved successful in some matters and almost impossible in others. Foreign policy, for obvious reasons, had to include the king and hardly concerned the Council at all. Developing plans for the administration could also be handled while on campaign, especially during periods when not much was happening in the war. Charles XII, together with some of his closest advisors, spent much time devising a number of important administrative reforms that were to be implemented by the Council back home. For instance, in 1713 he gave orders that the royal chancery was to be reorganised so that instead of consisting of one office that handled all sorts of matters, it was divided into a number of 'expeditions,' each with different responsibilities.[2]

More difficult for the king was domestic policy, both because his long absence made him lose touch with developments at home and because communication problems such as slow mail services sometimes prevented critical information from reaching him in time. The king's absence from political matters at home over time became an increasing problem, leaving the Council to do much more than was planned when the war began.[3] The question of the Council's level of authority has to be understood in a wider perspective than the matter of its handling domestic political matters during this time of war. The reason for the king's reluctance to yield any power to the Council has to do with a struggle for domination that dates back several centuries. The King's Council in Sweden was established in the middle ages and had had varying degrees of power. During the years of regency for Charles XI that power had reached its peak, but after the king had come of age and assumed the throne, the Council was stripped of much of its authority and lost many of its members.[4] Charles XI had dealt with the Council without any bloodshed, whereas a century earlier Charles IX had ordered the execution of a number of Council members whom he considered disloyal.

Against this background it is understandable why Charles XII apparently distrusted the Council and seems to have made an effort to keep it weak in his absence. During the Great Northern War, the Council consisted of a fairly small number of people. When the war began there were ten members who stayed in Stockholm, but they were mostly quite old and in 1705 already five of the ten had passed away. Charles XII was reluctant to appoint new Council members and when he did, several of those appointed were high-ranking military officers who were on campaign during the war. They could therefore not participate in the Council's work in Stockholm, which instead came to include a small group of members who by then had been holding their positions for a long time. There was, for example, Fabian Wrede (in the Council from 1685 to 1712), who was president of the Budget Office (Statskontoret) and the Chamber Audit College (Kammarkollegiet), and Nils Gyldenstolpe, a member of the Council from 1690 to1709, who among other things was chairman of the committee that was preparing a new legal code for the realm. A newcomer during the war years was Arvid Horn, who was appointed Council member in 1705. After the death of Charles XII he became one of the most influential members.[5]

As the Great Northern War progressed, the Council gained, or rather had to take, more power. After the Battle of Poltava in 1709 when Charles XII was in Bender, it sometimes took up to a year for a letter from him to arrive in Sweden. Thus, waiting for orders from the king was not an option when pressing situations arose. And there were many such instances in the aftermath of Poltava, not least because there were foreign powers that wanted to exploit the perceived weakness of the Swedes after the defeat. In 1709, Denmark attacked southern Sweden and in the following year Russia began to move in on Finland. There was much unrest in Sweden and the country suffered several years of famine and an epidemic of the plague as well. In other words, the emergencies were many and demanded that actions be taken by the Council. Apart from this, a constant top priority was to get resources for the war. More soldiers and more tax money were badly needed and it was the duty of the Council to devise ways to obtain more of both.[6]

## ■ Hard Times at Home

The king continually showed displeasure with what he saw as a lack of effort by the Council to allocate resources to the war. Nonetheless, Swedish society carried a heavy burden when it came to paying taxes and providing soldiers for the army. There was

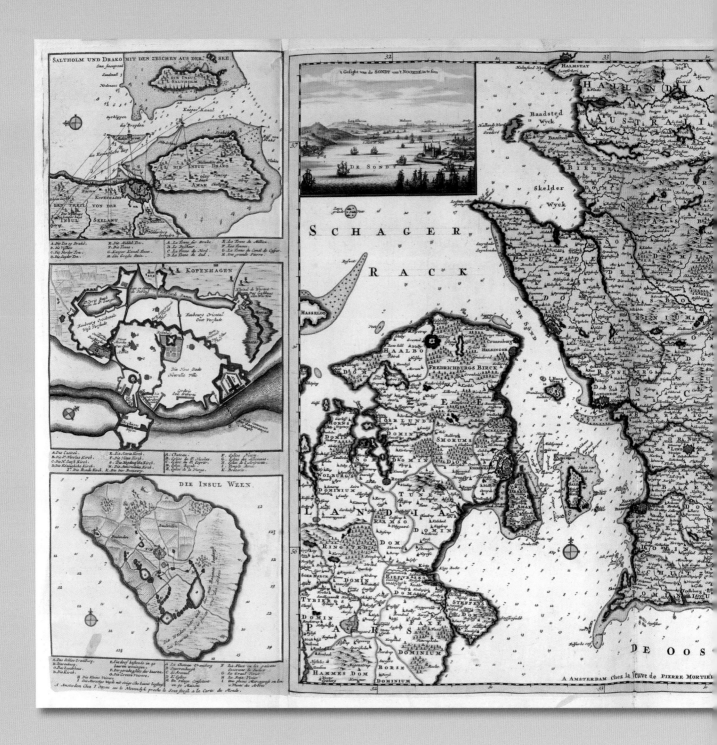

a constant need for men to replace those who died during the campaigns, either in battle or from diseases that plagued the camps. It has been estimated that about 200,000 Swedish soldiers died during the Great Northern War, which means that a fairly large proportion of the adult male population lost their lives away from home.[7] With so many men gone, the responsibility for farming, taking care of cattle, doing all other sorts of work needed to provide for families, and  being able to pay taxes, fell on those who remained at home, not least women and the elderly. Sweden's success as

*Map of Sweden, with details of some nearby islands and fortifications.*

Hand-coloured engraving by Reinier Ottens (1698-1750), ca. 1719-25. University of Amsterdam, Amsterdam, the Netherlands. Bijzondere Collecties, Universiteit van Amsterdam, plaatsnummer (OTM: HB KZL XX G 74 of OTM: HB KZL 1808 A 6).

a military power was partly owed to these women who took care of much of the work at home, making it possible for the Crown to use so many men as soldiers.[8]

The war years were in many ways difficult even apart from the war itself and the burdens that came with it. For most ordinary people the end of the seventeenth century and the first decades of the eighteenth century were harder than usual. During the years 1694-98, harvests had failed in many parts of Sweden, including the Baltic provinces, which led to many thousands dying of starvation. Historians have estimated that in Finland at least 20 per cent of the population died because of this famine. In the following years, food shortages continued to be a problem, particularly in Finland where crop failures were extensive in the first decade of the eighteenth century.[9]

Then, after several years of famine, in the year 1710 the plague started to spread in Sweden. It first came to Stockholm with refugees fleeing from Russian raids in Livonia and hit the capital in the late summer, with severe consequences. The death toll for Stockholm was somewhere around 22,000, which makes it more than a third of the population of the city at that time. Also, many people fled the city and settled elsewhere waiting for things to get better at home. This may have saved the lives of some who left, but many of them were already infected by then. Their escape was too late to save them and by leaving Stockholm they may have contributed to the rapid spread of the disease.[10]

How serious the situation caused by the plague was during the years after Poltava, is clear from Council minutes at that time. For instance, at a meeting in September 1710, the mayor of Stockholm presented a list of everyone in the city who had died in the last week. The number for that particular week was 569, which meant that people were dying at a quick pace. This was bad news not just because it meant that the disease continued to cause death, but also because of all kinds of practical problems associated with the handling of plague victims, either dead or still alive. With so many people having passed away and many others leaving the city there was almost nobody left who could take care of all the dead bodies. Most of the gravediggers had been infected and died. 'The dead are lying in the streets,' stated the mayor.[11]

While the plague was a big problem for the Council, it was only one of many pressing matters. At the same meeting in September 1710 there were discussions about the several thousand Swedish prisoners of war who had been brought to Russia after the Battle of Poltava. They now needed help with money and all sorts of practical matters. Another issue was organising and financing the defence of Stockholm, a city that was in special need of protection, being the capital and also the place where the royal family normally resided. During ordinary times, the people of Stockholm were paying for the defence of their city, but at this Council meeting the mayor stated that this was no longer possible. The Council declared it unacceptable to leave the capital without military protection, especially since Russian attacks on Finland earlier that year had made it clear that Stockholm was in a very vulnerable position. As the mayor explained, however, the problem was that a large part of the citizens had fallen victim to the plague or fled the city. There were too few people left to finance the defence of Stockholm, which meant that another solution had to be found. A third very serious matter discussed at the same meeting was a local rebellion that needed to be taken care of before it might spread.[12]

Just one of these issues was serious enough; together, they created a situation that was very unstable and that most definitely needed to be addressed without delay. Because of the plague, the Council relocated in 1710 to the city of Arboga for a short while. As the number of extremely serious situations continued to increase at an alarming rate, the responsibility of maintaining authority came to rest heavily on its members. The king spent the years after Poltava in the Ottoman Empire, mostly in the city of Bender, not coming back to Sweden until 1714. For the Council this was an additional difficulty because it created uncertainty all around the country. Of course, ordinary people would most likely never meet the king in person, but his absence still mattered to them and was something that caused a lot of unrest. There were even persistent rumours that the king in fact was dead and that this news had not been released to the public yet. For the Council it became an important task to find ways to convince people in every part of Sweden that the king was alive and that he had not stopped caring for those who remained at home.[13]

Religion was one way to address people's concerns and to ensure that they would continue to be able to endure the hardships during the war. The reign of Charles XII was in many ways characterised by Lutheran orthodoxy at its peak, giving everything a religious interpretation. All through the Great Northern War a number of special 'prayer days' (*böndagar*) were designated every year by the Church. In the early years they were often devoted to the Swedish victories on the battlefield, but as the war continued they gradually adopted a darker tone. This war, like all others, was seen as a punishment from God for the sins of the people, and this was emphasised during the prayer days. From this perspective, things grew gradually much worse, with the great losses at Poltava, the king having to spend years in exile in non-Christian territory, in addition to the plague and famine at home.[14]

## ■ Attacks on the Swedish Mainland

As if the problems with bad harvests and the plague were not enough, the war came much closer to home than before as it entered its second decade. While the battlefields of the Great Northern War were mostly located abroad, it must not be forgotten that there were many attacks on Swedish territory. Even if large parts of the Swedish realm were untouched by the acts of war, others were attacked or even occupied for a while. In the Battle of Poltava in 1709, the Swedish army suffered enormous losses and was far away from home. Sweden was seemingly left unprotected by its military, a situation that its enemies were quick to exploit. For people in many parts of Sweden the next decade was filled with terror, when Danish and Russian forces constantly attacked and burned settlements along the Swedish coasts.

A Danish attempt in 1709 to recapture the province of Scania in southern Sweden culminated in the Battle of Helsingborg in early 1710. Losing that battle, Denmark had clearly failed yet again to regain its lost provinces, but the attacks on Sweden did not stop just because of this. Although there were no new battles or organised Danish attempts to regain sovereignty over this area, in the years that followed many coastal villages were repeatedly raided by the Danish navy. The attacks were not directed against any military targets; instead, ordinary people living in Scania were taken prisoner or saw their houses plundered and burned down.[15]

In the eastern parts of Sweden, Russian attacks began in 1710, and in 1713 all of Finland was occupied until the war ended in 1721. For almost a decade, Finland was under Russian rule, a period that has been named *stora ofreden* (the great unrest). Following the Russian takeover, at least 14,000 people fled across the Baltic Sea to seek refuge. Together they made up about one-tenth of the population in Finland at this time. Many of them left to escape the Russians, but also because they had lost their homes. Several Finnish cities were burned down by the Russians, who were spreading death and terror as the troops moved along. Some of the destruction, however, came from the Swedish side, in an attempt to make the Russian takeover more difficult. For instance, when it became clear that Helsinki could no longer be defended, the city (including its grain storage) was burned down by the Swedish authorities in order to prevent it from falling into Russian hands.[16]

The Finnish refugees settled in many different parts of Sweden, even if a majority of them chose to stay in Stockholm or any of the cities along the northeastern coast. In all of Sweden, churches collected money to support the refugees, many of whom had fled without being able to take with them any of their belongings. Special 'refugee commissions' (*flyktingkommissioner*) were set up to distribute allocations to those in need, something which turned out to be a task of big proportions not least because it was difficult to keep track of all the refugees.[17]

Apart from Finland and Scania, the Baltic provinces were also under heavy attack several times during the war. There, small-scale Russian raids had been going on since the beginning of the war. This was especially bad since the people there had not yet fully recovered from the severe famine in the decade before. Piece by piece the territory was captured by Russia, never again to be returned to Sweden. In the years 1702-03 the province of Ingria and the city of Nyen (today's Saint Petersburg) were lost, and in 1704 the city of Dorpat (Tartu). A large number of people living in the captured territories were deported to Russia, where they were forced to work at large estates owned by the Russian nobility.[18]

The last of the Swedish strongholds on the Baltic coast was the city of Riga, which fell into Russian hands in 1710 after a lengthy siege, which meant several months of terror for its inhabitants. Apart from the Russian sieges, which brought with them violence and starvation, an epidemic of the plague also hit this area and took an unprecedented number of lives. It has been estimated that in the province of Livonia about 126,000 persons died, leaving only 90,000 survivors in the whole province. The high number of plague victims together with the number of people who were either killed or deported by the Russians, left the Baltic countryside in some places almost empty.[19]

After the death of Charles XII, the Great Northern War took one last turn, with Russia focusing its attention on the Swedish east coast. The aim was to put pressure on Sweden before the impending peace negotiations. With the Swedish army occupied elsewhere, this part of the country was left almost without protection. In the summers of 1719, 1720, and 1721 Russian ships repeatedly attacked towns and villages along the coast, plundering and burning houses and all kinds of ships and boats. At sea, the Swedish navy did its best to fight back, but was unable to stop the Russian raids altogether. For Sweden the main focus was to protect Stockholm, which it managed to do. But for many people living along the east coast there was simply no defence and nobody to help them. This situation turned out to last three years, with a seemingly indefatigable enemy incessantly on the attack.[20]

HOLMIA, REGIA SEDES ET CAPUT TOTIUS SUECIÆ, CUM OMNIBUS SUBURBIIS, CIRCUMJACENTIBUS INSULIS AC PROFLUENTIBUS. SUMMA CURA INLUCEM EDITA AB REINERO OTTENS, AMSTELÆDAMENSI GEOGRAPHO.

NAAUKEURIGE AFTEKENING VAN DE KONINGLYKE ZWEEDSCHE HOOFT EN RESIDENTIE-STAD STOCKHOLM MET ALLE DES ZELFS VOORSTEDEN, OMLEGGENDE EILANDEN EN STROOMEN UITGEGEVEN DOOR REINIER OTTENS TE AMSTERDAM.

The Russian raids were a hard blow against people who were already very poor. For two decades people had had to survive starvation and the plague, while also paying high taxes and sending large numbers of soldiers to the war. And when the war at last was threatening their own homes, there was nobody to protect them. This caused a lot of indignation and disappointment, especially now that the king was dead and the anger of ordinary people could be expressed more freely without risk of being seen as an act of disloyalty towards him. In some places discontent was expressed on a level that seemed downright dangerous from the Crown's perspective. In the county of Östergötland in southeastern Sweden, a group of 600 people decided to swear loyalty to the Russian tsar, because they felt that they had been betrayed and abandoned when the Russians had attacked them. The Crown had to act swiftly in order

*'A precise diagram of the royal Swedish capital city and residence of Stockholm...'*

*Hand-coloured engraving by Reinier Ottens (1698-1750), ca. 1719-25. University of Amsterdam, Amsterdam, the Netherlands. Bijzondere Collecties, Universiteit van Amsterdam, plaatsnummer (OTM: HB KZL XX G 74 of OTM: HB KZL 1808 A 6).*

to put down this act of insurgency. After a thorough examination eighteen men were condemned to death for treason, although after showing proper remorse all except one of them were pardoned.[21]

For the Crown it was of the greatest importance to act quickly and show determination in this situation. There were rumours that people in other counties were also planning to change their allegiance, perhaps hoping to be spared if the Russians attacked in the future. It has to be remembered that in the second half of the Great Northern War Finland (which was a large part of the Swedish territory) was occupied by Russia, and that this was fairly close to home for people living on the Swedish east coast, just across the Baltic Sea. They could not know when or how the war would end. People living in Sweden do not seem to have made any serious attempts to change sides, but the events in Östergötland show that it was something that the Crown considered a risk.

## ■ Financing the War

While all of this was happening, the Crown still needed to mobilise resources for the war, no matter how poor people were. In the army, the ranks had to be filled with new men as many soldiers did not survive very long. At the Battle of Poltava and on several other occasions many soldiers were taken prisoner. About 25,000 of them were brought to Russia, where they had to stay until the conditions for their return to Sweden were established in the Treaty of Nystad in 1721. Many of the soldiers had to spend years in remote places in Siberia or other parts of Russia, having to work hard in mines, shipyards, or at construction sites.[22]

To a large extent it was the local communities that were required to provide more and more men throughout the war. New soldiers had to fill the ranks all the time. This was a burden not only because it meant a loss of manpower that otherwise could have been doing work at home, but also because a soldier needed equipment, weapons, a uniform, and other such things, all of which was quite expensive. With soldiers dying in battle on foreign soil or being taken to faraway places as prisoners, any items they had had with them were most likely lost as well. Therefore, the cost of equipping a new soldier had to be paid each time by the local community in which he was recruited. The pressure this caused was felt for instance in the parish of Rättvik in the county of Dalecarlia, which was the home of the Rättvik company of the regiment Dalregementet. This company, consisting of 72 men, was set up at the beginning of the Great Northern War and sent off on campaign with the rest of the Swedish army. It took part in some battles before it ended up in Poltava, where it was completely lost along with most of the other companies that were engaged in the same battle. Back in Rättvik, a new company was at once set up and then sent off to Germany, where it was lost again, this time during the siege of Tönning in 1713. Soon afterwards, the people of Rättvik had to recruit new soldiers for the third time during the same war.[23]

Besides the responsibility for soldiers and the regular taxes that had to be paid, there were many other burdens. A number of extra taxes were devised and peasants were obliged to perform certain tasks such as supporting regiments travelling through their county. The burden of financing the war did not rest solely on the ordinary tax-paying people of Sweden, though. There were other sources, such as subsidies paid, or promised, by Sweden's allies. Nevertheless, getting as much as possible from the people at home was always an objective for Charles XII, who was ever eager to find ways to secure more income from taxes. All along, he was very critical of the efforts made by the Council, which he saw as lenient and not effective enough. Within the Council, the members were not always unanimous as to what course of action was to be followed. Especially when it came to handling the problem of insufficient resources there were major conflicts, both with the king and between different factions of the Council members.[24] While the king aimed to limit the powers of the Council, at the same time other government bodies were given more authority. This applies especially to the Budget Office, which was given a highly independent position. It had orders to allocate all available funds and give highest priority to the needs of the army, the navy, and the fortifications.[25]

The 'regulation of contributions' (*kontributionsförordningen*) of 1712 illustrates how Charles XII acted with regard to devising new forms of taxation. To explain its effort to obtain more resources for the military, the Council in 1711 sent a letter to the king, who by then resided in Bender, proposing a number of new taxes, including one that was to be paid by anyone renting a house. The king did not agree at all and, instead, decided on a property tax that could be levied each year.[26] The handling of this tax is typical of the reign of Charles XII, in that the idea and the design of this regulation came from him and his field office, while it was the Council and the administration at home that had to carry out his wishes. The officials in Sweden had to do this to the best of their abilities, but with the king so far away it could be difficult to know exactly how to execute the orders. More often than not, Charles XII seems to have been displeased with the handling of matters back home.

One method of cutting costs that the Budget Office resorted to was to pay only a part, or nothing at all, of the salaries to civil servants. Not being paid on time was far from unusual for anybody in Sweden who was employed by the Crown, since this often happened when finances were strained. But during the Great Northern War this method of saving money was used more than ever before. As early as the year 1700, it was decided that all civil servants would from then on get only half of their salaries. Exceptions were made for some of the lowest-ranking and poorest officials, but apart from them ordinary bailiffs were included as well as Council members. This was only the beginning; in the year 1711 orders were given that only a quarter of the salaries would be paid. Finally, in the year 1715, the Budget Office declared that there was no money at all to pay civil servants.[27]

This way of handling state finances was of course controversial, but did not meet much open protest at the highest level of government. Everybody knew that the king expected drastic measures to allocate resources for the war. Moreover, the Council would not protest against cutting salaries for officials as its leading member, Fabian Wrede, was head of the Budget Office and therefore the one who had made the decision. The Chamber Audit College was responsible for many of the officials who would not receive their salaries, but would hardly voice any complaints either since Fabian Wrede was president there as well.

Not being paid had obvious economic consequences for everybody employed by the Crown. But priorities were enforced even in situations where this could become a threat to national security. A good example is the regiment of the King's Guard (Livgardet), which had the responsibility to defend Stockholm. That the capital would have a military force as its protection was considered necessary, even if the front line in the war was far away. Also, from 1709 onwards the hostile attacks began to come ever closer, first in Scania and then across the Baltic Sea in Finland. From that perspective, it seemed foolishly dangerous to make cutbacks that hit the soldiers in Stockholm, but this was done anyway. As noted above, in the aftermath of the plague that hit Stockholm in 1710, its citizens could no longer finance the King's Guard. This meant that payments for Stockholm's military defence had to come from somewhere else. In the end, the solution was very typical for this period: the soldiers had to go without pay. During 1713 and 1714, they received no money at all for months on end. Colonel Gabriel Ribbing of the King's Guard complained desperately to the Council, claiming that soldiers were literally dying of starvation at their posts. Because of malnutrition and disease many of those who survived were not strong

Labels within the engraving:
Neu Schifsholm, Trabanten Stall, Königl. Admiralitæts haus, Franzisk., Blockhusholm, Hofman Hus

Fransiscus oder Ritterholms Kirch, Ritter haus

enough to perform their duties, so they could hardly have been a very effective force in protecting the capital during these years.[28]

Because of famine, the plague, and the generally very hard times, conditions were certainly not appropriate to demand the high taxes that the Crown wanted. But even though many people fell victim to the horrors that occurred during the war, there were enough people who somehow were able to pay their dues. Obviously some fared better than others, or at least not everybody suffered so much that they were completely ruined. In the early twentieth century a topic for intense debate in Swedish historical research has been the question of how heavy the tax burdens for ordinary peasants really were during the Great Northern War. The positions in the debate ranged from one side claiming that taxes were so high during those difficult times that it caused a downturn in the economy. The other side, however, argued that this was not the case, that peasants were obviously able to pay their taxes, and that therefore they could not have been as poor as has sometimes been suggested. Maybe the persistent complaints about extreme poverty were exaggerated in an attempt to reduce the tax demands. No definite answer to the question has been presented and

*View showing the Nordermalm and Sodermalm districts in Stockholm.*

*Hand-coloured engraving by Reinier Ottens (1698-1750), ca. 1719-25. University of Amsterdam, Amsterdam, the Netherlands. Bijzondere Collecties, Universiteit van Amsterdam, plaatsnummer (OTM: HB KZL XX G 74 of OTM: HB KZL 1808 A 6).*

the debate is complicated by the fact that interpretations of the sources are affected by the different views on Charles XII that historians have taken. Those with a negative attitude towards him tend to see the tax burdens as far heavier for the peasants than historians who have seen the king in a more positive light. Clearly, the Swedish economy suffered heavily because of the long and expensive war.[29]

## ■ Corruption among State Officials

If there was discontent with the war or with the handling of state finances, including taxation, this was not something that could be voiced. The king would not tolerate any opposition and for anybody who dared protest, the consequences would be severe. Still, the reign of Charles XII was filled with unrest in many parts of Sweden. Protests or sudden outbursts of violence were always said to have a specific cause, though, or to come from certain persons, instead of stemming from general displeasure with the king's politics. Yet, even if it was never stated openly, the pressure of the war was an underlying factor of the greatest importance.

One major problem during the Great Northern War that the king directed the Council to handle, was the large number of complaints from peasants all over Sweden about corruption in local administrations, especially with regard to tax levies. There was great dissatisfaction among the people around the country with the manner in which tax officials handled their duties. Many of the complaints concerned bailiffs forcing peasants to pay taxes that were too high and then keeping the extra money themselves. For the king and the Council this was a big problem, in more than one way. If people were indeed able to pay even more taxes than the prescribed amount, this was something that the Crown, rather than some bailiff, should benefit from. Also, general dissatisfaction with local officials could easily grow into more serious protests. The last thing that the king and the Council wanted in the already difficult situation during the war years was a rebellion in some part of the country.

Corruption was not easy to fight because in this particular period there was a rather delicate reason for it. When, as noted above, the Budget Office for many consecutive years withheld payments to all civil servants, it was maybe not so strange that some of them took matters into their own hands. At one Council meeting, Fabian Wrede said that their behaviour was regrettable, but that one must 'sometimes condone such things, because they are not paid all of their salary.'[30] With this forgiving attitude he implicitly defended both the corrupt government officials and the policy of the Budget Office, where he was the president and which had adopted the policy of withholding payments. But even if there were reasons that made corruption understandable, many people found it very upsetting. The Council heard disturbing rumours of discontent and this seemed to be a problem all over Sweden.

Popular displeasure with corruption did present an opportunity for the Council, because helping people who saw themselves as victims of this kind of abuse could be beneficial for the Crown. Therefore, in the years 1707-13 so-called commissions were appointed to investigate problems within the local administration in different parts of the country. They consisted of specially appointed men who were said to have been dispatched on direct orders of the king to perform this task. The commissions would visit different provinces, holding meetings where ordinary people could file formal complaints against local civil servants. This proved to be a very popular course of action and many thousands of complaints about officials, mostly bailiffs, were submitted. At the same time, the commissions became a means to legitimise the power of the king: by their very existence they showed that even if he was far away, Charles XII could still offer protection and care to his people. In order to make sure that nobody would fail to get this message, the commissions were always careful to point out to all the people they met that they were acting on behalf of the king. This was especially important in those parts of Sweden that were threatened by invasions either from Denmark or Russia, and the Council found it especially important to send commissions to Scania, to the counties on the Swedish west coast, and to Finland, where attacks occurred in 1709, 1711, and 1712.[31]

## ■ Discontent and Unrest

As explained above, there was much unrest in many parts of Sweden during the war years largely because many ordinary people were not sure who was actually governing the realm. Although the absence of the king did in reality not make much of a difference to the average peasant, the presence of the absolute king was of great psychological importance. When he was gone, many seem to have thought or at least suspected that nobody at all was left to care for the problems of ordinary people. They did not know whether the king would ever return, or whether he had already died somewhere in a distant foreign country without news of it having reached the people at home. The Council, no matter how vague and unclear its orders, had to be viewed as a body that was upholding the authority of the king and show decisiveness in whatever stressful situations arose. Otherwise the uncertainty and discontent among the people could escalate into something that would soon be very dangerous.

One such occasion happened in March 1710, in the county of Skaraborg in the western part of Sweden. There, local peasants had been called up to help protect southern Sweden from Danish attacks. Men from the parish of Vadsbo, however, refused to take part in this, claiming that according to the law they could be asked to protect their own county, but that since they were not soldiers the Crown had no right to force them to go anywhere else to fight. They had threatened the county governor (*landshövding*), Carl Gustaf Soop, who claimed that he had fled fearing for his life. So did the district judge (*häradshövding*) Aurell, who was chased away by an angry mob of men. Soop and Aurell managed to escape the situation. The bailiff, John Warenberg, was less fortunate. He had, to no avail, tried to plead with the Vadsbo men and give them all the money he had on him, but was beaten to death.

For the Council this was bad news, not only because of what had actually happened, but also because the reasons behind it turned out to be rather complicated. The perpetrators had to be punished, in order to set an example and make sure that the authority of the Crown not be contested. Attacks on state officials could not be tolerated, especially when they involved someone in as high a rank as the county governor, and killing a bailiff was bound to result in the hardest punishment possible. After a very carefully organised trial those who were seen as instigators were punished by decapitation and breaking on the wheel (*stegel*), which were the harshest methods of punishment. As the situation was deemed to be unsafe, there was a military presence nearby both during the trial and the executions.

But the reasons behind the violent outburst of the Vadsbo peasants had to be taken into consideration, not least to prevent that the same thing would happen again somewhere else. Therefore a thorough examination was ordered by the Council. The peasants claimed that their anger had been lingering for a long time, because of the bad treatment they had received, especially from the bailiff Warenberg, whom they accused of having pressed them for money. If this was true, then it was extortion that had led to violence and death in this case. It was clear that indulgence with the missteps of officials could lead to more problems.

The events in Vadsbo are interesting also because they shed light on the relationship between king and Council. In the aftermath of the events, they blamed what had happened on each other. The Council wrote to Charles XII that a major reason behind the violence had been the uncertainty created by his absence. He responded by saying that it had been a really bad idea to order the peasants to help with the defence of Scania. Gathering men who were already angry and telling them to bring weapons was asking for trouble. Thus, in the king's view, the Council was to blame for what had happened.

### ■ The King Returns

In 1715 Charles XII returned to Sweden and took up residence in Scania. As the war was still going on, he first sought to reclaim lost German and Baltic provinces. Then, in 1716 he left again on a new campaign, this time in Norway. Coming back to Stockholm to step back into the more regular role of ruler was not yet on Charles XII's agenda, and as things turned out his life ended in Norway before he was able to bring the war to a close. While the king was back in Sweden, the Council had to step back, because its services were no longer needed in the same way as before and because of the king's dissatisfaction with its work during his years of absence. Instead, Charles XII appointed the Holstein minister Georg Heinrich von Görtz to take care of both the state finances and foreign politics. It was not until after the death of the king in 1718 that the Council once again could strengthen its authority, only this time in a different context. The change on the throne meant a loosening of the hard grip that the absolute kings Charles XI and Charles XII had had on the Council. It now was the Council and Parliament that took the initiative, while the new Queen Ulrika Eleonora and King Fredrik had to step back and let go of their power.

### ■ Conclusion

During the Great Northern War it had been problematic for the Council to try to handle matters at home, not least because Charles XII never agreed with its chosen paths of action. This situation was far from ideal, except from a scholarly perspective: the king's absence is a positive factor with regard to the accumulation of source material about Sweden's government during that time. The large distance between him, the Council, and other officials in Sweden meant that instead of discussing matters in person, they wrote letters discussing the issues at hand. A big problem in studying Charles XII is, however, that he rarely expressed his opinions, thus making it hard to know why he made certain decisions or how he felt about things that happened around him. Yet, because of his correspondence with the Council during the war years it is actually possible to follow in detail how, despite his long absence, he was trying to rule Sweden from a distance.

# CHAPTER 8

# The Impact of the Great Northern War on Trade Relations with the Baltic

by Werner Scheltjens

The devastating immediate effects of the Great Northern War (1700-21) on Baltic trade are undeniable to the extent that it might seem superfluous to deal with them. The long-term economic consequences of the war, however, even if limited only to their impact on the structure of European trade relations, are far less apparent. Significant background information as well as at least a basic knowledge of this structure *before* the outbreak of war are necessary prerequisites for any effort to identify and assess these long-term consequences.

The present chapter will focus on the impact of the Great Northern War on Baltic export trade relations, rather than on the war's economic consequences in general. An important reason for this restriction lies in the fact that the source material available to study this specific impact has benefited significantly from the digitalisation of the Danish Sound toll registers, a unique source in pre-industrial economic history, containing an almost uninterrupted series of ships and their cargoes that were registered when passing through the Sound at Elsinore upon entering or leaving the Baltic, starting in 1497 and lasting until 1857, when the Sound dues were abolished.[1] Although this source has been known to economic historians for several generations thanks to a compilation of part of the extensive full text of the original records in seven volumes of highly aggregated statistics,[2] the limitations of the published statistics have (perhaps) prevented these resources from being used for a long-term analysis of the economic consequences of the Great Northern War on the structure of Baltic trade.

The description and analysis in this chapter will be presented in four sections. The first one introduces the subject matter and the 'mercantile background' of Sweden's rise in the seventeenth century.[3] The second section focuses on the structure of Baltic trade in the closing decades of the seventeenth century, the main characteristics of Sweden's foreign trade, and its role in maintaining and strengthening the Empire's great power status. This will be followed by a description of changes in the structure of Baltic trade during the Great Northern War, while the final section summarises these changes before, during, and after the Great Northern War on the basis of the specific example of Reval (present-day Tallinn).

## ■ The 'Mercantile Background' of Sweden's Rise in the Seventeenth Century

From as early as the Peace Treaty of Stolbovo (1617), which confirmed Muscovy's loss of the Baltic provinces of Ingria, Estonia, and Livonia,[4] but more intensively from the

*The port at Riga.*

*Painting by unknown artist, second half of the seventeenth century. Museum of History and Navigation, Riga, Latvia.*

1640s onwards, Sweden made significant efforts to dominate the Baltic Sea, not only by using (or at least threatening to use) its naval and military force[5] but, more important, by trying to influence and control major international trade flows in the Baltic, a continued effort in which the diversion of Russian trade flows towards the Swedish Baltic ports rather than Archangel played a decisive role.[6] Sweden developed a mercantilist transport policy with regard to Russian trade, in which the potential fiscal income from controlling Russian trade with England and the Dutch Republic was more important than direct Russo-Swedish trade.[7] Thus, as Kotilaine maintains, '[t]he existence of an international border between the old Novgorod lands and the Baltic littoral introduced a political dimension to the commercial exchange with all the complications that this entailed. Trade inevitably became an important bargaining chip in Swedish-Russian diplomacy, given that the historic dependency of the north-western Russian cities on Baltic trade was only matched by the Swedish ambitions of turning their Baltic possessions into thriving centers of commerce . . . .'[8] Despite these ambitions, which find expression in Sweden's mercantile policies, it is worth noticing that Sweden was not a mercantile state, like England or the Dutch Republic. The Swedish Empire was based on military power and on the control and taxation of foreign capital for the benefit of increasing the state's fiscal revenue.[9]

In the second half of the seventeenth century, when part of Pomerania had been put under Swedish rule (1648), Sweden fought a war with Denmark and Poland-Lithuania (1655-60) and withstood a failed offensive initiated by Muscovy (1656-58), which aimed at restoring the latter's long-lost access to the Baltic and even led to the temporary reconquest of Nyen.[10] In the Treaties of Oliva (1660), Kardis (1661), Pljussa (Plyse, 1666), and Andrusovo (1667), the territorial boundaries of the parties involved in Baltic trade were set for the decades to come. Sweden's economic aspirations in the Baltic were clearly reflected in these treaties, which were drawn up at the peak of Sweden's great-power status within the emerging European system of states.[11] At the same time, they might be seen as the basis for a gradual turning of the tide against Sweden; hence, relations between Sweden and Russia (Muscovy) after 1661 constituted a 'hostile coexistence' at best and were unsustainable in the long run. It was a question of waiting for the right time before an anti-Swedish coalition of neighbouring states would take shape and take action.[12]

Sweden's primary economic interests in the Baltic underwent structural changes as a consequence of the growing importance of Russian transit trade via Swedish ports in the Baltic, the rise of England as a significant trading partner, and the general dissatisfaction of competing powers (especially France and England) with the dominance of Dutch shipping in northern European waters, which found its expression in the implementation of mercantilist economic policies in several European states, including Sweden (see above). In fact, the growing discontent with the commercial dominance of the Dutch, who had successfully replaced the Hanse as mediator of trade relations between the Baltic and North seas in the course of the sixteenth and during the first half of the seventeenth century, much to the frustration of France and Britain alike, had already led to naval warfare around the mid-seventeenth century (First Anglo-Dutch War of 1652-54) and to the subsequent opposi-

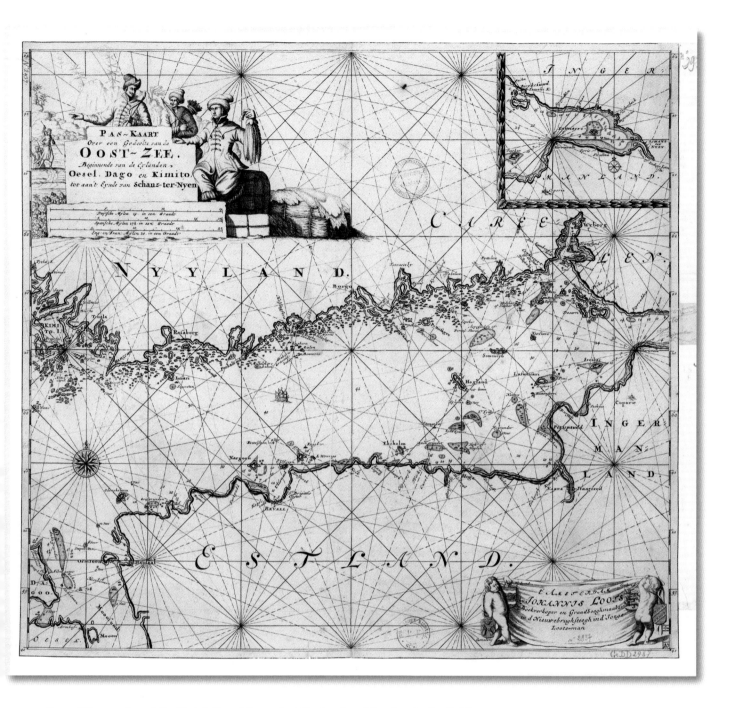

tion of Denmark and the Dutch Republic against England and Sweden in the Baltic.[13]
The dualism of *dominium maris baltici* (Sweden), on one hand, and access to the
Baltic (Denmark), on the other, is expressed clearly in Anderson's description of the
state of naval affairs in the Baltic in 1658: '. . . on finding that the Dutch intended to
side with Denmark, the English Government decided to send a fleet to help Sweden.
It was almost as disadvantageous for England as for the Dutch Republic that the
Baltic should become a Swedish lake, but it would be even worse for it to pass into
the power of the Dutch and Danes.'[14]

Both Sweden's efforts to establish itself as a European Great Power through the attain-
ment of *dominium maris baltici* and France's (failed) attempt to liberate its Baltic com-

merce from the dominance of the Dutch through the foundation of the Compagnie de Commerce du Nord (1661)[15] are indications of the growing significance of the Baltic as an area of international political economy. This should not be overrated, though: in England, the contribution of imports from northern Europe (including the Baltic) around 1700 was limited to about 10 per cent of total foreign trade; that of exports to northern Europe was even smaller, amounting to only about 5 per cent of total English exports.[16]

## ■ The Structure of Baltic Trade in the Closing Decades of the Seventeenth Century

Between 1670 and 1700, Sweden's economic policies towards its Baltic provinces, which were fed by domestic concerns as well as by the commercial attractiveness of transit trade with Muscovy, led to the sustained interest in the easternmost part of the Baltic Sea of merchants from the Dutch Republic and England and to the gradual introduction of novel timber production techniques along the shores of the Gulf of Finland.[17] Meanwhile, the main point of gravity in Baltic trade remained in the Polish city of Danzig, where the Dutch commercial system continued to dominate grain exports, even though the first signs of long-term decline, both of the port of Danzig and of the Dutch commercial system, had started to become apparent after 1670. Finally, the tax-free status of Swedish ships in the Sound is of particular importance for the development of its maritime transport and trade in the second half of the seventeenth century. In this chapter, an attempt is made to estimate the volume of Swedish tax-free shipping through the Sound, based on the following rationale: tax-free Sound passages by Swedish ships were in fact registered in the Sound toll registers, even though they did not have to pay taxes. These registrations allow calculating the total number of tax-free Sound passages by Swedish ships. Luckily—at least from our perspective—the tax-free status seems to have been subjected to limitations on several occasions. As a result, 'complete' registrations are available for several years in the period between 1670 and 1720. Using these 'complete' data, for most Swedish domiciles active in maritime transport through the Sound it is possible to estimate the average tonnage of one shipload exported from (or imported to) the Baltic. The multiplication of the average tonnage of one shipload of exports (or imports) by the number of ships from each Swedish domicile passing the Sound annually results in a tonnage estimate of the volume of tax-free shipping for each Swedish domicile, which could easily be aggregated. However, these calculations do not inform us about the products that were imported or exported. Consequently, the survey of the commodity structure of exports from Sweden relies exclusively on the data for registered exports (carried by Swedish and foreign ships) in the Sound toll registers.

A brief stagnation in 1688-89 and 1691-92 notwithstanding—due to a combination of a series of crop failures in the Baltic provinces[18] and the outbreak of the Nine Years' War of the Grand Alliance with France—the volume of Swedish exports from the Baltic experienced an almost uninterrupted increase between 1672 and 1694, with exported volumes rising from an estimated 43,295 tonnes in 1672, of which 29,251 tonnes were shipped tax-free, to 195,444 tonnes in 1693 (of which 53,219 tonnes were tax-free) and 195,057 tonnes in 1694 (of which 51,877 tonnes were tax-free). During the same period, Sweden's share in the total volume of exports from the Baltic rose from about 20 per cent to almost 50 per cent. The share of Swedish tax-free exports through the Sound increased strongly during this period and flourished in particular during the first phase of the Nine Years' War. Even though it was possible to estimate tax-free exports based on the registered average volumes of ship loads carried by shipmasters domiciled in Swedish ports, it is unlikely that the Sound toll registers have captured all of Sweden's exports from the Baltic during this period. Moreover, a relatively small part of Sweden's export trade did not leave the Baltic. Variable quantities of grain produced in these provinces were exported to the Swedish mainland (mostly Stockholm), especially in times of crop failure, or when the needs of the Swedish army had to be met urgently.[19] Likewise, about one quarter of all registered Swedish iron bar production went from Stockholm to various destinations in the Baltic.[20]

The commodity structure of Swedish exports from the Baltic in the final decades of the seventeenth century was composed of two major categories: foodstuffs, comprising different types of grain, of which rye was by far the most important, and raw materials, predominantly iron, hemp, flax, hempseed, flaxseed, tar, pitch, and timber. Whereas iron was exported almost exclusively from Stockholm, sufficient quantities of grain, hemp(seed), flax(seed), tar, or pitch were harder to find on the Scandinavian Peninsula.[21] Thus, it is clear from the outset that exports from the Swedish Baltic provinces, which had become part of the Empire in 1617, were of primary importance for the establishment and strengthening of Sweden's role in Baltic trade.

*Graph 1: Swedish exports from the Baltic, 1670-99. In tonnes, including estimated volume of Swedish tax-free exports. Share of Sweden in total exports from the Baltic on right axis.*

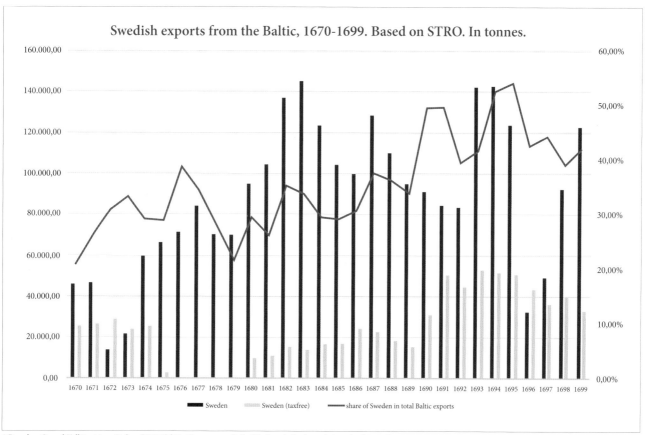

*Based on Sound Toll Registers Online (STRO) http://www.soundtoll.nl/index.php/en/over-het-project/str-online*

Table 1: The commodity structure of
Swedish exports through the Sound,
1670, 1680, 1690, and 1700. Based on
STRO. In tonnes.

| Category | Product | 1670 | 1680 | 1690 | 1700 |
|---|---|---|---|---|---|
| foodstuffs | rye | 11,874.72 | 33,226.94 | 34,840.39 | 8,825.80 |
| | wheat | 4,647.53 | 903.71 | 3,904.77 | 148.07 |
| | barley | 1,630.41 | 2,234.14 | 3,158.22 | 34.95 |
| | other | 2,542.35 | 947.02 | 1,284.53 | 790.79 |
| raw materials | timber | 4,865.02 | 6.019,60 | 7,751.17 | 27,151.13 |
| | tar & pitch | 10,355.11 | 9,000.38 | 5,370.88 | 10,765.06 |
| | iron | 379.28 | 11,495.73 | 2,107.38 | 13,674.45 |
| | hemp & flax | 3,293.16 | 11,949.43 | 11,519.12 | 6,443.78 |
| | hemp- & flaxseed | 1,156.97 | 12,047.23 | 14,993.67 | 2,512.24 |
| | other | 3,242.23 | 3,283.68 | 3,084.35 | 3,623.95 |
| other products | | 2,116.72 | 4,272.18 | 3102,86 | 1317,94 |

The principal ports from which the main products were exported from Sweden through the Sound, provide valuable insights into the functions of these ports as well as into the role of their respective hinterlands (i.e., the geographical areas where goods exported from a certain port could originate), all of which is important in view of the changes that took place during and immediately after the Great Northern War. Riga and Reval, the two major ports in the Swedish Baltic provinces, served as the main outlets for the grain produced on large Livonian, Estonian, and Lithuanian estates. With 48.72 and 31.57 per cent respectively, they accounted for some 80 per cent of total rye exports through the Sound between 1670 and 1700. During the same period, Stettin maintained a share of 8.90 per cent in the exports, while the contribution of other ports in the Swedish Baltic provinces, like Arensburg (Kuressaare), Pernau (Pärnu), Narva, or Nyen was more limited and probably affected strongly by external circumstances such as crop failures, export limitations, or outright prohibitions.[22] Such prohibitions and other external circumstances also had a significant impact on trade at Riga and Reval. On the eve of the outbreak of war in 1700, Riga's exports were almost non-existent (565 tonnes), whereas about 2,000 tonnes of rye (22.9 per cent) were exported from Nyen in the Neva delta instead. An impressive 86.60 per cent of all grain exported from the Swedish Baltic provinces through the Sound between 1670 and 1700 had Amsterdam as its destination.

In the second half of the seventeenth century, Riga was also the main port for the exportation of hemp, flax, and hemp-/flaxseed, alongside Reval and Narva. These products came from the vast hinterland of these Baltic ports, which spread well into Muscovy. Thus, these raw materials, which (alongside timber) are commonly referred to as 'naval stores,' were a vital part of Swedish-Russian transit trade in the seventeenth century.

Quite differently, the exportation of iron, tar, pitch, and timber was dominated by various clusters of ports on the Swedish mainland—with Stockholm, Norrköping, Kalmar, and Västervik as its main outlets—in the Gulf of Finland, and on the island of Gotland. Stockholm had a share of 90.96 per cent in (registered) iron exports. The dominant destinations for Swedish iron between 1670 and 1699, i.e., before the war broke out, were located in England and Scotland: London (39.62 per cent), Hull (12.83 per cent), Newcastle (3.95 per cent), Leith (3.36 per cent), Glasgow (3.13 per cent), as well as Dundee, Borrowstounness (Bo'ness), and the King's Lynn with shares between 1 and 2 per cent. Amsterdam was registered as the destination of only 19.79 per cent of all (registered) Swedish iron exported through the Sound. Tar and pitch exports were divided almost equally among Stockholm (35.89 per cent) and nearby Trångsund (4.70 per cent), on one hand, and the northeastern shores of the Gulf of Finland, with Vyborg (37.51 per cent) and Helsingfors (Helsinki) (5.25 per cent) on the other. (Nyen exported a significant quantity of tar and pitch in the year 1700, but was of marginal importance before that time.) Additionally, a small share of Swedish tar and pitch production was exported from Västervik (3.51 per cent), Kalmar (4.14 per cent), and Visby (2.23 per cent), which served as outlets for the forest-rich areas in southeast Sweden and on Gotland. The main destinations of Swedish tar and pitch exported through the Sound were Amsterdam (64.18 per cent), London (17.16 per cent), and a few other English ports, like Hull (1.55 per cent), Newcastle (1.28 per cent), Bristol (1.11 per cent), and Yarmouth (1.06 per cent), i.e., some of the main centres of Dutch and English shipbuilding in the second half of the seventeenth century. Whereas the ports of destination for Swedish timber exported through the Sound were comparable to the destinations for tar and pitch, but with an even stronger predominance of Amsterdam (78.62 per cent), the main export ports of timber only partly overlapped. Almost 70 per cent of Swedish timber was exported from Pernau (30.99 per cent), Narva (25.46 per cent), and Nyen (9.11 per cent) in the Swedish Baltic provinces; a secondary centre of timber exports was located in southern Sweden, in the hinterland of the ports of Västervik (12.75 per cent), Kalmar (5.59 per cent), and Visby (4.11 per cent), which, as was mentioned above, also had a small share in tar and pitch exports.

In addition to hemp(-seed), flax(-seed), and timber, which were the foremost important constituents of Russian transit trade via ports in Sweden's Baltic provinces (Estonia, Livonia, Ingria), a significant trade of other Russian goods, like wax, tallow, *jufti* (Russia leather), skins, and hides can be traced in the Sound toll registers. As could be expected, most of these goods were exported from Riga, Reval, Narva, and Nyen, although *jufti* seem to have had partly distinct distribution patterns: they were exported regularly and in the largest quantities from Narva (share in total *jufti* exports of 73.88 per cent), with additional, more irregular, exports from Riga (18.31 per cent), Reval (2.00 per cent), and Nyen (0.81 per cent). The exportation of hides through the Sound was less important and concentrated mostly in Riga (54.18 per cent), Reval (27.57 per cent), and Narva (9.81 per cent). Skins seem to have taken a more complex route, partly overland and partly by sea: between 1670 and 1700 the highest shares in the exportation of skins were held by Stettin (63.69 per cent) and Wolgast (18.36 per cent), which at that time were part of Swedish Pomerania. Riga and Narva were far less important in this respect. It may be assumed that these skins were transported overland via the Polish system of fairs,[23] probably to Frankfurt on the Oder, from where they were shipped out via Stettin or Wolgast. Remarkably, the exportation of skins via Stettin and Wolgast disappears after 1691 to return only in 1700.

This brief overview of the structure of Swedish exports from the Baltic between 1670 and 1700 has highlighted its main features: (1) the importance of the Swedish ports in the

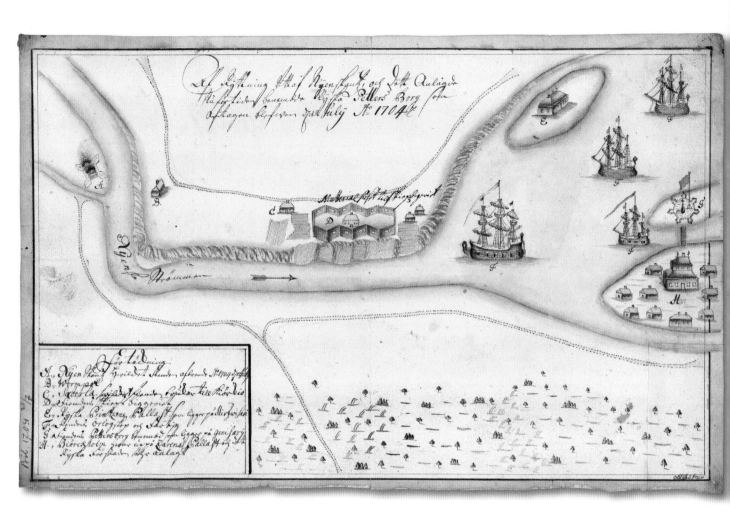

*A Swedish spy map of Saint Petersburg.*

*Pen and ink with watercolours by unknown artist, 1704. The Swedish Military Archives, Stockholm, Sweden. Defensionskommissionen 1700 AAAA:00004.*

Baltic provinces, in particular Riga, Pernau, Reval, Narva, and Nyen, for the exportation of grain from Lithuanian, Livonian, and Estonian estates, as well as for the exportation of products of Russian transit trade, such as hemp, flax, tar, pitch, timber, *jufti*, hides, tallow, and wax; (2) the significance of Stockholm and its immediate surroundings in the exportation of Swedish iron; (3) the existence of at least three smaller, additional centres of raw materials exportation in southeast Sweden (Västervik and Kalmar) and on Gotland (Visby) for tar, pitch, and timber exports; on the northeastern shores of the Gulf of Finland (Vyborg and Helsingfors) for tar and timber exports from Karelia; and, finally, in Swedish Pomerania (Stettin and Wolgast), although it should be noted that Swedish Pomerania did not play a major role in the international trade streams of the second half of the seventeenth century[24]; (4) the dominance of the Dutch in most of Swedish exports (except iron) through the Sound, and of the English in iron exports.

### ■ Changes in the Structure of Baltic Trade during the Great Northern War

Whereas Swedish exports from the Baltic, and particularly Swedish-Russian transit trade, had experienced a few good years at the close of the seventeenth century, a downward trend had already set in prior to 1700 (see graph 1). In the years immediately following the start of the war between Sweden and Russia in 1700 this trend turned into the total collapse of Baltic trade. The volume of tax-free and registered exports through the Sound from Sweden declined from 84,141 tonnes in 1700 to only 29,240 tonnes in 1709 (see graph 2).

Between 1701 and 1709, the geographical structure of the rapidly diminishing Swedish exports was subject to several changes. In 1701 and 1702, the largest volumes were shipped from Stockholm, Riga, Pernau, Nyen, Vyborg, and Stettin (1701) or Wolgast (1702). Between 1703 and 1706, the volumes exported from Stockholm became much lower and were surpassed by exports from Riga, Pernau, and Vyborg. Nyen was destroyed in 1703. Exports from Swedish Pomerania were handled through Stettin, Anklam, Wolgast, Greifswald, and Stralsund, in volumes that fluctuated widely from year to year. In the dramatic year 1709 there was almost no trade through the Sound. Together with the general decline of trade in the first decade of the eighteenth century, Sweden's share in total exports from the Baltic diminished as well, from more than 35 per cent in 1700 to just below 20 per cent during this same period (see graph 2). The peaks in 1710 and 1715 notwithstanding, Sweden's share in total exports from the Baltic recovered only for a short time in the next decade, thus marking the impact of the loss of its Baltic provinces to Russia.

In 1709, the defeat of the Swedes at Poltava heralded a new episode in the ongoing Russo-Swedish war. The Russian Empire started to get the upper hand and managed to consolidate its positions around the Baltic Sea. Almost immediately following the Battle of Poltava, economic, administrative, and infrastructural reforms were introduced at a great pace in the nascent Russian Empire. Most significant were the foun-

*Graph 2: Swedish exports from the Baltic, 1700-20. Based on STRO. In tonnes.*

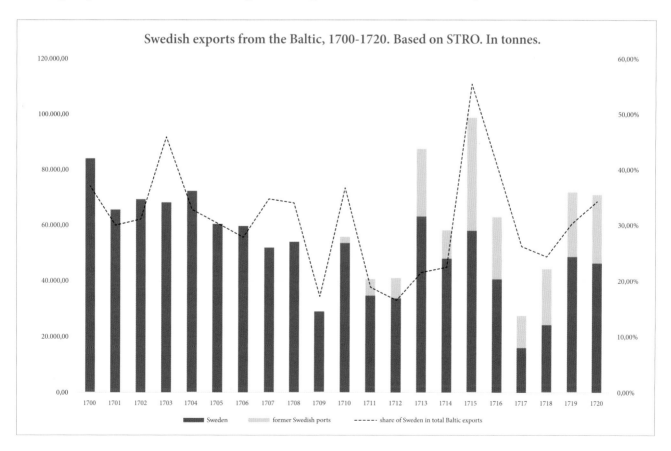

Swedish exports from the Baltic, 1700-1720. Based on STRO. In tonnes.

dation of the Senate in 1711 and the designation of Saint Petersburg as the Russian Empire's new capital in 1712.[25] The Empire's centre of power clearly moved towards the Neva estuary.

From 1710, exports through the Sound recovered, although volumes were at best only half the size of the volumes shipped in the final years of the seventeenth century. The recovery of Swedish exports after 1710 was interrupted briefly between 1716 and 1718, due to renewed warfare in the Baltic,[26] on one hand, and the effects of a series of Russian economic policy measures applied to the ports in the Baltic and Archangel, on the other (see below). By 1710, all of the formerly Swedish ports in the Baltic provinces had been conquered by the Russians; Nyen in 1703, Narva in 1704, Vyborg in 1709, and Riga and Reval in 1710. Whereas warfare largely prevented Peter the Great during the first decade of the eighteenth century from taking structural measures to restore trade in the now Russian-controlled ports in the Baltic, he nevertheless chose to found Saint Petersburg on the islands at the very mouth of the Neva delta, a few kilometres downstream of where the fortress of Nyenšanc (Nyenskans) and the trading city of Nyen used to be before they were destroyed by Russian troops.[27] Although at least three Dutch shipmasters are said to have entered Saint Petersburg shortly after its foundation on May 27, 1703,[28] it would take another decade before trade actually took off at the port. In the meantime, what little was left of Swedish exports was shipped mostly from Stockholm, Västervik, Stettin (for the time being), and a number of smaller ports on the Swedish mainland. Together with the loss of the significant ports in the formerly Swedish Baltic provinces, the commodity structure of Swedish exports from the Baltic drastically changed and almost immediately obtained the rather monotonous character for which Sweden's exports in the rest of the eighteenth century are known in historiography.[29]

The formerly Swedish ports in the Baltic provinces also resumed their trade, albeit at a lower level. Sweden's former transit trade with Russia as well as Vyborg's

| Port | Product | 1710 | 1715 | 1720 |
|------|---------|------|------|------|
| Stockholm | iron | 22.622,40 | 14.873,50 | 16.375,28 |
| | timber | 1.546,40 | 969,75 | 757,39 |
| | tar & pitch | 8.536,87 | 677,00 | 1.028,21 |
| | other | 1.522,45 | 825,91 | 629,85 |
| Kalmar | iron | 61,53 | 0,00 | 0,00 |
| | timber | 1.168,01 | 420,74 | 100,41 |
| | tar & pitch | 69,12 | 280,56 | 89,83 |
| | other | 29,14 | 215,40 | 96,09 |
| Vestervik | iron | 27,11 | 84,57 | 303,59 |
| | timber | 993,84 | 186,86 | 238,61 |
| | tar & pitch | 1.020,59 | 187,04 | 233,80 |
| | other | 471,03 | 38,40 | 465,33 |
| other ports | | 13.353,93 | 5.587,65 | 9.124,69 |

*Table 2: The commodity structure of Swedish exports through the Sound, 1710, 1715, and 1720. Based on STRO. In tonnes.*

export trade of goods from its Karelian hinterland had now de facto become Russian export trade. An impressive complex of domestic and foreign economic policy measures, some of them resembling ad hoc decision-making rather than a balanced development strategy,[30] was designed to create the appropriate circumstances for newly founded Saint Petersburg to become the Russian Empire's 'New Amsterdam.' Three policy axes can be discerned. The first was concerned with the position of Archangel in the Russian trade system, the second with the re-establishment of the formerly Swedish ports in the Gulf of Finland, and the third with the development of industries on the Russian mainland. As long as warfare disturbed trade and shipping in the Baltic Sea, policy measures were mainly concerned with the position of Archangel, but from 1718 onwards, their focus expanded to the newly conquered ports in the Gulf of Finland. The cumulative impact of these measures can be seen as a process of polarisation that affected the Russian Empire's governmental structure as a whole and that of northwest Russia in particular, while in a larger sense it also affected distant regions in Russia's interior as well as the role of the traditional centres of trade, Novgorod and Pskov.

At first, the policies concerned the role of Archangel as opposed to Saint Petersburg. As a direct consequence of continuous warfare in the Baltic,[31] trade at Archangel flourished like never before in its history. The annual turnover at Archangel rose from 1.5 million rubles in 1704 to 2.3 million rubles in 1717.[32] The number of Dutch ships calling at its port would reach its 'all-time high' in 1716, when 89 Dutch shipmasters were registered in Amsterdam to join the early and late convoys destined to Archangel.[33] However, as early as November 1713, Tsar Peter the Great initiated a long series of laws and regulations designed to promote Saint Petersburg at the expense of Archangel.[34]

Indeed, in the years 1714-20, several attempts were made to limit exports from Archangel in favour of Saint Petersburg. At the same time, merchants in Narva retained their rights to conduct trade according to previous Swedish regulations until 1718.[35] In 1714 it was decided that one-fourth of all *jufti* produced in Russia had to be transported to Saint Petersburg, that merchants could choose between Archangel and Saint Petersburg for hemp exports, and that other exports had to be handled via Archangel.[36] The same *ukaz* (decree) stated that in 1715 equal quantities of all goods had to be exported from Archangel and Saint Petersburg.[37] In the following years, the distribution of goods between Archangel and Saint Petersburg would be subject to continuous alterations, all of them in favour of the latter.[38]

In November 1717, the tsar published a new arrangement for 1718: two-thirds of all goods destined for exportation would have to be shipped via Saint Petersburg and only one-third via Archangel. Merchants from Novgorod and Pskov reacted to the new regulations with a request to allow them, because of their proximity to Saint Petersburg, to abandon the Archangel route altogether. As this request suited Peter the Great perfectly, it comes as no surprise that permission was granted immediately. Merchants of Kargopol, however, who—because of the large distance to Saint Petersburg—asked permission to continue sending their goods to Archangel, received a negative answer from the Senate.[39] The year 1718 was the first since the foundation

of Saint Petersburg in which the number of Dutch shipmasters that appeared in the eastern part of the Gulf of Finland was greater than the number of those active on the Archangel route. The Archangel trade had lost its significanc. Goods that, until then, would have to be shipped via Archangel, could now also be handled in the Russian ports of the Baltic. Reorientation became inevitable for the Dutch shipmasters. From 1718 until the introduction of the new customs tariff in 1724, trade regulations in Narva underwent several fundamental changes, which without exception were

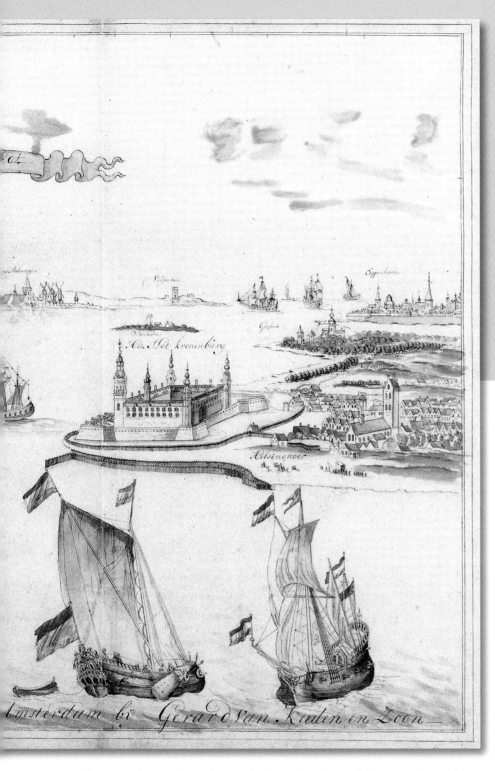

**A bird's-eye view of Öresund, as seen from the north. Kronborg Castle is on the right.**

Pen and ink with watercolours by G. van Keulen and son (1678-1726), 1726. The Scheepvaartmuseum, Amsterdam, the Netherlands.

inspired by Peter the Great's wish to make Saint Petersburg the Russian Empire's main port. The growth of trade via Narva continued to be a matter of concern, and measures were taken to protect trade in Saint Petersburg from being disturbed by Narva.[40] Similar policies were applied to Reval (see below).

Until 1721, Russia's economic policy measures were marked by the continued existence of state monopolies in the export of potash and tar and of state regulations with regard to strategic products like grain and tobacco, which were subject to change depending on external circumstances.[41] A 1718 *ukaz* stated that foreign merchants were required to import flax, hemp, and *jufti* to Narva, while they also had to make their ships available to local merchants for the exportation of goods abroad.[42] Importation of salt was prohibited in 1719.[43] Though these measures aimed to stimulate trade through Narva, their impact was limited because of the more profitable measures that were applied to Saint Petersburg. In 1720, Russian merchants sending goods coming from the Russian interior to Saint Petersburg were to pay a 3 per cent tax as opposed to 5 per cent if they went elsewhere. Moreover, if the goods transported to Saint Petersburg were exported, Russian merchants were exempted from paying any tax.[44] This measure clearly served the double goal of stimulating the development of a Russian merchant community and of promoting the port of Saint Petersburg. A groundbreaking *ukaz* of 26 November, 1721 literally redesigned the hinterlands of the Russian ports in the Baltic and of the port of Archangel, creating considerable comparative advantages for the port of Saint Petersburg.[45]

By that time, the increasing attention being paid to the establishment of a Baltic fleet had already resulted in the foundation of a number of ship wharfs and additional industries (manufactures): shipbuilding and timber production, weaponry, metallurgy and iron industry, and textile industry.[46] The stimulating effect of these industries on Russian exports can hardly be overestimated. In addition to state-controlled shipbuilding wharfs, a number of regional centres for the production of timber arose in the first decades of the eighteenth century. In 1706, the first fine-blade sawmill was put into use in the area around Archangel, soon followed by sawmills in Narva and in the surroundings of Novgorod, along the Sias and near Vyšnij Voloček, both located along waterways that led directly to Saint Petersburg.[47] The iron industry, at that time organised and controlled by the government, developed quickly in the first decades of the eighteenth century and was located in the Olonets Region (north of Lake Onega) and in the Ural Mountains.[48] The production supplies in the Urals appeared to be profitable and of good quality. Problematic, however, was the difficulty to transport iron from the Urals to the Russian capital because of the large distance: originally there was no direct connection over water between the two regions. Between 1703 and 1709, a canal was dug between the Tsna and the Tvertsa rivers close to Vyšnij Voloček. From 1710 onwards, iron could be transported over water to Saint Petersburg, though this remained time-consuming (up to five months) and difficult (especially on Lake Ladoga).[49]

From 1721, only goods originating in Pskov and its district could be transported to Narva for export.[50] Goods transported via the Gžackaja Pristan' and closer to Velikie Luki had to be sent to Saint Petersburg instead of Riga; Riga's hinterland was restricted to West-Russia and Ukraine.[51] The hinterland of Archangel was limited to the areas in the districts along the northern Dvina that had an immediate connection with Archangel via this river.[52] Export goods that were transported previously to the Jug River or other rivers, or to Vologda via the winter route, now had to be transported to Saint Petersburg instead. In 1722 merchants of Pskov obtained the freedom to send their goods to Narva or Saint Petersburg according to their needs,[53] which subjected Narva once more to severe competition from Saint Petersburg. In the same year, Narva was put under the rule of the governor of Saint Petersburg[54] after which both Saint Petersburg and Narva obtained a tax advantage of 2 and 1 per cent respectively as opposed to other ports in the Baltic Sea.[55]

## ■ Summary: The Example of Reval

The economic consequences of the Great Northern War were manifold; they had a lasting impact on northern Europe's international trade and Sweden's role therein. The structure of Russia's foreign trade was profoundly affected by the far-reaching economic policy measures it took to establish itself firmly on the shores of the Baltic Sea. In a few years' time, Archangel's turnover dropped from 2.3 million rubles on average in the years 1717-19 to only 120,000 rubles in 1725. In the same period, the value of exports via Saint Petersburg exploded: from 233,000 rubles in 1718 to 2,035,200 rubles in 1725. The relative positions of Saint Petersburg and Archangel in the value of goods exported from Russia in the first half of the eighteenth century would remain fairly constant: turnover at Saint Petersburg was up to ten times higher than at Archangel.[56] Foreign merchant communities were forced to adapt their activities to the changes in the Russian economy. Many Dutch merchants in Saint Petersburg originally started their 'Russian' businesses in Archangel. They had lived and worked there as long as Peter the Great's economic policy did not disturb their activities.[57] The decline of trade through Archangel immediately had its impact on the size of the Dutch merchant community in Saint Petersburg. From 1718 onwards, several Dutch merchants moved from Archangel to Saint Petersburg; others would follow after the Great Northern War.[58] Unfortunately, no sources are available that could provide us with the necessary details to fully understand this relocation, but according to an analysis of the Dutch historian Jan Willem Veluwenkamp, at least 16 out of 43 merchants who signed a cooperation agreement in Saint Petersburg in 1722 had originally started their activities in Russian trade in Archangel.[59]

Similarly, the changing role of Reval, a port of the formerly Swedish province of Estonia, provides a good example for summarising the impact of the Great Northern War on Sweden's commercial relations with western Europe, the relations of the Swedish mainland with its Baltic provinces, and the changing geographical structure of Russian trade.[60] Although Reval was certainly not the biggest port in the Baltic, it had played a significant role. During the period of Sweden's dominance in the Baltic, and especially from 1660 onwards, Reval was one of Sweden's ports for the exportation of grain supplies from the Baltic provinces to western Europe and the Swedish mainland (see above). In 1699 the great majority of ships leaving the port of Reval set sail for destinations in the Swedish Empire, especially Stockholm (77 ships), but also Narva (14), Riga (9), Helsingfors (3), Gothenburg (10), Stettin (3), Wismar (11), Stralsund (2), and smaller ports in Finland and Sweden (36). Other ports in the Baltic and western Europe were less prominent: eight ships went to Amsterdam, five to Lübeck, one to Königsberg, and six to Eckernförde. In 1727, however, most ships leaving Reval set sail for Saint Petersburg (30) and other Russian ports in the Baltic, like Riga (4), Vyborg (6),

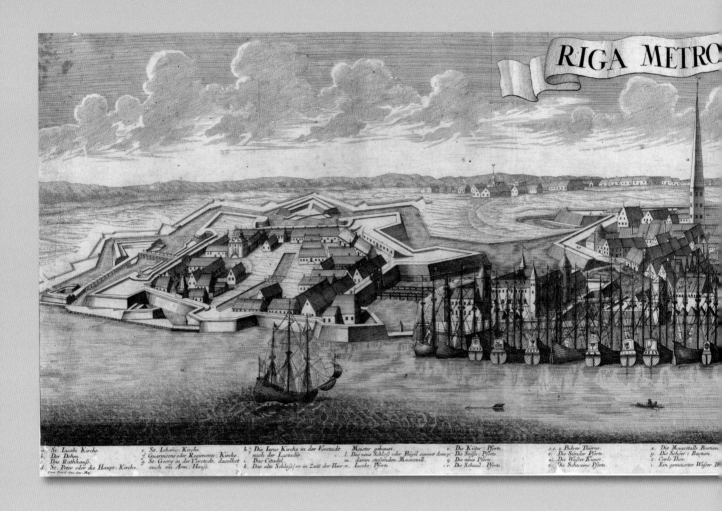

*A panorama showing Riga about 1710.*

*Engraving by unknown artist, 1710. The Swedish Military Archives, Stockholm, Sweden. Utländska stads- och fästningsplaner, Riga, SE/KrA/0406/28/041/040.*

and Narva (2). In 1727, only six ships left for Stockholm and nine went to smaller Finnish and Swedish ports; again other destinations were less important: only one ship went to Amsterdam, six to Lübeck, and four to Danzig.[61] Not only are these numbers indicative of the decline of Reval's trade during the Great Northern War,[62] the *portorium* books of Reval indicate that the city's import and export trade literally changed directions under the impact of the foundation of Saint Petersburg and the various policy measures that were taken to make Russia's Baltic ports subordinate to the Empire's brand-new capital.[63]

■ **Closing Remarks**

When the young Charles XII became king of Sweden in 1697, the time had come for his adversaries—Denmark, Poland-Lithuania, and Russia—to try to break Swedish dominance in the Baltic. Their attempts were unsuccessful at first, but Peter the Great's persistence gradually turned the tide in favour of Russia. After the decisive Battle of Poltava (1709) it was clear that the balance of power had shifted from the Scandinivian Peninsula to the continent. Whereas until that time Sweden had

managed to maintain its control over Livonia, Estonia, and Ingria on the east coast of the Baltic, its vital economic strongholds were now lost. With them, considerable tax income and a major source of grain supplies for the Swedish army went into foreign hands, thus effectively marking the end of Swedish 'era of great power' in the history of northern Europe.

The economic impact of the Great Northern War was felt long after Charles XII passed away in 1718. In fact, in the eighteenth century the Baltic's role in the European economy would become a very different one. To a large extent this was the result of the changing status of the Baltic Sea in international power relations during the final decades of the seventeenth century. From a largely peripheral supply area of grain and some raw materials, which was exploited mostly by Dutch and, to a lesser degree, English shipmasters, the Baltic turned into an object of international power politics, in which economic considerations, such as the control over strategic supply and distribution channels, started to play an increasingly important role. It is hardly a coincidence that the changes in the structure of Baltic trade before and during the Great Northern War occurred against a background of widespread mercantilist discourse, in Sweden as well as in Russia and several other European countries. This, too, is part of the experience of the Great Northern War.

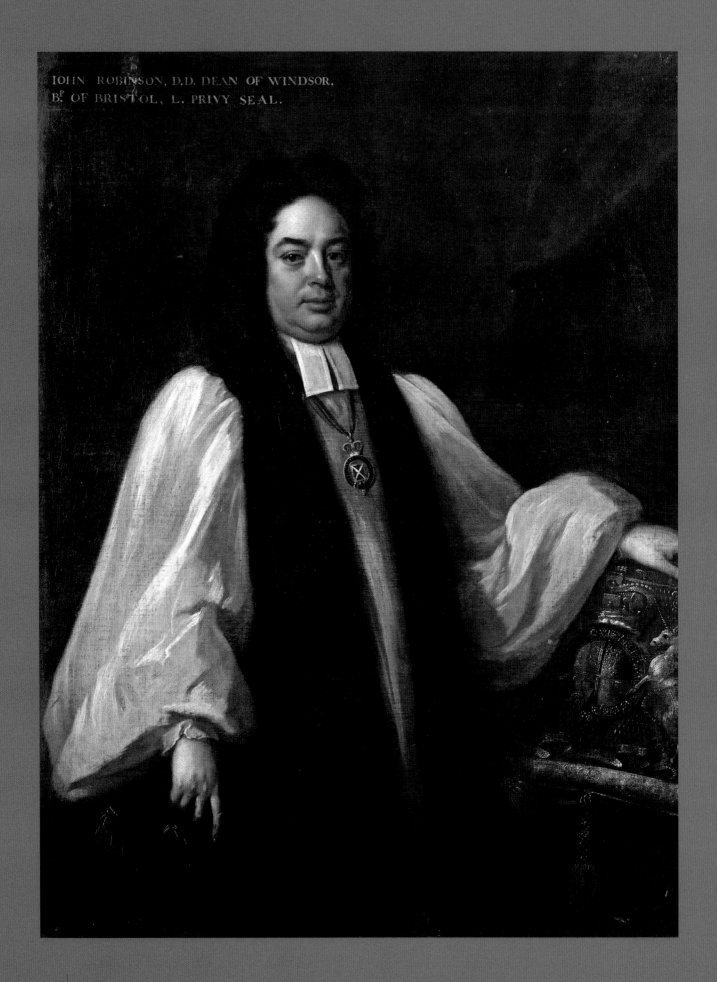

IOHN ROBINSON, D.D. DEAN OF WINDSOR.
B.P OF BRISTOL, L. PRIVY SEAL.

CHAPTER 9

# British Policy towards Sweden, Charles XII, and the Great Northern War, 1697-1723

by John B. Hattendorf

Britain's vital interests in Scandinavia were commercial and economic ones, not political. The most important commodities that Britain valued and needed to acquire from this region were iron, copper, timber, pitch, tar, hemp, and flax. Together these items comprised the category known as naval stores, the necessary materials for British industry to construct ships. As a vital economic interest upon which merchant shipping and naval power depended, British access to the Baltic Sea and the protection of this trade was a continual concern from the mid-seventeenth century to the end of the sailing ship period.[1]

International politics, the depredations of privateers, and wars created threats to the security of these all-important economic interests that, from time to time, required British diplomatic and naval responses. Oliver Cromwell took the first step, during the First Anglo-Dutch War in 1653-54, to obtain a treaty for reciprocal trading privileges[2] and regular diplomatic exchanges.[3] Following the restoration of the monarchy in England, this agreement was replaced in April 1661 with a new treaty that remains in effect 350 years later.[4]

Charles XII's rule in Sweden spanned the reigns of three different sovereigns in England and Great Britain: William III, Anne, and George I. Each of them faced distinctive international and internal issues in regard to relations with Sweden, but at the same time the basic underlying consistency in British economic interests remained.

## ■ English Relations with Sweden under William III, 1697-1702

Charles XII's accession to the throne in 1697 occurred at a critical moment in European international relations. Between the death of Charles XI on 15 April 1697 and the new 15-year-old king's declaration of self-rule, the Peace of Rijswijk was signed on 20 September 1697, ending the Nine Years' War. During that war, France and the Maritime Powers—England and the Dutch Republic—had actively vied for Swedish support. King Charles XI had played a careful hand to maintain neutrality between the rival international blocks and the internal factions supporting one side or the other. His success as a neutral made the belligerents invite him to be the mediator at Rijswijk. While this perpetuated Sweden's ambitions to maintain her reputation as a European power in the tradition of Gustav II Adolf, in fact she had become much weaker and more vulnerable in the half century since the Peace of Westphalia. Even though Charles XI did not

*Portrait of John Robinson, Bishop of Bristol.*

*Painting by Michael Dahl (1659-1743), 1712. Charterhouse, Sutton's Hospital, London, UK.*

live to carry out this role at Rijswijk, Swedish diplomats did take his place, but without the panache and acclaim that the king's personal presence might have brought. This situation at the opening of Charles XII's reign established some key factors that carried through the subsequent war. First, Swedish mediation at Rijswijk reflected the western European powers' tacit agreement that it was important for European stability to maintain Sweden's international reputation and position. The fact that the role of mediator was a cosmetic one and that Louis XIV and William III had made the real decisions secretly in advance between themselves, reflected this assessment. Second, Charles XI's prevarications to maintain neutrality had left a legacy of mistrust and the expenditure of significant sums of money by the rival powers to influence senior Swedish officials.[5]

After Rijswijk, the first topic to emerge pertained to commercial maritime relations. One of the unresolved issues from the Nine Years' War was the Anglo-Dutch policy of interrupting maritime trade with France. The dispute involved differing definitions of neutral trade compounded by activity that was clearly illegal. When John Robinson returned to Sweden as English *chargé d'affaires* in 1696, William III formally directed him to resolve the matter,[6] but Robinson found 'There is no probability any new measures can be taken with this Crown, before this difficulty about their ships be one way or another remov'd, which will hardly be without the expense of a good sum of money.'[7] The issue became the stumbling block that prevented English and Dutch diplomats from getting an alliance with Sweden in 1699 to maintain stability in the north while also trying to maintain the peace of western Europe.

Another legacy of diplomacy in the north during the Nine Years' War led the Maritime Powers to become involved in the complicated dynastic rivalry between Sweden and Denmark over the Holstein-Gottorp lands in Schleswig. In order to align Sweden against France, the Maritime Powers and Hanover had become guarantors of the Treaty of Altona in 1689, supporting the Swedish interpretation of the dispute that recognised the independent sovereignty of the duke of Holstein-Gottorp.[8] A month after Charles XI's death in 1697, Denmark announced plans to destroy the forts protecting Holstein-Gottorp that had been authorised as part of the 1689 agreement. The guarantors convened a conference at Pinneberg, near Hamburg, to try to resolve the issue. William III's initiatives for peace proved fruitless as Denmark seized a large part of the duchy of Holstein and demolished the forts.

William III ordered a combined Anglo-Dutch fleet under the overall command of Admiral Sir George Rooke, with the Dutch contingent under Lieutenant-Admiral Philips van Almonde, to the Sound to carry out their responsibilities as guarantors of the Treaty of Altona. In early June 1700, the sixteen English and eighteen Dutch warships arrived off Gothenburg, Sweden, while diplomats demanded that peace be restored and Danish troops be removed from Holstein-Gottorp. Denmark's refusal led Rooke to move the Anglo-Dutch fleet closer to Copenhagen and to develop cooperative links with Admiral-General Hans Wachtmeister, commanding the Swedish fleet. With the Danish fleet blocking the main channels of the Sound, Wachtmeister left his largest ships behind when he joined up with the Anglo-Dutch squadron. Rooke and Almonde rejected the Swedish proposal that Wachtmeister take overall command of a combined Anglo-Dutch-Swedish fleet, but they agreed to cooperate. John Robinson served as mes-

senger between the fleet, Charles XII, and Swedish commanders ashore and afloat. With orders to prevent the operation from becoming a general conflict and to keep it under control as a demonstration to Denmark of allied armed solidarity, Rooke refrained from attacking the Danish fleet and allowed it to withdraw into protected harbours at Copenhagen. Rooke's forces moved forwards to bombard the city of Copenhagen on 19-20 and 25-26 July, but caused relatively little damage. To put more pressure on Denmark, Rooke and Almonde agreed to the Swedish proposal that the Anglo-Dutch squadron support a Swedish amphibious landing at Humlebæk on the east coast of Zealand, north of Copenhagen. With Swedish forces blockading Copenhagen by sea, the operations began on 4 August with the landing of 4,000 troops under Anglo-Dutch naval protection.

While Swedish and Anglo-Dutch naval forces were in full control of the Sound, Swedish leaders wanted to collect the Sound Toll from ships passing through the waterway as the Danes had historically done. John Robinson opposed this as an unacceptable injustice that was no better than what the Danes were doing to Holstein-Gottorp.[9]

By 12 August more than 10,000 Swedish troops were ashore and organising to march on Copenhagen. Before that could happen information arrived that King Frederik IV of Denmark-Norway was willing to agree to a peace. On 23 August, Rooke received the report that the treaty was signed at Travendal. Celebrating the occasion, he ordered the warships under him to display all their flags and pennants during the day and to fire guns in the evening.[10] Charles XII requested that Rooke's forces assist in evacuating the Swedish invasion force from Denmark. When that task was completed, Rooke's squadron sailed on 12 September 1700.[11]

After leaving Denmark, Charles XII moved quickly to reinforce Swedish forces in the Baltic provinces and in Germany in order to counter-attack the forces of King Augustus II of Poland, who had invaded the Swedish territory of Livonia. The news that Tsar Peter had made peace with the Ottoman Empire was not immediately understood as the harbinger of a Russian declaration of war against Sweden.[12] At the same time, the gradual realignment of European states in relation to France over the Spanish Succession issue had clear implications for Sweden.

With Charles XII's departure, officials in London quickly saw need for reliable information on what the king and his army were doing, but this was difficult as Charles had banned foreign diplomats accompanying the army. The Maritime Powers were concerned that the French might be successful in attracting Sweden to their cause. In October 1701, the Dutch had learned that French agents had obtained 600,000 crowns in Amsterdam to bribe Swedish officials. On receiving this information, John Churchill, Earl of Marlborough, who was both captain-general of English forces at home and abroad and the English ambassador to the States General, moved swiftly to sign a treaty with Swedish representatives, not even waiting for approval from London. He and Grand Pensionary Anthonie Heinsius planned this as a temporary measure by which Sweden would agree not to ally with any enemies of the Maritime Powers.[13] King William's secretary, William Blathwayt, explained to Robinson, 'this treaty, you see, is not intended to be final, but only introductive of a more solid and substantial alliance between the two Crowns and the States.'[14] The treaty was some assurance that France would not use Sweden to disrupt the Grand Alliance led by the Maritime Powers and Austria over the Spanish Succession.

At this point, the allies intended to bring Sweden into that alliance, not only to use her troops and military skill, but to tie Charles XII firmly to the allied cause.

## ■ English Relations with Sweden under Anne, 1702-14

The year 1702 was a turning point for Anglo-Swedish relations with the death of William III and the accession of Anne, followed immediately by the outbreak of the War of the Spanish Succession. From the English perspective, Sweden now became an active threat to the allied strategic position in the war against France. In December 1702, Queen Anne ordered John Robinson, recently promoted to the rank of envoy and plenipotentiary, on a mission to Poland and Sweden. The queen instructed him to assure Charles of 'that friendship that is already between us, and of Our resolution to maintain all treaties and guarantees We are engaged in to him,'[15] particularly that of Travendal. England wanted 'a peace in the North . . . and an accommodation'[16] between Sweden and Poland, for which she offered mediation. At the same time, the queen renewed invitations for Sweden to join the Grand Alliance and to furnish troops.

The ministry in London wanted further information and ordered Robinson to get Charles's permission to stay with him. Robinson had left the English mission in Stockholm to Robert Jackson's care as commissary in charge of affairs, when Robinson and his wife with several servants sailed from Karlskrona in January 1703 for Stralsund. Then, going overland via Danzig and Warsaw, they arrived at Charles's headquarters on 9 March near Lublin in southeastern Poland. Among those with Robinson was his new private secretary, James Jefferyes, the son and namesake of an English army brigadier general and knight, who was governor of Cork, Ireland. Jefferyes was born in Stockholm about 1680 and spent the first ten years of his life in Sweden, where his father was in the Swedish army. In 1697, the boy was enrolled at Trinity College, Dublin, where he earned his Bachelor of Arts degree in 1701. Known to be fluent in Swedish, the young Jefferyes became useful to Robinson. Years before, King Charles XI had called Robinson 'a good Swede' in acknowledgement of his fluency in the language.[17]

Immediately on arriving at Charles's headquarters, Robinson sent Jefferyes to Count Carl Piper to request an audience. Rebuffed, Jefferyes was told that the army would march the next day. Robinson persisted and called on Piper personally, but the latter refused saying that the king would not see any foreign diplomats. Robinson replied that he had not come as a diplomat, but to carry personal letters from Queen Anne and from the royal family in Stockholm. On this information, Piper granted an audience.

On 12 March along a snow-covered road outside Lublin on the way to his planned audience, Robinson met Charles XII on horseback coming in his direction. Alighting from his carriage, Robinson was accorded a four- or five-minute audience with the king mounted on his horse. As Robinson recalled 'on my part it was a very odd audience, for I had on a very large robe with furs turn'd outwards, a great fur cap in my hand, and a very sorry periwig on my head.'[18] Although he made no progress in achieving English diplomatic objectives, Robinson and Jefferyes visited the Swedish army's camp and the king's field chancery several times and made useful contacts. At this time, Robinson arranged to send Samuel Åkerhielm to Oxford for three years at English expense. Åkerhielm's father had been in charge of foreign relations in Charles's field chancery until his death in 1702. One of his sisters had married Josias Cederhielm, while another married Olof Hermelin, both secretaries in the king's field chancery with whom Robinson did business.[19]

Robinson travelled on to Warsaw, where he joined in the proposals that allied ministers were making for peace between Poland and Sweden. The King-Elector Augustus II granted Robinson an audience in June 1703 and assured him of his interest in peace, but refused to relinquish the Polish throne. Robinson moved on to Danzig. From this vantage point, he was able to assist local officials with the relations to the Swedish army as well as to help frustrate French ambitions for trade with the city of Danzig. At the same time, Robinson made people aware of allied victories by sponsoring public celebrations to mark Blenheim in 1704 and Ramillies in 1706.[20] In August 1703, Sweden and the Maritime Powers signed a 'treaty of stricter alliance and for the tranquillity of Europe,' by which Sweden obtained a guarantee from England and the Dutch Republic of the Treaty of Travendal. In return, Sweden vaguely agreed to enter into negotiations for admission into the Grand Alliance and promised to supply 10,000 troops when the war against Poland and Russia had ended.

The issue of improving Anglo-Swedish trade relations continued unresolved and nearly broke into open conflict. As the War of the Spanish Succession progressed, naval stores remained critical to the English war effort, but Sweden continued to refuse to allow pitch or tar to be sold unless it was carried in Swedish ships, while refusing to place any limitations on her trade with France. In 1703, the Swedish Tar Company raised its prices by an exorbitant amount. An Act of Parliament in 1704 relieved the situation by subsidising naval stores acquired in North America and by moving to obtain such supplies from Russia, forcing Swedish merchants to lower their prices to remain competitive.[21]

A variety of threats to Swedish merchant shipping brought Swedish warships from the Baltic into the North Sea while English and Dutch warships were engaged with French threats. In late July 1704, Commodore William Whetstone with a squadron of eight 50-gun warships was on patrol off Orfordness, Suffolk, when he encountered a fleet of Swedish merchantmen under the convoy of Captain Gustav von Psilander in the 50-gun Swedish warship *Öland*. Although massively outnumbered, Psilander refused to give the customary salute to the English warships in recognition of England's claim to sovereignty of the British Seas. A four-hour battle followed in which Whetstone captured *Öland*, seized the merchant ships, killed and wounded a number of Swedish seamen, and took Psilander ashore, where he was imprisoned.[22] The Swedish envoy in England, Christoffer Leijoncrona, quickly took steps to defuse the situation. Agreeing, Secretary of State Robert Harley wrote to Robinson '. . . if it is necessary to have a Breach, it may be upon a much better foot, and with much better grace than on this occasion; Althô You know very well the Sovereignty of the Seas is very popular in England, and the Swede's Conduct therein not very acceptable to our Nation.'[23] Nevertheless, both sides took precautions to avoid a repetition of the incident.

Charles XII's activities continued indirectly to threaten the allies in the War of the Spanish Succession.[24] In this, the complications and interrelation of the various allied theatres of that war can be seen when, after the victory at Blenheim, the duke of Savoy asked officials in Vienna for an augmentation of 12,000 Imperial troops for service in

Italy. It did not seem possible for the Austrians to undertake that unless they could persuade some other ally, most likely Prussia, to supply 8,000 new troops. At the same time, Denmark and Saxony-Poland were working to persuade Prussia to join their war against Sweden. In this situation, the king in Prussia, concerned about a Swedish attack on Brandenburg-Prussia lands, was unwilling to release troops to fight in Italy unless the Maritime Powers could guarantee military assistance to Prussia in case of a Swedish attack.[25] In November 1704, the renewal of the 1701-02 troop subsidy agreement between the Maritime Powers and Prussia contained a secret article by which Queen Anne promised to use her best efforts to prevent Prussian involvement in the Great Northern War and agreed to encourage the States General to assist in making peace in the north.[26] Prussia's insistence on recalling troops from allied service if in danger of an attack from Sweden was disturbing and reinforced the Anglo-Dutch policy of keeping things quiet in the north so 'that no part of the forces of the allies may be diverted from pursing the interest of the common cause.'[27] Reinforcing England's neutral stance, Secretary of State Robert Harley told the Swedish resident in London:

> *Her Majesty at the same time that she is ready to perform all acts of friendship to the King of Sweden can not but consider the Czar of Muscovy as a Prince in Amity with her Majesty and treat him accordingly.*[28]

While England had no intention of involving herself directly in the north, the death of the bishop of Lübeck-Eutin in 1705 and the subsequent move by Denmark to displace the Swedish-backed candidate and take possession of that territory became a matter of direct concern to the allies. The cabinet in London saw that this could not only provoke war between Sweden and Denmark, but disrupt the allied grand strategy of the war with France. With this in mind, the diplomatic effort turned to 'prevent the Swedes from engaging in this broil.'[29] The Maritime Powers offered to recompense the Danish candidate if he would return the bishopric to the Holstein-Gottorp candidate, but the emperor initially failed to confirm the arrangement.[30]

With the allied successes in the war against France, Charles XII saw little reason to continue to refrain from attacking Saxony. Meeting hardly any resistance, the Swedish army pressed beyond Leipzig and moved towards Dresden. On this news, the allies became extremely concerned that Denmark, Prussia, and Hesse would withdraw their troops in allied service in order to carry out their treaty obligations to Saxony.[31] To mollify the concerns within the Grand Alliance, Charles XII assured all that he would not prejudice the allied war effort against France.[32]

At Schloss Altranstädt, not far from the battlefield of Lützen where the Swedish King Gustav II Adolf had been killed in 1632, Saxon officials agreed to Charles's demands in a secret agreement on 24 September 1706, by which Augustus would be dethroned and Stanislaw recognised. In October, Augustus defeated a Swedish army at Kalisz. In response, Charles announced the details of their secret agreement on 15 November to try to stop Augustus's double-dealing.[33] When Charles demanded that other European powers recognise Stanislaw as king of Poland, Louis XIV quickly did so. From the allied perspective the presence of the Swedish army in Saxony seemed to be advantageous to the French side as it posed the potential danger of a Swedish

*Portrait of John Churchill, the 1st Duke of Marlborough.*

*Painting by Godfrey Kneller (1646-1723), 1712. Althorp House, Northampton, UK. The Collection at Althorp.*

attack on the forces of the new emperor, Joseph I. To avert difficulties, the Maritime Powers began negotiations at The Hague to bring Saxon troops into allied service.

In the meantime, Robinson and his Dutch colleague, Johan van Haersolte, left Danzig together and travelled to Leipzig, where they arrived on 12 November.[34] By that time, Charles had eased his ban on foreign diplomats allowing them to maintain contact with his army in winter quarters. On 24 December 1706, Charles granted Robinson an audience and he was finally able to present his credentials, issued four years earlier, as envoy extraordinary. Robinson continued his quiet diplomacy with Sweden, which the king seemed to acknowledge when he conversed for half an hour in Swedish with Robinson's Yorkshire-born wife, Mary. As Robinson reported, 'It is esteeme'd a greater grace than ever His Majty show'd to any stranger before.'[35] Meanwhile, French diplomats were busy using to their advantage the delay over recognition to draw Sweden into their camp. Officials at The Hague and in London were particularly concerned that if Charles's army crossed into Austria, Sweden would, in effect, be supporting Louis XIV. This would directly affect allied military plans for 1707 and force allied armies onto the defensive in Flanders.[36] Sweden, Prussia, and Hanover also wanted to create a Protestant 'Evangelical Pact' that would strengthen Sweden's position in northern Germany and, if realised, would also weaken the position of Austria in the Grand Alliance against France.

Queen Anne ordered the duke of Marlborough with full diplomatic powers to meet Charles XII personally at Altranstädt to discuss allied concerns. Just before Marlborough left The Hague, Grand Pensionary Heinsius and Simon van Slingelandt, the secretary of the Council of State, advised Marlborough that the Dutch had intercepted French letters indicating that nearly every official around Charles XII, except Count Piper, was in French pay.[37] Despite such suspicions and the feeling that Charles was an unpredictable figure whose fate was uncertain, Queen Anne and English officials were secretly considering the possibility that Charles XII might be the most acceptable person to act as mediator between France and the allies to end the War of the Spanish Succession. Marlborough was told to judge the feasibility of giving Charles this future role, 'But,' as Lord Godolphin warned, 'the nicety of it seems to lie in this: that it may be too dangerous to give him a handle to press the peace and the mediation of it.'[38]

Marlborough arrived at Altranstädt on 26 April 1707 and had long conversations with Charles XII the following day, with Robinson translating when Marlborough was not using French. Their meetings were fruitful. Concerned about the threat of Russia, Charles declined the role of mediator in the War of the Spanish Succession as he would be fully engaged against Russia. At the same time, Charles assured Marlborough that he would not act in any way that would harm the allies, and that he would support the Maritime Powers when the time came to negotiate a peace with France. Marlborough confirmed England's support for Sweden's concerns about Holstein-Gottorp and Austria, recognition of Stanislaw as king of Poland, and as a guarantor of the Treaty of Altranstädt with Saxony. In addition, Marlborough quietly promised gifts to key Swedish officials. Count Piper was given a pension of £1,500 per year, while the two secretaries in the king's field chancery, Hermelin and Cederhielm, each got £500 per year. But Marlborough made no progress with either England's continuing desire to hire Swedish troops or with Sweden's entry into the Alliance. Charles's promise of neutrality and secret tacit support had to suffice.

Marlborough explored the idea that Robinson might be allowed to accompany Charles in his coming campaigns, but he found that Robinson's status as a diplomat made that impossible. Instead, Swedish officials agreed that Robinson's secretary, James Jefferyes, was allowed to accompany the Swedish army in the guise of a volunteer, but actually serving as an English agent with allowances for his equipage and expenses paid from London. Jefferyes would keep London directly informed and, in the event that the Swedes defeated the Russians, be on the spot to make the case that Swedish troops be sent to fight France.[39] As Marlborough was leaving a meeting with Charles, King Stanislaw arrived at Schloss Altranstädt and gave Marlborough the opportunity to talk with him personally.

Augustus II sent word that he had just arrived at Leipzig, just eleven kilometres away, where he invited Marlborough to confer with him on 28 April. Through this meeting,

Marlborough was able to expedite the deployment of Saxon troops to Flanders and to encourage the Austrians to take other Saxon troops into their pay.[40] Marlborough returned to The Hague, meeting en route with King Friedrich I in Berlin and Elector Georg Ludwig in Hanover. Pleased by his meetings with four kings, Marlborough remarked privately to his wife, 'They seem to be all very different in their kindes. If I was obliged to make a choice it should be the youngest, which is the king of Sueden.'[41]

Meanwhile in London, on 12 May 1707, the independent sovereign kingdoms of Scotland and England, which since 1603 had shared their sovereign in a personal, dynastic union, agreed to the Act of Union, joining together to form Great Britain. From this point, what previously had been termed English policy and diplomacy now became British.

Marlborough left Robinson to follow up. In late July 1707 Robinson and his Dutch colleague mediated an agreement between the Swedes and the Austrians over the Saxon troops and the rights of Protestants in Silesia to practice their religion.[42] In early July, the various parts of the Swedish army began to move against Russia. Robinson remained accredited to Charles XII, but moved to Hamburg to take up actively Britain's role as a guarantor of the 1700 Treaty of Travendal, an issue that was the foremost in Charles's conversations with Marlborough and Charles's particular request that Robinson undertake.[43] The British fear of a war between Austria and Sweden was removed by the second Treaty of Altranstädt, by which the emperor agreed to the Gottorp candidate for the Lübeck-Eutin bishopric and Britain joined in compensating the Danish candidate.[44] At this point, British relations with Sweden were cordial. Robinson remained in communication with Charles's field chancery and his communications to London were supplemented by reports from James Jefferyes to the secretary of state sent via Robinson[45] and by letters from Count Piper to Marlborough.[46] With these connections established, British worries over the situation in the north momentarily melted away.

All this came to an end in 1709. On 8 July of that year, the Russian army defeated Charles XII's troops at Poltava. Count Piper and Josias Cederhielm were captured, and Robinson's third contact, Olof Hermelin, disappeared. Jefferyes was also captured. Taken to Moscow, he was a prisoner until the British envoy there, Charles Whitworth, was able to gain his release. Writing from Poltava, Jefferyes reported that although King Charles and several thousand men had escaped, 'this strange reverse of fortune has wholly chang'd the face of affairs in these parts.'[47] The Russians were reportedly ready to march into Livland, invade Poland, and restore Augustus to the throne. If Prussia and Denmark should join in this, Jefferyes reported,

> . . . 'tis more than probable that Sweden by this long and tedious war is exhausted of men and money will be forc'd to succumb. I need not mention to Y:r Hon:r the great projects the Muscovites have maid to extend their dominions in the East Sea, all along the Nieper, over Crimm and the Black Sea to the Mare Caspium . . . .[48]

When Marlborough heard the news of Poltava, he sadly reflected on how such a battle could so quickly ruin a king and his country. '. . . I am extremely touched with the misfortun of this young King,' Marlborough wrote Godolphin. 'His continued successes, and the contempt he had of his enemys, has been his ruin.'[49] In late August, officials in London recalled Robinson to become bishop of Bristol and lord privy seal. Soon thereafter, Robert Jackson became minister resident at Stockholm in 1710. Jefferyes returned to London in early 1710 and a year later, with Robinson's encouragement, became minister resident to Charles XII in Turkey.[50] The broad strategic situation also changed as Augustus of Saxony reassumed the Polish crown and joined Denmark and Russia in a renewed league against Sweden. Denmark prepared to invade Sweden and to withdraw her troops from allied service. To prevent this, as well as to maintain their troop strength against France, the Maritime Powers retained the Danish troops in allied pay.[51] In order to alleviate the threat from the north to the war against France, England took the initiative to prevent further threats of troop withdrawals. In March 1710, representatives of the queen, the emperor, and the States General signed a declaration guaranteeing the neutrality of the Empire and Germany in the Northern War. Six months later, these diplomatic words were given military backing when the three allies, along with Prussia, the bishop of Münster, the elector of Mainz, the duke of Wolfenbüttel, the duke of Mecklenburg, and the landgrave of Hesse-Kassel all agreed to detailed plans for an army of neutrality of 12,000 to 15,000 men that could act in countries bordering on the Elbe or Oder rivers as a deterrent to any attack from the north. [52]

With Charles now in Ottoman-controlled territory, British policymakers were concerned about Charles's presence having a possible impact on the already existing tension between Hungary and Austria. This was further complicated by the change of government in Constantinople, with an anti-Russian government coming into power. The Ottoman declaration of war against Poland and Russia in November 1710 caused great concern to British diplomats that neutrality in the north might be imminently compromised.[53] The British government having no desire to become directly involved, gave orders for British diplomats to concur in all matters that the States General and Dutch diplomats judged necessary, being 'best and earliest informed' of such matters.[54]

At about this time, Bishop Gilbert Burnet was writing the *History of his Own Time* and asked Robinson for material about Sweden. Among other things, Robinson told Burnet that Charles '. . . has all along wished well to the Allies, and not at all to France which he never intended to serve by any step he has made.'[55] With that understanding in mind, Queen Anne instructed Jefferyes in early 1711 to confirm British friendship with Sweden. Swedish privateering captures of British ships trading to the Baltic became a mounting irritant as Baltic naval stores remained a vital need. Between 1710 and 1713, while the war with France was in progress, the allies could not spare warships to protect the Baltic trade.[56] Jefferyes could only argue, 'free ships make free goods in all cases but contraband.'[57]

In all this, Britain was negotiating a fine line. Henry St. John explained to Jefferyes:

> . . . it would not be for our advantage entirely to disoblige the northern confederates, or that the king of Sweden should be in a condition of hurting the common cause of the allies by the invasion of Saxony, so on the other hand it is very far from being the general interest to have the balance of power in the north entirely destroyed and the protestant religion in Germany deprived of so great a support as it must necessarily be by an absolute conquest of the Swedish provinces.[58]

*Portrait of Admiral Sir John Norris.*

*Painting by Godfrey Kneller (1646-1723), 1711. National Maritime Museum, Greenwich, London, UK.*

Secretary of State for the Northern Department in the earl of Oxford's new Tory government, St. John soon expressed doubts about recent British policy in the north and blamed the Dutch for a lack of resolution. He believed that the Treaty of Altranstädt was a solemn promise to maintain Stanislaw on the Polish throne.[59] As the Danes, Poles, and Russians pressed to use the army of neutrality to crush the Swedes, British and Dutch leaders resisted these attempts.[60] Despite previous mishandling, St. John believed that the best course for Britain was to temporise and keep the northern princes in the best humour as possible towards the allies.[61] During the remainder of Anne's reign, Britain showed little direct concern for Sweden, leading Charles to protest to the queen that Britain had 'grown cold,' but she reassured the king of her continuing friendship.[62]

As the Utrecht negotiations led to peace in the War of the Spanish Succession in 1713, the continual erosion of Sweden's strength led Britain to propose an international congress to promote the welfare of Sweden and prevent the kingdom's complete collapse. Charles repeatedly rejected the proposals, stymieing all efforts for negotiation, peace, or mediation. Nevertheless, Jefferyes remained in close contact with Charles, following him from Bender to Adrianople and Constantinople in 1713, and then to Stralsund in 1714-15.

In May 1714, with the War of the Spanish Succession over and in the very last months of Anne's reign, the queen protested to the tsar, 'we cannot see the total ruin and overthrow of a nation with whom we have such alliances and in the preservation of which the interests of our people are so deeply concerned.'[63]

## ■ British Relations with Sweden under George I, 1714-23

At Stralsund on 30 November 1714, Jefferyes formally notified Charles of George I's accession to the British throne. Charles XII greeted the news with compliments, but understood George's situation in his dual role of elector in Hanover and king of Great Britain. First, George needed to counter the opposing Jacobite claims to the British throne and then balance Hanoverian interests and ambitions in Germany, while at the same time dealing with the broad European and global issues that Utrecht established. Reminiscent of William III before him, George I's accession to the throne had created a type of composite state, but as elector George had a much stronger role as a ruler than William had as stadholder. The affairs of Britain and Hanover were handled through separate governments and sets of ministers, whose politics and policies were sometimes complementary, competing, or entirely opaque to one other. This was reflected in divisive political forces within the internal politics of both Hanover and Britain.[64]

Hanover had been an ally of Sweden since the 1680s, but also had an interest in territorial expansion that was awakened after 1709 by the weakening Swedish control over her German provinces. Additionally, Hanover was competing with Denmark and Prussia. When Denmark took Stade in 1712, one of Sweden's four fortified cities in Germany, and occupied the duchy of Bremen, Hanover moved to occupy Swedish Verden as her first move to try to control both duchies.[65] These tensions were reduced following the accession of George's nephew and son-in-law, Friedrich Wilhelm I

as king in Prussia. In a complex set of bilateral agreements Denmark, Prussia, and Hanover agreed to Hanover's purchase of Bremen and Verden from Denmark and Sweden in 1714-15, while allowing Denmark to absorb Holstein-Gottorp's lands in Schleswig.[66] However, the cost of Hanover's gain was for George (as elector, but not king) to join Denmark and Prussia in declaring war against Sweden.[67]

After the Utrecht peace released navies from their earlier operational commitments, an Anglo-Dutch naval expedition sailed to the Baltic in 1715, under the overall command of Admiral Sir John Norris with a Dutch contingent under Rear-Admiral Lucas de Veth. The orders for the two admirals were inconsistent. Those for the Dutch were designed strictly as defensive protection of neutral trade. The British Admiralty's instructions were similar, but allowed reprisals against Sweden for British losses. In addition, George I's private orders authorised Norris to join the Danish fleet as a means to protect trade. Yet, when Prussia encouraged this, Norris refused to separate from the Dutch squadron. It was only when Denmark joined in the demand that George found ways for the Royal Navy to be used for Hanoverian objectives. In September 1715, Norris sailed for England and left an eight-ship detachment under Captain Edward Hopson in Danish waters to make a political statement. It had no direct effect on the fall of Stralsund and Rügen. A number of diplomats had hoped that Charles would agree to a peace or a ceasefire to prevent the total loss of his lands. When that failed to happen, Hanover openly declared war on Sweden on 15 October 1715. Upon his return to Sweden in December 1715, Charles responded by actively creating the impression that his country supported Jacobite plots against George after the failed 1715 insurrection in Scotland.[68]

Part of Charles's strategy for his campaigns in Norway in 1716 appeared to be making a threat towards Britain that was meant to keep the Royal Navy on the defensive in home waters and not assist Charles's enemies in the Baltic. In response to the Swedish move against Norway, Denmark and Russia actively considered a pincer attack on northern and southern Sweden that would involve the use of a combined British-Danish-Dutch-Russian fleet, convoying soldiers across the Baltic. However, Tsar Peter's marriage alliances with Courland and Mecklenburg-Schwerin for his nieces, followed by rapid movement of Russian troops into those duchies, created indecision and delays that provoked suspicions on all sides. The Anglo-Dutch squadron was not able to join the Danes in the eastern Baltic until early August, by which time the tsar abandoned the plan. George felt betrayed by the tsar's decision and was deeply worried about expanding Russian actions affecting British access to naval stores. Amidst mutual suspicion, the northern alliance against Sweden disintegrated.[69]

In Britain, these events played into internal politics and led to political changes that first split the Whig Party and then brought James Stanhope forward as George I's chief minister and the key figure for British foreign relations from July 1716 until his death in February 1721. Stanhope made an aggressive series of interconnected policy changes. First, in order to establish a wider European basis for foreign policy, he agreed with the French to create the long-lasting Triple Alliance that soon became a foundation for British policy. While creating a basis for a broad pacification of Europe, it also removed French support for any Jacobite threat in

*Portrait of James Stanhope.*

*Painting by Johan van Deist (1695-1757), ca. 1718. The National Portrait Gallery, London, UK.*

France. Although the Dutch Republic was part of the Alliance, Stanhope de-emphasised that longstanding relationship, as Dutch priorities for neutrality began to clash with Britain's new policies.[70]

To further public support for the shift in British policy, the ministry used intelligence of the correspondence of the Jacobites with the Swedish ambassador in London, Count Carl Gyllenborg, and Baron Georg von Görtz, Sweden's minister at large on the continent, making it appear as though these letters involved a plot for a renewed Jacobite invasion of Scotland. The British ministry published the letters, imprisoned Gyllenborg in London, and prevailed on the Dutch to imprison Görtz. This orchestrated event was intended to influence British public opinion into support for George's Hanoverian policies against Sweden. In retaliation, Charles XII broke diplomatic relations with Britain. After a brief detainment, Robert Jackson returned to England in October 1717.[71] With the fear of war between the two countries, Britain did not send a convoy to the Baltic in 1717 and depended on Dutch merchants to bring naval stores from the region.[72]

While Britain's main focus turned to resolving the international situation in southern Europe, the north was overshadowed but not forgotten. The Jacobites had been actively attempting to bring about a separate peace between Russia and Sweden that could threaten both Hanover and Britain. George I thought this unlikely. He steered another course and pursued peace initiatives through Hanover, as Swedish military operations in Norway suggested possible attacks on Scotland or on Hanover through Denmark.[73]

In 1717, Admiral Norris went on a diplomatic mission to Amsterdam. There, he and the British diplomat Charles Whitworth conferred with Tsar Peter, but they rejected Peter's demand for 15 British warships to be placed annually under Russian command as a prerequisite for a commercial treaty. Norris saw 'the Czar by his situation, numerous army, and disposition towards the water, to be the most dangerous enemy our country can have.'[74]

Britain's failure to agree with Russia required a different emphasis towards Sweden. In 1718, when Norris sailed for the Baltic, his orders made no mention of Russia, but directed him to join with the Danes to annoy the Swedes, hinder them from leaving the Baltic, while encouraging Sweden to open commerce with British merchants. Shortly after Norris's arrival at the Sound, where the Dutch joined him, the Russians put to sea their largest naval force up to that time. Misinterpreting Russian intentions, the British, Danish, and Dutch thought that a Swedish-Russian peace was at hand and that Russian naval forces would join with Sweden's to oppose them. To prevent this, Norris joined the Danes to blockade the main Swedish naval base, Karlskrona, leaving the Dutch to convoy merchant trade. Norris's departure for home in late October relieved the pressure on Sweden, freeing Charles for his Norwegian campaign, which, if it had been successful, might have secured a strategic position that could have obtained more acceptable peace terms from Russia and Hanover.[75]

Charles XII's death in Norway on 11 December 1718 created a fundamental change that became evident to Britain in early 1719. In the initial accounts from Stockholm, Robert Jackson reported that Queen Ulrika Eleonora would have a joint monarchy along the model of England's William and Mary, with her prince consort, Friedrich, the hereditary prince of Hesse-Kassel. Soon he predicted correctly that Ulrika Eleonora would abdicate in favour of her husband to rule as King Fredrik I of Sweden.[76]

Spain's leading minister, Cardinal Alberoni, had been directing the efforts to undo the Utrecht settlement in the Mediterranean and was also actively supporting a Jacobite restoration in Britain. A Spanish expedition set out in March 1719 under the duke of Ormonde to invade Scotland, but a storm in the Bay of Biscay scattered it. After the Jacobite threat receded, George I ordered Lord Carteret as Britain's ambassador to Sweden. Britain's objectives at this point were to restore trading relations, renew the defensive alliance of 1700, and support Sweden against Russian conquests, while also encouraging Sweden's release of territories in Germany.[77]

The first step towards Britain's plan to create a balance of power and general peace in the north was the preliminary treaty between Hanover and Sweden signed in Stockholm on 22 July 1719. Carteret promised British naval support to defend against Russian raids on the Swedish coasts, while Sweden, in return, agreed to sell Bremen and Verden to Hanover. The various states worked out a complex series of further treaties to divide up Swedish territories. In a key agreement, Prussia agreed to leave her alliance with Russia in order to obtain a portion of Pomerania. Through French diplomacy, Denmark agreed to relinquish claims to Swedish territory in Germany in order to retain the Holstein-Gottorp territories. Then, Sweden needed to be persuaded to accept this dismemberment. To do this, Carteret falsified the date of the agreements between Prussia, Hanover, and Britain in order to make Swedish leaders think that they had been reached before the news of the Swedish-Hanoverian pact. At the same time, Carteret threatened to deny Sweden British naval assistance against Russia unless she agreed to relinquish her territories.

Circumstances prevented Britain from implementing her full plan. The financial turmoil surrounding the South Sea Bubble, combined with the continuing need for British naval forces in southern Europe, meant that the British forces available in the north were insufficient to compel Russia into making concessions that would allow Sweden to recover Livonia and Estonia. To conclude the war, Britain used further pressure to gain the Peace of Nystad in 1721, paying £20,000 to Russian court officials and the same amount to the Swedish king to encourage their approvals, with the promise of another £100,000 if George as king and elector were included as a participant in the peace.[78] To George's disappointment, neither Hanover nor Britain was included.[79]

Peace allowed Britain to return to her fundamental commercial and economic interests in the Baltic region. Her solid support for Sweden in the years following Charles XII's death, combined with the rise of Russia, resulted in bringing significant commercial gains to British merchants in the north. At the same time, the results of the War of the Spanish Succession and the Great Northern War combined to make Great Britain and Russia the two leading powers of Europe.

CHAPTER 10

# How to Handle a Warrior King
## *The States General and Its Policies in Regard to Charles XII of Sweden*

by Augustus J. Veenendaal, Jr.

Generally, two main themes, one mercantile and one military, governed the policies of the States General of the Republic of the United Netherlands—Dutch Republic for short—in respect of Sweden and the rest of the Baltic area. The mercantile theme emphasised the importance of the Baltic trade for the Dutch economy, especially that of the province of Holland proper. Trade could prosper only in peacetime, when Dutch merchants and shippers could safely follow their mercantile interests; hence the need for peace in the Baltic. The focus of the military theme was on the availability of Danish, Holstein-Gottorp, Brandenburg-Prussian, Saxon, and Swedish soldiers as auxiliaries to the army of the States to help fight for the allied cause against the ever-threatening French monarchy. Connected with this last issue were the attempts to keep a conflict in the north separated from the wars against France.

## ■ The All-important Baltic Trade

Dutch interest in Sweden was first and foremost commercial. In the Dutch Republic the Baltic trade had always been known as the *moedernegotie*, the mother of all trade. Rye and wheat from Poland and Russia, timber from Sweden and Finland, hemp, peck, tar, and other naval stores were imported in great quantities, and Sweden was also very important for its metallurgical industries. Dutch entrepreneurs like Trip and De Geer had set up extensive ironworks and cannon foundries in Sweden. Even more important was the concession granted by the Swedish Crown for the export of copper in exchange for a guarantee from De Geer and Trip of Dutch loans to the Crown, giving these men an almost complete monopoly.[1]

In return, Dutch merchants supplied the Baltic area with salt from France, Portugal, and Spain, wine from France, Spain, and Germany, and luxury and colonial goods from around the globe. When not enough outbound freight was available they ballasted their ships with bricks and tiles, which explains the large number of brick-built houses in port cities such as Danzig or Stralsund.[2]

Although the Dutch share of the Baltic trade was slowly diminishing after 1680, it remained very important. For Amsterdam, figures are known: an absolute low was reached in 1709 when only 212 ships arrived there from the Baltic, mostly from Königsberg and Elbing in East Prussia. By 1724 the number had again increased to 677 ships; but the now Russian ports on the Baltic had meanwhile become the chief ports of departure, with 232 ships, against 160 from Danzig and 106 from Königsberg.[3]

Archangel, Russia, on the White Sea, where a Dutch colony of traders had existed since the early seventeenth century, was another important centre. After Tsar Peter took the Swedish fortification of Nyenskans in Ingermanland—then not much more than a simple earthen redoubt—and founded Saint Petersburg there, he required the foreign—mostly Dutch and English—merchants to transfer their business to his future grand city on the Neva River. His measures to enforce this move were, however, half-hearted and could not be fully implemented. In 1713, he ordered that half of the Archangel trade was to be carried through Saint Petersburg, and two years later this order was extended. But the ongoing war and resulting lack of safety in the Baltic prevented Dutch and English traders from sailing to Saint Petersburg in sufficient numbers, so in 1718 the tsar rescinded the 1715 order. Henceforth one-third of all Russian trade was to pass through Archangel, and two-thirds through Saint Petersburg. The latter became the official centre of Russian trade after the Peace of Nystad (1721), although Dutch merchants kept up a strong presence in Archangel.[4]

It should be emphasised that the Dutch Republic had no clear-cut mercantile policy. In a fragmented government such a policy had proven to be well nigh impossible because of the conflicting interests of Holland—and to a lesser degree Zealand and Friesland—with the land provinces. But almost everyone agreed on one aspect: free trade was generally seen as the best solution for the open economy of the Republic. Yet, mercantile policies of competing states such as England and France, combined with protective measures of others, often nullified the States General's attempts to keep routes open. The traditional carrying trade and the entrepôt function of Holland came under increasing pressure in the last quarter of the seventeenth century, and the first twenty years of the next century promised to be even worse.[5]

## ■ The States General and the Freedom of the Sound

For Dutch merchants and shippers free passage through the Sound was of supreme importance. The nuisance of paying tolls to the Danish Crown was acceptable, as long as they were reasonable and not fluctuating with political and military circumstances. Denmark's gradual withdrawal from the Swedish mainland in the 1650s and 1660s was seen as an insurance against arbitrary acts of a government with fortifications on both sides of the Sound. A balance of power in the Sound was essential to free trade in the Baltic.

The States General had already interfered—somewhat reluctantly—in earlier struggles between Denmark and Sweden, every time because vital Dutch trade interests were threatened. In 1658, when King Charles X of Sweden was fighting in Poland, Denmark sought to profit from his entanglement there by declaring war on him, hoping to regain some of its lost possessions on the other side of the Sound. However, the Swedish king suddenly broke off all engagements in Poland and turned his forces against Denmark, easily overrunning the country and even laying siege to Copenhagen. Only then, when the Swedes refused to pull back and open the Sound to neutral shipping, did the States General send a naval squadron, under the command of Jacob Baron van Wassenaer-Obdam, to force the Swedes to retreat. The Dutch destroyed a number of Swedish ships and relieved Copenhagen. England was not happy with this forced *Pax Neerlandica* and the following year ordered a fleet to assist the Swedes and keep the Sound open to all. The States General then sent Admiral Michiel de Ruyter with a large squadron to reinforce the ships sent earlier, but with orders to avoid actual combat with the English. The latter did not want to fight either against a superior enemy and withdrew. De Ruyter then landed his forces, threw the Swedes out of their last strongholds on Danish soil, and forced King Charles X to come to terms. He evacuated all Danish territories and, possibly more important for the Dutch, lowered the tolls on Dutch merchantmen in Swedish ports.[6]

The mercantilist policies of Sweden were not abolished easily, and in 1673, when the heart of the Dutch Republic was still being threatened by the French armies, the government of King Charles XI, in league with France, again laid heavy duties on wine and salt not shipped in Swedish vessels or vessels of the countries of origin, i.e., France or Portugal.[7] As soon as England had withdrawn from the alliance with Louis XIV, thereby lifting the danger of an enemy landing on the Dutch coast, and with Denmark finally aligning itself with Holland against its eternal foe Sweden, the States General sent a large naval squadron to the Sound. The combined Dutch-Danish fleet destroyed the Swedish navy in June 1676 and even landed troops on the Swedish mainland. The Dutch-Swedish maritime treaty of 1679 put an end to all restricting measures in Swedish ports and, from that year on, tension between the two countries lessened. Two years later, with a new Dutch-Swedish agreement, Sweden broke with France and became good friends with the States again.[8] Sweden's presence, in the person of Ambassador Nils Eosander, Count Lillieroot as mediator at the Rijswijk peace negotiations, several years later, is a clear proof of the changed circumstances. Personally, Charles XI had been more in favour of making sure that the friendship with France would not be endangered, and the simultaneous treaty with Louis XIV is proof of that. But the treaty between France and Sweden of 1698 was as much an empty shell as the one with the Maritime Powers.[9]

## ■ A New King: An Enigma

Alas, this happy state of affairs did not last long. King Charles XI died in 1697 and with the accession of Charles XII things were to change fundamentally. Young, vigorous, and warlike, the new king was an unknown quantity. Sweden's position did not look strong in view of the anti-Swedish forces, Russia, Denmark, and Saxony, allies since 1699. However, Charles XII was willing to strengthen the bonds between Sweden and the Maritime Powers, and in 1699 negotiations began between his government and the Dutch and English. Under strong pressure from Stadholder-King William III and Grand Pensionary Anthonie Heinsius, Sweden agreed to guarantee all clauses of the Treaty of Rijswijk that pertained to the Maritime Powers. Charles XII could hardly be called neutral after the signing of the Triple Alliance with England and the States General in January 1700.[10]

Charles needed help from the Maritime Powers. Problems had arisen about the duchy of Holstein-Gottorp, always on friendly terms with Sweden, on Denmark's hard to defend southern border. Danish troops invaded the duchy and laid siege to Tönning. The Danes did not believe that the Maritime Powers would be willing to support Sweden with naval squadrons, but in this they were to be very wrong. Heinsius was said to be well informed of Danish plans through his correspondence with Ferdinand Wilhelm, Duke of Württemberg-Neustadt, the Danish commander-in-chief.[11] The Danish government counted on French support, ignored warnings from London and The Hague, and started to move into Holstein-Gottorp. Everything seemed lost for Sweden but Charles XII now could, and did, implore help from the Maritime Powers. Both London and The Hague maintained that they only acted as guarantors of the 1689 Treaty of Altona providing for the return of the lands taken by Denmark to the duke of Holstein-Gottorp, and not as parties in the conflict.[12] More important for them, the unhindered passage through the Sound was in danger.

And maybe even more pressing, the question of the Spanish succession after the expected death of Carlos II was to be settled as soon as possible and Swedish troops on German soil might eliminate the chances of hiring German auxiliaries during the impending conflict with France. Brandenburg and the emperor had to be placated, so haste was required. The allies responded by sending a strong fleet under the overall command of George Rooke—with sixteen ships—and Philips van Almonde—with eighteen ships—to help the Swedish cause. The Danish fleet was easily overcome and Copenhagen bombarded for a short time. The allies were careful not to damage Danish interests too much, as they knew they might need Danish auxiliaries in the war with France that was bound to come. The new King Frederik IV of Denmark was quick to give up and the Treaty of Travendal was signed on 18 August 1700, leaving Holstein-Gottorp pretty much independent of Danish influence.[13]

In a new treaty of February 1702 Charles XII even went further in his support of the English and Dutch. He now promised actual military help in case one of the Maritime Powers were attacked, but with the caveat: 'as soon as his own war would enable him to do so.' And to the disappointment of London and The Hague, his own war never enabled him to give actual help. The allies, rightly or wrongly, lost confidence in him and felt left in suspense. As it turned out, though, Charles waited to attack his most hated foe, Augustus II of Saxony-Poland, until 1706, when the allies in the west had strengthened their position against France sufficiently.[14] Despite the 1702 treaty, Amsterdam merchants supplied Tsar Peter with thousands of flintlocks, hundreds of cannon, tons of ammunition, and many men-of-war without the States General actually intervening.[15] Had political leaders already lost faith in the arrival of Swedish troops in support of their own war effort? In a government as loosely organised as that of the Dutch Republic such things were possible. Amsterdam was always inclined to follow its own policies even when they clashed with the interests of the United Provinces as a whole.

As Charles's plans were still unclear to allied diplomats, both London and The Hague had trouble determining their position. What did the move of the Swedish king into Poland mean, and what would be his next step? Above all, the Maritime Powers wanted to keep the Northern War separate from the war they were just starting to wage against Louis XIV. As long as the Swede did not threaten to invade the Empire, much-needed auxiliary troops to fight France could be raised among the German principalities.

### ■ The Importance of Auxiliary Troops

The desperate need for auxiliary troops for the impending military conflict with France was recognised early, even before the actual declaration of war. Already in 1701, England and the States General had contracted with the Danish king for no fewer than ten regiments of infantry, eight of cavalry, and one of dragoons. The States General assumed the cost for eight of the infantry and two of the cavalry, and with these ten regiments in Dutch pay—if complete some 10,000 men altogether—the army of the States seemed to be well set for the struggle against France. Some of these regiments, such as the Horse Life Guards (Liv-Regimentet til Hest) or the Life Guards on Foot (Livgarden til Fods), formed the pick of the Danish army and were considered well-trained, well-equipped, and dependable fighters. However, in the course of the War of the Spanish Succession a problem arose when the Danish government started to recall the by now experienced officers to home service and replace them with less accomplished men. As the Danish officers in Dutch service held no commission—an official appointment—from the States General, contrary for instance to those from Hesse-Kassel or Holstein-Gottorp, this was perfectly legal and formally correct. The Dutch authorities complained repeatedly, but to no avail.

With Denmark established as the most important supplier of troops by far, this was not all. A convention between the States General and the duke of Braunschweig-Lüneburg-Celle was signed in the same year for two regiments of horse and four of foot, while at the same time a similar agreement with the duke of Braunschweig-Lüneburg-Hanover strengthened the army of the States General with three regiments of foot and four of cavalry. Of the other possible northern belligerents, Holstein-Gottorp supplied one regiment of dragoons and one of foot in 1704, and the same number to England. Mecklenburg-Schwerin in 1701 contracted with the States General for two regiments of infantry.

Other, more southern German states also supplied a large number of troops but the need for more was always felt; hence the importance of keeping the theatre of the Northern War removed from that in the west. In 1707, the States General, together with Great Britain, acquired a large number of troops from the elector of Saxony, of which no fewer than five regiments of infantry and three of cavalry went into Dutch service. They were a welcome addition to compensate for the losses in the field.[16] With these regiments in service from so many different powers, the importance of a possible contribution by seasoned Swedish troops becomes clear. Heinsius and Marlborough closely cooperated in their efforts to keep the auxiliaries, for both were aware of their great importance for the allied cause.[17]

An unexpected possibility to get more soldiers in the field presented itself when Feodor Alekseevic, Count Golowin, Russian minister of war under Peter the Great, wrote to Heinsius from Wologda in May 1702, offering the States General 4,000 marines for the coming war against France as a reward for the attempts at mediation by the States General in the person of its envoy, Johan van Haersolte-Cranenburg, between the tsar and the Swedish king. Believing that these attempts would continue, the tsar was also willing, in case of a reasonable peace, to let the States have several thousand men of 'well-regulated foot soldiers' for the struggle against France. Heinsius knew Golowin personally, as the latter had accompanied Tsar Peter the Great during his tour of Holland and England in 1697-98, when Heinsius was one of the commissars for the reception of the tsar, and he and Golowin had had several talks in The Hague.

Heinsius's answer to this letter was guarded, but very friendly and full of thanks for the tsar's positive opinion about the mediation efforts and for his good intentions towards the States General and its subjects. Yet the offer had to be declined, as the season for naval operations had almost ended and marines were no longer needed. However, the grand pensionary suggested that the Russian ambassador in The Hague,

Andrej Artamonovic Matveev, be charged with conducting negotiations about foot soldiers for the next campaign. Nothing came of it, as the tsar could not miss several thousand of these soldiers during his war with Charles XII.[18]

## ■ After Poltava

Marlborough heard details of the Battle of Poltava sometime in August 1709 and wrote to Heinsius about it on the 26th, without further comment.[19] However, he was very much afraid that the possibility of a general war in the north would affect the position of the allies in the struggle against France in the Dutch Republic. Heinsius agreed wholeheartedly and wrote to Marlborough that the States were trying to dissuade the Danish king from beginning hostilities against Sweden and that Heinsius himself had spoken to the Danish envoy, Iver Rosenkrantz.[20] The Swedish army corps under Ernst Detlof von Krassow in Mecklenburg seemed a threat to the Danish position, however, and the British and Dutch governments were slowly thinking of giving some sort of guarantee so that Krassow would remain inactive. The northern allies, Denmark, Saxony, Prussia, and Russia, wanted a solid guarantee and proposed a kind of army corps, supplied by the Maritime Powers, to guarantee the neutrality of the Swedish possessions in the Empire. Johan Palmquist, Swedish envoy in The Hague, proposed that the allies take these Swedish troops into their service. Both Heinsius and Marlborough seemed to fancy the idea but were also aware of the potential impact on keeping Danish troops in allied service. Charles XII, at least according to Palmquist, was positive about letting his troops enter the service of the allies, and ultimately Marlborough was agreeable to the proposal as well. This way the need for a neutrality corps would be obviated and the allies would be strengthened with 8,000 experienced men.[21] But it all came to nought: rumours that Charles XII would refuse to accept the neutrality convention, agreed upon by the emperor, the Maritime Powers, Hanover, Denmark, Saxony, Prussia, and Russia, were already circulating in November 1710 and proved to be correct in March 1711.[22] No Swedish troops ever entered the service of the allies. Palmquist made Sweden's refusal officially known to the States General on 31 March 1711, whereupon the northern allies pressed London and The Hague to supply the promised twelve battalions at once. Experienced troops could hardly be spared in the continuing struggle against France. An agreement with the elector Palatine stipulated, however, that eight regiments of his troops in allied service were to be kept ready for dispatch to the north.[23] Nothing came of it in the end.

## ■ Charles XII in Turkey

News about the aftermath of Poltava, with many details of the Swedish defeat, was also sent by Jacobus, Count Colyer, the Dutch ambassador in Constantinople, as early as 1 August 1709. Charles XII was reported to have saved himself in Osu—modern-day Oschakov on the Black Sea at the mouth of the Dnieper—with a small group of Swedes and Cossacks. At the end of the same month Colyer wrote again, confirming the fate of the Swedish king and his situation as 'guest' of the Porte, the central Ottoman government.[24] Colyer kept Heinsius and the States General informed about Charles XII's move to Bender and about the audiences of his representative, Martin Neugebauer, but could tell little of the Porte's plans regarding the distinguished but unwelcome guest. Rumours of an impending rupture between the Porte and the tsar, about the possibility of Ottoman support for Charles's return to his dominions through Russian-held Poland, flew around, yet nobody actually knew exactly what was going to happen.[25] Policies of the Ottoman court were always unpredictable, to say the least, and the sudden appearance of a foreign prince in need of help clearly was a challenge. Rumours of the Swedish king having ordered five capital ships from Sweden for his return were contradicted by Neugebauer, who was on friendly terms with the representatives of Great Britain and the States General. Neugebauer even hinted at a much longer stay of his master in Bender and at pressure from Charles on the Porte to force a rupture with the tsar. At the same time the Ottoman government sounded out Colyer about the States General's willingness to send several warships to escort the Swedish king to his country.[26]

Pressure from the Porte on Charles to return to his dominions slowly mounted, but the Ottoman government had to move carefully lest it should forfeit the money advanced to the king for himself and his men. Colyer estimated this sum at six million guilders, possibly more, which the Ottomans hoped to get back from the Swedes once international relations returned to normal.[27] Colyer heard the first rumours about the attack on the Swedish compound at Bender, the *Kalabalik*, in Pera on 20 February, and he confirmed them a week later, but in much exaggerated form, with hundreds of men allegedly killed and wounded on both sides, and the king himself severely injured. Johan van Haersolte-Cranenburg, Dutch envoy to Saxony and Poland, also confirmed the attack but gave a much more moderate report, as heard from a Polish officer who had just returned from Bender.[28]

After this incident the Ottoman authorities held the king in a light form of confinement, but Colyer and other diplomats believed that this situation could not last. Somehow his return to Sweden was going to be planned, in great secret, and in September 1714, just before Charles actually started on his spectacular ride, everybody expected his return.[29] However, news of the actual passage of the king through Habsburg lands travelled slowly, and it was not until 1 December that Van Haersolte and Hendrik Willem Rumpf were both able, independently of each other, to report the king's safe arrival in Stralsund.[30]

## ■ Renewed War in the Baltic

The return of the king to Swedish territory opened up a new set of possibilities and most European governments had to readjust their position regarding the conflict in the north. The States General and Heinsius as the political leader were at a loss over the course to be taken. This is illustrated by a letter from Heinsius to Robert Goes, who had advanced a number of ideas for ending the war: 'So far I see so many uncertainties and apparent instabilities that I cannot make any positive decisions

in respect of your suggestions.'[31] After the Peace of Utrecht the need for auxiliary troops was no longer of any importance, and other problems seemed more pressing. The ongoing negotiations in Antwerp with the emperor about the Barrier in the Southern, now Austrian, Netherlands, and especially the financial side, proved to be a hard nut to crack without adequate British support, although the British government, as a result of the recent treaty with the States General, was obliged to provide support on this issue. It was not until 1715 that Heinsius, by making a commitment to supply military assistance to George I against the Stuart Pretender in Scotland, managed to put so much pressure on the king that strong British support was forthcoming. With six of the crack regiments of the army of the States actually helping the Hanover cause in Scotland, the British king could not do otherwise than give all help possible to the Dutch negotiators in Antwerp.

However, at the time of Charles XII's return to Stralsund, Heinsius and the other leaders of the Dutch Republic had to act. On 4 December 1714, with the news from Stralsund still fresh, Heinsius contacted his colleague Willem Buys, pensionary of Amsterdam and now the first Dutch ambassador to Louis XIV after the Peace of Utrecht, about what to expect from the French court in this regard.[32] The entire traditional system of alliances had to be rethought and renegotiated.

In 1714, in view of the problems encountered with Swedish privateers in the Baltic, influential merchants in Amsterdam had already pressed for the sending of a naval squadron, jointly with Britain, but to no avail. The simple reason was lack of money. In 1715 the same request was repeated and no fewer than thirty-two ships were deemed necessary, twenty from Britain and twelve from the United Provinces.[33] But even the equipment of these twelve ships proved to be a great problem, as the coffers of the three Holland Admiralties were still empty. Only the loan of a large sum provided by the Amsterdam Chamber of the Dutch East India Company made it possible to fit out the necessary ships, nine by the Amsterdam Admiralty, two by that of Rotterdam, and one by the Northern Quarter of Holland. The Admiralties of Zealand and Friesland were completely broke and took no part in this effort. This impotence of the Holland Admiralties was a sure sign of the terrible financial situation of the province of Holland; Heinsius was shocked at the inability of the States to put up the necessary money.[34] For a time the French government seemed to be inclined to join in the efforts of the Dutch Republic, as the new French ambassador, Pierre-Antoine de Castagnéry, Marquis de Châteauneuf had hinted to Heinsius. Willem Buys was instructed to sound out the French government, but neither he nor Heinsius was much inclined to press the subject. Working with just one ally was going to be difficult enough![35]

Another problem arose over the instructions for the commanding officer, Rear-Admiral Lucas de Veth, when he was told to join the British squadron under Vice-Admiral Sir John Norris, and help protect Dutch, British, and neutral shipping against the Swedish privateers that were infesting the Baltic and the North Sea. Norris was, among other things, instructed to claim damages for ships already taken and sold, and if no compensation were forthcoming, he could stop all Swedish shipping from entering or leaving Swedish harbours and take Swedish ships as reparations.[36] De Veth did not get such an ample instruction: he was to escort, in cooperation with the British commander, the Dutch and British merchant ships to their several destinations in the Baltic and back, and prevent Swedish or Russian privateers or men-of-war from attacking or hindering allied navigation. He was to return on 1 September. Not a word about exacting compensation for ships taken earlier.[37]

This was not all, however, for in the final instructions for Norris nothing was purported to have been said about exacting compensation. The British government assured Arent van Wassenaer-Duvenvoorde, the Dutch ambassador in London, that Norris's instructions were exactly the same as those for De Veth, but when in early June the two squadrons joined forces in the Sound, it became clear that Norris was openly instructed to retake English vessels earlier seized by privateers and force compensation. Moreover, his orders comprised that he take action against Swedish warships if deemed necessary. The two admirals, both old hands at this game, worked out a plan that would not compromise the Dutch. When a Swedish squadron would seem to threaten British ships, Norris would wait until being actually attacked, and if that happened, De Veth, according to his orders, would be allowed to help his ally and join the fight. Heinsius was not pleased with this development as he felt that the Dutch had been misled on purpose. In the future more precautions should be taken, according to the grand pensionary, to avoid this kind of complication.[38]

The Swedish government, although happy that the Dutch squadron was not going to retake merchant ships seized by privateers, did complain that the Russian government had purchased one man-of-war of 74 and two of 54 guns in Amsterdam, loaded them with munitions and other necessities, and had them sent to Saint Petersburg under protection of the Dutch squadron under De Veth.[39] This was contrary to all declarations that strict neutrality was to be maintained in respect of all belligerents. No action was taken, as these things happened too often, and the orders from the States General against the export of war material to belligerents were circumvented or just ignored in Amsterdam. However, Jean de La Bassecour, second pensionary of Amsterdam, asked Heinsius if it would not be better to order all towns and Admiralties to stop recruiting officers and sailors for Russian service. Four ships had already been purchased, five more were expected, and once enough crew had been recruited, the tsar would have a formidable navy able to withstand any enemy.[40]

No shot was fired in anger by the Dutch in 1715 and all merchantmen were safely conducted to their destinations, without being hindered by the Swedes. De Veth reported that while anchored on the Reval (present-day Tallinn) roadstead, he was regaled by the tsar on board the Russian flagship, together with Norris. The next day the tsar inspected De Veth's flagship, the 74-gun *Gelderland*, from top to bottom and had found everything in good order. The tsar opined that he thought the ship a bit short in relation to its width, something De Veth did not agree with, but he was too diplomatic to say so.[41] Norris had left eight of his ships for service with the Danish navy, clearly demonstrating British policy on behalf of the elector of Hanover, the king of Great Britain. The Dutch government did not want to be drawn into the Northern War to further the interests of King George as elector.[42]

The year 1716 showed the same urgency to send a British-Dutch squadron into the Baltic. The initiative was taken by the British government in February, as reported by Van Wassenaer-Duvenvoorde. While Heinsius agreed with the need for a naval presence in those waters, he warned that the necessary funds would be hard to find. In the end only the Admiralty of Amsterdam participated in equipping six ships, and the 400,000 guilders needed had to be raised on the Amsterdam money market. Again, the instructions to the respective commanders, Norris and Captain Hendrick Grave, caused problems.[43] Heinsius and Duvenvoorde suspected that Norris was, this

*Model of a 74-gun Dutch warship, dating from the early eighteenth century. Similar to the* Gelderland, *the flagship of Admiral de Veth in 1715.*

*Mixed media by unknown maker, ca. 1700-25. The Scheepvaartmuseum, Amsterdam, the Netherlands.*

time also, ordered to give active support to the Danes against Swedish naval operations, while Grave had to maintain absolute neutrality, although this could well mean that Dutch merchantmen ran the risk of being attacked by both warring parties. By the middle of June Grave set sail for the Sound with his six ships and some 300 Dutch merchantmen, while Norris had already arrived before him with about 50 English vessels.[44] Again, no shots were fired and most Dutch merchantmen reached their destinations safely, but Grave complained to Robert Goes, the Dutch envoy in Copenhagen, that Norris had been busier helping the Danish navy against possible Swedish attacks than protecting the allied vessels. As an afterthought the parties in Amsterdam that were involved in the Baltic trade, suggested in November 1716 that Grave on his way home could be ordered to attack any Swedish privateer found in the North Sea. These privateers roamed freely along the coast of Holland and Friesland and formed a serious threat to shipping. Amsterdam Pensionary Willem Buys was in favour of such measures and even Heinsius was not averse, but the Amsterdam Admiralty refused to give the necessary orders. Moreover, the season was already too far advanced and Grave almost back in home waters.[45]

## ■ Tsar Peter in Holland

That same year 1716 also brought Tsar Peter on a tour to Holland, another nuisance for the authorities. In early October Heinsius learned about the forthcoming visit. Being the ambitious monarch of a fast-growing empire and an important trading partner, the tsar had to be kept in a friendly mood, as Heinsius and his colleagues knew all too well. Of course, the grand pensionary had met the tsar during his earlier visit in 1697 and he must have known what to expect. A committee from the States of Holland was assembled, of which Arnold Joost van Keppel, Duke of Albemarle, a good friend of Heinsius, was the most prominent member. Tsar Peter arrived in Amsterdam on 16 December 1716 and was regally entertained by the committee and the city's burgomasters. The interests of trade and shipping must have been foremost in everybody's mind when wining and dining such a distinguished but difficult to please guest. Unfortunately Peter fell ill and had to stay in Amsterdam until early March. There he was joined by his wife Catherine, who had given birth to a baby boy on 13 January 1717 in Wesel, just across the border in Prussian territory. The boy had died the next day. By mid-March, the imperial couple was in The Hague, but there is little evidence of any real business being conducted by the tsar and the representatives of the States or Heinsius, although the tsar stayed for some time and did indeed meet with the grand pensionary again.[46] Next, Peter left for Flushing, where he boarded ship for Antwerp, travelling from there to Brussels. In early May he arrived in Paris, where he stayed until 20 June. He then slowly travelled north again to Spa, taking the waters there before returning to Amsterdam on 2 August. Meanwhile his spouse had spent the whole summer in that city. Many a sigh of relief must have been heard when the couple finally left the United Provinces in September 1717, travelling on the Rhine into Prussian territory. All towns that the tsar passed in his barge saluted him with cannon fire from the walls on orders of the States General.[47] In late September he was in Berlin and he finally returned to Saint Petersburg on 20 October 1717. Apparently Peter could afford to be absent from his dominions and the theatre of war for such a long time. Although the tsar's visit was deemed a success, the growing Russian influence in northern Germany and the Baltic was seen as a danger to the mercantile interests of the Dutch, but the States General did not know how to react.[48]

## ■ Friction with Great Britain

In 1717 the policies of King-Elector George I hardened towards Sweden and the British government aimed at a complete stop to all transports of grains and other vital cargoes to Sweden in an attempt to bring King Charles to reason by starving his country. The Dutch Republic was asked to comply, but Amsterdam Pensionary Willem Buys did not consider these measures adequate to bring the Swedes to their knees. Great Britain equipped a strong naval force under Admiral George Byng to support the Danish navy, but this time the Dutch did not cooperate at all. Supplies of grain and other foodstuffs in the Amsterdam storehouses were sufficient for another year, so Dutch shipping to the Baltic came to a virtual halt. If need be, new supplies could be found by way of Archangel, avoiding the troubled Baltic waters. Yet there are indications that some well-equipped and well-manned Dutch frigates were operating in the Baltic in 1717.[49] For 1718 a different course was taken. The London government now was more interested in the Mediterranean and Spain's aggression against the emperor, and a large fleet under Byng was sent out to southern waters. For the Baltic, only a small squadron, again under Norris, remained. This opened the way for the Dutch to protect their trade in the usual way without having to reckon with British policies that could conflict with Dutch aims. Sending a squadron of no fewer than thirty ships was first mooted in the winter of 1718 but there was a lot of opposition, as it was considered too expensive and too large for the purpose of protecting trade. So in the end only eleven ships of the line and two frigates were equipped, three by the Rotterdam Admiralty and the rest by Amsterdam. Originally Lieutenant-Admiral Jan Gerrit van Wassenaer-Rosenburg was appointed to command the large fleet, but when only eleven ships were deemed sufficient he backed out and an officer of lower rank was appointed. Jacob van Koperen, rear-admiral of the Rotterdam Admiralty was chosen, although Amsterdam would have preferred an officer of its Admiralty. Van Koperen sailed in June and was successful in protecting the Dutch mercantile interests, without clashing openly with Norris and his twelve ships.[50] Before the Dutch squadron actually sailed, the Amsterdam burgomasters petitioned the States General and Heinsius to use two or three ships of this squadron already fully equipped and manned, to sail and find two Swedish privateers which were reportedly roaming the North Sea. Buys recommended allowing the request but administrative complications prevented it.[51]

*Portrait of Georg Heinrich, Freiherr von Schlitz, genannt von Görtz – a Swedish official and confidant of Charles XII.*

*Portrait miniature by unknown artist, late seventeenth century – early eighteenth century. Nationalmuseum, Stockholm, Sweden.*

## ■ The Unfortunate Affair of Baron von Görtz

An ugly affair that soured the relations between the States General and Sweden and with Great Britain at the same time was the arrest of Baron von Görtz in 1717 in Arnhem, the capital of the province of Gelderland. Georg Heinrich, Freiherr von Schlitz, genannt von Görtz, was a nobleman from Holstein in Swedish service and highly regarded by Charles XII. He had come to The Hague and Amsterdam in the summer of 1716 to negotiate a large loan for the purpose of buying warships for Sweden. At the same time he was ordered to promote a separate peace between Charles XII and Tsar Peter. Amsterdam bankers were hesitant to advance money, although Görtz managed to sign an agreement with them which stipulated that funds would become available in 1717. After that, he went to France and was successful in obtaining money from Jacobites around the regent, the duke of Orléans. He crossed over to England early in 1717, had talks with Jacobites there, and became a regular visitor of the Swedish minister in London, Count Carl Gyllenborg. In contacting these would-be insurgents he double-crossed his own king, as Charles did not want to become involved in conspiracies of any kind. The British government got wind of this attempt to reinstate the House of Stuart, supposedly organised by Gyllenborg and Görtz with the help of disgruntled Jacobites who still resented the unfortunate outcome of the Jacobite rising in Scotland in 1715. Gyllenborg was arrested in his house in London on 12 February 1717 and naturally the affair caused a diplomatic scandal. Görtz, who had left England, was arrested by the Dutch authorities at the request of the British government, just before he could cross into Prussian territory on 21 February. This was a sensitive move, as Görtz was empowered to give—and had already sold—free passes to Dutch merchantmen as safeguards against reprisals by Swedish privateers, and Dutch ship owners had profited from this.[52] Heinsius was not pleased with either the affair or the arrest, and wanted more information from King George. The Holstein and Swedish ministers in The Hague urged the States General to release him. Rumours of a Swedish landing in Scotland, the apparent pretext for the arrests, were not believed by anyone. In Stockholm Rumpf, for instance, wondered how the hard-pressed Swedish navy would ever have been able to launch such an attack. Pressure mounted for the release of Görtz, even in the States General, since proof of his complicity remained weak. In June 1717, the States General requested permission from King George to release the baron, but the British government refused. Yet the losses of shipping in the Baltic continued to grow as Swedish privateers had stepped up their actions against Dutch ships, and finally the States General in early August 1717 went its own way and offered a man-of-war to bring Görtz back to Sweden. Even before this offer could be implemented, the baron was released by the States of Gelderland, without authorisation from The Hague. Albemarle, Heinsius's friend, was at his country house at Voorst, not too far from Arnhem, and distrusted Görtz's intentions. He complained to Heinsius that Görtz had gone to the former palace of William III, Het Loo, where he had met Tsar Peter as the latter was passing by. Albemarle strongly suspected that the meeting of the two bode no good for the Republic: 'It is strange that we have to witness these intrigues in our own country. In God's name, what will become of this Baron Görtz; will he remain here forever?'[53] Albemarle could soon feel relieved: Görtz departed at the end of August from Gelderland on his way to Sweden.[54] The immediate danger was over, but the uncertainty about the baron's intentions remained.

## ■ Death of a King

The news of Charles XII's death on 11 December 1718 reached Holland quickly. Grand Pensionary Heinsius wrote to his friend Adolf Hendrik van Rechteren, Heer van Almelo on 3 January 1719 with correct details about what had actually

*Portrait of Count Carl Gyllenborg, Swedish representative in London.*

*Painting by Lorens Pasch the Elder (1702-66), eighteenth century. Nationalmuseum, Stockholm, Sweden.*

happened: '. . . The most important event is the death of the king of Sweden in the trenches before Fredrikshald, shot dead through the head.'[55] Heinsius was hopeful that Princess Ulrika would succeed Charles and that the presence of her husband, Friedrich of Hesse-Kassel, would greatly help advance the interests of the Dutch Republic. After all, Friedrich was colonel of a regiment of cavalry on the payroll of the province of Holland and general of cavalry in the army of the States General.[56] He was well known to Heinsius and had been a regular correspondent of the by now aged pensionary. As early as 1 January 1715, when he had just arrived in Stralsund, Friedrich had announced to Heinsius his plan to marry Ulrika, and Heinsius had expressed his pleasure in a most friendly answer to the prince.[57] Heinsius was right about the beneficial influence of the prince after Charles's death: Hendrik Willem Rumpf, the Dutch envoy in Stockholm, was again admitted to the court and all restrictions imposed on him were lifted.

Indeed, Rumpf set great store on the presence of Friedrich at the side of the Swedish queen to see to the interests of the States General and those of its subjects harassed by Swedish privateers.[58] The States General, prompted by Amsterdam, at once sent a special envoy without character to Sweden to convey the feelings of the States, while an official ambassador of higher rank was to be despatched later. The choice for the first fell on Jacob de Bie, Dutch resident in Moscow from 1711 to 1718, and well versed in the affairs of the north.[59] After a difficult journey overland with many contretemps as a result of bad weather, De Bie arrived in Stockholm on 30 March 1719 and went to work immediately. He was of the same opinion as Rumpf that the prince seemed to be most favourable in his attitude towards the States and that he promised repeatedly to do his very best to further the interests of the Dutch merchants and skippers. The prince even told De Bie jokingly that he had acted for a whole week as minister of the States General to reach that goal.[60] In a letter to the prince, Heinsius acknowledged his great help in straightening out the conflicts between Dutch and Swedish interests and thanked him for his continuing support of the Dutch Republic.[61]

Indeed, Friedrich had been successful in lifting the Swedish embargo on Dutch merchant shipping in the Baltic, although trade with the former Swedish, now Russian ports remained forbidden until the very end of hostilities. De Bie and Rumpf, when asked for Dutch help to re-equip the Swedish navy argued that supplies of this kind—masts, tar, pitch, and hemp—had to come from exactly those forbidden ports, but no relief came until the Peace of Nystad.

## ■ Conclusion

Up until the Peace of Utrecht in April 1713, the first and foremost aim of the States General was to keep the Northern War separated from the War of the Spanish Succession. These efforts were reasonably successful; no doubt because of the forceful assistance of the British government whose aims were the same. French diplomacy was, of course, countering these policies but without real success. The authorities in The Hague, Grand Pensionary Anthonie Heinsius foremost, were always more focused on the war against Louis XIV than on the northern conflict. When the conflict with France finally ended in 1713, this position hardly changed. Despite regular and sometimes very shrewd reports from the Dutch ministers and envoys, politicians in The Hague simply failed to understand the way the Swedish monarch continued to wage war against superior forces, thereby ruining his country and its people. Of course, in this they were no exception, as most foreign politicians grappled with this problem without coming to solid conclusions. Attempts at mediation by Dutch envoys such as Robert Goes in Copenhagen and Christiaan Carel van Lintelo during the siege of Stralsund were ineffective, mirroring the weakened position of the States General in international politics. An added—internal Dutch—problem was that the interests of Amsterdam shipping circles were very different from those of the landed provinces, causing much friction in the States General. Amsterdam was already leaning more to Russia because of the growing trade between the two. It was not for nothing that Tsar

Peter during his 1717 visit stayed in Amsterdam at the house of Christoffel Brants, an important merchant with large interests in Russia.

After 1713 the mercantile interests in Amsterdam clamoured for protection of shipping to the Baltic. However, the financial exhaustion of the Dutch Republic precluded an active naval presence there in 1713 and 1714, and only in 1715, 1716 and 1718 did it become possible to equip squadrons for this purpose. Although the British and Dutch governments had collaborated reasonably well in respect to the Northern War until the Peace of Utrecht of 1713, a complication arose after that year, when the elector of Hanover ascended the throne of Great Britain. His interests as elector—the acquisition of Bremen and Verden—made him a participant of sorts in the hostilities against Sweden, while the Dutch Republic aimed at maintaining an absolute neutrality, further straining relations between London and The Hague. The presence in Stockholm of the hereditary prince of Hesse-Kassel, well known in The Hague, and his gradual assumption of power, were a godsend to the Dutch. The mission to Stockholm, in early 1719, of Jacob de Bie, a veteran Dutch diplomat, also helped establish good relations between The Hague and Stockholm, but all this took time. Even though the Peace of Nystad of 1721 came about without actual involvement of the Dutch Republic, indicating its diminished influence in international politics, it came as a relief to the Dutch authorities.

Dutch trade on the Baltic came back strongly after the peace, now that the seas were safe again. From an average of 880 ships annually during the troubled years 1711-20, the number of Dutch vessels passing the Sound almost doubled to an average of 1612 annually in the years 1721-30, and although the Dutch share was now less predominant, this number was still 42 per cent of the total of ships of all nations. Danzig, Elbing, and Königsberg remained important ports for Dutch skippers for the grain trade, but Reval and Riga, now Russian, were strong competitors. Sweden was no longer an exporter of grain as it had been during the seventeenth century, but became an importer, chiefly from its former Baltic provinces. The trade in Swedish iron, copper and such, however, remained solid and the worldwide business of the De Geer family retained a strong presence there. Apart from being grain exporters, the now Russian ports were most important, to the Dutch and British alike, for the trade in hemp, pitch, and tar for the shipbuilding industries. Despite the measures taken by Tsar Peter, Saint Petersburg remained a rather unimportant destination for Dutch ships trading on Russia. In the decade after the Peace of Nystad, only 24 ships—annual average—arrived there, while 22—annual average—still went to Archangel. In tons shipped the latter's preponderance was even greater, and that was to continue throughout the eighteenth century, even though the Archangel trade was only seasonal because of the severe winters up north.[62]

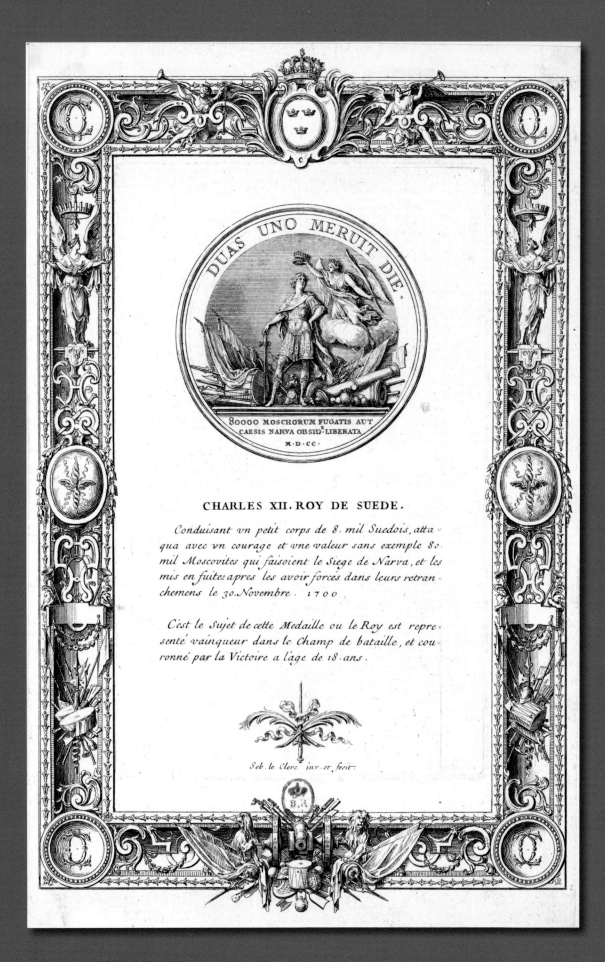

DUAS UNO MERUIT DIE

80000 MOSCHORUM FUGATIS AUT
CAESIS NARVA OBSID. LIBERATA
M·D·CC·

## CHARLES XII. ROY DE SUEDE.

Conduisant vn petit corps de 8. mil Suedois, atta-
qua avec vn courage et vne valeur sans exemple 80.
mil Moscovites qui faisoient le Siege de Narva, et les
mis en fuites apres les avoir forcés dans leurs retran-
chemens le 30.Novembre. 1700.

C'est le Sujet de cette Medaille ou le Roy est repre-
senté vainqueur dans le Champ de bataille, et cou-
ronné par la Victoire a l'âge de 18.ans.

Seb. le Clerc inv. et fecit.

# CHAPTER 11

# The French View of Charles XII
## *The King, the Soldier, the Man*

by  Eric Schnakenbourg

Throughout the reign of Louis XIV the provisions of the Treaties of Westphalia were fundamental to French policy in Germany, a policy in which Sweden played an integral part. In 1648 the Scandinavian kingdom was guarantor of the peace and held territories in the north of the Empire. Louis XIV, having been born in 1638, was raised on a foreign policy designed specifically for the Europe of the Westphalian order. In his estimation, Sweden's presence in Germany had earned its king the aversion of the Viennese court. Moreover, since he was convinced of a 'permanent enmity' between France and the Habsburgs, Louis XIV thought of Sweden as his natural ally.[1] Its role in the French strategy was to serve as an *allié de revers* (rear ally), igniting a backfire on the northern flank of the Empire, should war break out between Versailles and Vienna. Thus the absolute priority of Louis XIV's policy in the north was to preserve the Swedish king's 'footing in Germany,' in keeping with the provisions of the Treaties of Westphalia.[2]

This was the general context for relations between France and Sweden during the reign of Charles XII. Although in the early eighteenth century each country was engaged in its own war—the War of the Spanish Succession (1702-14) for France, the Great Northern War (1700-21) for Sweden—the court at Versailles kept a keen eye on Charles XII's activities, including his military successes in the early years of the Great Northern War, his defeat at Poltava, his Ottoman exile, and the offensives on the Swedish provinces of northern Germany. French diplomats sought to understand and anticipate the decisions of this often unpredictable monarch, who inspired everything from fascination to antipathy. The French king's agents were thus attentive observers of Charles XII, both as a king and as a man.

## ■ Rise of a New Alexander

The second part of Charles XI's reign was no doubt the seventeenth century's period of greatest tension in Franco-Swedish relations. Sweden's disastrous action in the Franco-Dutch War and its humiliating dependence on Louis XIV during the peace negotiations of 1679, led Charles XI to steer a new course in his foreign policy. He foreswore military ventures in order to set his kingdom on firm financial footing and consolidate his authority. The true kingpin of Swedish foreign policy was Chancellor (*Kanslipresident*) Bengt Oxenstierna, who feared Louis XIV's hegemony in Europe and favoured an alliance with England and the Dutch Republic.

*Medal celebrating the victory of Charles XII at Narva.*

*Engraving by Sébastien Leclerc (1637-1714), ca. 1700. Bibliothèque nationale de France, Cabinet des Estampes, Paris, France.*

In spite of all the trouble, the French continued to mind affairs at the court at Stockholm. Indeed, Louis XIV's ambassador to Sweden in the 1690s, Count d'Avaux, set aside political considerations to watch the health of Charles XI's son. In August and September 1693, with the eleven-year-old boy feverish for weeks on end, d'Avaux feared a case of tuberculosis and even evoked the possibility of an early death, writing warily, after several relapses, of the prince's 'exceedingly delicate complexion.'[3] The following year he reported that the young man had come down with smallpox.[4] He took an interest also in the prince's education, which had been entrusted to Nils Gyldenstolpe. Although he was considered to be in the French camp, d'Avaux had minimal confidence in this man who was in fact receiving money from all quarters.[5] The education that Prince Charles received opened him up to French culture. He learned French (although he would forever be a mediocre speaker), studied the life of Henry IV, and read the plays of Racine and Corneille.[6] As king he was filled with admiration for French culture and ordered the performance in Stockholm of ballets, plays, and other entertainments inspired by Versailles.[7]

D'Avaux tried to observe more closely once the prince became King Charles XII. In the very first weeks of the reign, the ambassador sketched character traits for Louis XIV. The young monarch is described as 'very discerning and witty'; he 'thoroughly enjoys violent exercise, and he has always shown an inclination toward war'; he seems to have 'every bit of his father's resolve'; and, especially, 'he is most favourably disposed toward France.'[8] D'Avaux was convinced that Charles XII held Louis XIV in high esteem, because he was reported to have said that Louis was 'Europe's greatest king, and [that] there is no safety but in solid alliance with him.'[9] The end of the regency, in December 1697, and the distribution of money and gifts to the members of the king's council (*Råd*) gave d'Avaux hope of seeing Oxenstierna isolated and France restored to the good graces of the Swedish monarchy, especially with conflict brewing over the Spanish succession. But his hopes were quickly dashed. His negotiations with Charles XII for a new Franco-Swedish alliance bore no fruit until 1698, and even then produced nothing but a toothless defence treaty. D'Avaux had failed to grasp that Charles XII was not, in fact, much of a francophile and was taking up the same principles of neutrality in European affairs that his father before him had espoused.[10]

The Great Northern War broke out just as Carlos II of Spain was on the verge of death. Louis XIV, who did not intervene in the north in order to avoid incurring the enmity of England or the United Provinces, allowed William III to step between Sweden and Denmark and impose the Treaty of Travendal (18 August 1700), which brought peace to the Sound. Louis nevertheless looked forward to good relations with Sweden. Reassured by his new ambassador, Count de Guiscard, he judged that the money and gifts he could distribute among the ministers would suffice to induce Charles XII to enter Germany if war broke out once again between France and the emperor.[11] Little by little, however, Guiscard realised that the Swedish king did not have the slightest desire to partake in the quarrels over the Spanish succession and intended to vanquish his enemies without any foreign mediation.[12] Guiscard deplored his 'dilatoriness and coolness' for the good offices of Louis XIV.[13]

Indeed, aside from the accusations of indifference and of partiality towards the House of Austria, both attributable to the influence of Chancellor Oxenstierna, the kings of France and Sweden held different priorities. Louis XIV's priority was to restore peace in the north as swiftly as possible, thus forging an *alliance de revers* against the emperor, whereas Charles XII's was to liberate his Baltic provinces from enemy troops. The astonishing victory at Narva, on 30 November 1700, convinced Versailles that Charles XII was next preparing an offensive against the elector of Saxony and king of Poland, Augustus II.

Having vainly attempted a rapprochement, Louis XIV now believed Charles XII favourably disposed towards his enemies. As noted by Marquis de Bonnac, whom Louis XIV had appointed ambassador to Sweden in late 1701, the war in the north was keeping Charles XII away from the conflict in the west: 'The more victories the Swedish king achieves, the more troops he will require to preserve his conquests; and the more he must preserve his troops for his own defence,'[14] the leaner his capacity to sustain France's enemies. The war in Poland was of interest to Louis XIV in yet another way. Since Charles XII's enemy in the conflict was both king of Poland and elector of Saxony, the French government hoped that the war in the north would spill over into the Empire, resulting in a formidable diversion of Swedish and Saxon armies coming to grips on German soil. The war could thus degenerate and spread into Habsburgian Silesia, all to the benefit of Louis XIV: 'I do not see how the emperor could remain a mere spectator to a war fought by two foreign princes on his own land.'[15] Some of the German troops arrayed by the emperor against the French would have to be withdrawn from the western front.[16] If he decided to enter Saxony, Charles XII would be acting as an *allié de revers* to the rear of the emperor, without the French having to incur any of the cost.[17] France's diplomats hoped to persuade Charles XII to pursue his war on the hereditary lands of Augustus II, but they could get precious little information to act on and struggled to fathom the Swedish king's intentions. Bonnac justly attributed the incessant reports on the offensive in Saxony to France's enemies, who were working to dissuade Charles XII from entering the Empire.[18] In 1706 the defeats and retreats of Louis XIV's armies in the Low Countries, Italy, and Spain allowed the Swedes to enter Saxony without entanglement in the War of the Spanish Succession. In late August the Swedish army camped at the small Saxon village of Altranstädt.

News of this, so long awaited at Versailles, led Louis XIV to believe that a breach was imminent between Charles XII and Emperor Joseph I.[19] The Swedish king's pilgrimage to Lützen, where Gustav II Adolf had died in 1632, rekindled memories of the happy Franco-Swedish alliance during the Thirty Years' War.[20] Seizing the opportunity, Louis XIV dispatched to Altranstädt a substantial contingent, consisting of no fewer than three informers and a negotiator, Baron de Besenval.[21] The baron was to get Charles XII either to serve as mediator in the War of the Spanish Succession or to break with the emperor, but he accomplished neither. The Swedish army's presence in Saxony proved to be of no benefit to Louis XIV. In 1707 Charles XII's troops withdrew from the Empire and headed for Russia, where the Swedish king sought to vanquish the last of his enemies.

The French, while considering the Swedish army's military valour more than sufficient to best Russia's troops, were not unaware of the difficulties inherent to an offensive in Russia. Like Louis XIV, Besenval thought the Swedish monarch would exhaust his army in the Russian vastness and his campaign would turn into an aimless, woeful march through hostile, devastated regions.[22] The scorched-earth campaign encountered by the Swedish army as soon as it had crossed Poland conjured up for the French government all the difficulties awaiting Charles XII, even if no one put any stock in his ultimate defeat. But over the course of 1708 the news reaching Versailles about the state of the Swedish army became ever more alarming, with tales of Russian harassment and disease striking down soldiers and horses alike. Analysis of Muscovite military capacity figures rarely in France's diplomatic correspondence of the time, but reflections on the struggles to which the Swedish king submitted his army grew increasingly common. By the autumn of 1708 both French agents in northeast Europe and the government at Versailles were agreed that Charles XII was caught in a deadlock. For Louis XIV, his ministers, and his diplomats the only question was how Charles XII could escape Russia without disaster. The Swedish army's eastern progress into Russia had made reliable information hard to come by. With neither an informer in Charles XII's entourage nor a diplomat posted to Moscow, Versailles was receiving its information through Poland or Stockholm, and two or three months after the fact. Thus the most varied rumours were flying.[23] In July 1709 Marquis de Torcy, Louis XIV's secretary of state for foreign affairs, wrote of receiving 'more and more opinions from different quarters all telling of an imminent accommodation between the king of Sweden and the Muscovites,'[24] whereas in fact Charles XII was at the time just laying siege to Poltava.

## ■ From Fallen Hero to Obstinate Monarch

News of the Swedish defeat reached Paris in mid-August 1709. Jean-Léonor de Grimarest, then working on the fourth volume of *Les Campagnes de Charles XII, roi de Suède*, noted: 'One struggled to credit the news of the Swedish king's defeat, though the newspapers of Holland took pains to publish it.'[25] In three dispatches, all dated 15 August 1709, Torcy asked his agents in Hamburg, Stockholm, and Danzig for more information on 'a dreadful bit of news that has been spreading over the past few days about a supposed defeat of the king of Sweden.'[26] In late August 1709 the *Gazette d'Amsterdam* reported from Paris that despite the spread of a detailed account of the battle that 'should render it believable, [the defeat] still has its doubters & we shall refrain here from adding to its credibility.'[27] It was two months after the battle that Louis XIV was at last convinced of the Swedish defeat,[28] and it took yet another few weeks to be sure what had happened to the king of Sweden himself, now a refugee in the Ottoman Empire.

Despite the defeat at Poltava and the troubles Sweden encountered after 1709, the French government maintained its confidence in Charles XII. According to Torcy, the king of Sweden would 'soon be fit to make his mark on the Empire as a great man' and to influence the powers of northeast Europe.[29] For the time being, however,

Charles XII was in exile some two thousand kilometres from his kingdom, leaving the field open for his enemies, who hastened to the Swedish provinces of the southern Baltics. In the weeks after the Swedish king's arrival in the Ottoman Empire Louis XIV's ambassador offered him passage aboard commercial ships to France, from where he could return in safety to his kingdom.[30] Charles XII was pleased by France's attitude but declined the offer, believing that he had the necessary resources to be reunited with his army in Poland.[31]

Although in dire straits, Sweden was still considered the guardian of Germanic liberties against the reputedly hegemonic designs of the Viennese court, and thus indispensable to the balance of power in Germany, the north, and Europe in general.[32] This is why, with the signing of the Treaty of Utrecht in 1713, Louis XIV was determined to safeguard Swedish Pomerania. Charles XII's return to the north, in November 1714, freed the hand of French diplomacy in the region. As soon as the Swedish king reached Stralsund the government at Versailles proposed a treaty for subsidies that would allow him to save his German provinces.[33] The new French ambassador, Count de Croissy, was to encourage Charles XII to save Pomerania and recover the duchies of Bremen and Verden, then under Danish occupation. But by late 1715 Sweden's enemies had managed to take possession of Pomerania. Louis XIV, who died in September, did not live to see the Swedes expelled from Germany. As his great-grandson, Louis XV, was only five years old at the time, the regency fell to his great-uncle Philippe, Duke of Orléans.

As of 1716 France's priority in foreign policy was to consolidate the peace in Europe through a rapprochement with Great Britain, whose king, George I, as elector of Hanover, was Sweden's enemy. In exchange, Philippe d'Orléans had to promise to persuade Charles XII to cede the duchies of Bremen and Verden to Hanover. This promise and, more broadly, the promotion of the interests of Great Britain's king, conditioned relations between France and the king of Sweden.[34] The negotiations that Baron von Görtz conducted in Paris in September 1716 and especially in January 1717 convinced Charles XII's right-hand man that no help was forthcoming from France. It was a misleading impression, for in truth Paris had not lost interest in the fate of Charles XII. In the estimation of Philippe d'Orléans and his chief minister, Abbé Dubois, the Swedish king must sacrifice certain possessions in the Empire in order to preserve others. Count de La Marck was dispatched to Lund, where he was to persuade Charles XII to accept French mediation for a separate peace treaty with Hanover. By paying the price for this treaty—the cession of Bremen and Verden— Charles XII would be able to focus his military efforts on the recovery of Pomerania and, later, the Baltic provinces. But these proposals discredited French mediation in the eyes of Charles XII, who considered that France, as guarantor of the Treaties of Westphalia, was under an obligation to help him recover all of his German possessions.[35] By late 1718, Franco-Swedish relations had reached their nadir. There was neither trust nor common interests nor real dialogue.

News of Charles XII's death before Fredrikshald, on the night of 11-12 December 1718, took three and a half weeks to reach Paris, arriving on 5 January 1719, doubtless via the news from Holland.[36] Restoring peace in the north became the issue of the day in the years 1719-21. France played an important role; Louis XV is the sole sovereign whose offices figure in every peace treaty. For the French government, the chief aim was to have Pomerania restored to Sweden. Hence the opposition of Philippe d'Orléans to the Anglo-Hanoverian peace plan, which called for the expulsion of the Swedes from the Empire in exchange for the restitution of Finland, Estonia, and Livonia. The government at London realised that it could count on France's support for the pacification of the north only if it agreed to restore Pomerania to Sweden, as James Craggs, secretary of state for the Southern Department, clearly stated: 'France is desirous to have the Swedes preserve a footing in Germany, in order to assist them as formerly, to disturb the Empire, whenever they shall think it necessary.'[37] Philippe d'Orléans carried the day, for during the peace negotiations between Sweden and Denmark the English agreed to press Frederik IV of Denmark to evacuate Pomerania[38] and the peace treaty of 1720 allowed the Swedes to recover it.[39] Although very active throughout the restoration of the peace in the western Baltics, France played only a limited role in talks between Sweden and Russia. Peter the Great would accept the mediation of Louis XV only if his conditions for peace were met in advance. The French, who conducted scarcely any trade with Baltic ports directly, were not opposed to letting the Baltics pass under Russian sovereignty. For them, the important issues lay elsewhere. Peace in the north would allow them to safeguard the essential thing: Sweden's footing in Germany.

## ■ The French View of Charles XII as a Man

Throughout his reign Charles XII was, as a king, the subject of much speculation by, and the object of many appeals from, the French government. He inspired much commentary, admiration, criticism, and reflection from many Frenchmen who had been able to approach him or who pondered his fate.

The Great Northern War, which resounded with its most spectacular events, especially the battles, did not go unnoticed in France. The young Swedish king's audacity at the Battle of Narva, on 30 November 1700, left all of Europe agape. 'The action is fine and grand for a king not yet eighteen years of age,' wrote Marquis de Dangeau in his *Journal*.[40] The Swedish envoy to Paris, Johan Palmquist, reported hearing cries of 'Long live King Charles' after the circumstances of the victory had been made public.[41] Engravings circulated in the capital to celebrate the success of the Swedish king, said to be walking in the footsteps of Gustav II Adolf, warrior king par excellence.[42] Charles XII had marked a return to the brilliant tradition of Swedish arms.

Charles XII's reputation was sustained by subsequent victories over the Saxons in Poland, victories that were not snatched from a composite Muscovite army of little experience but wrested from renowned German troops. With the victory at Kliszów (19 July 1702) over the troops of Augustus II, the myth of a new Alexander began to take shape.

France's diplomats in northern Europe were themselves impressed by the qualities of the young Swedish king and his army. Marquis du Héron believed after Kliszów that Charles XII could take Saxony in a couple of weeks.[43] Following the victory at Pułtusk (1 May 1703) Ambassador Bonnac was convinced that, if the Swedish

*Charles honoured with laurels of glory. Shown with a wig, this image was made after Arvid Karlsteen's image of Charles XII on the Riksdaler from 1705 (also called the 'Wig-Riksdaler').*

*Engraving by Simon Thomassin (1655-1733), ca. 1705. Bibliothèque nationale de France, Cabinet des Estampes, Paris, France.*

king continued as he was going, 'the whole Saxon army [would be] destroyed in less than two months.'[44] At Altranstädt Charles XII had reached the pinnacle of his glory. Basking in the glow of victories over the Danish, the Russians, the Poles, and the Saxons, the young sovereign had become the Hero incarnate. Wrote Saint-Simon in his *Mémoirs*: 'Glory has raised in Saxony a tribunal that lays down his law for all the world' and set him up 'to become the dictator of Europe.'[45] The French diplomatic archives contain an anonymous poem from the period; it begins: 'I have seen him, the hero that all admire; And I concur he is a demigod [. . . ].' In addition to being invincible, Charles XII was the most virtuous of princes, an enemy to pride and vanity.[46] Jean-Léonor Grimarest was beholden to the same fascination, publishing from 1706 to 1711 *Les Campagnes de Charles XII, roi de Suède*.[47] The work enjoyed

a certain success. The first two volumes were translated into German in 1707, and the whole work went through several editions, the last one published in The Hague in 1731. Grimarest paints a particularly laudatory portrait of the Swedish king, who is vigorous, firm yet affable, disdainful of luxury and splendour, and immune to passions. In addition to physical and moral qualities, he boasts a sharp wit and a sure judgment that confers on him 'a superior genius for war [. . .] . His army is his family. He cares for it, loves it, derives his pleasure from it. The soldier, the officer, for his part, devoted through duty and veneration, cherishes the prince, follows him, imitates him, and spills his blood with ardour and valour, convinced that whenever the conqueror wishes to strike he must vanquish.'[48] The man whom Grimarest several times calls a Hero seems modelled after the ideal of antiquity.

After the defeat at Poltava the king of Sweden retained his aura. Chevalier de Bellerive, captain of a company of dragoons in the service of Spain's king, re-signed his charge in 1711 to join Charles XII in the Ottoman Empire. He claimed to be attracted by 'the great name and astonishing adventures of the king of Swe-den,' who for him was the 'valiant lion of the North: the famous conqueror whose reputation has spread so far and wide.'[49] His meeting with the monarch did not disappoint. Bellerive noted his 'majestic and proud' bearing and the 'charming sweetness' of his countenance, and praised both his simplicity and his piety, concluding that Charles XII possessed the 'military and poetic virtues [. . .] of an Alexander in his audacity, of a Caesar in his courage, of a Pompey in his wisdom, but without any of their vices; he is an Alexander that takes no wine, a Caesar that harbours no ambition, a Pompey that abides no lethargy.'[50] Military theorist Jean-Charles de Folard also avowed great admiration for Charles XII after the victory at Narva. He considered the king of Sweden to be the greatest captain of modern times and, in 1715, dedicated to him his *Traité de la colonne*.[51] Count de Croissy, too, was impressed by Charles XII during the few weeks he spent with him in Stralsund in 1715. He noted his interlocutor's 'gallant air and pleasing visage' as well as his physical qualities; 'He is hardly ever at rest and covers much ground in little time, always swift like a man on the hunt.'[52] According to the count, Charles XII is worthy of admiration and 'combines wisdom and an ex-ceeding sweetness with a superior mind and much simplicity. His replies are apt and prompt.'[53] He concludes that in speaking with Charles XII he has the sense of speaking with a philosopher rather than a king.[54] The comparison of Charles XII to Alexander the Great was explicit during his lifetime, and his defeats did not diminish the enthusiasm of those who were convinced of his genius.

French opinion was nevertheless not unanimous, and many diplomats who dealt with the king of Sweden were less eager to give praise. His lack of interest in diplomacy, his taciturn nature, and his ceaseless travel made it particularly difficult for diplomats to carry out their duties. When, in October 1700, Charles XII went to Estonia he forbade foreign representatives to follow.[55] Louis XIV's ambassador, Guiscard, went nevertheless to Reval (present-day Tallinn), provoking Charles' ire and never getting an audience. Hence the diplomat's great relief on being recalled to France, and his acerbic judgment of the king: 'a young prince who is full of himself and obstinate in the extreme, believes himself above everything, and has neither education nor knowledge of foreign affairs.'[56] Guiscard's successor, Bonnac, who represented Louis XIV from 1701 to 1707, complained that his audiences with the king concerned only 'indifferent matters.'[57] During the Polish years of the Great Northern War French diplomats deplored the Swedish king's silence, which kept them from learning anything about a future offensive in Saxony: 'Indeed one cannot count on anything with a prince who comports himself like the Swedish king, who hews to no maxim nor to reason, and who abides by no rule but his own caprice,' observed French agent Philippe Groffey.[58] At Altranstädt, after much insistence, Besenval at last obtained an audience with Charles XII, but accomplished nothing whatsoever. The sovereign listened to the ambassador's compliments and then left the room without uttering a word.[59] Besenval bitterly expressed his disappointment: 'What say you of a country where one cannot approach the master and where the minister forever holds his tongue?'[60] These judgments of France's diplomats were largely conditioned on their incapacity to comprehend or sway the Swedish king during the rare audiences they managed to obtain with him. Thus Bonnac could say that he was unreasonable in his behaviour or not amenable 'to the force of argument.'[61] The French diplomats who approached Charles XII after the defeat at Poltava also showed much discouragement. Marquis des Alleurs, who would play an important role in relations between Charles XII and the Ottoman authorities, finally saw his patience run out, saying: 'fed up with the haughty, inflexible humour of the king of Sweden.'[62] In the final period of his reign things got worse under the influence of Baron von Görtz, 'the most deceitful, the most scheming, the most dangerous, and the most disparaged of all men' for Jacques de Campredon, who was in Stockholm at the time.[63]

It is apparent that those who knew the legend of Charles XII from afar or who were only briefly in his company had the most praise for him, whereas those who sought relations with him in a diplomatic capacity were highly critical. More generally, whereas Charles XII the war chief could command devotion and inspire admiration, Charles XII the strategist could prompt misgivings. He succumbed to hubris, believing he would always be victorious. In the weeks after the defeat at Poltava both Groffey and Bonnac emphasised that it was the conviction that his army was invincible that had led the Swedish king so carelessly to embark on the disastrous Russian campaign.[64] With the death of Charles XII the French diplomats in northern Europe considered the way open to a pacification of the Baltics. The king's utter obstinacy in pursuing war and refusing all compromise with his enemies revealed what Besenval called a 'lack of political qualities,' which had dragged Sweden into an abyss.[65]

The fate of Charles XII, from victorious new Alexander to defeated king in exile, inspired much reflection among his contemporaries. He became a figure of excess, and his story a cautionary tale for ambitious sovereigns. For example, one of the protagonists of the anonymous work *Dialogue entre le maréchal de Turenne et le prince d'Auvergne dans les champs Elysiens sur l'état des affaires de l'Europe vers la fin de cette année 1710* considers that Charles XII, having enjoyed triumph after triumph, had come to believe 'in immortality & in glory' and had 'in some way stripped himself of humanity,' but the natural movement that brings all human affairs into balance had led him to resounding defeats.[66] From the perspective of classical stoicism, which prescribes for the achievement of wisdom a life that accords with nature and reason, the adventures of Charles XII serve as a counterexample. This is particularly the case in Voltaire's *Histoire de Charles XII, roi de*

*Suède*, first published in 1731 and fourteen more times before the author's death, in 1778. In this text the fate of the Swedish king forms a basis for reflections on grandeur, decadence, and the ephemeral nature of military glory.[67]

Voltaire presents Charles XII as 'perhaps the most extraordinary man ever to walk the earth, who possessed all the great qualities of his forebears, and whose only flaw and misfortune was to have carried all of those qualities to excess.'[68] Several passages emphasise the Swede's uncommon qualities. He is so courageous as to be careless, so virtuous as to be austere, so determined as to be obstinate. The *Histoire de Charles XII* has a moral dimension that goes beyond the mere existence of the Swedish king. Man, it argues, must take his proper measure. Voltaire shows us a Charles XII who is as much a warrior king as a king of war, as much a commander-in-chief as a first among combatants who fails in the end. He is not a great sovereign combining the role of war chief with that of wise and magnanimous ruler. He is 'but a man,'[69] a 'knight errant [. . .] half hero, half madman.'[70] Charles XII does not govern; he makes war, to the eventual detriment of his country and subjects. For the Enlightenment *philosophes*, such as Voltaire and Montesquieu, the grandeur of a sovereign lies more in his capacity to foster the happiness of his people than in his military exploits, which earn him but a fleeting glory. From the perspective of a pedagogical history, the example of Charles XII, conqueror of useless things, ought to inspire reflection and 'cure the mad thirst for conquest.'[71] Tsar Peter, meanwhile, makes war to civilise his people and his country. Voltaire seeks to show that, contrary to common opinion, the 'Don Quixote of the north,' with his extravagant heroism, deserves less interest and praise than the 'Solomon of the north,' broad-minded legislator and founder of cities.[72]

At the apex of his glory, during the War of the Spanish Succession, Charles XII could have served as a formidable ally to France, but he turned out to be of no help. Worse, he became a burden to a French government that was striving to save whatever it could of the possessions Sweden had acquired at mid-century. The death of Charles XII, preceding by a few years the definitive decline of Sweden's power in the north, obliged the French to rethink their diplomacy in the region. Beyond the fate of the kingdom of Sweden, what fascinated contemporary Frenchmen was Charles XII's personality. To them he was a study in contrasts, inspiring admiration and praise for his military skill, drawing criticism and reproach for his political capacities.

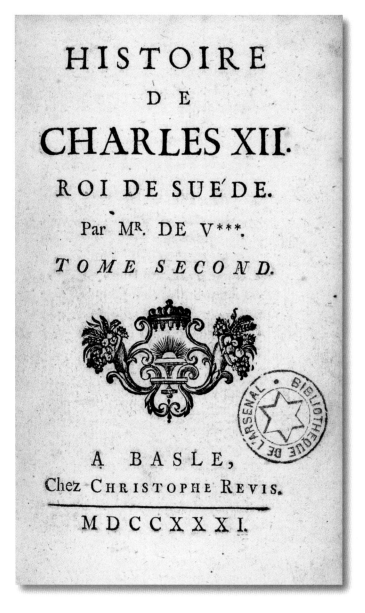

*Title page from the first edition of l'Histoire de Charles XII, roi de Suède by Voltaire.*

*Published by Christophe Revis, 1731. Bibliothèque nationale de France, Cabinet des Estampes, Paris, France.*

## CHAPTER 12

# 'The Mad Swede'
## *The Habsburg Monarchy and Charles XII*

by Michael Hochedlinger

### ■ Traditional Enemies

During most of the seventeenth century, relations between Sweden and the Habsburg Monarchy were characterised by a deep political and confessional antagonism. From Gustav II Adolf's invasion in 1630 to the Peace of Westphalia in 1648, Protestant Sweden was the Habsburgs' most dreaded political and military opponent, more dangerous even than Vienna's 'hereditary enemies': France and the Ottoman Turks.

During the Thirty Years' War, Swedish armies had repeatedly threatened and invaded Habsburg territory. The Swedish occupation of Lower Austria north of the Danube in 1645-46 was a traumatising episode in popular memory for centuries to come. Looting, destruction, and persecutions of all kinds made 'Swedish' a byword for terror and brutality, even if, in reality, the 'Swedish' tormentors were mostly German mercenaries.[1]

The peace treaty of 1648 put Queen Christina of Sweden, *pro feudo hereditario*, in possession of the secularised bishoprics of Bremen and Verden, the Mecklenburg city of Wismar, the islands of Usedom, Wollin, and Rügen, and mainland Western Pomerania, including the Oder estuary and Stettin. Thus, the Swedish monarch became a member of the Holy Roman Empire, with a seat and vote at the Imperial Diet.[2] Both within and outside the *Reich*, the Habsburg-Swedish antagonism continued to smoulder, especially after Charles, Duke of Pfalz-Zweibrücken, acceded to the Swedish throne in 1654 and, alongside France, supported the anti-Habsburg opposition in Germany. In order to prevent Sweden from sweeping Poland-Lithuania off the map in 1657-59, the emperor felt obliged to intervene militarily. Austria's weak neighbour was saved, but remained a dangerous political vacuum for the rest of its existence.

Over the following decades, Sweden, always in need of foreign subsidies, proved a reliable partner for the open-handed French. But its narrow escape from disaster during the Dutch War (1672-79) caused a sensational *renversement des alliances*: disgusted with his dependency on France, Charles XI of Sweden approached the emperor and, in October 1682, signed a treaty of alliance. Swedish troops even fought against Louis XIV in the early 1690s, after the French had occupied the Swedish king's German home country of Zweibrücken.

### ■ Vienna and the Coming of the Great Northern War

The Austrian Habsburgs' main concern at the time was the Great Turkish War, which began with the dramatic siege and relief of Vienna in 1683 and ended with an unex-

*Prince Eugene of Savoy, Imperial commander-in-chief, on horseback.*

*Painting by Jacob van Schuppen (1670-1751), ca. 1718. Deutsches Historisches Museum, Berlin, Germany. © bpk | Deutsches Historisches Museum / Arne Psille*

pected and total defeat of the Porte. By 1699, almost the entire kingdom of Hungary, for the most part in Turkish hands since the Battle of Mohács in 1526 and the capture of Buda in 1541, was liberated. The Turkish threat—which had hampered Vienna's freedom of action for nearly two centuries—was thus removed and largely disappeared as the main determinant of Habsburg foreign policy.

More than before, Austria was now a decidedly eastern European power. This shift was crucial for Vienna's involvement in the Great Northern War, which broke out just as the emperor's attention was entirely absorbed by a new international crisis: the extinction of the Spanish Habsburgs and the ensuing dispute over their succession.[3]

Geographically as well as mentally, Russia was far away and still seen as a semi-barbarian country. Poland, as an immediate neighbour, clearly needed more attention. To prevent the election of a French candidate, Vienna successfully supported the Saxon elector Augustus's conversion to Catholicism and his candidacy as king of Poland (1697). Austria's relations with her former eastern allies soon deteriorated. Tsar Peter felt betrayed when, in 1699, despite the Austro-Russian offensive alliance of February 1697, Emperor Leopold I together with Venice and Poland concluded a profitable peace treaty with the sultan and left Russia in the lurch. In June 1698, while on his first Grand Tour through western Europe, Peter had even rushed to Vienna to keep the Austrians in the war until Russia would have reached its war aims, but in vain. Bitter feelings remained. The subsequent reorientation of Russian foreign policy towards the Baltic aligned the tsar with Augustus of Saxony.

While Leopold I kept a sharp eye on the Baltic, the Swedes tried to exploit his fears of Franco-Swedish cooperation and extort a new treaty of alliance. However, the emperor refused to ratify far-reaching secret clauses guaranteeing Sweden's German provinces and Livonia and was also reluctant to include the duke of Holstein-Gottorp in the treaty or allow the secularised bishopric of Lübeck-Eutin to become a Holstein secundogeniture, which would have strained relations with Denmark. Just as Vienna seemed to change its mind in order to secure Swedish auxiliary troops against France, the concentric attack by Denmark, Saxony, and Russia put an end to the rapprochement.[4]

## ■ The Polish Question

The emperor was anything but happy with the turbulent situation in the Baltics, as the Spanish succession crisis was about to erupt into a full-scale war.[5] Vienna put pressure on Saxony to cease hostilities against Sweden and even threatened to concentrate an army of observation along the borders with Saxony and Poland. Such gestures seemed all the more justified as the overly ambitious elector-king was hatching sinister, if utterly unrealistic, plots against the Habsburg Monarchy. He conspired with France, contemplated the annexation of Silesia, and even coveted the crown of Hungary, where from 1701 discontent with the Habsburgs and their merciless tax regime was turning into open rebellion.

Charles XII's triumphant advance in Poland finally obliged Augustus to sign a subsidy treaty with Vienna on 16 January 1702, in which he promised Saxon troops for

Leopold's war against France. Understandably, the tangible benefits of the alliance remained modest at best, as Augustus was himself fighting a life-and-death struggle against Charles XII, whose declared goal was to depose him as king of Poland. The Swedish king even deliberately subordinated the defence of his Baltic possessions against the advancing Russians to his breakneck chase after Augustus.

By the same token, Austrian aid for the elector-king was half-hearted and largely limited to offering mediation between the two belligerents. At least the emperor granted free passage through Silesia to Saxon forces on their way to Poland. In a secret clause, soon sincerely regretted, Leopold promised to stand by Augustus as king of Poland, while the latter pledged not to support the Hungarian rebels. Openly backing the Saxon troublemaker against Sweden threatened to become a massive burden, as the Swedish forces, reaching Warsaw in June and Krakow in July 1702, were driving the Saxons before them, while, absurdly, the theatre of war itself, Poland, remained formally neutral.[6]

Ever since September 1700, Vienna had dreaded a Swedish attack on Saxony, as this would jeopardise the entire diplomatic and military mobilisation against France. Luring the Swedish war machinery into the *Reich*, therefore, was precisely the aim of the French, who in the summer of 1702 unsuccessfully offered Charles XII subsidies in return for invading Brandenburg, Saxony, or better still, the Habsburg Monarchy.

At the same time, the emperor's call for a speedy reconciliation with Saxony had fallen on deaf ears. Charles XII would not hear of peace negotiations, nor would he join the anti-French league, despite an official invitation by the emperor in November 1701 openly supported by London and The Hague. The Imperial envoy to Stockholm, Count Gotthard Helfried Weltz, had arrived in Reval in November 1700 but soon realised that Charles found foreign diplomats and their peace initiatives most annoying. The king forbade diplomats to follow him on his Polish campaign and reduced them to hinterland war correspondents.[7]

*Portrait of Emperor Joseph I.*

*Painting by unknown artist, ca. 1700. The Princely Collections, Vaduz, Liechtenstein. © Photo SCALA, Florence.*

For the allies, the interruption of ordinary diplomatic relations had the obvious advantage of paralysing Louis XIV's intrigues, with the French ambassador vegetating in far-away Danzig. A French mission to Moscow in 1702 responded to earlier Russian overtures for closer cooperation against the Habsburgs—including a diversion against Transylvania—yet failed to mediate peace between the tsar and Charles XII in order to free the Swedes for a strike against France's enemies. Russian signals had obviously been insincere.[8]

At roughly the same time, Russia also approached the emperor, but Peter's proposals, it appears, were not really taken seriously in the Austrian capital: between 6,000 and 20,000 Russian auxiliary troops, generous subsidies, and even a marriage between Tsarevich Alexei (to be educated in Vienna) and a Habsburg princess seemed a bit eccentric indeed. Similar offers were submitted in London and attempts made to bribe the duke of Marlborough to support Russia's admission into the Grand Alliance.

The semi-official channel through which negotiations were conducted, by the Livonian opposition leader Johann Reinhold Patkul, did not inspire confidence either. Patkul, who arrived in Vienna in August 1702, had—while in Saxon service in 1699—advocated a close partnership between Augustus and the emperor. In Russian pay since 1701, Patkul would not give up his pro-Austrian stance. His mission to the Austrian capital foundered among fears of his being either kidnapped or murdered by Swedish agents.[9]

There were even signals from Vienna that could be interpreted as openly anti-Russian. In 1700, Johann Georg Korb, who had been secretary to the Imperial diplomatic mission to Moscow in 1698-99, which had urged the Russians to double their war zeal while the Habsburg Monarchy was busy negotiating with the sultan, published a sensational 'diary.' The book contained important data on the tsar's war effort—including plans of fortresses—but also painted a drastic picture of Russia as a backward and cruel semi-Asiatic power. At Russian request, the publication was banned in 1702.

With the Swedes *ante portas* and seemingly invincible, the emperor's scope for action was dangerously shrinking. Hopes that considerable Swedish and Saxon forces would soon be available for operations against France were dashed, as Austro-Swedish relations became increasingly strained. Even Count Weltz, from his remote new headquarters in Riga, was fully aware that the Austro-Saxon alliance of January 1702 had deeply antagonised the Swedish king.

In May 1702, the emperor's Privy Conference decided, with a view of soothing Charles XII, to dispatch General Count Franz Ludwig Zinzendorf, not as a formally accredited diplomat, but as a semi-official military observer keen on studying the warrior king's exploits from close up. If the treaty with Saxony had proved a big mistake, Vienna was still determined not to let Poland fall into irresponsible—let alone French—hands. Both the Austrian envoy in Warsaw, Count Heinrich Stratmann, and Zinzendorf in the Swedish camp did their best to support Saxon peace feelers—all in vain.[10]

Charles XII finally dethroned Augustus as king of Poland in February 1704 and, in July 1704, replaced him with a young native puppet-king, Stanislaw Leszczyński, who found very little backing in the realm and remained dependent upon Swedish support. The anti-Swedish forces in Poland rallied in the Confederation of Sandomierz, concluded an alliance with Russia in August 1704, and declared war on King Stanislaw.

For the Swedish king, the Polish question had thus reached a dangerous dead-lock. It was clear that only a massive strike right into the heart of Augustus's power base, Saxony, would cut the Gordian knot. On 21 August 1706, from Rawicz, Charles XII marched into Silesia. On 27 August, his troops reached Saxon territory and were quickly spreading throughout the electorate. For an entire year, the modest manor house of Altranstädt near Leipzig was to serve the Swedish king as headquarters, not far from the battlefield of Lützen where Gustav Adolf had been killed in 1632 and which Charles XII visited in June 1707. 'I have tried to live like him. Perhaps God will grant me one day as glorious a death,' he exclaimed, according to Voltaire.[11]

To understand why, despite the new Emperor Joseph I's reputation as an energetic hotspur, Vienna's reaction to the flagrant violation of *Reich* and Habsburg territory was so chicken-hearted and its Swedish policy as tortuous as ever, a closer look at the problematic situation in Habsburg Hungary and its dangerous impact on the international system is necessary.

## ■ The Hungarian Diversion

From the start, the Swedish presence in neighbouring Poland had been an embarrassment for the emperor, because it necessarily encouraged the Hungarian rebels under Ferenc Rákóczi,[12] whose family had an impressive record of anti-Habsburg activities and of military cooperation with France and Sweden. In 1643 and again in the late 1650s, two Rákóczi princes of Transylvania, then a Turkish tributary, had allied with the Swedes against Vienna, and it was feared that their descendant would now do much the same.

After flirtations with Augustus and the francophile party among the Polish magnates had died away in 1703, Rákóczi found support, albeit moral rather than hands-on, from Louis XIV and eventually managed to set the rebellion ablaze. For the emperor the loss of control over large parts of Hungary between 1703 and 1711 was no side issue, since the Rákóczi rebellion not only made substantial tax income dry up, but also tied down Austrian forces urgently needed against the French in the west. For years to come Hungarian raiders were ravaging the eastern parts of Lower Austria and Styria; even Vienna's suburbs had to be walled in, to protect them against Magyar light cavalry.

Perhaps more dangerous, the revolt in Hungary threatened to become a massive stumbling block for the emperor's alliance with the Maritime Powers, for, at least until 1707, both London and the Hague showed one-sided sympaties for the Hungarians and what they believed to be a desperate fight against counter-reformatory excesses and absolutist oppression.

As expected, Rákóczi, in search of external support, soon turned to Charles XII, hoping to join an emerging Prusso-Swedish league against Vienna. In March 1704 a Hungarian delegation arrived at the Swedish headquarters. Closely watched by the Austrian envoy Zinzendorf, the Hungarians were not received by the king but obtained assurances that Sweden identified with the Protestant cause (which Rákóczi deliberately emphasised) and would offer mediation. Much the same happened in

Berlin, where the Hungarian mission turned up next. Both powers kept their promises. The Swedish representative in Vienna received orders to intervene on behalf of the Hungarian Protestants, but Leopold I, cleverly pretending that he had rejected a similar offer by the Saxon elector, refused in April 1704; a similar Prussian initiative was declined in summer 1704.

The anti-Saxon party in Poland seemed much more daring. In spring 1704, shortly before Charles XII forced them to elect Leszczyński, they offered the Polish crown to Rákóczi. The latter wisely refused, but only after long and careful consideration, despite the fact that the allied victory at Blenheim in August 1704 had finally destroyed all Hungarian hopes of effective military cooperation with France and its main German ally, the elector of Bavaria. The arrival of a French 'ambassador' and a tiny expeditionary force in 1705 were but modest consolation.

From a Swedish perspective, Rákóczi had nothing to offer and merely promised what French diplomacy was already busy working on: drawing the sultan into the war. Rákóczi's attempt in April 1706 to talk Augustus into bartering the Polish for the Hungarian crown, was not likely to change Charles XII's mind either.

The tsar, by contrast, showed himself far more obliging when in 1707 he began to court the Hungarian insurgents. Of course, they were only a means to another end. Peter's aim was to establish closer relations with France, which would then, hopefully, mediate peace between Sweden and Russia on moderate terms. Rákóczi, as Louis XIV's only eastern ally, seemed ideally suited to prepare the ground. In May 1707, a Russian secret mission signalled that the tsar and many Polish magnates would welcome the Hungarian prince as king of Poland.

Even if Russian advances probably accelerated the final rupture between Hungary and the Habsburgs, Rákóczi remained cautious, as he faced even more promising prospects. With the formal deposition of Joseph I by the secessionist Hungarian Diet in June 1707, Saint Stephen's crown itself became vacant. The exiled elector of Bavaria was brought into the play as a possible new king, while Rákóczi, as regent, was running the actual government business. Rákóczi even invited the tsar to join forces with Charles XII against the emperor, which would then have enabled him to accept the Polish crown.

Peter, naturally, had more than one iron in the fire, and Rákóczi was far from being the only Russian candidate for the Polish throne. In June 1707 the tsar, in order to secure the emperor's guarantee for his recent Baltic conquests, sent a mission to Vienna to assure the Austrians of his friendly attitude and offer not just 50,000 troops against Sweden and his son Alexei as a suitor for a Habsburg princess, but also the Polish crown to the emperor's commander-in-chief, Prince Eugene of Savoy. Understandably, the emperor would rather see Rákóczi installed in Warsaw than let his military genius go.[13]

However, the tsar's double-dealing did not stop the Russo-Hungarian rapprochement, especially after the Swedes had again left Saxony and were marching eastwards, while the military situation for the rebels became increasingly critical. In September 1707, against French objections, the tsar and Rákóczi concluded a treaty in which the Hungarian prince bound himself to accept the Polish crown, should he be chosen in free elections. Peter in turn promised what the insurgents needed: recognition of an independent Hungary and Transylvania, military aid, and money, which a dangerously weakened France would be unable to provide. The practical results of the agreement soon proved irrelevant. By 1708 Russian support for the insurgents had shrunk to an offer to mediate peace between the emperor and his rebellious subjects, even if Rákóczi supplied the Russians with secret reports about Swedish movements and established a rather useless diplomatic representation in Moscow. Despite their platonic character, Peter's fickle flirtations with the Hungarian opposition remained a significant obstacle for any serious cooperation between the tsar and the emperor—until the final defeat of the Hungarian revolt in early 1711.

## ■ Altranstädt

As Charles XII had hoped, his invasion of Saxony at once forced Augustus to give in. Shortly after the king's arrival at Altranstädt, the peace treaty was signed on 24 September 1706: the Saxon elector abdicated as king of Poland and renounced his alliance with the tsar. Despite this rapid success, the Swedish army did not march off against the only remaining enemy, Russia, but had obviously come to stay and suck Saxony dry. This was not just an effective way to weaken Augustus for the long term; the respite was simply imperative to recover energy for the final struggle in the east. Some 20,000 men, weak and weary after years of continuous fighting, had entered Saxony in August 1706; more than 30,000, well fed, in new uniforms, and with modernised equipment, left the country a year later. Relations with the local population were good, as the Swedes kept excellent discipline and paid cash. Still, it took more than ten years for Saxony to recover from the Swedish occupation.[14]

Vienna had no sympathy for Augustus of Saxony, but the longer the Swedes stayed in the electorate, the more Altranstädt was turning into a hotbed of international intrigue where foreign diplomats, now freely admitted, and even crowned heads such as Stanislaw and Augustus were gathering around the 25-year-old Charles, who set himself up as the arbiter of Europe. Sooner or later, the French would also appear on the scene, attempting to embroil the Swedish king into the War of the Spanish Succession. Even the *Reich* declared itself irritated. In late September 1706, the Imperial Diet at Regensburg lodged a formal complaint against the Swedish invasion and required the emperor to make Charles XII withdraw his troops from Saxony.[15]

It had been particularly inopportune that the Austrian liaison officer in the Swedish camp, Zinzendorf, fell ill in August 1706 and had to stay behind in Poland while the Swedes were marching into Saxony. Before Zinzendorf was able to join the Swedish headquarters again, Joseph I had decided to send the Bohemian Chancellor Count Johann Wenzel von Wratislaw on a special mission to Leipzig. The emperor's seasoned chief diplomat, a friend of Marlborough's and the political architect of the Blenheim campaign of 1704, had initially advocated armed resistance against Sweden, but his instructions now prescribed the utmost caution. They clearly reflected what Vienna tried to hide from Charles XII: that the emperor was lacking the necessary forces to confront the Swedes head-on. In October 1706, Wratislaw was fobbed off with the rather meaningless promise that the Swedish king would respect

the peace of the *Reich* and deny any support to the Hungarian rebels.[16]

The Austro-Swedish turbulences of 1707 have long been interpreted, especially on the Austrian side, as the result of Charles XII's legendary unpredictability, rashness, and pathological presumption. But one might just as well surmise that the Swedes simply used whatever pretext they came across[17] to humiliate the emperor and knock him out as a potential Russian ally in their back.

That Joseph I had so far refused to recognise Sweden's protégé Stanislaw Leszczyński as the new king of Poland—whose contacts with Rákóczi did not pass unnoticed—was the first bone of contention. Zinzendorf reported from Leipzig that Charles XII showed increasing signs of irritation. At first the Privy Conference in Vienna seemed unwilling to give in without a quid pro quo, but finally yielded to Swedish stubbornness in February 1707. The Swedish recognition, in return, of the emperor's brother, the Archduke Karl, as king of Spain could not be obtained, as Charles XII had already cast his vote in favour of the French candidate, Philippe d'Anjou.

This boded ill for the central question: was there danger of Franco-Swedish co-operation? The Swedes denied French sympathies, but in March 1707 a French envoy,

*The manor house at Altranstädt, where the negotiations with Charles XII took place.*

© *Photograph by Martin Geisler / Wikimedia Commons.*

Baron de Besenval, arrived in Leipzig and offered to mediate peace between Sweden and Russia. The mere fact that the king of Sweden, himself a member of the Holy Roman Empire, welcomed a representative of the French king, who had been formally declared an enemy of the *Reich,* shocked the Grand Alliance. The situation grew even more dramatic when the French broke through the allied defence lines in southern Germany and called upon the Swedes to join forces in Franconia!

In late April 1707, the duke of Marlborough paid Charles XII a visit in his Saxon headquarters to find out more about the king's attitude towards France.[18] Marlborough's trip to Altranstädt complicated matters for Austria's decision-makers. The English general had detected dangerous anti-Austrian feelings in the Swedish camp and strongly encouraged the Habsburg ally to make concessions whenever necessary so as not to undermine the common war effort. When Marlborough's advice arrived, three minor incidents had dangerously poisoned relations between the emperor and the king of Sweden. In early March 1707, Henning von Stralenheim, Swedish envoy to the Viennese court, felt obliged to box the ears of Count Max Adam Czobor, one of the emperor's gentlemen-in-waiting, whom he accused of having insulted the king of Sweden during a dinner. The well-connected Czobor had to be placed under house arrest and was transferred to Graz.[19] Stralenheim, who had served in the Imperial army against the Turks and had received a shot in the head during the storming of Belgrade in 1688 which left him with a speech defect, feared attacks by Czobor's relatives, but refused to settle the dispute in a duel. A show trial was started against the Hungarian nobleman, but Sweden demanded more: Czobor's death.

That was not all. To fill up their ranks the Swedes in Saxony were busy recruiting, especially in neighbouring Silesia where they met with considerable if illegal success. At Breslau, in February 1707, a Swedish recruiting commando clashed with the city guard. A Swedish corporal was killed and the rest maltreated and imprisoned. Charles XII felt deeply offended.

In April 1707, the Swedes spotted yet another offence which could be used against the emperor. The Treaty of Altranstädt obliged Augustus of Saxony to hand all Russian auxiliary troops over into Swedish captivity. A small contingent of 1,200 Russians had escaped to the Rhine, where, with the tsar's approval, they were used as garrison troops against France. This dispute threatened to escalate, when in late May 1707 it became apparent that the emperor, far from complying with Charles's ultimatum, had secretly allowed the Russian officers and soldiers to slip through his hereditary lands and join the tsar's army in Poland. The king of Sweden, it was reported, considered this an open breach of neutrality and seemed determined to retaliate by invading Silesia or even Bohemia. In July 1707, Charles sent four Swedish regiments, which the Russians had driven out of Poland, into quarters around Glogau and Sagan in Habsburg northern Silesia. Austrian protests went unheard and in August 1707 Prague began to prepare for a siege. Memories were still alive of the disaster of July 1648, when a Swedish army had captured and pillaged the capital of Bohemia, carrying off archives, libraries, and art treasures of immense value.

Regular diplomatic relations between Sweden and Austria had more or less ceased in May 1707 with the recall of Stralenheim, who joined his king at Altranstädt. Zinzendorf may have been overtaxed in the face of massive Swedish pressure and certainly did little more than pleading for concessions. In late July 1707, therefore, Count Wratislaw arrived in Leipzig for a second mission.

Negotiations were first conducted with the help of the English and Dutch representatives as mediators. The trivialities which had triggered the crisis could be ticked off the agenda quickly. Wratislaw had brought the troublemaker Czobor with him and, as a sign of the emperor's good will, handed him over to the Swedish king who sent him off to prison in Stettin. The responsible officer of the Breslau city guard had a similar fate and was put in a Swedish regiment, while the town paid damages.

What Charles XII really wanted was unclear. King Stanislaw, who sought to oblige the Austrians, was unable to discover the secret of the 'Swedish sphinx.' Joseph I remained convinced that Swedish aggressiveness was primarily meant to relieve the French and make the allies break off their ongoing invasion of southern France. The emperor must have felt confirmed in his view when the Swedish *chargé d'affaires* in Vienna, Johann Carl Stiernhöök, was unmasked as a French spy.[20]

At any rate the Swedish negotiators readily accepted what the Austrians and the Anglo-Dutch mediators offered: the long-awaited guarantee for the House of Holstein's aspirations to the bishopric of Lübeck-Eutin to which Denmark had renounced its rights in 1706, and a formal waiver of Sweden's obligation as a member of the *Reich* to furnish troops for the war against France. Free transit through Silesia, including free supply of provisions, was taken for granted.

The real escalation came in early August 1707, when the Swedes officially demanded the full restoration of the confessional status quo in Silesia as stipulated by the Treaty of Westphalia of 1648 and suggested that a formal convention be signed. When the English and Dutch diplomats, Robinson and Haersolte, seemed reluctant to proceed in this direction, the king took up direct negotiations with the Austrian side.

Ever since the passage of the Swedish army in August 1706 religious unrest in Silesia had been growing, and Silesian Lutherans were bombarding the Swedish king with protests against illegal counter-reformatory measures. These complaints were not unfounded, as Count Wratislaw admitted. The situation had been expected to improve with the accession of Joseph I, who unlike his father had a reputation for being open-minded in matters of faith. There were also economic reasons for religious tolerance in Silesia: thousands had left, reducing both the province's tax yield and the productivity of its important textile industry. The *Corpus Evangelicorum*, the union of Protestant members of the *Reich* at the Imperial Diet of Regensburg, officially supported Silesian Protestantism, but Charles XII went further by bringing the problem back to the centre stage of European politics.

Striving to win Sweden's friendship, the king of Prussia, then at loggerheads with Vienna, did not scruple to play the confessional card. In September 1706, he suggested a Protestant triple alliance between Sweden, Hanover, and Prussia to protect their co-religionists in Silesia, and even to support the Hungarians. Hanover, however, disapproved of the project's massive anti-Habsburg thrust and stayed away. The Prusso-Swedish defensive alliance signed in August 1707, even if it did comprise religious clauses, eventually remained a mere paper tiger.[21]

Joseph I had meanwhile begun to tackle the issue of Protestantism in Silesia. In May 1707, the emperor summoned Silesian deputies to Vienna, but Silesia's Protestants, playing for time, preferred to promote their cause in Altranstädt and Leipzig—with its famous university one of the centres of the German Protestant intelligentsia—and through the intermediary of the Swedish king, with whom they had established contacts.[22]

As the Swedes and their Silesian informants were driving Wratislaw into a corner, even the cool-headed, if dangerously obese, diplomat began to lose his nerve in the summer heat. Correspondence with Vienna could not keep pace with all the papers the Swedes put before him. This was not merely irresponsible sluggishness on the part of the emperor's ministers, as Wratislaw grumbled. Habsburg foreign policy needed to ponder whether it could assent without losing face. More than one voice favoured military preparations over an ignominious retreat. At the very least, the promulgation by the emperor of a 'declaration of tolerance' for Silesia should put an end to humiliating Swedish intervention in Habsburg internal affairs.

Joseph I's forces were engaged far away and very little could be expected from Austria's allies. Neither London nor The Hague would promise military aid in the event of a Swedish attack. The emperor had little doubt that his allies welcomed a confessional liberalisation in Silesia. Of course the Dutch Grand Pensionary Heinsius declared that justice was entirely on Joseph I's side but, nonetheless, saw no other solution than to back down. Nor would the *Reich* follow the emperor into a war against the champion of Protestantism. Relations with Prussia were tense and Augustus of Saxony was suspected of designs on Bohemia to compensate for his loss of Poland. Against this background, the tsar's efforts to accede to the Grand Alliance, while at the same time he concluded a treaty with Rákóczi and sought a rapprochement with France, were considered of little relevance.

In the face of Habsburg delaying tactics Charles and his ministers increased the pressure, and on 19 August 1707 the Swedish army began to break camp. This was the signal for the final showdown with Russia, but could also be interpreted as the first move for a strike against the Habsburg Monarchy and military cooperation with the Hungarian rebels who had long been pleading for a joint offensive against Silesia. When on 27 August the courier from Vienna finally brought instructions authorising Wratislaw to accept the Swedish conditions, the diplomat had already, at his own risk, agreed to the Swedish draft, albeit with substantial modifications. On 1 September 1707, at Liebertwolkwitz, where Charles XII was resting on his march to the east, Wratislaw signed the Convention of Altranstädt.[23]

On 12 September, near Görlitz, the Swedish king was presented with the emperor's ratification; the Swedish march through Silesia began the next day. Count Czobor and the unfortunate officer of the Breslau city guard were released. By 22 September the Swedes had left Habsburg territory, not without having caused expenses of fl. 950,000. Yet, Zinzendorf's cutting remark that this would cure even Silesia's Protestants of their Swedish sympathies was given the lie. The march of the Swedish army through Silesia provoked a kind of religious mass psychosis amongst Protestant children (*Kinderbeten*), commemorative medals were struck in great number, and broadsheets flooded the public sphere to hail Charles XII as a new Gustav II Adolf. Well into the twentieth century many Lutheran churches in Silesia, a Prussian province after 1742, remained decorated with portraits of the Swedish king.

The Convention, formally guaranteed by the Maritime Powers in November-December 1707, recorded the emperor's political concessions regarding Lübeck and Sweden's theoretical obligation to participate in the *Reich*'s war against France. But Altranstädt was, essentially, a religious treaty confirming the terms of the Westphalian Peace for Silesia.[24] Thus, among other things, Lutheran churches, schools, or properties had to be returned or reopened in those areas where the 1648 treaty had legalised them. In the rest of the duchy, where only private exercise was tolerated, the emperor, in addition to the existing churches, allowed six 'churches of grace' (*Gnadenkirchen*) to be built, but only under Swedish pressure and against handsome *douceurs*. Lutherans would henceforth be admitted to appointments within the administration of Silesia and Bohemia, at least on paper. Wratislaw had resisted more far-reaching Protestant claims, notably the inclusion of Silesia's Calvinists in the treaty, for which the king of Prussia, England, and the Dutch Republic were lobbying.

*Johann Wenzel Count Wratislaw, leading Imperial diplomat.*

*Engraving by unknown artist, ca. 1705. Austrian National Library Portrait Collection, Vienna, Austria.*

## ■ Aftershocks

The emperor had clearly suffered a moral defeat. True, a fusion of the War of the Spanish Succession and the Great Northern War had been prevented, but this came at a high price. Not only was the right of Protestant princes to intervene in Silesian affairs renewed, but, in a separate declaration on 1 September 1707, Charles XII also reserved the right to return to Silesia, should the Habsburg Monarchy fail to carry out its obligations within six months.

From his new observation post in Breslau, Baron Stralenheim, as Swedish watchdog, kept an eye on Austria's contractual fidelity. On the Austrian side, he faced a commission of exclusively Catholic government officials defending Catholic interests and, after a rough propaganda war, declared the implementation of the Altranstädt terms successfully completed, just before the term set by the treaty expired in March 1708. When overdue instructions from his king failed to appear, Stralenheim signed an agreement in February 1709 with his new counterpart, Count Zinzendorf, acknowledging that all issues had been settled once and for all. Altogether, 125 churches were handed back to the Lutherans.

On 5 August 1709, Zinzendorf, still at his listening post in Breslau, informed the emperor of the Swedish defeat at Poltava.[25] Soon ragged Swedish stragglers began to reach the town, while anti-Swedish pamphlets triumphantly derided Charles's fall.[26] Joseph I had little reason to rejoice. There was a grain of truth in Voltaire's anecdote that the emperor had told those who criticised his yielding to Sweden: 'You are very fortunate that the king of Sweden has not proposed to make me a Lutheran; because if he had, I do not know what I would have done.'[27]

Among those who had rejected the Convention of Altranstädt and refused any part in its execution, were the prince-bishop of Breslau, Franz Ludwig of Pfalz-Neuburg, the emperor's uncle, and Pope Clement XI himself, who in the struggle for the Spanish succession favoured the French party. The latter expressed indignation in a sharp letter to the emperor on 10 September 1707, without even knowing the exact wording of the final treaty. Joseph I and his advisors took their time before they reacted. In his reply of June 1708, the emperor asked for the Holy Father's understanding, protesting that he had sought advice from learned and pious men of the Church, and that there was no other solution to avert an even more worrisome scenario.[28]

At this point, the pope's and the emperor's forces in Italy were already on a collision course, although not over Silesia. In autumn 1708, the Imperialists invaded the Papal States and within three months forced His Holiness to capitulate. This did not stop the pope from insisting that the Convention of Altranstädt be cancelled.

## ■ Sweden's Decline

Charles XII's defeat and flight to Turkey in summer 1709 seemed to justify those such as Eugene of Savoy, who, so as not to irritate the tsar, had advised against the emperor's recognition of Stanislaw as king of Poland. After Poltava, the generalissimo was one of the first to congratulate the Russian envoy in Vienna on the victory.[29] Hardly had the news of Charles's disaster reached central Europe, when Augustus of Saxony returned on the Polish throne and resumed cooperation with the Russians. Denmark soon joined in and Prussia supported Sweden's enemies indirectly, while Hanover refused to renew its alliance with Stockholm and concluded provisional defensive treaties with Denmark and Russia. Habsburg foreign policy now faced the danger that Vienna's northern German allies against France might recall their contingents from the western front in order to annex Sweden's possessions in the *Reich*.

In March 1710, Britain, the Dutch Republic, and the Habsburg Monarchy, soon to be joined by other powers, including Saxony and Russia, signed a treaty to neutralise the north of the *Reich*, something that Stockholm had already requested after the shock of Poltava. This treaty was followed in August 1710 by a second agreement, stipulating the creation of an army of observation.[30]

With the death of Joseph I in April 1711, his brother Karl returned from Spain to be duly elected as Emperor Charles VI in October 1711. As if to deride Vienna's firm policy of neutrality, Augustus of Saxony-Poland had used the interregnum to launch, together with his Russian and Danish allies, a massive attack on Wismar and Swedish Pomerania in August 1711.

With the Swedes in great difficulty, Vienna now regarded the tsar as the most annoying troublemaker. The Russian autocrat, Eugene of Savoy complained, was even more arrogant and exasperating than Charles XII. Peter not only renewed his contact with the Hungarian rebels in spring 1710, as did Prussia, but was playing yet another trump card: his excellent relations with the Orthodox populations in the Balkans and, more dangerous, with the Orthodox Serbs who had fled into the Habsburg Monarchy in the 1690s and were showing clear signs of discontent. While the 'Orthodox and Slav international,' which the tsar tried to mobilise through several manifestos to the Balkan peoples did not provoke an uprising among the sultan's Christian subjects during Peter's war against the Turks in 1710-11, it was an additional sting in Austro-Russian relations.[31]

With the Habsburg Monarchy fully engaged in the War of the Spanish Succession, there was no reason to incur the sultan's wrath and sign the alliance which the tsar impetuously offered in 1711 and 1712. On the contrary, Austrian diplomacy did much to sabotage Russia's search for support against the Turks and even assured the sultan of the emperor's neutrality.[32] In 1711, tensions grew when Vienna refused to grant Peter the title of majesty. In August 1711, the tsar struck back by trying to win the Hungarian rebels over and granting them asylum in the Ukraine. Rákóczi refused, however, and moved to France, before taking up his last domicile in Turkey.

While secretly wishing for a Turkish victory, Vienna hoped, at best, for a protracted war that would keep Peter busy—but feared the worst: not only the Russian conquest of the Ottoman satellites of Moldavia and Walachia but even the capture of Constantinople.[33] Contrary to all expectations, the Turks saved the situation and defeated the tsar in a short campaign. Russian obtrusiveness in Vienna became even more insufferable after parallel Franco-Russian exploratory talks had clearly revealed that the Sun King would never abandon Sweden nor tolerate its expulsion from the *Reich*.

Curiously, the Habsburg Monarchy took up a similar position. In June 1712, the emperor's ministers ruled that a total Swedish defeat in Germany would merely strengthen potential Austrian rivals (Denmark, Saxony, Prussia, and Hanover). A large-scale redistribution of territories would only be tolerable if its beneficiaries handed earlier gains back and thus consented to a complete reversal of the 1648 settlement.[34] A complete Russian domination of the Baltic coast was not acceptable to the Maritime Powers, since it would encroach on their commercial and maritime interests in the east. It was rumoured in late 1710 that the tsar might try to obtain full membership in the Holy Roman Empire (*Reichsstandschaft*) by claiming that Livonia, promised to the Saxon dynasty but de facto in Russian hands, had been part of the *Reich* before 1561, but this proved to be a hoax.[35]

By December 1712, when Swedish forces, on their way from Pomerania to Holstein, invaded Mecklenburg and a Franco-Swedish alliance seemed to take shape, the emperor's Privy Conference had completely changed its mind: Sweden could not be trusted, it was declared in a moment of rare plain speaking, and should therefore be removed from the international stage—by others.[36]

Officially, Vienna remained more cautious. The emperor accepted a new Prussian neutrality plan based on the agreement of 1710, which he decided to discuss with other princes of the *Reich* at a congress in Brunswick. An army of neutrality was to ensure that Swedish, Danish, and Russian forces would disengage. Imperial decrees warned Denmark, Sweden, and Saxony-Poland to withdraw their troops from *Reich* territories that did not belong to them. The tsar received an admonition to the same effect.

Peter I responded by trying to pressure the emperor into signing an alliance and, against the mounting tensions between the Habsburgs and the Ottomans, met with a more favourable response. The anti-Swedish overtone in Austrian foreign policy did not imply, though, that the emperor, whose favourite role was that of impartial mediator, would declare war against Charles XII or would guarantee Russia's conquest of the Baltic seacoast. The Prussian king and the elector of Hanover, eager to gain Swedish territory, were less reticent. While Denmark, Saxony, Russia, Prussia, and Hanover were forming a huge anti-Swedish alliance, Stockholm was left with only a subsidy treaty with France (April 1715).

It was unfortunate for the hard-pressed Swedes that the emperor's attention remained distracted by other conflicts. After his triumph over the Russians the sultan turned against Venice and its remaining strongholds in Greece in December 1714. In compliance with the terms of the Holy League of 1684, the *Serenissima* called for military assistance that the emperor felt bound to grant.

## ■ The Return of the King

When Charles XII set foot on Turkish territory in July 1709, no one imagined he would stay for five years. Quite the reverse: in early 1710 a request by the Swedish resident in Vienna led the emperor's ministers to expect the immediate return of the king through Habsburg territory, which they were perfectly willing to support. There was reason to presume that the Swedish monarch would, as Eugene put it, soon cause trouble again and prevent the final collapse of the Swedish Empire.[37]

Nothing came of this first initiative, but the Turks gradually lost patience and, from 1711, increased their efforts to get rid of the royal refugee whom they called 'iron head'. Neither intimidation nor the king's capture in Bender and transferral to Didymoteicho in February-March 1713 sped up Charles's return journey, for which the Habsburg representative at the Porte gave ample guarantees (December 1713). There was little else Vienna could or would do to save Sweden from imminent disaster.

By early July 1714, Vienna was informed of Charles's planned departure and began to ready a dignified reception. Furniture, cutlery, and tableware were sent to Transylvania and troops regrouped to ensure the king's safety. The emperor generously complied with Charles's request for a substantial cash advance.[38]

Leaving Didymoteicho in early October 1714, Charles XII entered Habsburg Transylvania through the Rotenturm Pass one month later. Contrary to Austrian expectations, he travelled incognito and successfully evaded the emperor's 'welcoming commissary', General Count Heinrich Wilhelm Wilczek, who was also the Imperial envoy to the Russian court and had strict orders to prevent Protestant agitation along the king's itinerary. It took Charles XII only eight days from the southern border of Transylvania—via Hermannstadt, Karlsburg, Klausenburg, Debrecen, and Pest—to reach Vienna, where he arrived around 16 November. Cold-shouldering the emperor's wish for a formal meeting, he quickly left the Austrian capital on horseback and arrived—via Regensburg, Nürnberg, Würzburg, Kassel, and Brunswick—at the gates of Stralsund in the night of 21-22 November 1714. The king's suite and the remnants of the Swedish army (still more than 1,000 men, though many had left long before or had been fighting side by side with the Hungarian malcontents) followed much later, yet still in time to lose their lives during the siege of Stralsund which ended with the town's capitulation in December 1715. Charles escaped the inferno by the skin of his teeth.

## ■ Splendid Inaction

Vienna may have considered this a punishment for the king's ingratitude and lack of tact. Even during his journey across Habsburg territory, Charles XII had tormented his Imperial host with intransigence over minor questions of protocol. Back home in Swedish Pomerania, the king impudently demanded that the emperor ensure—if necessary by force of arms—that the provinces Sweden had lost over the past decade be handed back unconditionally. To add insult to injury, Charles found no harm in annoying the Habsburg ruler by upholding Protestant interests in the Palatinate against the confessional moratorium which France had enforced in the Treaty of Rijswijk in 1697.

More worrying was Charles's persistent refusal, against advice to the contrary, to send delegates to the Brunswick congress.[39] The summit had reassembled in December 1713 and clearly served the Austrians to keep the 'northern question' in abeyance, yet even Sweden's fiercest enemies attended.

In March 1715, the emperor's ministers declared themselves shocked by the blatant disobedience against the head of the Holy Roman Empire. By July 1715, it seemed clear that Vienna was no longer in a position to delay Sweden's expulsion from German soil against massive pressure from Hanover and Prussia, and that it would be best to have an eye on the emperor's own interests before the booty was shared. Such pragmatic insight came too late and the Habsburg Monarchy was now put off with fair words. Habsburg foreign policy *in nordicis* had no alternative but to commit itself to a wait-and-see attitude. 'Caesar attendat, non implicet se' was to be the motto for the years to come.[40]

The northern crisis affected the emperor's moral, feudal, and jurisdictional authority in the *Reich*, but not his immediate political interests. The Turkish War that broke out in June 1716 became the more burning issue. Austria's alliance with Venice, concluded in April 1716, had reserved a place for the tsar to join in, and indeed, a Russian proposal was not long in coming. Yet after Eugene's first battle triumph in August 1716, Vienna showed no enthusiasm for potential cooperation with Peter, whose commitment and Orthodox supporters in the Balkans aroused suspicion. Additionally, the emperor would never allow either Sweden's German territories to be partitioned or guarantee Russia's conquests in the Baltic without his or the *Reich*'s consent.

The tsar soon found a more amenable partner. In April 1716, the Russians signed a treaty with Duke Karl Leopold of Mecklenburg-Schwerin, once an ardent

admirer of Charles XII, who had fought in the Swedish army before succeeding his brother in 1713. For decades, the Mecklenburg dukes had been trying to enforce an absolutist regime and a standing army against fierce opposition from their provincial estates. Under Karl Leopold the conflict reached its climax. While the duke, just married to the tsar's niece, sought Russian military aid to silence his domestic enemies, Peter wanted to turn Mecklenburg into a Russian power base in the western Baltic. In summer 1716, a huge Russian army marched into Mecklenburg and began to support the duke's measures.[41]

But the tsar had gone too far. The Imperial Aulic Council in Vienna had been examining the Mecklenburg case since 1664, but now, in 1716, the escalation of the conflict forced the *Reich*'s Supreme Court to pass judgment on the duke and, indirectly, on the tsar, who simply ignored repeated exhortations by the emperor to withdraw his troops from Mecklenburg. When the tsar finally sounded the retreat in June 1717, it was only due to British pressure. In October 1717, Charles VI commissioned Hanover and Brunswick-Wolfenbüttel to restore order in Mecklenburg, but it took more than a year to put this into effect.

At this point, Austro-Russian relations were approaching an all-time low. This had much to do with the tsar's wrecked family life. Peter had repeatedly tried to marry his son and heir to the throne, Alexei, to some Habsburg archduchess. Eventually, in 1710, Vienna had become amenable, for this seemed the only way to prevent Russia from supporting the Rákóczi rebellion. But nothing came of the project, and the tsarevich finally wed a Brunswick princess, the sister of the emperor's wife. In November 1716, Alexei, fleeing from his dreaded father, sought refuge in Vienna, thereby endangering Austria's timid 'neutrality' in the Northern War.

There could be little doubt that the tsarevich was mentally deranged and morally depraved, but Charles VI, who despised Tsar Peter and had only just declined yet another Russian attempt at rapprochement, felt obliged to help his brother-in-law by hiding him. In August 1717, however, a Russian special envoy was allowed to see Alexei and persuaded him to return to Russia where, in February 1718, under torture, he promptly accused the emperor and his ministers of having promised support to dethrone Tsar Peter. In summer 1718, diplomatic relations between Austria and Russia were finally broken off amidst mutual recriminations. The war against the Turks had ended with a Habsburg triumph that pushed the borders far down into the Balkans, and Charles VI saw little need to treat the unsteady Russian autocrat with indulgence.[42]

Again, the emperor was given no respite to rest on Prince Eugene's laurels. In the summer of 1717, Spain attacked Habsburg Sardinia before invading Sicily in July 1718. It took three years and the massive military and naval might of Britain, Austria, and France to put Spain out of action. In desperate need of allies, Madrid established contact not only with the exiled Rákóczi, but also with Charles XII. It was hoped that alongside the Jacobites the warrior king would play a decisive role in an anti-Habsburg alliance between Spain, Prussia, Sweden, and Russia. The scheme was not entirely absurd, for Sweden and Russia, during their peace talks of summer 1718, did consider military cooperation against George I, while the alliance between France, Russia and Prussia signed in August 1717, though in reality stillborn, produced additional confusion.[43] Understandably, London was irritated when even the emperor appeared to favour the Jacobite cause, if only by conniving at the escape of the 'Old Pretender's Polish fiancée from her protective custody in Innsbruck in April 1719.

## ■ Sweden's Downfall

After the king of Sweden's death in December 1718 efforts favouring the pacification of the north increased. London seemed determined to end the war against Sweden and stop Russian expansion in the Baltic. British support also helped speed up effective *Reich* intervention in Mecklenburg. In early January 1719, George I, as elector of Hanover, Augustus of Saxony-Poland in his capacity as elector of Saxony—now fearing Russia more than the Polish opposition—and Charles VI signed the Treaty of Vienna to facilitate the long-awaited military solution to the Mecklenburg question.[44] The liberation of Poland from Russian control was accomplished when the Russians evacuated the country voluntarily in 1719.

In autumn 1719, a Swedish secret mission, supported by the British representative in Vienna, tried to talk the Austrians into sending 16,000 troops against the Russians in Livonia. Yet in December 1719 and January 1720, the emperor's ministers, even if they wished the Moscovites back into the wilderness, left little doubt that they considered such plans entirely absurd and an open conflict with Russia something to be avoided.[45]

The Habsburg Monarchy with its '*usitata indifferentia*,' as the emperor's councillors euphemistically called their irresolution, had gained nothing from Sweden's downfall. Charles VI proved incapable of preventing the most shameless acts of territorial 'self-service' in the northern parts of the *Reich,* committed by potential rivals or, as in the case of Prussia, declared opponents of the House of Austria. The emperor reciprocated gladly by questioning the legality of all the haggling and by delaying the formal enfeoffment of Hanover and Prussia with their new territories. This could not alter the fact that the territorial rearrangements were at once implemented—without the consent of the emperor as feudal overlord. A serious confessional struggle within the *Reich* kindled by Hanover contributed to heating up the conflict.[46]

Worse still, the Russian giant was much more dangerous (especially for Austria's vital interests in Poland and in the Balkans) than faraway Sweden had ever been. Habsburg foreign policy had little choice but to find a modus vivendi with the new great power in the east. British insistence that an anti-Russian league was still indispensable met with little sympathy; manoeuvring between the front lines seemed more promising.[47]

Austro-Russian relations were resumed in 1720, but remained problematic. Charles VI was still perfectly unwilling to grant his Russian counterpart the title of emperor. It was absurd, Vienna argued sarcastically, that Christendom should have two or even more secular heads.[48] It was only after the tsar's death that Vienna and Saint Petersburg eventually signed a treaty of alliance, in August 1726.[49]

## ■ Obituary for a Knight-Errant

When news of Charles's death reached Vienna in early 1719, the dictates of chivalry forbade any official expression of malicious joy. It was logical for Prince Eugene of Savoy to praise the late king's heroic military exploits.[50]

The assessment of the nordic mischief-maker and his hyperactivism in foreign policy had been quite different when Charles XII was still alive and unnerving the Austrians. As late as 1716, the pro-Russian Imperial Vice-Chancellor Schönborn bluntly called him the 'mad Swede' (*der dolle Schwed*).[51] This, to be true, was an epithet which Austrian diplomacy awarded very generously to all those crowned heads (and there were many of the kind at the period) whose passionate and often brutal policies contrasted sharply with the Austrian way of acting and the cumbersome collegial decision-making process that made Habsburg foreign policy so cautious and hesitant. Peter the Great, Friedrich Wilhelm of Prussia (the Calvinist 'worm of the *Reich*'), let alone Augustus of Saxony-Poland, received no better press than the king of Sweden.

Austria's view of Charles XII's character and political system was to a large extent influenced by Count Wratislaw and the unpleasant experience the emperor's leading diplomat had had during his thorny mission to Leipzig-Altranstädt. Even though he seems to have had little direct contact with the king—notoriously inaccessible to foreign diplomats—and transacted his business mainly with the Swedish ministers who, in his eyes, were corrupt and taciturn, had no influence on their master, and knew very little about his plans, Wratislaw's portrayal of the monarch was unequivocal and anything but flattering, showing a 'wild' and unreasonable man ('to say no more of an anointed head') with whom regular negotiations were virtually impossible (August 1707).[52]

Wratislaw was even more candid in his private correspondence with Marlborough, to whom he poured out his heart during and after the Altranstädt episode. In early August 1707 his hostility towards Charles XII was political. He strongly recommended resolute measures against Sweden. 'It is necessary,' he wrote, 'to take measures in the future that this king does not become more powerful and, as a result, is not able to shake all of Europe when the fancy takes him.'[53]

One month later, after Austria's diplomatic defeat had become bitter reality, Wratislaw's verdict was as personal as it was devastating:

> *The king is a young prince, full of vanity and vainglory inflated by the happy results of random accidents and extraordinary success without interruption. . . .*
> *Anger is the dominant passion that drives him most of the time in everything he did and does. This passion goes so far that we sometimes see him foaming with rage, and people who approach nearest him fear he will become furious, and if the prince were not so sober and bereft of wine, perhaps he would already be so. . . . This young king is spoiled by all the flattery and indignities that most of the princes of Europe have alternately given him. . . . This gave him an insufferable pride. . . . The greatest evil of all evils, in my opinion, is that this prince has no rule or policy and cares nothing for his life or for his states, he thereby becomes dangerous to all neighbours. . . . He was often heard to say that the war must go on for another 13 years.*[54]

# Charles XII at the Centre of Ottoman-Swedish Diplomacy

by Bülent Ari and Alptug Güney*

Following its defeat at the gates of Vienna in September 1683, the Ottoman Empire remained involved in a long and wearisome war. For the next sixteen years, some of the major European states joined the Holy League against the Ottomans in a conflict that changed the balance of power across the continent. It bled the Ottoman Empire militarily and financially dry and culminated in its defeat. The image of Ottoman invincibility was shattered and after this debacle on land, the empire was dragged into a turmoil which lasted for a long time. Henceforth the role of diplomacy in the foreign affairs of the Ottoman Empire would increase and at the same time it became more difficult to convince the Sublime Porte (central government) that a war would be more advantageous.[1] As the war ended with the signing of the treaties of Karlowitz[2] (1699) and Constantinople[3] (1700), a struggle for power developed between the military and civil authorities in Constantinople.[4]

In this power vacuum, after war and revolts had fractured the state, the task of re-establishing order was given to government officials such as Kalaylıkoz Ahmed Pasha and then Çorlulu Ali Pasha. These two grand viziers pursued a program of strengthening the government and the army and avoiding a war while putting down revolts in Constantinople.[5] Just at this time, with the impact of historical and strategical factors, the Ottoman Empire became part of two international issues. First, in 1703, the Hungarian independence movement in the Austrian Empire led by Ferenc II Rákóczi erupted. Although the Ottomans hoped for the success of this rebellion, they avoided showing open support and managed to stay outside the conflict between the insurgents and the Austrian government.[6]

## ■ Charles XII as Guest of the Sultan

Events took a different turn, however, in the second issue—the relationship with Russia—when Charles XII sought refuge on Ottoman territory after his defeat at Poltava.[7] There was a powerful group, a 'war party,' within the Ottoman Court which was uncomfortable with the Treaty of Constantinople and the presence of the Russian fleet in the Black Sea. The Swedes found in this war party a strong ally against those determined to mediate the conflict with the Russian tsarist government through diplomatic means.[8] By 3 August 1709, when Charles reached Bender, Sultan Ahmed III had put down all rebellions and curbed the disorders in Constantinople following the unrest at Adrianople. Çorlulu Ali Pasha was appointed grand vizier and he pur-

*Sultan Ahmed III's entry into Constantinople.*

*Painting by Jean Baptiste Vanmour (1671-1737), ca. 1700-13. Uppsala University Library, Uppsala, Sweden.*

sued a policy of strengthening the state through reforms and by staying out of armed conflicts.[9] To heal the wounds of war and revolt, the new grand vizier gave priority to reforming the army, to providing armament factories with modern technology and to re-equipping the dockyards. He wished to avoid implicating the empire in any war whatsoever before repairing the injuries of the latest wars. For this reason, when the Hungarians offered an alliance against the Austrians in 1706 with very favourable terms for the Ottomans, he left the matter unresolved and expressed only a diplomatic interest.[10] The grand vizier was wary of putting the hard-won peace with the Habsburgs in danger.[11] The unexpected arrival of the Swedes did not change his position on peace. In view of the state's traditions, its inclinations in foreign affairs, and also in consideration of the obligations of war and the king's physical condition, the king and his entourage were taken under Ottoman protection. They were allowed to stay as guests at the Bender encampment until the king's wounds were healed.[12] In a letter written by Charles to Çorlulu Ali Pasha he seemed to acknowledge that once he would have regained his health, he would return to his own country.[13]

On 10 August 1709, when Charles XII learned that the remnants of the Swedish army, now under the command of Adam Ludwig Lewenhaupt, had surrendered to the Russians at Perevolochna on 11 July and that the route through Poland was now in Russian hands, the Swedish king had to change his plans for his return. Up to that time the Swedes had attempted to draw the Sublime Porte into the war against Russia as an ally, now they had no choice but to rely on Ottoman support. Charles wasted no effort in countering Russian lobbying behind the scenes, even trying to exert influence on the proponents of peace, if necessary.[14] To convince the Sublime Porte to engage in war with the Russians, first the government in Constantinople, then the representatives of states not directly involved in the Northern War, such as Great Britain and the Dutch Republic, would have to be persuaded.[15] At his arrival at Bender, Charles had appointed Martin Neugebauer as his envoy to the Sublime Porte, but by early September Neugebauer had still not been able to obtain any result in favour of Sweden in his audiences with the grand vizier. This probably was due to overly cautious conduct of both sides towards one another, and to Neugebauer's lacking, as he said, 'any exact notion of what the king's full intentions might be.'[16] When the king realised that he was not the best man to defend the Swedish interests at the court of Constantinople, Neugebauer was replaced by the Polish general in Swedish service, Stanislaw Poniatowski.[17]

## ■ Russia and the Ottoman Empire

Russia's growing power in eastern Europe had raised concerns in conjunction with the terms of the Treaty of Constantinople and the recognition that with the capture of the Azov fortress the Russians had a clear road to the Black Sea.[18] The Crimean khan, Devlet Giray, was among those officials who were aware of the Russian aggression. Taking advantage of the distraction created by the Northern War, Grand Vizier Daltaban Mustafa Pasha had sought to recapture Azov from the Russians and destroy the fortifications built in that area in violation of the treaty's provisions. His efforts were stymied by the secret machinations of the Russian ambassador, Pjotr Andreyvic Tolstoy, at the Sublime Porte and an intervention could not be organised in due time. Russia's attempts to reach the Black Sea coasts were followed with mounting fears in Constantinople throughout the final quarter of the seventeenth century.[19]

Diplomatic exchanges between Bender, Kiev, and Bahçesaray in late August and early September 1709 are proof that the Ottoman government was aware of the importance of the Russian threat to northern Ottoman provinces, the Swedish issue, and the situation in Poland. The warden (*muhafız*) of Bender, Yusuf Pasha was following the developments in Poland through his spies, while the Crimean khan was monitoring Russian operations in Ukraine and Poland as well as Russian military attempts at the shores of the Black Sea.[20] Those who saw this as dangerous found it difficult to convince Constantinople that the threat of Russian escalating operations against the Ottomans could not be eliminated through diplomatic efforts. Grand Vizier Çorlulu Ali Pasha and his close political friends *Reisülküttab* (head of chancery) Abdülkerim Efendi and *Şeyhül-İslam* Ebezade Abdullah Efendi held Ottoman domestic and foreign politics in their hands. They did not believe that it would be advantageous to the empire to become involved in military adventures until diplomatic attempts were exhausted. Moreover, this approach assured them of the sultan's confidence.[21] Çorlulu Ali Pasha was well aware that the treaty with Russia was in need of a revision, but he believed that he could use the Swedes as bargaining chip in future diplomatic exchanges. For this reason, he left the settlement of disputes—e.g., Russian treaty violations such as the continuing reinforcement of its troops and the construction of new fortifications on the Black Sea coast—to be dealt with at the negotiation table.[22]

## ■ War or Peace with Russia

Çorlulu Ali Pasha's peace policy was based on an eventual revision of the treaty in favour of the Ottomans and on Russian recognition of absolute Ottoman sovereignty over the Black Sea. Many statesmen, however, argued that the tsar would not withdraw from Crimea and the Black Sea without war and they altogether rejected Çorlulu Ali Pasha's policy. To them, the Russian military initiative against Azov and its surroundings was clear evidence that their view was correct. Köprülüzade Numan Pasha, scion of the noblest Ottoman families, led this opposition. Following the revolt at Adrianople (1703) he gained support from the Janissaries, whose rejection of the grand vizier had diminished the latter's power, and from the *ulema,* the religious establishment. Now, Charles XII also joined this opposition group.[23]

Wary of his adversaries, Çorlulu Ali Pasha had brokered an agreement with the Russians, and in January 1710 he renewed the treaty of 1700. It basically was a confirmation of the Treaty of Constantinople, but new was the stipulation that the Swedish king would be free to return home through Russian or Russian-occupied countries. For Çorlulu Ali Pasha, once the treaty was renewed the presence of the Swedes was no longer advantageous. On the contrary, their presence had given the impression of Turkish non-compliance with the treaty and was a cause of constant tension along the Turkish-Russian border.[24]

Determined to pursue a more forceful policy, Charles was angered by Çorlu-lu Ali Pasha's reneging on his promise to him by making peace with the Russians, Charles sent Poniatowski to Constantinople on 8 February 1710. His task was to appeal directly to the sultan and to explain to him how the grand vizier was acting against Ottoman interests, with the ultimate goal of having Çorlulu Ali Pasha removed from power in a diplomatic manner.[25] Thus, the idea was developed, both in the Swedish encampment and among the members of the Ottoman opposition, that the peace advocates' failure to inform the sultan directly of the Russian danger had been a major shortcoming of the empire's foreign policy. For four years this opinion would be aired, sometimes as a genuine conviction, sometimes as a diplomatic cover for the Swedes.

As a matter of fact, already before the Battle of Poltava, Russian shipbuilding along the Azov coast had unsettled Ahmed III, who had sent a letter to the tsar regarding the Treaty of Constantinople and inquired about the intention of these activities:

> *What need is there to create along the shores of the Voronezh and the Don River a fleet for the Sea of Azov? The Black Sea is entirely within our power and due to the amity found between our two realms, our Supreme State would allow no foreign power passage across the Black Sea—who then do you fear? How is it conceivable that these ships could pass from the Sea of Azov to another sea and that they would be on their way to some other destination than the Black Sea?*[26]

Although in this royal missive (*nâme-i hümâyun*) the sultan broke with the spirit of two centuries of state policy regarding the Black Sea, he clearly wanted to make sure that the treaty's terms would be honoured.[27] Then, as tensions mounted following the Battle of Poltava, it appears that the Russian envoy, Tolstoy, shifted his diplomatic efforts because he was aware of the unease caused by his country's construction program along the Black Sea.[28]

In order to counter the anti-Swedish atmosphere created by Çorlulu Ali Pasha, a letter prepared by Poniatowski explaining Charles XII's opinion and assessment of recent developments was presented to the sultan at the Friday Prayers procession on 17 April 1710. This direct communication with the sultan was the first heavy blow to Çorlulu Ali Pasha's position.[29] Furthermore, on 18 April Devlet Giray, the Crimean khan, came to Bender for a meeting with Charles. From these developments it is clear that the sultan maintained contact with both sides of the Swedish issue and remained in control of the grand vizier's policy-making.[30]

On 15 May, by order of the sultan, the *Reisülküttab* met with Poniatowski. Regardless of what outcome was intended or what may have been said unexpectedly, the statement issued afterwards precisely reflected the views of Grand Vizier Çorlulu Ali Pasha:

> *His Royal Highness the Magnanimous King of Sweden seeks in vain to drag us into war. According to the present state of affairs as well as sound judgment, it is contrary to our civil and religious laws to engage in a war. Although the Sublime Porte has availed itself of every means and opportunity to please the king and return him to his country, the king has spurned all and sundry without reason or explanation. The king will not even deign to listen to any proposal made on his be-*

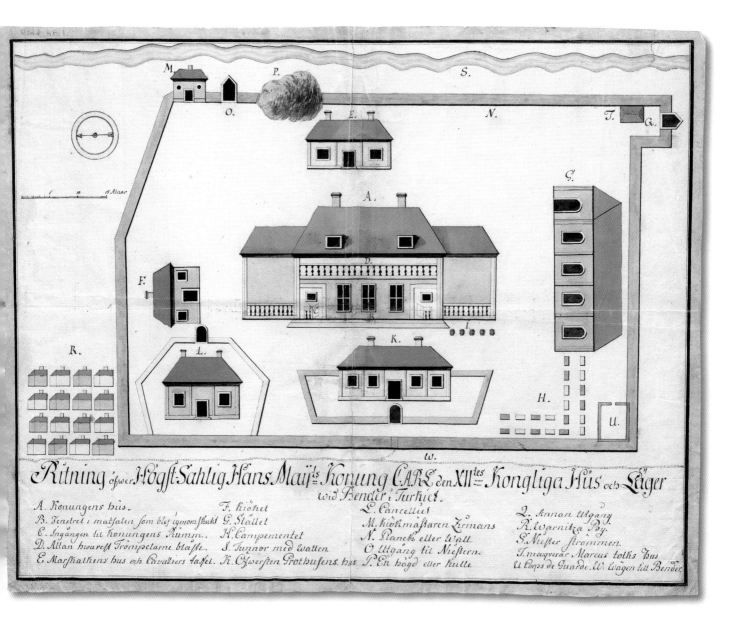

Ritning ofwer Högst Sahlig Hans Maij:ts Konung CARL den XII:tes Kongliga Hus och Läger wid Bender i Turkiet.

A. Konungens hus.
B. Fenstret i matsalen som blef igenomskuhtit.
C. Ingången til konungens Rumin.
D. Altan hwareft Trompetarne blåste.
E. Marshalkens hus och Cavaliers tafel.
F. Kiökiet
G. Stallet
H. Campementet
I. Tunnor med watten
K. Öfwersten Grothusens hus
L. Cancelliet
M. Kiökmastaren Zirmans
N. Planck eller Wall
O. Utgång til Niestern.
P. En högd eller kulle.
Q. Annan Utgång
R. Warnitza Poij.
S. Niester strommen.
T. marqvar Marcus toths hus
U. Corps de Guarde. W. Wägen til Bender.

*The yard of Charles XII's house in Varnitza.*

*Pen and ink with watercolours by unknown artist, ca. 1700-49. The Swedish National Archives, Stockholm, Sweden. Stafsundsarkivet, Autografsamlingen, 0003:00001*

*half. How could such a state of affairs not wear out the good graces of the Sublime Porte? If such is indeed the case, then the king can stay anywhere he so desires in the vast and ample ranges of our country.*[31]

Although the meeting appeared to have yielded no tangible result, the Swedes broke the grand vizier's dominance over foreign affairs by working surreptitiously behind the scenes. The interview, so desired by the Swedes, may well have been the grand vizier's final chance. Through his so-called secret confidant (*mahrem-i esrar*) among the courtiers at the palace, Poniatowski was fully informed about what was said at the sultan's audiences and now a channel of communication was established between the sultan and Poniatowski.[32] Following two meetings, one on 25 May 1710 at Bender between Gustav Henrik von Müllern, the king's chief minister, and *Küçük Mirahur* (junior stable master) Türk Mehmed Ağa,[33] an envoy sent from Constantinople, and a second meeting on 1 June, between the king and Devlet Giray, peace talks with the tsar were started, focusing on recognition of Augustus II as rightful king of Poland in lieu of Stanislaw Leszczyński. Although the meetings may have appeared to be consistent with the grand vizier's policy, the Swedish issue was in fact closely monitored by the sultan himself as well. Suspicious of the protection Charles XII received from the Ottomans, Augustus II sent General Franz von der Goltz to Constantinople as ambassador plenipotentiary. He stayed there and in Adrianople from 1712 to 1714, lobbying extensively on behalf of Augustus. The result was the signing, on 22 April 1714, of a concordat affirming the essence of the Treaty of Karlowitz. Von der Goltz returned to Warsaw, where on 1 February 1715 he submitted an exhaustive report of his activities to Augustus II.[34] Letters sent from Bender, as well as official reports from the palace to the empire's border regions, revealed that the Swedes were right about Russian involvement and that Çorlulu Ali Pasha's Russian policy placed the empire in grave danger. On 15 June 1710, two months after the Swedish memorandum had been presented to the sultan, Çorlulu Ali Pasha was dismissed. Köprülüzade Numan Pasha was appointed to replace him.[35]

## ■ A New Grand Vizier Takes Charge

Upon assuming his duties, Numan Pasha immediately summoned Tolstoy and minced no words expressing his discomfort with Russia's activities, demanding an immediate withdrawal of Russian troops. His subsequent meeting with Poniatowski to discuss the dispersal of Swedish forces in Europe and to inquire about his views on Russia filled the Swedish faction with excitement. Yet, while the new grand vizier distanced himself from Çorlulu, he sought to focus on domestic policy, a sign that foreign affairs would take a backseat in the empire.[36] Numan Pasha was an esteemed scholar, not a statesman, and he was inexperienced in politics. As he began preparations for his term in Constantinople, negative rumours were spread by those upset by his appointments and dismissals, as well as by his success in changing the sultan's mind on fiscal matters, and as a result of these counter movements the seal of the vizierate passed from the Köprülüzâde to Baltacı Mehmed Pasha, long trusted by the sultan.[37] Despite a clear possibility of war with Russia, the sultan and his statesmen were deliberately waiting for reports from the borders. The sultan was concerned that he might be overthrown in the event of war and, wanting to keep the army fully loyal to him, chose Baltacı Mehmed Pasha because he considered him to be a man of pliable disposition.[38] Coming from Aleppo to the capital, the new grand vizier felt that the time to make a decision for a military campaign was not yet ripe due to a lack of reports, and on 27 September 1710 he postponed the preparations.[39] Soon, however, disturbing news began again to arrive and it was clear there was no longer any reason for delay. On 3 November 1710 Devlet Giray arrived in Constantinople and made his views on Russia known to the sultan:

> If faith is placed in the enemy's words of peace and understanding and no heed paid to the news arriving from your borders, Crimea will be lost, the lands of the Emperor's European territories will be overrun forthwith by his enemies. The Rus-

*sians head south with a single goal—to descend on Constantinople. It is for this reason that they cooperate in unity with your non-Muslim subjects. Therefore, it is necessary to proceed with great care.*[40]

A comparison between Devlet Giray's words and Poniatowski's comments presenting the Swedish king's considerations shows the extent to which the Swedes agreed with Crimean policy. In a meeting with Numan Pasha, Poniatowski had said:

*Prior to the various talks taking place, the Ottoman Empire was subject to danger, which we brought to the attention of the grand vizier and the minister, as required. This danger, the growth of the Muscovite state and the collusion between the tsar and Augustus II to divide Poland between them, was the reason we spoke out. Russian occupation of the provinces of Podolia, Lithuania, and Volhynia thoroughly confirms our claims. With the approval of their neighbours, Moldavia and Wallachia, the Russians could gain dominion over the Tatars. On the one hand, since the Russians have already set foot in Crimea, the situation is clear. Once the tsar has seized such a strong nation, none can halt his advance on Constantinople. On the other hand, if the Sublime Porte were to turn a blind eye to King Augustus II's usurpation of the Polish throne, the Porte could be sure that he will unite his forces with the Great Tsar and wage war against the Ottoman Empire. For Augustus II is the tsar's inseparable friend and ally. He will not hesitate to give up half of what does not belong to him in order to gain the remaining half.*[41]

## ■ War with Russia Again

On 20 November 1710, a Grand Council, or conference of advisors (a *Büyük Divan* or *Meşveret-i Azime*), was held, attended by religious authorities and senior military officers, and including officials and commanders from the border regions as well.[42] They determined that the Russians had violated the Treaty of Constantinople; that their current operations along the border were preparations for an attack; that they were constructing fortresses and ships along the coast of the Sea of Azov; and that, as the Swedes had taken sanctuary in Ottoman lands following the Battle of Poltava, an attack across the border would be in contravention of the peace treaty (*ahidname-i hümayun*) and an act of war. According to the papers of the French ambassador, Charles d'Argental de Ferriol, the sultan also touched on the Swedish issue:

*Eighteen months ago, I promised I would return the king of Sweden to his own country. Fulfilling this promise is not only a matter of honour and pride but at the same time in the best interests of the state.*[43]

The Grand Council's declaration of war on Russia was met with elation in Bender. Tsar Peter wrote one more time, at the beginning of November, exploring the possibility of peace; his letter received no reply.[44] Tolstoy was imprisoned at the Yenikapı dungeons.[45] On 5 March 1711, as the tsar's edict declaring war on the Ottoman Empire was read out in Moscow's Cathedral of the Dormition (Uspenski Cathedral), the Ottoman vanguard began its first raids on the Ukrainian interior.[46]

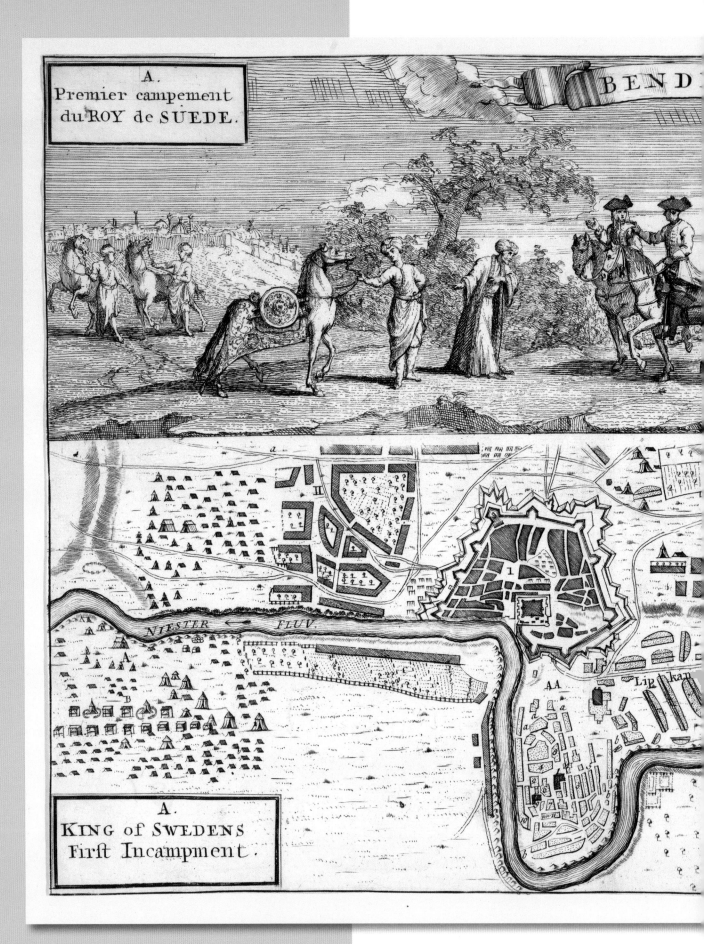

A.
Premier campement
du ROY de SUEDE.

BEND.

NIESTER FLUV.

Lip kan

A.
KING of SWEDENS
First Incampment.

Inside the engraving:

**AA.**
Second Campement du ROY de SUEDE

1. Sa Majesty.
2. M. le. Gen. Sparre
3. M. le. Gen. Dahldorff.
4. M. le. Gen. Hohle
5. M. le. Gen. Poniatowsky.
6. M. le. Chan. Mullern.
7. Le. Cons. Fisf.
8. M. le. March. Dubens.
9. M. le. Col. Grothusen.
10. M. L'Envoye Fabrice.
11. M. le. Col. Funk.
12. M. le. Col. Mentzer.
aa. Drabants ou gardes du Roy.
bb. garde Turque.

V. Hogarth. Inv.t et sculp.

**AA**
KING of SWEDENS Second Incampment.

1. His Majesty.
2. Gen. Sparre.
3. Gen. Dahldorff.
4. Gen. Hohle.
5. Gen. Poniatonsky.
6. Chan. Mullern.
7. Couns. Fisf.
8. Marsh. Dubens.
9. Col. Grothusen.
10. Envoy Fabrice.
11. Col. Funck.
12. Col. Mentzer.
aa. Drabants
bb. Turkish guards.

Scala Pas.
100  500  1000

*Charles XII at Bender. From Aubry de La Mottraye's 'Travels throughout Europe, Asia and into Part of Africa […]'.*

*Engraving by William Hogarth (1697-1764) and S. Parker (active 1720), 1723-24, The Metropolitan Museum of Art, New York, USA.*

At this juncture a new development, a new direction can be seen in Ottoman foreign policy, which, notwithstanding Charles's best efforts, aimed solely at preventing Russian access to the Black Sea, as was publicly proclaimed from the onset of the war. Wary of having to enter a war on two fronts, Baltacı Mehmed Pasha felt obliged to send a delegation to Vienna. It was led by Seyfullah Ağa and had several duties: to explain the tension in Ottoman-Russian relations, to placate the Austrians' sensitivities to Turkish posturing with regard to Poland, to ensure that no revisions would be made to the treaties of 1699 and 1700, and to confirm compliance with the provisions of those treaties as written.[47] Prince Eugene was of the same opinion as the Turks regarding the unfavourable direction of Russian policy. The idea of Turkish and Tartar troops entering Poland also unsettled him, however. As his letter to the grand vizier indicates, the prince was apparently persuaded that no interference with Poland was in the offing, nor any entanglement of the issue with the ongoing War of the Spanish Succession, so that peace would prevail as long as the Ottomans did not undertake to enter Poland.[48]

Throughout the negotiations in Vienna of April 1711, it is clear that the Ottoman wars were considered completely separate from those of the Swedes. In the Northern War, a Russian army had kept Swedish forces confined to Pomerania, and thus the Ottomans could not expect any assistance from the Swedes.[49] In fact, in order to avoid provoking a political crisis with either Austria or Poland, they tried as best they could to keep Sweden out of the conflict.

Calculating the intensification of political contacts between Constantinople and his encampment in case of a war, Charles XII now dispatched Poniatowski to Baltacı Mehmed Pasha, who was with the troops in the field, and he appointed Thomas Funck as his representative in Constantinople, to defend Swedish interests effectively.[50]

On 18 June 1711, Baltacı Mehmed Pasha invited Charles to the encampment at Isaccea for consultations arranged by Poniatowski. A week later, however, the king decided to decline any affiliation with the Ottoman army. He probably was concerned about matters of protocol. A sovereign could only be incorporated into another sovereign's war camp, not into one of a lower rank, as that of a grand vizier.[51] The king's rebuff of the commander-in-chief's invitation was seen, though, as arrogance by the Ottomans and was met with anger.[52] The king's conduct eliminated any opportunity to influence the strategy of the Ottoman army and the Swedes remained entirely outside the war council established at the encampment. Moreover, when on 21 July 1711 the Russian army—surrounded by the Ottomans at the Pruth and faced with total destruction—asked for a truce and consented to all demands of the Ottomans for the sake of survival, the Swedish-Polish issue was not on the agenda at the negotiations.[53] Furthermore, in the peace agreements resulting from negotiations between the Russian representative Pjotr Pavlovic Shafirov and Osman Ağa, the Swedish issues and concerns were left unresolved. This was not a question of a temporary contradiction in Ottoman foreign policy, if we take the talks in Vienna into consideration. The opposition in Constantinople was quick to respond. In its view, the Russian army had exploited the negligence of Ottoman officials.[54]

Despite objections of Khan Devlet Giray and Poniatowski, Baltacı Mehmed Pasha agreed to conditions according to which the Russians would only cede the fortresses at Azov and Kamianka-Dniprovska and be guaranteed a safe passage for the withdrawal of their troops. As a result, the Treaty of the Pruth was considered a diplomatic victory for the Russians rather than for the Ottomans. Yet, the peace deliberations restored Azov to the Turks, the Russian border fortresses would be demolished, and the Russians also recognised Stanislaw Leszczyński as king of Poland. Even more important, Russian troops were to be withdrawn from Poland, giving Charles XII a clear road to his own country.[55]

On the evening of 22 July the Swedish king received the news that negotiations had been concluded and that the Russians were leaving the battlefield. Even if he had departed for the grand vizier's headquarters immediately, it would have made no difference as agreements had already been reached. The king was, however, of the opinion that the opportunity to follow and destroy the Russian army was still present and he wanted to meet with the grand vizier to change his decision. Baltacı Mehmed Pasha rejected the king's proposals and dismissed any action that would risk losing the peace made with the Russians. In response to the criticism that the Turks must keep their promises and specifically those made to the Swedes, the grand vizier recalled that Swedish forces in Pomerania had not attacked the Russians as promised from the moment the war started. In the grand vizier's opinion, the Turks had only sought war to further their own interests and it was out of the question to go to war with Russia in order to fulfil a promise made to the Swedes. Although before the war it had been suggested that it was too dangerous for the king to return to Sweden via Poland, the victory at the Pruth had nullified this threat; the king was free to return to Sweden with an escort of Turkish forces of any size of his own choosing.[56]

### ■ New Swedish Hopes for War with Russia

Poniatowski immediately began negotiations, setting his sights on returning Charles to his country as soon as possible under the protections of the Treaty of the Pruth. No results were achieved, however, in his talks with İbrahim Efendi, deputy of Kâhya Osman Ağa, and, subsequently, Nicolas Mavrocordato, the dragoman of the Imperial Council. Justifiably, the general was convinced that relying on Russian guarantees to cross Russian territory without a large escort would be a terrible mistake. He wanted a force of 40,000 men to accompany the king across Poland.[57] In light of the peace treaty, the Turkish authorities saw no need for an escort of that size. The grand vizier did not ask for the king's opinion and, instead, tried to dictate terms in such a way that uproar could be avoided.[58] Meanwhile the viceroy of Rumelia, Hasan Pasha, was sent to Bender, commanding a cavalry force of 3,000 in order to make the king's situation a *fait accompli*. The grand vizier sent Poniatowski back to Bender without the king's permission. He was carrying a letter to Charles advising the conclusion of an immediate peace with the Russians. Baltacı Mehmed Pasha had also sent letters to several Polish notables to ensure that the king could return unharmed to Sweden via Poland. Charles, however, preferred rejection of the peace treaty which had not yet been approved by the sultan, and continuation of the war by seeking the grand vizier's dismissal. To that end, he sent the necessary orders to Funck, his delegate in Constantinople.[59]

Funck's efforts did not meet with success except to stir up further negative rumours about Baltacı Mehmed Pasha. On 6-7 August 1711, correspondence in Constantinople between Funck and high-ranking Ottoman officials continued to suggest that measures might once again be adopted to revise the treaty, although the sultan had already ratified it and had sent it to the imperial army.[60] Thereupon Funck returned once more to the army in order to oversee preparations for the king's homeward journey. As Charles XII would have to leave as soon as possible, it was brought to Funck's attention that no time should be wasted sending the king's envoys to make peace with the Russians. Since Funck did not have the king's permission to negotiate these issues, a request for clarification was immediately sent to Bender.

Charles detained Funck in Bender in order to learn whether it would be possible for Sweden to acquire some of the spoils, assuming that this topic might be found in the provisions under which peace had been made with the Russians. Accompanying Funck as far as Bender, the chief gatekeeper (*Kapıcıbaşı*), Mehmed Ağa, delivered a letter from the grand vizier to the Swedish king. In it, Baltacı Mehmed Pasha sternly admonished the king and asked him to complete his preparations for the journey within three days of receiving the letter. In the afternoon of 13 September the king gave his reply, saying 'his decision was to go through Poland in the shortest possible time.'

Over the course of his residency in Bender Charles had acquired burdensome debts and before leaving intended to 'answer them in the same manner of graciousness that the sultan has shown heretofore.' In order to leave Bender with his local debts paid, he made, however, a request to the Sublime Porte for a loan of 1,200 purses. The grand vizier firmly rejected the proposal and warned Charles against leaving immediately under these circumstances. As always, it was impossible to change the king's mind. To the issue of the escort troops was now added the issue of money. Sent to determine the state of affairs in Poland, Karl Törnskiöld, a Swedish diplomat, returned to Bender on 24 September and reported that the situation there favoured the Swedes and that the Poles would be no hindrance to the king's passage. Thus, the Swedes could be expected to set out as soon as their issues of money and escort forces could be resolved.[61]

The following days, the cold war between the two sides gained speed. Time was against the grand vizier and in the king's favour. Following the demonstration of his insufficiency and the mismanagement of developments after the Battle of the Pruth, Baltacı Mehmed Pasha attempted to undermine the king's position by blaming him for breaching the conditions of the treaty with the Russians. Furthermore, as the Russians wished, he aimed to send the king back to Sweden via Russian territory without protection.[62] In Constantinople the sultan was displeased with the grand vizier's decisions and misrepresentations to the Swedes and sent him a letter of reprimand.

On 25 September, Gustaf Celsing, secretary of the Swedish embassy, presented to the sultan a memorandum outlining Sweden's position and misgivings. It seems that the memorandum had positive effects. Baltacı Mehmed Pasha changed his disposition towards the Swedes when on 5 October an official brought a personal edict of the sultan (*hatt-ı hümayun*) to the imperial army. Five days after having received

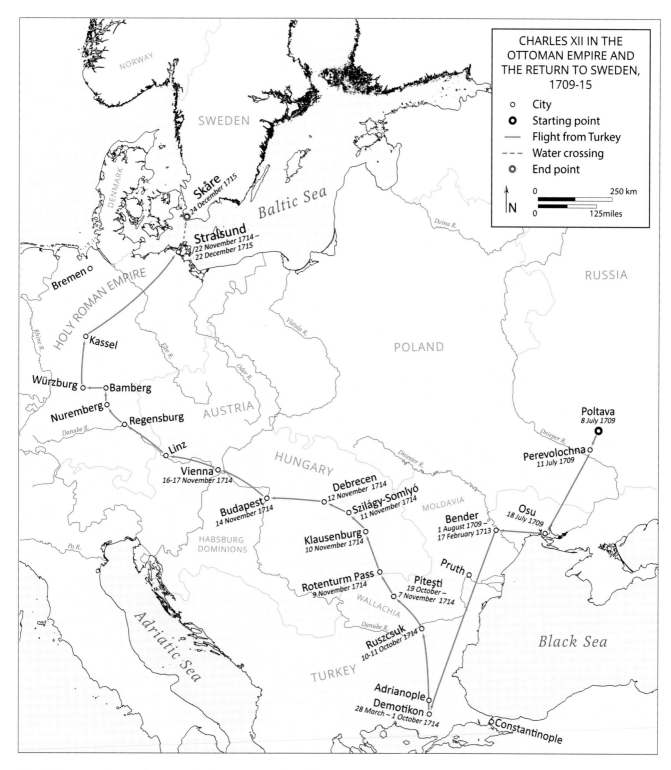

Funck, the grand vizier determined that cutting off the allowance paid for the expenses of the Swedish king and his retinue had been a disastrous misunderstanding and immediately sought to correct his mistake.

Careful to circumvent the grand vizier's henchmen at the court, Charles sent a memorandum to his dragoman Giovanni Baptista Savary in Constantinople detailing at length the missed opportunities and the dire situation of the Russians at the Pruth. The letter was translated into Turkish at the French embassy and submitted to the sultan on 30 October. Due to the unexpected nature of this memorandum, the sultan offered Savary the opportunity to meet personally and went incognito to an imam's house. It was rumoured that at this meeting the sultan cautioned the dragoman, saying 'he must be prudent because the Swedes have so many enemies,' an indication to the diplomatic circles of Constantinople, as well as the Ottoman elite that the delicate situation of the Swedes was seen to be the cause of the war with Russia.[63] At the same time, the sultan sent his grand vizier furious and threatening missives, telling him the Russians were using the Swedish issue merely as a pretext to avoid evacuating Azov.[64] Returning the Swedes to their country was not a matter of urgency; only after reaching a favourable agreement with Russia would the matter be placed next on the agenda.[65] This letter of the sultan, however, did not dissuade Baltacı Mehmed Pasha from the idea of sending the Swedes back as soon as possible. For this heedlessness, the grand vizier was dismissed and sent into exile at Mytilene on 20 November 1711. In July 1712, he was sent to the island of Lemnos, where he died two months later.[66]

## ■ Another Grand Vizier

Thus Charles XII had been the cause of the ouster and downfall of two Ottoman grand viziers. When the chief of the Janissaries, Yusuf Pasha, received the privy seal on behalf of the sultan, Charles was advised to write nothing on the Russian issue or other previous concerns and to try, for his own sake, to cultivate a mutual friendship with the new grand vizier.[67]

From this date onwards, the principles guiding Ottoman foreign policy were clear. The primary goal was to expel the Russians from Azov and keep them far from the Black Sea. From the Ottoman viewpoint, because of their weak military force, the Swedes had no role in this crisis, besides serving as leverage with the Russians. Despite the king's memoranda, which were important insomuch as they touched on the Russian issue, the Swedish issue would remain of secondary importance. Appointment and dismissal of grand viziers did nothing to change that situation.[68]

Ottoman statesmen were in favour of resolving the issue through diplomatic negotiations despite all the threats of war directed towards Russia. Talks began between the Ottomans and the Russians, mediated by the British and Dutch ambassadors. Former *Reisülküttab* Abdülkerim Efendi and Grand Chamberlain (*Kapıcılar Kethüdası*) Mehmed Ağa, who both had followed the Swedish issue closely right from the start, represented the Ottomans. Neither Poniatowski's memorandum to the sultan advising him of the pressing and alarming problems that avoiding a decision could cause, nor the money that Charles XII offered the khan were sufficient to change the course of Ottoman policy towards Russia. The Sublime Porte was willing to put less pressure on the Azov problem for the sake of peace with the Russians. As negotiations continued, Ebezade Abdullah Efendi was appointed *Şeyhülislam* and succeeded the deceased Paşmakçızade, and Abdülkerim Efendi returned as *Reisülküttab*. Thus, the line of thinking during Çorlulu Ali Pasha's viziership returned to the Ottoman foreign office. Meanwhile, with Russian acceptance of Ottoman terms and their surrender of the fortress of Azov in February 1712, peace was attained. According to the treaty's terms, Poland would be evacuated, the Cossacks would remain far from the province, and under the auspices of Turkish forces the Swedish king would return to his country by way of Poland.[69]

One of the three great wounds of the Karlowitz catastrophe having been healed—namely by retaking territories lost to Russia—the recovery should now continue with the retaking of the Morea. As the circumstances of this issue with Venice gained importance, the prolonged nature of the Swedish king's situation created unease. Financially speaking, Charles himself was the biggest problem because he owed money to everyone in Bender, from the merchants to the Janissaries, and was unable to pay. The Sublime Porte's absolute refusal to underwrite these debts stirred up more discontent with the presence of the Swedes, who continued to call for war. Following Russian assent to the terms, Charles, on 21 April 1712, in the presence of İsmail Pasha, the warden (*muhafız*) of Bender, announced that he had decided to return to Sweden via Poland. A former chief bailiff (*çavuşbaşı*), Mehmed Ağa said the following to Poniatowski, which reflects the average Turkish official's impression of the Swedes:

> Your situation is like a boorish guest who overstays his welcome; the guest stays too long and the host wants to kick him out, but I suppose it's not right either when the guest tries to exasperate his host and imposes himself by force![70]

Upon concluding the treaty with Russia, everyone, from the sultan to all dignitaries of the Ottoman state, thought that the time had come for the Swedish king to return to his country. The order sent to the khan and the Bender warden (*muhafız*) was that the Swedes were to return to their own country in the summer of 1712 and it was emphasised that it must be made scrupulously clear that the matter was settled, without any more negotiations.

Türk Mehmed Ağa arrived in Bender on 17 May and presented the sultan's missive to the king on 23 May. This personal letter of the sultan said that the king would be able to return to his country through Poland and stated that the Crimean khan and the *muhafız* would aid him on his journey. In other words, the sultan himself enjoined the king to leave without delay.

King Charles's letter, written by Colonel Christian Albrecht von Grothusen and sent to his representative in Constantinople, Funck, ordered the latter once more to save no efforts for the dismissal of the grand vizier.[71] Apparently the king still failed to understand that alteration of grand viziers did not alter Ottoman foreign policy. Once the safety of the Black Sea was assured, no Ottoman statesman favoured a war in the north. The major determinant political actors in the Ottoman geography were Austria, Poland, Venice, and Russia. The influence of an outside element, such as Sweden, could not be accepted. The policies which the king had tried to impose on the grand viziers, frustrated other government dignitaries and the intrigues and factitiousness of the Swedes had caused them to lose credit.

## ■ The *Kalabalik*

Even thereafter the spectre of another Ottoman-Russian war raised its head. When the Russians at Azov were close to breaking the treaty terms, the sultan immediately urged the Swedes' departure from the country. Yet, information about Russian manoeuvres in Poland arrived in Constantinople via Salahor Ahmed Ağa's reports from Poland and Türk Mehmed Ağa's from Bender. All preparations for the king's departure came to a halt because the Russians had not withdrawn from Poland as they had promised. Because of this, at a meeting of the Divan on 11 November 1712, the grand vizier incurred the wrath of Ahmed III. The decision was made to declare war on Russia, and Yusuf Pasha was removed from the vizierate the following day. In his place was appointed the less knowledgeable and less experienced Abaza Süleyman Pasha. While these events may have given hope to the Swedish party, they did not change Ottoman policy towards Sweden. The sultan sent the Crimean khan, who was leaving from Adrianople, a personal letter indicating that the king certainly must return to his country that winter and giving instructions for immediate payment of the requested 1,200 purses in preparation of the journey.[72] In order for the Swedes to take full advantage of the war and the presumed Ottoman victory, Charles created various pretexts to postpone his departure, yet for the Ottomans the decision to end the Swedish sojourn was a *fait accompli* and the king's efforts to prolong his stay at Bender exhausted their forbearance.[73] A missive from Ahmed III, sent to Bender and handed to Charles on 7 January 1713, demanded in threatening terms that he set out at once, adding that otherwise there would be various unpleasant consequences. The letter gave the Crimean khan authority to intern the king in Saloniki.[74] Because Charles ignored even the sultan's orders, the grand vizier convened a meeting of the Divan on 1 February, during which it was decided to offer the king peace, but to inform him as well that, if he were to oppose what had been offered, his blood would be on his own head and his men would be put to the sword.[75] Even though it had been intended to be a temporary measure, it was deemed exceedingly incorrect to have given Ottoman sanctuary to a sovereign ruler. Orders were given to capture the king if he resisted leaving, although he was not to be harmed. On 12 February 1713, Turkish and Tartar forces surrounding the Swedish camp staged a dramatic intervention to capture Charles, carrying him off to Bender. In Turkish sources, due to the turmoil and chaotic manner in which the Janissary and Tartar forces had gathered around the Swedish camp, this incident was called *Kalabalık* ('the Tumult'). Charles had come to Bender as a refugee king and now was a captive king. The Swedes taken prisoner by the Turks and Tartars were released the following day. As for the king, Ismail Pasha was his host for four days in order to make him forget these unfortunate attacks on his honour, before he departed for Didymoteicho, where he arrived on 28 March. A month later he was transferred to the Timurtaş Pasha Palace near Adrianople.[76]

The *Kalabalık* incident was not appreciated by the embassies of foreign nations, nor was it was among many Ottomans.[77] There was agreement among both groups that the treatment of a crowned sovereign who had taken sanctuary with the Ottomans had not been consonant with the prestige of the empire. This action had been ordered by the sultan, and ambitious political players in Constantinople immediately sought to use it against members of the government and state officials, first of all the grand vizier. Before Charles had even arrived in Didymoteicho, a *firman* was issued regarding restitution of all goods looted from the Swedes and the release of all captives. One dismissal followed another. *Şeyhülislam* Ebezâde Abdullah Efendi,

*Kizlar Ağası* Uzun Süleyman Ağa, *Büyük Mirahor* (grand stable master) Mehmed Ağa, *Çavuşbaşı* Türk Mehmed Ağa, *Bender Muhafızı* İsmail Pasha, Devlet Giray, the khan of Crimea, all were removed from their positions.[78] Soon after, on 4 April 1713, Grand Vizier Süleyman Pasha was also dismissed and replaced by Kel İbrahim Hoca, who maintained that he could resolve the Swedish issue and would assume total responsibility.[79] Yet, he lost the seal as soon as he had obtained the vizierate: his attempt to regain influence with the sultan by starting a dispute with the influential *Silahdar* (sword bearer) Damat Ali Pasha led to his tenure lasting only 22 days. In the event that the Russians did not immediately agree to peace terms, Kel İbrahim Hoca had decided to go to war against Russia and planned to send the Swedes back to their country through Poland, accompanied by a great number of troops. Despite all the appeals of the sultan and his close circle, he showed no understanding at all of the views of those who never wanted war with Russia and Poland, and the situation swiftly gave cause for his murder.[80] In his place was appointed the last grand vizier Charles XII would see in Turkey, Silahdar Damat Ali Pasha.

With the clear policy program of a clever, powerful statesman like Silahdar Damat Ali Pasha in the vizierate, Ottoman policy statements became unambiguous after a succession of weak grand viziers. To settle the Russian and Polish problems, and deal with Austria and Venice, Ali Pasha concluded a 25-year peace treaty with the Russians on 27 June, on previously agreed terms.[81] 27 August found Funck in Adrianople and Poniatowski was given orders to join the king. Thus, the Swedes no longer had any official emissary to the Sublime Porte. For the Ottomans, it was not necessary that an ambassador be sent directly by the king, because the king would soon leave the Ottoman territory; relations with the Swedes were established via the French ambassador. On 14 November 1713, on orders from the grand vizier, Charles and his entourage were transferred back to Didymoteicho. Ali Pasha's determination to establish peace in eastern Europe and his domination of the mechanisms of government appeared to eliminate any means of obtaining a political advantage for the Swedes. The king and his entourage in the Timurtaş Palace and in Didymoteicho, as well as the Swedish soldiers at Bender, were in an unendurable state of physical and psychological crisis. The Swedish senate immediately summoned the king to return to Sweden, convinced that there no longer remained any achievable chance of success for him among the Ottomans.[82]

Charles left Didymoteicho on 1 October 1714 with his entourage, joining the Swedish troops at Piteşti, on the border between Ottoman Walachia and Habsburg Transylvania, or Siebenbürgen as it was then known.[83] On 27 October, they crossed the border and passing through Hungary and Austria, arrived at Stralsund the night of 21-22 November. Thus ended the most intensive period of Turkish-Swedish relations, a first chapter that had lasted longer than five years.

## ■ Settlement of the Swedish Debts

Charles XII had promised to pay his debts to the Ottoman treasury upon returning to his country. He did indeed owe large sums to the Ottoman government as he had been living on its allowances. When this promise was considered insufficient, he sought a loan from the Ottoman government and the Sublime Porte agreed to lend him 400,000 *kuruş*. The Divan appointed a steward (*kethüda*) and sergeants (*çavuşlar*) to disperse 206,000 *kuruş* to the king's emissary between 14 August 1710 and 12 January 1711. From the total of 403,939 *kuruş*, 3,939 *kuruş* were deducted for expenses at Bender that had not been assessed with the loan. As 800 purses did not suffice, another 200 purses (100,000 *kuruş*) were lent: 100 purses as travel allowance and the other 100 to pay off creditors. If 100 purses were not enough to cover payment to these people, the king would send the balance after arriving home. If creditors would not accept this proposal, the Bender treasurer (*defterdar*) and the governor of the Dnieper River province (*Özi Valisi*) would serve as guarantors. The king certified receipt of the sum with his seal.[84] Some time after Charles's death in 1718, Grand Vizier Damat Ibrahim Pasha drew attention to the debts during audits. Kozbekçi Mustafa Ağa was sent to Stockholm in November 1727 to collect the money. After nine months in Sweden, he wrote a letter to Damat Ibrahim Pasha on 19 August 1728 requesting an extension for Sweden because of the country's poor financial situation.

Instead of collecting money, Mustafa Ağa returned to Constantinople with numerous expressions of gratitude and appreciation from Sweden. In the second year following Mahmud I's accession to the throne (October 1732) rumour spread in Constantinople that Sweden was indebted by treaty to Russia. Grand Vizier Hekimoğlu Ali Pasha sent *Sipahiler Kâtibi* (secretary of the cavalry) Mehmed Said Efendi to investigate the matter. After the Ottoman emissary had met with King Fredrik, payment of the debts to the Ottomans was extended. Receiving assurances that Sweden was not indebted to Russia, Mehmed Said Efendi returned to Constantinople on 17 November 1733.

Upon his departure, Charles had left the Ottoman government authorities promissory notes worth 2,000 Rumî purses (one *kise-i Rum* being equal to 500 *kuruş*). In 1737, however, the Swedish government, still trying to maintain friendly relations with the Ottoman Empire, appealed to the government in Constantinople and sought an agreement to pay off the debt in kind, with 'copper-tipped armaments,' including 30,000 muskets worth 200,000 *kuruş* and a 72-gun warship worth 600,000 *kuruş*. The Sublime Porte accepted the offer.[85] Unfortunately, the Swedish warship carrying the weapons to Constantinople sank off the Spanish coast near Cádiz. Another Swedish ship, loaded with gunpowder and 10,000 muskets, arrived safely in Turkey. When the Swedes delivered 6,000 additional muskets, the debt was considered paid.[86]

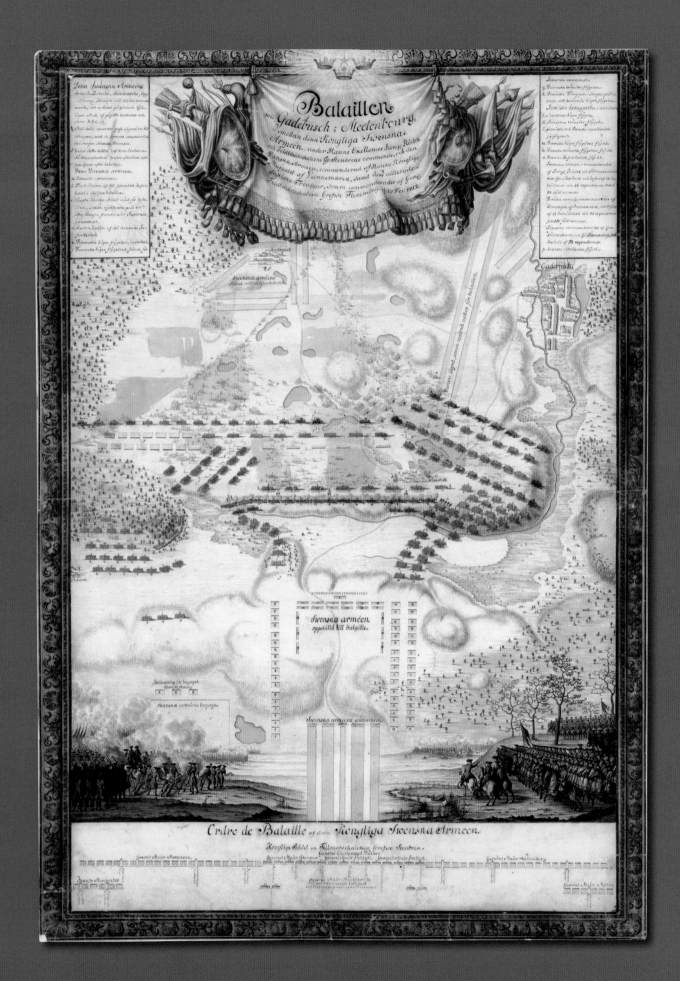

## CHAPTER 14

# Warmonger or Benefactor?
## *Charles XII and the Kingdom of Denmark-Norway*

by Knud J.V. Jespersen

### ■ A Great Power under Threat

Charles XII (1682-1718), Sweden's last king to command an army in the field, was a first cousin of King Frederik IV (1671-1730) of Denmark and Norway. Charles came to the throne in 1697 and Frederik became king in 1699. However, any feeling of kinship that may have existed between the two cousins took second place to an overriding pursuit of their separate political interests, and their close family relationship did not deter them from presiding over the last major confrontation between these nordic nations, the Great Northern War of 1700-21.

Sweden's status as a great power (from 1630 to 1700, approximately) was, to some extent, a consequence of external factors and was more attributable to the weakness of neighbouring states, including Denmark and Norway, than to any inherent strength. It emerged as a leading regional power because of its ability to mobilise its own resources for the conduct of war and to skilfully exploit any weakness in a neighbouring country whenever the opportunity arose.[1]

Throughout this period, Sweden was dependent on external subsidies and other material support and was not in a position to guarantee its own security without foreign help. In this sense, it was not a great power. Sweden was never in the same league as France, England, or even the Dutch Republic. Its overseas interests on the continent were open and vulnerable, and, apart from the Lutheran Church, the inhabitants of the Swedish Empire had little in common.

This remarkable empire was largest in the 1650s during the reign of Charles XII's grandfather, Charles X Gustav. His death in 1660 brought an end, however, to the desire and capacity for further territorial expansion and, from that time, there was an emphasis on defending the territories that had been gained and on avoiding any new conflicts. These were the key elements in Charles XI's foreign policy during his reign from 1660 to 1697 and it can best be described as a cautious balancing act and a policy of neutrality, as opposed to the aggressive and expansionist ambitions of his father. Charles XI devoted his energy to internal consolidation, and through extensive social, economic, administrative, and military reforms he systematically improved the country's internal resources so that it became possible to defend both Sweden and its overseas interests. By the time of his death in 1697 he had established a considerable naval fleet and an army of 90,000 men, largely recruited locally and therefore

*The Battle of Gadebusch, 1712.*

*Pen and ink with watercolours by Magnus Rommel, 1712. The Swedish Military Archives, Stockholm, Sweden. Sveriges Krig 13:014.*

with less dependence on overseas mercenaries and foreign subsidies. During the latter part of his reign there was a gradual emergence of some balance between Sweden's external interests and its internal strengths. This balance, so laboriously achieved, was destroyed during the Great Northern War by his son and heir, Charles XII, and its loss led to the eventual collapse of the Swedish Empire.

Denmark's increasing weakness during the seventeenth century opened the door for Sweden's emergence as the leading regional power. Denmark continued to govern Norway and controlled the seaways leading into the Baltic, but it found itself in a state of permanent siege as a consequence of Swedish possessions in northern Germany immediately to the south of the country's borders. This prevailing sense of being besieged was aggravated by constant problems with the duchy of Holstein-Gottorp, which had gradually become a Swedish enclave within the Danish monarchy and, not surprisingly, was regarded as the gravest threat to the country's security. In 1700, the elimination of this threat by severing the links between Holstein-Gottorp and Sweden was therefore a priority.[2]

Repeated unsuccessful attempts during the latter part of the seventeenth century to resolve this problem in a way that was acceptable to Denmark had shown quite clearly that it was impossible to win the support of the west European powers. France regarded the nordic countries as part of its *barrière de l'est* in its struggle with the German princes; and the naval powers of England and the Dutch Republic—which from 1689 had been allied under Stadholder-King William III—traditionally supported a balance of power in the Baltic to secure the greatest possible freedom of trade in that region. Both of these views dictated political calm and, for different reasons, the western powers had been ready to twist the arm of the Danish government whenever it had sought to make some decisive move in the delicate Holstein-Gottorp problem. This impasse was the underlying reason for a comprehensive reassessment of Danish foreign policy from 1698—the year after the succession of Charles XII in Sweden.[3]

With a young inexperienced king on the throne in Sweden—Charles was not quite 15 at the time of his succession—those countries that had been forced to cede territory during Sweden's expansion saw a unique opportunity for revenge and possibly an end to Swedish domination in the region, provided they acted quickly and decisively. First and foremost these were Denmark-Norway, Poland-Lithuania, and Russia, whose direct access to the Baltic since the early part of the seventeenth century had been blocked by territory taken by Sweden. But it was also an opportune time to strike because the western European powers, which were otherwise inclined to interfere in the nordic region, were preoccupied by conflicts that, in 1701, led to the War of the Spanish Succession, the final scene in Louis XIV's insatiable appetite for expansion. And so, in the years up to 1700, these three Baltic powers formed a military alliance whose ultimate objective was to drive Sweden back to within its original borders. But, in doing so, they grossly underestimated Charles's ability to negotiate difficulties and his powers of leadership.

Apart from this shared and overriding objective, the aims of the three powers were quite different. The Danish king was primarily concerned to destroy the troublesome Swedish alliance with Holstein-Gottorp—an alliance that had been strengthened in 1698 by the marriage of Friedrich IV, Duke of Holstein-Gottorp, and Hedvig Sofia, the sister of Charles XII of Sweden—and also to recapture the province of Skåne in southern Sweden. For Poland-Lithuania, whose king from 1697, Augustus II ('the Strong'), was a first cousin of both Charles XII of Sweden and Frederik IV of Denmark, the objective was to take possession of Livonia, with its important harbour of Riga, whilst the ambition of the Russian tsar, Peter the Great, was to achieve access to the Baltic and thereby transform Russia into a major maritime power as part of his plan for the modernisation and westernisation of Russia. And so the objectives of the partners in this alliance were very different. Their only bond was a common enemy, and these very different ambitions characterised the muddled plan of campaign which emerged in the prelude to the Great Northern War, without effective strategic coordination.

## ■ The Short War of 1700—A Danish Fiasco

After a series of diplomatic feelers between Denmark, Poland-Lithuania, and Russia in 1698-99, a formal agreement was reached early in 1699 for a joint attack on Swedish interests in the Baltic and Germany. According to that agreement, King Frederik IV of Denmark would attack Holstein-Gottorp and the Swedish possession of Bremen-Verden to the southwest, thereby removing the Swedish threat in northwest Germany, while the other two partners in the alliance would concentrate on the Swedish provinces in the eastern Baltic.[4]

In February 1700, in accordance with that plan and without a declaration of war, Frederik IV led his army into Holstein-Gottorp. At first all went well, but then it started to go badly wrong. An essential element of the plan was that it should be a lightning strike which would present the western powers with a *fait accompli* before they could react. However, the military challenge proved to be much greater than the Danes had expected. Before the attack, the duke's army had received considerable Swedish reinforcements and the Danish troops met strong resistance. The Danish command was hesitant and indecisive, and what had been planned as a swift military offensive became a drawn-out siege lasting through the spring of 1700.

This setback gave the Maritime Powers time to respond. They were extremely concerned that this attack would almost certainly develop into open conflict between Denmark and Sweden, which they were eager to avoid, especially at a time when they were on the verge of a final reckoning with France. Their reaction was therefore immediate and resolute.

On the orders of William III, a squadron of warships from England and the Dutch Republic was despatched to Danish waters with the purpose of placing the Danish government under the maximum pressure. In June this fleet reached the Sound, between Denmark and Sweden, where it was joined by a Swedish flotilla, while the Danish fleet retreated to the safety of the harbour in Copenhagen. From 20 to 25 July the combined fleet carried out a bombardment of Copenhagen, and although there was little material damage, there was considerable panic. And shortly afterwards, the Danes experienced, for the first time, the young Swedish king's ability to outmanoeuvre his enemies.

In response to these developments, Charles XII assembled an expeditionary force of about 10,000 well-trained soldiers on the west coast of Skåne, south of Helsingborg and within sight of Denmark. On 4 August, under the protection of the allied navies, this army crossed the Sound to Humlebæk, on the east coast of Zealand, where it met little resistance from a Danish force of a few hundred men, the majority of the Danish army being in Holstein-Gottorp. From this beachhead, with Charles XII in command, his invasion force headed south down the coast of the Sound, again meeting little opposition, and within a few days it had reached Rungsted, only 30 kilometres to the north of Copenhagen.

The panic-stricken Danish government feared that this invasion had all the signs of a repeat of the nightmare of 1658 when Charles X Gustav, almost without opposition, occupied Zealand and encircled Copenhagen, which then suffered the privations of a year-long siege until, in 1660, a humiliating peace accord was achieved. There can be no doubt that Charles XII—if he had been at liberty to do so—would have tried to capture the city, which was something his grandfather had failed to do. But he was overtaken by diplomatic events which, simultaneously, were unfolding in Holstein-Gottorp.

On 18 August, at Schloss Traventhal in Holstein-Gottorp, the desperate Danish government agreed to a demand from William III for an immediate end to hostilities. The peace treaty obviously required the withdrawal of Swedish forces from Zealand, but in all other ways it was a total victory for Sweden and the duke of Holstein-Gottorp, who was restored to power with all his sovereign privileges and 260,000 Reichstaler in reparation. Charles XII was able to celebrate his first military victory, albeit under the protection of the western navies, but his immediate reaction was one of disappointment. Later, when the Danes entered the deserted Swedish encampment at Rungsted, they found a bear chained to a pole, and just out of its reach lay a dead horse. The message was quite clear—the bear represented the young warrior king, and the chains were the western powers that, on this occasion, had deprived him of the spoils of victory. After this, the Danish government was in no doubt that in Charles XII they faced a formidable opponent, and he was militarily unchallenged by the Danes until after his crushing defeat at the Battle of Poltava in 1709.[5]

## ■ Charles XII's Incursions into Eastern Europe

So far as Frederik IV was concerned, the short, undeclared war in 1700 was a harsh demonstration of the inevitable consequences of underestimating an opponent and of diplomatic miscalculation. He learned the hard way that his young cousin in Sweden was a formidable adversary and that his alliance with Poland and Russia was of little value. Still licking his wounds he decided there was no alternative but to make a fresh start, to pull out of the alliance, and to conclude an agreement with William III and Emperor Leopold for mutual military support in the event of an attack. Frederik agreed to supply the Holy Roman Empire with 8,000 troops for the war against France. With England and the Dutch Republic, he signed a convention in June 1701 for the transfer of eight regiments of cavalry, one of dragoons, and ten of infantry. Of these nineteen regiments, ten were taken into Dutch service and remained there until 1713 with the remainder going into English service.

This brief conflict in 1700 could have marked an end to the Northern War and it would have entered the history books as just another episode in the almost unending conflict between Denmark and Sweden over Holstein-Gottorp, if it had not been for Charles XII who, unlike his father, had no intention of allowing his enemies to live in peace. After being compelled to withdraw from Zealand, he almost immediately embarked at the head of a large expeditionary force to the eastern Baltic to wreak havoc on the other partners in the disintegrating alliance, and the conflict then became a widespread war, which was something the coalition had always hoped and planned for. The ensuing military campaign in eastern Europe caused long-lasting changes to the balance of power in the entire Baltic region and, in particular, to the relative strengths of Denmark and Sweden.

For many years, Charles XII's long drawn-out campaign was an unqualified success and the young monarch became known as a brilliant military commander with an army that was almost invincible. From 1700 to 1706, in a series of engagements, he first of all defeated the Russians, thereby forcing Peter the Great to retreat from the Baltic coast—at least for the time being. He then set about Poland where King Augustus was first removed from the throne and then, in 1706 after further defeats in Saxony, was forced to agree to humiliating peace terms and to withdraw from the alliance with Russia. By 1706-07, Charles XII was the supreme military leader in the region, with a reputation throughout Europe as an indomitable warrior.[6]

For a short period at this time it seemed that the war in eastern Europe and the War of the Spanish Succession could become a single widespread conflict. Both sides in the Spanish war were eager to secure the support of the Swedish king, but he believed that Swedish interests were not threatened in any way by the conflict in western Europe; nor was he concerned to conclude a peace agreement, even on

the favourable terms that were offered by his enemies. The preceding years had convinced him that he was in his element on the battlefield.

There was also a problem with Russia in that, although it had suffered a setback, it had not been defeated and remained a threat in the Baltic. Charles was eager to remove that threat and, in 1708, at the head of an army of 40,000 battle-hardened troops, he invaded Russia with the ultimate objective of capturing Moscow. However, things did not go quite according to plan. In fact, his overambition led to a catastrophic defeat at Poltava in July 1709—a defeat that almost brought an end to the Swedish military presence in eastern Europe. King Charles fled over the border to the Ottoman Empire, to Bender in Moldavia, where he remained for more than five years, increasingly under a form of house arrest. Throughout this long period he was effectively out of the picture and the stage was left to the original parties in the alliance against Sweden—Peter the Great of Russia, Augustus of Saxony, who after the Swedish defeat at Poltava had been restored to the Polish throne, and Frederik IV of Denmark.

## ■ Danish Military Rearmament, 1700-09

After his humiliation in 1700, Frederik began to reinforce Denmark and Norway's army in anticipation of a final confrontation with Sweden, a confrontation that most regarded as inevitable. In 1701, he established a permanent militia—a standing army conscripted from the large estates—and this immediately increased his existing army of about 20,000 men by 16,000. His main reason for doing so was the appalling military weakness in Zealand which had been exposed during the short war of 1700 when Charles XII had enjoyed almost complete freedom of movement close to the Danish capital. There could be no repetition of that debacle and the new militia was intended primarily for local defence but, when fully trained, could also become part of the regular army. Their lack of experience and limited training meant that they would never be the equal of regular soldiers on the battlefield; nevertheless, the militia served with honour and was an important reserve force in the Great Northern War.[7]

In this way, and through a number of other military reforms during the first decade of the eighteenth century, Denmark became one of the most militarised countries in Europe. Its total force of 70,000 men when the country re-entered the war against Sweden in 1709 was equalled only by Brandenburg and Sweden. Military costs during those years of peace amounted to at least half the total government expenditure, and in the ensuing time of war they reached about 80 per cent. It was a state of affairs that, as early as 1694, prompted the English diplomat Robert Molesworth to liken the autocratic Danish society to 'a monster that is all head and no body, all soldiers and no subjects.'[8] This level of militarisation was tangible evidence of Denmark's permanent rivalry with Sweden, and a clear indication that the Danes believed a final confrontation with Charles XII was inevitable.

In 1708-09, this military rearmament was followed by renewed diplomatic efforts to breathe new life into the alliance of 1700. When Charles XII attacked Russia, Peter the Great implored his former coalition partners to help in what was a desperate situation, but neither Denmark nor Saxony was prepared to respond immediately. To some extent they wanted a clear idea of the likely outcome of the Swedish offensive, but they were also concerned about the possible reaction of the western powers to this renewed outbreak of war, having in mind their recent intervention to the advantage of Sweden.

From the point of view of England and the Dutch Republic, however, the situation in 1708-09 was very different from that in 1700. Together with Emperor Joseph I, they were now in the middle of a decisive war with Louis XIV, and Charles XII's invasion of Russia removed the risk of Sweden entering that war on the side of France. They were therefore inclined to support Denmark and Saxony, in the belief that this would not necessarily provoke a military response from Sweden. Furthermore, Russia's emergence as a Baltic power—made evident by the foundation of Saint Petersburg and the naval base at Kronstadt in 1703—meant that, in their opinion, Russia had become an important factor in the European political arena. For that reason alone, there were limits to the Maritime Powers' willingness to act against Russian interests, the foremost of which, in 1708-09, was to involve Denmark and Saxony in the struggle against Charles XII. Consequently the attitude of England and the Dutch Republic was to maintain the status quo in the Baltic because of their mercantile interests, but a revival of the alliance between Russia, Saxony, and Denmark against Sweden would be less of a provocation than in 1700 and, in fact, it would be rather welcome.

This mild approval became strong support with the news of Charles XII's comprehensive defeat at Poltava in July 1709. This was regarded throughout Europe as the beginning of the end for Sweden as a great power and, as a result, Swedish interests were no longer of great importance. With the full support of the Maritime Powers and the Holy Roman Empire, the earlier alliance between Denmark, Saxony, and Russia against Sweden was revived in the late summer of 1709; and to avoid any possible conflict with the anti-French coalition, Denmark and Saxony issued a joint declaration that they would not interfere with Swedish interests in northern Germany and Holstein-Gottorp, provided those areas were not used as bases for Swedish aggression. For some time at least, the coalition forces ranged against France secured a degree of calm to their rear during the last confrontation with Louis XIV, and the scene was now set for a combined Danish, Saxon and Russian attack on the Swedish heartland and a final reckoning with a fading power. From his exile in Moldavia, Charles XII was a powerless bystander as his disastrous policy of expansion was reduced to a struggle for the survival of his Swedish empire.[9]

### ■ The Unsuccessful Invasion of Skåne, 1709-10

The main objective of the alliance, which was shared by all the partners, was to 'contribute towards Sweden's burial,' as it was delicately expressed during the course of their negotiations. Russia would do so by invading Finland and the Swedish possessions in the eastern Baltic, and Augustus of Saxony would seek to regain control over Poland. A declaration of neutrality by the Swedish dominions in northern Germany forestalled an attack on Holstein-Gottorp, at least for the present, and so Frederik IV planned a direct attack on the Swedish heartland.

After years of military rearmament, the Danish king felt able to risk a trial of strength; but there seems little doubt that the deciding factor was a strong feeling that, if Denmark was ever to face Sweden on the battlefield, this was the right moment. After Poltava, Sweden was militarily weakened as never before. Russia was on the charge in the east and, since 1703, had emerged as a powerful force in the Baltic region. The western powers, normally so inclined to intervene, were for the time being fully occupied elsewhere and, if their war with France came to an end, there was no way of knowing how they would react to an attack on Sweden. Taken together, it was a unique opportunity to exact revenge for years of humiliation by the Swedes, and possibly even to recover former Danish territory on the other side of the Sound. The conclusion reached by the king was expressed very clearly on the supply wagons that subsequently rolled into Skåne with the Danish invasion force after the declaration of war on 28 October 1709. On the tailboard of the wagons was painted '*aut nunc, aut nunquam*'—now or never.

The Danish operation plan for the invasion of Sweden was formulated in strict accordance with agreements that had been made with Saxony during the summer, and it respected the undertakings that had been given to the anti-French coalition not to mount any attacks in northern Germany. The intention was that Norwegian troops would cross the Norwegian-Swedish border and strike at the heart of Sweden. At the same time, a Danish expeditionary force would land on the coast of Skåne in southern Sweden with the objective of retaking the former Danish possessions.

On 12 November a Danish invasion force of 15,000 men landed on the coast of Skåne at the little fishing village of Råå to the south of Helsingborg. At first everything went according to plan—the Swedish defence forces retreated from Skåne and, in a few months, it was totally in the hands of the Danish army.

However, as early as January 1710, the situation changed dramatically. The Norwegian advance was delayed because of poor leadership and inadequate planning, and the Swedish commander-in-chief, General Magnus Stenbock, had sufficient time to get reinforcements and, from central Sweden, to mount a counter-attack against the Danish army in Skåne. During February 1710, he completely outmanoeuvred the occupation forces, which then retreated to the area around Helsingborg. It was there, on 10 March 1710, that the last decisive battle over Skåne took place, and it ended in a total defeat for the Danes. During the following days, Frederik IV's surviving soldiers retreated from the whole of Skåne and they never returned. The Danish attempt to recapture the lost provinces had gone horribly wrong and, quite clearly, the answer to the slogan on the supply wagons at the start of the campaign was '*nunquam*'—never, so far as the recovery of Skåne was concerned. It was some small comfort that the remnants of the Danish army managed to return to Zealand without substantial loss.[10]

For Denmark, the first phase of the renewed war against Sweden had been an unmitigated disaster. The Danes had optimistically expected that Sweden would be defeated on the home front at a time when their king was at a safe distance in the Ottoman Empire. But this hope was crushed by a combination of Swedish tactics and Danish military incompetence.

However, the Danish invasion did divert large Swedish forces from elsewhere, to the advantage of the Russian tsar, who seized the opportunity to consolidate his control over the former Swedish provinces to the south of the Gulfs of Riga and Finland and at the same time, to advance north of the latter. The regions adjoining the Gulf of Finland thereby came under the total control of Russia, not only removing an important cornerstone in the Swedish overseas dominions, but also finally establishing Russia's new status as a Baltic power.

Denmark was paralysed and sombre after a campaign that had begun with great expectations and ended in disaster. If Sweden had not been so stretched, its military commanders would almost certainly have kept to their usual practice and followed their success with a counter-attack. But they were prevented from doing so by an outbreak of bubonic plague in the nordic region in 1710 which claimed the lives of many soldiers and civilians. In Copenhagen alone, this last major outbreak of the plague in the area caused the deaths of about one-third of the inhabitants. In these circumstances, there could be no Swedish counter-offensive, nor could there be any question of a renewed invasion of Skåne by the Danes—an uphill task that, in any event, had proved to be beyond their ability. The remainder of 1710 was therefore a time of military calm, during which the Danes gathered strength and prepared a new offensive against Sweden. Their focus shifted to northern Germany, where, in 1711, the next act in this long struggle between nations took place.

### ■ The War in Northern Germany, 1711-16

As we have seen, when the alliance was revived in 1709, Denmark and its allies gave an undertaking not to interfere with Swedish interests in northern Germany. That guarantee was followed, in 1710, by a declaration of neutrality by those provinces—a declaration that was underwritten by the emperor, the western powers, Prussia, Hanover, and, subsequently, by Saxony and Russia. The signatories guaranteed the neutrality of these Swedish territories, provided they were not involved in Swedish military operations. The attraction of this declaration, from the point of view of the anti-French coalition, was that it would secure calm in north Germany during the last phase of the war against France.

However, when the declaration was presented to Charles XII in Bender, he flatly refused to sign. In his opinion it would ruin his ambitious plan for a two-pronged attack on Poland, from Turkey and Swedish Pomerania, which he hoped to put into effect with the support of the Ottoman Sultan Ahmed III. This blunt refusal put Charles at loggerheads with his earlier allies in western Europe, and their reaction was to let it be known that they would show great forbearance towards Sweden's enemies and that they would not interfere if Denmark and its allies encroached on the Swedish possessions in north Germany. With that assurance, Denmark, Saxony, Poland and Russia felt free to mount an offensive.[11]

In 1711, with the wind in this new direction, the allies embarked on their next joint attack, which, on this occasion, was directed against the Swedish provinces of Pomerania and Rügen. Final agreement for the attack was reached in June. In July, a Danish army was mobilised in Holstein. Led by Frederik IV, it crossed the border into Mecklenburg on 9 August, on the way to Swedish Pomerania, where, together with forces from Saxony and Russia, it began a long siege of the garrison at Stralsund.

This stalemate continued for the remainder of the year but, in 1712, the campaign became rather more eventful in terms of gains and losses.

In the summer of 1712, Danish forces invaded Bremen-Verden. After the defeat of the Swedish garrison, the province remained under Danish occupation until 1715 when, in accordance with an agreement between Frederik IV and George I of Great Britain and Hanover, it was handed over to Hanover on payment of 30,000 Reichstaler and a British-Hanoverian acknowledgement of the Danish king's sovereignty over the whole of Schleswig, including Gottorp. In the long term, and from the Danish point of view, this was the most important achievement of the war: it offered a permanent solution to the problem of Gottorp, a problem that for many years had endangered Denmark's security. Another important development in 1712, which also had long-term consequences, was the re-appearance in north Germany of General Magnus Stenbock, who had led the Swedish army to victory at Helsingborg in 1710.

With some reluctance, but on the direct orders of his king, who was still in Moldavia, Stenbock landed at Rügen in September 1712 at the head of a formidable Swedish army. His objective was to relieve the besieged garrison at Stralsund and to secure the Swedish province of Pomerania as a stepping-stone for an invasion of Poland, which was one of the key elements in Charles XII's grand design for a joint Swedish-Turkish attack on Poland and Russia. However, that plan soon became unworkable. Charles never obtained the Turkish support that he had expected and, at the same time, most of the sea-borne supplies for Stenbock's expeditionary force were lost in a series of engagements with a superior Danish navy which had effectively blockaded supply lines from Sweden. Stenbock's situation under siege at Stralsund was fast becoming desperate. He was forced to act and, in a classic Swedish manoeuvre, chose to go on the offensive.

The campaign directed against Poland, as originally planned, was no longer feasible. Stenbock therefore decided he would defeat his enemies one by one, starting with the weakest. For that reason he directed his forces towards the west, where the Danish army was based, and hoped that the armies of Russia and Saxony would stay put. He also believed that the area towards Hamburg was the best location for obtaining supplies for his hard-pressed troops. By adopting this course of action, Stenbock was disobeying orders from his king and, not surprisingly perhaps, incurred the royal displeasure, a situation that persisted until his death in 1717. But he acted out of necessity and, at the time, there were very few viable alternatives.

And so, on 1 November 1716, at the head of an army of 16,000 men and under the nose of the besieging forces, he broke out of Stralsund and headed to the west. At that time the main force of the Danish army was positioned in the area around Hamburg but when Frederik IV heard that Stenbock was advancing, he immediately turned towards him with the intention of intercepting the Swedes as far to the east as possible. At the same time he persuaded his allies to join up with the Danish army at the small town of Gadebusch to the south of Wismar. Stenbock's plan to defeat his enemies one by one was therefore stillborn.

The first large engagement between the opposing forces took place at Gadebusch on 20 December 1712, when Stenbock, by the skilful use of his field artillery, narrow-

ly defeated a larger Danish-Saxon army and the Danes, having suffered considerable losses, retreated to the west. However, Stenbock's victory at Gadebusch was the last in the long string of military successes that had so characterised the Swedish era as a great power. It was also a Pyrrhic victory in that it led directly to the destruction, one year later, of Stenbock's army—the last outstanding Swedish military force on the continent.

Yet, this victory at Gadebusch encouraged Stenbock to pursue the Danish army into Holstein because he assumed that the alliance forces had been so weakened that Russia and Saxony would not come to the aid of the Danes. He was quite wrong. Frederik IV was again able to persuade his allies to pursue Stenbock, who, with no possibility of defeating his enemies separately, fell into a trap. The allied armies forced him further and further to the west and, from 14 February 1713, his army was encircled at the duke of Holstein-Gottorp's stronghold at Tönning, by the mouth of the river Eider, where, on 16 May 1713, after a three-month siege, he and his entire army surrendered. Stenbock remained a Danish prisoner until his death in 1717, and the dukedom of Holstein-Gottorp was once again occupied by Danish forces.

So far as Sweden was concerned, Stenbock's capitulation was a disaster of nearly the same magnitude as the defeat at Poltava. It meant an end to Sweden's long military presence in north Germany, although Wismar did not fall until 1715 and the garrison at Stralsund survived until 1716. The fate of the former Swedish possessions was thereafter in the hands of Denmark, Prussia, and Hanover, the latter being united since 1714 with Great Britain through George I. For Denmark, the

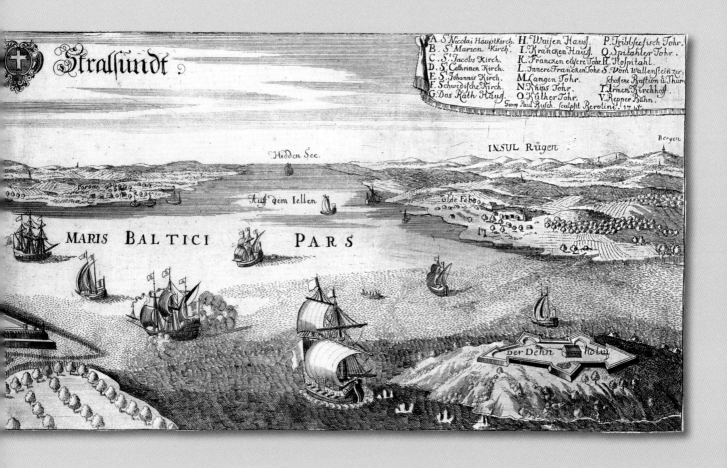

The city of Stralsund.

*Engraving by Georg Paul Busch (d. 1756), 1715. Sächsische Landesbibliothek Kartensammlung, Dresden, Germany.*

Swedish capitulation was much needed retribution for the defeats at Helsingborg and Gadebusch, both of which had been orchestrated by Stenbock. At the same time, and at long last, Holstein-Gottorp was divested of the Swedish support that had been the underlying reason for the disproportionate influence of the duke.

The only remaining Swedish stronghold on the continent was the heavily defended garrison at Stralsund. That was also on the point of collapse when, on 22 November 1714, Charles XII unexpectedly appeared after a breathtaking ride of 16 days across Europe from his place of exile in Moldavia. He had hoped that his presence would rally the defence forces and, characteristically, his original intention had been to go on the offensive. However, his plan came to naught because, in the meantime, the Danish navy had become all-powerful in the Baltic, Stralsund was cut off from Sweden and Charles was without supplies. The garrison's defeat was therefore only a matter of time.

The critical moment came on 15 and 16 November 1715, when a combined expeditionary force from Denmark and Saxony captured Rügen from the seaward side after a bitter struggle in which the Swedish forces were led by Charles himself. Stralsund was thereby deprived of its hinterland and, totally cut off from the outside world, the garrison was inevitably close to collapse. For the allies, the greatest prize would have been the capture of the Swedish king, thereby bringing an end to his activities. A considerable prize was offered for his capture—10,000 Reichstaler and 'unlimited preferment'—but, once again, Charles XII was underestimated.

During the night of 21 and 22 December 1715, despite the Danish blockade, he managed to escape across the Baltic in a small boat and, on the morning of 24 December, he set foot on Sweden at the fishing village of Skåre after an absence of 15 years. To some extent, Charles XII's dramatic flight from Stralsund symbolised Sweden's banishment from the continent. Stralsund capitulated shortly afterwards and the long drawn-out war entered its last phase when it moved to Scandinavia and, in particular, to the Norwegian-Swedish border region, where the last of the Swedish kings to lead his troops in battle finally met his end.

## ■ The Final Act: Norway, 1716-18

The last phase of the war was hastened by the western powers' growing desire for peace. After the War of the Spanish Succession was brought to a close in 1713, they were eager to see an end to the conflict in the Baltic region. Britain and the Dutch Republic were particularly concerned about Russian expansion in the eastern Baltic, which threatened their long-established naval supremacy in the area. In 1717, this led Britain to declare war on Sweden. This was followed by a dramatic increase in British and Dutch naval activity in the Baltic.

At the same time, after years of cooperation, the anti-Swedish coalition began to fall apart as the partners in that alliance increasingly pursued their separate political interests. Russia was eager to strengthen its hold on the territories it had gained in the Gulf of Finland and, given certain concessions, it was increasingly willing to conclude a separate peace agreement with Sweden. With growing support from Great Britain, Denmark wanted an end to the war and to exchange its territorial gains for some form of permanent security on its southern border. Although Augustus II of Poland-Saxony tended to sympathise with Denmark and Great Britain, he felt so threatened by the proximity of Russia that he maintained a diplomatic silence.

These splits in the alliance first began to appear in the summer of 1716 when a planned invasion of Skåne by combined forces from Denmark and Russia came to nothing when, at the last moment, the tsar withdrew Russian military support because there had been an unexpected breakthrough in highly confidential negotiations he was conducting with Sweden which were aimed at achieving a separate peace deal. Under the terms of that agreement, the tsar would have provided support for a Swedish invasion of Norway in return for Sweden's renunciation of any claims to its former Baltic provinces. In addition, the tsar had indicated a willingness to remove Augustus II from the Polish throne in return for territorial gains in Poland.[12]

But this devious plan foundered when it was presented to Charles XII for approval because, with his usual obstinacy, he flatly refused to relinquish his claims to what was left of his overseas territories. To some extent this was because of his natural reluctance to negotiate from a position of weakness. A more important consideration was his understanding that a surrender of those territories would set the seal on Sweden's decline from a major power to a minor state, which would have been quite unacceptable to him. Rather than concluding an agreement with Russia, he decided, very typically, on an immediate and unilateral invasion of Norway. He had recovered strength since his escape from northern Germany; the negotiations with Russia had clearly demonstrated the fragility of the alliance opposed to Sweden; and he was thereby encouraged to throw his forces at Norway as some compensation for all that had been lost. And so, in the closing years of the war, the conflict moved to Norway which, until that time, had been relatively calm, not least because most of the troops from both sides in the conflict had been active in north Germany.

Charles XII's first attempt to invade Norway was in 1716 when, at the head of a hastily mobilised army, he crossed into the southern part of the country and in no time reached Christiania, although the city's main fortress, Akershus Castle, did not fall. Danish reinforcements for the beleaguered city eventually arrived; Swedish supply lines were overstretched because of poor logistical planning; and Charles was forced to retreat to the area around the border fortress of Fredriksten, which was still in the hands of the Norwegians. Fredriksten and the adjoining town of Fredrikshald were the key to control over southern Norway, and the Swedes began a methodical siege. It was short-lived, however, because the Danish navy effectively cut the sea-borne supply route from Gothenburg and Charles had no alternative but to withdraw to Sweden. Perhaps he understood that, on this occasion, he had been badly prepared and too fast off the mark.

The new campaign in Norway, and thereby the final chapter in what had become an interminable war, began in the autumn of 1718 when Charles XII was better prepared and more conscious of the strength of the opposing forces. His plan was based on a large-scale pincer movement that would force Norway into submission. The south and the more northerly regions would be attacked simultaneously by overwhelming Swedish forces. The king would lead the southern army, which would advance on Christiania via Fredriksten. The northern army, under the command of an experienced general, Carl Gustaf Armfelt, would advance across the Swedish-Norwegian border and capture the region of Trøndelag and its capital, Trondheim. This northern campaign began in September 1718, and Armfelt met only light resistance. With little difficulty he advanced to the area around Trondheim but, at that point, his army came to a halt because of the habitual problems with supply lines.[13]

The southern army began its invasion somewhat later but, in November, the Norwegian border defences were put to rout and the Swedes resumed the siege of Fredriksten, which they had abandoned two years earlier. However, this turned out to be Charles's last military act because, during the evening of 11 December, he decided to carry out an inspection of some new military installations and, while crawling from a trench, was shot in the head. He died instantly, meeting his end on the battlefield, which was where he had spent so much of his 36-year lifetime. It has never been established beyond doubt that the bullet was fired from the Norwegian garrison or from within his own lines.[14]

Just as his grandfather's sudden death in 1660 led to a speedy resolution of a previous conflict between Sweden and Denmark, Charles XII's violent end led to the immediate collapse of the Swedish offensive. The southern army began to withdraw and when the news of the king's death reached the northern army, it followed suit. As those overstretched and undersupplied soldiers retreated through the mountains and the valley of Gudbrandsdalen on their way to Jämtland in Sweden, they were met by the most frightful blizzard. It persisted for three days and cost more Swedish lives than the entire campaign. During that retreat 4,000 men from a total force of 5,000 died from the cold, from hunger, and from sheer exhaustion. It was, of course, a military tragedy and, in a macabre way, also symbolised the sudden and final collapse of the Swedish Empire.

## ■ Peace at Long Last

Charles XII, with his boundless energy, had been the driving force behind the many military encounters that occurred during the final years of the Swedish Empire and, with his death, there was no longer the motivation to continue hostilities. The empire was in a state of collapse, and the Swedish populace was demoralised by the many heavy burdens that the fighting had caused. There was an urgent desire for peace, not just in Sweden, but also amongst her enemies, including Denmark and Norway which had been in a constant state of war for about ten years.

The final peace agreement was signed at Frederiksborg Castle in north Zealand on 14 July 1720. It was largely the outcome of British diplomatic mediation, as is evident from the extent to which the British interest of establishing a counter-balance to Russian expansion in the Baltic was accommodated. The peace terms were not entirely what the Danish government might have hoped for—particularly in the aftermath of recent military success – but they did reflect what was politically possible at the time.[15]

There was no provision for any Danish territorial gains, and absolutely no question of the former Danish provinces in Skåne being returned because, so far as the western sea powers were concerned, the ideal outcome was for the Sound to be bordered by two different countries. Denmark was required to return those lands it had captured—in other words, Rügen, part of Pomerania, Wismar, and Marstrand—and, as compensation, was awarded 600,000 Reichstaler. Sweden had to give an undertaking not to assist Holstein-Gottorp in any way that would harm Danish interests—an important concession to Denmark's security. Sweden was also compelled to relinquish its right to free passage of the Sound, which was exactly what the British wanted because they had no wish to trade on unequal terms in the Baltic. Finally, Great Britain and France guaranteed the Danish monarchy's unqualified rights to the duchy of Schleswig, while the remaining southern part of Holstein-Gottorp was restored to the duke.

Apart from Denmark's understandable regret that it did not secure one of its most important objectives in the war—the return of the provinces in Skåne— the overall outcome was not unsatisfactory from the Danish point of view. Denmark's other main objective—the severance of links between Sweden and Holstein-Gottorp—was achieved. As mentioned earlier, the Danish king had relinquished his ancestral rights to Bremen and Verden to the benefit of Hanover but the feudal chaos in the duchies had been set to rights, and Denmark's southern border at the river Eider was more secure than at any time in the past. On the whole, it was a strong basis for a lasting peace.

Of no less importance from a Danish perspective was that the war had reduced Sweden from a major threat to a nation similar in strength to Denmark-Norway. The balance of power in the north was thereby restored, with all that this conferred in terms of better security. Thereafter, that balance could only be adversely affected by

Russia, and on this one issue the former archenemies were united. In the long term, the peace accord after the Great Northern War transformed Denmark and Sweden from long-standing adversaries to peaceful allies, with a joint interest so far as Russia, the new Baltic power, was concerned. This placid coexistence is something that has characterised the nordic countries for the last few centuries and, in many respects, the foundations were laid with the peace accord in 1720, which finally brought an end to the aggressive appetite for expansion exemplified by the Swedish warrior kings.

## ■ Charles XII and Denmark-Norway

Charles XII succeeded to the throne of a great military power, a power that had been gradually and methodically strengthened by his immediate predecessors, not least through his father's internal reforms and shrewd diplomacy. At the time of his accession, in 1697, the Swedish Empire had reached its fulfilment, but its strength was insecure, as became clear when, from 1700, those nations that had lost territory to Sweden over the course of time began to join forces in order to overthrow their common enemy.

Charles XII's response to that threat was the only course of action he understood—the exercise of military power. His apparent conviction that there was no other way to safeguard his empire led him to embark on an endless series of military conflicts, collectively known as the Great Northern War, in which Sweden was almost invariably the aggressor. This uncompromising approach, and the reckless nature of many of these campaigns, led to impossible military adventures in Poland and Russia which proved to be completely beyond Sweden's military capability and drained Sweden of resources. As a consequence, Charles XII hastened the decline and fall of Sweden as a great power. Given that empire's underlying weaknesses, it was inevitable that, sooner or later, it would have collapsed in any event. However, the fact that this defeat was so complete and so sudden must be attributed to Charles and his ill-conceived attitude of all-or-nothing. He strained after everything with restless energy, but ended with nothing.[16]

In one sense, Charles XII was a blessing in disguise for Denmark-Norway. Since the second half of the seventeenth century, Sweden's emergence as a major power represented the greatest threat to the twin monarchy and, for a short time in 1660, it could well have become part of a large Swedish Empire. Charles XII's belligerence at the beginning of the eighteenth century more than suggests that this remained a Swedish ambition, and it was not abandoned until he overplayed his cards in the ensuing conflicts and lost. It was only then that relations between Denmark-Norway and Sweden could be put on a normal footing, and the relationship gradually became one of peaceful coexistence to the benefit of both nations. Although that transition was to a very limited extent a result of Denmark's strengths and statesmanship, it had much more to do with the fact that the international situation during these years was favourable to Denmark. When all is said and done, it was also Denmark's good fortune that, at the critical time, Sweden was ruled by an autocratic young monarch who was politically tone-deaf and who would only listen to the sound of the cannon.

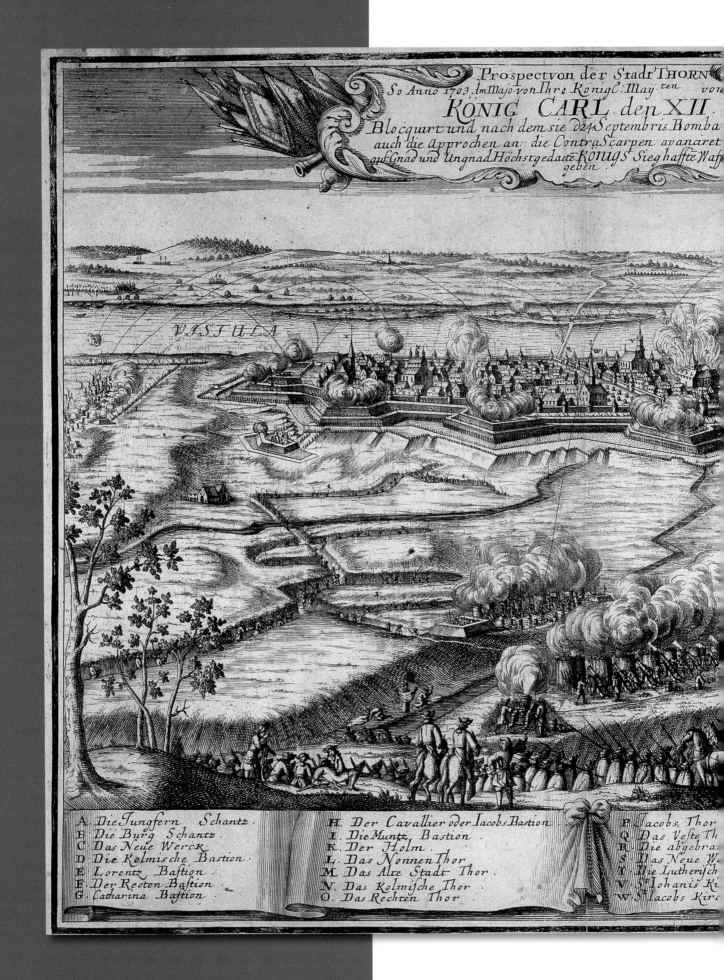

Prospect von der Stadt THORN
So Anno 1703, im Majo von Ihre Königl: May ten voi
KÖNIG CARL den XII.
Blocquirt und nach dem sie d24 Septembris Bomba
auch die Approchen an:: die Contra Scarpen avanciret
auf Gnad und Ungnad Höchstgedacte KÖNIGS Sieg haffte Waf
geben.

VISTULA

A. Die Jungfern Schantz.
B. Die Burg Schantz.
C. Das Neue Werck.
D. Die Kolmische Bastion.
E. Lorentz Bastion.
F. Der Rechten Bastion.
G. Catharina Bastion.

H. Der Cavallier oder Jacobs Bastion
I. Die Muntz Bastion.
K. Der Holm.
L. Das Nonnen Thor.
M. Das Alte Stadt Thor.
N. Das Kolmische Thor.
O. Das Rechten Thor.

P. Jacobs Thor
Q. Das Veste Th
R. Die abgebra
S. Das Neue W
T. Die Lutherisch
V. Johanis Ki
W. Jacobs Kirc

en
beschoße
Octobr

FLUVIUS

X. Die Dominicaner Kirch.
y. St. Catharina Kirch.
z. Das Rahthaus so unter der Bombardi-
   rung gantzlich zu aschen gemacht.
1. Die Schwedische Approchen.
2. Die Batterien.
3. Die Mortiers.

## CHAPTER 15

# A Polish View of Charles XII and the Great Northern War

by Gabriela Majewska

*The 1703 siege of Toruń, from 'Prospect von der Studt THORN So Anno 1703 im Majo von Ihro Königl. Mayten von schweden KÖNIG CARL den XII blocquirt [...]'.*

*Engraving by John Lithen, ca. 1706. Muzeum Okręgowe w Toruniu, Toruń, Poland.*

Baltic politics, and in particular the question of Livonia, became one of the fundamental problems of the union between the Polish-Lithuanian Commonwealth and Saxony, formed in 1697 when Friedrich August Wettin, Elector of Saxony, acceded to the Polish throne as Augustus II. The politics of Poland's new monarch had extensive dynastic objectives: protecting the territories of Poland-Lithuania from foreign interference, recovering Livonia, and making the Polish throne hereditary for the House of Wettin while also strengthening the position of the monarch. And there were economic objectives as well: pursuing independent commercial policies and extending control of overland transit trade between the east and the west. These objectives were linked to Augustus II's military expansiveness aimed at gaining a firm foothold on the Black Sea and Baltic coasts: in Livonia and Estonia. The pursuit of these plans implied the inevitable prospect of conflict with Sweden and Turkey. War with Turkey was averted—a treaty signed in January 1699 bringing to an end years of struggle against the Ottoman Empire. The plan to reclaim Livonia remained in place, and with it hopes of establishing a rival on the eastern Baltic coast to counter Gdańsk's monopoly on Baltic commerce. Creating conditions for trade in agricultural produce would also undermine competition in this market from Sweden.[1] The Saxon court contemplated the possibility of swapping membership of the Holy League for participation in a league of northern states. Augustus II's plans resulted in a network of alliances (with Denmark in March 1698 and September 1699; with Russia in November 1699, confirmed in February 1701; and with Brandenburg in February 1700), which evolved into an anti-Swedish coalition known as the Northern League. Its aim was to divide up Sweden's lands. Augustus II wanted to conquer Livonia.[2] At the same time, the Polish monarch attempted to take a stand on the War of the Spanish Succession. He held talks regarding cooperation with Louis XIV, while simultaneously pledging to side with the *Reich* against France. What is more, his main preoccupation was actually war with Sweden, making the chances of his involvement in the war in the west even less likely. When these events came to light they worsened opinions in Europe about Augustus II. The virtues of the Polish king as an ally were widely questioned.[3] Charles XII, Peter I, and Emperor Joseph I would accuse him repeatedly of duplicity, hypocrisy, and a lack of credibility.

### ■ Poland-Lithuania in the Face of the Great Northern War and Charles XII

The Wettin court's plans for war did not gain sufficient support either in Saxony or in the Polish-Lithuanian Commonwealth. Each attempt to increase the king's authority and restrict the nobility's privileges met with strong opposition from the magnates and their obedient nobles. The vast majority of nobles did not condone war with Sweden and feared it—memories of the losses and destruction inflicted by the Deluge (the Swedish-Polish conflict of 1655-60) were still fresh in people's minds. Augustus II also defied his election promise of reclaiming lost lands, failing to win over Polish politicians, led by Cardinal Michał Radziejowski, to the idea of a war over Livonia. The nobility's thoughts were preoccupied with the left bank of the Dnieper River and the recovery of those lands in the Ukraine that Poland had lost to Russia when the Truce of Andrusovo had been signed in 1667.[4]

The initiator and perpetrator of the war was undoubtedly—as stated by Jacek Staszewski, biographer of Augustus II—the king of Poland and elector of Saxony. Augustus II intended to wage an 'easy war,' but the consequences of his decisions were among the causes of the conflict known as the Great Northern War. According to Staszewski, its course was affected by mistakes made in planning the war campaign and by other errors on the part of Poland's monarch. It was a mistake to rely on the help of the Sapieha clan or their opponents in Lithuania, and to believe the assurances of Johann Reinhold Patkul, head of the Livonian nobility, that Riga could be captured by surprise after the popular uprising that would ensue in Livonia once it became known that the armies of the king of Poland had crossed the river Daugava. Help from the Lithuanians proved to be illusory; Riga was not captured. Errors were made by signing agreements with third countries and by accepting commitments concerning war or peace without the knowledge and consent of representatives from the countries ruled by Augustus II.[5]

The Great Northern War occupied the period from 1700 to 1719 in the history of the Polish-Lithuanian Commonwealth. It can be divided into three main phases. The first played out during 1700-03, when Swedish successes against the armies of Augustus II were accompanied by an escalating internal crisis which sowed the seeds of civil war. The second phase, 1704-09, was a period of chaos caused by military action, civil war and its attendant lawlessness, the collapse of central and regional state structures, the dethronement of the rightful king, the coronation of a new ruler, and, additionally, an outbreak of the plague. The third phase took place during 1710-19, when military operations in Poland were coming to an end, but the Commonwealth was bearing the burden of their huge cost and Augustus II, having been returned to the throne, was using the armies of Saxony to try to implement reforms that would strengthen his rule. This was the period when the Commonwealth became subject to Russian protection and interference. The end date of the war is defined by the withdrawal of Russian troops.[6]

Theoretically, at the beginning of the eighteenth century Poland-Lithuania was still the leading power in central-eastern Europe; in reality the Commonwealth was in a state of profound crisis. This political crisis coincided with a demise in the art of Polish warfare. As pointed out by a military historian, at the time of the Swedish invasion the Polish-Lithuanian army had only 18,500 soldiers and the Saxon army 20,000, whereas at the end of 1700 the Swedish army numbered around 87,000.[7] By the late seventeenth century, the crisis had become apparent in the Polish army's high command and among its officer corps. Poland's army commanders feared fighting a pitched battle against the enemy. When the time came, they favoured defensive military action. The crisis in the upper ranks resulted in poorer training for soldiers, a collapse in morale, and a loss of faith in victory.[8] Augustus II could not rely on help from Saxony in fight-

ing Charles XII. Recruitment there met with passive resistance from the target population and from the authorities who were meant to carry out this task. Hence, fearing the loss of his own soldiers, the king avoided clashes in the field, opting for a 'war of pursuit,' in which he compelled the enemy to chase his army, thus exhausting the opposition and depriving them of supplies, which were used up by the king's troops. Although this system of warfare depleted both forces, it was usually the local populations of the places through which the armies passed, that suffered most acutely.[9]

The outbreak of the Northern War began with the Saxon army entering Livonia in February 1700, but the Commonwealth only became an active theatre of operations in 1701, when the armies of Charles XII crossed the borders of Courland, placing the country in a new situation. At that point, it became apparent that Charles would pursue Augustus on Polish territory. Meanwhile, the Commonwealth was not prepared for war. The army was small and lack of funds prevented any rapid mobilisation of troops. Even worse was the internal split caused by Augustus II's policies. Those opposed to the king were prepared to embroil the country in war and negotiate with Charles XII, urging him to intervene in the internal affairs of the Commonwealth, hoping that the hated monarch would be overthrown.[10]

Up until November 1700, the most important factor in the war was the rivalry between the Sapieha clan and their opponents in Lithuania over which of the groups would support the king. The Lithuanian noble levy summoned by the commanders of the anti-Sapieha movement defeated the Sapiehas (November 1700) and engaged in the war against Sweden as allies of Saxony without the knowledge or consent of the Commonwealth.[11] Meanwhile, the victories of Charles XII intensified the resentment and hostility of the nobility in Poland and Lithuania towards Augustus II, which had been suppressed since the Saxon monarch's accession to the throne. The Sapieha clan surrendered themselves to the protection of Charles XII.[12] These events marked an internal collapse in Lithuania and posed a threat to the union with Poland, which did not want war. The Commonwealth was not formally at war with Sweden, though its ruling monarch was engaged in the conflict. In reality, the nature of the military operations, the tactics of the army, and the ways in which it was provisioned made it impossible to maintain neutrality.

Augustus II was prompted to take steps to try to make peace with Sweden after the failure of the Saxon armies in Livonia, including their unsuccessful assault on Riga in September 1700 and their defeat at the Battle of Riga in July 1701,[13] in addition to the Commonwealth's lack of support for the war and Denmark's and Brandenburg's withdrawal from it. Charles XII, however—whose actions were motivated by his desire to break up the relationship between Poland and Saxony because of its potential danger to Sweden—was only willing to enter into talks with the Commonwealth if the Polish king were dethroned. Furthermore, the peace which Augustus was eager to secure did not guarantee that he would not launch another attack on the Swedish army in exchange for Russian

*Portrait of King Augustus II of Poland.*

*Painting by Louis de Silvestre (1675-1760), ca. 1718. Staatliche Kunstsammlungen, Dresden, Germany. © bpk | Staatliche Kunstsammlungen Dresden | Elke Estel | Hans-Peter Klut.*

subsidies.[14] For the implementation of his plans Charles XII was counting on the support of Poles opposed to the Wettin king and also on that of the Sapiehas, who in March 1702 openly chose the Swedish side.[15] Thus, enemies of Augustus II transferred their allegiance to the king of Sweden. Some nobles referred to him as the defender of Polish liberty, a friend of Poland and ally against Russia.[16]

In the autumn of 1702, a meeting of the senate council in Toruń, attended also by representatives of the nobility, voted against dethroning him and for war with Sweden, but when it became clear that Augustus II's plans to fight Charles XII were based on cooperation with Moscow, resentment grew against the king. Nevertheless, the Sejm (the highest authority of the nobility-governed state) convened in Lublin in June-July 1703, ended in success for Augustus, the nobility agreeing to cooperate with Russia to defend the country.[17] Yet, although the king appeared to have gained support, political wrangling escalated and the process of bringing together Augustus's opponents began. Kazimierz Jarochowski, nineteenth-century historian and scholar of the Saxon period, observed that the Commonwealth was capable of defeating Charles XII: with the Poles' united resolve the Swedish king would inevitably have suffered the fate of his grandfather, Charles X Gustav, but this was prevented by the magnates' private interests.[18] The situation was all the more serious as by May 1702 Sweden's armies had captured Warsaw without resistance. Their subsequent defeat of Augustus II at Kliszów and the conquest of Kraków, followed by the capitulation of Toruń in October 1703, demonstrated the extent of the state's impotence. Moreover, the confederation treaty signed by the Wettin king's opponents in July 1703 in Środa Wielkopolska posed a significant threat, not only to his position but to the state's stability as well.[19]

The provisions of this treaty were conducive to Charles XII's plans regarding Augustus II's dethronement, which was proclaimed at a general confederation called in February 1704 in Warsaw. This, however, did not herald the breakthrough that Charles had hoped for. The Warsaw confederates were a minority, acting under Swedish coercion and backed by Swedish bayonets. The act of dethronement provided an opportunity for pro-royal nobles to reassert their support for Augustus, by forming a general confederation in Sandomierz on 30 May 1704 in the king's defence, endorsing the alliance with Russia against Sweden, and declaring all pro-Swedish factions enemies of the state.[20] While this marked a success for the Wettin king, it initiated the disintegration of the nobility's moral foundations. The Warsaw and Sandomierz confederations were to divide the Commonwealth into two camps and spark a civil war that would inflict greater losses than those caused hitherto by the Great Northern War. The fighting would bring with it the collapse of all authority, in particular that of the king, and bring into question the validity of sworn pledges.

After Augustus II had been deposed, the Swedish monarch was eager to have a new king elected as quickly as possible. Out of several candidates, he chose the *wojewoda* (palatine) of Poznań, Stanisław Leszczyński. Charles favoured a submissive candidate whose loyalty and obedience would be guaranteed. The contrast in personality and character between Charles and Leszczyński was aptly highlighted by Kazimierz Jarochowski:

*There may never have been two natures as dissimilar as those of Charles XII and Leszczyński. The first was valiant to the point of madness, seeking out danger, laconic and opposed to all manner of excess and ostentation; the second: a man of peace and counsel, anything but a soldier, eloquent and loquacious, with a fondness for the courtliness and comforts to which Polish magnates of the time were accustomed.*[21]

The nobility's opinion about the selection in July 1704 of Sweden's candidate for the Polish throne is very well conveyed by a contemporary diarist. Erazm Otwinowski wrote that Leszczyński was 'chosen as king of Poland by the king of Sweden and residents of the palatinates of Poznań, Kalisz, Łęczyca, Rawa, Mazovia, and Podlasie compelled by [Swedish] muskets.'[22]

Leszczyński's election provided blatant evidence of the Swedish king's interference in the Commonwealth's internal affairs and sparked numerous protests among the Polish nobility. One of those present in the field where the election took place called out: 'Let us not leave future generations the example of electing a king amidst foreign armed forces, submitting to the will of a foreign power.'[23]

Supporters of Augustus II reacted to Leszczyński's election by signing a treaty with Russia in Narva on 30 August 1704, on the strength of which Poland became an ally of Peter I, on a par with Saxony, and formally entered the war. The Narva treaty drew the Commonwealth into the Great Northern War, but it also halted the process of Lithuania's separation from Poland and violation of the principles of the Polish-Lithuanian union.[24]

The election of the new king failed to meet the expectations of Charles XII and his Polish adherents. The Swedish monarch had wanted it to serve as a means of procuring peace and gaining a level of security before the start of a campaign against Peter I; instead, it embroiled him in a hard-fought battle against Augustus and, according to the historian Jarochowski, an authority on the history of the Saxon period, it became one of the causes of his defeat at Poltava.[25] The Polish nobility who had been involved in the election of the anti-king were counting on an eagerly anticipated end to unrest, bringing with it a peace treaty and an alliance with Sweden in the hope that this would eradicate or reduce the substantial contributions levied on them, the ruthless methods used to exact them, and the Swedish lawlessness in Poland. In contrast, the country was plunged into even greater turmoil, and the looting of Polish property by Swedes continued unabated.[26] King Stanislaw tried to exempt from contributions those loyal to the Swedish king; he also attempted to remonstrate against the doubling of contributions levied by the Swedish General War Commissariat. To no avail. The Swedes relentlessly adhered to the principle that the lands of the Commonwealth had to provide for the upkeep of the Swedish army. In addition, all sides involved in the Northern War continued to apply the tactics of damaging and destroying their opponents' property. Shortly after the election, the armies of Russia marched on Wielkopolska, damaging and destroying the properties of Leszczyński and his followers. Charles XII gave the order to burn down the palace in Puławy which belonged to Hetman Adam Sieniawski, a follower of Augustus II.[27] Henceforth, these methods were used by all those involved in the struggle for the Polish throne: Augustus II, Charles XII, Peter I, and Stanislaw. This led the nobility to pledge their support to whichever contender held the upper hand, but these declarations were largely forced, insincere, transient, and rapidly changing with the arrival of enemy troops.[28] The aim was to try to survive.

By 1705 Swedish rule in Poland was almost nationwide. The peace treaty signed at the end of the year (26 November 1705), which the Poles had longed for, and the resultant alliance between Sweden and the Commonwealth failed to live up to expectations. It laid bare that Poland and Stanislaw Leszczyński were entirely dependent on Charles XII. In addition to numerous economic advantages and privileges for Swedish commerce, the king was granted the right to maintain an army in Poland, and to conduct marches and recruitment. The treaty prohibited the Commonwealth from making any other alliances without Sweden's consent. In short, it threatened the Commonwealth's sovereignty, of which Polish historians have no doubt.[29]

All attempts to defeat Augustus II in Poland proved futile. Wherever he fled from the Swedes new units assembled around him, while resistance in the occupied areas of the country grew. It was for this reason that the Swedish monarch, despite the reservations of his advisers and generals, decided to make a direct strike on Saxony and thus force Augustus into irrevocably abandoning the Polish throne. Augustus was more concerned with protecting Saxony from the ravages of war than he was with retaining the Polish crown and so decided to begin peace negotiations with Charles XII before the Swedish army crossed the borders of the electorate. However, the decision to invade Saxony was made before Augustus's envoys had reached Charles XII.[30] In early September 1706, the Swedes entered the territories of the electorate and by 24 September they had signed a peace treaty in Altranstädt, which was in essence a Swedish diktat. At the behest of the Swedish king, Augustus relinquished the Polish throne, withdrew from the war, and acknowledged Stanislaw Leszczyński as king. Saxony was also to pay high war contributions and agree to the indefinite stay of Swedish forces in its lands.[31] Augustus's approach had been full of ambiguities and angered Peter I. The Wettin king renounced the Polish crown while at the same time assuring Russia of his intentions to remain within the alliance.[32]

After the abdication, Augustus II lost many of his supporters. Representatives of the most powerful magnate families now surrounded Leszczyński, and the nobles at the head of the Confederation of Sandomierz were eager to mend fences with the new king while, of course, retaining their offices and titles. It seemed that Stanislaw, who was willing to compromise and win over his opponents, had an opportunity to effect a reconciliation and be the focal point for the splintered Commonwealth. Standing in his way, however, was Charles XII's resolve to defeat his adversaries in a decisive manner. The central authorities of Poland and Lithuania were taken over by supporters of King Stanislaw with the Swedish monarch's backing.[33] Thus Stanislaw lost his best opportunity of getting the nobility on his side.

After Altranstädt, Stanislaw gained a stronger position in Poland, though this did not alter the balance of his relationship with Charles XII to one of greater equality. The nobility still regarded Leszczyński as an imposed king sustained by a foreign ruler, and a Lutheran at that.[34] His demeanour towards the Swedes received a very negative appraisal from Władysław Konopczyński, an expert on eighteenth-century Polish-Swedish relations, who remarked that:

*Portrait of Stanislaw Leszczyński, King of Poland.*

*Painting by Antoine Pesne (1683-1757), ca. 1736. Schloss Charlottenburg, Berlin, Germany. © bpk | Stiftung Preussische Schlösser und Gärten Berlin-Brandenburg.*

> *The kind-hearted Leszczyński brought back from Altranstädt not even a smidgen of royal spirit: he cowered before the nation and humbled himself before the Swedes to the point of kissing Piper's hands and inducing in them feelings of pity and revulsion.*[35]

Józef Feldman, an authority on the times of Augustus II, described the relationship between Leszczyński and Charles XII in the same vein: '. . . throughout his reign Leszczyński played the role of vassal, if not slave, to the Swedish protector.'[36] In a letter to Charles, Leszczyński himself best described his situation: 'since I am entirely dependent on Your Royal Majesty, I beseech you send instruction regarding my person.'[37]

Sweden's defeat at Poltava altered the situation in Poland and in Saxony. It paved the way for the expulsion of the Swedish army. In August 1709 Augustus II returned

*The marriage of Karl Leopold, Duke of Mecklenburg-Schwerin, to Peter I's niece, Princess Ekaterina Ivanovna, in 1716, Gdańsk. The marriage was performed by the bishop of Moscow.*

*Engraving by unknown artist, ca. 1716. Biblioteka Gdańska PAN, Gdańsk, Poland.*

to Poland, and Saxony re-entered the Northern League, embarking on military action in Swedish Pomerania. Saxony, however, did not regain the position it had held in the first phase of the war. It was now clearly inferior to Russia. Relations between Augustus and Stanislaw were not resolved until December 1712; the latter relinquished the throne and returned the act of abdication to Augustus II in exchange for retaining his royal title, while his followers were to be granted amnesty.[38]

The Commonwealth did not participate in this phase of the war. Yet, the only potential advantages laid out before Poland throughout the entire course of the Great Northern War were associated with the campaign in Swedish Pomerania. Its conquest would have facilitated control of Prussia, created favourable export conditions for Wielkopolska, and, not least, changed the Commonwealth's foreign policy, steering it away from affairs in the east. The idea of relocating the battle to Pomerania even found support among Poland's nobility, as the peace which they had demanded after the restoration of Augustus II had proved impossible because of Swedish resistance. However, the interests of Saxony took precedence over those of the Commonwealth. After its subjugation, Pomerania was to be taken over by Augustus as elector of Saxony, not king of Poland. The potential participation of Polish troops in the fighting was disregarded. The Pomeranian campaign ended in defeat in 1714. Swedish Pomerania was ceded to Prussia.[39]

After the victory at Poltava, Peter I's position in relation to Poland became far more dominant. Augustus's restoration to the Polish crown by Peter simply confirmed the Wettin king's subordination to the tsar. Polish-Russian relations were regulated by a treaty of alliance signed in October 1709, which was supposed to be directed against Charles XII and Leszczyński, but in reality sanctioned Peter I's supremacy over Augustus II.[40] Otwinowski characterised the tsar's wilfulness:

> It was the Muscovite tsar and protector who ruled rather than the king, for he elevated and humiliated whomsoever he pleased. He posted the army wherever he pleased and in whatever numbers he pleased, and betrayed the Polish nobility into slavery.[41]

In 1715 the tsar acted as an armed mediator between the anti-Saxon confederates and the armies of Saxony. Russian forces swept through the territories of the Commonwealth looting and burning, seizing crops and cattle. Gdańsk, whose economic and military potential the Russian tsar intended to utilise in the war against Sweden, was badly affected. From February to May 1716, Peter I and his wife Catherine resided in the city of Gdańsk. It was there that Peter's niece Ekaterina was married to Karl Leopold, Duke of Mecklenburg-Schwerin, with whom the tsar had forged an alliance.[42] Meanwhile, Augustus II's duplicity continued: officially he stood by Russia while secretly conducting a campaign against it. In January 1719 he entered into a treaty guaranteeing Saxony's and Poland's inviolability, which was signed by Saxony, Austria, and Great Britain, and he also negotiated with the Swedish minister Görtz in an attempt to achieve peace with Sweden. The tsar's reaction was to make a series of agreements against Augustus II, the most important of which was the treaty concluded in Potsdam in 1720 between Russia and Prussia, committing the two sides to block any constitutional changes in Poland.[43]

The Commonwealth and Saxony, on which the Northern War had inflicted a huge burden, were excluded from the pacification of the north. Although these countries did not suffer any territorial losses, neither did they receive any compensation for the economic devastation and destruction they had suffered. The war activated processes which led to the marginalisation of the Polish-Saxon union, opened the Commonwealth to Russian influences and governance, and, as noted by Konopczyński, put the partition of Poland (in various configurations) firmly on the agenda.[44]

## ■ Impact of the Great Northern War on the Economy and the Political System of the Commonwealth

The Great Northern War caused immense devastation in the Polish-Saxon state, triggering the disintegration of economic life and a crisis of state structure. Although research carried out to date does not allow for a detailed assessment of the war's economic and demographic impact, the opinion that it caused huge material losses and laid waste to the population appears to be well founded. The Northern War differed from earlier ones. It was the first time that foreign armies

(Swedish, Saxon, and Russian) alternately occupied the entire country, and they each introduced new ways of exploiting the occupied territories. The experience of the Thirty Years' War and the premise that 'war feeds war' were influential factors, as well as the Swedish war economy, the activities of the Saxon war commissariats, and the Russian armies' exploitation of occupied lands. War economy measures were also used by Polish forces connected with competing political factions. The frenzied pillaging typical of wartime hostilities in the seventeenth century was replaced by planned operations. During certain periods of the war, the armies active in the Commonwealth numbered over 100,000 individuals within a single year.[45] These armies had to be sustained, provided with equipment, and paid for their services. The situation was complicated by the country's horrendous devastation and the material impoverishment that had affected everyone. Disputes about tax rates and collection methods became a theoretical problem, as there was no one to pay taxes and no way to collect them. The plague carried by Swedish troops, which spread across the Commonwealth from 1705 to 1713, was accompanied by crop failure and famine.

The destructive nature of this war did not stem as much from the consequences of military action as from the protracted campaigns, the unrelenting passage of marching armies, the rigorously enforced payment of high contributions, and the pillaging, looting, and murders committed by foreign as well as domestic and allied forces. Looting affected farms of both the peasantry and the nobility, huge contributions and pillaging crippled towns and cities, and many industrial facilities were destroyed.[46] Both the allies and the enemies treated the Commonwealth like a 'roadside inn,' where their armies could take up lodgings as they set about ravaging the country.[47] Pillage, rape, famine, and epidemics wreaked greater devastation than pitched battles.

All of this took place against the backdrop of a weakened, failing state apparatus that had been divided as a result of the dual kings, and the creation of two or more centres of state power. The state apparatus not only repeatedly failed to fulfil its basic duty of protecting the country and its inhabitants but frequently became the instrument of their rack and ruin as well.

The extent of the financial and material costs incurred nationwide during the Northern War is not known. Nevertheless, partial data can be used to illustrate the scale of the problem. Loss estimates, even if they are exaggerated, provide evidence of massive devastation. Foreign armies managed to extract around 60 million thalers from the Commonwealth in contributions alone. The sums demanded by soldiers in army pay arrears pre-dating 1717 amounted to around 100 million zlotys, while the provinces' grievances against military forces concerning a plethora of abuses were calculated as 293 million zlotys in contributions.[48]

Cities were hit hard. Because of its economic and military potential, Gdańsk became a focus of interest for both Peter I and Charles XII. The city's defences were strong enough to prevent its capture by any army. However, foreign forces repeatedly demanded ransoms and payments in kind from Gdańsk under threat of destroying its countryside estates. During the course of the Northern War,

Saxon, Swedish, Polish, and Russian armies arrived at Gdańsk's estates demanding provisions and accommodation for their soldiers, as well as supplies of military equipment and large sums of money. In 1703 the city was to pay General Magnus Stenbock 100,000 thalers in exchange for assurances that Sweden would not make any new demands. Yet by mid-1704 the city had to pay Sweden another 67,000 thalers.[49] The Swedes undeniably perfected the practice of draining economies and implementing contribution systems. When Gdańsk was drawn into the orbit of Russian influence during the final phase of the war, actions by Swedish privateers against the city's ships and shipping intensified. Gdańsk's shipping suffered when Russian warships began to control the movement of vessels in an attempt to force the city to sever its commercial ties with Sweden.[50] Within the space of a year, from May 1716 to July 1717, Swedish privateers captured and confiscated ten ships from Gdańsk.[51]

Other cities suffered heavily. Toruń incurred damages estimated at 1.5 million zlotys as a result of being besieged and captured by the Swedes in 1703.[52] Properties were destroyed when its suburbs were burned down, the city was barraged with artillery fire, and its town hall was set ablaze. After its capitulation, the Swedes elicited ransoms and other payments, seized the city's armaments, destroyed its principal fortifications, and sequestered its horses.[53] The contributions and various payments in kind made to the Swedes during 1703-10 by Elbląg were worth 3.84 million zlotys.[54] Poznań incurred severe damages. In 1703 the armies of Saxony marched on the city, while in 1704 it was besieged by the Swedes. A plague epidemic broke out in 1709, and in 1711 the armies of Russia entered the city. In 1712 it was estimated that 60 per cent of the buildings in Poznań had been destroyed or damaged, while siege warfare and the passage of troops through its suburbs had reduced them to ruins and left them almost entirely deserted. In outlying villages nearly 40 per cent of farms were completely destroyed and 38 per cent were partially destroyed between 1693 and 1705. The Poznań city authorities estimated the overall cost of losses and damages at 2.84 million zlotys.[55]

The contributions levied on Kraków were so high that they brought about the ruin of even its wealthiest burghers. Apart from having to pay ransom money, the city was obliged to provide supplies for the Swedish army: a single district of Kraków—Kleparz—had to provide 200 barrels of beer per day, the whole city having to supply 600,000 pounds of meat and the same amount of bread, 12,000 pounds of fatback, 10,000 pounds of snuff, as well as horseshoes, mattresses, and bed linen. The city commandant, Magnus Stenbock, ordered the collection of a poll tax.[56] In Kraków itself the Swedes also committed acts of pillage, sparing neither churches nor monasteries, their recklessness resulting in a fire that ravaged Wawel Castle. Otwinowski noted that after the Swedes had left the city, Kraków resembled a village.[57] The city's situation was made even worse by the presence of soldiers of the Crown. The commandant of the garrison stationed in Kraków levied contributions, extorted payments from shops, confiscated fish, meat, beer, and candles. The billeting of soldiers in the homes of Kraków's burghers led to many townhouses being abandoned, their residents fleeing, unable to tolerate the army's abuses.[58] Warsaw suffered less at the hands of Charles XII's army, even though contributions were levied on the city. Troops occupied the Royal Castle and opened up its treasury, but found nothing there of any value.[59]

In addition to the direct losses and damages caused by the war and its attendant disasters, the Commonwealth suffered huge indirect losses from the impact on its productive forces and the resultant drop in production and halt in manufacturing and trade. The economic difficulties which the war generated in Gdańsk, led to a reduction in ship traffic in the city's port. During 1701-20 the number of ships sailing from Gdańsk to destinations in the west dropped by 42 per cent in relation to the 1691-95 period, with an annual average of 337 ships during 1691-95, falling to 197 during 1700-20.[60]

The collapse of the agricultural economy led to a decline in trade, as evidenced by grain exports from Gdańsk—grain having been Poland's principal export commodity. During 1701-05 and 1716-20 the amounts exported were half of those recorded during 1691-95, with a sharp downturn taking place in 1714 and continuing until 1718.[61] The reduction in grain exports was not only attributable to the destruction wreaked during the Great Northern War but also to crop failure and to the reduced demand for Polish grain in western Europe.[62] Furthermore, the decline in trade was caused by fiscal exploitation on the part of the nobility-governed state. Attempts were made to solve the state's growing financial difficulties by introducing new customs duties and taxes on merchants. Indirectly the war also contributed to volatility in monetary relations. The fact that the reduction in exports coincided with the levying of cash contributions had a restraining effect on monetary transactions in the country.[63] The devastation resulting from warfare, combined with natural disasters, meant that less grain arrived at the port of Gdańsk. In comparison with the period from 1691 to 1695, the amount of grain being brought to Gdańsk in the early eighteenth century dropped by around 25 per cent.[64]

The effects of the war were felt acutely by smaller towns as well. The wartime occupation of Elbląg and its properties by foreign armies led to a reduction in trade turnover at the town's port. In comparison with the late seventeenth century, it fell by one-fifth during 1701-10 and by almost one half during 1711-20.[65] Chełmno in Royal Prussia was left with only 50 burghers in 1713 after the plague had thrice swept through the town. Chełmża was destroyed by fire, only a quarter of its houses survived, the population was decimated by the plague, and the town was mired in debt. In Tolkmicko only 36 burghers survived and 49 houses stood locked up and derelict. No fairs were held and there was no prospect of making beer, as the neighbouring forests had been cut down by the Elbląg garrison. In Tuchola and Kowalewo there were no more than 20 burghers, with only a handful left in both Łęczyca and Sieradz. In Biecz just 18 houses remained in 1717, and there were no skilled tradesmen at all.[66] The war years clearly formed the greatest period of decline among towns and cities of the Commonwealth. A very small number of historical sources record that, despite the devastation of war, production continued at ironworks in the Staropolskie

Zagłębie (Old Poland Industrial Basin), mostly focusing on military demands.[67]

The Great Northern War affected royal and ecclesiastical estates, the properties of the nobility and magnates, as well as peasant farms throughout the Commonwealth. Pillaging armies led people to flee, depopulating entire villages. Estates cultivated by serf labour felt the effects of a depleted workforce. Contemporary writers noted that the presence of armed forces meant that villages remained abandoned. The Żuławy Malborskie region was deserted and over 40 of the best estate farm managers belonging to the town of Chełmno emigrated to Prussia. The bishop of Płock complained that he had villages without peasants and fields without crops. Regional and district court records are full of grievances about the total depopulation of villages and the lack of income from farms.[68] An eyewitness reported that on hearing the news that army units were approaching, peasants fled their homes in panic and went into hiding.[69] The impoverishment of rural populations contributed to an increase in the numbers of vagrants and beggars. Discontent led to peasant rebellions against the nobility.[70] The huge losses and scale of damage to agricultural properties are reflected in the surveys of royal estates dating from 1710 to 1715. The surveyors frequently recorded the absence of essential farm equipment, the lack of seed grain for sowing purposes, damage to buildings, and population losses.[71] Agricultural production fell. Research to date tells us little about global levels of grain production. We know from surviving accounts books that in part of the estates belonging to the Lubomirski family (at their Sandomierz properties) the amount of grain sown during 1710-12 fell by half in comparison with that sown during 1659-61.[72]

Wartime losses were further exacerbated by plagues and other natural disasters, floods, droughts, hailstorms, and fire causing even more damage, crop failure, and starvation. The severity of these disasters increased during the Great Northern War. It is estimated that in the first two decades of the eighteenth century, fire, acts of war, famine, and pestilence (plague epidemics) reduced the overall population of the Commonwealth by a quarter, though in towns and cities by half.[73] The most tragic period was 1712-14, which saw three consecutive years of catastrophic crop failure. Famine led to deaths even among the military. The situation became so desperate that in order to ensure food supplies for his army Augustus II tried to stop grain being shipped down the Vistula to Gdańsk.[74] Crop failure resulted in higher living costs; for example, in Warsaw a loaf of bread cost twice as much in 1715 as in 1709-12.[75]

Saxony also felt the effects of the war. The Swedish invasion and the year-long stay of Charles XII's army brought huge economic losses to the electorate. Costs were incurred because a new army had to be raised after the crushing defeat of the Saxon forces at the Battle of Fraustadt and because of the enormous war contributions levied on Saxony. The task of extracting money from the occupied country fell to Magnus Stenbock, who had proved effective in the same role in Poland. Saxony was obliged to pay Sweden 500,000 riksdalers per month in cash, and this financial exploitation was accompanied by enlistment into the Swedish army. However, in contrast to what had happened in Poland, in Saxony

Charles XII gave orders categorically forbidding his soldiers to plunder and loot under threat of severe penalties, including death. The king did this in an attempt to ensure peace and order in the country and to restore discipline in the army: the Swedish invasion of Saxony had been preceded by news of the atrocities committed in Poland and led to an outbreak of panic. Roads leading westwards became swamped with refugees.[76]

In some ways, the hardships of the Swedish occupation were less acute for the inhabitants of the electorate, as contributions paid to Sweden were recovered in the guise of profits earned from the sale of equipment for the new army being formed by Charles XII. The demand for modern armaments and uniforms gave rise to a boom in artisan workshops and manufactories. Production in Saxony supplied uniforms and weapons not only to the domestic market but also to other armies in Europe, thus allowing economic recovery in the electorate to proceed apace.[77]

In the Commonwealth, economic ruin was accompanied by political disintegration, as all of the rights and privileges of the nobility were violated. During the Great Northern War several precedents were set which undermined the Commonwealth's internal governance, striking at the very core of its political structure. The most significant were the dethronement of Augustus II by the Confederation of Warsaw, the election of Stanislaw Leszczyński under blatant pressure from Sweden, and the abdication contrary to Polish law of Augustus II.[78]

The war had both a direct and an indirect impact on the Commonwealth's system of government during 1700-19, on the range of reforms implemented during 1716-17 and, thus, on its further development. The civil war which accompanied the Northern War led to the collapse of the political system. The competition among the numerous political circles and centres of command (the courts of Augustus II and Stanislaw; Sweden and Russia; ministers of the Commonwealth, war commissariats, and individual commanders) created unfettered chaos.[79] The ostensible restoration of state unity following the return of Augustus II in 1709 did not bring an end to the negative effects of war. The actions of the allied Saxon and Muscovite armies broke up the structure of the slowly recovering political system. This resulted in the Sejm ceasing to function. During 1700-17 only three regular sessions took place. In addition, many of the Sejm's decisions which were not flouted remained unimplemented, particularly fiscal and military resolutions.[80] These circumstances led to the decentralisation of the state, governance passing into the hands of *sejmiki* (regional assemblies). The members of the nobility who attended these meetings came to hold sole authority in all state matters. This decentralisation facilitated foreign interference, which ultimately worked against the nobility. The levying of contributions or extra charges was easier to force through at the *sejmik* of a single province than at the General Sejm. The war also contributed to the loss of authority of the state's highest-ranking officials. The unstable political situation meant that many senators, in attempting to avoid responsibility, limited their participation in political life: they avoided *sejmik* sessions and meetings of the nobility. Ministers either lost or regained their influence depending on the successes of the warring factions.[81]

During the war both sides made use of various political mechanisms that enabled the state to continue functioning, if only to a limited extent. The senate council and a general council including deputies elected from the nobility were meant to partially take on the role of the Sejm in both foreign and domestic affairs, as well as make it easier for the king to centralise power.[82] The *sejmiki* proved to be a key factor in the political system, their activity increasing during 1700-16. One of their principal aims was to try to safeguard against being excessively burdened with taxes and contributions. When faced with immediate threats from foreign armies, the *sejmiki* organised their own system for collecting and distributing money and food. During the war the *sejmik*'s executive bodies—marshals, treasury commissions, and special commissions to deal with specific issues—became increasingly important. This was a way of trying to prevent abuses and destruction and instil a sense of order despite the pandemonium caused by war.[83] In practice, however, the use of these political defence mechanisms often proved ineffective. The main problems were lack of coordination on a nationwide scale and the presence of hostile foreign armies.

## ■ Charles XII and His Troops in the Eyes of the Commonwealth's Inhabitants

The wars fought between the Commonwealth and Sweden in the late sixteenth and seventeenth centuries, and in particular the wars of 1626-29 and 1655-60, when Swedish forces directly invaded Polish territories, created a very negative picture of the soldiers of Gustav II Adolf and Charles X Gustav. Swedish armies pillaged and burned the country, murdering its population, and Swedish troops became synonymous with invaders, murderers, looters, and—because they were Protestants—with heathens and heretics. Not only was this image perpetuated in the early eighteenth century, but contemporaries asserted that the cruelty of the Swedes during the Great Northern War was even greater than it had been during the years of the Deluge (1655-60). Notably, the resentment towards Swedish troops was levelled at all residents of Sweden.[84] The strength of this antipathy is reflected in inscriptions found in churches and on roadside crosses from the sixteenth to the early eighteenth centuries: 'Lord, deliver us from fire, sickness, and Swedes.'[85]

The nobility, though divided between 'Sas' and 'Las' (the respective supporters of the Saxon elector and Leszczyński) were in virtually total agreement on this one issue. The blame for all of the evils, disasters, and misfortunes which beset the Commonwealth, as well as the flouting of the nobility's rights and privileges (tantamount to a cardinal sin), lay squarely with foreigners—specifically Swedes, Saxons, and Russians.[86]

The prolonged warfare, which gave rise to terror and chaos in the occupied territories, was recorded in diaries, chronicles, memoirs, and notes written by witnesses to the events, and reminders were printed in newspapers of the period.[87] They told of the havoc wreaked by ruthless and avaricious ransacking by Swedish soldiers, the theft of horse fodder, food, and valuables, the contributions unlawfully imposed on towns and villages, the burning of peasant farms and manorial demesnes, enforced recruitment to the army, and the desecration of churches and monasteries.

The insecurity and anguish that are always associated with war, were most acutely felt by civilians, who quite rightly feared the arrival and billeting of soldiers, even if officially they were not the enemy. The very worst of fears and apprehensions were raised among the residents of Warsaw by news of the Swedish army advancing on the capital in the spring of 1702. In contrast, at the start of their sojourn, the troops had made a positive impression overall, giving a good account of themselves as allies. The piety of the Swedish army was also admired by the capital's residents.[88] However, after victory at the Battle of Kliszów in July 1702, they revealed a different side: ruthlessness, greed, and savagery. These were considered to be the dominant traits in the behaviour of the Swedish army up until the end of its stay in the Commonwealth. Swedish soldiers were referred to as the 'wolves of the north,' as they were judged to be unsurpassed in committing acts of pillage, rape, and looting.[89]

During his first stay in Warsaw, in May 1702, Charles XII—the Lion of the North—made a generally good impression according to the historian Julian Bartoszewicz. Residents liked his demeanour, his piety, humility, and easy manner, as well as the respect he showed to earlier Polish rulers, in particular John III Sobieski.[90] The simplicity and modest needs of the king of Sweden contrasted sharply with the hedonism and depravity of Augustus II and his court. Charles XII also compared favourably with Charles X Gustav, who, as Bartoszewicz observed, had been feared by everyone in Warsaw. Charles XII inspired confidence. Yet, Poles saw a radically different picture of the Swedish king and his army emerge several months later, after his victory at Kliszów. The Swedes gave vent to their avarice and began to pillage.[91] Charles XII's conduct in the occupied Polish territories proved to be wholly at odds with the friendly assurances and declarations he had made to the Commonwealth; hence the accusations of treachery and dishonesty.[92] In his wartime diary, Wawrzyniec Rakowski, a captain of cavalry, recorded that '. . . under the guise of sweet serenity, HM the King of Sweden is plotting something quite different and wants to destroy our state and the prerogatives of right-minded citizens.'[93] Acts of rape, pillage, and debauchery by his troops made Charles XII appear to Poles not as the friend and saviour to free them from the reign of the treacherous Augustus but as another Attila, whose impoverished and starving soldiers were turning the 'promised land' to ruins and ashes.[94] A different opinion of Charles was provided by one of his followers—the soldier, politician, and diarist Krzysztof Zawisza, who regarded the Swedish monarch as Poland's friend and ally, as someone who loved the Poles.[95]

This 'polonophile' sovereign ruthlessly quashed not only those who opposed him but also their compatriots. He exacted exorbitant contributions with an iron fist, flouting all pre-election promises. Pleas to revoke or reduce contributions were not only futile but elicited the king's resentment and anger. Wilfulness, obstinacy, aloofness, and disregard for everyone and everything made him many enemies.[96] Thus, it is no surprise that the news of Charles's death was met with joy by both the royal court and the nation. Even Zawisza commented on the fact as follows: '. . . whose [Charles's] death will bring relief not only to Poland, but to Sweden itself,' while 14 years after the event Otwinowski remarked that the king's death helped Sweden regain its liberty.[97]

Swedish generals operating in the occupied Polish territories mostly had a bad reputation. They were widely feared and notorious for their cruelty, ruthlessness, greed, and rapacity.[98] Magnus Stenbock, who was deemed the most ruthless in exacting contributions, perfecting this system of extortion to an unprecedented level, became a symbol of oppression, abuse, and lawlessness in Poland.[99] In a letter written to his wife in August 1702, he even referred to himself as the devil of Kraków.[100] Exerting extreme pressure and employing terror tactics were methods recommended to Swedish commanders by Charles XII. In a letter to Field Marshal Carl Gustav Rehnskiöld in June 1703 the king wrote:

> *Seize and deliver by whatever means, let the nation suffer as it may, . . . .*
> *Whosoever shows the very least hesitation, or is otherwise at fault in whatsoever petty way—show him no mercy, extort and burn . . . . And he who is absent from his home, or has even the slightest inclination to take to his horse—on him above all, inflict fire and utter ruination.*[101]

These instructions were diligently followed by Stenbock, as attested in his report to the king:

> *In carrying out the orders of my most merciful king I organised an expedition into the mountains to destroy the Polish nests of resistance. . . . I marched with torch in hand, and on encountering any villages that had not paid contributions, I set fire to them on all four sides; several peasants were consumed by flames on these occasions.*[102]

Given this situation, it is no wonder that Swedes were hated in Poland. Stenbock, in a 1704 letter to Charles XII, wrote at length about the difficulties involved in recruiting soldiers in Gdańsk.[103] The general's ruthlessness and cruelty were even remarked on by Zawisza, who, as noted above, looked favourably upon the Swedes. He recorded in his memoirs that:

> *Generał Stenbock, a great soldier, greatly experienced in war, with the ingenuity to build bridges on water and make crossings, a man of great piety, a dancer, a dandy, but with it wild and severe towards his fellow man, caused Poland much anguish.*[104]

Zawisza held a better opinion of another of Charles XII's outstanding commanding officers, the aforementioned Rehnskiöld, whom he described as 'an old and obedient soldier, who treated common people well and was not severe to his fellow man.'[105] Other accounts are not so kind to this general. The army under his command pillaged and looted almost everything around Kraków, and harshly exacted contributions from the province of Pomerania.[106] In his war diary, Rehnskiöld himself provides very negative testimony of his time in Poland, writing about the imprisonment, torture, and execution of its inhabitants.[107] Zawisza provides character sketches of Swedish generals, some of whom he knew personally, noting many positive features. He highlights their commitment to the soldier's craft, their bravery and courage, but also their kindliness and forbearance. These last two qualities, coupled with mercy, were said to characterise the Swedish commandant of Poznań, Colonel Liljehök.[108] It is probably thanks to this officer that Swedes were regarded unusually favourably in this city. When comparing the Swedish presence of 1704 with the stay of Charles X Gustav's army, the city's residents deemed Liljehök's soldiers to be less oppressive.[109]

The Swedish army did not spare Poland's churches and monasteries. Vandalising and looting their fixtures and fittings, the army was accused of desecrating places of worship. Nuns were desperately afraid of drunken soldiers, who beleaguered convents demanding food, treasures, and weapons.[110] The army's negative image as a pillaging occupying force was compounded by the acute religious tension of the Counter-Reformation period, which was marked by a process of linguistic and religious polarisation in Poland: Pole—Catholic, Swede—Lutheran. Otwinowski accused the Swedes of heresy, referring to them mockingly as 'Luthers.'[111] Monarchs from the north invading Poland were suspected of being in league with the devil, and it was said that Charles XII owed his victories to unclean forces (the devil's help).[112] Thus, the Swedish soldier was perceived as a heretic and devil combined, an individual causing grave harm to people and acting to the detriment of the Catholic faith.

At the beginning of the eighteenth century, Sweden and Poland were not only divided by military rivalries, religious, political, and socioeconomic differences, but also by cultural disparities, different everyday customs, and different mentalities. The Sweden of the early modern era was associated by inhabitants of the Commonwealth with poverty, privation, and primitivism. Swedes were accused of lacking manners and culture and of 'wild,' barbaric customs. The soldiers of Charles XII who gained control of Kraków were deemed boors. Chronicles record that it was impossible to communicate with them—they did not speak Latin—and that drunken troops broke into convents.[113] Popular opinion maintained that the impoverished Swedish nation subsisted mainly through fishing and was invading Poland driven by the desire to pillage. Swedes themselves were referred to as 'stinking herrings,' as they were considered to smell of fish and seawater.[114] Charles XII and his marauding soldiers featured as antiheroes in early eighteenth-century satirical works.[115]

Despite the fact that the presence of Charles XII's troops in the Commonwealth had most unpleasant connotations for Polish society, the positive traits of the Swedish soldiers were also discerned. Otwinowski noted their bravery and courage, their high morale, and faith in victory, though he also remarked that the Swedish army in Lithuania in 1702 looked very shabby, its soldiers 'haggard, half-naked and riding emaciated nags.'[116] Stanisław Leszczyński appreciated the high levels of training and discipline of Charles XII's army, while the author of a Carmelite convent chronicle recorded in 1702 that the army accompanying Charles XII when he invaded Poland, was small but well trained and disciplined.[117] News periodicals published in Warsaw noted that discipline and rigour were maintained in the Swedish army and that its soldiers did not disturb the peace with gunfire, only ever making requests for food, which they did without committing any abuses.[118] Residents of Poland also recognised the soldiers' strength and stamina in enduring the discomfort and hardships of war, as well as their piety, given voice by their public singing of psalms.[119] Even in the late eighteenth century opinions about the valour and discipline of Swedish soldiers were still being mentioned in Polish journalistic writing.[120]

How big an influence the events of the Great Northern War had on the Commonwealth's inhabitants is demonstrated by the fact that subsequent generations passed down the memories of this tragic period. Even in the late eighteenth century, in political writings, memoirs, and addresses made at the Four-Year Sejm they were being used as deterrents and cited as the reason for numerous negative phenomena.[121] The enduring strength of memories about cruelty and battles involving Swedish soldiers is evidenced by folk songs and sayings noted in the nineteenth and even in the twentieth century. They include allusions to the rapacious behaviour of Swedish troops and their despicable nature, for example: 'as bad as a Swede,' 'filthy as a Swede,' 'the Swedes left Poland in need,' and 'as numerous as Swedes' (i.e., vastly abundant).[122]

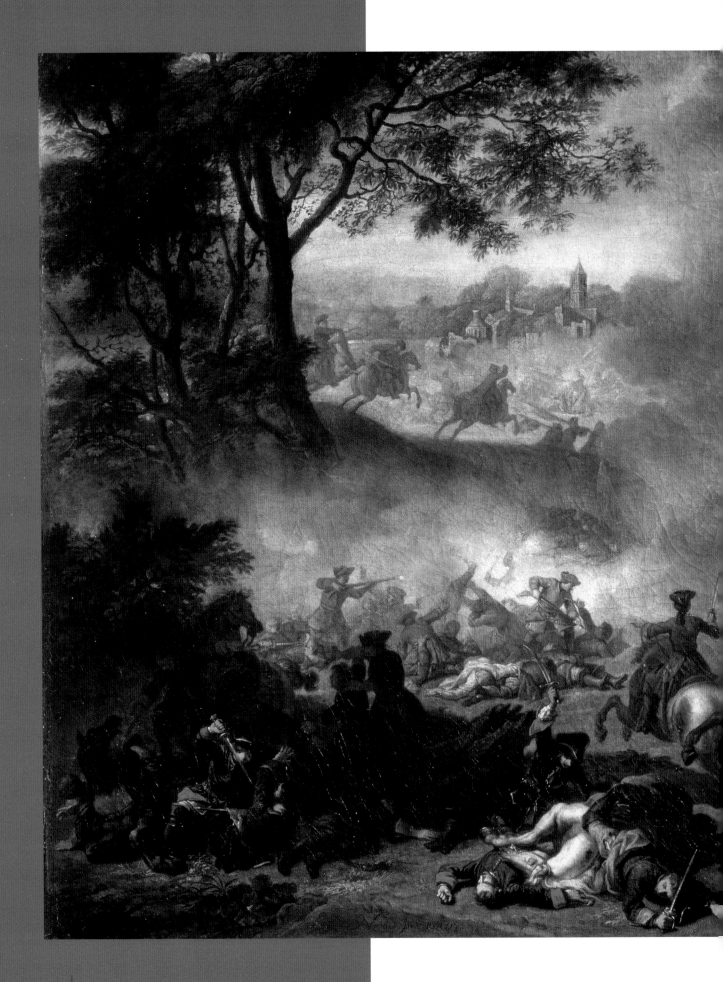

# CHAPTER 16

# Russian Views
# of Charles XII

by Pavel A. Krotov*

The Great Northern War of 1700-21 completely altered the balance of forces in northern and eastern Europe. The kingdom of Sweden, formerly the greatest power in the Baltic region, ended up succumbing to Russia. The central figures whose activities in this historical process caused the political map of Europe to be redrawn, were King Charles XII of Sweden and Tsar Peter I—Peter the Great.

Thanks to an efficient administration the Swedish kingdom had a strong army, a fleet, mighty border fortresses, universities, and well-developed industries. Yet, when this highly militarised state clashed with backward Muscovy it would eventually lose a war that dragged on for 21 years. When the war with Sweden started, Russia was only taking its first steps towards reforms. A small naval fleet had appeared on the Sea of Azov in 1696 and work had begun on establishing a large regular army in 1699. There were few large industrial enterprises, even paper had to be imported; there was a lack of professional learning and not a single university. Much depended on the head of state. Both Charles and Peter were educated in the spirit of an age in which the heroes of Antiquity—such as Alexander the Great and Julius Caesar—were held up as examples. But their endeavours were to have very different results.

How did Peter I and his circle see Charles XII? How did Russia's foreign policy manipulate different aspects of his character? Charles established his name in Europe as an outstanding commander almost immediately. In July 1700 the 18-year-old king landed his forces near Copenhagen in what seemed a highly risky undertaking. Some 4,800 Swedes arrived in the first two days alone, supported by an English-Dutch fleet, and eventually a total of 10,800 made the crossing.[1] The king moved decisively towards the Danish capital. With insufficient troops to protect Copenhagen, Denmark withdrew from the war, making peace at Travendal on 18 August.

In November of the same year a small Swedish army of 10,500 men and 37 cannon[2] inflicted a heavy defeat on the Russian army (33,384 men as of late October 1700)[3] beneath the walls of the Swedish fortress of Narva. One Russian contemporary, Fyodor Soymonov, recalled the impressions left by the Swedish victory: 'Then very uninformed regarding the finer points of military matters, the people could not understand how the Swedish king could, with such a small number of troops, overcome their own forces, far superior in number.'[4] Thus, did Charles XII first appear in Russian history.

Both the Russian ruling elite and the people had suffered a great shock, creating ideal conditions for conclusion of a peace on terms extremely advantageous to the Swedes. But Charles was to prove to be a man of unusual character and war between Russia and Sweden continued until 1721. In October 1700, William III of England put to Peter I a ceasefire proposal, with England acting as mediator. William's letter to Charles XII pointed out that this was a good moment to conclude peace. But the Swedish king wished to continue the war, to utterly crush his enemy.[5] In the soldier-king's refusal of mediation we may see a manifestation of key personality traits: maximalism, underestimation of the opponent, and a preference for war as a tool in resolving all issues. One might also conclude that Charles feared Russia's potential and wanted to crush it before it became too dangerous. Eventually, though, Charles XII would make miscalculations that helped the tsar achieve his goals.

Russia's rulers quickly came to understand the workings of the mind of the young Charles XII and were thereafter ready to take these into account. The Swedish king's obstinacy, his lack of flexibility, and his vindictiveness were noted by many contemporaries and even during his lifetime came to be seen as the 'Lion of the North's' defining qualities. Henry St. John, first Viscount Bolingbroke (1678-1751), politician and political philosopher, recalled Charles XII in 1736 as one 'who sacrificed his country, his people, and himself at last, to his revenge.'[6]

In a work published in Amsterdam in 1747, *L'Aveu sans exemple, ou Mémoires de Constantin de Tourville*, some common contemporary views of Charles are reflected. There is a claim, for instance, that the attitude of some in the royal entourage might have contributed to the king's belief in a divinely preordained fate and encouraged him to think that 'he alone was applauded, he alone was great; it was his valour and his genius that created the destiny of his arms.'[7] Furthermore it was noted that Charles was obstinate in seeking revenge, that he was driven by 'too inflexible a desire for vengeance.'[8] At Bender, after the defeat at Poltava, Charles XII stated before many witnesses that: 'Either I shall find happiness here or I shall no longer be king.'[9] The historian Sverker Oredsson emphasised aspects of Charles's character that are vital for any assessment of his military skills: his fatalism, his belief in divine predestination, and his tendency towards extreme, radical decisions.[10] Another authoritative historian, John B. Wolf, made the following assessment:

> Charles probably never understood clearly the high politics of his era. He was thrust into the responsibility of power before experience had ripened his understanding and, like many well-intentioned men, he entertained naïve ideas which he regarded as principles and which he tried to apply to all men and all circumstances. His early victories reassured him of his wisdom and invincibility, and made him reluctant to listen to advice. The dreary years in Saxony, the fiasco in Russia, the humiliating stay in Turkey, and the final climax of his career in the north all illustrate his stiff-necked adherence to fixed ideas regardless of the realities.[11]

After his convincing victory at Narva, Charles XII withdrew to Dorpat to recoup his forces, then on 19 July 1701 crossed the western Dvina—doing battle on the way—and repelled the Saxon troops besieging Riga. In January 1702 he moved his army into Lithuania, thereby adding Poland to the number of states with which Sweden was at war, and putting into practice the principle of 'war feeds itself.' He gained resounding victories over weak opponents (for instance, on 19 July 1702—the anniversary of his victory on the Dvina near Riga—when he won another glorious victory near Kliszów, not far from Kraków), all of which added to his fame as the Alexander the Great of modern history. In Poland it looked indeed as if Charles wished to resemble his great predecessor in ejecting kings from their thrones and handing out crowns: in July 1704 he forced the Polish *szlachta*, which had been summoned to Warsaw, to declare Stanislaw Leszczyński the new king of Poland. Yet, even though during the campaigns of 1702-04 Charles XII occupied a number of towns in Poland—Warsaw, Kraków, Lwów, and Toruń—and even though the Swedish army could have taken any other Polish town, it was unable to keep control of the whole territory.

Meanwhile, Peter I had set out to fulfil his underlying purposes. He wanted to reclaim even a small part of the shore of the Baltic Sea where he could then establish a port. This was vital for the further development of direct trade with European countries and cities, above all with the Dutch Republic, Great Britain, Hamburg, and Lübeck. There were two further aims: to establish a city that would become the capital of a Russian empire—Saint Petersburg, city of the Holy Apostle Peter—and to commence construction of a mighty naval fleet.

Believing that it was rather easy to predict the Swedish king's action, the tsar and his aides conceived, accordingly, a strategic programme for the military campaigns of 1702 and 1703. In April 1702 the tsar and half the Russian Guards would move from Moscow to Archangel. This demonstrative secession of military initiative was intended to reinforce Charles XII's view of the Russian monarch as weak and cowardly (on the eve of the Battle of Narva the tsar, then officially a mere captain in the Guards, had left his army to hasten the reserves). Russia sought to convince Charles that Peter took his troops off to the far north because he feared the invincible 'Swedish lion.' Otto Anton Pleyer, the Emperor Leopold I's *chargé d'affaires* in Moscow, wrote on 26 April 1702 that he had 'been reliably in-

*Portrait of Count Fedor Alexeevich Golovin, Russian minister.*

Engraving by Martin Bernigeroth (1670-1733), 1706. Österreichische National-bibliothek, Vienna, Austria.

formed that this was but a pretext and the true idea was to again attack Narva, although some tried to convince the tsar to move against Nysenskans' [Nyenskans was a Swedish fortress near the river Neva's debouching into the Baltic Sea].[12] The tsar's idea was that 'when he reached Arkhangelsk [Archangel] the enemy would be confident that he was simply passing time there but he meanwhile intended to move quickly through Arkhangelsk on to Novgorod and Pskov and continue the campaign towards Narva.'[13] Russian interpretation of the Swedish king's thought processes proved correct.

By 1703 Russian troops had indeed gained the access to the Baltic Sea that was so vital to its success. Russia now controlled the length of the Neva, a convenient waterway leading to the Baltic. A small naval fleet had been created and in 1703 Saint Petersburg had been founded. Russian troops had taken the mighty Swedish fortresses of Narva and Dorpat in Livonia (1704). On 2 October 1704 members of the Rådet or Council in Stockholm wrote to the king describing the Russian victories that 'have opened the route from Ladoga to the Baltic Sea, after which they also established a

port by their outlet onto the sea with a superb shipbuilding wharf . . . they founded and erected there a mighty fortress, have built and made ready a large number of ships and . . . galleys . . . from England and Holland come a large number of naval officers and simple seamen . . . they have taken the town of Dorpat and but a few days ago the extremely important and fortified site of Narva and Ivangorod.'[14]

Seeking to avoid direct conflict with Charles XII's main army, the tsar was ready to conclude peace even if Russia would only be left with a small part of the shore. Under no circumstances, however, was Peter ready to cede the Neva, the city of Saint Petersburg, or the fortifications on Kotlin Island. The arrival in Moscow in March 1705 of the English envoy extraordinary, Charles Whitworth, was seen as a propitious opportunity to start peace negotiations. Fyodor Alexeevich Golovin, head of Russian foreign policy, informed Whitworth of his country's desire that England assume the role of intermediary.[15] Whitworth, however, had been given no such powers. Moreover, the outcome of the War of the Spanish Succession was still not clear. England, the emperor, the Dutch Republic, and others of the Grand Alliance were deeply engaged in conflict with France and considered Sweden's preoccupation with wars against Russia, Poland, and (soon) Saxony to be a reliable guarantee that Sweden would not come to France's aid, despite the alliance concluded between these two countries in 1698.

In August 1706 Charles XII occupied Saxony, not without some resistance, and spent the next year there building up his main army. From this location he could influence wider European politics. Several diplomats could still remember the not-so-distant experience of the Thirty Years' War (1618-48), when Swedish commanders devastated the German lands, supported by their alliance with France. According to Peter I, the French called the Swedes 'the scourge of the Germans.'[16]

Russian diplomatic missions dispatched to Britain and Saxony at the turn of 1706 and 1707 reveal just how far Peter was ready to compromise on his military successes in order to avoid the risk of all-out conflict between the Russian and Swedish armies, seeing full battle as 'an extremely dangerous affair.'[17]

*Portrait of Andrey Matveev, envoy to The Hague.*

*Painting by Hyacinthe Rigaud (1659-1743), 1706. The State Hermitage Museum, Saint Petersburg, Russia. © The State Hermitage Museum / photo by Vladimir Terebenin.*

France meanwhile was suffering setbacks in the war against the Grand Alliance and, in hopes of getting Swedish support, was also interested in peace between Russia and Sweden. A French general, Morell, was dispatched to Saxony to bring Jean-Victor de Besenval de Brünstatt, French representative at the court of Charles XII, the Russian proposal.[18] Peace was to be offered in exchange for nearly all the Russian conquests on the Baltic. As a last resort, Russia was ready to keep only Ingria, which had been part of its territory from the ninth century right up to its seizure by the Swedes in 1612. It was here that Saint Petersburg was under construction, a city that Peter saw as symbolising his entire reform programme. But the Swedish king refused even to let the French envoy put the Russian proposal to him. His ministers reasoned 'with great pride and swearing' that the Swedish monarch would sign a peace only in Moscow, that he would depose Tsar Peter I and divide Russia up 'into small principalities,' would ensure the disbanding of the newly formed regular troops, rescind the order to wear only European-style clothing, and force Russians to wear beards once more.[19]

A new attempt to reach peace with Charles XII on the basis of mutual interest and reasonable compromise was undertaken in 1707, when the talented diplomat Andrey Artamonovich Matveev was dispatched from The Hague to London as envoy extraordinary and plenipotentiary. His instructions were to ask Queen Anne to force Sweden to sign a treaty of compromise with Russia. It was hoped that Britain could do this by recreating the conditions which had led to the removal of Denmark from the Northern War in 1700: British and Dutch fleets should enter the Baltic Sea and cut off communication between the main Swedish army and Stockholm. It would then be possible to demand that Charles sign a peace with the Russian monarch. Peter I was prepared to promise to join the Grand Alliance and to offer it 12,000 to 15,000 Russian troops without subsidy, and up to 30,000 after the signing of an agreement with Sweden. The extent of Matveev's powers is clear from the last clause in the instructions for this diplomatic mission. If the great powers of the anti-French coalition—the Holy Roman Emperor, Great Britain, the Dutch Republic—would agree in writing to demand peace between Russia and Sweden, leaving the former only a single port on the Baltic, while the rest of the conquests would be returned to the Swedes, Matveev was simply to ask for time to pass this on to the tsar. If they demanded an immediate answer, then Matveev was to sign such an agreement, having first ensured there was no alternative (on pain of death if he was found to be mistaken).[20]

It was not in the British interest, however, to put an end to the Great Northern War at this time. Matveev's embassy ended in failure just as had Morell's mission to Charles XII. The tsar had been seen, though, to be flexible, ready to make vast concessions, while Charles, in contrast, demonstrated obstinacy and arrogance, refusing to recognise that in the wake of Peter I's transformations Russia was already manifesting its immense potential to the world. Arguably, concerns about Sweden's security—precisely because of Russia's growing importance—may also have played a role in Charles's refusal to conclude a peace treaty.

At last the Russian side was convinced of the Swedish king's uncompromising approach. Not only did he wish to eject Russia from the Baltic Sea and humiliate

Peter I with a shameful peace treaty, he wanted much more. This was brought home to the Russian monarch by information from a variety of sources. In January 1707 Franz Ludwig von Zinzendorf, ambassador to Charles XII on behalf of Emperor Joseph I, recorded his understanding of the king's intentions gained from conversations with Swedish diplomats:

> Since he has no trust in Moscow, come what may the king of Sweden is tempted by peace with this potentate [Peter I], but he will not agree until all the methods of this state and its neighbours that are dangerous both in civil and military terms are radically altered, and until the Swedish Crown has ensured itself true safety through the forcible weakening of this power.[21]

Peter's agent abroad, Heinrich van Huyssen, wrote in June 1707 that Charles XII 'has no wish to come to any agreement with the tsar . . . nor will he conclude peace with him until Moscow has been reduced to a state in which it can no longer cause any harm to Sweden.'[22]

Such was the firm attitude of Charles XII and his immediate circle. In 1708 the king's privy counsellor Carl Piper responded to Emperor Joseph I's offer of mediation by saying that even the return of all the lands taken by the tsar would be insufficient to ensure Sweden's future safety. To prevent further attacks it was necessary to utterly destroy the Russian army, so reinforced by 'foreign discipline.' Those around the Swedish king felt that 'there can be no peace more advantageous nor more lasting than a peace concluded in Moscow itself.'[23]

Peter responded with a strategy of simply wearing the Swedish army out. In spring 1707 he resolved that general engagement should be permitted 'only when great need shall require it.' Retreating Russian forces should 'tire the enemy out' with small skirmishes, destroying food supplies and horse fodder in the path of the advancing Swedish army.[24] In September 1707 the Swedish army left Saxony and moved towards Moscow, but it was not in Moscow that their advance came to a halt. Charles would be forced to seek safety in Turkey.

Russian victory was brought closer by a number of serious miscalculations on the part of the Swedish king. His apparent underestimation of the enemy's abilities and his self-confidence meant that he did not go to meet the 13,000-strong Swedish force led by General Adam Ludwig Lewenhaupt. Rapid manoeuvres by Russian troops under Peter I allowed them to crush the Swedes near the village of Lesnaya (9 October 1708). Only half of the Swedish soldiers, minus their wagons and artillery, could join the main army led by Charles XII. After facing the remains of Lewenhaupt's corps, the king allegedly started to suffer from insomnia; he refused to undress at night, and even in May 1709 spent hours asking ensign R. Petre for details of the battle.[25] He failed to see, however, that the Russian army had changed completely since its defeat at Narva in 1700.

On 24 June 1709, two weeks before the decisive battle at Poltava, in response to Major-General Axel Sparre's statement that people were praying for peace in Sweden, Charles XII made clear his preference for continuing military action:

> . . . is it not all the same . . . if we don't smash them today, we'll do it tomorrow, if not tomorrow then the day after, and if we don't manage it this week then we'll do

*it a year from now, if not a year from now then five years from now, and if we don't*
*do it in five years we'll do it in ten . . . any peace must be honest and since that's the*
*case then war, it seems, can be conducted without end.*[26]

Total defeat of the Swedes came at Poltava on 8 July 1709. The troops of the
great reformer-tsar far outnumbered the Swedes. He concentrated 60,000 regular
Russian troops on the battle, along with 20,000 Cossacks, Kalmyks, and Moldavi-
ans, and 310 cannon.[27] Charles XII's army consisted of 24,300 combatants (and
another 2,250 sick and wounded),[28] plus up to 10,000 Ukrainian Cossacks of the
former Hetman Ivan Mazepa.[29] His artillery counted 41 field guns but had no
charges for 7 of them.[30] Three days after the battle, the remains of the Swedish army
surrendered on the Dnieper without a shot being fired and were taken prisoner.
The king himself fled to the Ottoman Empire. Such were the consequences of his
ambitious plan. Were it not for Charles's character and assumptions, there would
likely never have been such a battle as the one at Poltava, one with disastrous
results and far-reaching consequences—the total disappearance of a magnificent
army, with minimal losses on the Russian side. Adherence to his risky plan led to
catastrophe. If Charles XII had not lost the all-out engagement at Poltava, he would
surely have gone down in history as a great military leader and Peter I might never
have been remembered as a great tactician. It was Charles XII's stubbornness and
uncompromising approach that helped make Russia great.

Immediately after the Battle of Poltava the tsar ordered that conditions for
peace be sent to Charles XII and to the Rådet in Stockholm. They had changed
radically. Now the Swedish king was asked to cede not only Ingria but Karelia
with the town of Vyborg and the whole of Livonia with the towns of Reval (Tallinn) and Riga. Vyborg, Reval, and Riga had not yet been occupied by Russian
troops but such an occupation was the inevitable next step in the tsar's campaign.[31] Vice-Chancellor Pyotr Pavlovich Shafirov spoke of this to Piper, now
a prisoner of war, in the presence of another prisoner, Cabinet Secretary Josias
Cederhielm, and Major-General Johan August Meijerfelt, sent by the Swedish
king to conduct negotiations. Shafirov wanted them to explain to Charles that
nothing could stop the tsar from taking these Swedish provinces and that Denmark and Poland would now join the war against Sweden. Charles XII rejected
the proposed peace 'and showed no desire for reconciliation.'[32]

The programme of new conquests, announced in the Russian camp at
Poltava, was a necessary pre-condition for Russia to achieve the status of great
European power. Henceforth, the more the king refused to conclude peace, the
more Sweden had to lose—and the more Russia and its allies had to gain. Yet,
Peter I was far from wishing to destroy Sweden. In a secret instruction to Boris
Ivanovich Kurakin, Russian ambassador at the court of the elector of Hano-
ver, Georg I Ludwig (from 1714 George I of Great Britain), we find details of
Russian policy on Sweden. Dated 3 November 1709, the instruction reads: 'His
Royal Majesty has no intention of seeking the further final destruction of the
Swedish king, as the latter sought to do with His Royal Majesty, but wishes to
be moderate and to agree on this with his allies.'[33] The instruction also declared

that after the Battle of Poltava the tsar felt the need to consider, both for his own benefit and for the security of neighbouring states, how to restrain the Swedish king so that he could no longer harm neighbouring powers.[34]

Charles's new refusal to sign a peace forced Peter to re-establish his alliance with Denmark and Saxony and move the war further into Swedish territory, to clear Poland of Swedish troops and—with the aid of Danish, Saxon, and then Prussian and Hanoverian troops—seize Swedish lands in northern Germany. In 1710 Russian troops took Vyborg, Reval, Riga, and Kexholm—Livonia and Karelia were now in the hands of Russia, as she continued on the way to becoming a great power.

Again and again Charles XII thought that all could ultimately be decided in the field by the sword and musket, scorning anything that diplomacy could offer. Thus he refused to observe a convention on neutrality within the Holy Roman Empire. Signed in The Hague on 31 March 1710 by representatives of three great powers, the Empire, Great Britain, and the Dutch Republic, its purpose was to protect the German lands since Sweden was no longer able to control them. Under the terms of this convention the allies agreed not to enter the Empire to seize Swedish lands. Shafirov later wrote: 'Although this was much against the highest interests of His Royal Majesty and his allies, to show the world his moderation he deigned to agree with his allies and to persuade them to accept the suggestion, though it was harmful to their interests.'[35] The convention was approved by the Rådet in Stockholm but repudiated by Charles XII, who declared that it had been concluded without his consent.

During his years in exile in the Ottoman Empire, Charles plotted military and political revenge but his plans enjoyed only modest success. The ploy to destroy the Russian army using the Turkish forces during the war between the two lands (1710-13)—of which he was the ideological author—failed. Charles's forced expulsion from Turkey by an army of Crimean Tartars and Janissaries [Turkish elite units], through the lands of Poland to Pomerania—part of the lands around the southern shore of the Baltic belonging to the non-existent Swedish Empire—became a very real possibility. If he were expelled, he would become a hostage to the military and political machinations of others, in a highly insecure situation with no clear outcome, a situation on which he could have little or no influence. He might well be taken prisoner by the Russians or the Poles, for instance.

Charles's personal qualities were clearly manifested in an episode that has gone down in history under the Turkish name of *Kalabalik*, which means 'commotion.' At the start of 1713 he was in the village of Varnitza in Moldavia, not far from the town of Bender. To force the haughty king of Sweden to bow to their will, Tartars and Turks under the Crimean Khan Devlet II Giray advanced to storm the building in which he had taken shelter with his modest circle. Unique details of Charles XII's actions in this conflict are found in a document discovered by this author. Foma Mitlushenko, a Zaporozhye Cossack, stated that he lived in Varnitza in the house of the Swedish Hof-Chancellor Gustaf Henrik von Müllern. Thus, he found himself at the very centre of events and provided a vivid description of Charles's refusal to leave and head for the Polish border. The king, 'utterly disregarding . . . the Turks, said with great choler that he wished to die here, that he would not go, let them attack him and he would defend himself.' Mitlushenko then provided details of the actual storming of the building. The Swedes lost thirty men in the rifle crossfire on the first day. The following day the same house was surrounded with straw and set on fire, after which the storming recommenced. Rifle in hand, Mitlushenko fought alongside the king. His description of the end of the battle and the capture of the Swedish monarch is striking:

> When they set fire to the straw and the roofs burned, the ceilings started to fall in. The Turks increased their fire. The king, seeing that three Swedes had already died of suffocation and that flames were beginning to touch him, leapt out of the window, his right arm wounded by a Janissary's bullet below the elbow and with a scratch on his left cheek. Seizing the king, the Janissaries took him to the tent of the Pasha, who

*respectfully asked him to be seated on a chair, but he spat in the Pasha's beard and immediately lay down on his bed and cursed him . . . .*[36]

Mitlushenko's report was sent to Saint Petersburg in May 1713, to Peter I and Chancellor Gavrila Ivanovich Golovkin.[37] Although its importance may not have been recognised immediately, Peter was much interested to receive information about Charles's despairing actions in Moldavia. Another participant in the battle, a captured Turkish Janissary, Ali Abdullah, was also sent to Peter for questioning.[38] Of course, Mitlushenko's evidence must be used in the context of other sources. The clerk Johan Henrik von Kochen, also at Varnitza with Charles XII, wrote that the king was slightly wounded in the neck and that the second wound was inflicted 'in the left arm by a Janissary, whom he killed with his own hands.'[39] Such minor differences are unimportant, for the episode clearly illustrates certain fundamental aspects of the soldier-king's personality.

The Turkish sultan saw the king's brave but despairing fight to the last as a manifestation of his honour, dignity, and free will ('for the dishonourable events at Bender the king is greatly respected by the sultan'[40]). At Varnitza Charles XII was prepared to obey only one who was his equal in status, Sultan Ahmed III, sovereign of the Ottoman Empire. On no account would he submit to the sultan's vassal, Devlet II Giray. Charles again declined the opportunity to retain through diplomacy some of his territories, though—in hindsight—this could yet have saved Sweden. The king could have counted on the support of a number of states at the Brunswick peace conference which was set by Emperor Charles VI to commence in 1713. Charles XII's preliminary condition for the start of these negotiations was that Sweden's neighbours return all the lands they had taken. That this was unrealistic was clear to all (save perhaps Charles?). Charles VI continued to raise the question of a conference at Brunswick right up to 1720. First it was deferred because the Swedes refused to take part. Then it was ignored by the Russians, who saw it as giving the Swedish king a respite and making it possible to bring the negotiations under the control of a cartel of European powers. Such a turn of events in no way suited a now mighty Russia during the last years of the Great Northern War.[41] Charles XII missed his chance once more.

The king stubbornly rejected opportunities created for him by British diplomacy to preserve the remains of gains made by earlier Swedish kings. Britain had no interest in any further weakening of Sweden. Lord Strafford, London's envoy to The Hague, set out British policy on Sweden in some detail. In early 1713 he declared to Boris Kurakin, now Russian envoy in The Hague, that: 'Naturally England will never wish to see the Swedish Crown ruined and helpless. It is England's true intention that the northern powers be held in balance.'[42] The British diplomat identified the political obstacle: Russia's desire to hold on to all its conquests, while Charles XII refused to cede anything. It was Strafford's idea that Livonia, occupied by Russian troops, should remain in the hands of Sweden and Russia should be satisfied with the acquisition of Ingria including Saint Petersburg. Narva was equally necessary to both powers, so this port might be the subject of negotiation.[43] From 1714, however, Sweden ratcheted up its privateering war in the Baltic with the aim of hindering trade between Britain, the Dutch Republic, and other countries with ports now under Russian control: Vyborg, Narva, Reval, Riga, and Saint Petersburg.[44] Charles XII repulsed his only ally, Great Britain, a situation that Russian diplomats immediately put to their advantage.

Moreover, Peter I made use of the division between George I's interests as elector of Hanover and as king of Great Britain and was not opposed to having the Swedish bishopric of Bremen and the principality of Verden, seized by Denmark in 1712, handed to the elector of Hanover in 1715. Henceforth George I had a vital interest in a rapid end to the war between the northern allies and Sweden and in the ratification of these new acquisitions for his hereditary German lands. On 15 October 1715, he declared war on Sweden, in his role as elector, and sent a body of 6,000 men to Pomerania.[45] Under the terms of the Treaty of Greifswald between Russia and Hanover, concluded 28 October 1715, George undertook to guarantee Russia's Swedish conquests—Ingria, Karelia, and Estonia with the town of Reval—in return for Peter's promise to establish the legal foundation for Hanover's possession of Bremen and Verden.

The relatively minor advantages gained by the Swedes from the activation of privateering in 1714-15—for which they were responsible—were negated by the fact that Britain joined the powers of the northern alliance in defending the sea trade in the Baltic. In effect, the Swedish king found himself in total international isolation. By the end of 1715, Tsar Peter saw an opportunity to end the war in his favour, but in order to do so he needed the assistance of his allies. He had armies in the Ukraine, Finland, and northern Poland, but needed assistance of nearby western powers to bring Sweden's military operations to a complete halt. Because he had been ill for some time, his medical advisors had recommended that he take the cure at Bad Pyrmont in the principality of Waldeck, close to Hanoverian territory. The necessity of making a journey for his personal health coincided with the plans for the marriage of his niece to the duke of Mecklenburg-Schwerin, and with his desire to mobilise allies to join his plans. Peter's influence was essential for the elector of Saxony to fulfil his desire to be king of Poland. Russian naval forces controlled the Baltic and, in combination with the Russian army, the tsar was in a position easily to take control of East Prussia, dividing Brandenburg from its elector's hereditary land. With the geopolitical strategic situation in his favour, Peter now needed to convince Brandenburg-Prussia, Denmark, the Dutch Republic, Hanoverian Britain, and France that this was the best opportunity to end the war. For these various reasons, Peter made his second personal visit to western Europe in 1716-17. A highly publicised journey, it contrasted with his first trip in 1697-98, when he had travelled incognito to the Dutch Republic and England.

Departing from Saint Petersburg in February 1716 with a large retinue, the tsar travelled at a leisurely pace, making lengthy stays en route. First he went to Danzig, where he remained for two months and witnessed the marriage of his niece, Ekaterina Ivanovna, the daughter of Tsar Ivan V, to Duke Karl Leopold of Mecklenburg-Schwerin on 19 April. This union brought Mecklenburg-Schwerin under Peter's dependence and allowed him to put Russian troops in occupation of the duchy. Peter had not anticipated that the marriage would cause great concern among the northern German rulers, particularly Hanover, who began to be much more suspicious of Peter's motives and, from then on, became more reticent than he had expected to join his plans.

From Danzig, Peter travelled to Bad Pyrmont, where he took the waters during a three-week-long cure. Next, from early July to mid-October 1716, he was in Denmark, where he and the tsarina were warmly received and honoured. During the first part of the summer, Peter was involved in organising the arrival of some 29,000 Russian troops to join with Danish forces in a planned invasion of southern Sweden. To facilitate this amphibious operation, the Russian and Danish fleets united to form a combined fleet led by Peter, and on 13 August 1716 he had under his command around the island of Bornholm 17 Danish ships (1,136 cannon; 8,610 men), as well as frigates and other vessels. The Russian fleet dispatched to Bornholm was also impressive: 15 ships of the line (786 cannon; 5,590 men) and frigates.[46] A Dutch squadron (4 ships of the line with 220 cannon and 2 frigates) had already set off to the east.[47] The Dutch admiral had strict orders, however, to avoid hostilities and to confine himself to the protection of Dutch mercantile shipping. While 17 English ships of the line (990 cannon; 5,190 men) were also in the area, the Swedes were able to arm just 23 ships of the line (1,436 cannon), which were tucked away in the harbour of Karlskrona—a far inferior force.[48]

There had been numerous delays in readying the Danish and Russian forces, but eventually it was agreed that their landing in southern Sweden would take place on 21 September. Four days prior to this date, however, Peter cancelled the operation, having decided that it was too late in the season to complete it successfully.

Departing from Copenhagen in mid-October, Peter and Catherine travelled through Holstein to meet with Friedrich Wilhelm I, the Prussian king, allowing Prussia to fulfil a long-desired objective to send troops to seize the Swedish Baltic port of Stettin at the mouth of the Oder River, which further upstream was connected by a canal to the Havel River and, thus, Berlin. This agreement was formalised with the Treaty of Havelberg in which Peter guaranteed Friedrich Wilhelm's control of Stettin, while, in turn, Prussia paid Russia 400,000 thalers and guaranteed Russia the control of Ingria, Estonia, and Livonia.

Next, Peter travelled to Altona to meet Hanoverian representatives. The tsarina being pregnant, he decided not to return to Saint Petersburg but to go to the Dutch Republic, which he had last visited in 1698. Leaving her to travel more slowly, Peter went ahead alone, passing through Hamburg, Bremen, Amersfoort, and Utrecht, before arriving in Amsterdam on 17 December 1716. The tsarina had a difficult journey and stopped at Wesel, where she gave birth to their son Pavel on 2 January 1717, who only lived a day. Catherine eventually joined Peter and they spent most of their time privately in Amsterdam. Although he met government officials, among whom Grand Pensionary Heinsius was the most important, no political agreements were reached as the States General adhered to a policy of strict neutrality in the Northern War. In March 1717, the tsar went to the Southern, then Austrian, Netherlands, where he spent the spring, then stayed in Paris and Versailles until June 20. There, he met the seven-year-old future Louis XV and his negotiators managed to reach an understanding with the government of the regent, Philippe d'Orléans. The actual agreement

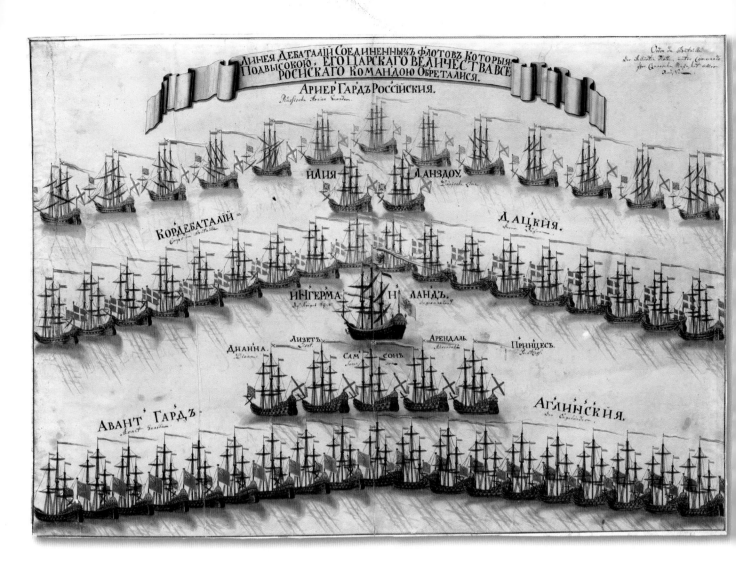

ЛИНЕЯ ДЕБАТАЛИИ СОЕДИНЕННЫХ ФЛОТОВЪ КОТОРЫЯ ПОДВЫСОКОЮ. ЕГО ЦАРСКАГО ВЕЛИЧЕСТВА ВСЕ РОСИСКАГО КОМАНДОЮ ОБРЕТАЛИСЯ.

АРИЕРГАРДЪ РОССИЙСКИЯ.

ИЛИЯ   ЛАНЗДОУ.

КОРДЕБАТАЛИЙ   ДАЦКИЯ.

ИНГЕРМА   Н   ЛАНДЪ.

ДИАННА.   ЛИЗЕТЪ   АРЕНДАЛЬ.   ПРИНЦЕСЪ.

САМ   СОНЪ.

АВАНТ ГАРДЪ   АГЛИНСКИЯ.

*The battle line of the combined allied Russian, Danish, and British fleet near Copenhagen on 13 August 1716.*

*Pen and ink with watercolours by unknown artist, ca. 1743. The Swedish Military Archives, Stockholm, Sweden.*

between Russia, Prussia, and France—the practical results of which were minimal—was only signed in Amsterdam after the tsar's return to the Dutch Republic in August 1717. There, his only political involvement was his meeting with the Swedish Baron von Görtz, just released from a Dutch prison, at Het Loo, the palace of the late Stadholder-King William III. This contact caused a lot of unrest in government circles in The Hague and London as Görtz was seen as an intriguer and suspected of double-dealing. Only in September 1717 did the tsar leave the Dutch Republic for good. His prolonged stays there had been primarily related to business. He needed ships, munitions and artillery, shipwrights, naval officers and seamen, artists and artisans, and in this he succeeded quite well. The Swedish ambassador complained about the large shipments of war material from Amsterdam and his hosts there must have been content. Politically he did not reach any agreement with the States General, who continued to consider themselves neutral in the conflict but were careful not to ruffle the feathers of the tsar too much.

In the end, Peter's ambitions for peace were stymied by the Dutch Republic's neutrality and Britain's increasing suspicions of Russia, caused by the latter's control of the Baltic, the potential threat to Hanover of Russian troops in Mecklenburg, and the Hanoverian rivalry with Denmark over control of Bremen and Verden. Also, there was a rising suspicion in western Europe that Peter was making a separate peace with Sweden that would exclude other powers.

Charles XII's common sense at last started to assert itself. From spring 1717 there were indeed direct contacts between Russian and Swedish diplomats regarding conclusion of a peace.[49] Russian propaganda machine expended considerable efforts on demonstrating that it was Charles XII's obstinacy and his lack of desire to negotiate a peace, which had caused the Northern War to drag on for so long. A book published in Saint Petersburg in 1717 was intended to have international resonance. Written by Vice-Chancellor Pyotr Shafirov and first published in a German version (from which it was translated into English), it had a long title of quite clear meaning: *A Discourse concerning the Just Causes why His Royal Majesty Peter the First . . . started the war against King Charles XII of Sweden in 1700 and which of these two potentates showed, during his time at war, greater moderation and readiness for peace, and which is most guilty in its continuation of the greatest spilling of Christian blood and the devastation of many lands, and by which of the warring countries this war was conducted according to the rules of Christian and political peoples.* The title page also notes the transfer of the capital from Moscow to the northwestern part of the Russian lands—'printed . . . in the reigning city of Saint Petersburg'—yet another indication to Europe of the irreversible changes that had taken place during the war, both in terms of Russia's international status and the country's inner workings. One of the key conclusions of this book was that 'the Swedish king alone is guilty of the beginning and the continuation of this still ongoing war, and the shedding of Christian blood, and the devastation of subjects. By contrast, his Royal Majesty's peace-loving nature and moderation in all such actions is well known to the world.'[50]

By the last year of Charles XII's life the relationship between the demographic, military, and economic potential of Sweden and Russia had altered radically. According to its first 'revision' or census of 1719, Russia had some 15,700,000 inhabitants,[51] whereas Sweden's population, by 1718, after all the losses of land on the other side of the Baltic, had been reduced from 2,500,000 to 1,247,000.[52] In the spring of 1718 the Swedish army consisted of just 40,000 poorly equipped regular troops and 25,000 to 30,000 members of the militia.[53] According to army lists for 1711, Russia had 171,000 regular troops[54] as well as Cossacks. The campaign of 1718 first demonstrated that the Russian fleet had joined the strongest navies of the Baltic powers, superior in force to both the Danish and Swedish fleets. At that time 25 ships of the line put to sea, with 1,436 cannon and 9,198 men[55] and on 1 September 1718 some 121 Russian galleys took part in training manoeuvres amidst the skerries near Åbo.[56] The Swedish fleet, just 15 ships of the line, was at Karlskrona and went into action only in April, limiting itself to the area around Bornholm.[57]

In December 1717 an offer arrived in Saint Petersburg from the first minister to the Swedish king, Georg von Görtz, proposing the start of Russo-Swedish peace negotiations.[58] Subsequently, a congress opened on 21 May 1718 on the Åland Islands. Now, it seemed, Charles XII trusted his former inveterate enemy. He sent the main part of his regular troops, some 20,000 men, to Norway to do battle with the Danes while the Russians refused to engage in any active fighting that year. Peter personally added a meaningful note to the official history of his reign, characterising the restraint shown by the Russians in 1718:

> *In this campaign we might have undertaken whatever great action we wished, since there was no Swedish fleet and the troops had been sent to Norway (and although the congress was taking place there was no peace). But they were not undertaken, in order not to hinder the tendency towards peace that the Swedish king then had.*[59]

By August 1718 the main details of the draft peace treaty had been agreed. Russia was to keep the whole of Livonia with Riga and Reval, plus part of Karelia with Vyborg and Ingria. Finland and the greater part of Karelia were to be returned to the Swedes. Russia was to provide Sweden with an auxiliary force of 20,000 soldiers to help win back the former Swedish territories of Bremen and Verden from the elector of Hanover,[60] although this did not mean that Russia was entering the war on Sweden's side. It was also foreseen that Sweden would compensate the lands ceded to Russia through the conquest of Norway. At the moment of Charles XII's death, 11 December 1718, these peace negotiations had ground to a halt. The tsar gave the Swedes an ultimatum: the treaty must be signed by the end of December.[61]

Once again Peter had demonstrated maximum flexibility, a readiness to make significant compromises. The signing of a peace treaty under such conditions would have been, in essence, a 'diplomatic revolution.' From an enemy Russia would have been transformed into an ally of Sweden, supporting it (although without a declaration of war) in its actions against Denmark, Saxony, and Hanover. The tsar was ready to come to an agreement with Charles XII and had no wish to utterly destroy Sweden. There was no chance of Sweden regaining Finland either alone or with the help of other powers, yet Peter was ready to make this truly 'royal' gift to the king in order to achieve peace. He well understood the character of Charles XII: the Swedish monarch—who had not been in the capital once since the start of the Great Northern War—was prepared to enter Stockholm only in triumphant mode. Charles now understood what was evident to all—that he, with his small army, could never defeat the mighty Russian state and Tsar Peter I. Peter gave his 'brother' Charles the chance to be a triumphant victor once more by taking Norway from Denmark. But the conquest of Norway by the now weak Swedish army demanded time, if it were indeed to be at all possible. It is quite clear why Charles XII put off signing the peace agreement with Russia: he wanted first to have some major military success in Norway. But there was to be no victory, and as 1718 drew to its close the conclusion of a peace agreement with Russia in exchange for the hope of a military annexation of Norway at some time in the future seems not to have appealed to the Swedish king. In such a case his 'triumph' would not have been evident: the Swedish losses under the proposed treaty would have been quite real, whereas the acquisition of Norway remained a shadowy illusion, promising a Sweden already exhausted by war yet further endless conflict with Denmark, Great Britain, Hanover, and other states.

Towards the end of the Northern War Charles XII rethought his attitude to Peter I. The Swedish king was a man of honour. He remained true to his word, once given,

*Peter I as commander of the four allied navies.*

Painting by Louis Caravaque (1684-1754), After 1716. The Central Naval Museum, Saint Petersburg, Russia.

and had great respect for military success. Both monarchs found common ground. It is indicative that Peter I saw an alliance with Sweden as key to stability in the Baltic region. But it was not until 1724 that Emperor Peter the Great at last managed to conclude a defensive alliance—with the new Swedish king, Fredrik I.

## ■ Conclusion

Specific aspects of Charles XII's character and his intransigent anti-Russian policy were among the main factors that helped turn Russia into a great European power over the course of the Great Northern War. The Russian state made extensive territorial gains in the strategically important Baltic region, gains of which Peter I could not even have dreamed when the war started—at that time he sought merely a single port on the Baltic Sea. By the end of the war, it was clear that Charles XII had played a significant role, both in shaping Russia's destiny and in turning Peter himself into one of the great rulers of world history. In a communication from Saint Petersburg dated 20 January 1719, French maritime consul H. de La Vie described the following incident. Some time ago the tsar had drunk to the health of the Swedish king (his death was not yet known in Russia) and one of his favourites asked why. His Majesty replied: 'It was in his own interests, since as long as the king lived he would forever be arguing with everyone.'[62] When news of Charles's death was received in Saint Petersburg, Friedrich Christian Weber, the resident of Hanover, asked the tsar at an assembly: 'Were congratulations in order or an expression of sympathy with respect to this great event?' The monarch shrugged his shoulders and replied: 'I don't know myself.'[63] His response seems to have been utterly sincere.

In truth, the path of Russia's history did not depend exclusively on the actions of the tsar. Any war with so mighty a state as Sweden demanded full mobilisation of all of Russia's resources and required extensive reforms. Russia needed a great ruler who could rapidly modernise the army, create a strong naval fleet in the Baltic, set in train rapid industrialisation, create an effective state administration, increase the income to the treasury several times, establish new educational institutions and systems of learning, and encourage the work of professional scholars. It was Peter I who was able to take on this role, and in the end it was largely Sweden's strength, and Peter's need to fight it, that led to Russia's great reforms.

In Charles XII fate sent the tsar a charismatic opponent. His character, his stubborn years-long war with Peter I, requiring that he muster all of Sweden's resources, facilitated the emergence of an adequate counterbalance in the form of the Russian Empire. It was no easy matter to destroy the mighty state created by Swedish kings over the course of the seventeenth century. Only an absolute Swedish monarch could do it, one who had no need to listen to advisers, who believed in his own magnificent destiny, who forgot to be careful, who took risks. Charles XII repeatedly created the conditions necessary for the success of state reform in Russia, 'assisting' Tsar Peter I in his transformation into Emperor Peter the Great. After his brilliant victory at Narva in 1700 Charles made no effort to conclude an advantageous peace treaty with his shocked enemy. In early 1702 the king entered Poland, with which he was not at war, thereby gaining a new enemy and transforming this extensive state into the main theatre of prolonged military action. This put an end for many years to come to any threat that the main Swedish army would enter Russia, with the consequence that Russian troops did battle with the Swedes not only on the latter's own territory but also in the lands of Poland, and later Germany. Moreover, Russia gained several years of breathing space during which it could reinforce the state and speed up reforms. It was only in September 1707 that the Swedish army set off from Saxony on the long march to the Russian border. In the same year Charles created the necessary conditions for total collapse of the Swedish Empire when he turned down Russian offers of peace which demanded only that Sweden cede the small province of Ingria, a territory that had belonged to Russia until 1612. Next, in 1710, he repudiated the Act of Neutrality, the purpose of which had been to preserve Swedish lands in northern Germany. He refused to use the Brunswick conference to his own ends. Little good came of his time in the Ottoman Empire, from the destruction of his army at Poltava right up to the end of 1714, while during these years, in the absence of an effective government in Sweden, Russia managed to reinforce its position significantly. Although it was not his intention, by his actions the king created a Russia that was truly great. Peter I's attitude towards Charles XII is best characterised by the fact that when official news of the king's death was received from Queen Ulrika Eleonora, the tsar, his wife Catherine, and all their courtiers donned mourning 'in memory of the Swedish king.'[64]

CHAPTER 17

# Brandenburg-Prussia and the Northern German States
## *amicus sed non vicinus*

by Linda S. Frey and Marsha L. Frey

Just as the colours and patterns in a kaleidoscope shift, coalesce, and change, so too did the fortunes of war for the belligerents in the Great Northern War (1700-21). What had been said of Denmark in 1692 was equally true of Sweden: 'Between the King of Denmark and most of his neighbours it may be said in general that there is always a reciprocal jealousy and distrust, which often breaks out into open hostilities; with those nearer more frequently, with the remoter more seldom . . . .'[1] The northern German powers, committed to the War of the Spanish Succession (1702-14), feared the merger of these two great conflicts as did their allies. In any case, the northern German powers and Denmark might withdraw troops from the struggle against Louis and deploy them in the north.[2] At least one of the protagonists in the Great Northern War, Tsar Peter, however, celebrated the outbreak of the War of the Spanish Succession, for it shifted attention away from the conflict in the north: 'Long may it last, God willing.'[3] The Russo-Turkish war of 1711, the Imperial elections of 1705 and 1711, the Triple Alliance of 1717, and the Quadruple Alliance of 1718 complicated the international scene for all the combatants.

What was said of Brandenburg-Prussia—that the elector-king was caught between and threatened by two powerful storms from both the east and the west—was also true for the other northern German powers.[4] Brandenburg-Prussia held one of the most tenuous positions because of the widespread dispersion of its territories from the shores of the Baltic to the banks of the Rhine. The distance of the East Prussian lands from the bulk of the Hohenzollern dominions meant that they could hardly be successfully defended against either Poland or Russia, especially if a sizeable number of troops were deployed elsewhere. The distance of the lands in the west, such as Cleves, made them equally difficult to protect against allied threats. The brilliant Prussian foreign minister, Heinrich Rüdiger von Ilgen, saw neutrality in the north as the only viable option for Brandenburg-Prussia to pursue while she was engaged in the west.[5] Holstein-Gottorp's position was even more precarious. Because her territories were intermingled with those of Denmark in Schleswig and Holstein, she had most to fear from the Danes and accordingly sought a strong alliance with Sweden.[6] The elector of Saxony and king of Poland was involved in both wars. Poland and Saxony felt threatened by their common neighbour, Brandenburg-Prussia, and in addition worried about the formidable armies of Sweden and Russia.

*Coronation of Friedrich I as king in Prussia.*

*Painting by Henrik Schildt, ca. 1701. Herzog Anton Ulrich Museum, Braunschweig, Germany.*

Mecklenburg was vulnerable to both sides in the Great Northern War and feared Denmark and Sweden in particular. To Mecklenburg's west lay the Swedish territories of Bremen and Verden as well as the duchy of Holstein-Gottorp, a Swedish ally; to the north, Scania, and to the east, Stettin, Stralsund, and Hither Pomerania, all Swedish. Wismar, an important Swedish port, was located inside Mecklenburg's territory. During the Thirty Years' War Gustav Adolf regarded Mecklenburg as *jure belli* Swedish.[7] Friedrich Wilhelm of Mecklenburg (1675-1713) retained as a necessity the Swedish alliance. His successor, Karl Leopold (1713-47), however, strove to increase ties with Russia to bolster his precarious position.[8] Hanover feared Danish ambitions and the expansion of Russian power.[9] None of the northern German powers, especially Hanover, Mecklenburg's southern neighbour, sanctioned the Russian alliance and the establishment of a Russian outpost in Mecklenburg-Schwerin later in the war.[10] These northern German states, particularly Brandenburg-Prussia, Holstein-Gottorp, and Mecklenburg-Schwerin, also worried about the movement and possible depredation of troops across their lands. Mecklenburg-Schwerin complained of depredations from the Danes as late as 1712 and went so far as to request military assistance from Prussia and the emperor.[11]

## ■ The Swedish Blue and Yellow Flag

One historian has aptly described the Great Northern War as a 'late sprout' of that earlier devastating conflict, the Thirty Years' War, in which a more powerful Sweden emerged and acted as guarantor of the treaty.[12] After this conflict the Swedes enjoyed a much stronger presence on the Baltic and in northern Germany. They had acquired Bremen, a Free Imperial City and an important Hanseatic port, and Verden, also a Free Imperial City; Wismar, a flourishing Hanseatic city as well as the former residence of rulers of Mecklenburg; and two Hanseatic cities, Stralsund and Stettin, in Pomerania. These territories gave the Swedes control of three strategic river mouths: the Weser, Elbe, and Oder. The Swedish blue and yellow flag also controlled the Neva and the Dvina (Daugava). Only the mouth of the Vistula, that flowed through Poland and emptied at Danzig, was not Swedish. Through these possessions, Sweden acquired seats in the Imperial Diet at Regensburg and periodically led the Lower Saxon Circle.[13] Because of their strategic position, the Swedes could deploy troops within striking distance not only of the northern German states, but also Denmark, the Low Countries, Poland, and the Habsburg lands. Sweden's desire to control the Baltic brought her into conflict with the Danes, who had lost control of the Sound, and also with Poland and Brandenburg-Prussia, because they held strategic ports on the Baltic. Denmark, whose enmity was 'prescriptive and unquenchable,'[14] was the Swedes' bitterest and most irreconcilable enemy, but they also had to worry about the permanently covetous Hanoverians. The treaties that concluded the War of the North (1655-60) had recognised Swedish possession of Scania, Blekinge, Bohuslän, and Halland, as well as Livonia, and forced the tsar to concede Swedish control of the Baltic provinces. By 1700, Sweden found herself surrounded by ambitious neighbours: the Danes, the Poles, the Hanoverians, the Brandenburg-Prussians, and the Russians.

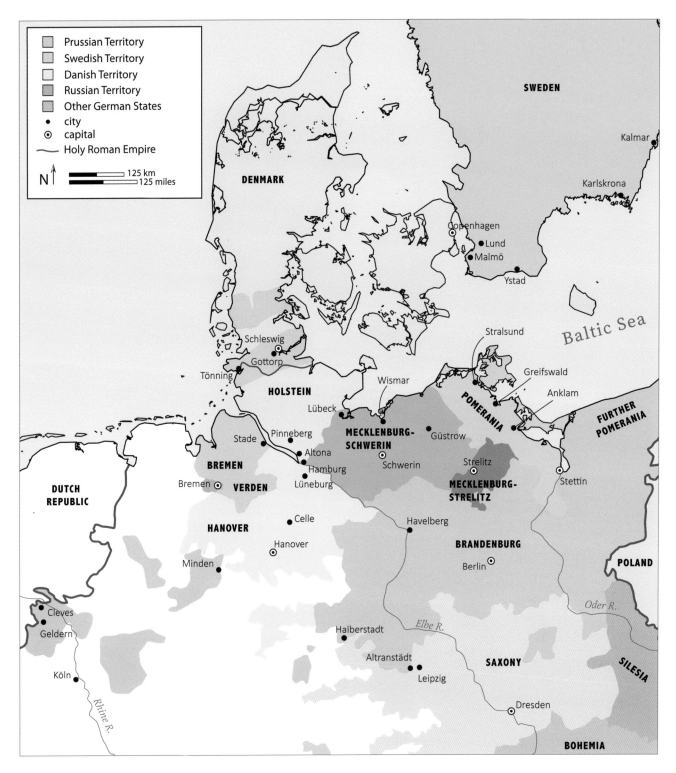

## ■ 'Religion Is an All-important Matter' (Napoleon)

Religiously, the Swedes shared a Protestant confession with the Danes and the northern German powers.[15] This evangelical alliance tightened the bonds among the latter and came to the fore when confessional issues roiled the Holy Roman Empire. For example, when the elector of Saxony converted to the Catholic faith, many contended that he could no longer head, as his predecessors had done since the sixteenth centu-

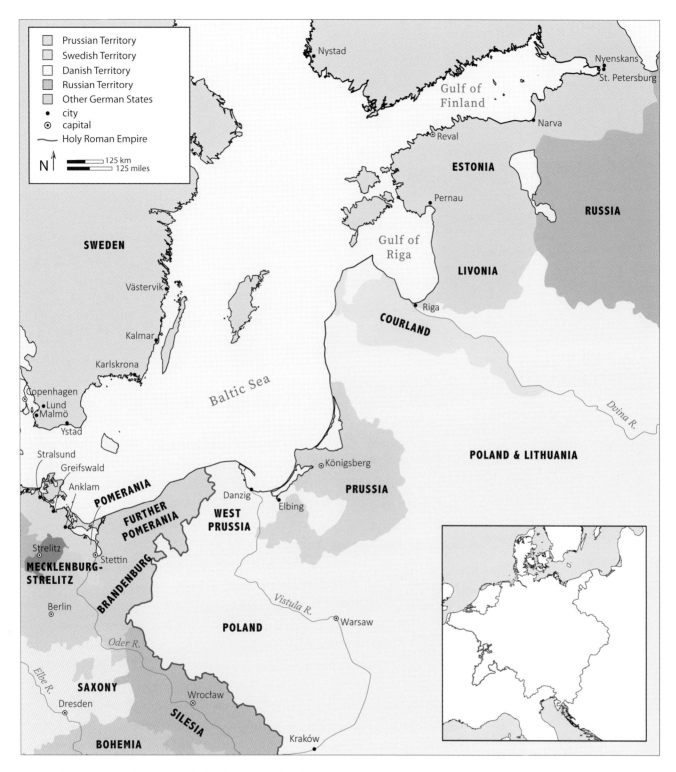

ry, the *Corpus Evangelicorum* in the Holy Roman Empire. Two northern states vied for that honour: Brandenburg-Prussia and Hanover.[16] The Protestants, including the Swedes, had jointly and ineffectually protested the persecution of the Protestants in the Empire and in Hungary.[17] In particular, they also objected to the policies of Karl Philipp, Elector Palatine, a Catholic, who persecuted Protestants in his domains. In reprisal, Friedrich Wilhelm I of Prussia, who vaunted his toleration policies, targeted his Catholic subjects in Minden and Halberstadt. The Brandenburg-Prussians in August 1707 even signed an evangelical alliance with Sweden to protect the faith.[18] Prot-estantism, however, did not always unite the powers. The third wife of Friedrich of Brandenburg-Prussia, Sophie Luise of Mecklenburg, was a Lutheran but an intolerant one. She frankly told her husband, a Calvinist, that as such he was incapable of going to heaven. Her rigid and uncompromising views led to frequent quarrels at court and hardly enhanced relations between the two states.[19]

While the Russians were heavily Orthodox, the Swedes felt most threatened by the Catholic Poles, who championed the Counter-Reformation in the north[20] and whose ruler espoused an ambitious foreign policy that sought to limit Swedish power. The newly elected king of Poland, Augustus II, the Saxon elector Friedrich August, aptly named the 'elusive eel' because of his known duplicity, intended to reinvigorate Poland.

## ■ 'Ambition Can Creep as Well' (Burke)

Sweden had a far-flung empire with no natural boundaries and faced enemies on three sides: the Baltic, the south, and German states. Hanoverian fear of Danish pretensions and rivalry with Brandenburg-Prussia, Mecklenburg's internal turmoil, the Swedish alliance with the dukes of Holstein-Gottorp, and the Holy Roman Em-pire's commitment to the Nine Years' War (1688-97) and later the War of the Spanish Succession (1702-14) had mitigated the danger for the Swedes as did other scarcely concealed regional rivalries. These foes harboured territorial ambitions that conflict-ed with those of Sweden. Poland coveted Lithuania and Riga, the elector of Branden-burg desired Swedish Pomerania and Stettin, and Hanover was after the duchy of Bremen and the principality of Verden and did not want it to fall into the hands of the Danes. Should the latter acquire these two territories they would have a land bridge to Oldenburg and Delmenhorst as well as full control over the mouths of the Elbe and Weser.[22] The elector also hoped to erect a stronger barrier against Denmark. To counter Danish strength, Hanover supported the duke of Holstein-Gottorp. In both 1688-89 and 1699-1700, Hanover was willing to amass troops with other powers to restore the duke to lands which Denmark had occupied.[23] Hanoverian-Danish hostility was deep-seated. Underlying the personal enmity was the Danish oppo-sition, shared by Brandenburg and Saxony, to Hanover's elevation to an electorate. Hanover's rulers had fought fiercely and intrigued shamelessly for this long-coveted status, which Denmark only agreed to recognise at the Peace of Travendal (1700).[24] The Swedes could also exploit Prussian-Polish rivalry in Pomerania. What was true of France at this time was equally true of the northern German powers: *amicus sed non vicinus*, or 'friends, but not neighbours.'

## ■ Dynasties Make Alliances. Others Wage War?

Sweden understandably sought marriage alliances with the northern powers, most particularly with the dukes of Holstein-Gottorp, whose lands acted as a barrier against a Danish advance.[25] Several marriages strengthened the bonds between

Sweden and the duchy. The queen mother in Sweden, Hedvig Eleonora, was the sister of Christian Albert, Duke of Holstein-Gottorp. Her daughter, Charles XII's eldest and beloved sister, Hedvig Sofia, married a cousin, Friedrich IV of Holstein-Gottorp, and Charles's cousin Albertina Frederica married Christian August of Holstein-Gottorp. When they were younger, the two cousins, Charles and Friedrich, although separated by six years, engaged in what contemporaries euphemistically termed 'the Gottorp folly,' wild and dangerous pranks. Charles also sought closer ties elsewhere. His younger sister, Ulrika Eleonora, married Friedrich of Hesse-Kassel, later to become King Fredrik I of Sweden. The marriages of Charles's sisters frustrated Hanoverian ambitions.

Sweden's natural enemies were also concluding dynastic alliances: Peter I married his daughter Anna to Karl Friedrich of Holstein-Gottorp and his niece Ekaterina Ivanovna to Karl Leopold of Mecklenburg-Schwerin. In 1711, Peter's son Alexei married Charlotte of Brunswick-Wolfenbüttel, whose sister was married to Emperor Charles VI. The houses of Brandenburg and Hanover also intermarried. Yet, the hope that marriage alliances would strengthen the ties between neighbours was not always realised. The incompatibility of the spouses may have exacerbated the rivalry. Friedrich I of Brandenburg-Prussia married Sophie Charlotte of Hanover (his second wife), and his son Friedrich Wilhelm I married his cousin Sophia Dorothea of Hanover, the sister of Georg of Hanover (later George I of Great Britain). Both marriages arguably increased the rivalry of the two neighbouring powers. Friedrich I of Prussia had earlier wed his beloved cousin Elisabeth Henriette of Hesse-Kassel, strengthening ties with the landgrave.[26] Their daughter Louise Dorothea Sophie married Friedrich of Hesse-Kassel (as his first wife), further cementing the alliance. Friedrich's third marriage, however, to Sophie Luise of Mecklenburg-Schwerin, 'the Venus of Mecklenburg,' designed to tighten the bonds between those two northern German powers, proved problematic, as was noted above. The rigidly Lutheran and increasingly reclusive queen alienated not only her husband, but also the rest of the court. Unbending and intolerant, she became increasingly melancholy and was ultimately sent home, where she died insane.[27] Friedrich Wilhelm of Mecklenburg-Schwerin also sought to strengthen ties with other German princes; he married Sophie Charlotte of Hesse-Kassel.

## ■ Imperial Politics: 'Confound Their Politics, Frustrate Their Knavish Tricks'

In addition to this complex and interwoven web of marriage alliances, Imperial politics roiled the northern German powers. The Hanoverian elevation to the electorate increased the tension among the powers as did the Hohenzollern acquisition of a crown and the Saxon election to the Polish kingship. In addition, the extinction of the Güstrow line with the death of Duke Gustav Adolf of Mecklenburg-Güstrow in 1695 had triggered an inheritance dispute between Friedrich Wilhelm of Mecklenburg-Schwerin and his uncle, Adolf Friedrich, Duke of Mecklenburg-Strelitz.[28] The Danish occupation of the duke of Holstein-Gottorp's lands in 1688-89 and 1699-1700 had also ratcheted up tensions as did the later Russian occupation of Mecklenburg.

# ■ 'Dragged into War by the Hair'

Into this toxic brew of dynastic and personal rivalry, ambition, and enmity, the Northern
War erupted in 1700.[29] As Henry St. John—later famous as Viscount Bolingbroke—pointed out so poetically: 'We have our eyes fixed on Northern affairs, but like People who gaze
on a storm at Sea, we are rather filled with horror at the sight . . . .'[30] Charles XII faced a
bevy of natural enemies who sought to seize Swedish lands. He noted somewhat cynically
that 'it is curious that both my cousins, Frederick [Denmark] and Augustus [Saxony-
Poland], wish to make war on me.'[31] Charles's father had urged him to keep the peace 'unless you are dragged into war by the hair,'[32] but so he was. Sweden's supremacy in the Baltic
had been dependent on the weakness and division among her natural enemies. When
Denmark, impatient to try yet again to annex the Holstein-Gottorp lands and regain
southern Sweden, joined with Augustus II of Poland, eager to take Livonia and Riga from
Sweden, and Peter of Russia, avid to seize Swedish lands around Ingria, the Northern War
erupted. Frederik IV of Denmark attacked Holstein-Gottorp in March of 1700 with 16,000
men and besieged the town of Tönning; Augustus invaded Livonia; and Peter, Ingria and
Estonia. Only Sweden's German lands remained as yet uncontested.

But the allies, and the Danes in particular, who pejoratively labelled the Swedish
sailors 'farm hands dipped in salt water,'[33] had underestimated Charles. Early in the
war, with aid from the Maritime Powers, he landed a Swedish army in Danish Zealand, threatened Copenhagen, and with an armed force some 20,000 strong under the
leadership of Hanover and Celle, the guarantors of the ducal lands of Holstein-Gottorp through the Treaty of Altona, forced Denmark to make peace and to return the
territories seized.[34] Charles later succeeded in getting Augustus deposed as king—albeit
temporarily in 1704—and expelling the Saxon troops from Poland. He did not attack
the electorate of Saxony at that time because of his promise to the Maritime Powers not
to enter the Empire and out of gratitude for their help early in the conflict. Other than
the invasion of Holstein-Gottorp, the march of Hanoverian and Celle troops through
Hildesheim,[35] and the ultimate expulsion of Danish troops, the northern German states
had so far remained relatively free of war. The main casualty in the north early in the
war was the death of a valued ally and brother-in-law, the duke of Holstein-Gottorp,
who was killed fighting with the Swedes at Kliszów in 1702.

The confederates who were fighting in the War of the Spanish Succession, the
British in particular, regarded the Northern War, in the words of John Churchill, Duke of
Marlborough, the allied commander, as a 'monstrous irrelevancy.'[36] Although Brandenburg-Prussia and Hanover wanted to force Sweden out of the Empire, neither yet went
to war. Hanover was so thoroughly committed to the war against Louis XIV that the
Maritime Powers reduced the rate they agreed to pay Hanoverian troops and did little to
win the elector over other than promise to pressure France to recognise the electorate.[37]

# ■ Between the Hammer and the Anvil

The elector of Brandenburg-Prussia, like the other northern German states, had sent
troops to fight in the War of the Spanish Succession. He was bound to the allies by

monetary ties, by the allied guarantee of his neutrality in the north, and by promises of future gains.[38] If Friedrich withdrew his troops, the allies feared that others, notably the Holsteins, the Danes, the Hanoverians, and the Saxons, would recall theirs as well and imperil the Grand Alliance. At the very start of the conflict Stadholder-King William III threatened to invade Cleves if Friedrich allied with Sweden's enemies.[39] This was not an idle threat as Cleves was the farthest western outpost of the Hohenzollern lands and perilously near—actually too near—the United Provinces. Indeed Cleves remained a concern for the king throughout the war.[40] Ensuring Friedrich's commitment to the struggle against Louis XIV and guaranteeing his neutrality in the north would best secure and further allied interests.[41] The allies, however, often found him unreliable; Marlborough later condemned what he thought of as the 'fickleness' of the court of Berlin.[42] The Prussian minister, Ilgen, continually manoeuvred among the combatants in the north, prompting the English minister at Berlin, Thomas Wentworth, Baron Raby and Earl of Strafford, to deprecate their irresolution. Following their designs, he noted, was 'like following a pack of hounds which were not staunch, for the minute a fresh hare starts they leave the former to follow that and immediately that for another; so that one has no way of catching anything.'[43] Friedrich I's territorial ambitions and strategic concerns made him an opponent of both Sweden and Russia. The conflict between Augustus and Charles threatened to spread into the lands of Friedrich, who realised that neither Sweden nor Poland were 'sure friends of his.'[44] He did not trust the combatants, Augustus in particular, who was known for his gargantuan appetite for wine, food, women, and gain, not necessarily in that order, as well as for his duplicity and cynicism. Brandenburg-Prussia had most to fear from Charles because of the strength of his army, his geographical position in northern Germany and on the Baltic, and his alliance with the House of Lüneburg.

Fearful of Swedish intentions and with his scattered territories in an exposed position, Friedrich was militarily vulnerable. He had concluded a treaty with Charles in 1703, by which the Swede had recognised him as king in Prussia in exchange for a promise of neutrality.[45] Friedrich, however, refused to recognise Stanislaw as king of Poland. This treaty countered Augustus's manoeuvrings in Saxony and Poland and mitigated Friedrich's fears of the Swedes,[46] whose possession of Stettin meant that Charles could easily and quickly march to Berlin, a mere 150 kilometres. The Swedish garrisoning of Elbing in Poland in December 1703 was done in order to prevent Friedrich's seizure of the city, and the stationing of Swedish troops in the bishopric of Warmia (also known by its German name Ermland) for winter quarters alarmed him. In addition, he feared that Charles might seize Danzig, an important Hanseatic port and Free Imperial City, and cut off communications between Brandenburg and the kingdom of Prussia. Without consulting his allies, Friedrich concluded a treaty with the city that guaranteed Danzig's independence and provided 2,000 Prussian troops in case of attack and free passage for Prussian troops. One of the English diplomats at the time, Alexander Stanhope, condemned the Danzig magistrates' attempts to justify the treaty as plastering over 'a very Scurvy business in a Slovenly manner.'[47] Such actions only fuelled allied distrust of the king. Friedrich's concurrent attempts to act as mediator in the northern struggle also occasioned unease, now with Sweden.

Brandenburg-Prussia continued to jockey among the combatants in both wars. As the conflict escalated, Friedrich, worried about the growing threat to his lands, especially from the Russians, mobilised more troops.[48] Despite his treaty with Charles, he continued to negotiate with Charles's enemies. However, he did not move against the Swedes, who were between him and his troops in Prussia. And although he continued to negotiate with the rulers of both Russia and Saxony, he did not commit to either because he did not have a large enough army or could not move against the strong position the Swedes held. A Prussian alliance, however, with either Sweden or Saxony was impossible because neither power was willing to cede West Prussia to the Hohenzollerns as both were endeavouring to win over the Polish nobility.

By 1704, the Maritime Powers and the emperor were pressing Denmark and the northern German powers, Brandenburg, Hanover, and Hesse in particular, to consign more troops to the war effort against Louis XIV, but managed to convince only Brandenburg-Prussia.[49] By obtaining this agreement they hoped to tie down a large number of troops in Italy and reinforce their recently acquired ally, Vittorio Amedeo II, Duke of Savoy.[50] Friedrich's decision to dispatch 8,000 troops to the Italian front in 1704, in accordance with his treaty of 28 November 1704, reflected his commitment to the Grand Alliance. Denuded of so many troops, the Prussian king then did not have the resources to get involved in the Northern War. By 1706 he had fewer than 8,000 effective fighting men in Prussia. Marlborough used both charm and threats to convince the king to remain neutral in the north. He warned him that the allies would deal with Prussia, should he get involved in the Northern War, as they had dealt with Denmark in 1700, when the Anglo-Dutch fleet had supported Charles XII.[51] In return for his neutrality, the Maritime Powers guaranteed the inviolability of the king's Prussian lands. The allied victory at Blenheim on 13 August 1704 that had forced Bavaria out of the war, may also have influenced the king and underscored allied power. Friedrich was militarily vulnerable in Prussia and understandably feared Swedish intentions in Courland and Poland. Moreover, he had allowed the transit of Saxon troops through his lands while denying the same to the Swedes.

In the midst of the war in 1705 yet another dispute arose—over the contested succession of the Lübeck-Eutin bishopric, traditionally held in turn by the king of Denmark-Norway and the duke of Holstein-Gottorp. When the bishop died in 1705, initially neither the emperor nor Frederik IV of Denmark would recognise the claim of Holstein-Gottorp, Sweden's ally. Friedrich of Brandenburg-Prussia, however, supported this claim[52] and, later in 1706, so did Frederik IV and, in 1707, Emperor Joseph I. But this dispute further increased tension and reflected Prussia's growing support of Charles, especially after Friedrich discovered that Augustus was willing to join Charles and force him out of Prussia. Friedrich continued to offer his mediation, but unsuccessfully, as Charles refused to rely on the sincerity of Augustus, the most scheming double-dealer of his day.[53] As late as 1705, Charles Whitworth, the British representative to Russia, thought that Friedrich I seemed resolved 'to quench rather than increase the flame' in the north.[54] That was cer-

*Ekaterina Ivanovna, Duchess of Mecklenburg-Schwerin and niece to Peter I of Russia.*

*Painting by Louis Caravaque (1684-1754), mid-1710s. The State Russian Museum, Saint Petersburg, Russia.*

tainly the view from Berlin, but the elector of Brandenburg advised his son and successor to 'keep his lands in peace and calm and to avoid as long as possible war and disturbance.' It was hardly a light thing, 'to draw the sword and harder still with honour and advantage to sheathe it again.' He emphasised that the present war in the north 'could easily be fatal to us and our house.'[55]

Friedrich was also concerned about the Orange inheritance, continually pressuring the allies to guarantee those lands in return for giving up his ambitions in the north. The allies succeeded in convincing Friedrich to renew the treaty in 1705, 1706, and 1708, despite his bitter altercations with the States General over the Orange inheritance and with the emperor. From 1706 to 1708 Friedrich delayed in dispatching his troops to the allied fronts and considered a potential triple alliance with Hanover and Sweden. The victories of Ramillies on 23 May 1706, Turin on 7 September 1706, and later Oudenaarde on 11 July 1708, however, cemented allied strength, bound Friedrich more firmly to the alliance, and changed the calculus in the north.

## ■ Invasion of Saxony: A Furious Surprise

Although Charles had earlier respected the allied prohibition of an invasion of the Holy Roman Empire in part because he did not want to lose the Maritime Powers' guarantee of Travendal, by 1706 the balance had clearly shifted to the allies' favour. After campaigning in Poland for five years, Charles invaded Saxony in August. He intended to force Augustus to renounce the Polish throne and his Russian alliance. The Swedish occupation was by all accounts not punitive but did exact contributions to support the men, who commingled with the local population, allegedly leaving enough illegitimate children behind to staff a regiment.[56] This invasion was 'a furious surprise' and not a pleasant one for the court of Berlin.[57] In response to this growing threat, Friedrich signed yet another alliance, which provided that Sweden and Brandenburg-Prussia would mutually guarantee each other's territories, furnish 6,000 troops if the other were attacked, and protect the Protestants as stipulated in the Treaty of Westphalia.[58] Friedrich continued to manoeuvre among the combatants without committing to so problematic a struggle. Denmark, who neither could nor would understand his policy of neutrality, viewed it as emblematic of Prussian friendliness towards Sweden.[59] In return for English recognition of Stanislaw, Charles allayed allied concerns that he would intervene in the War of the Spanish Succession.

Still the Swedish occupation of Saxony remained a threat and underscored the possibility of the merging of the two conflicts. Emperor Joseph I, who had alienated Charles and aided Augustus by granting passage for the Saxons via Silesia, by siding with Denmark in the Lübeck-Eutin dispute,[60] and by negotiating with the tsar, found himself powerless to do anything as his armies were fighting in Hungary (the Rákóczi insurrection) and in the south and the west. One minister aptly voiced allied uneasiness when he noted that the emperor 'apprehends the worst, but is obliged to dissemble . . . lest he should provoke and draw upon himself the Lyon, which is broke lose, and is at Liberty (as the Empire is now composed) to devour any part of it without Restraint.'[61] Joseph feared that Charles might become a second Gustav Adolf and pose a real threat to Catholicism.[62]

To appease Sweden the emperor offered free transit to the Swedish army through Silesia, gave up the claim to an Imperial contingent which Charles owed as a German prince, sanctioned the Gottorp candidacy to the Lübeck-Eutin bishopric, and guaranteed the reinstatement of the religious rights of 1648 to the Silesian Protestants.[63] These extensive concessions underscored the threat the Swedes posed to the German lands. The allies for their part worried that the emperor might withdraw troops from the war to deal with the Swedish threat[64] and accordingly did all they could to avoid a rupture with Charles.[65] Marlborough personally visited Charles to extract a promise that he would remain neutral in the War of the Spanish Succession.[66]

## ■ After Poltava: 'Too Dangerous to Do Anything'

The defeat of the Swedes, outnumbered four to one, at Poltava in July 1709, changed the calculus of the war, prompted the Saxons to re-enter the war, and increased the possibility of a Prussian or Hanoverian alliance with the tsar and Augustus. The Branden-burg elector hoped to attain valuable territories from either Peter or Augustus without actively participating in the war. In short, he opted to gamble: risk little and possibly gain a good deal. The Maritime Powers continued to pressure their allies, particularly Denmark, Hanover, and Prussia, to remain committed to the conflict against France.[67] Although the allies feared the outbreak of war in the Empire, no government took ac-tion. As Godolphin candidly wrote to Marlborough in September 1709: 'I am perswad-ed the whole Alliyance is engaged in interest not to suffer a war to begin in the north (of which nobody can foresee the consequences or the end) before the conclusion of the present warr, in which they have already been so long engaged.'[68]

Friedrich I refused to break openly with the Swedes, whose army had retreated towards Swedish Pomerania and crossed Friedrich's frontier, traversing the Neumark. He was forced to accept this *fait accompli* because his troops were committed to the war in the south. Ilgen felt that the king could not break with Sweden because he would have 'neither troops nor money.' Moreover Ilgen still hoped to benefit from the peace with France.[69] The greatest danger to Prussia, he thought, would come from a war on two fronts.[70] But Friedrich was becoming increasingly disillusioned with his allies and considered withdrawing some or all of his troops from the Low Countries, even the rumour of which, Marlborough warned the king, would deliver a 'mortal blow' to the allies.[71] By 1709, approximately three-fourths of his 44,000-man army were in the service of the allies. Friedrich tried to tack between the adverse political winds of the east and west. He sought to have his recent kingship acknowledged, fulfil his obligations to the emperor and the allies, maintain good relations with the Maritime Powers, champion Protestant interests in the Empire, and at the same safe-guard his own interests in the east.

Hanover, committed to the war against France and initially a strong ally of Swe-den and enemy of Denmark, was eager to capitalise on Swedish weakness. In particu-lar the elector sought to wrest the duchies of Bremen and Verden from Sweden and refused to sanction Danish possession. Georg, like Friedrich of Prussia, temporised, balancing the pro-Swedish faction against the anti-Swedish one, headed by the pow-erful and skilful Andreas Gottlieb von Bernstorff. On 14 July 1710, though, Hanover concluded a defensive alliance with its old foe, Denmark, after Charles, understand-ably, had refused Georg's offer of a sizeable loan in exchange for Hanoverian occupa-tion of the two critical duchies for 25 years. Still committed to the War of the Spanish Succession, the elector could do little but wait for the fortunes of war to turn.[72]

The duke of Holstein-Gottorp, Charles's ally, found his lands overrun yet again by the Danes. The parties that guaranteed Travendal were occupied with the war against France and did nothing in spite of pressure from Sweden. The British contin-ued to urge both the Danes and the Swedes not to send troops into the Empire. The Danes, in particular, had been warned by England not to pursue a plan which would send Russian troops across Mecklenburg, Brandenburg, and Holstein.[73]

Friedrich of Prussia, caught 'between a hammer and an anvil,'[74] pressed for a neutrality convention, that is, neutralisation of the Swedish possessions in the Em-pire, which meant that these lands could not be invaded or used as a base for attack by the northern belligerents.[75] The convention of neutrality of 31 March 1710, concluded by representatives of the emperor, the Maritime Powers, Denmark, Saxony, Hanover, Prussia, and Russia, in effect isolated the Northern War from the ongoing conflict to the south.[76] Charles XII, however, opposed this agreement and formally rejected the so-called Neutrality Act in March of 1711 because it denied him his German base and interned his Pomeranian army, yet at the same time gave an advantage to his enemies, who would be protected in the Empire while prosecuting the war elsewhere. St. John aptly described the allied policy as one of 'shifts and expedients.' For him it was 'like living by the peace of Cordials; an artificial strength opposes the distemper for the present, which returns complicated upon us in a little time and the effects of the polluting medicine form a new disease.'[77] In St. John's view, it was 'too dangerous to the common cause to do anything' and yet 'impossible to do nothing.'[78]

## ■ The Summer of 1711: 'Keep the Fire out of the Empire'

Once the Russians had signed a peace with the Turks in July 1711, the tsar refused further concessions to either Prussia or Hanover. The allies' fear that troops would be withdrawn from the conflict in the west and sent to the north was realised in the summer of 1711 when Augustus II withdrew three Saxon regiments and dispatched them against the Swedes and those of her ally, Holstein-Gottorp, which also had deployed a considerable number of troops for the ongoing war against Louis. As late as October 1711 the English were trying, in the words of Secretary of State Henry Boyle, 'to keep the fire [that is, the Northern War] out of the Empire.'[79] Nonetheless, by 1712 the British had concluded that the 'northern troubles are become such a maze of errors, and the character of the partys are so bizarre, that the Queen hardly sees a way thro them.'[80]

From 1709 to 1711, Friedrich of Prussia had remained loyal to the allies in spite of his anger over the neglect of Prussian interests in the Barrier Treaty and the May peace preliminaries because of the promise of Britain's future support.[81] It is true, as Droysen has contended, that he pursued 'im Osten Politik ohne Krieg' or 'politics without war in the east,'[82] but given the problematic nature of his position and his commitment to the allies it is difficult to criticise his actions. Furthermore his territorial ambitions towards Swedish Pomerania antagonised Sweden just as his desire to acquire western Prussia and Warmia to connect electoral Brandenburg and East Prussia, brought him into conflict with Poland and Russia.

## ■ 'An Infamous Peace'

After the British withdrawal from the War of the Spanish Succession, Friedrich fought on without British subsidies. 'I would,' he wrote, 'rather hazard all than agree to such an infamous peace.' The 'stench' of the British abandonment angered him.[83] After the Treaties of Utrecht ended the war for most of the combatants—including the king in Prussia—Friedrich Wilhelm I, son of the late king, fought on as elector of Brandenburg until the Treaty of Baden of 7 September 1714 ended the war for the Empire. Friedrich Wilhelm I reaped certain benefits: he acquired Spanish Guelderland, Moers, Lingen, and Neuchâtel, and the acknowledgment of his kingship. His father had managed to keep his lands relatively free from the devastation of war in spite of his tenuous geographical position between the Great Northern War and the War of the Spanish Succession.[84]

## ■ A Scramble for Spoils

As the war against Louis XIV was drawing to a close, Hanover, eager to seize vulnerable territory, occupied Verden, claiming to be 'safeguarding' it for Sweden. This occupation prompted Brandenburg-Prussia in turn to sequester Stettin in 1713. Friedrich Wilhelm, who refused to be a junior partner in the alliance with Denmark,[85] had in effect 'appropriated Swedish territory under the guise of friend-ship,'[86] as had Hanover. In 1714, Friedrich Wilhelm I and Georg of Hanover—now also George I of Great Britain—joined together to serve the 'German mission' and expel the victor of 1648 from the Empire. Georg was determined to bring both Britain and Hanover into the war and make Hanover the leading northern German power by making its neighbour to the west, Mecklenburg, a dependency and by acquiring Bremen and Verden. Those acquisitions would give the electorate access to both the Baltic and the North Sea and command of the estuaries of the Elbe and the Weser. Hanover received a guarantee of the possession of both Bremen and Verden by agreeing to betray the duke of Holstein-Gottorp and sanction Danish seizure of Holstein-Gottorp's lands in Schleswig.[87] In May of 1715, Brandenburg-Prussia declared war on Sweden and in October, Georg, as elector, did as well. The coalition, however, was fraught with difficulties and competing ambitions. To counter these moves Charles concluded a dynastic alliance with the ambitious Friedrich of Hesse-Kassel, who married his younger sister, Ulrika Eleonora, in 1715.

Mecklenburg got drawn into in the war not only because of Hanoverian ambitions but also Russian ones. Karl Leopold of Mecklenburg-Schwerin concluded a pact with Denmark guaranteeing him the tolls from Warnemünde as well as possession of Wismar, the former residence of his family and a Swedish enclave within Mecklenburg's borders. At the same time, Denmark concluded alliances with both Hanover and Prussia guaranteeing the establishment of Wismar as a Free Imperial City.[88] In 1716 Karl Leopold came to an agreement with Russia according to which the duke married Peter's niece, Tsarevna Ekaterina Ivanovna, and Peter in turn guaranteed Wismar and Warnemünde, in effect creating a Russian outpost in northern Germany. Peter also agreed to intervene in Mecklenburg's internal politics, assisting the duke in a quarrel with the nobility-dominated estates, and occupying Mecklenburg. In addition, Russian merchants had the right to reside and trade in Mecklenburg and Russian troops were guaranteed free passage. This pact infuriated Mecklenburg's neighbours, the Danes and the Hanoverians. The duke had acquired another wife and the Russians had another base which their troops pillaged. Peter also planned—futilely as it turned out—to dig a canal through Mecklenburg to the Elbe, and thereby get direct access to the sea.[89] The greater fear

for many northern German states, and the emperor as well, was the possibility of Russia acquiring a permanent footing in the Holy Roman Empire. In the words of Stanhope, George strove to 'divert the tsar from attempts which would immediately throw all Germany into flame.'[90] Ultimately, this alliance did not benefit the duke, for the Russians, under diplomatic pressure, were compelled to withdraw. The duke was forced from his lands by the Hanoverians under an Imperial 'execution' for illegal activities. His lands were put under sequestration by Hanover and Prussia, even though the latter had earlier promised to come to his aid.[91]

Mutual antagonisms and conflicting territorial ambitions fractured the allied coalition into Russia and Prussia on one side and Hanover and Denmark on the other. Friedrich Wilhelm I shared the Russian desire to keep Poland weak and worried about the vulnerability of his East Prussian lands. Also underlying that alliance was Friedrich Wilhelm I's detestation of his brother-in-law. Augustus of Poland-Saxony aligned with neither side.

## ■ Peace in the North: Russia, 'Closer and Closer to Our Lives'

The death of Charles XII at the siege of Fredrikshald in December 1718 yet again changed the character of the war. Hanover now pursued both an anti-Swedish and anti-Russian policy. In January 1719, George concluded a treaty with Charles VI, the new Holy Roman Emperor, and Augustus II of Poland aimed against both Russia and Prussia. This compact convinced Friedrich Wilhelm to abandon Russia, and Russia, in turn, to withdraw troops from Poland. In November 1719, Sweden made peace with Hanover, which acquired Bremen and Verden,[92] and, in 1720, with Prussia, which gained Stettin and part of West Pomerania and thus control of the river Oder.[93]

Only in June of 1720 did Sweden conclude a peace with Denmark, which received the Holstein-Gottorp lands in Schleswig.[94] Brandenburg, however, continued to fear a Russian attack on East Prussia until the Swedes ultimately made peace at Nystad with that power in 1721 and ceded Livonia, Estonia, Ingria, Kexholm, and part of Karelia.[95] Peace between Augustus and Sweden was not made until 1731.

Swedish influence in northern Germany had undoubtedly declined. The Swedes did retain some strongholds in the Holy Roman Empire: they kept Wismar, Stralsund, and the Greifswald area in Pomerania. Russian influence in Poland and northern Germany increased. Peter supported the duke of Holstein-Gottorp, marrying his daughter, Grand Duchess Petrovna, to Karl Friedrich, who unavailingly protested the loss of his lands. Holstein-Gottorp emerged as one of the main losers in northern Germany, for the Danes retained the Gottorp lands in Schleswig. The duke of Mecklenburg-Schwerin lost as well, for his lands, already ravaged by the Russian occupying force, were sequestered and he was reduced to the possession of Dömitz in southern Schwerin.

The northern German states, Hanover and Prussia, emerged stronger from the conflict, for they both had acquired new and lucrative lands. Friedrich Wilhelm I, like his father, had been unwilling to enter the conflict and only did so in the later stages. His goal, always, was to 'have powerful friends, but not powerful neighbours.'[96] Uncomfortable with the vagaries of eighteenth-century politics and lacking the subtlety and gift for dissimulation necessary to succeed in the international arena, Friedrich Wilhelm built up his army, igniting the hostility of Charles VI, who presciently considered it both excessive and suspect.

Throughout the war, the northern German powers had constantly manoeuvred ruthlessly, whether it be by marriage alliances or defensive/offensive alliances, and in the Great Northern War the belligerents submitted their quarrels 'to the judgment of cannon.' One contemporary French officer acerbically observed: 'There is no judge more equitable than cannon. They go directly to the goal and are not corruptible.'[97] The balance in the north had shifted to Russia. As a Hanoverian official noted at the end of the war, 'Germany and the entire North have never been in such grave peril as now, because the Russians should be feared more than the Turks. Unlike the latter, they do not remain in their gross ignorance and withdraw once they have completed their ravages, but, on the contrary, gain more and more science and experience in matters of war and state, surpassing many nations in calculation and dissimulation and are gradually advancing closer and closer to our lives.'[98] The northern German powers no longer faced a threat from a powerful Sweden, but from an even more formidable foe: Russia.

*AMICUS SED NON VICINUS*

# CHAPTER 18

# Charles XII
## *A King of Many Faces*

by Inga Lena Ångström Grandien

The broad interest in Charles XII made him the subject of artistic scrutiny literally from the day he was born till the day he died, and the very large number of portraits of him produced during his lifetime is, in the case of Swedish kings, only surpassed by the many portraits of Gustav II Adolf. In certain fields, as for example that of medals, there are more specimens with his likeness than there are of the latter's.[1] This chapter discusses mainly the painted portraits, the space available not allowing mention of more than a handful of medals and graphics.

Despite all the portraits it is, for several reasons, not an easy task to say what the king looked like—either as a child, a youth, or as a grown man. In the case of the young prince, Charles is almost always depicted in an allegorical scene or in a family portrait with a dynastic message in which his features are greatly idealised. The artist behind most of these early images of the king-to-be was David Klöcker Ehrenstrahl, who has been called the father of Swedish painting. It is no exaggeration to say that it was he who shaped the image of the young Charles, as he had also shaped that of his father, Charles XI.[2]

Ehrenstrahl was born in Hamburg in 1628 as David Klöcker. His first contacts with Sweden were as a writer for the itinerant Swedish chancery at the peace negotiations in Osnabrück at the end of the Thirty Years' War. When they were completed in 1648, he went to Amsterdam to study with the portrait and animal painter Jurian Jacobsz. In 1651, Carl Gustaf Wrangel, governor of Swedish Pomerania, employed him to paint portraits of his family at their residence in Wolgast. When the Wrangels returned to Sweden in 1652, Klöcker came with them and was in the same year hired by Queen Dowager Maria Eleonora. It is interesting to note that Maria Eleonora, rather than Queen Christina, used his services, the latter's taste already shaped in another fashion than the north-German/Dutch style in which he was working at this time.

In early 1654, Klöcker went on a study trip to Italy, where he was to spend long periods in Venice and Rome. With the intent of becoming a court painter at the Swedish court he left Italy in 1659, on his return journey visiting both France and England. By the time he reached Stockholm in 1661 and was appointed painter to the royal court, the Dutch Abraham Wuchters, painter by appointment to the king of Denmark, was already there. Although much appreciated for his realistic portraits in the Dutch tradition, he was soon outmanoeuvred by Klöcker,

*Portrait of Charles XII.*

*Painting by Michael Dahl (1659-1743), ca. 1710-17. Private collection. © Photograph by Philip Mould Ltd, London / Bridgeman Images.*

who did not hesitate to spread rumours of his bad drawing and lack of insight in composition, i.e., composition in the new, fashionable style of European portraiture which Klöcker had learned on his travels. The splendour-loving French baroque and the portrait style of the age of Louis XIV in particular had left a lasting impression on him and would dominate his portraits throughout the rest of his life.

In 1674, Charles XI raised Klöcker to the nobility by giving him a knighthood (this is when he named himself Ehrenstrahl), with the intent to separate him 'from the common crowd of painters,' according to his charter of nobility.[3] This was the first time a painter was knighted in Sweden, but in doing that, the king was only echoing what Charles I of England already had done for Anthony van Dyck, and Felipe IV of Spain for Velázquez when he made him a knight of Santiago.[4]

The Swedish royal family could not have acquired a more loyal servant than Ehrenstrahl, who became the perfect artist for the visual expression of Swedish absolutism, basing his ambition to glorify the royal family on a quasi-religious conviction.[5]

### ■ Great Expectations

From the very beginning, the images of the king-to-be reflected the great expectations there were of him. His birth was commemorated by two medals made after drawings by Ehrenstrahl. On both, he is depicted as a gift from heaven, and on both, classical mythology, cosmic symbolism, and religious ideas come together.[6] One is engraved by Arvid Karlsteen.

*Allegorical scene related to Charles XII's birth.*

*Watercolour by Andreas von Behn (1650-1730) after David Ehrenstrahl, ca. 1682. Nationalmuseum, Stockholm, Sweden.*

*Medals commemorating the birth of Charles XII.*

*Silver medals by Arvid Karlsteen (1647-1718) and Anton Meybusch (1645-1702), 1682. Kungl. Myntkabinettet, Stockholm, Sweden. © Photograph by Gabriel Hildebrand.*

It depicts the parents as Juno and Jupiter, the royal couple of Olympia, who gently lower a small naked boy down to a segment of the earth on which Sweden's three crowns are drawn.[7] As Martin Olin has pointed out, the medal is also a tribute to Queen Ulrika Eleonora for having given birth to an heir to the throne.[8] On the other medal, engraved by Anton Meybusch, the child sits on a bed of clouds above the polar star, from which he is lowered down to the ground.[9] God's all-seeing eye shines over the scene as a reminder that the regent is his representative on earth.

The first time Prince Charles appears in a painting by Ehrenstrahl is in an allegory on his birth, a painting that survives only as a miniature by Andreas von Behn (see pages 342-43).[10] The scene is set in a forest or a park, and, as indicated by two huge columns, in front of a temple of sorts. In the centre is a high pedestal with acanthus-decorated legs on which the child is half-sitting on a cloud-like cushion, raising his hand as in a blessing. Elegantly dressed women with garlands on their heads and in their hands surround the child: virtues that have come to offer their gifts to the newly born. One of them is about to put a small wreath on his head but holds it in such a way that it looks like a glory.

The three women behind the child are Maria Eufrosyne De la Gardie, the wife of Magnus Gabriel De la Gardie and a sister of Charles X Gustav; the child's mother, Queen Ulrika Eleonora; and Queen Dowager Hedvig Eleonora. A man, half-hidden behind a pillar, is possibly the father, Charles XI.

The painting evokes the atmosphere of a *tableau vivant* and could be an illustration of the panegyric poem 'Swea Frögde-Roop' [Mother Sweden's Shouts of Joy], written by Christian Torner in celebration of the prince's birth.[11] In this poem, apart from the emphasis on dynasty, the prince's remarkable virtues are detailed and he is promised a temple of eternal glory, as the virtues were closely connected to the symbolism of eternity.[12]

In Ehrenstrahl's group portrait of the royal family from the second half of 1683[13]—the so-called Pfalz portrait, referring to the Pfalz-Zweibrücken line of the Vasa dynasty that had become the Swedish royal house in 1654—the now circa 15-month-old prince, his nakedness only partly hidden behind fluttering blue veils, sits on a red cloud-like cushion on a table covered by golden-lace-fringed red velvet. Next to him on the table is his sister Hedvig Sofia in a pink-orange dress, putting a crown of laurel leaves on his head. Queen Dowager Hedvig Eleonora, in an ermine-trimmed gold-brown cloak adorned with Swedish royal crowns, is seated to the left (for the viewer) of the table and points to the prince. Slightly leaning on the back of her chair, is Charles XI, clad in a brown-black costume, while Queen Ulrika Eleonora, in a blue gold-embroidered dress, stands to the right with one arm around Hedvig Sofia, holding the prince's hand with the other. Maria Eufrosyne De la Gardie, dressed in black, stands behind the group, under an oval painting-within-the-painting showing Charles X Gustav, the first of the Swedish Palatine kings.

The prince is lifting one arm, a gesture that in connection to his 'coronation' by Hedvig Sofia could be interpreted as an imperator's gesture in classical times, but also has Christian connotations: it occurs in paintings of The Holy Family and in the, to Ehrenstrahl familiar, Venetian tradition where the Christ child is depicted as *salvator mundi*.[14]

The portrait otherwise follows the same scheme as French family portraits by Pierre Mignard, Charles Le Brun, and Jean Nocret, painters who in turn built on a tradition developed by the Flemish Anthony van Dyck in England: monumental

*King Charles XI of Sweden with his family.*

*Painting by David Ehrenstrahl (1628-98), 1683. Nationalmuseum, Stockholm, Sweden.*

(Opposite page) *The royal children playing with a lion.*

*Painting by David Ehrenstrahl (1628-98), 1684. Nationalmuseum, Stockholm, Sweden.*

*Prince Charles at four years of age.*

*Portrait miniature by Elias Brenner (1647-1717), 1686, Nationalmuseum, Stockholm, Sweden.*

group portraits in settings of heavily draped classical architecture—where often a painted portrait of a deceased family member can be seen, screened off by drapery.[15] Notwithstanding the apparent intimacy of the scene, this painting can hardly be called a family portrait; it rather is a dynastic tableau proclaiming the continuity of royal succession. Why was a painting with such ostentatious emphasis on the young prince commissioned in 1683? In January of that year the government had made a decision which introduced absolute power in Sweden. Charles XI had come into possession of both the full military and economic power, and the painting served undoubtedly as an instrument to legitimise the dynastic continuity of the royal family and to establish the idea of the Swedish Palatine family as the holder of absolute power, subordinate only to heavenly power.[16] The painting conveys the great expectations one had of the prince. He was to guarantee the dynasty's continuation while simultaneously being thought of as a bringer of peace. In spite of this rather heavy burden on his small shoulders, the painting has, as pointed out by Allan Ellenius, an optimistic or even a triumphant air about it.[17]

The commission for the painting may have come from Queen Dowager Hedvig Eleonora, who also may have had a say in its composition; her place in the portrait, between Charles XI and Prince Charles, and closer to the latter than his mother is, points to this. As emphasised by Lisa Skogh, the queen dowager was the most important woman in the royal family. From 1654 until 1680 and from 1693 to 1715 she was the only queen in the Swedish realm; although never a reigning queen, she did have two votes in the Council during her regencies, and for 55 years she was the eldest member of the Swedish royal family.[18] Therefore it is she, not Ulrika Eleonora, who usually is clad in ermine, the most 'royal' of outfits.

In June 1683 a new prince, Gustav, was born and sometime in the first half of 1684 Ehrenstrahl painted him and the other royal children playing with a lion.[19] The scene takes place on a terrace, covered by an oriental carpet and overlooking a park with large trees and a fountain. On the horizon the red light of dawn can be seen. Behind the children, half-hidden behind thick drapery, are two fluted columns and between these a large urn decorated with reliefs.

To the left Hedvig Sofia, in an orange gown; behind her a fluttering orange veil holds the royal pet in a thin satin ribbon, while the tiny Gustav is crawling naked between the lion's paws, taking a firm grip on one of its enormous fangs. Charles himself, in the same light costume as in the Pfalz portrait, is sitting astride the state symbol, triumphantly raising a palm twig: the lion, symbol of power, has thus been tamed by Charles with the help of the other children.

The painting is a congenial image of all the hopes that were set on the young prince, the allusions to the triumphing Christ and the promise of resurrection being almost overly explicit, but paralleled by the enthusiastic formulations in the complimentary literature. Through his birth, God had placed the foot of the state on solid ground.[20] In several paintings of Charles XI Ehrenstrahl had already represented the Swedish Lion, the symbol of Sweden, as a living animal, resting next to the throne. How he got the brilliant idea of letting the royal children play with it

'as if it were a large, trustworthy St. Bernard,'[21] we do not know. The composition has,
however, certain similarities to a painting from 1634 by Anthony van Dyck showing
the five children of Charles I of England standing around a large dog (a mastiff), a
painting which Ehrenstrahl might have seen on his visit to the English court.

*Prince Charles with his sister, Princess Hedvig Sofia.*

*Painting by David Ehrenstrahl (1628-98), 1687. Nationalmuseum, Stockholm, Sweden.*

*(Opposite page) Queen Ulrika Eleonora and the royal children.*

*Painting by David Ehrenstrahl (1628-98), 1689. Nationalmuseum, Stockholm, Sweden. Photograph by Andreas Svensson.*

As mentioned above, there were other painters at the court, one of them the miniature painter Elias Brenner.[22] In his miniature from 1686 the prince wears a full-bottomed wig, a light blue cavalier coat and round his neck a red rosette; although only four, he is dressed as a grown-up but at the same time looking more the child he really is than in Ehrenstrahl's portraits.[23]

The difference between Brenner's and Ehrenstrahl's way of depicting the prince is obvious when comparing the miniature to a painting by Ehrenstrahl from the following year showing Charles taking Hedvig Sofia for a walk. That the youngster, holding hands with his sister and in his other hand carrying a commander's baton, is only five is hard to believe. The siblings are standing on a terrace in front of a rock that makes a dark background to their light features and shimmering clothes: Charles in a yellow tunic and a blue mantle—the Swedish colours—and a sword at his side; Hedvig Sofia in a long white dress dotted with small yellow flowers and a fluttering orange veil behind her.

Karin Sidén has compared this work to Anthony van Dyck's 1641 painting of William II, Prince of Orange, and Princess Mary of England.[24] In both, the children are holding hands, but whereas in Van Dyck's painting this symbolises the forthcoming wedding in the same year of the two portrayed, in Ehrenstrahl's it represents love between siblings in general and mirrors also the genuine affection Charles and Hedvig Sofia always felt for each other.

The royal family suffered terrible losses when, within a period of a few months in 1685, the small Princes Gustav, Ulrik, and Fredrik died one after another. And that was not all. A new prince, Karl Gustav, born in December 1686, died after only a few weeks in February 1687. Sometime later that year Ulrika Eleonora gave instructions to Ehrenstrahl for a painting which would symbolise that, with the help of her deep belief in God, she had accepted their deaths. She is sitting by her desk and in front of her is a paper with the words 'Dein Wille geschehe' [Thy will be done]. In the painting's left upper corner the four deceased princes float like angels on their way from the heavy and dark life on earth to heaven.[25]

In 1689 Ehrenstrahl painted a more formal version in which the three living royal children are also represented (Ulrika Eleonora had been born in February 1688).[26] They are grouped around the queen, who is sitting in an ermine-trimmed dress on an upholstered bench with gilded legs. Although she is placed in the centre, the self-assured position of Prince Charles at her side, clad in yellow and blue and one arm akimbo, makes him the painting's main character.[27]

In Ehrenstrahl's group portrait of the royal family from 1697, Prince Charles, coming in from the right, is leading Princess Hedvig Sofia by the hand, as in the artist's painting from 1686 but now as a self-assured young cavalier. Next to Charles, Princess Ulrika Eleonora is kneeling, in a pose reminiscent of Mary Magdalene in front of the cross. Queen Ulrika Eleonora, who had died in 1693, is represented in an oval-shaped portrait among the curtains with on its frame four hardly visible medallions containing the names and portraits of the deceased princes. Beneath the portrait, King Charles XI is standing next to Queen Dowager Hedvig Eleonora, who wears the same ermine-trimmed dress as in the Pfalz portrait. But although she occupies the painting's midst, it is again Prince Charles—with one hand on his hip—who is the dominant figure, something which the subordinate body language of the dog crawling by his feet and of Ulrika Eleonora helps to underscore.[28]

As argued by Allan Ellenius, this group portrait makes the strongest possible contrast to the Pfalz portrait. The colour scheme is more subdued, the shadows isolate the figures from one another; the triumphant tone has been changed for one of guarded dignity.[29]

## ■ The King

The portraits of Charles XII as king are more varied but also more contradictory, partly as a result of there being more artists and also some gifted amateurs around. The very first portraits of him as king were made by Ehrenstrahl, who by now had left all allegorical requisite behind him.[30] After his death in the autumn of 1698, all portraits of Charles prior to his departure from Sweden in 1700 were executed by David (von) Krafft (1655-1724), Ehrenstrahl's nephew and successor as painter to the Swedish royal court. He had grown up in Hamburg. In 1675 his uncle invited him to come to Stockholm as his assistant and apprentice. After some years he was appointed drawing master to Queen Ulrika Eleonora, who in 1684 bestowed a yearly pension on him for which he should go abroad and study, 'especially in Italy,' but first he had to go to the Danish court and paint portraits of her family. After a year spent in Copenhagen and some time in Germany he arrived in 1687 in Italy, where he was to spend one year in Venice, three years in Rome—where he visited the academy of Queen Christina—and one in Bologna. After another two years in Paris he was called back to Stockholm and to his aging uncle Ehrenstrahl's studio, in 1696.

Krafft was not automatically thought of as Ehrenstrahl's successor as court painter, having returned from his study trip as a good enough portrait painter but not the full-fledged, versatile one in the grand, continental manner that had been hoped for. Instead, a Swedish portraitist based in London, Michael Dahl, was asked to become court painter.[31] When he declined, attempts were made to find a French artist, but when these also failed, Krafft was appointed painter to the Swedish court by mid-1699.

In Italy he had learnt to paint using a delicate colour scheme in the spirit of the late baroque and also a severe drawing style, which meant that he returned with artistic ideals that were different from Ehrenstrahl's. This did not prevent him from once again adapting himself to the latter's style, so that the changeover from one court painter to another was hardly noticeable, his first portraits of Charles XII building strongly on Ehrenstrahl's late renditions, only the colours being less vivid.

Some late portraits from Ehrenstrahl's studio might have been finished by Krafft, for example *Charles XII in Coronation Costume* (see page frontpiece). Maybe he also had a hand in the group portrait of 1697. Through *ad vivum* studies of the young king, Krafft slowly developed a portrait type of his own, the main difference lying in the rendering of the head, which he gave a more elongated shape.[32]

*(Opposite page) Charles XII on horseback at the Battle of Narva.*

*Mezzotint by Georg Philipp Rugendas (1666-1742), 1701. Nationalmuseum, Stockholm, Sweden.*

The equestrian portrait was as a genre primarily reserved for kings, and the first such portraits of Charles XII were, indeed, only created after he had become king, in that way marking his new position and showing who was now 'holding the reins.' Documentary evidence establishes that Krafft painted at least six large equestrian portraits in 1698-99. Of these, one was sent to the Russian court, two to Holstein, one to Poland, and one to August Wilhelm, Hereditary Prince of Braunschweig-Wolfenbüttel.[33]

In several private collections in Sweden and abroad there is an equestrian portrait of the young king dressed in a long gold-fringed skin coat under a shining cuirass, his head proudly thrown back. On top of his full-bottomed wig he wears a tricorne.[34] Horse and rider are performing a pesade, a popular motif in equestrian portraiture of the period. The horse is, accordingly, made to rear but the movement is totally controlled by the rider as proof of the king's consummate horsemanship and—in an extension—his qualities as a ruler.[35]

Some of these, both undated and unsigned, portraits could have been executed by Ehrenstrahl prior to his death in 1698 but, although clearly inspired by this artist's equestrian portraits of Charles XI, they have a distinctive character of their own and give proof of Krafft's more modern strivings to keep the forms within definite planes.

The king's head is also, as described above, more elongated than in Ehrenstrahl's portraits, showing that Krafft has based his portraits on *ad vivum* studies. Of course he did not know that for the following fifteen years he would be in the unusual situation for a courtier painter of having to create portraits of his king after other artists' *ad vivum* studies, executed at Charles XII's various whereabouts. These would, furthermore, not come directly to Krafft's studio. First they would have to pass through the needle's eye of a 'jury' consisting of the king's grandmother, Queen Dowager Hedvig Eleonora, and his sisters, Hedvig Sofia and Ulrika Eleonora, the latter being the only judge after the deaths of her sister in 1708 and of the queen dowager in 1715. It was only by their permission that an image would be used as a model for reproduction by Krafft and his assistants, and they would surely not have given one such if they had not seen something of the young man they remembered in the portrait, though it must have become increasingly difficult, as the years passed by, to tell if an image was a good likeness or not.

Then there were also the portraits of the king that never came to the Stockholm court, painted by artists who often had been able to sell them straight off the easel, so great was the demand for a likeness of Charles XII. These were copied in turn, used as models for engravings or on articles for everyday use such as glass goblets, tankards' lids, and plates, rings, and lockets.

*Charles XII on horseback.*

*Painting by Johann Heinrich Wedekind (1674-1736), 1701. Arménuseum, Stockholm, Sweden.*

## ■ A King with an Unusual Appearance

In the autumn of 1700, after having left Sweden and before the Battle of Narva, Charles radically changed his appearance by putting the wig away and beginning—in the phrase of the time—'to wear his own hair.' This he would keep short and combed upwards like a crown around his head. Removal of the wig was initially done for better comfort in the field, but he soon became used to going without one.[36] He also exchanged the expensive courtly dress from the early equestrian portraits for a grey coat (but with lynx-trimmed lapels), under which he wore a steel cuirass. This was in turn soon replaced by a plain blue coat with brass buttons common among his troops, a yellow waistcoat of chamois leather or cloth, a black taffeta cravat wound several times around his neck, and elk-skin breeches. On his feet he had stiff top boots and iron spurs. On his head he wore a tricorne, with a large brass button on the left, but more often than not he went bareheaded.

After the Swedish victory at Narva but before the king's new appearance became known at the court, David Krafft, clearly inspired by Coysevox's relief of Louis XIV *en empereur romain vainqueur* in the War Salon in Versailles, created a portrait type where Charles, with a plumed helmet on his full-bottomed wig and in a vermin mantle, comes riding across fallen enemy soldiers.[37] The type soon became popular thanks to a print made by Georg Philipp Rugendas in Augsburg, who added the figure of Fama reaching down from the sky to crown the victorious king.[38] The horse has all four legs in the air as it jumps over a fallen enemy soldier and his horse, both looking equally terrified. In the dark background we see a whole array of men, horses, and weapons.[39]

The first painter to portray the king without a wig was Johann Heinrich Wedekind (1674-1736) from Reval (present-day Tallinn), who had been trained as a portraitist by Ernst Wilhelm Londicer.[40] When Londicer died in 1697, Wedekind wrote to the Swedish Council, petitioning to be allowed to keep Londicer's privileges to practice his art 'unlimited by the guild's rules both in Stockholm and in other prosperous Swedish towns,' something he apparently was granted since he turned up in several places in the Swedish realm during the following decades, Reval however remaining his base until in 1720, when he moved to Saint Petersburg to become court painter to Peter the Great.

Wedekind painted two portraits of the king without a wig. Probably the first one is a knee piece, unsigned but convincingly attributed to him. In it, the bareheaded young king is standing next to a table with the Swedish regalia on it, the detailed rendering of which is typical of the painter's early work.[41] Charles is dressed in a dark blue-grey coat over a leather waistcoat and has a broad, embroidered belt round his waist. His outfit, typical of his first period 'without a wig,' is proof that the painting may have been executed during the week he spent in Reval in October-November 1700 or perhaps at the winter camp at Lais (Laiuse), Estonia, in 1700-01.

Wedekind may also have painted it in Riga in the summer of 1701, as a preliminary study for his signed equestrian portrait of Charles XII depicting

*(Opposite page) Portrait of Charles XII.*

*Painting by Johann Heinrich Wedekind (1674-1736), 1700-01. Private collection, Tallinn, Estonia. Photograph by Jaanus Heinla, owner AS Restor Company, Tallinn.*

*Portrait of Charles XII.*

*Painting by Axel Sparre. (1652-1728), 1701. Arménuseum, Stockholm, Sweden.*

*Portrait of Charles XII.*

*Painting by François de la Croix (1653-1713), 1702. Nationalmuseum, Stockholm, Sweden. © www.rojalist.se | photograph by R. Wesslén.*

*(Opposite page) Portrait of Charles XII.*

*Painting by Johan David Swartz (1678-1740), 1707. Nationalmuseum, Stockholm, Sweden.*

the defeat of the Saxon army of King Augustus on the Dvina (also known as Daugava) River, 19 July 1701.[42] It is undated, but documentary evidence suggests that it was executed later in July that year.

The king and his horse—brown, with a splendid white tail—take up the main part of the canvas (see page 352). The battle is shown in the lower part; the Swedish halberdiers in blue goldsmith uniforms, the Saxons in red. The king wears the same outfit as in the painting described above, the only difference being the tricorne on his head. In the background the river and the city of Riga can be seen. The cloud-covered sky opens miraculously behind the king, allowing the sun to shine on his face and waistcoat.[43]

Neither of these two Wedekind paintings reached Stockholm and it is generally agreed that the first portrait to show the court in Stockholm what Charles looked like without a wig was a small gouache, painted by Count Axel Sparre, a field marshal in the Swedish Army as well as a skilful miniature painter, at the camp near Bauskė in Courland in the autumn of 1701.[44] The faintly smiling king is bareheaded with his hair combed back. Over a cuirass he wears a blue coat lined with lynx skin, which is open to the waist and held together by a jewel-buckled belt. At first, the portrait shocked the people at court, unused to seeing Charles like this as they were—the women were also convinced that it would render him susceptible to colds—but it would soon be used as a model for miniatures, engravings, and woodcuts, and for the title page of Charles XII's Bible of 1703.[45]

A portrait by François de La Croix of May 1702 in Warsaw illustrates in an interesting way the common knowledge that contemporary but differently trained artists may render a totally different image of one and same person. Wedekind's portrait, in which the king is shown distant and aloof, has not much in common with that of François de La Croix, one of the many artists of the day who spread the French portrait style of Rigaud and de Troy throughout Europe. On a visit to La Croix's studio, the king had seen a portrait of his enemy King Augustus.[46] It seemed to him true to life and he commissioned a portrait of himself. The finished painting became an intimate and psychologically direct, lively, and striking portrait, in which we see for the first time some of the charm for which Charles was known, but also a hint of brutality, his face expressing greater security and command than in earlier portraits.

The portrait exists in a couple of slightly different versions. In one, the king is depicted in armour, not in skin coat and cuirass as here, but the dazzling white shirt collar, probably put there for contrast, appears in both, as well as the flowing blue draperies, decorated with crowns and the king's monogram. It is

*(Opposite page) Full-length portrait of Charles XII.*

*Painting by David von Krafft (1655-1724), 1707. After David Swartz, 1707 (original). Nationalmuseum, Stockholm, Sweden.*

*Portrait of Charles XII.*

*Painting by Daniel (1679-1753) and Robert (1682-1766) Gardelle, 1708. Bibliothèque de Genève, Geneva, Switzerland.*

not known from any contemporary copies in Sweden,[47] nor do we know if it was shown at the Swedish court. Even if it was, it is uncertain that 'the jury' would have accepted it as a likeness of the king; the three royal women might have been shocked by its directness.

In the summer of 1707 the Swedish portrait painter Johan David Swartz executed a series of studies and paintings of Charles XII at Altranstädt.[48] Of these, a knee piece and a full-length are regarded as the most reliable, as far as Charles's likeness is concerned, of all the portraits of the king that have survived. A letter written in Altranstädt[49] allows us to date these paintings to early August 1707, only a few weeks before the Swedish army set off on the disastrous campaign against Russia (thus, the inscription on both—'Swartz fecit 1706'—is incorrect).

In the knee piece (see page 357) he stands in the opening of his tent, with the camp's tent in the background. His face is full of personal characteristics; even the measles scars are there (although hardly visible). He smiles his typical smile, giving the expression of having been depicted right in the middle of an unstrained conversation with one of his confidants. On a table—where, in traditional portraits of a ruler, the regalia are placed—lies a soldier's hat. The discreet crown pattern on the tablecloth and a baton are the only indications that here stands a king.

The full-length portrait shows Charles in classical contrapost in an undefined room devoid of royal attributes. He stands with his right arm akimbo, his hat on his hip, and his left hand firmly on the sword hilt.

When the two portraits arrived in Stockholm, in the autumn of 1707, some people at the court were shocked by their realism. Yet, in a letter apologising for the portrait, which he had sent home and which his wife had found 'badly executed,' one of the king's generals explained that Charles had sat beside the painter and had encouraged a true likeness, not one thought polite or in fashion.[50]

For years to come, these two paintings would serve as the basic models for portraits of the king, and they would be reproduced over and over by Krafft and his assistants. But while the knee-length was used as a

model for paintings distributed among people at the court and Council members, the full-length became a model for official portraits of the king, that is to say, in David von Krafft's version of it. The king stands in the same position as in Swartz's original but his face is touched up and his features have been softened. In another version of the portrait, Krafft has included a table with the regalia.[51]

But would any portrait be a true likeness of the king? A Swedish student named Alstrin, who visited the camp in Altranstädt in May 1707, states his opinion on the matter in a letter to his uncle in Uppsala: 'he is very difficult to portray for painters since no portrait I ever saw of the king looks like him, among the hundreds I have seen and of which the whole world is full, all book-shops, all artists' studios and houses as well as houses of others.'[52]

We also have an interesting verbal description of the king from this period. In the spring of 1708, during the campaign against Russia, Charles XII spent some days at Korolny, the estate of a Polish magnate in Lithuania, whose then 11-year-old daughter Pana Onjuchowska many years later told of her impressions of the king: 'He, that put the whole world to fright, was mild as a lamb and shy as a nun. Of a fairly tall, fit and slender figure, his face was small in relation to the body. He was not beautiful, but one could not call his face, scarred by smallpox, ugly, and his dark blue eyes shone like diamonds. He did not wear a wig. His chestnut brown hair was slightly powdered, short and combed back. He looked very youthful.'[53]

La Bibliothèque de Genève, Switzerland, has a painting that almost to the word fits in with this description, signed '10/1708' by the brothers Robert and Daniel Gardelle from Geneva and given to the library by Robert Gardelle.[54] The king is shown in a commanding position in a terrain filled with greenery. He looks very youthful indeed, his dark blue eyes shining 'like diamonds.' With his left hand around the sword hilt he holds his hat under his left arm and makes a commanding gesture with his right arm.[55] Below his right elbow four soldiers can be seen riding towards a large house with high gables.

The directness of the portrait makes one suspect an *ad vivum*, but that would be impossible: in the autumn of 1708 the king was far into Ukraine and Robert Gardelle alternated between the courts in Berlin and Kassel. Unless he or his brother had managed to portray the king while in Saxony, the portrait must have been copied after another painter's unknown original.

From letters written both by Axel Sparre himself and others we know that Sparre, who had had such a success with his Bauskė portrait, early in 1712 executed a portrait of the king in Bender that was sent to the royal ladies in Stockholm, who probably were eagerly waiting for one since they had not seen a new likeness of the king for five years.[56] In a letter to Hedvig Eleonora, Sparre boasts that he 'so well has managed to catch the likeness of His Majesty's mild face, that everyone on the spot as well as the king himself have found it to be very much alike.'[57]

In Hedvig Eleonora's bedchamber at Gripsholm there is an oil painting of Charles XII in cuirass, long yellow waistcoat and blue coat, leaning against the mouth of a canon. He is thin-haired and somewhat corpulent, his face a remarkable high co-lour with the measles scars clearly visible. The painting has for long been regarded as

*Charles XII at Stralsund.*

*Painting by anonymous painter, 1715. Head probably after Axel Sparre (1652-1728), 1715. Nationalmuseum, Stockholm, Sweden.*

identical to Sparre's Bender portrait, but as shown in 1973-75 by Heribert Seitz, this attribution has to be revised in the light of a restoration made in 1922, which among other things proved the inscription on the reverse of the canvas—'Axel Sparre pinxit in Bender 1712'—to be apocryphal.[58] Behind the king there also appeared a long-hidden fortified town in flames, which Seitz identified as Stralsund under siege, his conclusion being that the painting was executed by an unknown artist after the king's unsuccessful defence of Stralsund in the autumn of 1715, probably in the beginning of 1716.[59]

That at least the royal head could be based on Sparre's Bender portrait tends to be confirmed by its reappearance—though, as put by Axel Sjöblom, 'in French translation, ruddy, well fed as after a splendid dinner party and with an air of supreme self-satisfaction'—in Hyacinthe Rigaud's portrait of Charles XII in armour from the first half of 1715, painted on commission by Erik Sparre, Axel Sparre's half-brother, who had been appointed Swedish ambassador to France and needed a representative portrait of his sovereign to adorn his Paris residence. From one of Sparre's letters we learn that he had lent Rigaud a copy of the Bender portrait made by Axel Sparre himself in the form of a gem, to serve as a model for the head.[60]

As Pontus Grate has pointed out, the dryness of the execution proves the painting was executed by Rigaud's workshop. It follows his standard *mise en scène*; the same pose and armour and the same battlefield in the background recur in several other Rigaud portraits. The result became, in Grate's words, 'a far cry from reality.'[61] None of his soldiers would in this image of a posing salon hero have recognised his king, and it is rather ironic that this portrait in which Charles XII is depicted so victorious, was executed while he was spending a not-so-glorious time in Stralsund, where he had arrived in November 1714.

The king's face in the painting has not such high colour as in the Gripsholm painting, in which the yellow-red facial colour was seen by August Hahr as a sun tan, a result of long days on horseback under the influence of weather and wind. Now that the burning town has re-emerged in the painting it could well be explained as a reflection from the fires.[62] Accordingly, the original behind these paintings may have had a somewhat lighter facial complexion.

As is apparent from the above, Sparre made a replica of his original painting in the form of a gem, i.e., a miniature, for his brother, which suggests that his Bender portrait could well have been a miniature.[63]

Another of Sparre's replicas may have found its way to England, to Ham House in Surrey.[64] Maybe this is the nearest we shall come to his praised portrait of the king in Bender. Interestingly enough, the king's face is coloured by a light suntan. We also note that it stands quite far from the two portraits discussed above, especially from Rigaud's, but that can be explained by this painter's professionalism; the transformation of Sparre's miniature into a representative portrait was an easy task for him.

Sometime between 1710 and 1717 the above mentioned Michael Dahl in London, on commission by the Swedish envoy, Count Carl Gyllenborg, executed a portrait of the king against a sky darkened by smoke from a burning town in the background

*(Opposite page) Portrait of Charles XII.*

*Painting by Hyacinthe Rigaud (1659-1743), 1715. Nationalmuseum, Stockholm, Sweden.*

*Portrait of Charles XII.*

*Portrait miniature by Axel Sparre (1652-1728), ca. 1712. Ham House, London, UK. © National Trust / Christopher Warleigh-Lack.*

(see page 380).[65] He stands in the pose of a general with his baton on a plinth next to him, his gloved left hand grasping his sword hilt. The face is probably based on one of the prints of the king that circulated, and, because of the clothes—a yellow vest under a fur-lined dark blue-grey uniform coat—possibly one of the Bauskė type. Elegant and sentimental, Dahl's painting, which already in 1764 came to the Royal Collections in Stockholm, was especially pleasing to the nineteenth-century romantic taste, corresponding as it does to the young hero of Esaias Tegnér's poem (see page 379, 382, 386). Sometime later, Dahl made a new version (see page 340), which has always been kept in private collections in England and has never been shown in Sweden. It shares only the head with his first painting. The details of costume have been generalised and the belt taken off, but with the introduction of the cuirass and the employment of the classic stance of commander, Dahl has gained a considerable impact. The swift brushstrokes that make up the night sky, now much lighter, show a verve that is lacking in the first version.

■ The Last Portraits

In December 1714, shortly after the king's arrival in Stralsund, Axel Löwen,[66] another gifted dilettante among the king's officers, executed a small ink drawing of Charles XII in a room with decorated walls and a drapery. Because of the seemingly exaggerated traits, especially the protruding jaw, the drawing has been judged a 'near caricature' but since the death mask[67] (see page 368) also has a heavy jaw, this simple portrait is probably quite realistic, conveying the image of a deeply troubled man, his 'petrified face' marked, as observed by Strömbom, 'by gloom and steadfastness.'[68]

The first portraits of the king after his return to Sweden in December 1715 were executed in Ystad by Wedekind, who happened to be there on his tour of Swedish garrison towns.[69] There is a signed miniature dated 'Visby, 27 December 1715,' and a signed oil painting dated '1715.' The miniature, which gave rise to the 'Ystad type,' shows Charles XII now almost completely bald except for a thin wisp of hair in the middle of his crown.[70]

The head reappears in the painting, a half-length portrait showing the king against a snowy landscape. To the left there is a snowed-in village with a church in its midst; to the right lies the barge *Snappopp* on which he was taken out of Stralsund.[71] The rising sun colours the sky red, adding a touch of Christian symbolism to the portrait: 'the Saviour' has arrived.

In the autumn of 1717 David von Krafft finally got the opportunity to paint the king *ad vivum* again, after having had to reproduce other artists' originals for years. It happened in Lund, where he had come at the request of Princess Ulrika Eleonora, who

*(Opposite page) Portrait of Charles XII with Snappopp in the background.*

*Painting by Henrik August Ankarcrona (1831-1917). After Johan Heinrich Wedekind, 1715 (original). National-museum, Stockholm, Sweden.*

*Portrait of Charles XII.*

*Painting by Axel Löwen (1686-1772), 1714. Nationalmuseum, Stockholm, Sweden.*

*Portrait of Charles XII in* Konung Carl den XII:tes historia, *by J.A. Nordberg.*

*Engraving by Eric Geringius (1707-47), 1740. Private collection. © Photograph courtesy of Magasin 5, Stockholm, Sweden.*

*(Opposite page) Portrait of Charles XII.*

*Painting by David von Krafft (1655-1724), 1717. Château de Versailles, Versailles, France. © De Agostini Picture Library / G. Dagli Orti / Bridgeman Images.*

at her meeting with Charles in August 1716 in Vadstena, had asked for his portrait.[72] During Krafft's sojourn in Lund an interesting incident occurred, witnessed by his assistant, the 16-year-old Lorens Pasch (the Elder).[73] The king came to the studio when the artist was not there; after silently looking at the painting, he took out his knife and shredded the face to pieces. Only then did he see young Pasch, who burst into tears. This amused Charles and his men greatly, but after asking for his name, he patted him on the shoulder and promised 'he would remember him.'[74] The same anecdote is told by Adlerfelt, who claims the king shredded the face not because it did not look like him but because he found it an exact likeness—and did not like what he saw.[75] But the duke of Holstein, who was in Lund at the time, had Krafft make a replica of it, 'just as good and similar,'[76] and it did not take long until it was accepted by the king and his sister.

As the last official portrait it became the most widespread of all portrait types and is to be found in Swedish royal castles, in churches, and in manors owned by the descendants of Charles XII's men. Countless also are the copper prints that spread the Lund type to private dwellings all around the country.[77] To this day it is the most common image of the king, reproduced in school books, history books, and articles, and it is no exaggeration to say that the 'Lund type' has formed the image of Charles XII for generations of Swedes.

In composition and movement scheme it stands close to Swartz's full-length Altranstädt portrait, while the tall, stiffly turned head is closer to Wedekind's Ystad type. The modelling of the head in broad, firm planes is, however, totally Krafft's own.

The painting the king shredded was repaired and is today in Versailles, France.[78] A comparison between this and the replicas and copies reveals that his traits are made younger in the copies and the posture more energetic and elastic. But there is another difference. The face in the original painting is angular and harsh, in Hatton's words 'giving an impression of cruelty and inhumanity, in spite of, or perhaps because of a vague smile that is nearly a sneer.'[79] This is probably what the king saw and what angered him so much, but all of this has vanished in the copies. In spite of the baldness and the marked face we see a forever youthful hero full of defiant courage and heroic strength.[80]

## ■ The Caroline Chapel[81]

The mortal remains of Charles XII were put to rest in the Caroline Chapel in the Riddarholmen Church in Stockholm, the 'Swedish Pantheon' as it sometimes

*Charles XII's sarcophagus.*

Riddarholmen Church, Stockholm, Sweden. © The Royal Court, Sweden/ photo Alexis Daflos.

**Charles XII's death mask.**

Plaster cast by unknown maker, copied from the eighteenth-century original in 1930. In 1917, a comparison of the mask with the king's skull proved that the mask was not a direct cast of his face. Livrustkammaren, Slottsbacken, Stockholm, Sweden.

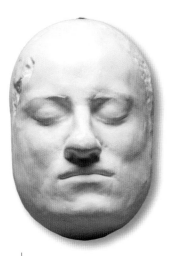

has been called because of the many grave vaults and chapels and the hundreds of gravestones that make up the floor. Several medieval kings have been buried here—its founder Magnus Ladulås (d. 1290) being the first one—but none of the Vasa kings.[82] With the burial of Gustav II Adolf (d. 1632) the Riddarholmen Church was reinstituted as a royal burial church, and with the exception of Queen Christina, whose grave is in St. Peter's in Rome, all succeeding rulers of Sweden up to Gustav V (d. 1950) are buried here; the grave of Gustav VI (d. 1973) is in the Haga Park, north of Stockholm.

Already in 1673, a design for a chapel in classical style by Nicodemus Tessin the Elder had been approved, but the Caroline Chapel was not finished until 1743 when the roof was completed after a design by Carl Hårleman. The very first plans for a chapel had been made in the 1650s by Jean de La Vallée, who intended to rebuild the main choir into a grave chapel. It was Tessin's idea to build a freestanding chapel, as a pendant to the Gustavian Chapel on the opposite side of the church.[83]

Charles XII's sarcophagus of black marble was made in Holland, after designs by Nicodemus Tessin the Younger, the architect behind the decorations for the coronation in 1697 and also for the funeral service in the Riddarholmen Church in February 1719. Both events, though different in spirit, were characterised by great splendour since Tessin knew the king adhered to a grand ceremonial idiom around the notion of majesty. In the case of the sarcophagus, however, he seems to have tried to reflect the king's simple personal habits. Maybe Tessin also remembered the king's words in a letter to him that 'no figure sculpture should be allowed to disturb the devotion in a sacral building'; the finished sarcophagus became much simpler than any other church object he designed. On the smooth marble surface

*The Caroline Chapel, traditional burial site for Swedish royalty.*

*Riddarholmen Church, Stockholm, Sweden.*
*© Vadim Petrakov | Shutterstock.*

there are only the insignia that, in the words of Ragnar Josephson, 'tell that here lie a king and a hero.'[84]: crown, spire and sword, and Hercules's club and lion skin, all made of gilded marble. On a corner of the lion skin is written CAROLUS XII. Next to the sarcophagus were the keys to the fortress of Toruń in Poland, captured in 1703, beside a banner taken there by the king. They were later removed.

## ■ Two Posthumous Sculptures

Probably the best portrayal in terms of likeness came some thirty years after the king's death, a bust finished in 1747 by the sculptor Jacques-Philippe Bouchardon in Stockholm. People who had known the king praised it for being 'extremely alike.'[85] The likeness was due to the artist's careful preparations. He had been present at the opening of the king's grave in 1746 and made sketches, and he had also copied the death mask. Other models he used were Krafft's Lund portrait and a medal by Hedlinger.[86] Inspired by French sculpture tradition, from Coysevox to his own teacher Jean-Louis Lemoyne, he created a bust characterised by a forceful rhythm. The king wears a mantle draped over one shoulder, and in a proud movement turns his head to the side where the mantle sweeps up in a heavy fold, the dynamic impact of which contrasts with the simple uniform.[87] The bust was cast by Gerhard Meyer in plaster and at least four times in bronze. The idea for a bust had come from Meyer himself, who, knowing that a French bronze founder had been called to Sweden and considering his position threatened, wanted to show his skills. The first bronze copy was given to Crown Prince Adolf Fredrik and his wife Lovisa Ulrika.[88]

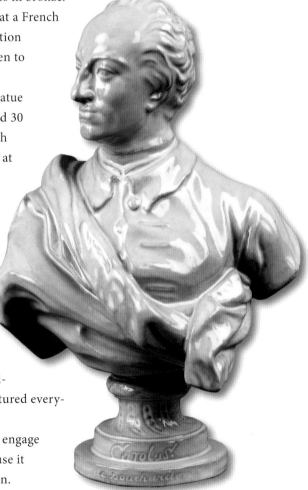

*Bust of Charles XII.*

*Ceramic with white glaze, copy after Jacques-Philippe Bouchardon (1711-53), 1747. Upplandsmuseet, Uppsala, Sweden. © Photograph by Olle Norling.*

Krafft's Lund type got its most monumental expression in the statue by Johan Peter Molin in Kungsträdgården in Stockholm, inaugurated 30 November, 1868, on the 150th anniversary (according to the Swedish calendar) of Charles XII's death. The idea of a statue had originated at a meeting arranged in Stockholm on the anniversary of Poltava in 1862. A collection was taken, bringing in 11,000 riksdaler, and a competition for a statue was announced.[89] This was won by Molin, who prepared himself as painstakingly as Bouchardon had done. He made sketches of Charles's clothes now in the Royal Armory, and had a studio built in the backyard of his house so that he could study his work in daylight.[90]

The king stands in his usual simple uniform with his drawn sword in front of him, one arm raised and a finger pointing towards the enemy of the east—Russia.[91] Though simple in contour and with few attributes, it congenially expresses the period's sentiments of the king as a man of action who bravely had ventured everything for his country.[92]

As no other statue of a Swedish king, this one has continued to engage people up to the present—not because of the statue itself, but because it represents the most controversial and debated of all kings of Sweden.

# A Literary Charles XII

by Nils Ekedahl

Bringing home the body of King
Charles XII of Sweden.

Painting by Gustaf Cederström (1845-
1933), 1884. Nationalmuseum,
Stockholm, Sweden.

*'Without a poetic sensibility, no one can conceive of Charles XII or any of his doings as anything other than a caricature.'*

– Bernhard von Beskow (1853)[1]

With his dramatic life and enigmatic personality, Charles XII has been an inviting literary subject, starting in his own lifetime. This has been particularly true in Swedish, in which language he has been portrayed by a long line of poets, playwrights, and prose writers, although his fate has also given authors in other countries pause, from Defoe and Voltaire to Byron and Pushkin, from Rilke to Borges. This literary production reached a peak in the nineteenth century, when the romantic heroic ideal was applied to Charles XII both in Sweden and across Europe, but in modern literature, too, he has been a recurring character, not least in the post-Second World War period.

The purpose of this essay is to give a sense of Charles XII's treatment in literary history, and to indicate how the picture of him changed over time, and in which contexts. A full survey of the vast literary production is impossible here. Neither is it possible to treat individual works, even the most important ones, in any detail. Instead, my ambition is to trace the broad sweep of literary developments, presenting what is perhaps best described as a précis of the historical themes, by drawing primarily on the Swedish tradition. The subject has been discussed by scholars working in a range of disciplines, but the only general survey to date is the Swedish literary historian Olov Westerlund's dissertation on Charles XII in Swedish literature until the early nineteenth century (*Karl XII i svensk litteratur från Dahlstierna till Tegnér*, 1951).[2]

Purely historical accounts are not treated here, neither are biographies. The focus is entirely on literary genres: poetry, plays, novels, and short stories, and of course feature films. When it comes to the earlier publications, however, 'fiction' is a misnomer, stemming as it does from a nineteenth-century aesthetic of originality, where it denoted a certain form of *belles lettres*. Before then, literature was written in the rhetorical context of classical genre poetics, which also comprised genres such as oratory, history, biography, epigrams, and panegyrics of various kinds. The earliest literary attempts consisted largely of panegyrics, naturally enough, and even though the literary scope of this essay excludes biographical and historical works, it must inevitably begin with panegyric and didactic texts.

Regardless of the period, it is difficult to draw an absolute distinction between history and fiction. The Charles XII of the literary writers has always been influenced by historians' assessments, yet even so his characterisation cannot be reduced to a pale reflection of historiographical trends. The literary accounts have their own tradition, and interplay of history and fiction has not been a one-way street.[3]

The theme most frequently seen, whether directly or indirectly, in literary works about Charles XII is that of the hero. What distinguishes the heroic mind? How best to judge a hero in a moral or political perspective? What was the significance of his actions in historical terms? Such questions arose frequently in texts, and the way they were treated reflects the transformation of the heroic ideal from the baroque period's magnanimous paragon of virtue to the nineteenth-century romantic hero, and on to the post-war distrust of rank heroic posturing. Where the Enlightenment view of Charles XII was ambivalent, the period spanning Romanticism to the Second World War was generally strongly heroising, while depictions since then have been characterised by an almost programmatic de-heroisation. Throughout, the picture of this divisive king was never unambiguous, and the hero cult always had its challengers. Even at times when admiration of Charles XII was at its greatest, some writers have regarded him and his actions with dispassion, if not distaste.

One might think that with so much that was self-contained and evasive about the king, more would have been done to attempt a probing psychological account. Yet it has not happened often. Very few authors have tried to truly empathise with his character and show the human face behind the mask of the warrior king. It is striking how often he has been used to illustrate accepted beliefs and positions, be it a dictator's mentality or the Swedish national character. And almost invariably Charles XII has been given one of two extreme roles: admired role model or object lesson. During the twentieth century especially, this polarisation has been great.

## ■ Heroic Virtue—Baroque Panegyrics to Charles XII

The genre that dominated the literary accounts of the king in his lifetime was a central feature of baroque political culture—the princely homage. Using it as their vehicle, different groups could make themselves heard and proclaim the values that they believed characterised the legitimate exercise of power, and although the lyrics often echoed a ruler's own propaganda, it is clear that the homage cannot be seen as merely a megaphone for state authority. Far from being opportunistic flattery, it is a genre that has to be read as an expression of political expectation, addressed directly to the monarch.

In both form and content, the Swedish panegyrics were traditional, showing an almost slavish adherence to classical and Renaissance models. The obligatory theme was *virtus heroica*, heroic virtue, which was thought to distinguish people of high birth. In Charles XII's case, this was said to have been evident from birth:

> *Now to the Northern hero and the realm of Svea's heroine,*
> *A precious prince is born, a noble princess.*
> *Now ascends a Carl to Your royal throne*
> *Who hereafter will sit in rule over the realm of Svea;*
> *In him shall your virtue and heroism be example,*
> *A perpetual immortal Temple of Honour.*[4]

By descent, even as a baby Charles XII was singled out for the highest honour and the poem shows how, from the very first, heroic ideals pervaded the panegyrics.

The notions of heroic virtue reached a pitch at the time of his accession to the throne, in 1697, which was presented as a cosmic drama in which death and life struggled against each other but ultimately yielded victory to Charles XII. His accession was depicted as the sunrise after a long night of despair, and the coronation marked the culmination in Sweden of baroque sun symbolism. Among the poets who chimed in the chorus of praise were Göran Josua Törnqvist, Israel Holmström, and Gunno Eurelius Dahlstierna.[5] With his *Kunga Skald* [Royal Stanzas], Dahlstierna made the single longest contribution, but the others produced voluminous works as well. One female poet who praised the king was Sophia Elisabeth Brenner.[6]

Another recurring element was biblical allusion. It was customary, given the theocratic discourse of the day, to compare contemporary princes with the Old Testament Israelite kings. In Charles XII's case, however, there were even messianic allusions. As a child he was shown in forms that brought to mind the portrayal of the Infant Jesus in baroque art, and at his accession he was regularly referred to as 'the Lord's anointed.'[7] The effect was to position him as a national saviour, to the extent that Dahlstierna made loyalty to the king an integral part of his subjects' Lutheran identity:

> *Give God thine heart; give the King thy faith:*
> *Give God thine soul; and give the King thy goods, thy life and blood:*
> *Give to God and King his own; lo! the Devil gets naught![8]*

The most high-flown allusions came later, in 1714, when the king's return from Turkey was equated to the birth of Jesus at Christmas in a poem entitled *Hosianna, eller Fägnefult glädie-rop* [Hosanna, or Delighted Cry of Joy]: 'Two kings at once now draw near to Sweden | With their dew of grace this frenzied dread to cool.' The parallel is a memorable backdrop to the millenarianism that contemporaries then associated with the king.[9]

Most of the panegyrics were in the high style, in Latin, full of comparisons with Hercules and Alexander the Great, the latter being a figure that Charles XII himself seems to have identified with.[10] However, there were also texts in a much simpler style. One such was *Giöta Kiämpa-Wisa* [Geatish Song of a Hero], a ballad-like poem by Dahlstierna about the Battle of Narva. As it was printed as a chapbook, it has been taken to be a form of baroque peasant romance or an attempt to meld political propaganda with popular verse, but it is also possible that in ballad form it was intended as an equivalent to the Renaissance poetry's neo-classicising *carmen heroicum*, considered the noblest of all genres, which makes its simplicity all the more conspicuous.[11] Dahlstierna returned to the ballad form with his *Saxa-Kalaas* [Saxon Feast], written after the Treaty of Altranstädt in 1706, but it was also used by other authors, such as the prolific propagandising poet Wilhelm Kruse.[12] Common to all the wartime Swedish-language panegyrics in the king's lifetime was the emphasis on a just peace—exhortations to the king to fight for honour and glory in war are rare.

Turn to Russia and one finds plenty of similar allusions to the Bible. As the enemy of Peter the Great and the Russians, Charles XII figured in the role of the giant Goliath in battle against righteous David, or as Pharaoh pursuing God's chosen people. On the continent, meanwhile, interest in Charles was stirred up by propaganda in Latin produced by the Swedish field chancery, which was intended to quash a flurry of libellous pamphlets.[13] In the anglophone world, the king's support for the opposition to the ruling Hanoverian dynasty found its critics, among them Daniel Defoe, who in 1715 published *The History of the Wars of His Present Majesty Charles XII*. Defoe was firmly opposed to absolute monarchy, and although he acknowledged that Charles XII had shown courage and perseverance, he censured him for his arrogance, brutality, and despotism.[14]

## ■ From Voltaire to Swedenborg

Today, Defoe's book is especially memorable for its part in prompting François-Marie Arouet, better known as Voltaire, to write *Histoire de Charles XII, roi de Suède* (1731), by far the most famous of all the biographies of the king. Voltaire wanted to be a historian and was determined to give as accurate a picture as possible. At the same time, his literary ambitions are clear, and although he put a great deal of effort into setting out the sequence of events, his account is more notable for its narrative than its political analysis. Since the point of the book—according to Voltaire himself—was to warn of the dangers of the *folie de conquête*, 'the folly of making conquests,' it should be read as being in the tradition of the moralising princely tract of the Renaissance.[15] With its elegant style, spiced with anecdotes and *bons mots* that have gone down in history, it should also be seen against the background of popular genres of the day such as panegyrics and vignettes.

For Voltaire, the king's character and actions were central, as was passing moral judgment on them. In best Enlightenment spirit, he explained that any prince who wanted to earn praise must above all strive to do well, show lenience, and be interested in the arts and sciences. None of these virtues could be said to have been Charles XII's strong suit. At the same time, the king had often shown courage, willpower, and patience in both good times and bad, as Voltaire conceded. He went on to argue, however, that these were virtues of conquerors and tyrants rather than of good rulers, and pointed out that the king lacked the wisdom of a true statesman. That fault had proved fatal:

> *Thus fell Charles XII, King of Sweden, at the age of thirty-six and a half, having experienced the extremes of prosperity and of adversity, without being softened by the one or in the least disturbed by the other. Almost all his actions, even those of his private life, were beyond credibility. Perhaps he was the only man, and until now the only king, who never showed weakness; he carried all the heroic virtues to that excess at which they become faults as dangerous as the opposite vices. . . . His great qualities, just one of which could have immortalised another sovereign, led to his country's misfortunes . . . he was a remarkable rather than a great man, and to be admired rather than to be emulated.*[16]

Voltaire believed that Charles XII's personal qualities had made him a remarkable man, but that they had also led him to destruction, and he made a distinction between the king as a person and as a politician. As the Swedish historian Karl-Gustaf Hildebrand said, this left the king as something of a paradox: the more that was made of the king's personal advantages, the stronger a warning example he became.[17] A political role model he was not. That much was plain when he was compared to Peter the Great, who, although according to Voltaire a primitive and brutal man, was described as a far more significant figure, because he fought for human progress in his attempt to civilise Russia.

Voltaire's biography was enormously popular—it was one of world literature's most widely spread works—and to this day the literary image of Charles XII still bears its stamp.[18] In Sweden, however, it was unpopular, for the picture it painted of the king was far removed from the popular revanchism in the lead-up to the war with Russia in 1741.[19] In the attempt to drum up public support for the war, the persona of Charles XII played an important role. Thus in the so-called *Sinclairsvisan* (*Sinclair Ballad*) his was the voice calling for revenge for the Russian-arranged murder of a Swedish officer in Poland. And the year before, the Caroline chaplain Jöran Nordberg issued an alternative biography on behalf of the Swedish government, with a series of sharp attacks on Voltaire. It was written as a chronicle in format and simple in style, but translated into French and German it reached international audiences. In response, Voltaire printed the sarcastic *Lettre à Mr Norberg* (1744).[20]

Someone who was clearly not reverent in his treatment of Charles XII was Emanuel Swedenborg. In his youth, he had courted the king with flowery, complimentary poems, and had even met him and won his admiration. What he thought then of the king is unknown, but his later dreams and spirit visions gave him a very jaundiced opinion of Charles. His notes on his experiences were for private use and without artistic ambitions, but as they were later published and played a significant role in Strindberg's *Charles XII*, they are not without literary interest. According to Swedenborg, Charles XII was more astute than most, but also domineering and violent, and one of the most stubborn people ever to have lived. Driven by boundless pride, behind his mask of virtue he had set himself up in opposition to God, and in Swedenborg's visions he figures among the worst offenders: even in hell he wants to make himself king in order to attack God and conquer heaven, which earned him the epithet 'a devil more than any other.' Like Voltaire, Swedenborg was prepared to admit that the king had a number of sterling qualities—not least intellectually—but as he had put them to such evil purposes, the final verdict could only be negative.[21]

## ■ The Charles XII of the Romantics—A Fettered Thundergod

While Enlightenment views on Charles XII were ambivalent, it became more common to take a positive line towards the end of the eighteenth century. Behind this was a romantic fascination with exceptionality and the lone protagonist, driven by his inner conviction to forge his own path through the world, which, taken with Kant's moral duty, was fertile ground for a new heroic ideal based on personality rather than noble birth. In this view, heroes and geniuses must be measured by their pursuit of loftier values and as a tool for the *Weltgeist*, the world spirit—they could not be judged solely according to utilitarian worth. As heroes, they stood above good and evil and the usual social norms, while they personified sentiment, drive, and idealistic devotion. Charles's intransigence was now seen not primarily as a lack of political sense, but as an expression of personal integrity and an example of the idealistic struggle against an unsympathetic world.[22]

According to the romantics, it was heroes who bound together the fate of the world and forged history, and it fell to the historians and poets to depict their lives and struggles. One who did so was the German-Swedish writer Ernst Moritz Arndt, who described Charles XII as the standard-bearer of idealism against overwhelming odds, even though he brought about his own downfall by forgetting the limits on the power of mankind.[23] This view was embraced wholeheartedly by Gustav IV Adolf of Sweden, who in the early nineteenth century adopted a hairstyle *à la Charles XII* and imitated his mode of dress. This did nothing, however, to bring him success in his war against Russia in 1808-09, something that Johan Ludvig Runeberg later underlined in his *Fänrik Ståls sägner* (1848, *The Tales of Ensign Stål*).

Sweden's loss of Finland in 1809 and the subsequent yearning for revenge against Russia created a need for Swedish heroes. The figure pressed into service was, of course, Charles XII, whose heroic status was now proclaimed by poets such as P.D.A.

Atterbom, Johan Olof Wallin, Erik Gustaf Geijer, and Esaias Tegnér. They painted a picture of a king who was not without flaws; a picture that shifted uneasily between vigorous sabre-rattling and reflections on the romantic hero's tragic destiny. The same was also true of individual authors: while Geijer in 'Karl den tolfte' [1811, Charles XII] had depicted the king as a bold commander, his elegy 'Viken, tidens flyktiga minnen!' [1818, Begone, Fleeting Memories of Time] had a more mournful tone.[24]

The most influential poems, however—Tegnér's 'Götha Lejon' [Geatish Lion] and 'Carl XII,' both written for the centenary of the king's death in 1818—concentrated on the young, victorious warrior. While the first poem does not mention the king by name, it is plain who is meant, especially given that the image of a lion sleeping with open eyes was known from a medal from the Caroline period and the poem talks of the lion driving the enemy before him on the far shores of the Baltic. The second poem depicts the 18-year-old king on the battlefield of Narva:

> *King Carl, the youthful hero,*
> *In smoke and dust he stood;*
> *He drew his belted longsword*
> *And into battle strode.*
> *'Come, let us try its war-bite,*
> *What Swedish steel may do.*
> *Make way, you Moscoviters,*
> *Fresh heart, the lads in blue!'*
>
> . . .
>
> *So great a heart was beating*
> *Within his Swedish breast,*
> *In gladness as in anguish,*
> *Alone for what is Just.*
> *Alike at flood or ebbtide,*
> *Too resolute to quell,*
> *The overlord of fortune,*
> *He fought until he fell.*[25]

The poem, much quoted, was extremely popular in its day, and continues to determine much of the popular image of Charles XII. With its political attack on Russia, the romantic heroic cult was very much to the fore, and the king was depicted as a 'beardless thundergod,' rising above the vicissitudes of fortune to remain true to the demands of justice and morality. In nineteenth-century Sweden, the poem was an almost mandatory element in any patriotic celebration, and, by dint of the pan-Scandinavistic student movement, it became known in the other nordic countries too.[26]

However, a determination to exact revenge from Russia was not the only explanation for the early nineteenth-century interest in Charles XII. There was also, in 1810, the election to the Swedish throne of one of Napoleon's marshals, Jean-Baptiste Bernadotte, who chose the regnal name Karl Johan. His recruitment, his name even, had natural connotations of the Caroline era, and following the Treaty of Kiel in 1814 and Sweden's subsequent union with Norway that autumn, the crown prince was heralded as a new Charles,

who would realise the old idea of uniting the two countries. 'Arise, Twelfth Charles! and see | complete and immortal | the great work that you started,' as J.O. Wallin versified.[27]

Once this union had become a reality, however, allusions to Charles XII were less appropriate, and for the next three decades the members of the Bernadotte dynasty went to striking lengths to distance themselves from their Caroline heritage, while they played up the Gustavian legacy.[28] They were driven to do this by their alliance with the Russian emperor, which Karl Johan signed in 1812 and which held throughout his reign. It formed a solid obstacle to any attempt at an official Charles XII cult and the parallel was soon dropped, even though Karl XIV Johan included Charles XII in the pantheon of statues of Charleses that were intended to legitimise his position as the Swedish monarch. When people marked the centenary of Charles XII's death in 1818, it was without royal sanction.[29]

Similarly, in nineteenth-century European literature, Charles XII played the role of a war hero. Byron portrayed him briefly in the narrative poem *Mazeppa* (1819), which begins with the king on the run with the Ukrainian Hetman Ivan Mazepa the night after the Battle of Poltava. Charles XII is depicted as unbroken, unbowed—a stoic hero:

> *Kinglike the monarch bore his fall,*
> *And made, in this extreme of ill,*
> *His pangs the vassals of his will;*
> *All silent and subdued were they,*
> *As once the nations round him lay.*[30]

Mazepa, too, was treated as a romantic hero by Byron. A completely different picture of him as a perfidious traitor is to be found in Alexander Pushkin's work, whose dramatic poem *Poltava* (1828-29) has been described as a panegyric to Russian imperialism: while Charles XII is treated respectfully as a heroic opponent of Peter the Great, it is made plain that the honour he was fighting for was false and that it was the tsar who had history on his side.[31] In nineteenth-century continental literature, the king was a recurring figure on the stage—for example, in an anonymous French vaudeville comedy with the title *Heure de Charles XII, ou le lion amoureux* [1839, The Time of Charles XII, or the Amorous Lion], in the German poet and dramatist Rudolf Gottschall's *König Karl XII. Geschichtliches Trauerspiel* [1866, King Charles XII: Historical Tragedy], and in a mini-drama (1897) by the Austrian comedian Rudolf Kutschar, *Karl XII:s Jugendliebe*, about Charles XII's love life as a young man.[32]

## ■ Liberalism's Charles XII—Freedom-loving Paragon of Civic Virtue

In Sweden, interest in Charles XII was renewed in the 1840s, when the king was enlisted as a liberal friend of freedom. The fact that the country's most extreme autocrat could be assigned that role seems astonishing to modern eyes, but must be understood in the light of the growing liberal opposition to Karl XIV Johan and the alliance with Russia. The tsardom was generally seen as a bastion of reaction and despotism, and the liberals believed that Karl XIV Johan's nepotism and eagerness to govern singlehandedly formed an 'internal Russia' in Sweden, inspired by his autocratic ally. Against this, they held up

Karl XIV Johan of Sweden is welcomed into Elysium by Charles XII.

Lithograph by Carl Andreas Dahlström
(1806-69), ca. 1844. Nationalmuseum,
Stockholm, Sweden.

the romantic ideal of the Charles XII who was emblematic of the struggle for civil liberty both at home and abroad. The student poet C.W.A. Strandberg treated this theme around 1840. Significantly, the king adorned the cover of his anthology of martial poems *Sånger i pansar* [1842, Songs of Armour], while Tegnér's Charles XII poem became something of a national anthem, much like the French Revolution's Marseillaise.[33]

This impression of Charles XII was strengthened by student pan-Scandinavism, the Crimean War of 1853-56, and the Polish uprisings of 1861-63. The finishing touch came in 1862, when Tsar Alexander II abolished all Russian victory celebrations—except its triumph at Poltava. In Sweden popular indignation was drummed up, and the same year the liberals organised a commemoration in Stockholm of 'the Swedish men, who by their death and captivity gave proof of their loyalty to this historic idea', i.e., the ideology of National Liberalism.[34] At heart, it was a celebration of Sweden's national freedom, with Charles XII described as 'the most Swedish of Swedes'. In speeches given by August Sohlman, editor of Sweden's leading liberal newspaper, *Aftonbladet*, the king's simplicity, piety, and 'morality' were set against the 'loose' morals of Charles's contemporaries, which supposedly characterised the *ancien régime*:

> I am not ashamed to confess that I feel my heart swell and my eyes fill with tears when, in the midst of this Rococo era, when all courts were the scene of the greatest debaucheries, the grossest duplicities, the most ridiculous codes of etiquette, and the dustiest old fogies, I see this noble Swedish figure rise up in all his magnificent simplicity, alone, with his sword and his Bible, his pure morality, his unfeigned piety.[35]

The Charles XII of the National Liberals was a man of the people, and having previously been used to stir up a lust for revenge for the loss of Finland to Russia, his mission was now extended to other peoples, whose national independence was said to have been anticipated by his anti-Russian and anti-Prussian policy. At the Stockholm party in 1862, salutations from Polish refugees on the run from the tsarist police were read out to loud cheers, as were those from Giuseppe Garibaldi, who was admired in liberal circles.[36]

The culmination of the liberals' enthusiasm for Charles XII came with the 150th anniversary of the king's death in 1868, when Johan Peter Molin's famous statue of the king was unveiled in the Kungsträdgården Park in Stockholm. At the inauguration, which was a public event on an unprecedented scale, a variety of popular plays were performed at theatres across the city. The recurring themes were the king's simplicity and 'morality', as well as his renunciation of personal happiness for the good of his people and his desire to protect his poorest subjects from their masters' bullying and arbitrariness. The inauguration was later the subject of literary treatment in a pocket novel.[37]

Further examples of how Charles XII was used to help shape Sweden's national identity are to be found in the *Läsebok för folkskolan* [Reader for Schools]. In this book, first published in time for the statue's inauguration and intended for use in all the country's schools, both Tegnér's 'Carl XII' and a detailed depiction of the Battle of Narva were included as central elements in a good, patriotic education.[38] The book bore similarities to the corresponding section in the Finnish writer and journalist Zacharias Topelius' immensely popular newspaper serial *Fältskärns berättelser* [A Military Surgeon's Tales], an account of a family's fate in Sweden and Finland during

Tr. hos Andersou.

Stig upp med Oss ur grus och natt,
O Carl! af Carlar förd ur striden
Dit upp, der hjeltars mål är satt,
Och segren palmbekröns af friden.

FRÅN KARL XII:s STATYS AFTÄCKNINGSFEST I STOCKHOLM DEN 30 NOVEMBER 1868. 1. Festplatsen när täckelset fallit. Teeknad af O. A. MANKELL och A. G. HAFSTRÖM.

*The unveiling of the statue of Charles XII in Stockholm on 30 November 1868 (Swedish calendar).*

*Print by O.A. Mankell (1838-85) and A.G. Hafström (1841-1909), 1868. Kungliga Biblioteket, Stockholm, Sweden. Ny illustrerad tidning 1868 s. 389.*

the seventeenth and eighteenth centuries, which cherished National Liberal ideals and a political system where the king ruled in person, but with a popular mandate.[39]

In comparison to the early nineteenth-century romantic image, liberalism's Charles XII was a moral leader. As before, the king was esteemed for his personal qualities, but instead of bravery and courage, virtues such as piety and simplicity came to the fore, making him the very pattern of civic virtue. Much was made of his sobriety; for example, in an otherwise hostile account, the views of the storyteller Anders Fryxell on the king's abstemiousness were coloured by liberal public morals. As a young, powerful, clean-living man, Charles XII became a popular figure in the temperance movement's songbooks, and when an academic temperance society was mooted in Uppsala in 1888, 30 November was chosen as the day of its foundation in order to commemorate 'the teetotal king.'[40]

Originally, the liberals' version of Charles XII had taken shape in opposition to an increasingly ossified Swedish monarchy. However, after the alliance with Russia collapsed, and after Sweden acquired a modern bicameral parliament and the monarchy embraced the National Liberal ideology, much of this oppositional character eroded.[41] Thus the royal family played an active part in the inauguration of the statue in 1868, giving the celebration an official character, and although there were protests from workers and others unable to afford tickets to the festivities, the left-wing press questioned neither the hero of the hour nor the party as such.[42] Support for Charles XII as a national symbol appears to have been widespread at the time. This was certainly the impression abroad, and Henrik Ibsen made fun of this popular enthusiasm for Charles XII in *Peer Gynt* (1867).

Historians were still critical, however. Fredrik Ferdinand Carlson, a leading liberal historian, described him as an adventurer, and said that his policies were fundamentally unsuccessful. This distance found its way into more literary works, as is evident from the patriotic commemorative poems by Carl Snoilsky in *Svenska bilder* [1881-97, Swedish Pictures]. Snoilsky was a poet of a *juste milieu* bent with close ties to the royal family; nevertheless his portrait of Charles XII was anything but sympathetic: for all the patriotic clichés, the king appears more as a warning example. Despite this, for the next half century the poems were required reading in Swedish schools.[43]

## ■ The Great Sacrifice—The National Romantics' Charles XII

During the last decades of the nineteenth century, the way the king was remembered took on a conservative, National Romantic gloss (see, for instance, the painting by Gustaf Cederström on pages 372-73). This was driven by schools, the Church, and the armed forces, who hailed him as a paradigm of patriotic duty and the unity of the Caroline era as the antithesis to Sweden's recent political divisions. Significantly, this was also the period that saw professional historians' acceptance of a more positive picture of Charles XII as a farsighted strategist, whose war policies were ultimately designed to safeguard European culture against Slavic barbarism.[44] The opposite line was taken by the labour movement, which thought the king a power-crazed adventurer who laid waste the country on a whim.[45] The tension between these approaches slowly mounted, culminating in the so-called Strindberg Feud of 1910-12.

Crucial to the early twentieth-century literary vision of the king was Verner von Heidenstam's narrative cycle *Karolinerna* [1897-98, The Carolines], one of the most controversial works about Charles XII, but also among the most fascinating, and one which to this day influences the literary image of the Caroline era. Given his aspirations to the role of national laureate, Heidenstam wanted to write a national epic with the Swedish people as the protagonists. The focus is on ordinary soldiers and ordinary people, and the account covers the whole of Charles XII's reign, albeit with an emphasis on the difficult years following Poltava. Linguistically, the stories are told in a slightly archaicising style, with a tendency towards grandiose pathos and a moralising tone.

Heidenstam's main theme is the relationship between the king and his subjects, the starting point being the people—the Carolines of the title—and their experiences, although the king also serves as the volumes' focal point because of the sheer power of his personality: even those who complain and curse him are enthralled when his will is revealed to them. The king's will thus becomes the will of the people. The king also personifies the people's temperament. Heidenstam had previously discussed the nature of Swedishness in the pamphlet *Om svenskarnas lynne* [1896, On the Swedes' Temperament], and in *Karolinerna* he used the king to symbolise the ambiguity in the Swedes' disposition: 'Not only for his foolhardiness and his ultimate poverty, but for almost any of his qualities, he remains an archetype for both the sunny side to the Swedish temperament and for all it encompasses by way of tragedy and broken genius.'[46] Charles XII's person was a mix of the adventurousness and frivolity as well as the melancholy, verging on monomania, that Heidenstam believed characterised the nordic temperament.

Heidenstam did not defend Charles's policies—if only because he was much influenced by Fryxell—and the king in his narrative is a largely unsympathetic figure: closed, arrogant, and indifferent to the suffering of others. Nevertheless, he emerges a hero. It was Heidenstam's belief that suffering and sacrifice could only ennoble the human condition, and in his stories he sought to show how the king instilled enthusiasm and a spirit of self-sacrifice in his subjects. It was through the trials and tribulations he imposed on the Swedes that they became aware of their greatness: 'It was our own secret will and desire which he preserved against our own indecision,' one of the protagonists concluded in the final story.[47] Even as the king devastated the country, he brought the Swedes to the point where they could do great deeds.

All in all, *Karolinerna* is a monument to a nation's self-abnegating submission to a charismatic leader. In the bleak light of twentieth-century totalitarianism, this sort of tragic heroism seems deeply questionable. Nevertheless, there is no doubt that it is tragedy that imbues *Karolinerna* with its artistic force. The romantics may have conjured up the idea that Charles XII's life had its tragic moments, but it was Heidenstam who made it central to his argument. Just how consciously he did so is shown by the related collection of essays, *Karl XII och det tragiska* [1898, Charles XII and the Tragic], in which he announced that the king could only be understood in the light of classical tragedy.

Where Tegnér portrayed Charles XII as a mighty, victorious demigod, Heidenstam had him as an also-ran who ultimately proved his heroism by sacrificing himself for a doomed cause. His soldiers, the whole Swedish nation even, shared the same fate, and their immense sacrifice for the nation was a recurring theme in Heidenstam's stories. It could be interpreted both morally and politically, but it really stemmed from an aesthetic choice: the struggle by the king and his armies could not be comprehended by reason, according to Heidenstam, but could only be experienced aesthetically, as tragic drama—the drama he depicted in his stories.[48]

Reception of *Karolinerna* was muted—the left disliked the jingoism, the right the king as a tragic figure—but the stories nevertheless had an enduring impact. They were followed by a series of other accounts, which served to consolidate Charles XII's position as symbol of Swedish nationalism: *Kungens blå gossar* [1900, The King's Boys in Blue] by the adventure storywriter Nils Hydén, or *En hjältesaga: Romantiserad skildring ur Magnus Stenbocks lif* [1902, A Hero's Tale: Romantic Sketches from the Life of Magnus Stenbock] by Iwan T. Aminoff (pseudonym: Radscha). Heidenstam's stories underpinned much of nationalism in public opinion, and were marketed at the outbreak of war in 1914 as appropriate reading for the young.[49]

Abroad, too, Heidenstam had his followers. The most famous was Rainer Maria Rilke, who, George C. Schoolfield has suggested, found in the Swede's work his inspiration for the poem 'Karl der Zwölfte reitet in der Ukraine' [Charles XII Rides in the Ukraine], published in *Das Buch der Bilder* [1902, The Book of Pictures].[50] Critics

Sic itur . . .

*teckning af P. Lindroth.*

STRINDBERG

'Sic itur…,' a caricature of Verner von
Heidenstam as Charles XII.

Pen and ink drawing by Per Lindroth
(1878-1933), 1911. Kungliga Biblioteket,
Stockholm, Sweden. Söndags-Nisse 1911.

may have dismissed the poem as 'really bad,' and it may occupy an obscure place in
the poet's oeuvre, but it still confirms that the notion of a tragic Charles XII had a real
hold on the imagination.[51] Rilke described the war as a colourful, intoxicating adventure. In the din of battle—contrasted with grey tedium of daily life—the king hears
things as they really are and sees the true nature of life: 'He had awakened to seeing:
| the beautiful battle | fawned upon his wilfulness.' After the battle, he rides away
on a grey horse, gazing greyly ahead, but happily content with the fighting.[52] When
compared to Heidenstam's majestic figure, Rilke's Charles XII appears superficial in
his aestheticisation, but the similarity in the authors' views on the king is palpable.

   Heidenstam's tragic-heroic image of Charles XII survived the First World War surprisingly intact. It had been stewarded by the educationalist Carl Grimberg, whose popular *Svenska folkets underbara öden* [1913-24, The Swedish Nation's Wondrous Fate] was a

runaway bestseller. Among the author's favourite heroes was Charles XII, who was given a lively account in the book.[53] Grimberg was also one of the driving forces behind the silent film *Carl XII*, with Gösta Ekman in the lead, which after many chops and changes finally went on general release in 1925. It was marketed as a history film, but the screenplay had been written by the novelist Hjalmar Bergman, who took his inspiration from not only Heidenstam and Grimberg, but also Topelius and Fryxell. The fact that it was based on literary works is evident from the intertitles, which have quotes from Tegnér's famous poem. The characterisation of the king was insipid, however, and completely lacked the complexity found in *Karolinerna*; instead, his relationship with women—which was described as interesting, but very chaste—was a recurring theme. The issue seems to have been of particular interest during the early decades of the twentieth century.[54]

The last hurrah for the National Romantics' Charles XII came in Frans G. Bengtsson's *Karl XII:s levnad* [1935-36, Charles XII's Life], written while the clouds of war were again gathering. According to Bengtsson, the king's fate could only be understood in mythological terms, and his account of the man has been described as 'hyper-romantic', in the sense that he made the king into a 'hero of God's grace', driven by nothing more than his own desire for adventure and glory.[55] Politics was far less interesting to Bengtsson, and he eschewed the more chauvinist brand of nationalism: his is an account of a moral hero. As such, the king is above mundane reality and, at least until Poltava, the war is depicted as a game and the main characters as fortunate knights. Yet, as one reviewer noted, this wore thin as the book progressed, and in the second part Bengtsson produced a king humanised by adversity. Although the narrative begun in an almost Tegnérian vein, with the king as a boyish demigod, it gradually elided into Heidenstam's doomed defier of fate.

With his broad brush, Bengtsson's monumental work marked the end in Sweden for both the romantics' bellicose Charles XII, eager for the fray, and the National Romantics' defiantly tragic hero. The echoes of the latter could still be heard, though, in the Argentinian poet Jorge Luis Borges's 'A Carlos XII' in *El otro, el mismo* (1964, *The Other, The Same*):

> *You knew that victory or defeat*
> *was indifferent in the face of Fate,*
> *that there is no other virtue than to be brave*
> *and that the marble will at last be forgotten.*
> *You burn ice-cold, alone like the desert.*
> *No one touched your soul and you are dead.*[56]

Borges was fascinated by Norse history and depicted the king as a warrior in the Viking mould. The portrait is not unequivocally heroic, however, and the complete loneliness that is the king's destiny has more than a touch of stoic endurance in the face of an arbitrary fate.

## ■ Mass-murderer and Ruination of the Nation—Charles XII after Strindberg

The National Romantics' heroisation of Charles XII did not go unchallenged. There was always criticism from certain quarters, especially the labour movement, and both the king's policies and his person came under attack. In the literary realm, this critical view was embodied by August Strindberg, who hated the 'era of the jubilee' that Charles XII was so much a part of. As early as *Röda rummet* (1879, *The Red Room*), *Svenska folket* (1881-82, *The Swedish People*) and *Svenska öden och äventyr* (1890, *Swedish Destinies and Adventures*) he had made himself its spokesman. It would not culminate, however, until his play *Carl XII*, which opened in 1902. The plot—to the extent that one can say this inner drama has a plot—is based on Fryxell's tales and is set in the Swedish county of Skåne and the Norwegian town of Fredrikshald. It is centred on the king and shows a closed, almost autistic protagonist who sacrifices everything in his pursuit of war. Strindberg believed Charles XII to be anything but a hero. He is described as a villain (*bov*), who lays waste the country by squandering his father's legacy and abandoning his subjects to suffering and destitution. In the play, Strindberg experimented with an expressionist style, so that in a dreamlike scene a soldier, who goes by the telling name of Starve, appears in the king's chamber. He had once saved the king's life in Russia, but instead of thanks was demoted because the king was too proud to accept help from others. The soldier regretted what he did: 'Yes—I was number fifty-eight, Starve, of Taube's Dragoons. And that I saved your life I now repent, for if you'd perished Poltava would never have happened, and we'd be enjoying six years of peace now!'[57] In contrast to Heidenstam, Strindberg underscored the wave of popular discontent with Charles XII and his war. He chiefly followed Swedenborg, who, he felt, gave 'a symbolist picture of the greatest tyrant who ever lived, *d'après nature*.'[58] At the same time, he noted his own similarities to the king—the loneliness of genius, the complex relationships with women, and the titanic struggle with God. It is this last aspect, as one scholar has noted, that the play shows as a steady vastation (*ödeläggelse*), as the king's imaginary greatness is peeled away piece by piece, so that when he is shot dead he is destitute and desperate.[59] In the final scene, it is intimated that the fatal bullet is sent by God.

The similarities between Strindberg's and Heidenstam's portraits of Charles XII are more numerous than the differences, yet even so the king would end up as the focus of the so-called Strindberg Feud of 1910-12, which came down to a bitter fight between the two authors for authority over the Swedish literary public. It was fought out in the newspapers, and began when Strindberg attacked the right's adulation of Charles XII, which he compared to the ancient Egyptian cult of the dead pharaohs. He jeeringly described the king as a hopeless commander and a leech who preyed on his own people, and the war as 'a plunderer's march for twice nine years, with no other visible purpose than adventure.'[60] The real enemies, however, were Heidenstam, Sven Hedin, the royal court, and the Swedish Academy, and gradually the debate shifted focus to other issues. The feud meant that an explicitly critical view of Charles XII was aired in public, and that the king's position as a national symbol suffered a serious blow.

Strindberg's debunking efforts have had a profound impact on the image of Charles XII in the century since. It was a long time in coming, however: it was only after the Second World War that it became the accepted view, when Heidenstam's and the National Romantics' hero worship of the tragic victim was finally discredited. True, the official cult's grip had slackened somewhat in the interim, and it should be noted that Charles XII never had a prominent place in Swedish literature during

World War II—not even when Sweden was assisting Finland during the Winter War of 1939-40 did he become a symbolic figure. Later in the Second World War, he disappeared almost completely from public view, for reasons that some scholars put down to the difficulty of reconciling an aggressor king with Sweden's policy of neutrality, quite apart from the uncomfortable allusions made by the nazis to the king's campaigns in their attempts to recruit Swedes to fight on the eastern front.[61]

After the war, there was no interest in the romance of war whatsoever: within the programmatically modernist social democracy, the king was viewed in a manner heavily influenced by Strindberg. Instead of being a hero, Charles XII quickly became a terrible warning of the insanity of war and the dangers of dictatorship and a leadership cult. As such, he has featured in a surprisingly large number of novels in the post-war period. One example is Peter Nisser's trilogy *Den röda mården*, *Vredens födelse*, and *Slaget* [1954-57, The Red Marten, The Birth of Wrath, and Battle]. Nisser had fought as a volunteer in Finland and wanted to use his own experiences to paint an unvarnished picture of the reality of war, without idealising the hardships. Charles XII only figures on the margins, but Nisser's dislike is clear. It is also found, more explicitly worded, in Gustaf Adolf Lysholm's *Röster från ödemarken* [1967, Voices from the Wasteland]: 'There is no nightmare that for horror compares with the terrifying reality that signed itself Carolus Rex.' Lysholm is known for his finely tuned, nostalgic portrayals of *fin de siècle* Stockholm, but with this novel he created a 'chorus of mourning' of Caroline troops who go through a bleak litany of human suffering during the campaign in Norway in 1718.[62] There are similar descriptions in Sven-Edvin Salje's *Natten och brödet* [1968, Night and Bread], the last in a series of novels about the Swedish county of Blekinge in the days of the Swedish Empire, and Gunnar E. Sandgren's *Fursten* [1962, The Prince], a story about Russian prisoners of war and their harsh treatment in Sweden during the Great Northern War.

In all these novels, the perspective known from *Karolinerna* was reversed: disillusioned by the atrocities of the twentieth century, authors now described Charles XII as a violence-obsessed mass murderer who ruthlessly sacrificed any and all in pursuit of his will, while his subjects were forced to bear the brunt of the disastrous outcome, and all of it described without a shred of enthusiasm for the king or the nation. Although a good deal of the subject matter and narrative technique was taken from their predecessors, the ideological distance is immense, and where there was once a national symbol one finds a man, without a scrap of heroism about him and in all essentials under challenge for both his person and his policies.

The same was true of Lars Widding's *Karolinersvit* [1974-77, The Caroline Series], which was a huge commercial success. Drawn on an epic scale, the action has much of the adventure novel about it as well as a distinct heroising tendency, and, like Topelius, it centres on the fate of a family whose members shed light on the war from different perspectives. The Swedish people and the king are polar opposites, with the king held personally responsible for the country's hardships. Yet he, too, falls victim to his own bloodlust, and ultimately Widding's protagonist, Pilfeldt, an officer in the royal guard, shoots the king at his own request—an ending that is reminiscent of Strindberg's play. Finally the king, too, is engulfed by the futility of war.

*The actor August Palme in the role of Charles XII for a play by August Strindberg.*

Photograph by unknown artist, ca. 1902. Strindberg Museum, Stockholm, Sweden. © Strindbergsmuseet.

For Widding, it is the ordinary people who are the real war heroes. Another example of this is Elsi Rydsjö's series *Karolinernas kvinnor* [1992-99, The Carolines' Women], which can be read as a female counterpart to Heidenstam's stories. The action begins the day after the Battle of Poltava, with one of the female protagonists thinking about the king as she searches for her husband among the dead and wounded:

> *The king, thought Karolina. The king was probably heading off [south]. In safety on his litter, the one protected by the Lifeguard halberdiers. They'd mount guard around him and take the bullets that should have hit him a long time ago. One single bullet hit its target, and it injured his foot!—if only, God willing, it had struck where it should have.*[63]

War here has nothing heroic about it. If there is anything to be celebrated, it is a group of vulnerable women and their camaraderie. Ordinary Swedes wish the king dead: it is certainly not far from soldier Starve's words to the king in Strindberg's play. Further examples of the way the Great Northern War features in recent Swedish literature are Björn Holm's factual novels (1977-92) about the adventures of the army scout Stephan Löfving in Russian-occupied Finland, and of course Peter Englund's *Poltava: Berättelsen om en armés undergång* (1989, *Poltava: The Story of an Army's Downfall*), an acclaimed account that blurs the boundaries between history and fiction. Together with Kristian Petri, Englund revisited the Great Northern War in the short novel *Jag skall dundra* [2005, I Will Thunder], a fictional account of the Swedes' war crimes against civilians in occupied Poland.

## ■ A Charles XII for Post-modern Neo-nationalist Times

In the early 1980s, it might have seemed that Charles XII was forever relegated to history's cabinet of curiosities. The last three decades, however, have seen the rise of Swedish ultra-nationalism, and neo-nazi groups have adopted the king as a symbol of Swedishness. At first glance, the effect has been to partially re-establish a much older, right-wing nationalist tradition, but in fact by linking the king with racism and xenophobia a brand-new, even more strongly polarised, picture of Charles XII has emerged. The element of provocation in this was obvious, to the extent that in the early 1990s the anniversary of the king's death attracted considerable media attention when it was used by various extremist groups to stage violent confrontations with the police.[64]

This mobilisation cannot be said to have made much in the way of a literary mark. There was a certain amount of rehashing, of course, with Tegnér's 'Kung Carl' recorded in the 1990s by the rock group Ultima Thule, which had ties to white supremacist groups. Similarly, there was a tendency to depict the king and his troops as steadfast warriors, waging a constant battle against an overmighty enemy in a manner that recalled Heidenstam's *Karolinerna*.[65] There are greater literary qualities to be found in the backlash to this new heroisation—for example, Ernst Brunner's novel *Carolus Rex—hans liv i sanning återberättat* [2005, Carolus Rex: His Life Truly Narrated], an account obviously designed to crush the heroic myths surrounding the king. Recounting his life story, Charles XII reveals himself to be a psychopathic mass murderer on a par with Hitler and Stalin, with a total disregard for soldiers' and civilians' lives alike.

On one level, Brunner's novel can be read as carrying on the Strindberg tradition, but even so it is hard to imagine it would have existed without the recent polarisation of Charles XII's legacy, for it appears to be almost a rebuttal of the ultra-nationalists' use of the king. Another response has been to highlight Charles XII's multicultural character, such as his long stay in Bender, his interest in other cultures, and the fact that his army consisted of soldiers from various countries. One writer who has sought to do so is the journalist Herman Lindqvist, who launched the idea of Charles XII as Sweden's 'first really multicultural king'; another is the playwright Nils Poletti, who in the summer of 2014 staged a play about the king in Riddarholmen Church in Stockholm, the traditional burial site for Sweden's monarchs, specifically to make him 'king of the whole of Sweden again,' not just the king of the nationalists and ultra-nationalists.[66]

The neo-nationalist use of Charles XII has not been limited to Sweden. As Russian nationalism has grown stronger, the king has increasingly been mentioned again as the doomed enemy of Peter the Great and the Russian Empire. As early as the 1990s, the poet Stanislav Kunjaev wrote about the king's fate, and in 2000 the novelist Sergei Tsvetkov published a fictional biography. Both works were influenced by the Great Russia tradition known from Pushkin, with Charles XII as a valiant warrior, fighting a losing battle for the wrong cause.[67] He was featured in a similar role in the film *Sluga Gosudarev* (2007, *The Sovereign's Servant*), written and directed by Oleg Ryaskov. This film, which ends in a bloody sequence showing the tsar's triumph at Poltava, illustrates the way history is used in the nationalist offensive that now characterises the Putin era, and is one of a series of violent adventure films to play up Great Russia aspirations in the past decade.

### ■ Conclusion

Evidently, the Charles XII of literary tradition was steeped in notions of heroism from the very beginning, so much so that it is fair to say that the king has become locked into playing his heroic part, even where writers have tried to dent his halo. At the same time, there is no straight line from role model to salutary object lesson, and even in the most recent portrayals the picture is ambivalent. In Swedish literature, however, one sees that the nature of that heroism changed in the mid-nineteenth century, as people's interest shifted from Narva to Poltava and the activist revanchism of the romantics gave way to a resigned contemplation of human cost exacted by Sweden's former superpower status. It is hardly an accident that the shift coincided with the definitive collapse of Sweden's dreams of empire, and it is tempting to see subsequent literary accounts of Charles XII as revealing the need to reflect on how a nation might cope with a traumatic experience that put every last citizen to the test. For other European countries, the past 150 years offer this and similar experiences to excess, but for Sweden they had to be sought further back in history. And so the Great Northern War has been pressed into service, providing the necessary experiences in post-war literature, used as a parallel to the Second World War, but the need was also reflected in Heidenstam's depictions of the Carolines' self-sacrifice, and indeed in Strindberg's descriptions of soldier Starve's fate. They take different approaches to the experience of war, but the one thing shared by all the literary accounts of Charles XII from the last 150 years is that they can be understood as mirroring Swedish neutrality.

# APPENDIX A
# A Chronology in Three Calendars

One of the major challenges and sources of confusion for an understanding of the European-wide chronology of events in the period covered by this volume is that three different calendars were in use: (1) the Julian or Old Style calendar, (2) the Swedish Style calendar, and (3) the Gregorian or New Style calendar. Historical literature in different countries and in different languages, and even by different authors, varies in its use of calendars to date events. References in the endnotes to original documents will vary according to the calendar of the original document. However, for the purposes of this volume and in order to better understand the chronology of events across Europe, all dates in the text have been standardised according to New Style, the same calendar that is in general use in Europe today.

**The Julian or Old Style Calendar.** Julius Caesar introduced this calendar in 45 BCE, hence its name. It was established on the principle that a calendar year consisted of 365 days. Every fourth year was to have an extra day to correct for the length of the year that astronomers calculated as 365 days and six hours. The sixth calends of March (i.e., 24 February) was the day that was doubled. In later practice, an error was made when calculating the four-year intervals. The current year was used in the calculation, making the 'leap year' occur every third year, instead of every fourth. This was corrected by the Emperor Augustus so that every fourth year was calculated from 4 CE. Over time, a further issue arose about the date on which the new calendar year began. For the Romans, January was the beginning of the civil New Year, with the solar year beginning on 1 January. Later, Christmas Day, 25 December, or the feast of the Annunciation, Lady Day, 25 March, was used to begin a new calendar year. By the middle of the seventeenth century most European countries had adopted 1 January as the beginning of the calendar year, except Britain, which until 1751 continued to use 25 March. For the span between 1 January and 24 March, many English and later British official papers and records used a double-dating system (for the year) that looked like a fraction, e.g., 15 February 1702/3. Of the countries discussed in the period covered by this volume, England, Scotland, Wales, and Russia used Old Style; Denmark, Norway, and the Protestant German states used it until 1700; Sweden used it before 1700 and after 1712; and five of the seven provinces of the Dutch Republic (Friesland, Groningen, Overijssel, Utrecht, and Protestant portions of Gelderland) officially used it until 1700-01— in daily practice, though, these provinces had adopted New Style long before 1700 because of the preponderance of Holland, which used New Style dates. The Ottoman Empire had a calendar that was exactly 584 years behind the Old Style calendar and the Ottoman year began on 1 March.[1]

**The Gregorian or New Style Calendar.** During the medieval period, scholars began to note that there was an increasing discrepancy between the length of the solar year and the length of the calendar year. By the sixteenth century, astronomers had discovered that the Julian calendar had overstated the length of one year by 10 minutes and 48 seconds. As a result of this observation, Pope Gregory XIII introduced a new calendar by the Papal Bull *Inter Gravissimus* of 24 February 1582. The pope had multiple purposes for this change. Not surprisingly, they were primarily related to the practices of the Roman Catholic Church, but the change also had a major effect outside that realm on all who used the calendar for practical purposes. By 1582, the 10-minute and 48-second difference between the lengths of the solar and calendar years had created a discrepancy of ten days. In order to resolve this, ten days were dropped from the 1582 calendar so that 4 October was followed immediately by 15 October. At the same time, it was decreed that the year would begin on 1 January. In order to adjust for future discrepancies, every fourth year was designated as a leap year, which meant that an extra day would be added to February. An exception to this rule was made for the centenary years, including the year 1700 that occurs in this volume: a century year had to be divisible by 400 to be a leap year in the New Style calendar; thereby the year 2000, for example, was a leap year but not the year 1700. The Old Style calendar continued to have leap years every fourth year. For that reason, the discrepancy between the Old Style and the New Style increased by one additional day in 1700 (as of 1 March) to 11 days, in 1800 to 12 days, and in 1900 to 13 days. From the late sixteenth century, countries such as England used a system of double dates to avoid confusion in official correspondence between the home government and representatives overseas. For example, a document might be dated 10/21 June 1706 to represent an Old Style date of 10 June and a New Style date, eleven days apart, of 21 June. If the date fell between January and 24 March, before the new calendar began, it would be shown as 15/26 February 1702/3. While most Catholic states adopted the new calendar quickly, there was a wide disparity in dates when states began to use it, and its use could change if territory was seized by a power that used another calendar. Of the countries discussed in the period covered in this volume, by 1700 New Style was used in Austria, Bohemia, Courland, Denmark, Norway,  France, the Catholic and Protestant German states, Hungary, Moravia, Poland, Transylvania, and in the Dutch Republic (Holland, Catholic Gelderland, and Zeeland; then Friesland, Groningen, Overijssel, Utrecht, and Protestant portions of Gelderland as of 1700-01).[2] As noted above, the preponderance of Holland within the Dutch Republic and the importance of its foreign relations insured that, de facto, New Style was used in all the provinces long before 1700, especially in official business within the Republic and in foreign relations.[3]

**The Swedish Style Calendar.** Sweden had adopted the New Style calendar in 1590, but had reverted to the Julian or Old Style dates in 1604. At the recommendation of Johannes Bilberg (1647-1717), professor of mathematics at Uppsala University and later bishop of Strängnäs, the Swedish government decided on 1 November 1699 to change gradually to the Gregorian or New Style calendar as of 1 March 1700 by eliminating the extra day in leap years over a period of eleven leap years, thereby eventually bringing the Swedish calendar into line with the New Style calendar by 1740. According to this plan, the Old Style date of 29 February became the Swedish calendar date of 1 March 1700. In the following years, with the king out of the country and the Great Northern War dominating events, the Swedish government failed to omit the extra day in February for both 1704 and 1708. On 1

January 1711, Charles XII, wishing to remedy the situation, decided that Sweden would return to the Old Style calendar in 1712. In order to accomplish this, it was necessary for the Swedish calendar for that year to have 367 days, by including both the normal additional day for a leap year in February 1712 and yet another day, 30 February, which marked the last day on which the Swedish Style calendar was used. With its reversion to the Old Style calendar, Sweden was eleven days behind the New Style. Of the countries discussed in the period covered by this volume, Swedish Style was used between 1700 and 1712 in Estonia, Finland, Livonia, and Sweden, and by Swedish forces outside these areas.[4]

Several of the contributors to the present volume are used to adhering to the Swedish calendar in their scholarly work. They have kindly agreed to adopt the New Style calendar in this particular instance, in order to provide consistency of dates throughout the volume.

These are the first and last dates on which the Swedish calendar was in use:

| OLD STYLE | SWEDISH STYLE | NEW STYLE |
|---|---|---|
| 29 February 1699/1700 | 1 March 1700 | 11 March 1700 |
| 29 February 1711/12 | 30 February 1712 | 11 March 1712 |

| EVENTS (in chronological order)[5] | OLD STYLE | SWEDISH STYLE | NEW STYLE |
|---|---|---|---|
| Birth of Prince Charles | 17 June 1682 | | 27 June 1682 |
| Treaty of Altona | 20 June 1689 | | 30 June 1689 |
| Death of Charles XI | 5 April 1697 | | 15 April 1697 |
| Treaty of Rijswijk | 10 September 1697 | | 20 September 1697 |
| Coronation of Charles XII | 14 December 1697 | | 24 December 1697 |
| King Christian V of Denmark dies, succeeded by Frederik IV | 15 August 1699 | | 25 August 1699 |
| Augustus II enters Livonia | 1 February 1700 | | 11 February 1700 |
| First bombardment of Copenhagen | 8-9 July 1700 | 9-10 July 1700 | 19-20 July 1700 |
| Second bombardment of Copenhagen | 14-15 July 1700 | 15-16 July 1700 | 25-26 July 1700 |
| Landing on Zealand | 24 July 1700 | 25 July 1700 | 4 August 1700 |
| Treaty of Travendal | 7 August 1700 | 8 August 1700 | 18 August 1700 |
| Death of King Carlos II of Spain | 21 October 1700 | 22 October 1700 | 1 November 1700 |
| King Louis XIV declares Philippe, Duc d'Anjou, as King Felipe V of Spain | 5 November 1700 | 6 November 1700 | 16 November 1700 |
| Battle of Olkieniki | 18 November 1700 | 19 November 1700 | 29 November 1700 |
| Battle of Narva | 19 November 1700 | 20 November 1700 | 30 November 1700 |
| Battle of Erastfer | 29 December 1701 | 30 December 1701 | 9 January 1702 |
| Elector Friedrich III of Brandenburg crowned Friedrich I, king in Prussia | 7 January 1701 | 8 January 1701 | 18 January 1701 |
| Swedes cross Dvina and enter Courland | 8 July 1701 | 9 July 1701 | 19 July 1701 |

| EVENTS (in chronological order)[5] | OLD STYLE | SWEDISH STYLE | NEW STYLE |
|---|---|---|---|
| Grand Alliance against France and Spain (Emperor, England, Dutch Republic) | 27 August 1701 | 28 August 1701 | 7 September 1701 |
| Death of Stadholder-King William III, succeeded by Queen Anne in England; no successor stadholder in Dutch Republic. | 8 March 1702 | 9 March 1702 | 19 March 1702 |
| England, Dutch Republic, and Empire declare war on France and Spain | 4 May 1702 | 5 May 1702 | 15 May 1702 |
| Battle of Kliszów | 8 July 1702 | 9 July 1702 | 19 July 1702 |
| Death of Duke Friedrich of Holstein-Gottorp, succeeded by Karl Friedrich | 8 July 1702 | 9 July 1702 | 19 July 1702 |
| Battle of Pułtusk | 20 April 1703 | 21 April 1703 | 1 May 1703 |
| Cardinal Radziejowski declares Interregnum in Commonwealth | 3 February 1704 | 4 February 1704 | 14 February 1704 |
| Sandomierz Confederation declares war on Sweden | May 1704 | May 1704 | May 1704 |
| Election of Stanislaw Leszczyński as king of Poland by Swedish supporters | 1 July 1704 | 2 July 1704 | 12 July 1704 |
| Battle of Jakobstadt | 25 July 1704 | 26 July 1704 | 5 August 1704 |
| Battle of Blenheim/Höchstädt | 2 August 1704 | 3 August 1704 | 13 August 1704 |
| Death of Emperor Leopold I, succeeded by Joseph I | 24 April 1705 | 25 April 1705 | 5 May 1705 |
| Battle of Gemäuerthof | 15 July 1705 | 16 July 1705 | 26 July 1705 |
| Peace treaty between Sweden and Poland | 15 November 1705 | 16 November 1705 | 26 November 1705 |
| Battle of Fraustadt | 2 February 1706 | 3 February 1706 | 13 February 1706 |
| Battle of Ramillies | 12 May 1706 | 13 May 1706 | 23 May 1706 |
| Charles XII with Army arrives at Saxon border | 26 August 1706 | 27 August 1706 | 8 September 1706 |
| Battle of Turin (Castiglione) | 27 August 1706 | 28 August 1706 | 7 September 1706 |
| Treaty of Altranstädt | 13 September 1706 | 14 September 1706 | 24 September 1706 |
| Battle of Kalisz | 18 October 1706 | 19 October 1706 | 29 October 1706 |
| Marlborough meets Charles XII at Altranstädt | 15-18 April 1707 | 16-19 April 1707 | 26-29 April 1707 |
| Marlborough meets Augustus II at Leipzig | 17 April 1707 | 18 April 1707 | 28 April 1707 |
| Union of England and Scotland to create Great Britain | 1 May 1707 | 2 May 1707 | 12 May 1707 |
| Convention of Altranstädt | 21 August 1707 | 22 August 1707 | 1 September 1707 |
| Battle of Oudenaarde | 30 June 1708 | 1 July 1708 | 11 July 1708 |

| EVENTS (in chronological order)[5] | OLD STYLE | SWEDISH STYLE | NEW STYLE |
|---|---|---|---|
| Battle of Holowczyn | 3 July 1708 | 4 July 1708 | 14 July 1708 |
| Battle of Lesnaya | 28 September 1708 | 29 September 1708 | 9 October 1708 |
| Battle of Poltava | 27 June 1709 | 28 June 1709 | 8 July 1709 |
| Swedish Army surrenders at Perevolochna | 30 June 1709 | 1 July 1709 | 11 July 1709 |
| Charles XII's arrival at Bender | 21 July 1709 | 22 July 1709 | 1 August 1709 |
| Battle of Helsingborg (Skåne) | 27 February 1710 | 28 February 1710 | 10 March 1710 |
| Neutrality Convention of The Hague | 20 March 1710 | 21 March 1710 | 31 March 1710 |
| Battle of Køge Bay | 23 September 1710 | 24 September 1710 | 4 October 1710 |
| Ottoman Empire declares war on Russia | 10 November 1710 | 11 November 1710 | 21 November 1710 |
| Death of Emperor Joseph I, succeeded by Archduke Karl, Carlos III of Spain, as Emperor Charles VI | 6 April 1711 | 7 April 1711 | 17 April 1711 |
| Treaty of the Pruth | 10 July 1711 | 11 July 1711 | 21 July 1711 |
| Dismissal of John Churchill, Duke of Marlborough, as Commander-in-Chief | 30 December 1711 | 31 December 1711 | 10 January 1712 |
| Swedish-Danish naval battle off Rügen | 18 September 1712 | | 29 September 1712 |
| Battle of Gadebusch | 9 December 1712 | | 20 December 1712 |
| Death of Friedrich I of Prussia, succeeded by Friedrich Wilhelm I | 14 February 1713 | | 25 February 1713 |
| Peace of Utrecht | 31 March 1713 | | 11 April 1713 |
| Stenbock defeated at Tönning | 5 May 1713 | | 16 May 1713 |
| Treaty of Adrianople | 16 June 1713 | | 27 June 1713 |
| Death of Duke Friedrich Wilhelm of Mecklenburg-Schwerin, succeeded by Duke Karl Leopold | 20 July 1713 | | 31 July 1713 |
| Treaty of Rastatt | 23 February 1714 | | 6 March 1714 |
| Secret agreement between Russia and Prussia | 2 June 1714 | | 13 June 1714 |
| Death of Queen Anne, succeeded by Elector Georg Ludwig of Hanover, as King George I | 1 August 1714 | | 12 August 1714 |
| Russian-Swedish naval battle of Hangö | 27 July 1714 | | 7 August 1714 |
| Treaty of Baden signed ratifications exchanged | 27 August 1714 17 October 1714 | | 7 September 1714 28 October 1714 |
| Charles XII's arrival at Stralsund | 10-11 November 1714 | | 21-22 November 1714 |
| Treaty of Vienna | 25 December 1714 | | 5 January 1715 |
| Naval battle at Fehmarn Belt (also, Action of 24 April 1715) | 13 April 1715 | | 24 April 1715 |

| EVENTS (in chronological order)[5] | OLD STYLE | SWEDISH STYLE | NEW STYLE |
|---|---|---|---|
| Treaty between Hanover and Denmark | 21 April 1715 | | 2 May 1715 |
| Swedish-Danish naval battle of Rügen | 28 July 1715 | | 8 August 1715 |
| Death of King Louis XIV; regency of Philippe, Duc d'Orléans | 21 August 1715 | | 1 September 1715 |
| Hanover declares war against Sweden | 4 October 1715 | | 15 October 1715 |
| Treaty of Greifswald | 17 October 1715 | | 28 October 1715 |
| Battle of Stresow | 5 November 1715 | | 16 November 1715 |
| Charles XII's return to Sweden from Stralsund | 13 December 1715 | | 24 December 1715 |
| Marriage of Duke Karl Leopold of Mecklenburg-Schwerin to Tsarevna Ekaterina Ivanovna, niece of Tsar Peter | 8 April 1716 | | 19 April 1716 |
| Treaty of Triple Alliance at The Hague | 24 December 1716 | | 4 January 1717 |
| Start of Russo-Swedish peace negotiations, on Åland Islands | 10 May 1718 | | 21 May 1718 |
| Treaty of Passarowitz | 10 July 1718 | | 21 July 1718 |
| Emperor joins Triple Alliance creating Quadruple Alliance | 22 July 1718 | | 2 August 1718 |
| Death of Charles XII, succeeded by Queen Ulrika Eleanora | 30 November 1718 | | 11 December 1718 |
| Treaty of Stockholm (Sweden and Hanover) | 9 November 1719 | | 20 November 1719 |
| Treaty of Stockholm (Britain, Sweden, and Prussia) | 21 January 1720 | | 1 February 1720 |
| Queen Ulrika Eleanora of Sweden abdicates, succeeded by Prince Friedrich of Hesse-Kassel, as King Fredrik I | 29 February 1720 | | 11 March 1720 |
| Treaty of Fredriksborg | 3 July 1720 | | 14 July 1720 |
| Death of Anthonie Heinsius, Grand Pensionary of Holland | | | 3 August 1720 |
| Treaty of Nystad | 30 August 1721 | | 10 September 1721 |

[1] Cheney, *A Handbook of Dates,* 1, 9, 12-13, 236-41.

[2] *Ibidem,* 17-19, 236-41.

[3] This statement modifies the established English language published source, *Ibidem,* and is based on the extensive archival experience in seventeenth-century Dutch documents by Augustus J. Veenendaal, Jr. and Jannie W. Veenendaal-Barth.

[4] Cheney, *A Handbook of Dates,* 236-41; Lodén, *Tid,* 154-55.

[5] This chronology is partially based on and expands that in Frost, *The Northern Wars,* 333-34.

# Gazetteer

Whenever appropriate, geographical names are in their modern, local, and national spellings. In some cases widely accepted modern anglicised forms are used, e.g., Battle of Blenheim, not Höchstädt; Gothenburg, not Göteborg; Hanover, not Hannover; Leghorn, not Livorno.

Other historical works, in different languages and national historical traditions, have used a variety of spellings and names for the same geographical places. Moreover, names have often changed significantly because of new national borders. In an attempt to avoid confusion, the editors have compiled a selection of the major alternative geographical names and transliterations for key places mentioned in the text.

| German-Dutch-English-Swedish | Present-day |
|---|---|
| Åbo | Turku (Finland) |
| Adrianopel, Adrianople | Edirne (Turkey) |
| Archangel | Arkhangel'sk (Russia) |
| Arensburg (on Ösel) | Kuressaare (Estonia) |
| Bachtschisarai, Bahçesaray | Bakhchisaray (Crimea) |
| Bender | Bendery (Moldova) |
| Birsen | Biržai (Lithuania) |
| Culm | Chełmno (Poland) |
| Culmsee | Chełmża (Poland) |
| Dagö (island) | Hiiumaa (Estonia) |
| Damm | Dabie (Poland) |
| Danzig | Gdańsk (Poland) |
| Demotikon, Demotika | Didymoteicho, Dhidhimótikhon, (Greece) |
| Dorpat | Tartu (Estonia) |
| Dünaburg | Daugavpils (Latvia) |
| Elbing | Elbląg (Poland) |
| Erastfer | Erastvere (Estonia) |
| Fraustadt | Wschowa (Poland) |
| Gemäuerthof | Mūrmiža (Poland) |
| Gnesen | Gniezno (Poland) |
| Gollnow | Goleniów (Poland) |
| Graudenz | Grodno (Belarus) |
| Hangö, Hanko, Gangut | Hankoniemi (Finland) |
| Hummelshof | Hummuli (Estonia) |
| Jakobstadt | Jekabpils (Latvia) |
| Jug (river) | Vyg, Yuga (river; Russia) |
| Kecksholm, Kexholm | Käkisalmi (Finland) |

| German-Dutch-English-Swedish | Present-day |
| --- | --- |
| Königsberg | Kaliningrad (Russia) |
| Krakau, Cracow | Kraków (Poland) |
| Ladoga (lake) | Ladozhskoye (lake; Russia) |
| Lais | Laiuse (Estonia) |
| Lemberg | L'viv (Ukraine) |
| Lesna, Lesnaja, Lesnaya | Lyasnaya (Belarus) |
| Libau | Liepaja (Latvia) |
| Marienburg | Malbork (Poland) |
| Memel | Klaipéda (Lithuania) |
| Memel, Njemen (river) | Neman/Nemunas (river; Belarus/Lithuania) |
| Noteburg, Nöteborg | Schlusselburg/Petrokrepost (Russia) |
| Nystad, Neustad | Uusikaupunki (Finland) |
| Ösel (island) | Saaremaa (Estonia) |
| Onega (lake) | Onezhskoye (Russia) |
| Perevolotjna | Perevolochna (Ukraine) |
| Pernau | Pärnu (Estonia) |
| Pleskau | Pskov (Russia) |
| Reval, Revel | Tallinn (Estonia) |
| Saloniki | Thessaloniki (Greece) |
| Stettin | Szczecin (Poland) |
| Thorn | Toruń (Poland) |
| Tuchel | Tuchola (Poland) |
| Velikie Luki | Velikiye-Luki (Russia) |
| Vilna, Wilna | Vilnius (Lithuania) |
| Vyborg, Viborg | Vyborg (Russia) |
| Vyšnij Volocek | Vyshniy Volochek (Russia) |
| Weichsel, Vistula | Wisła (river, Poland) |
| Wesenberg | Rakvere (Estonia) |
| Windau | Ventspils (Latvia) |
| Wologda | Vologda (Russia) |

# General Bibliography

*In Swedish and some other languages, the letters å, ä, and ö are considered additional letters of the alphabet and come in order after the letter z. Since English-language readers are unaccustomed to this practice, å is treated as equivalent to aa, while ä and ö are considered equivalent to ae and oe in the bibliography's Scandinavian and German names.*

## ARCHIVAL SOURCES

### Austria

Österreichisches Staatsarchiv Wien

Haus-, Hof- und Staatsarchiv

Staatenabteilungen Schweden

Staatenabteilungen Rußland I

Staatskanzlei Vorträge und Konferenzprotokolle

Reichskanzlei Vorträge

Reichskanzlei Friedensakten

Reichskanzlei Braunschweig

Habsburg-Lothringisches Hausarchiv Familienkorrespondenz A

Kriegsarchiv, Wien

Alte Feldakten

### Great Britain

London, British Library (BL)

Additional Manuscripts (Addit. Ms.)

Addit Ms. 35,105-06: Correspondence of the Rev. John Robinson, D.D., British Agent (from 1696 Envoy extraordinary) in Sweden with William Blathwayt, Secretary at War, acting as Secretary of State with King William during the king's journeys abroad; 1692-1701

Addit Ms. 34,677: Letters of Robert Harley, Secretary of State (cr. Earl of Oxford, 1711), to the Rev. John Robinson, British Resident at the court of Sweden; Whitehall, 30 May, 1704- 4/15 July, 1707

Addit. Ms. 61,146: The Blenheim Papers. Letters from the Rev'd Dr John Robinson

Addit. Ms. 61,260: Correspondence of the Duke of Marlborough with and about Charles XII

The National Archives, Kew (TNA)

SP 42/ State Papers, Domestic. Naval

SP 88/16-17: State Papers, Poland and Saxony

SP 95/11-25: State Papers, Sweden

SP 105: Treaties

### France

Archives des Affaires Etrangères, La Courneuve, Paris

Correspondance Politique, Suède, vol. 88-151, 1699-1721.

Pologne , vol. 114 à 124 : 1703-1710.

### Germany

Hannover Stadtarchiv

Merseburg, Zentrales Staatsarchiv

### Poland

Archiwum Główne Akt Dawnych w Warszawie

Archiwum Publiczne Potockich: Ms. no. 162, vol. 2; no. 163 a, vol. 31

Archiwum Radziwiłłów: dz. II, Ms. no. 1970, 1990

Archiwum Zamoyskich, Ms. no. 3030

Biblioteka Czartoryskich w Krakowie: Ms. no. 196

### Russian Federation

Archives of the Navy, St. Petersburg

F. 1331 (Atlases, maps and plans of Archives of Central maps production of Navy). Op. 1. D. L. 1. - The Swedish original map «Campement på Zeland wid Humblebäck». Signatures: Landscrona. 23 augustÿ 1700. Clas Rödken

Archives of Ancient Acts, Moscow

F. 9 (Cabinet of Peter the Great), Otd. 2, D. 39, L. 454

F. 198 (Menshikov, A.D.), Op. 1, D. 352, L. 164-166

### Sweden

Riksarkivet, Diplomatica, Gallica, Stockholm

Vol. 195-197, correspondance du résident Daniel Cronström, 1708-1719 Vol. 220-223, correspondance de l'ambassadeur Erik Sparre 1712-1717

### Turkey

III. Ahmed'in Baltacı Mehmed Paşa'ya Hattı, Topkapı Sarayı, E. 6073. Arşiv Kılavuzu, I. Fasikül, 138, Vesika IV (Istanbul, 1938)

## BOOKS and ARTICLES

Åberg, A., 'Soldaterna', in: *Rättvik. Del I:2, Socknen och kommunen* (Rättvik, 1967).

Ågren, M., ed., *Making a Living, Making a Difference: Work and Gender in Early ModernSwedish Society* (New York, 2017).

Ångström Grandien, I.L., 'Det profana måleriet', in: *Signums Svenska konsthistoria*, VI, Barocken (Lund, 1997).

_____, review of Ehasalu, P., 'Rootsiaegne maalikunst Tallinnas', in: *Konsthistorisk tidskrift*, 2009, 2.

_____, 'Hur såg Kristina ut? Några tidiga porträtt av drottning Kristina', in: Sandin, P., ed., *Bilder av Kristina – drottning av Sverige - drottning i Rom*. Livrustkammaren (Stockholm, 2013).

Åström, S.-E., *From Stockholm to St Petersburg. Commercial Factors in the Political Relations between England and Sweden 1675-1700* (Helsinki, 1962).

_____, 'England and the Baltic Naval Stores Trade in the Seventeenth and Eighteenth Centuries', in: *Mariners Mirror*, 58 (1972), 375-95.

_____, 'The Swedish Economy and Sweden's Role as a Great Power', in: Roberts, M., ed., *Sweden's Age of Greatness, 1632-1718* (London & Basingstoke, 1973).

_____, 'Technology and Timber Exports from the Gulf of Finland', in: *Scandinavian Economic History Review*, 23 (1975), 1-14.

_____, *From Tar to Timber: Studies in Northeast European Forest Exploitation and Foreign Trade, 1660-1860* (Helsinki, 1988).

Abou-El-Haj, Rifa'at Ali, *1703 Isyanı, Osmanlı Siyasasının Yapısı* (Ankara, 2011).

*Abrys domowej nie szczęśliwości wewnętrznej niesnaski, wojny Korony Polskiej i Wielkiego Księstwa Litewskiego pro informatione potomnym następującym czasom przez jedną zakonną oobę swiatu pokazany i z żałością wyrażony Anno 1721*, F.K. Kulczycki, ed. (Kraków, 1899).

Adler, F., ed., *Die Erinnerungen Axel von Löwens* (Stockholm, 1930).

Adlerfeldt, G. von, *Leben Carls des zwölften, Königs von Schweden* (Frankfurt & Leipzig, 1740).

Ahlström, W., *Arvid Horn och Karl XII 1710-1713* (Lund, 1959).

Ahlund, C., 'En mental militarisering. Den svenska litteraturen före och under första världskriget', in: *Samlaren* 124 (2003), 134-57.

Aili, H., 'Swedish War Propaganda in Latin, German, and Swedish', in: Moss, A., ed., *Acta Conventus Neo-Latini Hafniensis*. Medieval & Renaissance texts & studies 120 (Binghamton, NY. 1994), 271-83.

Aksan, V.H., *Ottoman Wars 1700-1870: An Empire Besieged* (Harlow, 2007).

Aktepe, M., '1711 Prut Seferi İle İlgili Bazı Belgeler', in: *Tarih Dergisi*, Sayı XXXIV, (Istanbul, 1984), 19-54.

_____, 'Baltacı Mehmed Paşa', in: *TDV Islam*

*Ansiklopedisi*, 5, 35-36.

_____, 'Çorlulu Ali Paşa', in: *TDV Islam Ansiklopedisi*, 8, 370-71.

Albion, R. G., *Forests and Sea Power: The Timber Problems of the Royal Navy, 1652-1862* (Cambridge, MA., 1926; reprinted Hamden, CT, 1965).

Aldridge, D.D., *Admiral Sir John Norris and the British Naval Expeditions to the Baltic 1715-1727* (Lund, 2009).

Allen, D.J., 'Bibliography of English Language Citations in Charles XII, King of Sweden', in: *Karolinska Förbundets Årsbok* (2002).

Altbauer, D., 'The Diplomats of Peter the Great', in: *Jahrbücher für Geschichte Osteuropas* N.F., 28 (1980), 1-16.

Amburger, E., *Ingermanland: Eine junge Provinz Rußlands im Wirkungsbereich der Residenz und Weltstadt St. Petersburg/Leningrad* (Köln & Wien, 1980).

Aminoff-Winberg, Johanna, *På flykt i eget land. Internflytingar i Sverige under stora nordiska kriget* (Åbo, 2007).

Anderson, M.S., *War and Society in Europe of the Old Regime 1618-1789* (Avon, 1988).

_____, *The Rise of Modern Diplomacy, 1450-1919* (London, 1993).

Anderson, R.C., *Naval Wars in the Baltic during the Sailing-ship Epoch 1522-1850* (London, 1910; reprint London, 1960).

Anisimov, E.V., *Gosudarstvennye preobrazovanija i samoderžavie Petra Velikogo v pervoj četverti XVIII veka* (St. Petersburg, 1997).

Anonymous, 'Karl XII:s hemfärd från Turkiet', in: *Historisk Tidskrift*, 13 (1893), 71-78.

Antonsson, O., 'Franska porträttskulptörer i Sverige under 1700-talet', in: *Nationalmusei Årsbok*, 1946.

Anusik, Z., *Karol XII* (Wrocław, 2006).

*Archiv kniazia F.A. Kurakina*, 2 (St. Petersburg, 1891); 6 (St. Petersburg, 1896).

Aretin, K.O. von, *Das Alte Reich 1648-1806. II, Kaisertradition und österreichische Großmachtpolitik 1684-1745* (Stuttgart, 1997).

Argıt, Betül İpşirli, *Rabia Gülnuş Emetullah Sultan 1640-1715* (Istanbul, 2014).

Arājs, J., 'Bitwa nad Dźwiną 9 lipca 1701 roku', in: Dybaś, B. ed., *Wojny północne w XVI-XVIII wieku. W czterechsetlecie bitwy pod Kircholmem* (Toruń, 2007), 197-209.

Artamonov, V.A., *Rossia i Rech Pospolitaya posle Poltavskoi pobedy (1709-1714)* (Moscow, 1990).

_____, *Poltavskoe srazhenie. K 300-letiyu Poltavskoi pobedy* (Moscow, 2009).

Artéus, G., *Krigsteori och historisk förklaring II: Karolinsk och europeisk stridstaktik 1700-1712* (Göteborg, 1972).

_____, *Svensk fältherrekonst* (Stockholm, 2005).

_____, 'Individ och kollektiv, metodik och geografi. Karl XII och hans armé', in: Oredsson, S., ed., *Tsar Peter och kung Karl*, 153-71.

Arwidsson, F., *Försvaret av Östersjöprovinserna 1708–1710* (Uppsala, 1936).

Asker, B., '"En nation som man bör visa tänderna". Svensk syn på Ryssland under Peter den store' in: Jonson, L., and Torstendahl Salytjeva, T., eds., *Poltava. Krigsfångar och kulturutbyte* (Stockholm, 2009).

Attman, A., *Swedish Aspiration and the Russian Market during the 17th Century* (Göteborg, 1985),

Auer, L., 'Austrian Political Attitudes towards the Polish Republic during the Great Northern War', in: *Sarmatia Europaea*, 2 (2011/12), 29-46 (online publication).

Backman, S., *Från Rawicz till Fraustadt. Studier i det stora nordiska krigets diplomatie 1704-1706* (Lund, 1940).

Backscheider, P.R., *Daniel Defoe: His Life* (Baltimore, 1989).

Bain, R.N., 'Charles XII and the Great Northern War', in: Ward, A.W., Prothero, G.W., and Leathes, S., eds., *The Cambridge Modern History*, 5 (Cambridge, 1908).

Bak, J.M., and Király, B.K., eds., *From Hunyadi to Rákóczi. War and Society in Late Medieval and Early Modern Hungary* (New York, 1982).

Balisch, A., 'Infantry Battlefield Tactics in the Seventeenth and Eighteenth Centuries on the European and Turkish Theatres of War: The Austrian Response to Different Conditions', in: *Studies in History and Politics*, 3, 1983-84; Reprint in: J. Black, ed., *Warfare in Europe 1650-1795* (Aldershot, 2005).

Ballagi, A., 'Zur Geschichte der Heimkehr Karls XII. und des schwedischen Heeres durch Ungarn', in: *Karolinska Förbundets Årsbok* (1931), 172-223; (1934), 144-87.

Bartoszewicz, J., 'Karol XII w Warszawie w 1702 roku', in: *Dzieła Juliana Bartoszewicza*, vol. VII, *Szkice z czasów saskich* (Kraków, 1880), 261-71.

Bartoszewicz, J., ed., *Pamiętniki Krzysztofa Zawiszy (1666-1721)* (Warszawa, 1862).

Baycar, A., ed., *Osmanlı Rus İlişkileri Tarihi, Ahmet Cavit Bey'in Müntehabâtı* (Istanbul, 2004).

Behre, G., Larsson, L-O., and Österberg, E., *Sveriges historia 1521-1809. Stormaktsdröm och småstatsrealiteter* (Stockholm, 1985).

Bell, G. M., *A Handlist of British Diplomatic Representatives, 1509-1688*. Royal Historical Society Guides and Handbooks, 16 (London, 1990).

Benda, K., *Le projet d'alliance hungaro-suédo-prussienne de 1704* (Budapest, 1960).

_____, 'The Rákóci War of Independence and the European Powers', in: Bak and Király, *From Hunyadi*, 433-44.

Berg, L.O., 'Peipuseskaderns fartyg. En tabellarisk framställning', in: *Forum Navale*, 22 (1965), 129-33.

Bergström, O., 'En maskeradbal på Stockholms slott 1692', in: *Personhistorisk tidskrift* (1907), 21-29.

Berner, E., *Geschichte des preußischen Staates* (Bonn, 1896).

_____, 'Die auswärtige Politik der Kurfürsten Friedrich III von Brandenburg, König Friedrich in Preußen', in: *Hohenzollern Jahrbuch*, 4 (1900), 60-109.

Berney, A., *König Friedrich I. und das Haus Habsburg* (München & Berlin, 1927).

Bespiatyh, Y.N., 'Tret'e «prishestvie» Petra I na Beloe more', in: Bespiatyh, Y.N., ed., *Arkhangelsk v XVIII veke* (St. Petersburg, 1997).

Beydilli, K., 'İsveç', in: *TDV İslam Ansiklopedisi*, 23, 407-14.

Beydilli, K., and İ.E. Erünsal, 'Prut Savaşı Öncesi Diplomatik Bir Teşebbüs, Seyfullah Ağa'nın Viyana Elçiliği (1711)', in: *TTK Belgeler*, XXII, 26 (Ankara, 2002), 1-33.

Beyme, K. von, 'Schwedisches Imperium im Deutschen Reich: Ein vergessenes Kapitel der Imperien- und Mythenbildung', in: Bluhm, H., et al., eds., *Ideenpolitik. Geschichtliche Konstellationen und gegenwärtige Konflikte* (Berlin, 2011), 71-88.

Biernat, Cz., *Statystyka obrotu towarowego Gdańska w latach 1651-1815* (Warszawa, 1962).

Birke, A.M., and K. Kluxen, eds., *England und Han-*

nover. *England and Hanover* (München, 1986).

Bittner, L, Gross, L., and Santifaller, L., eds., *Repertorium der diplomatischen Vertreter aller Länder seit dem Westfälischen Frieden (1648)*, 3 vols. (Berlin, Graz & Köln, 1936-65).

Bjerg, H.C., and Frantzen, O.L., *Danmark i krig* (København, 2005).

Björck, S., *Heidenstam och sekelskiftets Sverige. Studier i hans nationella och sociala författarskap* (Lund, 1946).

_____, *Karl XII:s stövlar. Notiser om dikt och annat* (Stockholm, 1954).

Black, J., *A Military Revolution? Military Change and European Society 1550-1800* (Basingstoke & London, 1991).

_____, *European Warfare 1600-1815* (New Haven & London, 1994).

_____, *Politics and Foreign Policy in the Age of George I, 1714-1727* (Farnham, Surrey, and Burlington, VT, 2014).

_____, 'Hanover and British Foreign Policy 1714-1760', in: *The English Historical Review,* 120, no 486 (April 2005), 303-39.

Boëthius, B., and Heckscher, E.F., *Svensk Handelsstatistik 1637-1737: Samtida bearbetningar / Swedish Statistics of foreign trade 1637-1737: Contemporary accounts* (Stockholm, 1938).

Bogucka, M., 'Sweden and Poland: Economic, Sociopolitical and Cultural Relations in the First Half of the 17th Century', in: Rystad, G., ed., *Europe and Scandinavia: Aspects of the Process of Integration in the 17th Century* (Lund, 1983), 161-67.

_____, 'Fairs in Early Modern Poland', in: Irsigler, F., and Pauly, M., eds., *Messen, Jahrmärkte und Stadtentwicklung in Europa / Foires, marchés annuels et développement urbain en Europe* (Trier, 2007), 243-51.

Bohlen, A., 'Changes in Russian Diplomacy under Peter the Great', in: *Cahiers du monde russe et soviétique*, 7 (1966), 341-58.

Boissonnade, P., and Charliat, P., *Colbert et la Compagnie de Commerce du Nord (1661-1689)* (Paris 1930).

Boles, L.H., *The Huguenots, the Protestant Interest, and the War of the Spanish Succession, 1702-1714* (New York, 1997).

Bolin, S., 'Wilhelm Kruse. Ett bidrag till kännedomen om den politiska agitationsdiktningen under kung Karl XII', in: *Karolinska Förbundets Årsbok* (1929), 118-51.

Bolingbrok, *Pisma ob izuchenii i pol'ze istorii* (Moscow, 1978).

Borkowska, M., Karkucińska, W., Wiesiołowski, J., eds., *Kroniki benedyktynek poznańskich*, (Poznań, 2001).

Brantly, S., 'The Formal Tensions in Strindberg's Carl XII', in: *Scandinavian Studies,* 62 (1990), 92-107.

_____, 'Att söka Sverige i Karl XII:s porträtt', in: *Horisont*, 46, 1, 2 (1999), 14-22.

_____, 'Heidenstam's *Karolinerna* and the fin de siècle', in: Ingwersen, F., and Norseng, M.K., eds., *Fin(s) de siècle in Scandinavian Perspective*, Studies in Scandinavian Literature and culture, 1 (Columbia, 1993), 69-77.

Braubach, M., *Der Aufstieg Brandenburg-Preußen (1640-1815)* (Freiburg im Breisgau, 1933).

_____, *Prinz Eugen von Savoyen. Eine Biographie,* 5 vols. (Wien, 1963-65).

Braudel, F., *Vardagslivets strukturer* (Stockholm, 1982).

Brenner, S.E., *Samlade dikter 1:1: Poetiske dikter 1713*, Lindgärde, V., ed., (Stockholm, 2009).

Bring, S.E., ed., *Karl XII. Till 200-årsdagen av hans död* (Stockholm, 1918).

Brink Pinto, A., *Trettionde november – kampen om Lund 1985-2008* (Lund, 2013).

Brinkman, K.G. von, and Andersson, G., eds., *Handlingar ur von Brinkmanska archivet på Trolle Ljungby*, vol. 1 (Örebro, 1859).

Brown, B., ed., *The Letters and Diplomatic Instructions of Queen Anne* (London, 1968).

Brown, C., *Van Dyck* (Oxford, 1982).

Brown, J., 'Enemies of Flattery: Velazquez' Portraits of Philip IV', in: Rothberg, R.I., and Rabb, T.K., eds., *Art and History: Images and Their Meaning* (Cambridge, 1988).

Browning, Oscar, *Charles XII of Sweden* (London, 1899).

Bruijn, J.R., *The Dutch Navy of the Seventeenth and Eighteenth Centuries.* Research in Maritime History no. 45 (St. John's, Newfoundland, 2011).

_____, 'The Anglo-Dutch Navies in Marlborough's Wars', in: Hattendorf, J.B., Veenendaal, A.J., Jr., and Hövell tot Westerflier, R. van, eds., *Marlborough: Soldier and Diplomat* (Rotterdam, 2012), 274-99.

Bruijn, J.R., Prud'homme van Reine, R., and Hövell tot Westerflier, R. van, eds., *De Ruyter: Dutch Admiral* (Rotterdam, 2011).

Brulin, H., *Sverige och Frankrike under Nordiska Kriget och Spanska Successionskrisen åren 1700-1701* (Uppsala, 1905).

_____, 'Österrike och det stora nordiska kriget före Karl XII:s infall i Sachsen 1700-1706', in:

*Historisk Tidskrift*, 29 (1909), 141-66, 197-242.

Buchholz, W., 'Schwedisch-Pommern als Territorium des deutschen Reichs 1648-1806', in: *Zeitschrift für Neuere Rechtsgeschichte*, 12 (1990), 14-33.

_____, 'Zwischen Glanz und Ohnmacht. Schweden als Vermittler des Friedens von Rijswijk', in: Durchhardt, H., ed., *Der Friede von Rijswijk 1697* (Mainz, 1998), 219-55.

Buchwald-Pelcowa, P., *Satyra czasów saskich* (Wrocław, 1969).

Burenstam, C.J.R., *Retour de la Turquie de Charles XII et des troupes suédoises par la Transylvanie, la Hongrie et l'Autriche en 1714-1715* (Brussels, 1874).

Bussemaker, Th., 'De arrestatie van Gyllenborgh en Görtz in 1717', in: *Tijdschrift voor Geschiedenis* 16 (1901), 65-85; 129-49; 193-218.

Byron, G.G. Lord, *The Complete Poetical Works,* 4, McGann, J.J., ed. (Oxford, 1986).

Carlquist, G., 'Karl XII:s ungdom och första regeringsår', in: Bring, S.E., ed., *Karl XII*, 43-86.

Carlson, E., ed., *Karl XII:s egenhändiga bref* (Stockholm, 1893).

_____, *Der Vertrag zwischen Karl XII. von Schweden und Kaiser Joseph I. zu Altranstädt 1707* (Stockholm, 1907).

_____, *Sveriges historia under konungarne af pfalziska huset 8:3: Sveriges historia under Carl den tolftes regering*, 3 (Stockholm, 1910).

_____, 'Karl XII:s ryska fälttågsplan 1707-1709: sedd i ljuset af nyare forskningar', in: *Nordisk tidskrift*, 12 (1889), 366–91.

_____, 'Karl XII och kejsaren 1707. Sveriges sista bragd som evangelisk stormakt', in: *Historisk Tidskrift*, 17 (1897), 75-96.

_____, *Kapten Jefferyes Bref till Engelska Regeringen från Bender och Adrianopel 1711-1714, från Stralsund 1714-15.* Historiska Handlingar, del 16, no. 2 (Stockholm, 1897).

Carlson, F.F., *Sveriges historia under konungarne af pfalziska huset 6–7: Sveriges historia under Carl den tolftes regering*, 1-2 (Stockholm, 1881-85).

Cavallie, J., *Från fred till krig: de finansiella problemen kring krigsutbrottet år 1700* (Uppsala, 1975).

Čerepnin, L.V., et al., eds., *Ėkonomičeskie svjazi meždu Rossiej i Šveciej v XVII v.: Dokumenty iz sovetskich archivov* (Moskva-Stockholm, 1978).

Chance, J.F., *George I and the Northern War: A Study of British-Hanoverian Policy in the*

*North of Europe in the Years 1709-1721* (London, 1909).

_____, ed., *British Diplomatic Instructions, Sweden, 1689-1727.* Camden Third Series, XXXII (London, 1922).

_____, ed., *British Diplomatic Instructions, Denmark, 1689-1789.* Camden Third Series, XXXVI (London, 1926).

Cheney, C.R., *A Handbook of Dates for Students of British History*, revised by M. Jones. Royal Historical Society Guides and Handbooks, 4 (Cambridge, 2000).

Childs, J., *Armies and Warfare in Europe 1648–1789* (Manchester, 1982).

Christensen, A.E., 'Der handelsgeschichtliche Wert der Sundzollregister', in: *Hansische Geschichtsblätter* (1934), 59.

Churchill, W.S., *Marlborough: His Life and Times*, 6 vols. (London, 1947); also *Marlborough: His Life and Times*, 2 vols. (Chicago, 2002).

Cieślak, E., *Stanisław Leszczyński* (Wrocław, 1994).

_____, 'Powojenne załamanie gospodarcze – pierwsze przejawy ożywienia gospodarczego w połowie XVIII wieku', in: Labuda, G., ed., *Historia Pomorza*, vol. II (Poznań, 1984), 50-122.

_____, 'W wirze wojny północnej', in: Cieślak, E., ed., *Historia Gdańska,* vol. III/1: 1655-1793 (Gdańsk, 1993), 485-508.

Cieślak, E., Trzoska, J., 'Handel i żegluga Gdańska w XVIII w.', in Cieślak, E., ed., *Historia Gdańska*, vol. III/1: 1655-1793 (Gdańsk, 1993), 357- 444.

Clausewitz, C. von, *Om kriget* (Stockholm, 1991).

Conrads, N., *Die Durchführung der Altranstädter Konvention in Schlesien 1706-1709* (Köln & Wien, 1971).

_____, 'Der Anteil des schwedischen Gesandten Stralenheim an der Entschlußbildung und Durchführung der Altranstädter Konvention von 1707', in: Conrads, N., *Schlesien in der Frühmoderne Zeit. Zur politischen und geistigen Kultur eines habsburgischen Landes* (Köln, 2009), 127-48.

Coroban, C., 'British Reactions to Charles XII's Stay in the Ottoman Empire', in: *Revista Română de Studii Baltice şi Nordice*, 3, 1 (2011), 29-63.

Coquery, E., 'Le portrait en tableaux', in: *Visages du Grand Siècle. Le portrait français sous le règne de Louis XIV 1660-1715.* Exhibition catalogue (Nantes, 1997).

Coxe, W., ed., *Memoirs of John Duke of Marlborough* (London, 1918).

Creveld, M. van, *Supplying War: Logistics from Wallenstein to Patton* (New York, 1977).

Čulkov, M.D., *Istoričeskoe opisanie rossijskoj kommercii pri vsech portach i granicach…* 7 vols. in 21 books (1781-88).

Dahlstierna, G.E., *Samlade dikter*, 1-2, in: Noreen, E., ed. (Stockholm, 1920-28).

Dalin, O., *Samlade skrifter 1:1: Swenska Friheten*, in: Carlsson, I., and Carlsson, G., eds. (Stockholm, 2010).

Davey, J., *The Transformation of British Naval Strategy: Seapower and Supply in Northern Europe, 1808-1812* (Woodbridge, 2012).

Davies, N., *God's Playground, A History of Poland*, vol. 1 (New York, 1982).

Dehing, P., *Geld in Amsterdam. Wisselbank en wisselkoersen, 1650-1725* (Hilversum, 2012).

Demarsy, A., ed., *Voyage du chevalier de Bellerive au camp du roi de Suède à Bender en 1712* (Paris, 1872).

Dixon, S., *The Modernisation of Russia 1676-1825* (Cambridge, 1999).

'Doneseniya frantzuzskogo konsula v Peterburge Lavi i polnomochnogo ministra pri russkom dvore Kampredona s 1719 po 1722 g', in: *Sbornic Imperatorskogo Russkogo Istoricheskogo obschestva* (St. Petersburg, 1884), 40.

Droste, H., *Im Dienst der Krone. Schwedische Diplomaten im 17. Jahrhundert* (Berlin, 2006).

Droysen, J.G., *Geschichte der preußischen Politik* (Leipzig, 1872).

Drozdowski, M., 'Działalność budżetowa sejmu Rzeczypospolitej w czasach saskich', in: *Roczniki Dziejów Społecznych i Gospodarczych,* 38 (1977), 116-28.

Dygdała, J., 'Upadek miasta w dobie wojny północnej (1700-1718)', in: Biskup, M., ed., *Historia Torunia*, vol. 2 (Toruń, 1996), 139-61.

Ehasalu, P., *Rootsiaegne maalikunst Tallinnas (1561-1710). Produktsioon ja retsepsioon. Painting in Tallinn during the Swedish Period (1561-1710): Production and Reception* (Tallinn, 2007).

Ehrenstrahl, D.K., *Die vornehmste Schildereyen, welche in denen Pallästen des Königreiches Schweden zu sehen sind. Inventiret, verfertiget und beschrieben von David Klöcker Ehrenstrahl* (Stockholm, 1694).

Ekedahl, N., *Det svenska Israel. Myt och retorik i Haquin Spegels predikokonst.* Studia Rhetorica Upsaliensia, 2 (Uppsala, 1999).

_____, 'Mot en modern mediemonarki', in: Ekedahl, N., ed., *En dynasti blir till. Medier, myter och makt kring Karl XIV Johan och familjen Bernadotte* (Stockholm, 2010), 283-301.

Ellenius, A., *Karolinska bildidéer.* Ars suetica 1 (Uppsala, 1966).

Ellinger Bang, N., and Korst, K., *Tabeller ovber skibsfart og varetransport gennem Øresund*, 7 vols. (Copenhagen & Leipzig, 1906-30).

Eng, T., *Det svenska väldet. Ett konglomerat av uttrycksformer och begrepp från Vasa till Bernadotte* (Uppsala, 2001).

Englund, P., *Poltava: Berättelsen om en armés undergång* (Stockholm, 1988).

_____, *Rasskaz o gibeli odnoi armii* (Moscow, 1995).

_____, *The Battle That Shook Europe: Poltava and the Birth of the Russian Empire* (London, 2002).

Erdmann, Y., 'Patkul und Wien. Seine Verhandlungen mit dem Wiener Hof und mit Gesandten und Unterhändlern in Wien', in: *Zeitschrift für Ostforschung*, 12 (1963), 266-93.

Erdmannsdörffer, B., *Deutsche Geschichte vom westfälischen Frieden zum Regierungsantritt Friedrich des Grossen, 1648-1740* (Berlin, 1893).

Ericson Wolke, L., *Lasse i Gatan. Kaparkriget och det svenska stormaktsväldets fall* (Lund, 2006).

_____, *Sjöslag och rysshärjningar. Kampen om Östersjön under stora nordiska kriget 1700-1721* (Stockholm, 2012).

_____, 'Riga 1710. Det svenska östersjöväldets fall', in: Ericson [Wolke], L., Hårdstedt, M., Iko, P., Sjöblom, I., and Åselius, G., *Svenska slagfält* (Stockholm, 2003).

_____, 'Mellan Poltava och Tönningen: svenska operativa förutsättningar och resursmobilisering 1709-1713', in: *Militärhistorisk tidskrift*, 10-11 (2009-10), 45-71.

Ericson [Wolke], L., Hårdstedt, M., Iko, P., Sjöblom, I., and Åselius, G., *Svenska slagfält* (Stockholm, 2003).

Ericson Wolke, L., and Hårdstedt, M., *Svenska sjöslag* (Stockholm, 2009).

Ericsson, P., 'Bilden av suveränen', in: Dahlgren, S., Florén, A., Karlsson, Å., eds., *Makt & Vardag. Hur man styrde, levde och tänkte under svensk stormaktstid* (Trelleborg, 1992).

_____, *Stora nordiska kriget förklarat. Karl XII och det ideologiska tilltalet* (Uppsala, 2002).

Eriksson, I., *Karolinen Magnus Stenbock* (Stockholm, 2007).

Evdokimova, S., *Pushkin's Historical Imagination* (New Haven, CT, 1999).

Fankidejski, J., *Klasztory żeńskie w diecezji chełmińskiej* (Pelplin, 1883).

Feigina, S.A., *Alandskiy congress. Vneshnaia politica Rossii v kontse Severnoi voiny* (Moscow, 1959).

Feldbæk, O., and Jespersen, K.J.V., *Revanche og neutralitet 1648-1814. Dansk Udenrigspolitiks Historie,* vol. 2 (København, 2002).

Feldman, J., *Polska w dobie wielkiej wojny północnej 1704-1709* (Kraków, 1925).

Ferretti, V.A., *Boreale Geltung. Zu Nördlichkeit, Raum und Imaginärem im Werk von Jorge Luis Borges.* Imaginatio Borealis – Bilder des Nordens 14 (Frankfurt am Main, 2007).

Fiedler, J., *Actenstücke zur Geschichte Franz Rákóczys und seiner Verbindungen mit dem Auslande,* 2 vols. (Wien, 1855-58).

Finkel, C., *Rüyadan İmparatorluğa Osmanlı, Osmanlı İmparatorluğu'nun Öyküsü 1300-1923* (Istanbul, 2012).

Florovsky, A.V., 'Russo-Austrian Conflicts in the Early 18th Century', in: *The Slavonic and East European Review,* 47 (1969), 94-114.

Forrest, A., 'The Logistics of Revolutionary War in France', in: Chickering, R., and Förster, S., eds., *War in an Age of Revolution 1775-1815* (Cambridge, 2010), 178-79.

Frantzen, O., and Jespersen, L., *Danmarks krigshistorie 700-2010* (Köbenhavn, 2010).

Frey, L., and Frey, M., *A Question of Empire: Leopold I and the War of the Spanish Succession, 1701-1705* (New York, 1983).

_____, *Frederick I: The Man and His Times* (New York, 1984).

_____, 'The Foreign Policy of Frederick I, King in Prussia, 1701-1711: A Fatal Vacillation?', in: *East European Quarterly,* 9, no. 3 (1975), 259-69.

_____, 'The Anglo-Prussian Treaty of 1704', in: *Canadian Journal of History,* 11, no. 3 (December 1976), 283-94.

_____, 'Rákóczi and the Maritime Powers: An Uncertain Friendship', in: Bak and Király, *From Hunyadi,* 455-66.

_____, eds., *The Treaties of the War of the Spanish Succession: An Historical and Critical Dictionary* (Westport, CT, 1995).

Frey, L., Frey, M., and Rule, J.C., eds., *Observations from The Hague and Utrecht: William Henry Harrison's Letters to Henry Watkins, 1711-1712* (Columbus, OH, 1979).

From, P., *Karl XII:s död: gåtans lösning* (Lund, 2005).

_____, *Katastrofen vid Poltava: Karl XII:s ryska fälttåg 1707-1709* (Lund, 2009).

Frost, R.I., *The Northern Wars: War, State and Society in Northeastern Europe, 1558-1721* (Harlow, 2000).

_____, 'Monarchy in Northern and Eastern Europe', in: Scott, H., ed., *The Oxford Handbook of Early Modern European History, 1350-1750* (Oxford, 2015), II, 385-417.

Fryxell, A., *Berättelser ur svenska historien,* 21-29 (Stockholm, 1856-59).

_____, *Min historias historia. Autobiografisk uppsats af Anders Fryxell* (Stockholm, 1884).

Gadd, C.J., *Det svenska jordbrukets historia. 3, Den agrara revolutionen: 1700-1870* (Stockholm, 2000).

Garde, H.G., *Den dansk-norske sømagte historie 1700-1814* (København, 1852).

Generalstaben, *Karl XII på slagfältet: karolinsk slagledning sedd mot bakgrunden av taktikens utveckling från allra äldsta tider,* 1-4 (Stockholm, 1918-19).

Gierowski, J., *Między saskim absolutyzmem a złotą wolnością. Z dziejów wewnętrznych Rzeczypospolitej w latach 1712-1715* (Wrocław, 1953).

_____, *W cieniu Ligi Północnej* (Wrocław, 1971).

Gierowski, J., ed., *Rzeczpospolita w dobie upadku 1700-1740, Wybór źródeł* (Wrocław, 1955).

Gierszewski, S., *Elbląg. Przeszłość i teraźniejszość* (Gdańsk, 1970).

Gipping, A.I., *Vvedenie v istoriju Sankt-Peterburga ili Neva i Nienšanc* (Moscow, 2003).

*Gistoria sveiskoi voiny* (Podennaya zapiska Petra Velikogo), 1; 2 (Moscow, 2004).

Glete, J., *Navies and Nations: Warships, Navies and State Building in Europe and America, 1500-1860* (Stockholm, 1993).

_____, *Swedish Naval Administration 1521-1721. Resource Flows and Organisational Capabilities* (Leiden & Boston, 2010).

Gökbilgin, M.T., 'Rákóci Ferenc II ve Macar Mültecileri', in: *Türk Macar Kültür Münasebetleri Işığı Altında II. Rákóczi Ferenc ve Macar Mültecileri Sempozyûmu* (31 Mayıs-3 Haziran 1976) (Istanbul, 1976), 1-17.

Goliński, J.K., 'Bellonae domus descriptio. Strach przed wojną pośród lęków doby saskiej', in: Stasiewicz, K., Archemczyk, S., eds., *Między barokiem a oświeceniem. Wojny i niepokoje czasów saskich* (Olsztyn, 2004), 152-60.

Goll, J., *Der Vertrag von Alt-Ranstaedt. Oesterreich und Schweden 1706-1707. Ein Beitrag zur Geschichte der österreichischen Politik während des nordischen Krieges* (Prag, 1879).

Górny, A., Piwarski, K., *Kraków w czasie drugiego najazdu Szwedów na Polskę 1702-1709* (Kraków, 1932).

Grandin, G., 'Den svenska sjömakten under den karolinska tiden', in: *Karolinska Förbundets Årsbok* (1988), 123-38.

Granér, M., 'Carl XII:s död i svensk diktning', in: *Samlaren,* ny följd 23 (1942), 43-60.

Grauers, S., 'Den karolinska fälthärens underhåll 1700-1703', in: *Karolinska Förbundets Årsbok* (1968).

_____, 'Den karolinska fälthärens underhåll 1704-1707', in: *Karolinska Förbundets Årsbok* (1969).

_____, 'Svensk och polsk krigsmakt i sina inbördes relationer under det stora nordiska kriget', in: *Karolinska Förbundets Årsbok* (1976).

Grimarest, J.L. de, *Les campagnes de Charles XII, roy de Suède,* 4 vols. (Paris, 1707-10).

Groth, A., 'Port, żegluga i handel morski Elbląga w XV-XVIII wieku', in: Długokęcki, W., ed., *Morskie tradycje Elbląga. Przeszłość, teraźniejszość, przyszłość* (Elbląg, 1996), 63-109.

Güler, M., '1150/1737 Osmanlı-İsveç Ticaret Anlaşması', in: *AKÜ Sosyal Bilimler Dergisi,* IX, 2, (Aralık 2007), 101-20.

Günther, A., 'Das schwedische Heer in Sachsen 1706-1707', in: *Neues Archiv für Sächsische Geschichte und Alterthumskunde,* 25 (1904), 231-63.

Guichen, Vicomte de, *Pierre le Grand et le premier traité franco-russe (1682-1717)* (Paris, 1908).

Guldon, Z., Wijaczka, J., 'Zarazy a zaludnienie i gospodarka Polski w dobie wielkiej wojny północnej', in: Muszyńska, J., ed., *Rzeczpospolita w dobie wielkiej wojny północnej* (Kielce, 2001), 199-215.

Gutmann, M.P., *War and Rural Life in the Early Modern Low Countries* (Assen, 1980).

Hårdstedt, M., *Om krigets förutsättningar: Den militära underhållsproblematiken och det civila samhället i norra Sverige och Finland under Finska kriget 1808-09* (Umeå, 2002).

Hahr, A., 'Karl XII-porträtten', in: *Ord och Bild* (1901).

Haintz, O., *König Karl XII von Schweden* (Berlin, 1958).

Hantsch, H., *Reichsvizekanzler Friedrich Karl von Schönborn 1674-1746* (Augsburg, 1929).

Hartley, J.M., *Charles Whitworth: Diplomat in the*

*Age of Peter the Great* (Aldershot, 2002).

_____, 'Changing Perspectives: British Views of Russia from the Grand Embassy to the Peace of Nystad', in: Hughes, L., ed., *Peter the Great and the West: New Perspectives* (Basingstoke, 2001), 53-70.

Hartmann, S., *Reval im Nordischen Krieg* (Bonn & Bad Godesberg, 1973).

_____, *Die Beziehungen Preußens zu Dänemark, 1688-1789* (Wien, 1983).

Hassinger, E., *Brandenburg-Preußen, Schweden und Rußland 1700-1713* (München, 1953).

Hattendorf, J.B., *England in the War of the Spanish Succession: A Study in the English View and Conduct of Grand Strategy* (New York, 1987).

_____, 'John Robinson's Account of Sweden, 1688: The Original 1688 Manuscript, edited and collated with the 1693 Manuscript and the Published Editions from 1694', in: *Karolinska Förbundets Årsbok* (1996), i-xlvi, 1-126.

_____, 'Robinson, John (1650-1723), Bishop of London and Diplomatist', in: Matthew, H.C.G., and Harrison, B., eds., *Oxford Dictionary of National Biography* (Oxford, 2004), 47, 360-64.

_____, 'Charles XII, 1682-1718: King of Sweden', in: Messenger, C., ed., *Reader's Guide to Military History* (London & Chicago, 2011), 90-91.

_____, ed., *The Journals of Sir George Rooke, Admiral of the Fleet, 1700-1704*. Publications of the Navy Records Society (London, forthcoming).

Hattendorf, J.B., Veenendaal, A.J., Jr., and Hövell tot Westerflier, R. van, eds., *Marlborough: Soldier and Diplomat* (Rotterdam, 2012).

Hatton, R.M., *Diplomatic Relations between Great Britain and the Dutch Republic, 1714-1721* (London, 1950).

_____, *Charles XII of Sweden* (London 1967; New York, 1969).

_____, *George I: Elector and King* (London, 1978).

_____, *Karl XII av Sverige* (Köping, 1985).

_____, 'Charles XII and the Great Northern War', in: Bromley, J.S., ed., *The New Cambridge Modern History*, vol. 6: *The Rise of Great Britain and Russia, 1688-1725* (Cambridge, 1969), 648-80.

_____, ed., 'Captain James Jefferyes's Letters to the Secretary of State, Whitehall, from the Swedish Army, 1707-1709', in: *Historiskt Magasin. Första volymen*. Historiska Handlingar, 35, 1 (Stockholm, 1954), 1-93.

_____, 'Gratifications and Foreign Policy: French Rivalry in Sweden during the Nine Years War', in: Hatton, R.M., and Bromley, J.S., eds., *William III and Louis XIV: Essays 1680-1720 by and for Mark A. Thomson* (Liverpool, 1968), 68-94.

_____, 'Louis XIV and His Fellow Monarchs', in: Hatton, R., ed., *Louis XIV and Europe* (London, 1976), 16-59.

_____, 'Presents and Pensions: A Methodological Search and Case Study of Count Nils Bielke's Prosecution for Treason in Connection with Gratifications from France', in: Mack, P., and Jacob, M.C., eds., *Politics and Culture in Early Modern Europe: Essays in Honour of H.G. Koenigsberger* (Cambridge, 1987), 101-17.

Haverling, S.-G., *Huvuddrag i svensk och antisvensk propaganda i Västeuropa på 1710-talet* (Stockholm, 1952).

Heckscher, E.F., 'De europeiska staternas finanser på Karl XII:s tid', in: *Karolinska Förbundets Årsbok* (1921).

_____, 'Öresundsräkenskaperna och deras behandling', in: *Historisk Tidskrift* (1942), 170-86.

Heidenstam, V. von., *Samlade verk*, Böök, F., and Bang, K., eds. (Stockholm, 1943-44).

Heiss, G., and Klingenstein, G., eds., *Das Osmanische Reich und Europa 1683 bis 1789: Konflikt, Entspannung und Austausch* (Wien, 1983).

Helander, H., *Neo-Latin Literature in Sweden. Stylistics, Vocabulary and Characteristic Ideas*, Studia Latina Upsaliensia 29 (Uppsala, 2004).

_____, 'Andreas Rydelius om vältaligheten och enväldet', in: Beskow, P., et al., eds., *Förbistringar och förklaringar. Festskrift till Anders Piltz* (Lund, 2008), 320-35.

Hellie, R., 'The Petrine Army: Continuity, Change, and Impact', in: *Canadian-American Slavic Studies*, vol. 8, no.2 (1974).

Hellmann, M., 'Die Friedensschlüsse von Nystad (1721) und Teschen (1779) als Etappen des Vordringens Rußlands nach Europa', in: *Historisches Jahrbuch*, 97/98 (1978), 270-88.

Hemmings, J., 'The Semiotics of Diplomatic Dialogue: Pomp and Circumstance in Tsar Peter's Visit to Vienna in 1698', in: *International History Review*, 30 (2008), 515-44.

Hildebrand, B., 'Casten Feif', in: *Svenskt biografiskt lexicon*, vol. 15 (Stockholm, 1956).

Hildebrand, B.E., *Sveriges och svenska konungahusets minnespenningar, praktmynt och belöningsmedaljer*, vol. I (Stockholm, 1874).

Hildebrand, K.-G, 'England och Sverige, 1707: Några Bidrag', in: *Karolinska Förbundets*

*Årsbok* (1937), 176-201.

_____, 'Till Karl XII-uppfattningens historia I: Från Voltaire till Fryxell', in: *Historisk tidskrift* (1954), 353-92.

_____, 'Till Karl XII-uppfattningens historia II: Från Beskow till Hjärne', in: *Historisk tidskrift* (1955), 1-46.

Hildebrand, S., ed., *Karl XI:s almanacksanteckningar* (Stockholm, 1918).

Hintze, O., *Die Hohenzollern und ihr Werk* (Berlin, 1916).

*Historia skrócona Karola XII, króla szwedzkiego z francuskiego na język polski przetłumaczona R. 1756* (Warszawa, 1756).

Hjärne, H., *Karl XII: omstörtningen i Östeuropa 1697–1703* (Stockholm, 1902).

Hjelmqvist, F., *Kriget i Finland och Ingermanland 1707 och 1708* (Lund, 1909).

Höbelt, L., 'The Impact of the Rákóczi Rebellion on Habsburg Strategy: Incentives and Opportunity Costs', in *War in History*, 13 (2006), 2-15.

Hoff, B. van 't, ed., *The Correspondence 1701-1711 of John Churchill First Duke of Marlborough and Anthonie Heinsius Grand Pensionary of Holland*. Werken uitgegeven door het Historisch Genootschap, 4e serie, no. 1 (Utrecht, 1951).

Hoffmann, G.E., Neumann, K., und Kellenbenz, H., *Geschichte Schleswig-Holsteins. Vol. V: Die Herzogtümer von der Landesteilung 1544 bis zur Wiedervereinigung Schleswigs 1721* (Neumünster, 1986).

Holm, N. F., 'Stralenheim och Zobor', in: *Karolinska Förbundets Årsbok* (1960), 98-104.

_____, 'Poltava-minnet och tillkomsten av Carl XII:s staty', in: *Karolinska Förbundets Årsbok* (1977), 43-56.

Holmquist, B.M., 'Johann Heinrich Wedekind – Karl XII:s målare', in: Dahlberg, A-M., and Tamla, T., eds., *Estland och Sverige* (Tallinn, 1993).

Holmström, I., *Samlade dikter II: Kunglig panegyrik, gravdikter, bröllopsdikter, supliker, politiska dikter*, Olsson, B., Nilsson, B., and Malm, M., eds. (Stockholm, 2001).

Holtrop, P., 'Hollandse Protestanten in Sint-Petersburg in de tijd van Peter de Grote', in: Holtrop, P., a.o., eds., *Twee Eeuwen Nederlanders in Sint-Petersburg. De Hollandse Kerk als sociaal en religieus middelpunt* (Zutphen, 2013), 41-57.

Horn, D.B., *British Diplomatic Representatives, 1689-1789*. Camden Society, XXXII (London, 1932).

Horstmeier, C., Koningsbrugge, H. van, Nieuwland, I., and Waegemans, E., eds., *Around Peter the Great: Three Centuries of Russian-Dutch Relations* (Groningen, 1997).

Hoszowski, S., 'Handel Gdańska w okresie XV-XVIII wieku', in: *Zeszyty Naukowe Wyższej Szkoły Ekonomicznej w Krakowie,* 11 (1960), 3-71.

Houtte, J.A. van, *An Economic History of the Low Countries 800-1800* (London, 1977).

Hughes, L., *Russia in the Age of Peter the Great* (New Haven, CT, 1998).

Hughes, M., *Law and Politics in Eighteenth Century Germany: The Imperial Aulic Council in the Reign of Charles VI* (Bury St. Edmunds, 1988).

İnalcık, H., 'Karadeniz'de Kazaklar ve Rusya: İstanbul Boğazı Tehlikede', in: Demir, M., ed., *Çanakkale Savaşları Tarihi*, I (Istanbul, 2008), 59-64.

_____, *Devlet-i Aliyye II* (Istanbul, 2014).

Ingrao, C.W., *In Quest of Crisis: Emperor Joseph I and the Habsburg Monarchy* (West Lafayette, IN, 1979).

_____, *Josef I. Der 'vergessene' Kaiser* (Graz, 1982).

Israel, J., *Dutch Primacy in World Trade, 1585-1740* (Oxford, 1989).

_____, 'Heinsius, Dutch Raison d'État and the Reshaping of the Baltic and Eastern Europe', in: Jongste, J.A.F. de, and Veenendaal, A.J., Jr., eds., *Anthonie Heinsius and the Dutch Republic 1688-1720: Politics, War, and Finance* (The Hague, 2002), 25-44.

Itzkowitz, N., 'The Ottoman Empire in the Eighteenth Century', in: Çiçek, K., ed., *The Great Ottoman-Turkish Civilisation*, I (Ankara, 2000), 376-77.

Jacobowsky, C.V., 'Svenska studenter i Oxford, ca. 1620-1740', in: *Personhistorisk Tidskrift* (1927), 105-33.

Jacobs, B., 'Strindberg and the Dramatic Tableau: Master Olof and Charles the Twelfth', in: *Scandinavica* 43 (2004), 53-95.

Jääskeläinen, J., *Paikallisyhteisö resurssina ja tuhojen kohteena: Venäjän armeijan logististen ratkaisujen seuraukset Suomen sodassa 1808-1809,* (Åbo, 2011).

Jägerskiöld, O., *Den svenska utrikespolitikens historia*, II: 2, 1721-1792 (Stockholm, 1957).

Jägerskiöld, S., *Sverige och Europa 1716-1718. Studier i Karl XII:s och Görtz utrikespolitik* (Ekenäs, 1937).

Jarochowski, K., *Dzieje panowania Augusta II od wstąpienia Karola XII na ziemię polską aż do elekcji Stanisława Leszczyńskiego(1702-1704)* (Poznań, 1874).

_____, *Oblężenie miasta Poznania przez Patkula. Epizod kampanii roku 1704* (Poznań, 1879).

_____, *Dzieje panowania Augusta II.,* Vol. I, *Od śmierci Jana III do chwili wstąpienia Karola XII na ziemię polską;* vol. II, *Od wstąpienia Karola XII na ziemię polską aż do elekcji Stanisława Leszczyńskiego (1702-1704),* Gajewski, A., ed. (Oświęcim, 2015).

Jeannin, P., 'Les Comptes du Sund comme source pour la construction de l'activité économique en Europe (XVIe-XVIIIe siècle)', in: *Revue Historique,* ccxxxi (1964), 55-102; 307-40.

Jespersen, K.J.V., 'Rivalry without End: Denmark, Sweden and the Struggle for the Baltic, 1500-1720', in: Rystad, G., Böhme K-R., and Carlgren, W.M., eds., *In Quest of Trade and Security: The Baltic in Power Politics, 1500-1990,* I (Stockholm, 1994).

_____, 'Warfare and Society in the Baltic 1500-1800', in: Black, J., ed., *European Warfare 1453-1815* (London, 1999), 180-200.

_____, 'Den sidste styrkeprøve 1700-1720', in: Frantzen, O.L., and Jespersen, K.J.V., eds., *Danmarks krigshistorie 700-2010* (København, 2010), 334-71.

Jörn, N., and North, M., eds., *Die Integration des südlichen Ostseeraumes in das Alte Reich* (Köln, Weimar & Wien, 2000).

Johannesson, K., *I polstjärnans tecken. Studier i svensk barock.* Lychnos-bibliotek 24 (Uppsala, 1968).

Johns, R., '"The British Caesar": John Churchill, 1st Duke of Marlborough, and the Visual Arts', in: Hattendorf, J.B., Veenendaal, A.J., and Hövell tot Westerflier, R. van, eds., *Marlborough: Soldier and Diplomat* (Rotterdam, 2012), 320-55.

Johnson, S., *The Complete English Poems* (Harmondsworth, 1971).

Jonasson, G., *Karl XII:s Polska Politik 1702-1703* (Stockholm, 1968).

_____, *Karl XII och hans rådgivare. Den utrikespolitiska maktkampen i Sverige 1697-1702* (Uppsala, 1960).

_____, 'Karl XII:s baltiska militärpolitik under år 1701', in: *Scandia* 29 (1963), 250-91.

Jones, A., *The Art of War in the Western World* (Urbana & Chicago, 1987).

Jones, R.E., 'Getting the Goods to St. Petersburg: Water Transport from the Interior 1703-1811', in: *Slavic Review*, 43, 3 (1984), 413-33.

Jongste, J.A.F. de, and Veenendaal, A.J., Jr., eds., *Anthonie Heinsius and the Dutch Republic 1688-1720: Politics, War and Finance* (The Hague, 2002).

Jonson, E., *Skärgårdskriget. Rysshärjningarna 1719.* (2nd ed., Stockholm, 1990).

Josephson, R., *Nicodemus Tessin d. y. Tiden – Mannen – Verket.* Sveriges Allmänna Konstförenings publikation XXXVIII (Stockholm, 1930).

_____, 'Karl XI och Karl XII som esteter', in: *Karolinska Förbundets Årsbok* (1947).

Kabuzan, V.M., *Narody Possii v XVIII v. Chislennost' i etnicheskiy sostav* (Moscow, 1990).

Kahan, A., 'Entrepreneurship in the Early Development of Iron Manufactories in Russia', in: *Economic Development and Cultural Change*, 10, 4 (1962), 395-422.

Kalinowski, R., ed., *Klasztory karmelitanek bosych w Polsce, na Litwie i Rusi,* vol. III (Warszawa & Kraków, 1902).

Kalisch, J., and Gierowski, J., eds., *Um die polnische Krone. Sachsen und Polen während des Nordischen Krieges 1700-1721* (Berlin, 1962).

Kamalov, İ., ed., *Tolstoy'un Gizli Raporlarında Osmanlı İmparatorluğu* (Istanbul, 2009).

Kamen, H., *The War of Succession in Spain, 1700-15* (London, 1969).

Kan, A., 'Den postsovjetiske Karl XII', in: *Karolinska Förbundets Årsbok* (2000), 215-17.

Kantemir, D., *Osmanlı İmparatorluğu'nun Yükseliş ve Çöküş Tarihi* (Ankara, 1980).

*Karl XII på slagfältet: Karolinsk slagledning sedd mot bakgrunden av taktikens utveckling från äldsta tiden* (Stockholm, 1918).

Karlsson, Å., *Den jämlike undersåten. Karl XII:s förmögenhetsbeskattning 1713* (Uppsala, 1994).

_____, 'Familjen Celsing och de svensk-osmanska relationerna under 1700-talet', in: Ådahl, K., ed., *Minnet av Konstantinopel. Den osmansk-turkiska 1700-talssamlingen på Biby* (Stockholm, 2003), 35-74.

_____, 'Hedvig Eleonora – kulturmecenat och landsmoder', in: *Karolinska Förbundets Årsbok* (2007), 9-23.

_____, 'Den tolerante enväldshärskaren? Karl XII och fördraget i Altranstädt 1707', in: *Karolinska Förbundets Årsbok* (2008), 203-13.

_____, 'Kungens intresse och undersåtarnas välfärd: Karl XII:s reformpolitik under 1710-talet', in: Göranson, U., ed., *Justitiekanslern 300 år* (Uppsala, 2013), 81-94.

Karlsson, Å., Kronberg, K., and Sandin, P., eds., *Karl XII och svenskarna I Osmanska riket*. Armémuseums Årsbok 2015 (Stockholm, 2015).

Keegan, J., *Krigets historia* (Stockholm, 2005).

Kemble, J.M., ed., *State Papers and Correspondence*, (London, 1857).

Kennedy, P., *The Rise and Fall of the Great Powers: Economic Change and Military Conflict from 1500 to 2000* (London, 1989).

Kent, H.S.K., *War and Trade in the Northern Seas: Anglo-Scandinavian Economic Relations in the Mid-Eighteenth Century* (Cambridge, 1973).

Kiss, G., 'Franz Rákóczi II., Peter der Große und der polnische Thron (um 1707)', in: *Jahrbücher für Geschichte Osteuropas*, 31 (1965), 344-60.

Kivelson, V.A., 'The Cartographical Emergence of Europe?', in: Scott, H., ed., *The Oxford Handbook of Early Modern European History, 1350-1750* (Oxford, 2015), I, 37-69.

Klinge, M., *Idyll och hot. Zacharias Topelius – hans politik och idéer* (Stockholm & Helsingfors, 2000).

Klopp, O., *Der Fall des Hauses Stuart und die Succession des Hauses Hannover in Gross-Brittannien und Irland*, 14 vols. (Wien, 1875-88).

Köpeczi, B., *La France et la Hongrie au début du XVIIIe siècle* (Budapest, 1971).

Kołłątaj, H., *Do Stanisława Małachowskiego … Anonima listów kilka*, vol. II, *O poprawie Rzeczpospolitej*, list II (Warszawa, 1788).

Kolosov, E.E., 'Artilleriya v Poltavskom srazhenii', in: Beskrovnyi L.G., et al., eds., *Poltava. K 250-letiu Poltavskogo srazheniia* (Moscow, 1959).

Koningsbrugge, J.S.A.M. van, *Tussen Rijswijk en Utrecht. De diplomatieke betrekkingen tussen Zweden en de Verenigde Nederlanden 1697-1713*. Baltic Studies 3 (Groningen, 1996).

_____, 'A Time of War: Dutch-Baltic Relations in the Years 1709-1711', in: Lemmink, J.Ph.S., and Koningsbrugge, J.S.A.M. van, eds., *Baltic Affairs: Relations between the Netherlands and North-Eastern Europe 1500-1800* (Nijmegen, 1990), 141-59.

_____, 'Der Niedergang der niederländischen Handels mit Rußland und dem Baltikum in den Jahren 1710-1721', in: Horstmeier, C., et al., eds., *Around Peter the Great: Three Centuries of Russian-Dutch Relations* (Groningen, 1997), 86-91.

Konopczyński, W., *Polska a Szwecja. Od pokoju oliwskiego do upadku Rzeczypospolitej 1660-1795* (Warszawa, 1924).

_____, *Dzieje Polski nowożytnej*, wyd. 3 (Warszawa, 1996).

Konovalchuk, P., and Lyth, E., *Vägen till Poltava. Slaget vid Lesnaja 1708* (Stockholm, 2009).

Korkiakangas, O., *Kaarle XII:n kenttäarmeijan huolto sotaretkellä vuosina 1700-1701 mannereurooppalaisten näkökulmasta*. Historiallisia tutkimuksia 89 (Helsingfors, 1974).

Koroluk, W. D., *Polska i Rosja a wojna północna* (Warszawa, 1954).

Kotilaine, J.T., *Russia's Foreign Trade and Economic Expansion in the Seventeenth Century: Windows on the World* (Leiden, 2005).

_____, 'Opening a Window on Europe: Foreign Trade and Military Conquest on Russia's Western Border in the 17th Century', in: *Jahrbücher für Geschichte Osteuropas*, Neue Folge, 46-4 (1998), 495-530.

Koźmian, K., *Pamiętniki*, Żupański, J.K., ed., vol. I (Poznań, 1858).

Kreutel, R., and Teply, K., *Kara Mustafa vor Wien. 1683 aus der Sicht Türkischer Quellen* (Graz, 1982).

Krotov, P.A., *Bitwa pri Poltave (k 300-letnei godovschine)* (St. Petersburg, 2009).

_____, 'Kalabalyk u Bender: archivnye materialy o pridnestrovskoi «zavaruche» Karla XII', in: Beril, S.I., et al., eds., *Severnaia voina v Pridnestrov'e: istoriia i sovremennost* (Tiraspol, 2010).

_____, 'Vospominaniya Konstantena de Tourvilia o pohode Karla XII v Rossiu', in: *Voprosy istorii*, 3 (1989), 125-33.

Kurat, A.N., *XII. Karl'ın Türkiye'de Kalışı Ve Bu Sıralarda Osmanlı İmparatorluğu* (Istanbul, 1943).

_____, *Prut Seferi ve Barışı*, 2 vols. (Ankara, 1951).

_____, 'Hazine-i Bîrun Kâtibi Ahmed bin Mahmud'un (1123-1711-Prut) Seferine Ait "Defteri'" (Berlin, Preussische Staatsssibliothek, Orientalische Abteilung, Nr. 1209), in: *Tarih Araştırmaları Dergisi*, IV, 6-7 (Ankara, 1968), 261-426.

_____, 'Leh Fevkalade Elçisi von Goltz'un Türkiye'deki Faaliyetine Ait Raporu (1712-1714)', in: *Tarih Vesikaları Dergisi*, 16 (Ankara), 225-65.

Kurat, A.N., ed., *The Despatches of Sir Robert Sutton, Ambassador in Constantinople (1711-1714)*. Camden Society, Third Series, vol. LXXVIII (London, 1953).

Kuvaja, C., *Försörjning av en ockupationsarmé: Den ryska arméns underhållssystem I Finland 1713-1721* (Åbo, 1999).

_____, *Karolinska krigare 1660-1721* (Helsingfors, 2008).

Kuylenstierna, O., 'Karl XII:s yttre', in: Bring, S.E.,

ed., *Karl XII* (Stockholm, 1925).

Labuda, G., and Michowicz, W., eds., *The History of Polish Diplomacy, X-XXc* (Warsaw, 2005).

Lagerroth, E., *Svensk berättarkonst: Röda rummet, Karolinerna, Onda sagor och Sibyllan*. Publications of the New Society of Letters at Lund, 61 (Lund, 1968).

Laidre, M., *Segern vid Narva: Början till en stormakts fall* (Stockholm, 1996).

_____, *The Great Northern War and Estonia: The Trials of Dorpat 1700-1708* (Tallinn, 2010).

Łakociński, Z., *Magnus Stenbock w Polsce. Przyczynek do historii szwedzkich zdobyczy w czasie wielkiej wojny północnej* (Wrocław, 1967).

Lambert, A., *War at Sea in the Age of Sail, 1650-1850* (London, 2000).

Lamberty, G. de, *Mémoires pour servir à l'histoire du XVIIIe siècle*. 14 vols. (La Haye, 1728-40).

Lamm, M., *Gunno Dahlstierna* (Stockholm, 1946).

Landberg, G., *Den svenska utrikespolitikens historia*, I: 3, 1648-1697 (Stockholm, 1952).

Landgren, B., *Mannen från Prag. Rainer Maria Rilke, hans liv och hans diktning* (Möklinta, 2011).

Larsson, O., *Stormaktens sista krig: Sverige och stora nordiska kriget 1700-1721* (Lund, 2011).

Lediard, T., *The Life of John, Duke of Marlborough* (2nd ed., 2 vols., London, 1743).

Legg, W, ed., *British Diplomatic Instructions, France, II, 1721-1744*, Royal Historical Society (London, 1925).

Leitsch, W., 'Der Wandel der österreichischen Rußlandpolitik in den Jahren 1724-1726', in: *Jahrbücher für Geschichte Osteuropas*, 6 (1958), 33-91.

Lengeler, J.P., *Das Ringen um die Ruhe des Nordens. Grossbritanniens Nordeuropa-Politik und Dänemark zu Beginn des 18. Jahrhunderts* (Frankfurt am Main, 1998).

Lennersand, M., *Rättvisans och allmogens beskyddare. Den absoluta staten, kommissionerna och tjänstemännen, ca 1680-1730* (Uppsala, 1999).

Leszczyński, S., 'Rzut oka na politykę i administrację narodową dla użycia Delfina', in: Lubicz-Niezabitowski, ed., *Rys życia i wybór pism Stanisława Leszczyńskiego, króla polskiego* (Warszawa, 1918).

Levey, M., *Painting at Court* (New York, 1971).

Lewitter, L.R., 'Poland, Russia and the Treaty of Vienna of 5 January 1719', in: *Historical Journal*, 13 (1970), 3-30.

Liljegren, B., *Karl XII. En biografi* (Lund, 2000).

_____, 'Om Frans G. Bengtssons Karl XII', in: Andersson, L., et al., eds., *På historiens slagfält: en festskrift tillägnad Sverker Oredsson* (Lund, 2002), 55-73.

Lindblad, J.Th., *Sweden's Trade with the Dutch Republic 1738-1795: A Quantitative Analysis of the Relationship between Economic Growth and International Trade in the Eighteenth Century* (Assen, 1982).

Lindegren, J., 'Karl XII', in: Florén, A., Dahlgren, S., and Lindegren, J., eds., *Kungar och krigare. Tre essäer om Karl X Gustav, Karl XI och Karl XII* (Stockholm, 1992).

Linderborg, Å., *Socialdemokraterna skriver historia. Historieskrivning som ideologisk maktresurs 1892-2000* (Stockholm, 2001).

Ljustrov, M.J., *Vojna i kul'tura. Russko-švedskie literaturnye paralleli épochi Severnoj vojny* (Moscow, 2012).

Lodén, L.O., *Tid: En Bok om Tideräkning och Kalenderväsen* (Stockholm, 1968).

Lööw, H., *Nazismen i Sverige 1980-1997. Den rasistiska undergroundrörelsen: musiken, myterna, riterna* (Stockholm, 1998).

Loewe, V., ed., *Preußens Staatsverträge aus der Regierungszeit König Friedrich I., Publikationen aus den preußischen Staatsarchiv,* 92 (1923).

Lossky, A., '"Maxims of State" in Louis XIV's Foreign Policy in the 1680's ', in: Hatton R.M., and Bromley, J.S., eds., *William III and Louis XIV, Essays 1680-1720* (London, 1970), 8-15.

Lund, E.A., *War for the Every Day: Generals, Knowledge, and Warfare in Early Modern Europe 1680-1740* (London, 1991).

Lundquist, L., *Council, King and Estates in Sweden 1713-1714* (Stockholm, 1975).

Lundström, H., 'Karl XII – Messias, en i utlandet omkring år 1718 omfattad trossats', in: *Kyrkohistorisk Årsbok,* 2 (1902), 1-18.

Lynn, J.A., *Women, Armies and Warfare in Early Modern Europe* (Cambridge, 2008).

_____, ed., *Feeding Mars: Logistics in Western Warfare from the Middle Ages to the Present* (San Francisco & Oxford, 1993).

_____, 'How War Fed War: The Tax of Violence and Contributions during the Grand Siècle', in: *The Journal of Modern History,* 65 (1993), no. 2.

Malettke, K., *Les relations entre la France et le Saint–Empire au XVIIème siècle* (Paris, 2001).

Mancall, M., *Russia and China: Their Diplomatic Relations to 1728* (Cambridge, MA, 1971).

Marklund, A., *Stenbock: Ära och ensamhet i Karl XII:s tid* (Lund, 2008).

Massie, R.K., *Peter the Great, His Life and World* (New York, 1980).

*Materialy dlia istorii russkogo flota,* 2 (St. Petersburg, 1865).

Matley, I.M., 'Defense Manufactures of St. Petersburg 1703-1730', in: *Geographical Review,* 71, 4 (1981), 411-26.

Matuz, J., *Das Osmanische Reich, Grundlinien Seiner Geschichte* (Darmstadt, 2006).

McKay, D., *Allies of Convenience: Diplomatic Relations between Great Britain and Austria 1714-1719* (New York & London, 1986).

_____, 'The Struggle for Control of George I's Northern Policy, 1718-19', in: *The Journal of Modern History,* 45, no. 3 (Sept. 1973), 367-86.

McKay, D., and Scott, H.M., *The Rise of the Great Powers 1648-1815* (London, 1983).

Mediger, W., *Mecklenburg, Rußland und England-Hannover 1706-1721. Ein Beitrag zur Geschichte des Nordischen Krieges,* 2 vols. (Hildesheim, 1967).

_____, 'Rußland und die Ostsee im 18. Jahrhundert', in: *Jahrbücher für Geschichte Osteuropas,* 34 (1968), 85-103.

Meidal, B., *Från profet till folktribun. Strindberg och Strindbergsfejden 1910-12* (Stockholm, 1982).

Merriman, R.D., ed., *Queen Anne's Navy: Documents Concerning the Administration of the Navy of Queen Anne, 1702-14.* Publications of the Navy Records Society, CIII (London, 1951).

Metasch, F., *300 Jahre Altranstädter Konvention. 300 Jahre schlesische Toleranz* (Dresden, 2007).

Mezgolich, E., 'Graf Johann Wenzel Wratislaw von Mitrowitz. Sein Wirken während des Spanischen Erbfolgekrieges'. PhD thesis, Universität Wien, 1967.

Michael, W., 'Ein schwieriger diplomatischer Fall aus dem Jahre 1719', in: *Historische Zeitschrift,* 52 (1902), 56-68.

Milne, J., 'The Diplomacy of Dr. John Robinson at the Court of Charles XII of Sweden 1697-1709', in: *Transactions of the Royal Historical Society,* Fourth Series, 30 (1948), 75-93.

Minha, C., 'Die deutsche Politik Kaiser Josephs I'. PhD thesis, Universität Wien, 1934.

Molesworth, R., *An Account of Denmark as It Was in the Year 1692* (London, 1694).

Moltusov, V.A., *Poltava – vändpunkten* (Stockholm, 2010).

Munthe, A., *Karl XII och den ryska sjömakten,* 1-3 (Stockholm, 1924-27).

Murray, G., ed., *The Letters and Dispatches of John Churchill, First Duke of Marlborough from 1702 to 1712.* 5 vols. (London, 1845; New York, 1968).

Murray, J.J., *George I, The Baltic and the Whig Split: A Study in Diplomacy and Propaganda* (London, 1969).

_____, ed., *An Honest Diplomat at The Hague: The Private Letters of Horatio Walpole, 1715-1716* (Bloomington, IN, 1955; reprinted, Freeport, NY, 1971).

_____, 'Scania and the End of the Northern Alliance (1716)', in: *The Journal of Modern History,* XVI, no. 2 (June 1944), 81-92.

_____, 'Sweden and the Jacobites in 1716', in: *The Huntington Library Quarterly,* VIII, no. 3 (May 1945), 259-76.

_____, 'Robert Jackson's 'Memoir on the Swedish Tar Company," December 29, 1709', in: *The Huntington Library Quarterly,* X (August 1947), 419-28.

_____, 'British Public Opinion and the Rupture of Anglo-Swedish Relations in 1717', in: *Indiana Magazine of History,* XLIV, no. 2 (June 1948), 125-42.

_____, 'Robert Jackson's Mission to Sweden (1709-1717)', in: *The Journal of Modern History,* XXI, no. 1 (March 1949), 1-16.

_____, 'An Eighteenth-Century Whitebook', in: *The Huntington Library Quarterly,* XIII, no. 4 (August 1950), 371-82.

_____, 'Sjömakternas Expedition till Östersjön 1715', in: *Karolinska Förbundets Årsbok* (1953), 134-96.

Naumann, E., 'Om centralförvaltningen under Karl XII:s tid', in: Bring, S.E., ed., *Karl XII.*

Naumann, M., *Österreich, England und das Reich 1719-1732* (Berlin, 1936).

Neumann, W., *Lexikon baltischer Künstler* (Riga, 1908).

Nikiforov, L.A., *Russko-angliyskiye otnoshenia pri Petre I* (Moscow, 1950).

_____, 'Poslednie gody Severnoi voiny i Nishtadtskiy mir', in: Kafengauz, B.B., and Pavlenko, N.I., eds., *Ocherki istorii SSSR. Period feodalizma. Rossija v pervoi chetverty XVIII v. Preobrazovaniya Petra I* (Moscow, 1954), 573-98.

Nisser, W., *Michael Dahl and the Contemporary Swedish School of Painting in England* (Uppsala, 1927).

Noorden, C. von, *Europäische Geschichte im*

*achtzehnten Jahrhundert*, 3 vols. (Düsseldorf & Leipzig, 1870-82).

_____, 'Die preußische Politik im spanischen Erbfolgekriege', in: *Historische Zeitschrift* (1867), 197-358.

Nordensvan, C.O., *Karl XII: synpunkter och betraktelser* (Stockholm, 1918).

Nordmann, C.J., *La crise du Nord au début du XVIIIe siècle* (Paris, 1962).

Nyblom, A., *Ryktbarhetens ansikte. Verner von Heidenstam, medierna och personkulten i sekelskiftets Sverige* (Stockholm, 2008).

Nycz, M., *Geneza reform skarbowych sejmu niemego (studium z dziejów skarbowo-wojskowych z lat 1697-1717)* (Poznań, 1938).

Öhman, J., 'Morgen kommt der Schwed…'. MA thesis, University of Göteborg, 1999.

Olander, G., *Studier över det inre tillståndet i Sverige under senare delen av Karl XII:s regering, med särskild hänsyn till Skaraborgs län* (Göteborg, 1946).

Olausson, M., 'Den stora rollen', in: Cavalli-Björkman, G., ed., *Ansikte mot Ansikte. Porträtt från fem sekel*. Nationalmusei utställningskatalog nr. 626 (Stockholm, 2001).

Olin, M., *Det karolinska porträttet. Ikonografi, ideologi, identitet* (Stockholm, 2000).

Olsson, H., *Carl Snoilsky* (Stockholm, 1981).

Olsson, S., *Olof Hermelin. En karolinska kulturpersonlighet och statsman* (Lund, 1953).

Oredsson, S., 'Karl XII', in: Oredsson, S., ed., *Tsar Peter och Kung Karl. Två härskare och deras folk* (Stockholm, 1998), 35-74.

_____, 'Karl XII och det svenska stormaktsväldets fall i historieskrivning och tradition' in: Oredsson, S., ed., *Tsar Peter och Kung Karl. Två härskare och deras folk* (Stockholm, 1998), 239-72.

_____, 'Livskraften hos Karl XII-forskningens 'nya skola'', in: Zetterberg, K., and Åselius, G., eds., *Historia, krig och statskonst. En vänbok till Klaus-Richard Böhme* (Stockholm, 2000), 45-70.

_____, 'Stormaktsdrömmar och stridsiver. Ett tema i svensk opinionsbildning och politik 19101942', in: *Scandia* (2008), 257-96.

*Osmanlı Rus İlişkileri Tarihi, Ahmet Cavit Bey'in Müntehabâtı*, Baycar, A., ed. (Istanbul, 2004).

Ostrowski, D., 'Peter's Dragoons: How the Russians Won at Poltava', in: Plokhyi, S., ed., *Poltava 1709: The Battle and the Myth* (Cambridge, MA, 2012), 81-106.

Ostwald, J., 'Marlborough and Siege Warfare', in: Hattendorf, J.B., Veenendaal, A.J., Jr., and Hövell tot Westerflier, R. van, eds., *Marlborough: Soldier and Diplomat* (Rotterdam, 2012), 122-43.

Otwinowski, E., *Dzieje Polski pod panowaniem Augusta II*, Mułkowski, A., ed. (Kraków, 1849).

_____, *Pamiętniki do panowania Augusta II*, Raczyński, E., ed. (Poznań, 1839).

Özcan, A., *Râşîd Mehmed Efendi; Çelebizâde İsmaîl Âsım Efendi, Târîh-i Râşid ve Zeyli* (Istanbul, 2013).

_____, 'Edirne Vak'ası', in: *TDV Islam Ansiklopedisi*, 10, 445-46.

_____, 'Karlofça', in: *TDV Islam Ansiklopedisi*, 24, 504-07.

_____, 'Köprülüzâde Nûman Paşa', in: *TDV Islam Ansiklopedisi*, 26, 265-67.

Papp, S., 'Ottoman Accounts of the Hungarian Movements against the Habsburgs at the Turn of the Seventeenth and the Eighteenth Centuries', in: C. Imber, ed., *Frontiers of Ottoman Studies*, II (London, 2005).

Parker, G., *The Military Revolution: Military Innovation and the Rise of the West 1500-1800* (Avon, 1988).

Parry, C., ed., *The Consolidated Treaty Series, 1648-1918*. 231 vols. (Dobbs Ferry, NY, 1969-81).

Parvev, I., *Habsburgs and Ottomans between Vienna and Belgrade 1683-1739* (New York, 1995).

Pastor, P., 'Hungarian-Russian Relations during the Rákóczi War of Independence', in: Bak and Király, *From Hunyadi*, 467-92.

Perjés, G., 'Army Provisioning, Logistics and Strategy in the Second Half of the 17th Century', in: *Acta Historica*, Journal of the Hungarian Academy of Science, XVI (1970).

Perlestam, M., 'Logistiska uppdrag och strider: Den karolinska armén 1701–1709', in: *Karolinska Förbundets Årsbok* (2011).

Persson, B., *Gud verkar med naturliga medel. Pestens härjningar i Skåne 1710-1713* (Lund, 2006).

Peterson, C., *Peter the Great's Administrative and Judicial Reforms: Swedish Antecedents and the Process of Reception* (Stockholm, 1979).

Petrov, P.N., *Istorija Sankt-Peterburga s osnovanija goroda do vvedenija v dejstvie vybornogo gorodskogo upravlenija po učreždenijam o gubernijach* (St. Peterburg, 1885).

Pettersson, I.-L., *Statens läsebok*, Litteratur-Teater-Film, Ny serie 18 (Lund, 1999).

Pilss, F., 'Die Beziehungen des kaiserlichen Hofes unter Karl VI. zu Russland bis zum Nystädter Frieden 1711-1721'. PhD thesis, Universität Wien, 1949.

*Pis'ma i bumagi imperatora Petra Velikogo* (Moscow, 1952), IX, 2.

Plokhyi, S., 'Poltava: The Battle That Never Ends', in: Plokhyi, S., ed., *Poltava 1709: The Battle and the Myth* (Cambridge, MA, 2012), XIII-XXV.

*Pochodnyi zhurnal 1718 goda* (St. Petersburg, 1913).

*Pochodnyi zhurnal 1719 goda* (St. Petersburg, 1913).

*Polnoe Sobranie Zakonov Rossijskoj Imperii, poveleniem gosudarja Imperatora Nikolaja Pavlovicha sostavlennoe*, 1st Series (1649-1825), 45 vols. (St. Petersburg, 1830).

Poraziński, J., *Epiphania Poloniae. Orientacje i postawy polityczne szlachty polskiej w dobie wielkiej wojny północnej (1702-1710)* (Toruń, 1999).

_____, 'Funkcje polityczne i ustrojowe rad senatu w latach 1697-1717', in: *Kwartalnik Historyczny*, 51:1 (1984), 25-45.

_____, 'Opozycja antysaska w Rzeczypospolitej za Augusta II jako problem polityczny i ustrojowy', in: *Acta Universitatis Nocolai Copernici, Historia XXVIII, Nauki Humanistyczno-Społeczne*, 28 (1993), 93-101.

_____, '"Od Sasa do Lasa" – czyli wojna w krzywym zwierciadle. Uwagi o satyrze politycznej czasów saskich', in: Stasiewicz, K., Archemczyk, S., eds., *Między barokiem a oświeceniem. Wojny i niepokoje czasów saskich* (Olsztyn, 2004), 90-97.

Porfiriev, I.E., *Peter I: Grundläggare av den ryska reguljära arméns och flottans krigskonst* (Stockholm, 1958).

Possieth, J., *Hosianna, eller Fägnefult glädie-rop/ öfwer twenne konungars […] annalkande til Swea rike* (Stockholm, 1714).

Prak, M., *The Dutch Republic in the Seventeenth Century: The Golden Age* (Cambridge, 2005).

Probst, N.M., 'Danish Perspectives on De Ruyter's Role in the Nordic Conflicts', in: Bruijn, J., et al., *De Ruyter: Dutch Admiral* (Rotterdam, 2011), 141-61.

Raczyński E., ed., *Pamiętniki do panowania Augusta II napisane przez Erazma Otwinowskiego* (Poznań, 1839).

Rado, Ş., 'Hazine-i Bîrun Kâtibi Ahmet bin Mahmud Efendi'nin Tuttuğu Prut Seferi'ne Ait Defterden Koparılan Sahifelerde Neler Vardı?', in: *Belleten*, vol. L, 198 (Aralık 1986), 812-13.

Rakowski, W.F., *Pamiętnik wielkiej wojny północnej,* Nagelski, M., Wagner, M., eds. (Warszawa, 2002).

Rappe, A., 'Karl XII:s plan för fälttåget mot Ryssland 1708 och 1709', in: *Kungliga Krigsvetenskapsakademiens Handlingar och Tidskrift,* 95 (1892), 321-44.

Rauch, G. von, 'Zur baltischen Frage im 18. Jahrhundert', in: *Jahrbücher für Geschichte Osteuropas,* 5 (1957), 441-87.

*Recueil des Instructions données aux Ambassadeurs et Ministres de France, depuis les Traités de Westphalie jusquà la Révolution Française* (Paris, 1884-): Pologne I-II; Russie I; Suède II; Turquie.

Redlich, F., 'De praeda militari: Looting and booty 1500-1815', in: *Vierteljahrschrift für sozialund wirtschaftsgeschichte,* Beiheft 39 (1956).

_____, 'Contributions in the Thirty Years War', in: *The Economic History Review,* XII, 2 (1959).

Redlich, O., *Das Werden einer Großmacht. Österreich von 1700 bis 1740* (2nd ed., Brno, München & Wien, 1942).

Reed, W.L., *Meditations on the Hero: A Study of the Romantic Hero in Nineteenth-Century Fiction* (New Haven & London, 1974).

Rehnskiöld, C.G., 'Carl Gustaf Rehnskiölds anteckningar och dagböcker', in: Quennerstedt, A., ed., *Karolinska Krigares Dagböcker,* vol. IX (Lund, 1913).

Reiling, J., and Rohde, C., eds., *Das 19. Jahrhundert und seine Helden. Literarische Figurationen des (Post-)Heroischen* (Bielefeld, 2011).

Reingrabner, G., ed., *Der Schwed' ist im Land! Das Ende des Dreißigjährigen Krieges in Niederösterreich* (Horn, 1995).

Rekola, K., *Lewenhauptin retkikunta vuonna 1708* (Helsinki, 1963).

Repin, N.N., 'Ot diskriminacii k fritrederstvu: pravitel'stvennaja reglamentacija torgovli čerez Archangel'sk v 20-60-e gody XVIII v. i ee rezul'tat', in: Bespjatych, J.N., ed., *Archangel'sk v XVIII veke / Arkhangelsk in the XVIII century* (St. Petersburg, 1997), 228-49.

_____, 'Izmenenie ob"ema i struktury éksporta Archangel'skogo i Peterburgskogo portov v pervoj polovine XVIII veka', in: *Promyšlennost' i torgovlja Rossii XVII-XVIII vv.: sbornik statej* (Nauka, 1983), 175-92.

Rill, B., *Karl VI, Habsburg als barocke Grossmacht* (Wien, 1992).

Ringoir, H., *Afstammingen en Voortzettingen der Cavalerie en Wielrijders.* Militair-Historische Bijdragen van de Sectie Krijgsgeschiedenis

nr. 3 ('s-Gravenhage, 1978).

Roberts, M., ed., *Swedish Diplomats at Cromwell's Court, 1655-56: The Missions of Peter Julius Coyet and Christer Bonde.* Camden Fourth Series, 36 (London, 1988).

Rodell, M., *Att gjuta en nation. Statyinvigningar och nationsformering i Sverige vid 1800-talets mitt* (Stockholm, 2001).

Rodger, N.A.M., *Command of the Ocean: A Naval History of Britain, 1649-1815* (London, 2004).

Rodger, N.A.M., Dancy, J.R., Darnell, B., and Wilson, E., eds., *Strategy and the Sea. Essays in honour of John B. Hattendorf* (Woodbridge, 2016).

Roider, K.A., *Austria's Eastern Question 1700-1790* (Princeton, 1982).

Roniker, J., *Hetman Adam Sieniawski i jego regimentarze. Studium z historii mentalności szlachty polskiej 1706-1725* (Kraków, 1992).

Rosen, C. von, *Bidrag till kännedom om de händelser, som närmast föregick det svenska stormaktsväldets fall: I. Sveriges ställning till Polen 1701-1704* (Stockholm, 1936).

Rosén, J., *Den svenska utrikespolitikens historia,* II: 2 1697-1721 (Stockholm, 1952).

Rothstein, A., *Peter the Great and Marlborough: Politics and Diplomacy in Converging Wars* (Basingstoke, 1986).

Rousset de Missy, J. de, *Le cérémonial diplomatique des cours de l'Europe,* published as vols. 4 and 5 of [Jean Dumont], *Corps Universel Diplomatique du Droit des Gens:* Supplément. 2nd ed., 5 vols. (Amsterdam & La Haye, 1739).

Ruuth, M., 'Karl XII i den mystiska separatistiska profetians ljus', in: *Kyrkohistorisk Årsskrift* 14 (1914), 434-48.

Rycaut, P., *Osmanlı İmparatorluğu'nun Hâlihazırının Tarihi (XVII. Yüzyıl)* (Ankara, 2012).

Rydsjö, E., *Karolinernas kvinnor* (Stockholm, 2001).

Rystad, G., *Karl XI: En biografi* (Lund, 2001).

_____, 'Vägen till fred', in: Askgaard, F., and Stade, A., eds., *Kampen om Skåne* (København, 1983), 399-420.

Sallnäs, B., *Samuel Åkerhielm d.y.: En Staatsmannabiografi* (Lund, 1947).

Samerski, S., 'Von der Trauer des Papstes. Die Reaktion Clemens XI. auf die Altranstädter Konvention', in: Wolf, J.R., ed., *Altranstädter Konvention,* 108-32.

Sandstedt, E., *Studier rörande Jöran Nordbergs Konung Carl XII:s historia* (Lund, 1972).

_____, 'Karl XII och Alexander-rollen', in: *Karolinska Förbundets Årsbok* (2000), 169-82.

Šarymov, A., *Predystorija Sankt-Peterburga / 1703 god: Kniga issledovanij* (St. Petersburg, 2004).

Schama, S., 'Royal Family Portraiture', in: *Art and History: Images and Their Meaning* (Cambridge, 1988).

Schartau, S., 'Om Sveriges inre tillstånd under Karl XII:s tid', in: Bring, S.E., ed., *Karl XII.*

Scheltjens, W., *De invloed van ruimtelijke verandering op operationele strategieën in de vroeg-moderne Nederlandse scheepvaart: Een case-study over de Nederlandse scheepvaart in de Finse Golf en op Archangel, 1703-1740* (Groningen, 2009).

_____, 'The Volume of Dutch Baltic Shipping at the End of the Eighteenth Century: A New Estimation Based on the Danish Sound Toll Registers', in: *Scripta Mercaturae,* 2009, 43 (1-2), 83-110.

_____, 'Maße und Gewichte. Konvertierungsmöglichkeiten am Beispiel der Sundzollregister', in: Rauscher, P., and Serles, A., eds., *Wiegen – Zählen – Registrieren: Handelsgeschichtliche Massenquellen und die Erforschung mitteleuropäischer Märkte (13.-18. Jahrhundert)* (Innsbruck-Wien-Bozen, 2015), 455-79.

Schilling, L., 'Der Wiener Hof und Sachsen-Polen 1697-1764', in: *Sachsen und Polen zwischen 1697 und 1765. Beiträge der wissenschaftlichen Konferenz 1997 in Dresden* (Dresden, 1998), 119-36.

Schmidt, Th., 'Geschichte des Handels und der Schifffahrt Stettins', in: *Baltische Studien,* 19, 2 (1863), 1-100.

Schnakenbourg, E., *La France, le Nord et l'Europe au début du XVIIIe siècle* (Paris, 2008).

_____, 'La chute de l'Alexandre du Nord: le gouvernement français et la campagne russe de Charles XII, 1706-1709', in: Åselius, G., and Caniart, V., eds., *Quatre siècles de coopération militaire franco-suédoise. Svenskt-franskt militärt samarbete under fyra sekler* (Paris, 2009), 265-82.

_____, 'Le regard de Clio: l'*Histoire de Charles XII* de Voltaire dans une perspective historique', in: *Dix-Huitième Siècle,* 40, 447-68.

_____, 'Les chemins de l'information: la circulation des nouvelles depuis la périphérie européenne jusquau gouvernement français au début du XVIIIe siècle', in: *Revue Historique,* 638, 291-311.

_____, '"Un pied en Allemagne": La diplomatie française et la présence suédoise dans le Nord de l'Empire, 1648-1720', in: Dessberg,

F., and Schnakenbourg, E., eds., *Les horizons de la politique extérieure française. Stratégie diplomatique et militaire dans les régions périphériques et les espaces seconds (XVIe-XXe siècles)* (Bruxelles, 2011), 237-54.

Schnath, G. *Geschichte Hannovers im Zeitalter der Neunten Kur und der englischen Sukzession 1674-1714.* Four vols. (Hildesheim, 1938-82).

Schnettger, M., *Der Spanische Erbfolgekrieg: 1701-1713/14* (München, 2014).

Schoolfield, G.S., *Young Rilke and His Time* (Rochester, NY, 2009).

Schutte, O., *Repertorium der Nederlandse vertegenwoordigers, residerende in het buitenland 1584-1810* ('s-Gravenhage, 1976).

_____, *Repertorium der buitenlandse vertegenwoordigers, residerende in Nederland 1584-1810* ('s-Gravenhage, 1983).

Scott, H., ed., *The Oxford Handbook of Early Modern European History, 1350-1750.* Vol. 1: *Peoples and Places.* Vol. 2: *Cultures and Power* (Oxford, 2015).

Seerup, J., 'Danish and Swedish Flag Disputes in the Channel', in: Rodger, N.A.M., Dancy, J.R., Darnell, B., and Wilson, E., eds., *Strategy and the Sea. Essays in Honour of John B. Hattendorf,* 28-36.

Seitz, H., 'Ett porträtt av Karl XII', in: *Livrustkammaren,* 13, 1973-75.

Selander, I., *Folkrörelsesång* (Stockholm, 1996).

Semenov, A., *Izuchenie istoricheskikh svedenii o rossijskoy vneshney torgovle i promyshlennosti s poliviny XVII-go stoletiya po 1858 god* (3 parts bound in 2 vols., 1859; reprint Newtonville, MA, 1977).

Sevinç, T., 'İsveç Karlı XII. Şarl'ın Osmanlı Devleti'ne İlticası ve İkameti (1709-1714)', in: *History Studies,* Vol. 6, 1 (January 2014), 139-59.

Shafirov, P.P., *Razsuzhdenie, kakie zakonnye prichiny Ego Tsarskoe Velichestvo Petr Pervyi... k nachatiu voiny protiv korolia Karola XII imel...* (St. Petersburg, 1717).

Sidén, K., *Den ideala barndomen. Studier i det stormaktstida barnporträttet* (Stockholm, 2001).

_____, 'Familjeporträttet', in: Cavalli-Björkman, G., ed., *Ansikte mot Ansikte. Porträtt från fem sekel.* Nationalmusei utställningskatalog nr. 626 (Stockholm, 2001).

Simms, B., *Europe. The Struggle for Supremacy: 1453 to the Present* (London, 2013).

Simms, B., and Riotte, T., eds., *The Hanoverian Dimension in British History, 1714-1837*

(Cambridge, 2007).

Sjebaldina, G., 'Karolinernas sibiriska dagböcker – om de egna och de andra,' in: Jonson, L., & Torstendahl Salytjeva, T., eds., *Poltava. Krigsfångar och kulturutbyte* (Stockholm, 2009).

Sjöberg, M., *Kvinnor i fält 1550-1850* (Hedemora & Möklinta, 2008).

Sjöberg, N., 'Några Karl XII-porträtt', in: *Personhistorisk tidskrift,* 1912, 121-23.

Sjöblom, A., 'Historien om ett porträtt', in: *Nationalmusei årsbok,* 1929.

Sjöström, O., *Fraustadt 1706: Ett fält färgat rött* (Lund, 2008).

Skrzetuski, W., *Historia Królestwa Szwedzkiego od panowania Waldemara to jest od roku 1250 aż do roku 1771* (Warszawa, 1792).

Skworoda, P., *Wojny Rzeczypospolitej Obojga Narodów ze Szwecją* (Warszawa, 2007).

Slottman, W.B., *Ferenc II Rákóczi and the Great Powers* (New York, 1997).

*Smärre dikter av Lejonkulans dramatiker,* Noreen, E., ed., Skrifter utg. av Vetenskaps-societeten i Lund 20 (Lund, 1937).

Smid, S., *Der Spanische Erbfolgekrieg: Geschichte eines vergessenen Weltkriegs (1701-1714)* (Köln, 2011).

Snapper, F., 'Veranderingen in de Nederlandse scheepvaart op de Oostzee in de achttiende eeuw', in: *Ondernemende geschiedenis. 22 opstellen aangeboden bij het afscheid van Mr. H. van Riel* ('s-Gravenhage, 1977), 124-39.

Snickare, M., *Enväldets riter: kungliga fester och ceremonier i gestaltning av Nicodemus Tessin den yngre* (Stockholm, 1999).

Snyder, H.L., ed., *The Marlborough-Godolphin Correspondence,* 3 vols. (Oxford, 1975).

_____, 'Communication: The Formulation of Foreign and Domestic Policy in the Reign of Queen Anne: Memoranda by Lord Chancellor Cowper of Conversations with Lord Treasurer Godolphin', in: *The Historical Journal,* XI, 1 (1968), 144-60.

Sörensson, P., 'En fransk ambassadörs omdöme om Karl XII. En bidrag till konungens karaktäristik', in: *Karolinska Förbundets Årsbok* (1910), 314-18.

_____, 'Kejsaren, Sverige och de Nordiska Allierade från Karl XII:s hemkomst från Turkiet till Alliansen i Wien 1719', in: *Karolinska Förbundet Årsbok* (1926), 147-238; (1927), 172-247; (1928), 209-72; (1929), 196-252.

Sokol, A.E., *Das habsburgische Admiralitätswerk des 16. und 17. Jahrhunderts* (Wien, 1977).

Soom, A., *Der baltische Getreidehandel im 17. Jahrhundert* (Stockholm, 1961).

Sowa, A., *Świat ministrów Augusta II. Wartości i poglądy funkcjonujące w kręgu ministrów Rzeczypospolitej w latach 1702-1728* (Kraków, 1995).

Soymonov, F.I., *Istorija Petra Velikogo* (St. Petersburg, 2012).

Spens, E., 'Sjömaktens inflytande på stride nom Vorpommern 1715', in: *Tidskrift I Sjöväsendet* (1939), 288-311.

Spicer, 'The Renaissance Elbow', in: Bremmer, J., and Roodenburg, H., eds., *A Cultural History of Gesture* (Padstow, 1991).

Srbik, H. Ritter von, ed., *Österreichische Staatsverträge: Niederlande,* vol. 1 (Wien, 1912).

Stamp, A.E., 'The Meeting of the Duke of Marlborough and Charles XII at Altranstadt, April 1707', in: *Transactions of the Royal Historical Society,* New Series, XII (1896), 103-16.

Staszewski, J., *August II Mocny* (Wrocław, 1998).

_____, 'Wojny XVIII wieku', in: Stasiewicz, K., Archemczyk, S., eds., *Między barokiem a oświeceniem. Wojny i niepokoje czasów saskich* (Olsztyn, 2004), 7-13.

Steneberg, K.E., *Kristinatidens måleri* (Malmö, 1955).

Stenroth, I., *Sveriges rötter. En nations födelse* (Stockholm, 2005).

Stenström, S., *Arvid Karlsteen. Hans liv och verk* (Göteborg, 1944).

_____, 'Karl XII:s dödsmask och Simon Josse', in: *Livrustkammaren* (1967), 107-46.

Stille, A., *Carl XII:s fälttågsplaner 1707-1709* (Lund, 1908).

Strindberg, A., *Tal till svenska nationen, Folkstaten, Religiös renässans, Tsarens kurir,* Samlade verk 68, Meidal, B., ed. (Stockholm, 1988).

_____, *Karl XII, Engelbrekt,* Samlade verk 47, Ollén, G., ed. (Stockholm, 1993).

Strömbom, S., *Lorens Pasch den yngre* (Stockholm, 1915).

_____, *Svenska kungliga porträtt. 1. Index över svenska porträtt,* 3 (Stockholm, 1943).

Sumner, B.H., *Peter the Great and the Ottoman Empire* (Oxford, 1949).

Süreyya, M., *Sicill-i Osmani* (Istanbul, 1996).

Święcicka E., 'The Collection of Ottoman-Turkish Documents in Sweden', in: Imber, C., ed., *Frontiers of Ottoman Studies,* II (London, 2005), 49-62.

Syveton, G., *Louis XIV et Charles XII au Camp*

de Altranstadt 1707. La mission du Baron de Besenval (Paris, 1900).

_____, 'Louis XIV et Charles XII', in: *Revue d'histoire diplomatique*, 12 (1898), 161-95.

_____, 'Au camp d'Altranstadt. Besenval et Marlborough', in: *Revue d'histoire diplomatique*, 12 (1898), 581-616.

Tängerstad, E., *Fredrik den store och Karl XII som stumfilmshjältar. Produktion och reception av filmerna Fredericus Rex och Karl XII* (Florens, 1997).

Tallett, F., *War and Society in Early-Modern Europe 1495-1715* (London & New York, 1992).

Targosz, K., 'Obraz wojen i zaraz początków XVIII w. w kronikach zakonnic', in: Stasiewicz, K., Archemczyk, S., eds., *Między barokiem a oświeceniem. Wojny i niepokoje czasów saskich* (Olsztyn, 2004), 122-37.

Tarschys, B., *Talis Qualis. Studentpoeten – miljö och idéhistoriska studier* (Stockholm, 1949).

Taylor, D., 'Russian Foreign Policy, 1725-1739: The Politics of Stability and Opportunity'. Unpublished PhD thesis, University of East Anglia, 1983.

Tegnér, E., *Samlade dikter 3: 1817-24*, Böök, F., and Lundquist, Å.K.G., eds., (Lund & Stockholm, 1975).

Thaler, P., 'Erbländische Protestanten und die protestantische Großmacht Schweden im 17. Jahrhundert', in: Wadl, W., ed., *Glaubwürdig bleiben. 500 Jahre protestantisches Abenteuer* (Klagenfurt, 2011), 261-83.

Thanner, L., *Revolutionen i Sverige efter Karl XII:s död. Den inrepolitiska maktkampen under tidigare delen av Ulrika Eleonora d.y:s regering* (Uppsala, 1953).

Thompson. A.C., *Britain, Hanover, and the Protestant Interest, 1688-1756* (Rochester, 2006).

Tomaszewski, D.B., *Nad Konstytucją i rewolucją dnia 3 maja roku 1791 uwagi* (Lwów, 1791).

Torbacke, J., *Carl Grimberg. Ett underbart öde?* (Stockholm, 1993).

Tornquist C.G., *Utkast till svenska flottans sjötåg* (Stockholm, 1788).

Trzoska, J., 'Sprawa kaprów królewskich w Gdańsku w polityce Augusta II i Piotra I (1716-1721)', in: *Rocznik Gdański*, 46 (1986), 23-48.

_____, 'Handel i żegluga gdańska w XVIII wieku', in: Cieślak, E., ed., *Historia Gdańska*, vol. III/1 (Gdańsk, 1993), 357-94.

_____, 'Zmienne koniunktury w handlu i żegludze gdańskiej', in: Cieślak, E., ed., *Historia Gdańska*, vol. III/1 (Gdańsk, 1993), 70-96.

_____, 'Zmiany w handlu bałtyckim i europejskim', in Cieślak, E., ed., *Historia Gdańska*, vol. III/1 (Gdańsk, 1993), 339-56.

_____, 'Gdański handel i żegluga wobec zmiany układu sił w Europie podczas wielkiej wojny północnej', in: *Słupskie Studia Historyczne,*16 (2010), 51-67.

Tuxen, A.P., and With-Seidelin, C.L., *Erobringen af Sveriges tyske Provinser 1715-1716* (Köbenhavn, 1922).

Uddgren, H.E., *Kriget i Finland 1713* (Stockholm, 1906).

_____, *Kriget i Finland 1714* (Stockholm, 1909).

_____, *Karolinen Adam Ludvig Lewenhaupt: hans krigföring i Kurland och Litauen 1703-1708*, 1-2 (Stockholm, 1919-50).

Übersberger, H., *Russlands Orientpolitik in den letzten zwei Jahrhunderten*, vol. 1: *Bis zum Frieden von Jassy* (Stuttgart, 1913).

Unger, G., *Karl XII och Östersjökriget 1715. En sjöhistorisk och strategisk studie* (Stockholm, 1928).

*Uppsala University Art Collections. Painting and Sculpture* (Borås, 2001).

Uppström, R., *Mysteriet Karl XII:s död* (Göteborg, 1994).

Upton, A.F., *Charles XI and Swedish Absolutism* (Cambridge, 1998).

Uzunçarşılı, İ.H., *Osmanlı Tarihi*, IV (Ankara, 2011).

Vassileff, M., *Russisch-französische Politik 1689-1717* (Gotha, 1902).

Veenendaal, A.J., Jr., ed., *De Briefwisseling van Anthonie Heinsius, 1702-1720*, 19 vols. ('s-Gravenhage, 1976-2001).

Veluwenkamp, J.W., *Archangel. Nederlandse ondernemers in Rusland 1550-1785* (Amsterdam, 2000).

_____, 'Dutch Merchants in St. Petersburg in the Eighteenth Century', in: *Tijdschrift voor Skandinavistiek*, 16 (1995), 235-91.

_____, 'The Purchase and Export of Russian Commodities in 1741 by Dutch Merchants Established at Archangel', in: Lesger, C.M., and Noordegraaf, L., eds., *Entrepreneurs and Entrepreneurship in Early Modern Times: Merchants and Industrialists within the Orbit of the Dutch Staple Market* (Den Haag, 1995), 85-101.

_____, 'Die "Sound Toll Registers Online" als Instrument für die Erforschung des frühneuzeitlichen Ostseehandels', in: Rauscher, P., and Serles, A., eds., *Wiegen – Zählen – Registrieren: Handelsgeschichtliche Massenquellen und die Erforschung mitteleuropäischer Märkte (13.-18. Jahrhundert)* (Innsbruck-Wien-Bozen, 2015), 365-84.

Villstrand, N.E., *Sveriges historia 1600–1721* (Stockholm, 2011).

Voltaire, F.M. Arouet de, *Histoire de Charles XII, roi de Suède*, (1731, éd. Leipzig, 1859; éd. Genève 1997); translated by A. Henderson as *The Life of Charles XII, King of Sweden* (London, 1734).

_____, *The History of Charles XII, King of Sweden*. Translated by A. White, with an introduction by R.M. Hatton (London, 1976).

Vozgrin, V.E., *Rossiia i evropeiskie strany v gody Severnoi voiny ( istoriia diplomaticheskikh otnoshenii v 1697-1710 gg.)* (Leningrad, 1986).

Vries, J. de, and Woude, A. van der, *The First Modern Economy: Success, Failure, and Perseverance of the Dutch Economy, 1500-1815* (Cambridge, 1997).

Waddington, A., *Histoire de Prusse*, 2 vols. (Paris, 1922).

Waegemans, E., *De tweede reis van Peter de Grote naar Nederland (1716-1717)* Baltic Studies 13 (Groningen-Antwerpen, [2013]).

Wästberg, P., *Gustaf Adolf Lysholm. Diktare, drömmare, servitör. En biografi* (Stockholm, 2013).

Wallace, D., 'Entrepreneurship and the Russian Textile Industry: From Peter the Great to Catherine the Great', in: *Russian Review*, 54, 1 (1995), 1-25.

Wałęga, S., 'Cudzoziemscy goście w osiemnastowiecznym Toruniu', in: *Rocznik Toruński*, 14 (1979), 261-304

Wallin, J.O., *Dikter 2:1810-1839*, Liedgren, E., and Malmström, S., eds. (Stockholm, 1963).

Wascher, A., 'Die außenpolitischen Beziehungen (1706-1707) zwischen Schweden und Österreich während des Großen Nordischen Krieges'. MA thesis, Universität Graz 1994.

Wennerholm, J.B.R., 'Karl XII och Lanchester - ett bidrag till frågan om den karolinska arméns effektivitet under Stora nordiska kriget', in: *Kungl. Krigsvetenskapsakademiens handlingar och tidskrift*, 202 (1998).

Wensheim, G., *Studier kring freden i Nystad* (Lund, 1973).

Werner, G., *Hjalmar Bergman som filmförfattare*. Skrifter utgivna av Hjalmar Bergman samfundet 1 (Stockholm, 1987), 129-56.

Wernstedt, F., *Kungl. Svea livgardes historia*. Vol. iv, 1660-1718 (Stockholm, 1954).

Westberg, L., 'Den sista striden under stora nordiska kriget. Sundsvall den 15 maj 1721', in: *Karolinska Förbundets Årsbok*, (1990), 94-116.

Westerlund, O., *Karl XII i svensk litteratur från Dahlstierna till Tegnér* (Lund, 1951).

Wetterberg, G., *Från tolv till ett: Arvid Horn (1664-1742)* (Stockholm, 2006).

Whitlocke, B., *A Journal of the Swedish Embassy in the Years 1653 and 1654* (London, 1855).

Whitworth, C., 'Dispatches', in: *Russkoe istoricheskoe obshchestvo sbornik*, 39 (1884); 50 (1886); 61 (1888).

Widéen, A., 'Mynt- och medaljbilder från 1600-talet hämtade från kopparstick', in: *Nordisk Numismatisk Årsbok*, 1954.

Widén, P., *Från kungligt galleri till nationellt museum. Aktörer, praktik och argument i svensk konstmuseal diskurs ca 1814-1845* (Hedemora, 2009).

Wijn, J.W., *Het Staatsche Leger*. VIII, Het Tijdperk van de Spaansche Successieoorlog 1702-1715, 3 vols. ('s-Gravenhage, 1956-64).

Wijnne, J.A., ed., *Négociations de Monsieur le comte d'Avaux*, 3 vols. (Utrecht, 1882-1883).

Williams, B., *Stanhope: A Study in Eighteenth Century War and Diplomacy* (Oxford, 1932).

Wilson, P.H., *German Armies: War and German Politics, 1648-1806* (London, 1998).

_____, 'New Approaches under the Old Regime', in: Mortimer, G., ed., *Early Modern Military History 1450-1815* (New York, 2004).

Wimmer, J., *Wojsko Rzeczypospolitej w dobie wojny północnej (1700-1717)* (Warszawa, 1956).

Wintle, M., *An Economic and Social History of the Netherlands, 1800-1920: Demographic, Economic and Social Transition* (Cambridge, 2000).

Wittram, R., *Peter I., Czar und Kaiser. Zur Geschichte Peters des Grossen in seiner Zeit*, 2 vols. (Göttingen, 1964).

Wolf, J.B., *The Emergence of the Great Powers, 1685-1715* (New York, 1951).

Wolf, J.R., ed., *1707-2007. Altranstädter Konvention. Ein Meilenstein religiöser Toleranz in Europa* (Halle, 2008).

Wolff, L., *Inventing Eastern Europe: The Map of Civilization on the Mind of the Enlightenment* (Stanford, 1994).

Yüksel, S., 'Rusların Karadeniz Yönünde Yapmış Oldukları İlk Yayılma Faaliyetleri (18. Yüzyılın Başlarına Kadar)', in: *SDÜ Fen Edebiyat Fakültesi Sosyal Bilimler Dergisi*, 28, (Nisan, 2013), 101-16.

Zander, U., *Fornstora dagar, moderna tider. Bruk av och debatter om svensk historia från sekelskifte till sekelskifte* (Lund, 2001).

Zawadzki, K., *Początki prasy polskiej. Gazety ulotne i seryjne XVI-XVIII wieku. Bibliografia*, vol. I (Wrocław, 1977).

Zernack, K., 'Imperiale Politik und merkantiler Hintergrund. Ein Dokument der schwedischen Rußlandpolitik im 17. Jahrhundert', in: Zernack, K., *Nordosteuropa: Skizzen und Beiträge zu einer Geschichte der Ostseeländer* (Lüneburg, 1993), 133-55.

_____, 'Handelsbeziehungen und Gesandtschaftsverkehr im Ostseeraum. Voraussetzungen und Grundzüge der Anfänge des ständigen Gesandtschaftswesens in Nord- und Osteuropa', in: Zernack, *Nordosteuropa*, 81-104.

_____, 'Schweden als europäische Großmacht der frühen Neuzeit', in: Zernack, *Nordosteuropa*, 203-28.

_____, 'Virtus politica im Militärstaat – Strukturprobleme der schwedischen Großmachtzeit', in: Zernack, *Nordosteuropa*, 229-44.

Zimmermann, F., 'Der Schweden Durchzug durch Siebenbürgen um das Jahr 1714', in: *Archiv des Vereins für siebenbürgische Landeskunde*, N.S. 17 (1883), 291-337.

Zinkeisen, J.W., *Osmanlı İmparatorluğu Tarihi*, V (Istanbul, 2011).

Zwierzykowski, M., 'Konsekwencje ustrojowe wielkiej wojny północnej dla Rzeczypospolitej', in: Dybaś, B., ed., *Wojny północne w XVI-XVIII wieku* (Toruń, 2007), 259-67.

# Reference Notes

## Introduction

[1] Hattendorf, Veenendaal, and Van Hövell, eds., *Marlborough*.

[2] Voltaire, *Charles XII* (1976), 29.

[3] Hatton, 'Introduction' to Voltaire, *Charles XII* (1976), 25.

[4] Johnson, *Complete Poems*, 88. Also printed in Hatton, *Charles XII of Sweden*, xiv-xv; Hatton, *Karl XII*, 19.

[5] Hattendorf, 'Charles XII,' 90.

[6] Hatton, *Charles XII of Sweden and Karl XII av Sverige*.

[7] Norberg, 'Inledning,' in Karlsson, et al., *Karl XII och svenskarna i Osmanska riket*, 18-19 and *passim*.

[8] Kivelson, 'The Cartographical Emergence of Europe?,' 55, based on Wolff, *Inventing Eastern Europe*, 148, 156-57, 166.

## 1 The Great Northern War (1700-21) and the Integration of the European States System

[1] I am grateful to Professor John Hattendorf, Dr. Derek McKay, and Baron Rolof van Hövell tot Westerflier, who all made helpful comments on a draft of this essay. During the period under review, Britain, Russia, and Sweden were following the Julian calendar. This was ten days behind the rest of the continent in the Swedish case and eleven for the other two countries. In the footnotes, such dates are designated O.S. [Old Style], while other dates are N.S. [New Style]. In the text itself, all dates are given in the New Style.

[2] His 'Instructions', dated 20 and 30 January 1707 N.S. are in *Recueil . . . Suède*, 217-46; on his mission, see more generally Syveton, *Louis XIV et Charles XII*, and Klopp, *Der Fall des Hauses Stuart*, XII, 368-82. Besenval took over when the diplomat originally named, Louis Gaspard de Ricous, was unable to travel because of illness. Count Erik Sparre, a Swede in French service, had been sent as an unofficial envoy with the same aim earlier in 1707, but his mission had had little impact: Hatton, *Charles XII*, 223.

[3] Besenval's 'Instructions', 226 ff and 236 ff.

[4] Frost, *The Northern Wars*, 226-300, is now the best brief anglophone account.

[5] Schnakenbourg, *La France, le Nord et l'Europe*, 281.

[6] Syveton, *Louis XIV et Charles XII*, 81.

[7] For French policy, see the major study by Schnakenbourg, *La France, le Nord et l'Europe*.

[8] Hatton, *Charles XII*, 224-27, provides a brief account.

[9] Snyder, *Marlborough-Godolphin Correspondence*, 738-45, and Lamberty, *Mémoires*, IV, 432-39, for the duke's travel difficulties: he was unable to cross over from England to the continent due to contrary winds. Guillaume de Lamberty was an 'Agent and Correspondent' (that is to say he reported on events but did not handle significant negotiations) of the electorate of Hanover in the Dutch Republic between 1706 and 1718: Bittner, *Repertorium*, I, 76; Schutte, *Buitenlandse vertegenwoordigers*, 297.

[10] Van 't Hoff, *The Correspondence*, 302. For the relationship between the two men, see Augustus J. Veenendaal, Jr., 'Marlborough and Anthonie Heinsius', in Hattendorf, Veenendaal, and Van Hövell tot Westerflier, *Marlborough: Soldier and Diplomat*, 172-91.

[11] Ostwald, 'Marlborough and Siege Warfare', in Hattendorf, Veenendaal, and Van Hövell tot Westerflier, *Marlborough: Soldier and Diplomat*, 122-43, is a valuable introduction.

[12] Snyder, *Marlborough-Godolphin Correspondence*, 668.

[13] *Ibidem*, 702, n. 4; Van 't Hoff, *The Correspondence*, 265. For the war in the Empire, see Bernhard R. Kroener, '"The only thing that could save the Empire"', in Hattendorf, Veenendaal, and Van Hövell tot Westerflier, *Marlborough: Soldier and Diplomat*, 216-48.

[14] This has recently been highlighted in a major study by Brendan Simms, *Europe: The Struggle for Supremacy*, 66, 69, and *passim*.

[15] Schnakenbourg, *La France, le Nord et l'Europe*, 12-13.

[16] Treaty of 26 September 1701 O.S./7 October 1701 N.S.: Snyder, *Marlborough-Godolphin Correspondence*, 36, n. 2. The Treaty is printed in Parry, *Consolidated Treaty Series*, XXIV, 29-31.

[17] Schnakenbourg, *La France, le Nord et l'Europe*, 66-67.

[18] There are accounts of his mission in Snyder, *Marlborough-Godolphin Correspondence*, 757-65; Klopp, *Der Fall des Hauses Stuart*, XII, 383-90; and Murray, *Letters and Dispatches*, III, 357-59. Voltaire, in his *History of Charles XII*, which was partly based upon interviews with surviving contemporaries, unearthed the story of the map of Russia on Charles XII's table, and it was then endorsed by the duke's first important English biographer, Thomas Lediard, who had actually accompanied Marlborough on his journey to Saxony: *The Life of John, Duke of Marlborough*, I, 463; for the mission to Altranstädt, *ibidem*, I, 453-72. See also Rothstein, *Peter the Great and Marlborough*, 75.

[19] This agreement is not mentioned or even hinted at in any of the British documents on the mission, but it was revealed by the king to his confidant, the Swedish officer Axel von Löwen (1686-1772), during an extended series of conversations when he visited Charles XII in spring 1712, during the king's exile in the Ottoman Empire, and it is credited by his most authoritative modern biographer: Adler, *Die Erinnerungen Axel von Löwens*, especially 36-40; Hatton, *Charles XII*, 225. For the career of Axel von Löwen, see Adler, *Die Erinnerungen Axel von Löwens*, 5-16.

[20] Snyder, *Marlborough-Godolphin Correspondence*, 1322 [written before news of Poltava was confirmed], 1331, 1334, 1343-44, and *passim*.

[21] Quoted by Rothstein, *Peter the Great and Marlborough*, 123.

[22] Van 't Hoff, *The Correspondence*, 467 (24 August 1709 N.S.).

[23] See the letters exchanged between Marlborough

and Heinsius in the early weeks of 1710: Van 't Hoff, *The Correspondence*, 469-82.

[24] Van 't Hoff, *The Correspondence*, 459, 467, 468, 469, 472, 475, 479, 480.

[25] It is printed in Parry, *Consolidated Treaty Series*, XXVI, 449-55; there is another copy, with helpful commentary, in Srbik, *Österreichische Staatsverträge, Niederlande*, I, 391-400; Lamberty, *Mémoires*, VI, 283-320 *passim*, is interesting on the negotiations, which were complex and prolonged, and has inside information derived from his position as a semi-official Hanoverian diplomat in The Hague; Hatton, *Charles XII*, 327, and Wittram, *Peter I.*, II, 221-25, are among the very few scholars who have appreciated the agreement's wider significance.

[26] Hatton, *Charles XII*, 331.

[27] Rothstein, *Peter the Great and Marlborough*, 143, 145.

[28] Hatton, *Charles XII*, 225 and n. 67, 329.

[29] Chance, *BDI . . . Denmark*, 27.

[30] This is clear from Van 't Hoff, *The Correspondence*, 467, 469, 472, 479-80; see also Lamberty, *Mémoires*, V, 442-43; VI, 297 ff.

[31] Lamberty, *Mémoires*, V, 442; VI, 283-84.

[32] Wilson, *German Armies*, 137 ff and ch. 5 *passim*.

[33] Lamberty, *Mémoires*, VI, 285; the Dutch declaration of December 1709 is printed in *ibidem*, V, 442-43; that of the Imperial Diet in January 1710 is in *ibidem*, VI, 285-86.

[34] Parry, *Consolidated Treaty Series*, XXVI, 452.

[35] *Ibidem*, 493-98.

[36] Van 't Hoff, *The Correspondence*, 507.

[37] Schnakenbourg, *La France, le Nord et l'Europe*, 93.

[38] Simultaneously the allies approached the Swedish Regency with a proposal that the troops in Pomerania should be hired by them and integrated into the army which was fighting France, but nothing came of this idea.

[39] His 'Instructions', dated 11 January 1711 O.S., are printed in Chance, *BDI . . . Sweden I*, 47-50. Jefferyes (1679/80-1739) had been born and brought up in Sweden and so had a good command of Swedish. Biographical information can be found in Hatton, *Letters from the Swedish Army*, 2-32; his necessarily intermittent letters during the mission to the Swedish

king are printed in Carlson, *Kapten Jefferyes bref till Engelska Regeringen*: see 1-17.

[40] Carlson, *Kapten Jefferyes bref*, 6.

[41] Quoted by Rothstein, *Peter the Great and Marlborough*, 183.

[42] Hatton, 'Charles XII and the Great Northern War', 671; Chance, *BDI . . . Sweden I*, 54-55.

[43] Aksan, *Ottoman Wars*, 90-98; Wittram, *Peter I.*, II, 224-25.

[44] Lamberty, *Mémoires*, VI, 314-15, 452.

[45] *Ibidem*, 442-43. Russia was represented by one of its most experienced diplomats, A.A. Matveev, in the Dutch Republic.

[46] E.g., Snyder, *Marlborough-Godolphin Correspondence*, 1600, 1621, 1641, 1667; Van 't Hoff, *The Correspondence*, 525-26; Lamberty, *Mémoires*, VI, 442-43.

[47] There are brief accounts of the final phase in McKay, *Rise of the Great Powers*, 86-93, and Hatton, *George I*, 184-92, 235-42; more detailed studies of importance include Hatton, *Charles XII*, 383-494 *passim*; Nordmann, *La crise du Nord*; and Wittram, *Peter I.*, II, 253-345, 406-74. Only the briefest outline is provided here.

[48] Schnakenbourg, *La France, le Nord et l'Europe*, 117-254, is an informative study of French policy during the war's final phase.

[49] Mediger, *Mecklenburg, Rußland und England-Hannover*, is a masterly examination of this issue.

[50] Mancall, *Russia and China*.

[51] Compare, e.g., the 'Instructions for the Sieur de Baluze', 28 September 1702, with those for M. de Campredon, 25 August 1721, for a French assessment of the scale of the transformation: *Recueil . . . Russie*, I, 94-99 and 233-45.

[52] Figures from Hartley, 'Changing Perspectives', in Hughes, *Peter the Great*, 61.

[53] 'Instructions for the Marquis de Monti', 5 May 1729, *Recueil . . . Pologne*, II, 2-3.

[54] Wittram, *Peter I.*, II, 315-20, and Schnakenbourg, *La France, le Nord et l'Europe*, 475-554, for the visit; *Recueil . . . Russie*, I, 170-95 *passim*, sets out the French attitude.

[55] E.g,. The 'Instructions' for the Marquis de Bonnac, 30 May 1716, *Recueil . . . Turquie*, 212-55, esp. 212, 235; 'Instructions' for the

Marquis de Châteauneuf, 5 January 1717, *Recueil . . . Russie*, I, 138-43; 'Instructions' for the Comte de la Marck, 7 March 1717, *Recueil . . . Suède*, 278-96, esp. 278, 281.

[56] Droste, *Im Dienst der Krone*, 84.

[57] Bohlen, 'Changes', *passim*.

[58] Bittner, *Repertorium*, I, 431-32, 434-47, 439-45, and *passim*; Anderson, *Rise*, 70-71. Simultaneously Poland-Lithuania underwent a similar evolution, though the personal union with Saxony added a distinctive twist. The number of permanent missions doubled in little more than a decade: from 16 in 1709 to 32 by 1723. These were not primarily conducted by diplomats from Poland-Lithuania itself, however. The first Saxon king quite consciously ran down the kingdom's diplomatic service, which conducted only relations with the Ottoman Empire together with frequent short-term embassies to Russia, and instead employed the electorate's foreign service to conduct the kind of expansive policy expected of a monarchy. Expenditure on diplomacy provides the best guide to this change: spending on the Polish-Lithuanian foreign service fell by over 70 per cent in a generation, from 340,000 zlotys (1697-1703) to 160,000 (1703-17), and finally to 92,000 (1717-33). By contrast, that on Saxon diplomacy increased by more than tenfold over the same period, from just under 15,000 thalers (1699) to 158,000 thalers by the time of Augustus II's death (1733). This meant that by the final decade of his reign, Saxony-Poland had a network of permanent embassies which rivaled that of most leading European powers. Augustus II's political ambitions were only slightly lowered by the reality of his subordination to Russian control. See Labuda and Michowicz, *History of Polish Diplomacy*, 247-67.

[59] Grabar, *History of International Law*, 40, 47, 51, and *passim*; Altbauer, 'Diplomats', 7.

[60] Altbauer, 'Diplomats', *passim*; Taylor, 'Russian Foreign Policy', 10-20.

[61] Dixon, *Modernisation*, 28.

[62] *Le cérémonial diplomatique des cours de l'Europe*, published as vols. 4 and 5 of [Jean Dumont], *Corps Universel Diplomatique du Droit de Gens: Supplément*, here V, 389 ff, 535 ff, 623 ff, 729 ff.

## 2 Charles XII: A Biographical Sketch

\* Professor Karlsson usually adheres to the Swedish calendar in her scholarly work. She has kindly agreed to use New Style dates in the present chapter.

1 This account of Charles XII's childhood is drawn primarily from Hatton, *Charles XII*, and Carlquist, 'Karl XII:s ungdom och första regeringsår'.

2 *Karl XI:s almanacksanteckningar*, 85. All translations are the author's own.

3 For Queen Hedvig Eleonora, see Karlsson, 'Hedvig Eleonora—kulturmecenat och landsmoder'.

4 *Karl XI:s almanacksanteckningar*, 150.

5 Carlquist, 'Karl XII:s ungdom', 46.

6 *Ibidem*, 46 ff., quote at 51.

7 *Ibidem*, 53, quoting the prince's curriculum.

8 *Karl XI:s almanacksanteckningar*, 298-99.

9 *Ibidem*.

10 Bergström, 'En maskeradbal på Stockholms slott 1692'.

11 For the coronation, see Snickare, *Enväldets riter*.

12 For the planned marriage, see Hatton, *Charles XII*.

13 Charles XII to Hedvig Eleonora, 14 December 1712, in Carlson, ed., *Karl XII:s egenhändiga bref*.

14 For Charles XII's first years on the throne, see Carlquist, 'Karl XII:s ungdom', 71 ff.

15 See the chapters by Åselius, Kuvaja, and Ericson Wolke in this volume.

16 See Lennersand's chapter in this volume.

17 Jonasson, *Karl XII och hans rådgivare*, 138 ff.

18 For the reforms and financial measures, see Karlsson, *Den jämlike undersåten: Karl XII:s förmögenhetsbeskattning 1713*.

19 For Feif, see Hildebrand, *Svenskt biografiskt lexicon*, xv, s.v. 'Casten Feif'.

20 Feif to Nicodemus Tessin, 27 April 1711, in Brinkman and Andersson, eds., *Handlingar*, I.

21 For the Chancery ordinances and the Principal Secretary, see Karlsson, 'Kungens intresse och undersåtarnas välfärd'.

22 *Idem, Den jämlike undersåten*.

23 For Charles XII's views on the east, see *idem*, 'Familjen Celsing och de svensk-osmanska relationerna under 1700–talet'.

24 For a detailed discussion, see Uppström, *Mysteriet Karl XII:s död*, and From, *Karl XII:s död: gåtans lösning*.

25 Thanner, *Revolutionen i Sverige efter Karl XII:s död*.

26 Voltaire, *The Life of Charles XII*, 161.

27 Strindberg, *Tal till svenska nationen*.

## 3 Charles XII as a Protagonist in International Perspective: An Overview

1 Upton, *Charles XI and Swedish Absolutism*, 260. See also Rystad, *Karl XI*, 240-79.

2 Except where otherwise noted, this and the following sections are based largely on Hatton, 'Charles XII and the Great Northern War', 648-80.

3 *Ibidem*, 661-62.

4 Many authors traditionally refer to this event as having taken place at Bender, but, in fact it took place at Varnitza (Varniţa), where Charles XII lived, 3-4 kilometers outside of Bender and a suburb of modern-day Bender (Tighina) in Moldova.

5 Bengt Liljegren, 'Kalabaliken I Varnitsen', in Karlsson, et al., *Svenskarna i Osmanska Riket*, 89-105.

6 Hatton, *George I*, 238-42.

7 Hatton, 'Louis XII and His Fellow Monarchs', 30.

8 Frost, 'Monarchy in Northern and Eastern Europe', 407.

## 4 Swedish Grand Strategy and Foreign Policy, 1697-1721

\* Professor Åselius usually adheres to the Swedish calendar in his scholarly work. He has kindly agreed to use New Style dates in the present chapter.

1 Villstrand, *Sveriges historia*, 32.

2 Lindegren, 'Karl XII', 180.

3 Fryxell, *Berättelser*; Carlson, *Sveriges historia*, 6-7; *ibidem*, 8.

4 Rappe, 'Karl XII:s plan', 321-44; Hjärne, *Karl XII*; Stille, *Carl XII:s fälttågsplaner*; Bring, *Karl XII*; Generalstaben, *Karl XII*.

5 Nordensvan, *Karl XII*; Munthe, *Karl XII*; for a recent analysis of perceptions of Charles XII, see Oredsson, 'Karl XII och det svenska stormaktsväldets fall'; *idem*, 'Livskraften'.

6 Artéus, 'Individ och kollektiv', 154.

7 Peterson, *Peter the Great's Administrative and Judicial Reforms*.

8 Kennedy, *Rise and Fall*, 99; for the Danish population, see Villstrand, *Sveriges historia*, 375.

9 Villstrand, *Sveriges historia*, 423-26.

10 Braudel, *Vardagslivets strukturer*, 49.

11 Gadd, *Det svenska jordbrukets historia*, 26.

12 Villstrand, *Sveriges historia*, 381-82.

13 Rosén, *Den svenska utrikespolitikens historia*, 51.

14 Heckscher, 'De europeiska staternas finanser', 57 n. 1.

15 Kennedy, *Rise and Fall*, 99.

16 Cavallie, *Från fred till krig*.

17 Glete, *Navies and Nations*, 241-44.

18 Landberg, *Den svenska utrikespolitikens historia*, 213-61; Jespersen, 'Rivalry without End', 163-64.

19 Landberg, *Den svenska utrikespolitikens*, 250-52; Jonasson, *Karl XII och hans rådgivare*, 112-20.

20 Rosén, *Den svenska utrikespolitikens*, 63-67.

21 Asker, '"En nation som man bör visa tänderna"', 313-16; Rosén, *Den svenska utrikespolitikens*, 67-70.

22 Jonasson, *Karl XII och hans rådgivare*, 168-99.

23 The Swedish plans as described by Quartermaster-General Carl Magnus Stuart to Chancellor Bengt Oxenstierna in June 1701 (published in Rosen, *Bidrag till kännedom*, 10 n. 6).

24 Jonasson, *Karl XII; idem, Karl XII:s polska politik*.

25 Hjärne, *Karl XII*; Frost, *The Northern Wars*,

280-82.

26 Jonasson, 'Karl XII:s baltiska militärpolitik'.

27 Rosén, *Den svenska utrikespolitikens*, 108-11, quote at 111.

28 Quoted in Ericson Wolke, 'Riga 1710', 314.

29 Quoted in Rosen, *Bidrag till kännedom*, vol. 1, 119.

30 An argument found in both Munthe, *Karl XII*, and Rosen, *Bidrag till kännedom*, vols. 1 and 2.

31 Uddgren, *Karolinen Adam Ludvig Lewenhaupt*.

32 The standard positions are adopted by Carlson, 'Karl XII:s ryska fälttågsplan', and Stille, *Carl XII:s fälttågsplaner*, for example.

33 Frost, *The Northern Wars*, 288.

34 The best account of Lybecker's invasion of Ingria is still Hjelmqvist, *Kriget i Finland*, while our understanding of Lewenhaupt's campaign and the Battle of Lesnaya has recently been nuanced by Konovalchuk and Lyth, *Vägen till Poltava*.

35 Carlson, *Karl XII:s egenhändiga bref*, 363.

36 Ericson Wolke, 'Mellan Poltava och Tönningen', 45-71.

37 The leading study of the Baltic conquest from a Swedish perspective is Arwidsson, *Försvaret*.

38 Rosén, *Den svenska utrikespolitikens*, 119-24; Wetterberg, *Från tolv till ett*, 168.

39 Ahlström, *Arvid Horn*; Wetterberg, *Från tolv till ett*, 180-88.

40 Artéus, 'Individ och kollektiv', 158-59.

41 Kuvaja, *Försörjning*.

42 For the conquest of Finland, see Uddgren, *Kriget i Finland 1713*, and idem, *Kriget i Finland 1714*.

43 Rosén, *Den svenska utrikespolitikens*, 127-28, 133-34.

44 For British naval activity in the Baltic, see Aldridge, *Admiral Sir John Norris*.

45 Rosén, *Den svenska utrikespolitikens*, 135-57.

46 Lindegren, 'Karl XII', 209-11.

47 Wensheim, *Studier*.

48 Jägerskiöld, *Den svenska utrikespolitikens historia*, 100.

49 Oredsson, 'Karl XII', 69; cf. idem, 'Karl XII och det svenska stormaktsväldets fall', 304.

# 5 Charles XII's Armies in the Field

*Professor Kuvaja usually adheres to the Swedish calendar in his scholarly work. He has kindly agreed to use New Style dates in the present chapter.

1 Lindegren, 'Karl XII', 181.

2 Artéus, 'Individ och kollektiv, metodik och geografi', 170.

3 Lindegren, 'Karl XII', 182, 185. See also Grauers, 'Den karolinska fälthärens underhåll 1700-1703', 111.

4 See Van Creveld, *Supplying war*; Lynn, *Feeding Mars*; Kuvaja, *Försörjning av en ockupationsarmé*; Hårdstedt, *Om krigets förutsättningar*; Jääskeläinen, *Paikallisyhteisö resurssina ja tuhojen kohteena*.

5 Lindegren, 'Karl XII', 186-87.

6 Kuvaja, *Försörjning av en ockupationsarmé*, 2-3; Forrest, 'The Logistics of Revolutionary War in France', 178-79.

7 Van Creveld, *Supplying War*, 6-8; Tallett, *War and Society in Early-modern Europe 1495-1715*, 55; Korkiakangas, *Kaarle XII:n kenttäarmeijan huolto sotaretkellä vuosina 1700-1701. mannereurooppalaisten näkökulmasta*, 23-24, 406-10; Parker, *The Military Revolution*, 75-76; Perjés, 'Army Provisioning, Logistics and Strategy in the Second Half of the 17th Century', 12-17; Lynn, *Women, Armies and Warfare in Early Modern Europe*, 27-28; Jones, *The Art of War in the Western World*, 273.

8 Korkiakangas, *Kaarle XII:n kenttäarmeijan huolto sotaretkellä vuosina 1700-1701*, 193, 409-10; Grauers, 'Den karolinska fälthärens underhåll 1700-1703', 116-17.

9 Ostwald, 'Marlborough and Siege Warfare', 124-25.

10 Von Clausewitz, *Om kriget*, 380-87; Keegan, *Krigets historia*, 348-51; Tallett, *War and Society*, 37, 53.

11 Kuvaja, *Karolinska krigare 1660-1721*, 130, 133-34, 237.

12 Von Clausewitz, *Om kriget*, 300, 303-04, 311; Tallet, *War and Society*, 121; Laidre, *Segern vid Narva*, 134-35; *Svenska slagfält*, 302.

13 Artéus, *Karolinsk och europeisk stridstaktik*, 29-31, 42-43, 50-52, 62-63, 111; Black, *European Warfare 1600-1815*, 38-41; Tallett, *War and Society*, 22-23, 30-31; Keegan, *Krigets historia*, 366-67, 370; Wilson, 'New Approaches under the Old Regime', 140-42; Hellie, 'The Petrine Army: Continuity, Change, and Impact', 239-40; Balisch, 'Infantry Battlefield Tactics in the Seventeenth and Eighteenth Centuries', 216-18.

14 Artéus, 'Individ och kollektiv, metodik och geografi', 168-69; Larsson, *Stormaktens sista krig*, 69.

15 Van Creveld, *Supplying War*, 24; Lynn, *Women, Armies and Warfare*, 27-28; Perjés, 'Army Provisioning, Logistics and Strategy', 14; Korkiakangas, *Kaarle XII:n kenttäarmeijan huolto sotaretkellä vuosina*, 57, 413-15; Jones, *The Art of War*, 215-16.

16 Eriksson, *Karolinen Magnus Stenbock*, 157.

17 Lynn, *Women, Armies and Warfare*, 12-14, 35-36, 118-26. See also Sjöberg, *Kvinnor i fält 1550-1850*.

18 Englund, *Poltava*, 261.

19 Childs, *Armies and Warfare in Europe*, 103, 160; Jones, *The Art of War*, 252; Anderson, *War and Society in Europe of the Old Regime 1618-1789*, 43; Lindegren, 'Karl XII', 185-86.; Lynn, *Feeding Mars*, 105, 139-42; Perjés, 'Army Provisioning, Logistics and Strategy', 17-18.

20 Van Creveld, *Supplying War*, 17, 20-21, 26-27; Korkiakangas, *Kaarle XII:n kenttäarmeijan huolto sotaretkellä vuosina*, 44-45, 48, 210-11; Jääskeläinen, *Paikallisyhteisö resurssina ja tuhojen kohteena*, 63–64; Hårdstedt, *Om krigets förutsättningar*, 58-59; Childs, *Armies and Warfare*, 113-14; Tallett, *War and Society*, 63-65. Redlich, 'De praeda militari', 63; Jones, *The Art of War*, 256; Perjés, 'Army Provisioning, Logistics and Strategy', 27-28.

21 Lynn, *Women, Armies and Warfare*, 27-28; Kuvaja, *Försörjning av en ockupationsarmé*, 47-48; Perjés, 'Army Provisioning, Logistics and Strategy', 14-15, 17-19; Parker, *The Military Revolution*, 76; Jones, *The Art of War*, 273.

22 Perjés, 'Army Provisioning, Logistics and Strategy', 10-11, 16, 44-45; Black, *A Military Revolution?*, 36-37; Black, *European Warfare 1600-1815*, 36-37; Korkiakangas, *Kaarle XII:n kenttäarmeijan huolto sotaretkellä vuosina*, 27, 45, 49, 293-95; Van Creveld, *Supplying War*, 19, 27.

23 Gutmann, *War and Rural Life in the Early Modern Low Countries*, 41, 69, 78; Lynn, *Women, Armies and Warfare*, 19-27, 30-32, 146; Childs, *Armies and Warfare in Europe*, 28-30, 150-58, 165-66, 172-73; Tallett, *War and Society*, 55-56, 76-77; Redlich, 'De praeda militari', 20-24, 58-59, 72-77; Jones, *The Art*

*of War*, 217-19, 252-54; Anderson, *War and Society*, 46-48, 54, 67-68, 137-38; Korkiakangas, *Kaarle XII:n kenttäarmeijan huolto sotaretkellä vuosina*, 18, 21-22; Black, *A Military Revolution?*, 45-46.

[24] Gutmann, *War and Rural Life*, 41-42, 62-64; Black, *A Military Revolution?*, 17; Lynn, *Women, Armies and Warfare*, 32-33; Redlich, 'De praeda militari', 45-48, 66-68; Jones, *The Art of War*, 215-16; Redlich, 'Contributions in the Thirty Years War', 251-52.

[25] Gutmann, *War and Rural Life*, 130; Childs, *Armies and Warfare*, 160; Tallett, *War and Society*, 159-60.

[26] Grauers, 'Den karolinska fälthärens underhåll 1700-1703', 119-20.

[27] Korkiakangas, *Kaarle XII:n kenttäarmeijan huolto sotaretkellä vuosina*, 149, 173-74, 215, 291, 420; Grauers, 'Den karolinska fälthärens underhåll 1700-1703', 119, 124-25; Grauers, 'Svensk och polsk krigsmakt', 22.

[28] Grauers, 'Den karolinska fälthärens underhåll 1700-1703', 126–27; *idem*, 'Den karolinska fälthärens underhåll 1704-1707', 110-11, 120-21; *idem*, 'Svensk och polsk krigsmakt', 24; Eriksson, *Karolinen Magnus Stenbock*, 127-28.

[29] Grauers, 'Den karolinska fälthärens underhåll 1700-1703', 133-35, 138-40; Marklund, *Stenbock*, 147-48, 167.

[30] Eriksson, *Karolinen Magnus Stenbock*, 115-23; Grauers, 'Den karolinska fälthärens underhåll 1700-1703', 136-37; *idem*, 'Svensk och polsk krigsmakt', 27; Sjöström, *Fraustadt 1706*, 44-46; Marklund, *Stenbock*, 149-56; Frost, *The Northern Wars*, 282-83.

[31] Eriksson, *Karolinen Magnus Stenbock*, 139-40;

Marklund, *Stenbock*, 156-60.

[32] Grauers, 'Den karolinska fälthärens underhåll 1704-1707', 118-19, 122-41.

[33] *Idem*, 'Den karolinska fälthärens underhåll 1700-1703', 140; Frost, *The Northern Wars*, 282.

[34] Eriksson, *Karolinen Magnus Stenbock*, 131, 139.

[35] Moltusov, *Poltava – vändpunkten*, 15-19, 21-22; Englund, *Poltava*, 34; Porfiriev, *Peter I*, 184-85.

[36] Liljegren, *Karl XII*, 151.

[37] From, *Katastrofen vid Poltava*, 79-80, 125-27; Liljegren, *Karl XII*, 153; Porfiriev, *Peter I*, 187-90.

[38] Rekola, *Lewenhauptin retkikunta vuonna 1708*, 48, 55-59, 71, 74, 92, 152-56, 160-61, 167; *Svenska slagfält*, 287-91; Konovaltjuk and Lyth, *Vägen till Poltava*, 32, 71-72, 202, 233.

[39] Liljegren, *Karl XII*, 155-59; Englund, *Poltava*, 37-39.

[40] From, *Katastrofen vid Poltava*, 202-05; Liljegren, *Karl XII*, 161-63; Porfiriev, *Peter I*, 198.

[41] From, *Katastrofen vid Poltava*, 223-25, 235, 240-41, 244-56, 260-63; Moltusov, *Poltava – vändpunkten*, 26, 29-33; Liljegren, *Karl XII*, 163-70; Englund, *Poltava*, 43-45; Porfiriev, *Peter I*, 198-99, 206, 209-12, 216.

[42] From, *Katastrofen vid Poltava*, 252.

[43] Kuvaja, *Karolinska krigare*, 35, 196, 202.

[44] Lund, *War for the Every Day*, 84-85.

[45] Sources for tables: Liljegren, *Karl XII*; From, *Katastrofen vid Poltava*; Marklund, *Stenbock*; Eriksson, *Karolinen Magnus Stenbock*; *Svenska*

*slagfält*; Kuvaja, *Karolinska krigare*.

[46] Kuvaja, *Karolinska krigare*, 130-37.

[47] *Ibidem*, 163-64, 203-05, 209-10, 234-35.

[48] Moltusov, *Poltava – vändpunkten*, 10-12, Marklund, *Stenbock*, 126.

[49] From, *Katastrofen vid Poltava*, 180-81.

[50] Eriksson, *Karolinen Magnus Stenbock*, 98, 108-09, 139-40; Liljegren, *Karl XII*, 112-13; From, *Katastrofen vid Poltava*, 186-88, 246.

[51] Larsson, *Stormaktens sista krig*, 145.

[52] Lindegren, 'Karl XII', 189-95; Grauers, 'Den karolinska fälthärens underhåll 1704-1707', 121.

[53] Perlestam, 'Logistiska uppdrag och strider', 71, 91-92; Marklund, *Stenbock*, 120-21; Lund, *War for the Every Day*, 73-76.

[54] Liljegren, *Karl XII*, 139.

[55] Eriksson, *Karolinen Magnus Stenbock*, 204-05, 270-71.

[56] Artéus, 'Individ och kollektiv, metodik och geografi', 161-62; Kuvaja, *Karolinska krigare*, 182; Frost, *The Northern Wars*, 276.

[57] Artéus, *Karolinsk och europeisk stridstaktik*, 36-41, 48-49, 56-60, 67-71, 112-13; *idem*, 'Individ och kollektiv, metodik och geografi', 165-69; Wennerholm, 'Karl XII och Lanchester'; Frost, *The Northern Wars*, 273-75.

[58] Kuvaja, *Karolinska krigare*, 182-83.

[59] Frost, *The Northern Wars*, 283.

## 6 Swedish Naval Power and Naval Operations, 1697-1721

\* Professor Ericson Wolke usually adheres to the Swedish calendar in his scholarly work. He has kindly agreed to use New Style dates in the present chapter.

[1] This essay is based on my book, *Sjöslag och rysshärjningar* (sea battles and Russian ravages), which is the result of extensive archival research.

[2] Eng, *The Swedish Empire*.

[3] Grandin, *Den svenska sjömakten*.

[4] *Ibidem*, 135, for both quotations.

[5] His last and very important book about these matters is *Swedish Naval Administration*.

[6] Ericson Wolke, *Sjöslag och rysshärjningar*, 79-82.

[7] *Ibidem*, 88-112; Berg, 'Peipuseskaderns fartyg', is also useful, as is Munthe, *Karl XII och den ryska sjömakten*, Del III.

[8] Lambert, *War at Sea in the Age of Sail*, 94.

[9] Ericson Wolke, *Sjöslag och rysshärjningar*, 113-24 and 146-73; see also Laidre, *The Great Northern War*.

[10] The most recent study of the privateering war is Ericson Wolke, *Lasse i Gatan*.

[11] Munthe, *Karl XII och den ryska sjömakten*, 556.

[12] Unger, *Karl XII och Östersjökriget*; Spens, 'Sjömaktens inflytande'; Frantzen and Jespers-

en, *Danmarks krigshistorie*, 358-60; for invaluable information about losses at Fehmarn Belt, see Tuxen and With-Seidelin, *Erobringen af Sveriges tyske provinser*.

[13] For this quotation and the one in the preceding paragraph, see Ericson Wolke, *Sjöslag och rysshärjningar*, 140-41.

[14] Unger, *Karl XII och Östersjökriget*, 126-28.

[15] Jonson, *Skärgårdskriget*, is still the best book about the devastating summer of 1719; see also Ericson Wolke, *Sjöslag och rysshärjningar*, 244-68 and other works mentioned there.

[16] Aldridge, *Admiral Sir John Norris*; Westberg, 'The Last Battle in the Great Northern War'.

## 7 The Absent King and Swedes at Home

[1] Lennersand, *Rättvisans och allmogens beskyddare*, 132-33; Karlsson, *Den jämlike undersåten*, 30-31.

[2] Karlsson, *Den jämlike undersåten*, 30-34; Naumann, 'Om centralförvaltningen under Karl XII:s tid', 546.

[3] Lennersand, *Rättvisans och allmogens beskyddare*, 132-33.

[4] Upton, *Charles XI and Swedish Absolutism*, 42-43.

[5] Lennersand, *Rättvisans och allmogens beskyddare*, 137.

[6] Lundqvist, *Council, King and Estates in Sweden*, 17.

[7] Ericson Wolke, *Sjöslag och rysshärjningar*, 75.

[8] Ågren, *Making a Living, Making a Difference*, ch. 7.

[9] Aminoff-Winberg, *På flykt i eget land*, 26-27.

[10] *Ibidem*, 29-30.

[11] Rådsprotokoll 24 September 1710, Riksarkivet Marieberg.

[12] *Ibidem*.

[13] Lennersand, *Rättvisans och allmogens beskyddare*, 157-63.

[14] Ericsson, *Stora nordiska kriget förklarat*, 92-103; Persson, *Gud verkar med naturliga medel*, 78-79.

[15] Ericson Wolke, *Sjöslag och rysshärjningar*, 125-26.

[16] Aminoff-Winberg, *På flykt i eget land*, 58-59.

[17] *Ibidem*, 113-14, 202-41.

[18] Ericson Wolke, *Sjöslag och rysshärjningar*, 153-55.

[19] Aminof-Winberg, *På flykt i eget land*, 27-29; Ericson Wolke, *Sjöslag och rysshärjningar*, 153-55.

[20] Ericson Wolke, *Sjöslag och rysshärjningar*, 244-60.

[21] Lennersand, *Rättvisans och allmogens beskyddare*, 259.

[22] Sjebaldina, 'Karolinernas sibiriska dagböcker', 44.

[23] Åberg, 'Soldaterna', 271-72.

[24] Lennersand, *Rättvisans och allmogens beskyddare*, 139.

[25] *Ibidem*, 139.

[26] Karlsson, *Den jämlike undersåten*.

[27] Lennersand, *Rättvisans och allmogens beskyddare*, 139.

[28] Wernstedt, *Kungl. Svea livgardes historia*, 599.

[29] Schartau, 'Om Sveriges inre tillstånd under Karl XII:s tid', 529; Olander, *Studier över det inre tillståndet i Sverige under senare delen av Karl XII:s regering*, 126.

[30] Lennersand, *Rättvisans och allmogens beskyddare*, 139.

[31] *Ibidem*, ch. 5.

## 8 The Impact of the Great Northern War on Trade Relations with the Baltic

[1] www.soundtoll.nl The data used in this chapter have been homogenised and standardised. Quantities of cargoes shipped have been converted to metric tonnes. The various steps of the conversion process have been described in Scheltjens, 'The volume of Dutch Baltic Shipping at the End of the Eighteenth Century: A New Estimation Based on the Danish Sound Toll Registers'; *idem*, 'Maße und Gewichte. Konvertierungsmöglichkeiten am Beispiel der Sundzollregister'.

[2] Ellinger Bang and Korst, *Tabeller ovber skibsfart og varetransport gennem Øresund*. For source criticism concerning the original records as well as the published Sound toll tables, see Heckscher, 'Öresundsräkenskaperna och deras behandlings'; Christensen, 'Der handelsgeschichtliche Wert der Sundzollregister'; Jeannin, 'Les Comptes du Sund comme source pour la construction de l'activité économique en Europe (XVIe-XVIIIe siècle)'; Veluwenkamp, 'Die "Sound Toll Registers Online" als Instrument für die Erforschung des frühneuzeitlichen Ostseehandels'.

[3] Zernack, 'Imperiale Politik und merkantiler Hintergrund. Ein Dokument der schwedischen Rußlandpolitik im 17. Jahrhundert', 134.

[4] Amburger, *Ingermanland: Eine junge Provinz Rußlands im Wirkungsbereich der Residenz und Weltstadt St. Petersburg/Leningrad*, 1; Kotilaine, *Russia's Foreign Trade and Economic Expansion in the Seventeenth Century: Windows on the World*, 146.

[5] On Sweden's military force and its structural problems, see Zernack, 'Virtus politica im Militärstaat – Strukturprobleme der schwedischen Großmachtzeit'.

[6] Čerepnin, *Ėkonomičeskie svjazi meždu Rossiej i Šveciej v XVII v.: Dokumenty iz sovetskich archivov*, 5-6; Attman, *Swedish Aspiration and the Russian Market during the 17th Century*, 18-29; Kotilaine, *Opening a Window on Europe: Foreign Trade and Military Conquest on Russia's Western Border in the 17th Century*, 499; Scheltjens, *De invloed van ruimtelijke verandering op operationele strategieën in de vroeg-moderne Nederlandse scheepvaart*, 22.

[7] Zernack, 'Imperiale Politik und merkantiler Hintergrund', 134.

[8] Kotilaine, *Russia's Foreign Trade*, 43. Similarly Zernack observed that '[a]us dem bloßen Handelsmarkt, den Moskau für die westeuropäischen Kommerzländer im 16. und frühen 17. Jahrhundert bedeutet hatte, war ein politischer Faktor geworden, der nicht länger eine quantité négligeable der internationalen Diplomatie darstellte'. See Zernack, 'Handelsbeziehungen und Gesandtschaftsverkehr im Ostseeraum', 103.

[9] Zernack, 'Schweden als europäische Großmacht der frühen Neuzeit', 214.

[10] Gipping, *Vvedenie v istoriju Sankt-Peterburga ili Neva i Nienšanc*, 239.

[11] Zernack, 'Handelsbeziehungen', 101-03.

[12] Idem, 'Imperiale Politik', 137.

[13] Anderson, *Naval Wars in the Baltic 1522-1850*, 71-103.

[14] *Ibidem*, 87.

[15] Boissonnade and Charliat, *Colbert et la Compagnie de Commerce du Nord (1661-1689)*.

[16] Åström, *From Stockholm to St.Petersburg: Commercial Factors in the Political Relations between England and Sweden 1675-1700*, 11; *idem*, 'The Swedish Economy and Sweden's Role as a Great Power 1632-1697', 58-101.

[17] Idem, 'Technology and Timber Exports from the Gulf of Finland'.

[18] Soom, *Der baltische Getreidehandel im 17. Jahrhundert*, 62-65.

[19] *Ibidem*, 70-72.

[20] For details, see: Boëthius and Heckscher, *Svensk Handelsstatistik 1637-1737*, 746.

[21] For a more detailed discussion of tar and timber production and exports in the seventeenth century, see Åström, *From Tar to Timber*, 12-32.

[22] Comprises a small proportion of cargo registrations as 'rye and barley'.

[23] Comprises *dehler* (deals), *balker* (balks), *laegter* (laths), and *braedder* (boards).

[24] Hartmann, *Reval im Nordischen Krieg*, 90-91.

[25] For a brief survey of the Polish system of fairs in the early modern period, see Bogucka, 'Fairs in Early Modern Poland'.

[26] Schmidt, 'Geschichte des Handels und der Schifffahrt Stettins', 45-49.

[27] Petrov, *Istorija Sankt-Peterburga s osnovanija goroda do vvedenija v dejstvie vybornogo gorodskogo upravlenija po učreždenijam o gubernijach*, 57.

[28] Anderson, *Naval Wars*, 162-93.

[29] Šarymov, *Predystorija Sankt-Peterburga / 1703 god: Kniga issledovanij*, 377-434.

[30] There is a protracted discussion about the name of the first shipmaster in Saint Petersburg. See Šarymov, *Predystorija Sankt-Peterburga*, 713-32.

[31] See, for example, Lindblad, *Sweden's Trade with the Dutch Republic 1738-1795*.

[32] In historiography, there is an ongoing debate about the nature of Peter the Great's reforms. Some scholars maintain that no long-term strategy can be observed in the rules and regulations issued by the tsar; others seem to be convinced of the opposite. Particularly revealing is Peterson's classic study on the Swedish antecedents of Peter's reforms. See Peterson, *Peter the Great's Administrative and Judicial Reforms*; Anisimov, *Gosudarstvennye preobrazovanija i samoderžavie Petra Velikogo v pervoj četverti XVIII veka*.

[33] Veluwenkamp, *Archangel*; Repin, 'Ot diskrim-

inacii k fritrederstvu: pravitel'stvennaja reglamentacija torgovli čerez Archangel'sk v 20-60-e gody XVIII v. i ee rezul'tat'; Čulkov, *Istoričeskoe opisanie rossijskoj kommercii pri vsech portach i granicach […]*, I, book 2, 107.

[34] Repin, 'Izmenenie ob"ema i struktury éksporta Archangel'skogo i Peterburgskogo portov v pervoj polovine XVIII veka'.

[35] Scheltjens, *De invloed*, 128.

[36] Čulkov, *Istoričeskoe opisanie rossijskoj kommercii*, I, book 2, 55-56.

[37] *Ibidem*, V, book 2, 100-03; 109; 111-12.

[38] Repin, 'Izmenenie', 181; Čulkov, *Istoričeskoe opisanie rossijskoj kommercii*, I, book 2, 46.

[39] Repin, 'Izmenenie', 181; Polnoe Sobranie Zakonov Rossijskoj Imperii [hereafter PSZ], V, nr. 2784.

[40] Čulkov, *Istoričeskoe*, I, book 2, 61; Repin, 'Izmenenie', 181; PSZ, V, nrs. 3051, 3115, 3268.

[41] Repin, 'Ot diskriminacii k fritrederstvu', 231; Čulkov, *Istoričeskoe*, I, book 2, 107.

[42] Čulkov, *Istoričeskoe*, V, book 2, 132.

[43] *Ibidem*, I, book 2, 103.

[44] *Ibidem*, V, book 2, 117-18.

[45] *Ibidem*, V, book 2, 118.

[46] Semenov, *Izuchenie istoricheskikh svedenii o rossijskoy vneshney torgovle i promyshlennosti s poliviny XVII-go stoletiya po 1858 god*, I, 56-57.

[47] PSZ, VI, nr. 3860; Repin, 'Ot diskriminacii k fritrederstvu', 231; Čulkov, *Istoričeskoe opisanie rossijskoj kommercii*, I, book 2, 103-05.

[48] Matley, 'Defense Manufactures of St. Petersburg 1703-1730'; Kahan, 'Entrepreneurship in the Early Development of Iron Manufactories in Russia'; Wallace, 'Entrepreneurship and the Russian Textile Industry: From Peter the Great to

Catherine the Great'.

[49] Matley, 'Defense Manufactures', 416.

[50] Kahan, 'Entrepreneurship', 401.

[51] Matley, 'Defense Manufactures', 420-23; Jones, 'Getting the Goods to St. Petersburg'.

[52] Čulkov, *Istoričeskoe opisanie rossijskoj kommercii*, V, book 2, 118.

[53] *Ibidem*, 174; Repin, 'Ot diskriminacii k fritrederstvu', 231; PSZ, VI, nr. 3860; Semenov, *Izuchenie istoricheskikh svedenii*, I, 58-59.

[54] The geographical location of the provinces is described as follows: '… Provincii, kotorye prilegli … k vodjanomu chodu Dviny *bez perevolok zemleju*'. This literally means that no passages over land (barrages) were allowed during transportation of goods to Archangel.

[55] Čulkov, *Istoričeskoe opisanie rossijskoj kommercii*, V, book 2, 118-19.

[56] *Ibidem*, 123-24.

[57] Semenov, *Izuchenie istoricheskikh svedenii*, I, 58.

[58] Repin, 'Izmenenie', 175-92; Repin, 'Ot diskriminacii k fritrederstvu', 228-49.

[59] Veluwenkamp, 'Dutch Merchants in St. Petersburg', 247.

[60] *Idem*, 'The Purchase and Export of Russian Commodities', 86-87.

[61] *Idem*, 'Dutch Merchants in St. Petersburg', 243.

[62] This summary is based on Soom, *Der baltische Getreidehandel*, 275-77, 286-93; Hartmann, *Reval im Nordischen Krieg*, 90-105.

[63] Hartmann, *Reval im Nordischen Krieg*, 96-97.

[64] *Ibidem*, 98.

[65] *Ibidem*, 100.

## 9 British Policy towards Sweden, Charles XII, and the Great Northern War, 1697-1723

[1] See for example: Chance, 'Introduction' to *British Diplomatic Instructions, Sweden, 1689-1727*, x.; Albion, *Forests and Sea Power*; Åstrom, 'England and the Baltic Naval Stores Trade'; Kent, *War and Trade in the Northern Seas*, 1-5; Rodger, *Command of the Ocean*, 191-92; and Davey, *Transformation of British Naval Strategy*, 13-24.

[2] Whitelocke, *A Journal*.

[3] Roberts, *Swedish Diplomats at Cromwell's Court*. For a full list of English diplomatic representatives in Sweden from 1535 to 1789, see Bell, *A Handlist*, 272-79, and Horn, *British Diplomatic Representatives*, 139-44.

[4] T.N.A., S.P. 108/518; Parry, *Consolidated Treaty Series*, VI, 469-94. Still in effect, the treaty was supplemented by the Convention of 25 July 1803,

renewed by article II with the Treaty of Örebro, 18 July 1812, and amended by the Declaration of 27 November 1911.

[5] Hatton, 'Gratifications and Foreign Policy', 93-94; Buchholz, 'Zwischen Glanz und Ohnmacht'; Upton, *Charles XI*, 211-12.

[6] Chance, *British Diplomatic Instructions, Sweden*, 16-17: 31 December 1696.

[7] BL, Addit. Ms. 35,105, fos. 133-34: Robinson to Vernon, 1 January 1698.

[8] The full text is printed in Parry, *Consolidated Treaty Series*. XVIII, 407-17: Treaty of Accommodation, etc., between Denmark and Gottorp, signed at Altona, 20/30 June 1689.

[9] BL, Addit. Ms. 35,106: Robinson to Blathwayt, 7 August 1700.

[10] Hattendorf, *The Journals of Sir George Rooke*. Entry for 12 August 1700 (O.S.).

[11] *Ibidem*. Entry for 1 September 1700 (O.S.).

[12] Hatton, *Charles XII*, 140.

[13] Snyder, *Marlborough-Godolphin Correspondence*, I, 36-37: Marlborough to Godolphin, 23 September/4 October 1701 and 26 September/7 October 1701.

[14] BL, Addit. Ms. 35,106, fo. 162: Blathwayt to Robinson, 8 October 1701.

[15] Chance, *British Diplomatic Instructions, Sweden*, 26-29: Instructions for Dr. John Robinson, 11 September 1702.

[16] *Ibidem*.

[17] Hatton, 'Captain James Jefferyes's Letters', 6-11; Horn, *British Diplomatic Representatives*, 140.

[18] T.N.A., S.P. 95/15: Robinson to Hedges, 14 March 1703; transcribed in Hattendorf, 'John Robinson's Account', xxxi.

[19] Hatton, *Charles XII*, 235; Stamp. 'The Meeting', 106; Åkerhielm's attendance at Oxford is attested to in Robinson's correspondence; Sallnäs, *Samuel Åkerhielm*, 11-12, 14-15; and in Jacobowsky, 'Svenska studenter', 129, based on a 1704 letter from him dated at Oxford. However, the Archives of Oxford University has no record of his matriculation in the university nor has any record of him been found in the archives of Robinson's college at Oxford, Oriel, where it is possible that Robinson might have made a connection for him. Possibly Åkerhielm was using some anglicised form of his surname, but none has been identified.

[20] Milne, 'Diplomacy of Dr. John Robinson', 80-84.

[21] Merriman, *Queen Anne's Navy*, 141-44, 158-65; Murray, 'Robert Jackson's Memoir', 424-26.

[22] Seerup, 'Danish and Swedish Flag Disputes with the British in the Channel', 31-32.

[23] BL, Addit. Ms. 34, 677, fos. 5-6: Harley to Robinson, 4/15 August 1704. Ericson Wolke and Hårdstedt, *Svenska sjöslag*, 153-54.

[24] Hattendorf, *England in the War of the Spanish Succession*, 122.

[25] Snyder, *Marlborough-Godolphin Correspondence*, I, 380, 381-83: Marlborough to Godolphin, 2/13 October, 6/17 October, and 9/20 October 1704; Murray, ed., *Letters and Dispatches*, I, 504: Marlborough to Harley, 13 October 1704.

[26] Hattendorf, *England in the War of the Spanish Succession*, 278-79, 286-87.

[27] T.N.A., SP 104/4, fo. 4: Hedges to Vernon, 17 October 1704.

[28] Riksarkivet, Stockholm, Anglica 536: Harley to Swedish resident, 18 July 1704.

[29] T.N.A., S.P. 104/72, fo. 121: Harley to Stanhope, 18 January 1706.

[30] T.N.A., S.P.104/39, fos. 95-96: Harley to Sunderland, 9 October 1705; S.P. 81/162, fo.16: E. Howe to Harley, October 1705; Snyder, *Marlborough-Godolphin Correspondence*, I, 516-17: Marlborough to Godolphin, 21 December 1705/1 January 1706 and 25 December 1705/5 January 1706; S.P. 195/77: Stepney to Raby, 15 January 1706; S.P. 104/4, fo. 19: Harley to Vernon, 2 April 1706; Brown, *Letters of Queen Anne*, 188: Anne to Godolphin, 4 June 1706.

[31] Hoff, *Correspondence of Marlborough and Heinsius*, 264-65: Heinsius to Marlborough, 4 and 6 September 1706; 266-67: Marlborough to Heinsius, 11 and 15 September 1706. Murray, ed., *Letters and Dispatches*, III, 129-30: Marlborough to the elector of Hanover, 11 September 1706.

[32] Murray, ed., *Letters and Dispatches*, III, 130: The elector of Hanover to Marlborough, 21 September 1706.

[33] Hatton, *Charles XII*, 212-15.

[34] Veenendaal, *Briefwisseling*. V, 650: Van Haersolte to Heinsius, Frankfurt (Oder), 5 November 1706; V, 668-69: Van Haersolte to Heinsius, Leipzig, 14 November 1706; V, 727-20: Van Haersolte to Heinsius, 16 December 1706, Leipzig.

[35] T.N.A., S.P. 88/17: Robinson to Harley, 15 February 1707, also quoted in Milne, 'Diplomacy of Dr. John Robinson', 85.

[36] Snyder, *Marlborough-Godolphin Correspondence*, II, 729: Marlborough to Godolphin, 16 November 1706.

[37] *Ibidem*, 747: Marlborough to Godolphin, 9/20 April 1707.

[38] *Ibidem*, 743: Godolphin to Marlborough, 1 April 1707.

[39] Hatton, *Charles XII*, 224-27; Snyder, 'Communication', 155-56; Stamp, 'The Meeting', 113-16, with transcriptions of T.N.A., S.P. 88/20: Robinson to Harley, 17/28 and 19/30 April 1707; Snyder, *Marlborough-Godolphin Correspondence*, II, 752, 757-62: Marlborough to Godolphin, 16/27 April and 29 April/10 May 1707; Hatton, 'Presents and Pensions', 104; Murray, ed., *Letters and Dispatches*, III, 347-48: Marlborough to Harley, 27 April 1707; Hildenbrand, 'England och Sverige, 1707'; Hatton, 'Captain James Jefferyes's Letters', 14-19;

[40] Snyder, *Marlborough-Godolphin Correspondence*, II, 747, 753, 761: Marlborough to Godolphin, 9/20 April, 16/27 April and 28 April/9 May 1707; Murray, ed., *Letters and Dispatches*, III, 347-48: Marlborough to Harley, 27 April 1707; Veenendaal, *Briefwisseling*, VI, 22: Van Haersolte to Heinsius, 12 January 1707, Leipzig.

[41] Snyder, *Marlborough-Godolphin Correspondence*, II, 762: Marlborough to the duchess, 29 April/10 May 1707.

[42] BL, Addit. Ms. 61,146, fos. 102-10: Robinson to Marlborough, 19/30 July 1707, enclosing 'Minutes of Conferences with Swedish Ministers'.

[43] Snyder, *Marlborough-Godolphin Correspondence*, II, 759, 764: Marlborough to Godolphin, 28 April/9 May 1707; Murray, ed., *Letters and Dispatches*, III, 359: Marlborough to Harley, 10 May 1707.

[44] BL. Ms Loan 29/45N: Harley to Lord Treasurer, 22 September 1707.

[45] Hatton, 'Captain James Jefferyes's Letters'; Carlson, *Kapten Jefferyes Bref*.

[46] BL, Addit. Ms. 61, 260, fos. 149-86b; letters from Jefferyes to Marlborough in 1711 are in BL, Addit. Ms., 61, 368, fos. 45-51.

[47] Hatton, 'Captain James Jefferyes's Letters', 76: Jefferyes to Secretary of State, 13 July 1709.

[48] *Ibidem*.

[49] Snyder, *Marlborough-Godolphin Correspondence*, III, 1331, 1334: Marlborough to Godolphin, 1/12 August with quote from 15/26 August 1709.

[50] See also Kurat, ed., *Despatches of Sir Robert Sutton*.

[51] T.N.A., S.P. 104/4, fos. 112v-113: Boyle to Pultney, 22 November 1709.

[52] T.N.A., S.P. 84/234, fos. 39-47: Declaration of 3 March 1710.

[53] T.N.A., S.P. 104/48: St. John to Palmes, and to d'Alais, 29 December 1710; BL, Addit. Ms. 37, 358, fos. 143-44: Charles Whitworth's 'Memorial of Affairs of North,' 11 January 1711.

[54] T.N.A., S.P. 84/241, fo. 18: St. John to Raby, 23 March 1711.

[55] Bodleian Library, Oxford, Ms. Add. D.23, fos. 67-68: Robinson to Bishop Burnet, undated, printed in Hattendorf, 'John Robinson's Account', 103-04.

[56] Rodger, Command of the Oceans, 175.

[57] Carlson, Kapten Jefferyes Bref, 4: Jefferyes to Queensbury, 18 May 1711.

[58] Chance, British Diplomatic Instructions, Sweden, 55: St John to Jefferyes, 21 August 1711.

[59] BL, Addit. Ms. 37, 358, fos. 193-94: St. John to Whitworth, 8 May 1711.

[60] Bodleian Library, Ms. Eng. Let e.4, fo. 63; St. John to Orrery, 24 July 1711; Houghton Library, Ms. Eng. 218.1F: Orrery to Bolingbroke, 28 July 1711.

[61] BL, Addit. Ms. 37, 358, fo. 365v: St. John to Whitworth, 7 August 1711; T.N.A., S.P. 105/5: St. John to Pultney, 10 August 1711 and 8 April 1712.

[62] T.N.A., F.O. 90/72: Charles XII to Anne, 15 May 1713; Anne to Charles XII, 1 October 1713.

[63] T.N.A., F.O. 90/72: Instructions to G. Mackenzie, 20 May 1714.

[64] McKay, 'The Struggle for Control', 367; Black, 'Hanover in British Foreign Policy', 303-09; Gibbs, 'English Attitudes toward Hanover and the Hanoverian Succession in the First Half of the Eighteenth Century', in Birke and Kluxen, England und Hannover, 35-36; Duchhardt, 'England-Hannover und der europäische Friede 1714-1748', in Birke and Kluxen, England und Hannover, 128-30; Black, 'Hanoverian Nexus', in Simms and Riotte, eds. The Hanoverian Dimension, 12-13; Black, Politics and Foreign Policy, 74, 77-78, 80-81, 119,

[65] Schnath, Geschichte Hannovers, III, 653-73.

[66] Ibidem, 696-705; Hoffmann, et al., Geschichte Schleswig-Holsteins, V, 249.

[67] Black, Politics and Foreign Policy, 67-68.

[68] Rodger, Command, 229; Hatton, Diplomatic Relations, 75-78; idem, Charles XII, 403-06; Murray, 'Sweden and the Jacobites in 1716'; idem, 'Sjömakternas Expedition'; idem, George I, The Baltic and the Whig Split, 161-89; Aldridge, Admiral Sir John Norris, 63-110.

[69] Hatton, Charles XII, 417-25; idem, George I, 189; Mediger, Mecklenburg, Rußland und England-Hannover, 270-366; Murray, 'Scania'; idem,

George I, The Baltic and the Whig Split, 216-84; Rodger, Command, 229-30; Aldridge, Admiral Sir John Norris, 111-61.

[70] Hatton, Diplomatic Relations, 136-44; Williams, Stanhope, 200-29; Murray, Honest Diplomat, 352-56: Walpole to Townshend, 14 October 1716.

[71] T.N.A., S.P. 95/21: Jackson to Secretary of State, 6 March 1716; 10 October 1717; Murray, 'An Eighteenth-Century Whitebook'; idem, 'British Public Relations'; idem, 'Robert Jackson's Mission'; Hatton, Diplomatic Relations, 147-59; Lamberty, Mémoires, X, 18-88.

[72] Hatton, George I, 218, 235.

[73] Ibidem, 222, 236-37.

[74] Aldridge, Admiral Sir John Norris, 176, quoting T.N.A., S.P. 42/75: Norris to Stanhope, 7 July 1717.

[75] Ibidem, 199, 210; Hatton, Charles XII, 463 ff.

[76] T.N.A., S.P. 95/23, fo. 25: Robert Jackson to Secretary of State, 20 February 1719; fos. 29-30: Robert Jackson to Secretary of State, 2 March 1719.

[77] Chance, British Diplomatic Instructions, Sweden, 116: Stanhope to Carteret, 22 July 1719.

[78] Ibidem, 159-60: Townshend to Finch, 9 August 1721; 163: Townshend to Finch, 10 November 1721; idem, George I. 483-84.

## 10 How to Handle a Warrior King

[1] Prak, The Dutch Republic in the Seventeenth Century, 123.

[2] Van Houtte, Economic History of the Low Countries, 184-86.

[3] Snapper, 'Veranderingen in de Nederlandse scheepvaart', 128-36, 271-73.

[4] Veluwenkamp, Archangel. Nederlandse ondernemers in Rusland, 153-58.

[5] De Vries-Van der Woude, The First Modern Economy, 500, 675, 714-15.

[6] Israel, Dutch Primacy in World Trade, 219-21; Bruijn, The Dutch Navy, 72; Probst, 'Danish Perspectives', in Bruijn, De Ruyter, 141-61.

[7] Charles XI had attained his majority in 1672; he died prematurely in April 1697.

[8] Israel, Dutch Primacy, 300-02; Bruijn, The Dutch Navy, 79; Hatton, Charles XII, 85-86

[9] Hatton, Charles XII, 85.

[10] Ibidem, 112-13. The dates provided by Hatton represent various calendars.

[11] Ferdinand Wilhelm, Duke of Württemberg-Neustadt (1659-1701), officer, first in Danish, then in Dutch service, major-general of infantry and colonel of the crack regiment of the Holland Guards since 1693; after the Peace of Rijswijk he returned into Danish service but kept his colonelcy of the Holland Guards in absentia. Veenendaal, Briefwisseling Heinsius, I, 202; Hatton, Charles XII, 117.

[12] Hatton, Charles XII, 128, 133.

[13] Frost, The Northern Wars, 228-29; Bruijn, 'The Anglo-Dutch Navies in Marlborough's Wars', 286-87.

[14] Hatton, Charles XII, 157.

[15] Van Koningsbrugge, 'Der Niedergang des niederländischen Handels', 87-88.

[16] For a survey of all foreign regiments in Dutch service, see Wijn, Staatsche Leger, III, 496-521.

The Scots and Swiss regiments were considered national troops, not hired for the war but in permanent service.

[17] See for instance Marlborough to Heinsius, Tournai, 5 August 1709; also Heinsius to Marlborough, 25 February 1710, in Van 't Hoff, The Correspondence, nrs. 768 and 831.

[18] Golowin to Heinsius, 3/14 May 1702, original in Russian and translation into Dutch; Heinsius to Golowin, 1 September 1702, copy in Dutch, in Veenendaal, Briefwisseling Heinsius, I, nrs. 332 and 811. It is not known at what time Heinsius received the letter from Golowin.

[19] Marlborough to Heinsius, 26 August 1709, in Van 't Hoff, The Correspondence, nr. 782.

[20] Heinsius to Marlborough, 28 September 1709, in ibidem, nr. 799: '. . . Nous déhorterons les Danois de toutes hostilitez contre la Suède, comme j'ay déjà fait en mon particulier à M. Rosekrans; et comme il est parti vers l'armée je vous prie de

faire de mesme, car la guerre du Nord ne nous conviendroit pas.'

21 Heinsius to Marlborough, 6 August 1710, in Van 't Hoff, *The Correspondence*, nr. 881; Marlborough to Heinsius, 11 August 1710: 'If it were possible to find mony for the entertaining the Sweedish troopes offered by M. Palmquist, it must have a very good effect all manner of ways, for it would dishearten France and at the same time strengthen the Allyes, and take off the necessity of assembling troops for the maintaining of the neutrallity of the North,' in *ibidem*, nr. 884; Ernst Detlof von Krassow (1660-1714), was a Pomeranian nobleman in Swedish service. Since 1708 he was colonel of a Mecklenburg-Schwerin regiment of infantry in allied service, on the payroll of the province of Holland; Wijn, *Staatsche Leger*, III, 515.

22 The neutrality convention was signed in The Hague on 31 March 1710; the second convention with the stipulation of a corps of 12,000 men was signed in December of the same year. Hatton, *Charles XII*, 327; she gives the size of the neutrality corps as 21,000 men; Dutch sources give 12,000, which seems more plausible. See also Van Koningsbrugge, *Tussen Rijswijk en Utrecht*, and idem, 'A Time of War: Dutch-Baltic Relations in the Years 1709-1711'.

23 Heinsius to Marlborough, 5 October 1710, in Van 't Hoff, *The Correspondence*, nr. 909; Hatton, *Charles XII*, 334; Wijn, *Staatsche Leger*, III, 8, 11.

24 Colyer to Heinsius, Pera, 1 August 1709, and same to same 31 August 1709, in Veenendaal, *Briefwisseling Heinsius*, IX, nrs. 235 and 441.

25 See for instance Daniel J. de Hochepied, Dutch consul in Smyrna, to Heinsius, 30 September 1709, in *ibidem*, IX, nr. 657.

26 Colyer to Heinsius, Pera, 18 November 1709; same to same, 15 December 1709, in *ibidem*, IX, nrs. 932 and 1065; same to same, 10 January 1710, in *ibidem*, X, nr. 45; also Heinsius to Marlborough, 24 September 1710, in Van 't Hoff, *The Correspondence*, nr. 904.

27 Colyer to Heinsius, Pera, 6 February 1713, in Veenendaal, *Briefwisseling Heinsius*, XIV, nr. 708.

28 Colyer to Heinsius, Pera, 20 and 27 February, 8 March 1713, in *ibidem*, XIV, nrs. 775, 806, and 847. Johan van Haersolte-Cranenburg to Heinsius, Warsaw 17 March 1713, in *ibidem*, nr. 905.

29 See for instance Hendrik Willem Rumpf, Dutch envoy in Stockholm, to Heinsius, 15 September

1714, in *ibidem*, XVI, nr. 387; also Colyer to Heinsius, Pera, 21 September 1714, in *ibidem*, nr. 401. Apparently Colyer did not yet know that the king had departed the day before.

30 Johan van Haersolte to Heinsius, Dresden, 1 December 1714, and H.W. Rumpf to Heinsius, Stockholm, 1 December 1714, in *ibidem*, nrs. 609 and 610.

31 Heinsius to Robert Goes, 7 November 1716, in *ibidem*, XVIII, nr. 129. The original Dutch text is: 'Maer ik vind daerin tot noch toe sooveel onseeckerheyt ende apparente wisselvallicheden, dat mij ontrent de vrage bij U W.E.G. gedaen noch niet wel positive souden konnen determineren.'

32 Heinsius to Buys, 4 December 1714, in *ibidem*, nr. 613.

33 Heinsius to de La Bassecour, second pensionary of Amsterdam, 3 February 1715, in *ibidem*, XVI, nr. 824. The ships deemed necessary were three of 74 guns, three of 63, three of 52, and two of 44 guns, plus one smaller.

34 Heinsius to Buys, 21 February 1714; Heinsius to Arent van Wassenaer-Duvenvoorde, Dutch ambassador in London, 5 March 1714; de La Bassecour to Heinsius, Amsterdam 9 March 1714, in *ibidem*, XVI, nrs. 882, 920, 941.

35 Heinsius to Buys, 8 February 1715; Heinsius to de La Bassecour, 8 March 1715; Buys to Heinsius, 8 March 1715, in *ibidem*, XVI, nrs. 844, 932, 935.

36 A. van Wassenaer-Duvenvoorde to Heinsius, 9 April 1715, in *ibidem*, XVI, nr. 1080; Hatton, *Charles XII*, 403.

37 The draft instruction for De Veth in Heinsius to Van Wassenaer-Duvenvoorde, 10 May 1715, in Veenendaal, *Briefwisseling Heinsius*, XVII, nr. 19.

38 Van Wassenaer-Duvenvoorde to Heinsius, 21, 28, and 31 May 1715; Lucas de Veth to Heinsius, 15 June 1715; Heinsius to Van Wassenaer-Duvenvoorde, 18 June, 2 July 1715, in *ibidem*, XVII, nrs. 51, 73, 81, 126, 132, 174.

39 H.W. Rumpf to Heinsius, Stockholm, 12 July 1715, in *ibidem*, XVII, nr. 209.

40 De La Bassecour to Heinsius, Amsterdam, 9 November 1715, in *ibidem*, XVII, nr. 598.

41 De Veth to Heinsius, Reval, 12 August 1715, in *ibidem*, XVII, nr. 307.

42 Bruijn, *The Dutch Navy*, 130.

43 The appointment of a captain instead of a rear-admiral meant of course a much lower pay

scale, again proving the extreme urgency of economy in Holland.

44 Van Wassenaer-Duvenvoorde to Heinsius, London, 14, 18, and 28 February; 14 April 1716; Heinsius to Van Wassenaer-Duvenvoorde 21 February, 31 March, and 21 April 1716, in Veenendaal, *Briefwisseling Heinsius*, XVII, nrs. 910, 915, 920, 937, 1016, 1026, 1051, 1060.

45 Buys to Heinsius, Amsterdam, 8, 12 November 1716, in *ibidem*, XVIII, nrs. 130 and 137.

46 Heinsius himself makes no mention of his meeting with the tsar in his correspondence.

47 Heinsius to Buys, 6 October; the Holland Commission to Heinsius 15 December 1716; Keppel-Albemarle to Heinsius 31 August 1717, in *ibidem*, XVIII, nrs. 81, 174, 519. See for the visit of Tsar Peter to Holland Waegemans, *De tweede reis van Peter de Grote naar Nederland*.

48 Israel, 'Heinsius, Dutch Raison d'État, and the Reshaping of the Baltic', 39, 41.

49 Bruijn, *The Dutch Navy*, 130; Heinsius to Buys, 12 March 1717; Buys to Heinsius, Amsterdam, 13 March 1717; Heinsius to Robert Goes, 16 March 1717, in Veenendaal, *Briefwisseling Heinsius*, XVIII, nrs. 302, 304, 307. About the Dutch frigates in the Baltic, Buys to Heinsius, Amsterdam, 5 October 1717, in *ibidem*, XVIII, nr. 554.

50 Robert Goes to Heinsius, Copenhagen, 8 February 1718; Heinsius to Adolf Hendrik van Rechteren-Almelo, 8 April 1718; Buys to Heinsius, Paris, 17 May 1718, in *ibidem*, XVIII, nrs. 692, 748, 787. Also Bruijn, *The Dutch Navy*, 130.

51 Amsterdam burgomasters to Heinsius, 6 May 1718; Buys to Heinsius, same date, in Veenendaal, *Briefwisseling Heinsius*, XVIII, nrs. 773 and 776.

52 Hatton, *Charles XII*, 437.

53 Albemarle to Heinsius, Voorst, 25 August 1717, in Veenendaal, *Briefwisseling Heinsius*, XVIII, nr. 508. Albemarle's original text in French is: 'Il est bien étonnant qu'il faille que nous soyons exposé à voir mener de telles intrigues dans nostre propre pays. Au nom de Dieu, que viendra-t-il donc de ce baron de Görtz: doit-il rester toujours icy?'

54 The story of Görtz's arrest is based on Bussemaker, 'De arrestatie van Gyllenborgh en Görtz in 1717', Hatton, *Charles XII*, 422, 438, and the following letters to or from Heinsius: René Saunière de l'Hermitage, Dutch agent in London, to Heinsius, 12 February 1717; Heinsius to Van Borssele van der Hooghe, Dutch ambassador in

London, 9 March 1717; H.W. Rumpf to Heinsius, Stockholm, 14 April and 5 May 1717; Borssele van der Hooghe to Heinsius, London, 8 May 1715; Van Wassenaer-Duvenvoorde to Heinsius, Duvenvoorde, 27 June 1717; Heinsius to Willem Buys, 8 August 1717, in Veenendaal, *Briefwisseling Heinsius*, XVIII, nrs. 256, 294, 347, 376, 428, 491.

⁵⁵ Heinsius to Almelo, 3 January 1719, in *ibidem*, XIX, nr.100. The Dutch text is: '. . . maer de grootste ende importantste tijdingh is de doot van de coning van Sweeden in de tranchee voor Fredricshal, door 't hooft door- ende dootgeschoten.' How Heinsius acquired this knowledge so soon is not clear, but reportedly his intelligence network was well organised.

⁵⁶ Friedrich, hereditary prince of Hesse-Kassel, was general of cavalry of the States General since 1704 and colonel of a cavalry regiment since 1710. He was to give up his rank and command only in November 1721. Ringoir, *Afstammingen en Voortzettingen Cavalerie*, 6.

⁵⁷ Friedrich of Hesse to Heinsius, Stralsund, 1 January 1715, and Heinsius to Friedrich of Hesse, 11 January 1715, in Veenendaal, *Briefwisseling Heinsius*, XVI, nrs. 699 and 739.

⁵⁸ H.W. Rumpf to Heinsius, 9 January 1719, in *ibidem*, XIX, nr. 116.

⁵⁹ Heinsius to Buys, 26 January 1719; Buys to Heinsius, 27 January 1719, in *ibidem*, nrs. 142 and 144.

⁶⁰ De Bie to Heinsius, 1 April 1719, in *ibidem*, nr. 253; the remark of the prince in same to same, 8 April 1719, in *ibidem* nr. 266: De Bie was called into the cabinet of the prince, when '. . . liefde te seggen dat de geheele week als Hollantsche minister hadde geageert en hoopte geavoueert te sullen worden.'

⁶¹ Heinsius to Friedrich of Hesse-Kassel, 12 December 1719, in *ibidem*, nr. 565: 'J'ay pourtant eu bien de la satisfaction d'entendre de temps en temps par les ministres de l'État en Suède que Vre. Altesse Royale, quoyque tant esloigné de nous, avoit toujours conferé la mesme amitié et la mesme affection qu'il nous a tesmoigné estant ici, et qu'elle avoit pris tant de soin de nos interests que des siens propres. Je vous assure que nous en serons toujours bien recognoissants.'

⁶² Bruijn, 'Scheepvaart', 209-48.

## 11 The French View of Charles XII

¹ 'Inimitié permanente.' *Mémoires pour l'instruction du Dauphin*, Paris, 1992, 70; Lossky, '"Maxims of State" in Louis XIV's Foreign Policy in the 1680s', 8-15.

² 'Un pied en Allemagne.' Schnakenbourg, '"Un pied en Allemagne": La diplomatie française et la présence suédoise dans le Nord de l'Empire, 1648-1720', 237-54.

³ 'Complexion aussi délicate.' D'Avaux to Louis XIV, 5 August, 2 and 9 September, 28 October 1693, in Wijnne, *Négociations de Monsieur le comte d'Avaux*, vol. 2, 344, 382, 390, 432, 481.

⁴ Archives des Affaires Étrangères, La Courneuve [hereafter A.A.E.], Correspondance Politique [hereafter C.P.], Sweden, vol. 75, fol. 414 and 432, d'Avaux to Louis XIV, 2 and 9 June 1694.

⁵ Ragnhild Hatton asserts that he was pro-French: *Charles XII*, 46; Lindström and Norrhem, *Flattering Alliances: Scandinavia, Diplomacy, and the Austrian-French Balance of Power*, 55. But d'Avaux once referred to Gyldenstolpe as a 'bad Frenchman' ('mauvais français'), in Wijnne, *Négociations de Monsieur le comte d'Avaux*, vol. 3, 64.

⁶ Liljegren, *Karl XII. En biografi*, 41, 45.

⁷ Nicodemus Tessin, in charge of court entertainments, affirmed that 'His Majesty is most eager to know of everything that happens at the French court' ('Sa Majesté est très curieuse d'être informé de tout ce qui se passe à la cour de France'), Liljegren, *Karl XII. En biografi*, 61.

⁸ 'Beaucoup de pénétration et d'esprit,' 'aime beaucoup les exercices violens, et il a toujours témoigné de l'inclination pour la guerre,' 'toutte la fermeté de son père à soutenir une résolution,' 'il est fort prévenu en faveur de la France.' D'Avaux to Louis XIV, 29 May 1697, in Wijnne, *Négociations de Monsieur le comte d'Avaux*, vol. 2, 139.

⁹ 'Le plus grand roy de l'Europe et [qu'] il n'a rien de seur que d'estre bien uny avec luy.' D'Avaux to Louis XIV, 8 January 1698, in Wijnne, *Négociations de Monsieur le comte d'Avaux*, vol. 3, 21. Barre, the secretary that d'Avaux left behind in Stockholm, also affirmed that Charles XII was 'entirely on France's side' ('entièrement porté pour la France'). A.A.E., C.P., Sweden, vol. 90, fol. 12, Barre to Torcy, 6 May 1699.

¹⁰ Jonasson, *Kark XII och hans rådgivare. Den utrikespolitiska maktkampen i Sverige 1697-1702*, 91.

¹¹ A.A.E., C.P., Sweden, vol. 89, fol. 55-56, Guiscard to Louis XIV, 3 July 1700.

¹² Brulin, *Sverige och Frankrike under nordiska kriget och spanska sucessionkrisen åren 1700-1701*, 116.

¹³ 'Froideur et lenteur.' A.A.E., C.P., Sweden, vol. 89, fol. 159, Louis XIV to Guiscard, 23 September 1700.

¹⁴ A.A.E., C.P., Sweden, vol. 93, fol. 176, Bonnac to Louis XIV, 16 December 1701.

¹⁵ 'Je ne vois pas comment l'Empereur pourra demeurer simple spectateur dans la guerre que deux princes étrangers se feront dans son pays.' A.A.E., C.P., Sweden, vol. 104, fol. 62, Louis XIV to Bonnac, 12 March 1705.

¹⁶ A.A.E., C.P., Poland, vol. 111, fol. 73, du Héron to Louis XIV, 9 June 1702. It was, moreover, incumbent upon Charles XII to supply troops in his capacity as duke of Pomerania.

¹⁷ 'So far the Swedish king's war has produced the same effect as if I had funded him to pursue it' ('La guerre du roi de Suède produit jusqu'à présent les mêmes effets que si je lui avais donné des subsides pour la continuer'). A.A.E., C.P., Poland, vol. 110, fol. 506, Louis XIV to du Héron, 30 March 1702.

¹⁸ Bonnac reported that Robinson had boasted of having 'obtained Charles XII's word that his troops would not enter Saxony' ('tiré la parole du roi de Suède qu'il ne ferait point passer ses troupes en Saxe'). A.A.E., C.P., Sweden, vol. 97, fol. 220, Bonnac to Louis XIV, 17 May 1703.

¹⁹ 'It is almost impossible with [Charles XII's forces] armed in the middle of the Empire, right next to the hereditary states of the House of Austria . . . for there not to arise between these two princes such reciprocal complaints as to bring affairs to a sudden, open breach ('Il est presque impossible qu'étant armé au milieu de l'Empire, dans le voisinage des États héréditaires de la maison d'Autriche . . . il ne s'élève bientôt entre ces deux princes des plaintes réciproques, capables de porter tout d'un coup les affaires à une rupture ouverte'). Instructions to Ricous, 20 January 1707; Geffroy, *Recueil des instructions aux ambassadeurs, Suède*, 225.

²⁰ A.A.E., C.P., Sweden, vol. 106, fol. 284-85, Bonnac to Louis XIV, 22 September 1706.

²¹ His mission has been studied in detail: Syveton, *Au camp d'Altranstädt (1707), la mission du baron de Besenval*.

22 A.A.E., C.P., Sweden, vol. 108, fol. 98, Louis XIV to Bonnac, 17 February 1707, and vol. 111, fol. 202, Besenval to Torcy, 27 August 1707.

23 Schnakenbourg, 'Les Chemins de l'information': la circulation des nouvelles depuis la périphérie européenne jusqu'au gouvernement français au début du XVIIIe siècle', 291-311.

24 'De plus en plus d'avis de différents endroits qui rapportent un prochain accommodement entre le roi de suède et les Moscovites.' A.A.E., C.P., Sweden, vol. 121, fol. 225, Torcy to Besenval, 18 July 1709.

25 'On ne voulait point croire la défaite du roi de Suède quelques soins que prissent les journaux de Hollande de la publier.' Grimarest, Les Campagnes de Charles XII, roi de Suède, vol. 4, 237.

26 'Une nouvelle funeste qui se répand depuis quelques jours d'une prétendue défaite de roi de Suède.' A.A.E., C.P., Denmark, vol. 73, fol. 151, Torcy to Poussin; C.P., Sweden, vol. 115, fol. 266, Torcy to Campredon; C.P., Poland, vol. 119, fol. 287, Torcy to Besenval.

27 'Devraient la rendre croyable, elle ne laisse pas de trouver encore des incrédules & on suspend ici d'y ajouter foi.' Gazette d'Amsterdam, Friday, 30 August 1709.

28 A.A.E., C.P., Poland, vol. 119, fol. 291, Louis XIV to Besenval, 5 September 1709.

29 'Bientôt en état de faire un grand personnage dans l'Empire.' A.A.E., C.P., Sweden, vol. 124, fol. 11, Torcy to Campredon, 11 June 1711, and vol. 123, fol. 245, Torcy to Campredon, 9 April 1711.

30 Riksarkivet, Diplomatica, Gallica, vol. 195, 'Mémoire présenté au Grand Vizir', by Ferriol, 19 August 1709.

31 A.A.E., C.P., Turkey, vol. 47, fol. 71, Müllern (the Swedish king's secretary of state) to Ferriol, 5 November 1709.

32 This paragraph rests on a memorandum titled 'Réflexions sur la Suède', written by Poussin, dated 26 February 1713, and addressed to Torcy. A.A.E., C.P., Sweden, vol. 125, fol. 372-80.

33 A copy of this treaty can be found in A.A.E., C.P., Sweden, vol. 134, fol. 81-87.

34 Riksarkivet, Diplomatica, Gallica, vol. 222, Sparre to Müllern, 14 October 1715 and 28 February 1716.

35 A.A.E., C.P., Sweden, vol. 140, fol. 36-37, 62, Campredon to Huxelles, 20 January and 5 February 1717; ibidem, vol. 139, fol. 271, La Marck to Louis XV, 18 October 1717.

36 According to Marquis of Dangeau, the regent made the news of Charles XII's death public on 5 January 1719. Dangeau, Journal, vol. 17, 454, 5 January 1719.

37 Craggs to Stair, 9 March (OS), or 21 March (NS), 1719 in Legg, British Diplomatic Instructions, France, vol. 2, 142.

38 T.N.A., S.P., 78/165, fol. 269 and 270, Stanhope to Dubois, 9 October 1719.

39 Jespersen and Felbæk, Dansk udenrigspolitik historie 2: Revanche og neutralitet, (1648-1814), 187.

40 'L'action est belle et grande pour ce jeune roi qui n'a pas encore 18 ans.' Dangeau, Journal, vol. 7, 466, 28 December 1700, and vol. 8, 3-4, 4 January 1701. The age is stated incorrectly; Charles XII was born on 17 June 1682 and was thus five months past his eighteenth birthday at the time of the Battle of Narva.

41 Laidre, Segern vid Narva. Början till en stormakts fall, 177.

42 The history of Gustav Adolf was taught to young Louis XIV. Cornette, Le Roi de Guerre, 182-84.

43 A.A.E., C.P., Poland, vol. 111, fol. 214, du Héron to Louis XIV, 18 August 1702.

44 'Toute l'armée saxonne sera détruite dans moins de deux mois.' A.A.E., C.P., Sweden, vol. 97, fol. 254, Bonnac to Louis XIV, 4 May 1703.

45 'La gloire a élevé en Saxe un tribunal qui impose ses lois à tout le monde,' 'en posture d'être le dictateur de l'Europe.' Saint-Simon, Mémoires, 799.

46 'Je l'ai vu ce héros que tout le monde admire; Et je conviens que c'est un Demi-Dieu [. . . ].' A.A.E., C.P., Sweden, vol. 103, fol. 414, anonymous.

47 Grimarest, Les Campagnes de Charles XII, roi de Suède, 4 vols., Paris, 1706-11.

48 'Un génie supérieur pour la guerre [. . .]. Son armée est sa famille, il en a soin, il l'aime, il en fait son plaisir. Le soldat, l'officier de son côté soumis par devoir et par vénération chérit ce prince, le suit, l'imite, et prodigue son sang avec ardeur et avec courage, persuadé que quand ce conquérant veut frapper, il doit vaincre.' Grimarest, Les Campagnes de Charles XII, roi de Suède, vol. 1, 13-17.

49 'Le grand nom et les surprenantes aventures du roi de Suède,' 'brave lion du Nord: ce fameux conquérant dont la réputation fait tant de bruit dans le monde.' Demarsy, ed., Voyage du chevalier de Bellerive au camp du roi de Suède à Bender en 1712, 7 and 9.

50 'Majestueux et fier,' 'charmante douceur,' 'vertus militaires et politiques . . . d'un Alexandre par son intrépidité, d'un César par son courage, d'un Pompée par sa sagesse, mais il n'a aucun de leurs vices; c'est un Alexandre sans vin, un César sans ambition, un Pompée sans mollesse.' Ibidem, 17.

51 Chagniot, Le Chevalier Folard. La Stratégie de l'incertitude, 70-72, 132 and 164.

52 'Bon air et [la] physionomie avenante,' 'il n'est guère en repos et fait beaucoup de chemin en peu de temps allant toujours au train d'un homme qui court le cerf.' A.A.E., C.P., Sweden, vol. 132, fol. 83, Croissy to Torcy, 27 May 1715.

53 'Concilie sagesse et douceur extrême, avec un esprit supérieur et beaucoup de simplicité. Ses réponses sont justes et promptes.' Ibidem, fol. 79, Croissy to Louis XIV, 27 May 1715.

54 For Croissy's mission, see Sörensson, En fransk ambassadörs omdöme om Karl XII. En bidrag till konungens karaktäristik, 314-18.

55 Laidre, Segern vid Narva. Början till en stormakts fall, 213.

56 'Un jeune prince rempli de lui-même, opiniâtre au dernier excès qui se croit au-dessus de tout, et qui n'a aucune éducation ni connaissances des affaires étrangères.' A.A.E., C.P., Sweden, vol. 92, fol. 229, Guiscard to Louis XIV, 15 September 1701.

57 'Des choses indifférentes.' A.A.E., C.P., Sweden, vol. 97, fol. 207, Bonnac to Louis XIV, 20 April 1703.

58 'On ne peut effectivement compter sur rien avec un prince qui fait comme le roi de Suède, qui ne suit ni maximes, ni raison, et qui n'a point d'autre règle de sa conduite que son caprice.' A.A.E., C.P., Poland, vol. 117, fol. 62, Groffey to Bonnac, 16 May 1706.

59 A.A.E., C.P., Sweden, vol. 110, fol. 74, Besenval to Louis XIV, 15 March 1707.

60 'Que dites-vous d'un pays où l'on ne peut approcher le maître et où le ministre garde un silence éternel?' Besenval to Pecquet, 15 March 1707, excerpt from the papers of Besenval's family, cited by Syveton, Au camp d'Altranstädt (1707), la mission du baron de Besenval, 65.

61 'À la force des raisonnements.' A.A.E., C.P., Poland, vol. 118, fol. 57, Bonnac to Besenval, 7 April 1707.

62 Cited by Le Corre, 'Les Relations franco-suédoises dans le cadre des conflits européens du début du XVIIIème siècle', 15.

63 'Le plus fourbe, le plus intrigant, le plus dangereux et le plus décrié de tous les hommes.' Sörensson, Sverige och Frankrike, 1715-1718, vol. 2, 41.

64 Groffey to Besenval and Bonnac to Groffey, 8 and 15 August 1709, B.N., French Manuscripts

division, Correspondence of Philippe Goffrey, vol. 10677, fol. 187 and 192.

[65] 'Défaut de qualités politiques.' A.A.E., C.P., Poland, vol. 164, fol. 219, Besenval to Dubois, 13 January 1719, and C.P., Prussia, vol. 61, fol. 216, Groffey to Dubois, 31 January 1719.

[66] 'À l'immortalité & à la gloire,' 'en quelque façon dépouillé de l'humanité.' *Dialogue entre le maréchal de Turenne et le prince d'Auvergne dans les champs Elysiens sur l'état des affaires de l'Europe vers la fin de cette année 1710*, 102-03.

[67] Schnakenbourg, 'Le Regard de Clio: l'Histoire de Charles XII de Voltaire dans une perspective historique', 447-68.

[68] 'L'homme le plus extraordinaire peut-être qui ait jamais été sur la terre qui a réuni en lui toutes les grandes qualités de ses aïeux, et qui n'a eu d'autre défaut ni d'autre malheur que de les avoir toutes outrées.' Voltaire, *Histoire de Charles XII*, 166.

[69] 'Qu'un homme.' Voltaire to Rolland Puchot des Alleurs, 26 November 1738, *Correspondance de Voltaire*, vol. 1, 1302.

[70] 'Un chevalier errant . . . moitié héros, moitié fou.' Voltaire to Pierre Robert le Cornier de Cideville, 16 February 1731, *Correspondance de Voltaire*, vol. 1, 264.

[71] 'Guérir de la folie des conquêtes.' Voltaire, *Discours sur l'histoire de Charles XII*, 153.

[72] Voltaire, *L'Homme aux quarante écus*, *Les Œuvres complètes de Voltaire*, 66, Henri Masson, dir., 409. Voltaire also wrote *Histoire de l'empire de Russie sous le règne de Pierre le Grand*. Part one appeared in 1760, part two in 1763.

## 12 The Habsburg Monarchy and Charles XII

[1] Reingrabner, *Der Schwed*; Öhman, 'Morgen kommt der Schwed . . . .'

[2] Buchholz, 'Schwedisch-Pommern'; Jörn and North, *Integration*; Beyme, 'Schwedisches Imperium'.

[3] There is no detailed and up-to-date diplomatic history of the period from an Austrian perspective. Redlich's *Werden einer Großmacht* remains the best introduction. Also see Braubach, *Eugen*. A synoptic analysis of Habsburg foreign policy during the first decades of the eighteenth century needs to be based on the massive archival material in the Austrian State Archives (ÖStA), Haus-, Hof- und Staatsarchiv (HHStA) in Vienna. The series Staatenabteilungen Schweden (boxes 10-14) contains important material on the Altranstädt negotiations of 1707 and a considerable amount of intercepted Swedish correspondence between Bender and Stockholm. Sweden's role in the protocols of the Privy Conference (Staatskanzlei Vorträge und Konferenzprotokolle) is rather modest, as Austria's attitude towards Sweden was largely determined by relations with other powers such as Prussia, Poland, Saxony, Turkey, and, increasingly, Russia. Part of Prince Eugene's correspondence *in nordicis* and Swedish intercepts are in ÖStA, Kriegsarchiv Alte Feldakten, boxes 271-74.

[4] ÖStA, HHStA Staatenabteilungen Schweden 10: *Relationes conferentiae*, 2 September 1698 and 6 April 1699.

[5] There is much general literature on the 'Baltic question' by German historians who pay comparatively little attention to the role of the Habsburg Monarchy, e.g., Rauch, 'Zur baltischen Frage'; Mediger, *Rußland*; Hellmann, 'Friedensschlüsse'; Zernack, 'Schweden als Europäische Großmacht der frühen Neuzeit'.

[6] Kalisch and Gierowski, *Um die polnische Krone*; Jonasson, *Polska Politik*; *Sachsen und Polen zwischen 1697 und 1765*, esp. the contribution by Schilling, 'Wiener Hof'; Auer, 'Austrian Political Attitudes Towards the Polish Republic During the Great Northern War'.

[7] Brulin, 'Österrike', is largely based on the Austrian diplomatic correspondence.

[8] Syveton, 'Louis XIV'; Brulin, *Sverige*. For France's relations with Russia, see Vassileff, *Russisch-französische Politik*.

[9] Erdmann, 'Patkul'.

[10] ÖStA, HHStA Staatenabteilungen Schweden: *Relationes conferentiae*, 3 May 1702 and 31 August 1702 and instructions to Zinzendorf, 19 May 1702.

[11] 'J'ai tâché de vivre comme lui. Dieu m'accordera peut-être un jour une mort aussi glorieuse.' Voltaire, *Histoire de Charles XII*, 64.

[12] Fiedler, *Actenstücke*; Benda, *Projet*; Kiss, 'Franz Rákóczi II' (extensive Hungarian bibliography); Köpeczi, *France*; Bak and Király, *From Hunyadi*, with contributions by Benda, 'Rákóczi War', Frey, 'Rákóczi', and Pastor, 'Hungarian-Russian Relations'; Slottman, 'Ferenc II Rákóczi'; Höbelt, 'Impact'.

[13] Braubach, *Eugen*, vol. 2, 203-05.

[14] Günther, 'Das schwedische Heer'.

[15] *Conclusum trium collegiorum Sacri Romani Imperii* (27 September 1706): ÖStA, HHStA, Staatenabteilungen Schweden 11. Unfortunately, the otherwise solid Minha, 'Deutsche Politik' has little to say about the impact of the Swedish threat on the *Reich* at large or on the Eternal Imperial Diet. Unsurprisingly, the Swedish envoy in Regensburg systematically

sided with the anti-Habsburg opposition, notably during the process against the Wittelsbach electors of Bavaria and Cologne. Aretin, *Das Alte Reich*, vol. 2, 255-62, is very disappointing.

[16] The best treatment of the Austro-Swedish negotiations at Altranstädt, based on the relevant manuscript sources in ÖStA, HHStA, Staatenabteilungen Schweden boxes 11-14, is by the Bohemian historian Jaroslav Goll, *Vertrag*. The detailed account by Noorden, *Europäische Geschichte*, vol. 2, 535-92, also draws on Austrian archival material. From a Swedish perspective see Carlson, *Karl XII*, and idem, *Vertrag* (published in Swedish and German), Rosén, *Utrikespolitikens Historia*, vol. 2/1, 106-11. Products of the tercentenary are Metasch, *300 Jahre*, Karlsson, 'Tolerante enväldshärskaren', and Wolf, *1707-2007*. Also see Mezgolich, 'Wratislaw', 163-90. Wascher, 'Beziehungen' consulted material in Vienna and Stockholm but can only be used with caution. Hatton, *Charles XII*, 212-27, pays little attention to the Austro-Swedish conflict. Ingrao, *Josef I.*, 71-77, 79-87, probably overstates the religious motivation on the Swedish side.

[17] According to King Stanislaw, Charles XII himself admitted: 'Res exigui momenti, sed nolumus ludi ab aula caesarea.' Zinzendorf's report (27 May 1707): ÖStA, HHStA Staatenabteilungen Schweden 12.

[18] Stamp, 'Meeting'; Syveton, 'Au camp d'Altranstadt'; Churchill, *Marlborough*, book 2, vol. 3, 220-28.

[19] The documents in ÖStA, HHStA Obersthofmeisteramt Ältere Zeremonialakten 21 show that Vienna took the affair very seriously indeed (protocols of 7 and 17 March 1707). Also see Holm, 'Stralenheim'.

[20] Significantly, the Swedish mission in Vienna was upgraded only in 1719 with the arrival of a minister plenipotentiary. The emperor reacted by dispatching an envoy extraordinary in late 1720.

[21] Prussia's (confused) foreign policy is covered by Berney, *König Friedrich I.*, 90-112, and in great detail by Hassinger, *Brandenburg-Preußen*, 193-223. For Prusso-Swedish relations see Backman, *Från Rawicz*.

[22] Relations between Austrian Protestantism and Sweden dated back to the Thirty Years' War: Thaler, 'Erbländische Protestanten'.

[23] There is no Swedish ratification of the Convention of 1 September 1707 and no engrossed copy of Charles's declaration of the same date in the Austrian State Archives. The same applies to the *Exekutionsrezess* of February 1709. Wratislaw's original declaration (*Promittitur*), signed at Liebertwolkwitz but dated from Altranstädt, is kept in the Riksarkivet Stockholm (printed in Carlson, *Vertrag*, 34-45, in Latin and German). Swedish proposals with Austrian corrections were published by Goll, *Vertrag*, 58-61. Drafts and copies of the treaty are in ÖStA, HHStA, Staatenabteilungen Schweden 11.

[24] See the exhaustive study by Conrads, *Durchführung*, and *idem*, 'Anteil'.

[25] ÖStA, HHStA Staatenabteilungen Schweden 11.

[26] Czobor gave his never-ending feud with Stralenheim the greatest publicity: Lamberty, *Mémoires*, vol. 6, 751-74. A counter-offensive is *Brieff des Herrn N.N. an seinen Freund den Bericht der Affaire des Graf Zobor mit dem Baron Stralenheim betreffend* (1711).

[27] 'Vous êtes bien heureux que le roi de Suède ne m'ait pas proposé de me faire luthérien; car s'il l'avait voulu, je ne sais pas ce que j'aurais fait.' Voltaire, *Charles XII*, 76.

[28] Samerski, 'Trauer des Papstes'.

[29] Braubach, *Eugen*, vol. 2, 186-88, 336.

[30] Srbik, *Staatsverträge*, vol. 1, 391-416; Braubach, *Eugen*, vol. 2, 369-72.

[31] Sumner, *Peter the Great*, 26-36, 45-49; Florovsky, 'Russo-Austrian Conflicts'.

[32] Roider, *Eastern Question*, 21-37; Parvev, *Habsburgs and Ottomans*.

[33] The most detailed account of Austro-Russian relations in the period is provided by Pilss, 'Beziehungen'. Übersberger, *Russlands Orientpolitik* is weak. Hantsch, *Schönborn*, 208-29, contains further details on Vienna's eastern policy, as relations with Stockholm, Moscow, Berlin, etc. fell within the remit of Schönborn's Imperial Chancellery (*Reichshofkanzlei*). Relevant reports to the emperor are in HHStA, Reichskanzlei Vorträge boxes 6a-6c.

[34] That was still the emperor's position when, in May 1717, he was confronted with an Anglo-Hanoverian peace plan to divide up the Swedish spoil and keep the Russians out of Europe. Vienna expected Saxony to hand back the two Lusatias (part of the kingdom of Bohemia until 1635) in exchange for gains further east: ÖStA, HHStA Staatskanzlei Vorträge 22.

[35] Wittram, *Peter I.*, vol. 2, 226-31.

[36] 'Sueco non fidendum, teste experientia, ideo sollte man ihm die Flügel stutzen und völlig übern Haufen werfen.' Protocol of the Privy Conference meeting of 2 December 1712 (quoted in Pilss, 'Beziehungen', 81).

[37] Braubach, *Eugen*, vol. 2, 370 (July 1710).

[38] The best (if rather confused) description of the king's homeward journey is by Ballagi, 'Geschichte' (based on a book in Hungarian published in 1922); Hatton, *Charles XII*, 384-89. But also see Burenstam, *Retour*; Zimmermann, 'Durchzug'; anonymous, 'Karl XII:s hemfärd'. Dates of the journey differ due to the use of different calendar systems. Charles's passage through Transylvania provoked a flood of legends and anecdotes which were all proved unfounded: the king simply had no time to rest and do what he was reported to have done. Prince Eugene's role in the business is illuminated by Braubach, *Eugen*, vol. 3, 296-301. Eugene's notes are in ÖStA, HHStA Staatenabteilungen Schweden 14. Vienna's irritation at the king's incognito and lack of politeness is obvious from *Protocollum conferentiae*, 30 September 1714: ÖStA, HHStA Staatskanzlei Konferenzprotokolle 19.

[39] Its history has not yet been written. Important material is in ÖStA, HHStA Reichskanzlei Friedensakten and Braunschweig.

[40] *Relatio conferentiae*, 10 March 1715 (quoted by Pilss, 'Beziehungen', 102); and 5 May 1715 (HHStA, Staatskanzlei Konferenzprotokolle 20). The fullest treatment of Habsburg-Swedish relations after 1714, drawing on Austrian material, is Sörensson, 'Kejsaren'. Jägerskiöld, *Sverige* has little to say on the Habsburg Monarchy.

[41] Mediger, *Mecklenburg*; Michael Hughes, *Law and Politics*.

[42] Hantsch, *Schönborn*, 229-35, based on important manuscript material in ÖStA, HHStA Staatenabteilung Rußland I 24, also used by Wittram, *Peter I.*, vol. 2, 346-405.

[43] Guichen, *Pierre le Grand*.

[44] Michael, 'Fall'; Naumann, *Österreich*; Lewitter, 'Poland'; McKay, *Allies*, 211-66.

[45] ÖStA, Staatenabteilungen Schweden 14; Braubach, *Eugen*, vol. 4, 97-108; Wittram, *Peter I.*, vol. 2, 409-10. The British envoy to Vienna reported in 1721 that the Austrians had '*la haine la plus marquée*' for the Russians. Braubach, *Eugen*, vol. 4, 408.

[46] *Relationes conferentiae*, 27 May 1719 and 5 January 1720: ÖStA, HHStA Staatskanzlei Vorträge 23. *Relatio conferentiae*, 11 January 1720 and Instructions for the new ambassador in Sweden, Count Fridag, 9 March 1720: *ibidem*, Staatenabteilung Schweden 14.

[47] *Relatio conferentiae*, 27 August 1720: ÖStA, HHStA Staatskanzlei Vorträge 23.

[48] Wittram, *Peter I.*, vol. 2, 470-71.

[49] Leitsch, 'Wandel'.

[50] Braubach, *Eugen*, vol. 4, 36 (April 1719). A libellous pamphlet circulated in Vienna sometime after the king's death (*Epitaphium Carolo XII . . . erectum*).

[51] Hantsch, *Schönborn*, 233.

[52] Wratislaw's bitter remarks are reproduced in Goll, *Vertrag*, 53, Redlich, *Werden*, 82/3 and Ingrao, *Josef I.*, 82. His confidential letters to Joseph I are in ÖStA, HHStA Familienkorrespondenz A 16.

[53] Wratislaw to Marlborough, 6 August 1707: ÖStA, HHStA Staatenabteilungen Schweden 14. 'Il faut prendre des mesures à l'avenir que ce roi ne devienne plus puissant et que par conséquent il ne soit pas en état de bouleverser toute l'Europe, quand la fantaisie le prend.'

[54] Wratislaw to Marlborough, 3 September 1707: ÖStA, HHStA Staatenabteilungen Schweden 14. 'Le Roy est un jeune Prince, plein de vanité et enflé d'une vaine gloire par une suite heureuse des accidens inopinés et par des prospérités extraordinaires et sans interruption. . . . La colère est la passion dominante qui le pousse la

plupart de tems à tout ce qu'il fait et entreprend. Cette passion va si loing qu'on le voit quelques fois écumant de rage, et les gens qui l'approchent le plus près craignent qu'il ne devienne furieux, et si ce Prince n'étoit pas si sobre et bevroit du vin, peut-être le seroit-il déjà. . . . Ce jeune Roy est gatté par toutes les flatteries et bassesses que la plupart des princes de l'Europe luy ont faites tour à tour. . . . Cecy luy a donné un orgueil insupportable. . . . Le plus grand mal de tous les maux selon moy est que ce Prince n'a aucune règle ni politique et ne se souciant ni de sa vie ni de ses états, il devient par là dangereux à tous les voisins. . . . On l'a ouï souvent dire qu'il doit faire encore la guerre 13 ans.'

## 13 Charles XII at the Centre of Ottoman-Swedish Diplomacy

\* Professors Ari and Güney usually adhere to the Swedish calendar in their scholarly work. They have kindly agreed to use New Style dates in the present chapter.

1 Inalcik, *Devlet-i Aliyye*, II, 71.

2 Özcan, 'Karlofça'.

3 The Treaty of Constantinople was not ratified by Tsar Peter until 1709 because of the war with Sweden. This is precisely the political crisis that the Battle of Poltava brought to the fore. See Kurat, *XII. Karl'ın Türkiye'de Kalışı ve Bu Sıralarda Osmanlı İmparatorluğu*, 80.

4 Insurrection broke out in Constantinople in 1703, and Mustafa II lost his throne to Ahmed III; Feyzullah Efendi, highly respected advisor of the sultan, was executed as the one chiefly held responsible for the misadministration. See Özcan, 'Edirne Vak'ası'; also, Rifa'at AliAbou-El-Haj, 1703 İsyanı, *Osmanlı Siyasasının Yapısı*, 86.

5 Itzkowitz, 'The Ottoman Empire in the Eighteenth Century'.

6 Occupied with the War of the Spanish Succession, the Austrians had no intention of going to war with the Ottomans. Meanwhile, the fast-growing Hungarian rebellion left Austria between two fires. Schnettger, *Der Spanische Erbfolgekrieg: 1701-1713/14*; Smid, *Der Spanische Erbfolgekrieg: Geschichte eines vergessenen Weltkriegs (1701-1714)*; Kamen, *The War of Succession in Spain, 1700-15*.

7 Hughes, *Russia in the Age of Peter the Great*, 38-41; Englund, *The Battle That Shook Europe: Poltava and the Birth of the Russian Empire*; Ostrowski, 'Peter's Dragoons: How the Russians Won at Poltava', 81-106; Plokhyi, 'Poltava: The Battle That Never Ends', XIII-XXV.

8 Beydilli, 'İsveç'; Święcicka, 'Ottoman Manuscripts in Europe', 50.

9 Aktepe, 'Çorlulu Ali Paşa'.

10 Papp, 'Ottoman Accounts of the Hungarian Movements', 43; Gökbilgin, 'Rákóci Ferenc II ve Macar Mültecileri', 6.

11 Matuz, *Das Osmanische Reich*, 193. For more information see Parvev, *Habsburgs and Ottomans*; Heiss and Klingenstein, *Das Osmanische Reich und Europa 1683 bis 1789*; Kreutel and Teply, *Kara Mustafa vor Wien, 1683 aus der Sicht Türkischer Quellen*.

12 Baycar, *Osmanlı Rus İlişkileri Tarihi, Ahmet Cavit Bey'in Müntehabâtı*, 166-67. Kurat, *XII. Karl'ın Türkiye'*, 152; Święcicka, 'Ottoman Manuscripts in Europe', 50.

13 Kurat, *XII. Karl'ın Türkiye'*, 112-13.

14 *Ibidem*, 93-94.

15 Coroban, 'British Reactions to Charles XII's Stay in the Ottoman Empire', 29-63.

16 *Ibidem*, 124-25.

17 Kurat, *XII. Karl'ın Türkiye'*, 56; Coroban, 'British Reactions', 38-39.

18 When earlier, in 1703, Grand Vizier Daltaban Mustafa Pasha together with the khan of Crimea had developed a plan to retake the Azov fortress, Tolstoy's energetic counter-diplomacy and the interference of Emetullah Gülnuş, the valide sultan (the sultan's mother) prevented it. Daltaban Mustafa Pasha was replaced by Rami Mehmed Pasha. See Kamalov, *Tolstoy'un Gizli Raporlarında Osmanlı İmparatorluğu*, 125-29. For more information on Emetullah Gülnuş see Argıt, *Rabia Gülnuş Emetullah Sultan 1640-1715*.

19 İnalcık, 'Karadeniz'de Kazaklar ve Rusya: İstanbul Boğazı Tehlikede', 59-64; Yüksel, 'Rusların Karadeniz Yönünde Yapmış Oldukları İlk Yayılma Faaliyetleri (18. Yüzyılın Başlarına Kadar)', 101-16; Kamalov, *Tolstoy'un Gizli Raporlarında Osmanlı İmparatorluğu*, 125-29; Rycaut, *Osmanlı İmparatorluğu'nun Hâlihazırının Tarihi (XVII. Yüzyıl)*, 144.

20 Kurat, *XII Karl'ın Türkiye'*, 100.

21 For the Crimean khan, see Süreyya, *Sicill-i Osmani*, II, 419.

22 Despite his peace policy, the grand vizier was strengthening the Ottoman army and navy.

Kurat, *XII. Karl'ın Türkiye'*, 208-09.

23 *Ibidem*, 183-84.

24 *Ibidem*, 164-65.

25 Zinkeisen, *Osmanlı İmparatorluğu Tarihi*, V, 276.

26 Aktepe, '1711 Prut Seferi İle İlgili Bazı Belgeler', 22. Quotation from: 6 numaralı Nâme-i Hümâyûn Defteri'nin 36'ncı sahifesinden alınan mektup örneğI ('sample letter taken from the 36th page of volume number six of the Nâme-i Hümâyûn').

27 Another reason to be wary of war with the Russians was the tsar's shepherding of the Slavic cause in the Balkans, as well as the appearance of Wallachian and Moldavian pro-Russian movements. Uzunçarşılı, *Osmanlı Tarihi*, 72.

28 Aktepe, '1711 Prut Seferi İle İlgili Bazı Belgeler', 23.

29 Kurat, *XII Karl'ın Türkiye'*, 196-97. One of the first examples of the sultan's loss of confidence in the grand vizier was, after he read the king's letter and learned its contents, the arrest of Silahdar Gedik Hasan Ağa, esteemed among Çorlulu Ali Pasha's men, for currying favour. *Ibidem*, 201.

30 *Ibidem*, 207-11.

31 *Ibidem*, 202. A day before the meeting, Poniatowski's secret confidant in the palace sent a messenger to report that the following conversation had occurred between the sultan and the grand vizier: 'The sultan asked the grand vizier if any news had been received from the Swedish king; the grand vizier answered that there was nothing new; the sultan then said "I believe that there is nothing new, because the emissaries sent by the king are not allowed to join the negotiations; for this reason they do not make their demands known." The grand vizier attempted to defend himself with the sultan, who took out the memorandum sent to him and extended it to the grand vizier.' The sultan's disposition notwithstanding, Çorlulu's reversal of his political ideas shows he was convinced that war with Russia would be pointless and a quite dangerous adventure.

32 Here Poniatowski was said to be the shah of 'secret informants' in Constantinople; he was

even given the famous epithet of *eksaporreton* taken from the (Constantinopolitan) Greek and given to no one after him, most likely by the chief dragoman of the palace, Nicolas Mavrocordato. However, *mahrem-i esrar* was a common expression at the time, and care should be taken with Poniatowski's use of it in this sense. See Kantemir, *Osmanlı İmparatorluğu'nun Yükseliş ve Çöküş Tarihi*, 486; Çiftçi, 'Bâb-ı Âlî'nin Avrupa'ya Çevrilmiş İki Gözü: Eflak ve Boğdan'da Fenerli Voyvodalar (1711-1821)', 27-48.

[33] Mehmed Ağa's successful negotiations and the reports he submitted on the Swedish issue during Baltacı Mehmed Pasha's vizierate were reasons for his advancement to *Kapıcılar Kethüdası* on 2 November 1710. Kurat, *XII. Karl'ın Türkiye*, 288.

[34] *Ibidem*, 217; for the full report in French see Kurat, 'Leh Fevkalade Elçisi von Goltz'un Türkiye'deki Faaliyetine Ait Raporu (1712-1714)', 225-65.

[35] At the end of May 1710, according to French ambassador Des Alleurs, the king borrowed 400,000 *kuruş* from a Constantinople Jew with the approval of the sultan. The grand vizier, however, knew nothing of this. Developments provide evidence that the grand vizier's fate had already been sealed by the talks held between Charles XII and Devlet Giray on 1 June. Kurat, *XII. Karl'ın Türkiye*, 225.

[36] *Ibidem*, 235-41.

[37] Kantemir, *Osmanlı İmparatorluğu'nun Yükseliş ve Çöküş Tarihi*, 514; Özcan, 'Köprülüzâde Nûman Paşa', 265-67; Kurat, *XII. Karl'ın Türkiye*, 246-48. Râşid's history offers no reason related to the affairs of state for Köprülüzade's dismissal. See Özcan, *Târîh-i Râşid ve Zeyli*, 839.

[38] Aktepe, 'Baltacı Mehmed Paşa', 36; Kurat, *XII. Karl'ın Türkiye*, 285; Kantemir, *Osmanlı İmparatorluğu'nun Yükseliş ve Çöküş Tarihi*, 504-14.

[39] Özcan, *Târîh-i Râşid ve Zeyli*, 866.

[40] Aktepe, 'Baltacı Mehmed Paşa', 24.

[41] Kurat, *XII. Karl'ın Türkiye*, 235-36. For a comprehensive evaluation of the history of Ottoman-Polish relations see Topaktaş, *Osmanlı-Lehistan Diplomatik İlişkileri*, 15-35.

[42] *Osmanlı Rus İlişkileri Tarihi, Ahmet Cavit Bey'in Müntehabâtı*, 168-70.

[43] Kurat, *XII. Karl'ın Türkiye*, 295.

[44] *Ibidem*, 306.

[45] Özcan, *Târîh-i Râşid ve Zeyli*, 846.

[46] Kurat, *XII. Karl'ın Türkiye*, 351, 355-62. Proclamation of war with Russia was delayed with the intention of gaining time to seek aid from the Maritime Powers. The tsar, evaluating the Swedish issue and war with the Turks, could not obtain any promise of support in case of conflict with the Turks from his diplomatic contacts. *Ibidem*, 376-78. The Battle of the Pruth was recorded by a secretary who participated in the campaign, the Janissary Hasan Kürdî (or Giridî), in his 'Tarih-i Moskof' (History of Moscow). Munich, Bayerische Staatsbibliothek, Cod.turc. 91; Topkapı Sarayı Müzesi, Hazine Kitaplığı, Nr. 233. See also Kurat, *Prut Seferi ve Barışı*.

[47] The delegation left Constantinople on 14 January 1711, arriving in Vienna on 7 April. See Beydilli-Erünsal, 'Prut Savaşı Öncesi Diplomatik Bir Teşebbüs, Seyfullah Ağa'nın Viyana Elçiliği (1711)', 2-4. The letter from Grand Vizier Baltacı Mehmed Pasha presented to Prince Eugene lays out the status of the Ottoman inland sea where on the shores of the Black Sea shipyards were found, a clear sign the Treaty of Constantinople had been violated, and signalled that the only obvious purpose of the journey was to put an end to Russia's infractions. For a copy of the letter, see BOA, *Nâme Defteri*, VI, 205-08. Beydilli-Erünsal, 'Prut Savaşı Öncesi Diplomatik Bir Teşebbüs', 37-45.

[48] Beydilli-Erünsal, 'Prut Savaşı Öncesi Diplomatik Bir Teşebbüs', 9. This development showed how Charles XII's war plans were utterly inconsistent with the state of affairs. The king believed that once Poland had been cleared of Russian forces, a combined assault on Russia from multiple directions would lead the way to Moscow. See Kurat, *XII. Karl'ın Türkiye*, 332-33.

[49] *Ibidem*, 345-46. Charles XII and Ahmed III declared on several occasions throughout the months of May and June 1711 that without mutual agreement neither Sweden nor the Ottoman Empire would make peace with Russia. *Ibidem*, 383-85.

[50] These changes took place mid-April; the full delegation of Ottoman diplomats sent to Vienna signals that the Ottoman and Swedish governments had very different political objectives. *Ibidem*, 386-87.

[51] Browning, *Charles XII of Sweden*, 254.

[52] Kurat, *XII. Karl'ın Türkiye*, 407-08.

[53] Hazine-i Bîrun Kâtibi Ahmet bin Mahmud Efendi's records on the Pruth expedition confirm that the Ottoman Empire was not able to take advantage of the favourable terms. According to Mahmud Efendi, never before in Ottoman history had so much ammunition and so many cannon been collected as this time from the Russian army surrounded at the Pruth, and the commander-in-chief, Tsar Peter, was forced into an unprecedented and unconditional surrender. Protocol, however, required an aloof and imperious attitude, and the substance of the treaty does not reflect well on the Ottomans, who missed a historic opportunity and allowed the Russian army to leave with all its equipment. The Russians, in order not to surrender their cannon, put forward the excuse that they required protection from Tartar attacks. That the Ottomans gave credence to this excuse and did not stand behind the Tartars is one of the most peculiar cases in Ottoman diplomatic history. Rado, 'Hazine-i Birun Kâtibi Ahmet bin Mahmud Efendi'nin Tuttuğu Prut Seferi'ne Ait Defterden Koparılan Sahifelerde Neler Vardı?', 812-13; Kurat, 'Hazine-i Bîrun Kâtibi Ahmed bin Mahmud'un (1123-1711-Prut) Seferine Ait Defteri'.

[54] In contrast, Şeyh ül-İslam Paşmakçızade Seyid Ali Efendi in replying to a letter from French ambassador Des Alleurs defended the peace at the Pruth, stating: 'I can confirm that the tsar truly is in a tight spot; however, it is undeniable that this pact concerns many of the Ottoman Empire's interests. Our laws (sharia) forbid drawing the sword on those who call for mercy. The tsar has asked for peace, and the grand vizier can make no move to the contrary without opposing this basic position; and the sultan, too, would not be able to do it without the approval and consent of the whole army as well as confirmation in writing from the minister rescinding the peace.' Kurat, 'Hazine-i Bîrun Kâtibi Ahmed bin Mahmud'un', 513-14.

[55] For more on the Pruth treaty, see *Osmanlı Rus İlişkileri Tarihi, Ahmet Cavit Bey'in Müntehabâtı*, 178-83.

[56] Kurat, *XII. Karl'ın Türkiye*, 459-68; also Browning, *Charles XII of Sweden*, 254-55.

[57] Kurat, *XII. Karl'ın Türkiye*, 476-78.

[58] That the Swedish representative at this meeting petitioned to borrow a sum of money was a sign of the Swedes' hopeless situation. As Mavrocordato mentioned, provisions and financial assistance could have been provided to the Swedes in the event of further delay. *Ibidem*, 478.

[59] *Ibidem*, 481-82.

[60] *Ibidem*, 516.

[61] *Ibidem*, 524-28.

[62] This decision unsettled Ahmed III, who wrote furiously to the grand vizier asking, 'Is it your intention to enslave the Swedes to Nalkıran or else to accursed Moscow?' See 'III. Ahmed'in Baltacı Mehmed Paşa'ya Hattı', *Topkapı Sarayı Arşivi, E. 6073*.

[63] Kurat, *XII. Karl'ın Türkiye'de*, 537-40.

[64] 'III. Ahmed'in Baltacı Mehmed Paşa'ya Hattı', Topkapı Sarayı Arşivi, E. 6073.

[65] Kurat, *XII. Karl'ın Türkiye'*, 545-46.

[66] Aktepe, 'Baltacı Mehmed Paşa'.

[67] Kurat, *XII. Karl'ın Türkiye'*, 550.

[68] As a matter of fact, the Russian surrender of Azov was linked to the Swedish departure from Ottoman territory with an ultimatum issued to Russia on 21 December giving them a 40-day period in which to evacuate Azov. Otherwise war would recommence. *Ibidem*, 555-58.

[69] *Ibidem*, 559-66.

[70] *Ibidem*, 582.

[71] *Ibidem*, 583-97.

[72] *Ibidem*, 604-09; *Târîh-i Râşid ve Zeyli*, 871.

[73] Charles XII claimed for himself the money sent to pay his debts and in order to depart in two weeks he tried to borrow an additional amount of 1,000 purses, reacting harshly to the conditions. Kurat, *XII. Karl'ın Türkiye'*, 621.

[74] *Ibidem*, 624.

[75] 'Krala ne güne muamele olunmak gerekdir diye müzakere olundukda: birkaç seneden beru diyarına gitmesi için teklifatına müsaade olundukda, kendüden taallul u huşunet müşahede olunub, Devlet-i Aliyye'ye zahmet vermeden gayrı bir fikri olmadığı zahirdir. Müsafir ise müddet-i müsaferet tamam oldu. Gidecek ise bir an mukaddem kalksun. Yok düşmenden havf ederim derse işte asker hazır u amade duruyor. Ve illa ferman-i aliye itaat etmeyüb bu halatın birini ihtiyar etmezse ahz olunub bu tarafa götürülmesi iktiza eder deyu ittifak ve Şeyhülislam Efendi fetva vermekle Bender Seraskeri Vezir İsmail Paşa'ya ferman yazıldı,' in Özcan, *Târîh-i Râşid ve Zeyli*, 874; Kurat, *XII. Karl'ın Türkiye'*, 625. An English translation of the text quoted above: 'We have been negotiating a long time with the king; for several years we have offered to allow him to go to his own land, to our own detriment, and it is clear that the Great Ottoman Empire has not been unharmed by these ideas. It is well for a guest to remain a while, if he is going to leave according to the precedent. If not, a soldier stands ready and prepared against the enemies of his people. If the *ferman* is not obeyed, which side it is necessary to ally with will be revealed, and the Şeh ül-İslam will give the fatwa to İsmail Pasha, the Seraskeri Vezir at Bender.'

[76] Kurat, *XII. Karl'ın Türkiye'*, 630-37, 654.

[77] Finkel, *Rüyadan İmparatorluğa Osmanlı*, 299.

[78] Kurat, *XII. Karl'ın Türkiye'*, 645-46.

[79] This appointment was the main factor allowing the Swedish issue to get out from under the Russian shadow. *Ibidem*, 651.

[80] *Ibidem*, 650-58.

[81] *Ibidem*, 661.

[82] Bearing letters of farewell and gratitude from the king, Grothusen arrived in Constantinople on 29 July as ambassador plenipotentiary. On 22 August, he came before the sultan's presence and tendered a letter detailing the king's route to his country through Austria, and appearing again in the sultan's presence on 27 August, he essentially received the sultan's permission for the king to travel. Despite his amicable reception, Grothusen's request for a loan of 1,200 purses was refused by Ali Pasha. The Sublime Porte, Des Alleurs, and the Swedes themselves each provided a portion of the money required for the king's return. *Ibidem*, 670-73.

[83] *Ibidem*, 680.

[84] See Sevinç, 'İsveç Karlı XII. Şarl'ın Osmanlı Devleti'ne İlticası ve İkameti (1709-1714)'.

[85] During the reign of Mahmud I a certificate was drawn up discharging the debt and dealing with the particulars of the Swedish-Ottoman agreement. *Başbakanlık Osmanlı Arşivi, Cevdet Hariciye*, 8634. The certification can be found at the end of the text. See Güler, '1150/1737 Osmanlı-İsveç Ticaret Anlaşması'.

[86] Finkel, *Rüyadan İmparatorluğa Osmanlı*, 299.

## 14 Charles XII and the Kingdom of Denmark-Norway

[1] In recent Swedish historiography there is a consensus that the Swedish period of great power was a cyclic phenomenon. See Rystad, 'Vägen till fred', in Askgaard and Stade, eds., *Kampen om Skåne*, 399-420, and Behre, Larsson, and Österberg, *Sveriges historia 1521-1809*, 184-88.

[2] A brief summary of the armed conflicts between Denmark and Sweden can be found in Jespersen's 'Warfare and Society in the Baltic 1500-1800', in Black, ed., *European Warfare, 1453-1815*, 180-200.

[3] Lengeler, *Das Ringen um die Ruhe des Nordens*, 31-41.

[4] For the alliance negotiations, see Feldbæk and Jespersen, *Revanche og neutralitet 1648-1814*, 170 ff., where the short war of 1700 is also covered.

[5] Jespersen, 'Den sidste styrkeprøve 1700-1720', in Frantzen and Jespersen, eds., *Danmarks krigshistorie 700-2010*, 341-44.

[6] A description of Charles XII as a field commander is given in Arteus, *Svensk fältherrekonst*, 7-28. Oredsson, 'Karl XII', in Oredsson, ed., *Tsar Peter och Kung Karl*, 35-74, gives a detailed account of the king's childhood and character.

[7] Jespersen, 'Den sidste styrkeprøve', 336-39.

[8] Molesworth, *An Account of Denmark*, 224.

[9] For the renewed alliance, see Feldbæk and Jespersen, *Revanche og neutralitet*, 180-82.

[10] The unsuccessful invasion of Skåne is fully covered by Bjerg and Frantzen, *Danmark i krig*, 190-99.

[11] For the war in northern Germany and its eventual outcome, see Jespersen, 'Den sidste styrkeprøve', 349-60; cf. Arteus, *Svensk fältherrekonst*, 65-76.

[12] Feldbæk and Jespersen, *Revanche og neutralitet*, 187-89.

[13] The final act in Norway is dealt with by Jespersen, 'Den sidste styrkeprøve', 363-66.

[14] The circumstances surrounding the death of Charles XII's are thoroughly dealt with by Uppström, *Mysteriet Karl XII's død*.

[15] Feldbæk and Jespersen, *Revanche og neutralitet*, 189-91.

[16] Oredsson, 'Karl XII', 64-69.

# 15 A Polish View of Charles XII and the Great Northern War

1 Gierowski, *W cieniu Ligi Północnej,* 24.

2 Skworoda, *Wojny Rzeczypospolitej,* 211-12.

3 Staszewski, *August II,* 133-134.

4 Otwinowski, *Pamiętniki do panowania Augusta II,* 19; Konopczyński, *Polska a Szwecja. Od pokoju oliwskiego do upadku Rzeczypospolitej 1660-1795,* 32.

5 Staszewski, *August II,* 93-108.

6 Zwierzykowski, 'Konsekwencje ustrojowe wielkiej wojny północnej dla Rzeczypospolitej', 260.

7 Wimmer, *Wojsko Rzeczypospolitej w dobie wojny północnej,* 41-44.

8 Anusik, *Karol XII,* 79.

9 Staszewski, *August II,* 147.

10 Anusik, *Karol XII,* 79.

11 Jarochowski, *Dzieje panowania Augusta II. Od śmierci Jana III do chwili wstąpienia Karola XII na ziemię polską,* I, 183-88; Staszewski, 'Wojny XVIII wieku', 9.

12 Otwinowski, *Dzieje Polski pod panowaniem Augusta II,* 31.

13 See Arājs, 'Bitwa nad Dźwiną 9 lipca', 197-209.

14 Jonasson, *Karl XII och hans rådgivare. Den utrikespolitiska maktkampen i Sverige 1697-1702,* 239, 250; Burdowicz-Nowicki, *Piotr I, August II I Rzeczpospolita 1697-1706,* 278.

15 Konopczyński, *Polska a Szwecja. Od pokoju oliwskiego do upadku Rzeczypospolitej 1660-1795,* 40; Feldman, *Polska w dobie wielkiej wojny północnej 1704-1709,* 11, 15.

16 Jarochowski, *Dzieje panowania Augusta II. Od wstąpienia Karola XII na ziemię polską aż do elekcji Stanisława Leszczyńskiego (1702-1704),* II, 9.

17 Konopczyński, *Polska a Szwecja. Od pokoju oliwskiego do upadku Rzeczypospolitej 1660-1795,* 42.

18 Jarochowski, *Dzieje panowania Augusta II. Od wstąpienia Karola XII na ziemię polską aż do elekcji Stanisława Leszczyńskiego (1702-1704),* II, 84.

19 Staszewski, 'Wojny XVIII wieku', 10.

20 Jarochowski, *Dzieje panowania Augusta II. Od wstąpienia Karola XII na ziemię polską aż do elekcji Stanisława Leszczyńskiego (1702-1704),* II, 366.

21 Quoted after Cieślak, *Stanisław Leszczyński,* 17: 'Nie było może dwóch mniej podobnych do siebie natur jak Karol XII i Leszczyński. Pierwszy waleczny do szaleństwa, szukający niebezpieczeństw, lakoniczny, nieprzyjaciel wszelkiej zbytku i wystawy; drugi, człowiek pokoju i rady, wszystko raczej niż żołnierz, wymowny i rozmowny, lubujący się w zwykłej magnatom polskim owej epoki dworności i wygodzie.'

22 Rakowski, *Pamiętnik wielkiej wojny północnej,* 16: '. . . obrany królem polskim od króla szwedzkiego, województwa poznańskiego, kaliskiego, łęczyckiego, rawskiego, mazowieckiego, podlaskiego pod flintami [szwedzkimi] przymuszonych.'

23 Jarochowski, *Dzieje panowania Augusta II. Od wstąpienia Karola XII na ziemię polską aż do elekcji Stanisława Leszczyńskiego (1702-1704),* II, 394: 'Nie zostawiajmy potomności przykładu wyboru króla wśród obcej siły zbrojnej, według woli obcego mocarstwa.'

24 Koroluk, *Polska i Rosja a wojna północna,* 363; Feldman, *Polska w dobie wielkiej wojny północnej 1704-1709,* 2.

25 Jarochowski, *Dzieje panowania Augusta II. Od wstąpienia Karola XII na ziemię polską do elekcji Stanisława Leszczyńskiego (1702-1704),* II, 396.

26 *Ibidem,* II, 396-97.

27 Cieślak, *Stanisław Leszczyński,* 51.

28 See Poraziński, *Epiphania Poloniae. Orientacje i postawy polityczne szlachty polskiej w dobie wielkiej wojny północnej (1702-1710).*

29 Konopczyński, *Polska a Szwecja. Od pokoju oliwskiego do upadku Rzeczypospolitej 1660-1795,* 50-52; Feldman, *Polska w dobie wielkiej wojny północnej 1704-1709,* 129; Cieślak, *Stanisław Leszczyński,* 47-50; Anusik, *Karol XII,* 138.

30 Anusik, *Karol XII,* 148-50.

31 Staszewski, *August II,* 165, 166; Anusik, *Karol XII,* 154.

32 Burdowicz-Nowicki, *Piotr I, August II i Rzeczpospolita 1697-1706,* 686,705.

33 Cieślak, *Stanisław Leszczyński,* 54.

34 *Ibidem,* 54; Konopczyński, *Polska a Szwecja. Od pokoju oliwskiego do upadku Rzeczypospolitej 1660-1795,* 59-61.

35 Konopczyński, *Polska a Szwecja. Od pokoju oliwskiego do upadku Rzeczypospolitej 1660-1795,* 59: 'Poczciwy Leszczyński nie przywiózł z Altranstädtu ani szczypty królewskiego ducha: tchórzył przed narodem, korzył się przed Szwedami, aż do całowania rąk Pipera, aż do wywoływania w nich samych uczucia politowania i wstrętu.'

36 Feldman, *Polska w dobie wielkiej wojny północnej 1704-1709,* 58: '. . . przez cały czas panowania Leszczyński odegrał w stosunku do protektora szwedzkiego rolę wasala, by nie rzec niewolnika.'

37 Quoted after Cieślak, *Stanisław Leszczyński,* 55: 'jako że w zupełności zależę od Waszej Królewskiej Mości, błagam zechciej przekazać mi dyspozycje co do mojej osoby.'

38 Staszewski, *August II,* 185.

39 Gierowski, *W cieniu Ligii Północnej,* 94, 95.

40 Budrowicz-Nowicki, *Piotr I, August II i Rzeczpospolita 1697-1706,* 738; Feldman, *Polska a sprawa wschodnia,* 8-11.

41 Otwinowski, *Dzieje Polski pod panowaniem Augusta II,* 165.

42 Cieślak, 'W wirze wojny północnej', 497.

43 Staszewski, *August II,* 206, 207.

44 Konopczyński, *Polska a Szwecja. Od pokoju oliwskiego do upadku Rzeczypospolitej 1660-1795,* 100.

45 Poraziński, '"Od Sasa do Lasa" – czyli wojna w krzywym zwierciadle. Uwagi o satyrze politycznej czasów saskich', 91.

46 Gierowski, *Między saskim absolutyzmem a złotą wolnością,* 9 ff.

47 Konopczyński, *Dzieje Polski nowożytnej,* 585.

48 Nycz, *Geneza reform skarbowych sejmu niemego (studium z dziejów skarbowo-wojskowych z lat 1697-1717),* 142, 263.

49 Cieślak, 'W wirze wojny północnej', 485-91; idem, *Stanisław Leszczyński,* 45.

50 Trzoska, 'Gdański handel i żegluga', 52-55; Cieślak, 'W wirze wojny północnej', 497-504.

51 Trzoska, 'Sprawa kaprów królewskich w Gdańsku w polityce Augusta II i Piotra I (1716-1721)', 24 ff.

52 Wałęga, 'Cudzoziemscy goście w osiemnastowiecznym Toruniu', 263.

53 Archiwum Główne Akt Dawnych, Archiwum Publiczne Potockich, Ms. no. 162, vol. 2: Z Torunia, 14.07.1703, 361; Otwinowski, *Dzieje Polski pod panowaniem Augusta II,* 53-54; Dydgała, 'Upadek miasta w dobie wojny północnej (1700-1718)', 143-44.

54 Gierszewski, *Elbląg. Przeszłość i teraźniejszość,* 153.

[55] Trzoska, 'Zmiany w handlu bałtyckim i europejskim', 339, 340; Guldon and Wijaczka, 'Zarazy a zaludnienie i gospodarka Polski w dobie wielkiej wojny północnej', 206.

[56] Górny and Piwarski, *Kraków w czasie drugiego najazdu Szwedów na Polskę 1702-1709*, 21-46; Łakociński, *Magnus Stenbock w Polsce. Przyczynek do historii szwedzkich zdobyczy w czasie wielkiej wojny północnej*, 32 ff.

[57] Otwinowski, *Dzieje Polski pod panowaniem Augusta II*, 35, 46-47; see *Rzeczpospolita w dobie upadku 1700-1740*, 23-24.

[58] Gierowski, *Między saskim absolutyzmem a złotą wolnością*, 29-30.

[59] Archiwum Główne Akt Dawnych, Archiwum Publiczne Potockich, Ms. no. 163a, vol. 31: F. Włoszkiewicz do S. A. Szczuki, Warszawa 25.05.1702, 515-17; Biblioteka Czartoryskich, Ms. no. 196: List z Warszawy z 26.05.1702, 267-69; Bartoszewicz, 'Karol XII w Warszawie w 1702 roku', 261-71.

[60] Calculation based on Trzoska, 'Zmienne koniunktury w handlu i żegludze gdańskiej', 90; Trzoska, 'Handel i żegluga gdańska w XVIII wieku', 382.

[61] Calculation based on Biernat, *Statystyka obrotu towarowego Gdańska w latach 1651-1815*, 88-92.

[62] Hoszowski, 'Handel Gdańska w okresie XV-XVIII wieku', 48.

[63] Gierowski, *Między saskim absolutyzmem a złotą wolnością*, 72, 76.

[64] Calculation based on Biernat, *Statystyka obrotu towarowego Gdańska w latach 1651-1815*, 280-81.

[65] Groth, 'Port, żegluga i handel morski Elbląga w XV-XVIII wieku', tab. 4.

[66] Gierowski, *Między saskim absolutyzmem a złotą wolnością*, 68-69.

[67] *Ibidem*, 71.

[68] *Ibidem*, 44, 57-58.

[69] *Abrys domowej nieszczęśliwości wewnętrznej niesnaski* , 62.

[70] Roniker, *Hetman Adam Sieniawski i jego regimentarze. Studium z historii mentalności szlachty polskiej 1706-1725*, 10.

[71] Nycz, *Geneza reform skarbowych sejmu niemego (studium z dziejów skarbowo-wojskowych z lat 1697-1717)*, 18.

[72] Guldon and Wijaczka, 'Zarazy a zaludnienie i gospodarka Polski w dobie wielkiej wojny północnej', 214.

[73] *Ibidem*, 202; see *Rzeczpospolita w dobie upadku 1700-1740*, 25-26.

[74] Gierowski, *Między saskim absolutyzmem a złotą wolnością*, 13.

[75] *Ibidem*, 15.

[76] Anusik, *Karol XII*, 152-60.

[77] Staszewski, *August II*, 172, 176.

[78] Poraziński, '"Od Sasa do Lasa" – czyli wojna w krzywym zwierciadle. Uwagi o satyrze politycznej czasów saskich', 92.

[79] Idem, 'Opozycja antysaska w Rzeczypospolitej za Augusta II jako problem polityczny i ustrojowy', 93-101.

[80] Drozdowski, 'Działalność budżetowa sejmu Rzeczypospolitej w czasach saskich', 116-28.

[81] Zwierzykowski, 'Konsekwencje ustrojowe wielkiej wojny północnej dla Rzeczypospolitej', 261-62; see Sowa, *Świat ministrów Augusta II. Wartości poglądy funkcjonujące w kręgu ministrów Rzeczypospolitej w latach 1702-1728*.

[82] See Poraziński, 'Funkcje polityczne i ustrojowe rad senatu w latach 1697-1717', 25-45.

[83] Zwierzykowski, 'Konsekwencje ustrojowe wielkiej wojny północnej dla Rzeczypospolitej', 263.

[84] *Klasztory karmelitanek bosych w Polsce, na Litwie i Rusi*, 22-23; Fankidejski, *Klasztory żeńskie w diecezji chełmińskiej*, 208-09; see Majewska, *Szwecja. Kraj, ludzie, rządy w opinii polskiej II połowy XVIII wieku*, 89-123.

[85] Odyniec, 'Obraz Szwecji i Szwedów w Polsce XVI w. (do 1587 r.)', 12.

[86] Poraziński, '"Od Sasa do Lasa" – czyli wojna w krzywym zwierciadle. Uwagi o satyrze politycznej czasów saskich', 95.

[87] See, for example, Otwinowski, *Dzieje Polski pod panowaniem Augusta II*; *Pamiętniki do panowania Augusta II napisane przez Erazma Otwinowskiego*; Rakowski, *Pamiętnik wielkiej wojny północnej*; *Pamiętniki Krzysztofa Zawiszy (1666-1721)*; *Abrys domowej nieszczęśliwości wewnętrznej niesnaski*; *Kroniki benedyktynek poznańskich*; Fankidejski, *Klasztory żeńskie w diecezji chełmińskiej*; Zawadzki, *Początki prasy polskiej. Gazety ulotne i seryjne XVI-XVIII wieku*, 297.

[88] Biblioteka Czartoryskich, Ms. no. 196: Doniesienie z Warszawy z 19. 06.1702, 351; Bartoszewicz, 'Karol XII w Warszawie w 1702 roku', 261-71.

[89] Wałęga, 'Cudzoziemscy goście w osiemnastowiecznym Toruniu', 263.

[90] Bartoszewicz, 'Karol XII w Warszawie w 1702 roku', 262, 265.

[91] Archiwum Główne Akt Dawnych, Archiwum Radziwiłłów, Dept. II, Ms. no. 1970: Uniwersał Karola XII z 1702.

[92] Otwinowski, *Pamiętniki do panowania Augusta II*, 103.

[93] Rakowski, *Pamiętnik wielkiej wojny północnej*, 11: '. . . pod pozorem słodkiego spokoju Król JM szwedzki co innego knuje i chce zburzyć państwo nasze i prerogatywy dobrze myślących obywateli.'

[94] Górny and Piwarski, *Kraków w czasie drugiego najazdu Szwedów na Polskę 1702-1709*, 46.

[95] *Pamiętniki Krzysztofa Zawiszy (1666-1721)*, 352.

[96] Cieślak, *Stanisław Leszczyński*, 44; Feldman, *Polska w dobie wielkiej wojny północnej (1704-1709)*, 60-61; Anusik, *Karol XII*, 98.

[97] *Pamiętniki Krzysztofa Zawiszy (1666-1721)*, 352 : '. . . z którego [Karola] śmierci nie tylko Polska wypocząć może, ale i sama Szwecja'; Otwinowski, *Dzieje Polski pod panowaniem Augusta II*, 333; idem, *Pamiętniki do panowania Augusta II*, 356.

[98] Górny and Piwarski, *Kraków w czasie drugiego najazdu Szwedów na Polskę 1702-1709*, 27; Goliński, 'Bellonae domus descriptio. Strach przed wojną pośród lęków doby saskiej', 152-61.

[99] Archiwum Główne Akt Dawnych, Archiwum Radziwiłłów, Dept. II, Ms. no. 1990: List Stenbocka do ordynata Zamoyskiego z 11.02.1703; Jarochowski, *Dzieje panowania Augusta II. Od wstąpienia Karola XII na ziemię polską aż do elekcji Stanisława Leszczyńskiego (1702-1704)*, II, 70; Łakociński, *Magnus Stenbock w Polsce*, 15; Górny and Piwarski, *Kraków w czasie drugiego najazdu Szwedów na Polskę 1702-1709*, 26.

[100] Jarochowski, *Dzieje panowania Augusta II. Od wstąpienia Karola XII na ziemię polską aż do elekcji Stanisława Leszczyńskiego (1702-1704)*, II, 70.

[101] Quoted after Konopczyński, *Polska a Szwecja. Od pokoju oliwskiego do upadku Rzeczypospolitej 1660-1795*, 46: 'Brać i dostarczać jak się da, niech kraj cierpi ile chce, . . . . Kto okaże choćby najmniejszą opieszałość, albo inaczej choć troszkę zawini – tego bez litości, jak najsrożej egzekwować i palić . . . . A kto w domu nieobecny, albo okazuje najlżejszą chęć wsiąść na koń – tego przede wszystkim spalić i zrujnować do szczętu.'

[102] Quoted after Łakociński, *Magnus Stenbock w Polsce*, 53: 'Wykonując rozkaz mego najmiło-

ściwszego Króla urządziłem wyprawę w góry dla zburzenia polskich gniazd oporu. . . . w marszu tam szedłem z pochodnią w ręku , a gdy na drodze znalazła się jakaś wieś, która nie zapłaciła kontrybucji, wtedy podpalałem ją ze wszystkich czterech stron; kilku chłopów upiekło się przy tej sposobności.'

[103] *Ibidem*, 95.

[104] *Pamiętniki Krzysztofa Zawiszy (1666-1721)*, 383: 'Generał Stenbock żołnierz wielki, doświadczenia wielkiego do wojny, pomysłów dobrych na wodzie do robienia mostów i przepraw przebywania, człowiek siła praktykujący, tanecznik, galantomo, ale z tym wszystkim dziki i ciężki na ludzi, dał się dobrze Polsce we znaki.'

[105] *Ibidem*, 384: 'Żołnierz stary, grzeczny, dobrze postępujący z pospólstwem, nie ciężki na ludzi.'

[106] Archiwum Główne Akt Dawnych, Archiwum Zamoyskich, Ms. no. 3030, document dated 07.09.1707, 111; Górny and Piwarski, *Kraków w czasie drugiego najazdu Szwedów na Polskę 1702-1709,* 51.

[107] Rehnskiöld, 'Generalen friherre Carl Gustaf Rehnskiölds anteckningar och dagbocker', 28, 30, 82.

[108] *Pamiętniki Krzysztofa Zawiszy*, 382-86.

[109] Jarochowski, *Oblężenie miasta Poznania przez Patkula. Epizod kampanii roku 1704,* 18-24.

[110] *Kroniki benedyktynek poznańskich*, 272; Fankidejski, *Klasztory żeńskie w diecezji chełmińskiej*, 155-56, 187, 208; Targosz, 'Obraz wojen i zaraz początków XVIII wieku w kronikach zakonnic', 122-36; Górny and Piwarski, *Kraków w czasie drugiego najazdu Szwedów na Polskę 1702-1709*, 29, 32; Łakociński, *Magnus Stenbock w Polsce*, 51.

[111] Otwinowski, *Dzieje Polski pod panowaniem Augusta II*, 69, 332.

[112] Bogucka, 'Sweden and Poland: Economic, Sociopolitical and Cultural Relations in the First Half of the 17th Century', 164.

[113] Targosz, 'Obraz wojen i zaraz początków XVIII wieku w kronikach zakonnic', 127-28.

[114] Biblioteka Czartoryskich, Ms. no. 197; Rozmowa Polaka ze Szwedem, 06. 04. 1703, 255, 256.

[115] Buchwald-Pelcowa, *Satyra czasów saskich*, 223-37.

[116] Otwinowski, *Dzieje Polski pod panowaniem Augusta II*, 78; idem, *Pamiętniki do panowania Augusta II*, 37: 'mizerni, wpółnadzy, na chudych szkapach.'

[117] Leszczyński, 'Rzut oka na politykę i administrację narodową dla użycia Delfina', 212; *Klasztory karmelitanek bosych w Polsce, na Litwie i Rusi,* 131.

[118] Biblioteka Czartoryskich, Ms. no. 196: Doniesienie z Warszawy z 19.06.1702, 531.

[119] Bartoszewicz, 'Karol XII w Warszawie w 1702 roku', 263, 264; Targosz, 'Obraz wojen i zaraz początków XVIII wieku w kronikach zakonnic', 123-31.

[120] Skrzetuski, *Historia Królestwa Szwedzkiego*, 299; Tomaszewski, *Nad konstytucją i rewolucją dnia 3 maja roku 1791 uwagi*, 21.

[121] Koźmian, *Pamiętniki*, 30; Kołłątaj, *Do Stanisława Małachowskiego*, list II, 24; see Majewska, *Szwecja. Kraj, ludzie, rządy w polskiej opinii II połowy XVIII wieku*, 117.

[122] Majewska, *Szwecja. Kraj, ludzie, rządy w polskiej opinii II połowy XVIII wieku*, 119: 'Zły jak Szwed,' 'Brudny jak Szwed,' 'Szwedy narobiły w Polsce biedy', 'Tyle co Szwedów.'

# 16  Russian Views of Charles XII

* In his scholarly work Professor Krotov generally adheres to the Julian calendar, which was used in Russia until 1918. He has kindly agreed to use New Style dates in the present chapter.

[1] Swedish manuscript map entitled 'Campement på Zeland wid Humblebäck', signed: 'Landscrona. 23 augustÿ 1700. Clas Rödken'. RGAVMF, Fund 1331, opis 1, delo 1, f. 1.

[2] *Karl XII på slagfältet*, vol. 3, 298-99, 318.

[3] Artamonov, *Battle of Poltava*, 34.

[4] 'Народ же бывший тогда в крайней не искусности в военных делах не мог понять, как шведский король с таким малым войском смог одолеть их силу, весьма многим числом превосходящую.' Soymonov, *History of Peter the Great*, 94.

[5] Nikoforov, *Russo-English Relations*, 24-25.

[6] Bolingbroke, *Letters*, 1752, 294.

[7] 'on n'applaudissoit qu'à lui seul, il n'étoit grand que par lui-même; sa valeur, son génie avoient fait le destin de ses armes . . . .' *L'Aveu sans exemple*, 182.

[8] 'Charles vouloit se venger, & une ardeur trop opiniâtre l'empêchoit . . . .'; 'un desir trop inflexible de vengeance.' *Ibidem*, 170, 183.

[9] *Letters and Papers of Emperor Peter the Great*, 1077.

[10] Oredsson, 'Tsar Peter and King Charles', 42, 69, 70.

[11] Wolf, *The Emergence of the Great Powers*, 56.

[12] Cited in Bespyatykh, 'The Third "Coming" of Peter I', 50.

[13] *Ibidem*, 51.

[14] 'Brefvexling mellan konung Carl XII och Rådet', 150.

[15] *Anthology of the Imperial Russian Historical Society*, vol. 39, 70.

[16] *History of the Swedish War*, issue 1, 209.

[17] *Ibidem*, 159.

[18] Shafirov, *A Discourse concerning the Just Causes . . .*, 39.

[19] *Ibidem*.

[20] Nikoforov, *Russo-English Relations*, 44-45, 50, 63.

[21] Cited in Vozgrin, *Russia and European Lands*, 204.

[22] Cited in *ibidem*.

[23] Haintz, *König Karl XII von Schweden*, vol. 1, 212.

[24] *History of the Swedish War*, issue 1, 134, 275, 278.

[25] Artamonov, *The Battle of Poltava*, 306.

[26] Cited in *ibidem*, 493.

[27] Krotov, 'Battle of Poltava', 158-81.

[28] Englund, *Poltava*, 55.

[29] Krotov, 'Battle of Poltava', 193.

[30] Kolosov, 'Artillery at the Battle of Poltava', 100-01.

[31] Vozgrin, *Russia and European Lands*, 252.

[32] Shafirov, *A Discourse concerning the Just Causes . . .*, 47-49.

[33] *The Archive of Prince F.A. Kurakin*, vol. 2, 23.

[34] *Ibidem*.

[35] Shafirov, *A Discourse concerning the Just Causes . . .*, 51.

[36] Krotov, 'Kalabalik at Bender', 121.

[37] *Ibidem*, 116.

[38] Artamonov, 'Russia and the Rzeczpospolita', 134-35, 183.

[39] Bring, 'Kanslisten Johan Henrik von Kochens berättelse', 201.

[40] Cited in Krotov, 'Kalabalik at Bender', 122.

[41] Nikiforov, 'The Last Years of the Northern War', 555.

[42] *The Archive of Prince F.A. Kurakin*, vol. 6, 168-69.

[43] *Ibidem.*

[44] Nikoforov, *Russo-English Relations*, 110.

[45] *Ibidem*, 122-24.

[46] RGAVMF, Fund 176, *opis* 1, *delo* 130, ff. 136v-137.

[47] Anderson, *Naval Wars*, 174, 175.

[48] *Ibidem*, 175-76.

[49] Feygina, *The Congress of Åland*, 187.

[50] Shafirov, *A Discourse concerning the Just Causes . . .*, 57.

[51] Kabuzan, *The Peoples of Russia in the Eighteenth Century*, 77.

[52] Åström, 'The Swedish Economy', 61; Feygina, *The Congress of Åland*, 204.

[53] Nordmann, *La crise du Nord*, 139-40.

[54] *Full Collection of the Laws of the Russian Empire*, 617.

[55] RGADA, Fund 9, *otdelenie* 2, *delo* 39, f. 454; Fund 198, *opis* 1, *delo* 352, ff. 164-66; *Materials for a History of the Russian Fleet*, part 2, 293-94.

[56] *Campaign Journal for 1718*, 4, 17.

[57] Anderson, *Naval Wars*, 185; Garde, *Den dansk-norske Sømagte historie*, 96; Tornquist, *Utkast till svenska flottans sjötåg*, vol. 2, 93.

[58] *History of the Swedish War*, issue 1, 469-70.

[59] *Ibidem*, 474; issue 2, 250.

[60] Nikiforov, 'Last Years of the Northern War', 579.

[61] Feygina, *The Congress of Åland*, 318-19.

[62] *Anthology of the Imperial Russian Historical Society*, vol. 40, 7-8.

[63] *Ibidem*, 9.

[64] *Campaign Journal for 1719*, 118.

## 17 Brandenburg-Prussia and the Northern German States

[1] Chance, *British Diplomatic Instructions, Denmark*, V.

[2] *Ibidem*, 22-23.

[3] Hughes, *Russia in the Age of Peter the Great*, 31.

[4] Berner, *Geschichte der preussischen Staates*, 228.

[5] Hartmann, *Die Beziehungen Preussens zu Dänemark*, 34.

[6] Bain, 'Charles XII and the Great Northern War', 584-615.

[7] Mediger, *Mecklenburg, Rußland und England-Hannover*, I, 4.

[8] *Ibidem*, I, 79, 86; ch. 2.

[9] Davies, *God's Playground: A History of Poland*, I, 492-96.

[10] Mediger, *Mecklenburg, Rußland und England-Hannover*, I, 221.

[11] Hartmann, *Die Beziehungen Preußens zu Dänemark*, 55.

[12] Quoted in Frey and Frey, *Frederick I*, 228.

[13] Schnath, *Geschichte Hannovers*, III, 629.

[14] Chance, *British Diplomatic Instructions, Denmark*, V.

[15] Thompson, *Britain, Hanover, and the Protestant Interest*; Boles, *The Huguenots, the Protestant Interest, and the War of the Spanish Succession.*

[16] Parry, *Consolidated Treaty Series*, XXXI, 93-96 for agreement of 17 January 1720 at Regensburg; Waddington, *Histoire de Prusse*, II, 398 says the agreement was never executed. See also Parry, *Consolidated Treaty Series*, XXXI, 171-76 for the treaty between Hanover and Prussia for the Protection of the Protestant Religion, signed at Berlin, 3 March 1720.

[17] See for example, T.N.A., S.P. Germany, 80/18: Stepney to Vernon, 24 March 1702; S.P. 105/65: Vernon to Stepney, Whitehall, 31 March 1702; S.P. 80/20: memorial of 10 September 1702; B.L., Add.Mss. 37,156, ff.83-84: memorial of 20 December 1701, f.129: memorial of 22 November 1702; Add.Mss. 7058, f.159: Hedges to Stepney, Whitehall, 15 December 1701 and Hedges to Stepney, 2 January 1703; ZSTA Merseburg, Repertorium I, Korrespondenz mit dem kaiserlichen Hof, 47 A 2, ff. 7-11: Bartholdi's memorial of 25 January 1702; Waddington, *Histoire de Prusse*, II, 397-98; Frey and Frey, *A Question of Empire.*

[18] Hatton, *Charles XII*, 222.

[19] Waddington, *Histoire de Prusse*, II, 150-51.

[20] For excellent coverage of the background to the war see McKay and Scott, *The Rise of the Great Powers*, 10-14; Bain, 'Charles XII and the Great Northern War'; Wolf, *The Emergence of the Great Powers*, esp. ch.3.

[21] Schnath, *Geschichte Hannovers*, III, 308-09.

[22] *Ibidem.*

[23] Hatton, *George I*, 82; Schnath, *Geschichte Hannovers*, III, 307.

[24] Schnath, *Geschichte Hannovers*, III, 309.

[25] *Ibidem*, III, 308.

[26] Frey and Frey, *Frederick I*, 30-32.

[27] *Ibidem*, 70, 140-41; Waddington, *Histoire de Prusse*, II, 149-52.

[28] Frey and Frey, *Frederick I*, 56-57, 188-89; Mediger, *Mecklenburg, Rußland und England-Hannover*, I, 7.

[29] For an excellent overview of the war see Hatton, 'Charles XII and the Great Northern War'.

[30] T.N.A., S.P. 104/123: St. John to Scott, 3 February 1713.

[31] Massie, *Peter the Great*, 318.

[32] Hatton, *Charles XII*, 127.

[33] Massie, *Peter the Great*, 320.

[34] Chance, ed., *British Diplomatic Instructions, Denmark*, X; Schnath, *Geschichte Hannovers*, III, 312.

[35] Schnath, *Geschichte Hannovers*, III, 327.

[36] Churchill, *Marlborough*, I, 647.

[37] Hatton, *George I*, 866-67.

[38] Frey and Frey, 'The Foreign Policy of Frederick I', 259-69. See also Braubach, *Der Aufstieg Brandenburg-Preußens*; Erdmannsdörffer, *Deutsche Geschichte*, III, part 7; Noorden, 'Die preußische Politik', 197-358; Berner, 'Die auswärtige Politik der Kurfürsten Friedrich III', 60-109; Hintze, *Die Hohenzollern und ihr Werk*, 275 and ff; Hassinger, *Brandenburg-Preußen, Schweden und Rußland*, 278.

[39] Hatton, *Charles XII*, 133.

40 Hartmann, *Die Beziehungen Preußens zu Dänemark,* 44-45.

41 T.N.A., S.P., Military Expeditions 87/2: Marlborough to Harley, Hanover, 4 December 1704. See also Marlborough to Heinsius, 26 September 1704, in Van 't Hoff, *The Correspondence,* nr. 221.

42 Murray, ed., *The Letters and Dispatches of John Churchill,* III, 203: Marlborough to Harley, 1 November 1706.

43 T.N.A., S.P. Prussia, 90/3/78: Raby to Harley, Berlin, 25 October 1704.

44 *Ibidem,* 128-29: Raby to Harley, Berlin, 6 December 1704.

45 Hassinger, *Brandenburg-Preußen, Schweden und Rußland,* 90 and ff;. Loewe, ed., *Preußen Staatsverträge,* XCII.

46 Noorden, *Europäische Geschichte,* II, 38.

47 T.N.A., S.P., Holland 84/227: Stanhope to Harley, 14 October 1704. For Heinsius' suspicions see Veenendaal, *Briefwisseling Heinsius,* IV, nr. 1127, Heinsius to Lintelo, The Hague, 4 November 1704.

48 Hartmann, *Die Beziehungen Preußens zu Dänemark,* 35.

49 Snyder, *The Marlborough-Godolphin Correspondence,* I, 528, Marlborough to Godolphin, The Hague, 25 April/6 May 1706.

50 Frey and Frey, 'The Anglo-Prussian Treaty of 1704', 283-94; Coxe, *Memoirs of John Duke of Marlborough,* I, 355, Marlborough to the duchess, 27 November 1704.

51 Churchill, *Marlborough* 1, 907. See also B.L., Add. Mss. 22196, fol.27: Raby to Cadogan, Berlin, 29 November 1704.

52 Hartmann, *Die Beziehungen Preußens zu Dänemark,* 30.

53 Hassinger, *Brandenburg-Preußen, Schweden und Rußland,* 49.

54 Whitworth, 'Dispatches', 164: Whitworth to Harley, from camp at Grodno, 13/24 September 1705.

55 Hartmann, *Die Beziehungen Preußens zu Dänemark,* 36.

56 Hatton, *Charles XII,* 216.

57 Lintelo to Heinsius, Berlin, 30 November 1706, in Veenendaal, *Briefwisseling Heinsius,* V, nr. 1338.

58 Waddington, *Histoire de Prusse,* II, 193-94.

59 Hartmann, *Die Beziehungen Preußens zu Dänemark,* 37-39.

60 Hatton, *Charles XII,* 213, 222.

61 Kemble, *State Papers and Correspondence,* 457: Stepney to Harley, Camp at Cambron, 24 October 1706.

62 Schnath, *Geschichte Hannovers,* III, 622, 625.

63 *Ibidem,* 627, 629.

64 B.L., Add.Mss.9100, fol. 119-21: Salm to Marlborough, Vienna, 10 August 1707; Hannover Stadtarchiv 16693: Raby to Robéthon, 26 February 1707; HHSA, England, Korr. 41, Berichte: Gallas to Joseph I, London, 2 September 1707.

65 Chance, *British Diplomatic Instructions, Denmark,* 24-25: Harley to Pulteney, Whitehall, 2/13 September 1707.

66 Hatton, *Charles XII,* 224-26; Hassinger, *Brandenburg-Preußen, Schweden und Rußland,* 201.

67 Chance, *British Diplomatic Instructions, Denmark,* 29: Boyle to Pulteney, Whitehall, 22 November 1709.

68 Snyder, *The Marlborough-Godolphin Correspondence,* III, 1379: Godolphin to Marlborough, Windsor, 17/28 September 1709.

69 Hartmann, *Die Beziehungen Preußens zu Dänemark,* 44.

70 *Ibidem,* 45.

71 Murray, *The Letters and Dispatches of John Churchill,* IV, 630: Marlborough to the king, 19 October 1709.

72 Hatton, *George I,* 184-85.

73 Chance, *British Diplomatic Instructions, Denmark,* 30: Boyle to Pulteney, Whitehall, 26 November 1709; 31: Boyle to Pulteney, Whitehall, 7 March 1709/1710.

74 Droysen quoted in Hartmann, *Die Beziehungen Preußens zu Dänemark,* 48.

75 Frey, Frey, and Rule, *Observations from The Hague and Utrecht.*

76 *Ibidem,* 134-35. See also Van 't Hoff, *The Correspondence,* nrs. 976 and 977.

77 T.N.A., S.P. Prussia 104/52: St. John to Raby, 17 March 1711.

78 St. John to Marlborough, 20 July 1711 quoted in Chance, *George I,* 23.

79 *Idem, British Diplomatic Instructions, Denmark,* 34-35: Boyle to Pulteney, Whitehall, 9 October 1711.

80 *Ibidem,* 36-37: Bolingbroke to Pulteney, Whitehall, 18 September 1712.

81 Frey and Frey, 'The Anglo-Prussian Treaty of 1704', 293.

82 Droysen, *Geschichte der preußischen Politik,* IV, part 1.

83 Frey and Frey, *The Treaties of the War of the Spanish Succession,* 169.

84 Frey and Frey, 'The Foreign Policy of Frederick I', 259-69; Frey and Frey, *The Treaties of the War of the Spanish Succession,* 167-70.

85 *Ibidem,* 65.

86 Hatton, *Charles XII,* 144.

87 Hatton, *George I,* 184-86.

88 Mediger, *Mecklenburg, Rußland und England-Hannover,* I, 120.

89 *Ibidem,* I, chs 3 and 4. See also Hughes, *Russia in the Age of Peter the Great,* 55.

90 Hatton, *George I,* 190.

91 Waddington, *Histoire de Prusse,* II, 394-97. See also Chance, *George I,* 147-49, 187, 224; Mediger, *Mecklenburg, Rußland und England-Hannover,* I, ch.7; Rill, *Karl VI,* 174-75.

92 Parry, *Consolidated Treaty Series,* XXXI, 81-91 for treaty signed at Stockholm on 9/20 November 1719.

93 *Ibidem,* 127-47 for treaty of peace between Prussia and Sweden signed at Stockholm, 21 January/1 February 1720.

94 *Ibidem,* 219-31 for treaty of peace between Denmark and Sweden, signed at Stockholm, 3 June 1720.

95 *Ibidem,* 339-55 for treaty of peace between Russia and Sweden, signed at Nystad, 30 August 1721.

96 Waddington, *Histoire de Prusse,* II, 401. See also Schnath, *Geschichte Hannovers,* III, 699.

97 Massie, *Peter the Great,* 302.

98 Hughes, *Russia in the Age of Peter the Great,* 56.

# 18 Charles XII: A King of Many Faces

[1] There exist about 250 medals commemorating the king. Strömbom, *Svenska kungliga porträtt*, 339.

[2] Ehrenstrahl's first portraits of Charles XI are from 1662, when the prince was seven years old, the same year in which Ehrenstrahl was appointed painter to the court. The very first portraits of Charles XI were executed by Abraham Wuchters. Sidén, *Den ideala barndomen*, 93.

[3] From 'dhen gemene Målare hopen.'

[4] Levey, *Painting at Court*, 124.

[5] Ellenius, *Karolinska bildidéer*, 22. In becoming a court artist he did not give up his independence altogether and was not, like Van Dyck in England, forever condemned to paint portraits. Among other things he also painted the ceiling decoration in Riddarhuset (The House of Knights) in Stockholm and two large religious compositions for the Royal Chapel (now in Storkyrkan, S. Nicolai, in the Old Town, Stockholm).

[6] Ellenius, *Karolinska bildidéer*, 107.

[7] Hildebrand, *Sveriges och svenska konungahusets minnespenningar*, 430-31; Stenström, *Arvid Karlsteen*, 178. Arvid Karlsteen (1647-1718), called 'the father of Swedish engraving,' was the first Swedish-born engraver to emerge.

[8] Olin, *Det karolinska porträttet*, 112.

[9] Stenström, *Arvid Karlsteen*, 178; Sidén, *Den ideala barndomen*, 102.

[10] Sidén, *Den ideala barndomen*, 102-03, 300; Strömbom, *Svenska kungliga porträtt*, 103. Andreas von Behn (b. 1650 probably in Kristianopel, Sweden – d. after 1713 probably in Vienna) studied abroad, mainly in London, where he learnt the art of enamel painting. In 1677 he was appointed cabinet painter to Hedvig Eleonora and came in the same period in contact with Ehrenstrahl, from whom he received private instruction. He painted portraits, biblical compositions, and allegories in oil on copper, often in small formats, and miniatures in enamel. In 1693 he was made a drawing teacher to Prince Charles and also a court miniaturist, an appointment which was withdrawn in favour of Elias Brenner, who had complained to the king. After having left Sweden, he resided for some time in London. He was last heard from in Vienna in 1713. *Svenskt Konstnärslexikon*; Nisser, *Michael Dahl*, 67.

[11] Sidén, *Den ideala barndomen*, 102; Ellenius, *Karolinska bildidéer*, 108-09; see also p. 345 in this volume.

[12] Sometime between December 1682 and January 1683, Ehrenstrahl painted a portrait of the prince.

The Stockholm castle accounts for 1714 state that David von Krafft that year copied a portrait by Ehrenstrahl showing the prince, as a child at six months of age, against a drapery painted with 'feinen Ultramarinen.' The copy was sent to King Stanisław Leszczyński of Poland. In 2007 a portrait called *Portrait of a Young Prince* came on the art market. Inscribed in an oval, painted frame within the painting it shows a boy-child with short, curly blond hair and rosy cheeks, dressed in loosely fitting, white-lace-fringed blue garments, held together in the front by a pearl broche. He is sitting upright on a red cushion with golden tassels against an ultramarine fond framed by heavily falling, yellow-reddish drapery. With one hand he lifts a sword, in the other he holds a commander's baton. It is tempting to see the painting as Ehrenstrahl's long-lost portrait (or a copy of it) of the six-month-old prince. The sword and baton reveal the child's royal descent, and the young boy could very well be about six months old. There is also an overall likeness to Ehrenstrahl's portraits of other children, while the head and face have distinctive similarities to the prince's in Ehrenstrahl's painting of him playing on a silver kettledrum from 1684 (see p. 35).

[13] It is dated following Ehrenstrahl's description in *Die Vornehmste Schildereyen*, 19, where it says that Prince Charles is one and a quarter of a year old in the painting. Cf. Ellenius, *Karolinska bildidéer*, 92.

[14] Ellenius, *Karolinska bildidéer*, 105. See also Sidén, 'Familjeporträttet', 64-65.

[15] Schama, 'Royal Family Portraiture', 163.

[16] Sidén, 'Familjeporträttet', 65.

[17] Ellenius, *Karolinska bildidéer*, 183.

18    Skogh, 'Politics of Possession', 3.

[19] It has been dated to the first half of 1684, since Prince Ulrik, born in July 1684, is not present in the painting.

[20] Ellenius, *Karolinska bildidéer*, 108.

[21] '. . . Kungabarnen, som leka med svenska lejonet, som vore det en stor pålitlig S:t Bernhards-hund.' Strömbom, *Svenska kungliga porträtt*, 348.

[22] Elias Brenner (Storkyro, Finland, 1647-Stockholm, 1717) was married to Sophia Elisabet Brenner, one of Sweden´s first female writers.

[23] Sidén, *Den ideala barndomen*, 104. Strömbom, *Svenska kungliga porträtt*, 348. Some replicas of this miniature exist.

[24] Sidén, *Den ideala barndomen*, 104, 300; cf. Brown, *Van Dyck*, 228.

[25] To depict dead infants as angels draws on Dutch and Flemish group portraits of the period. See Schama, 'Royal Family Portraiture', 160; cf. Robinson, 'Family Portraits of the Golden Age', 494-95. The same theme recurs in Ehrenstrahl's painting *Allegory over the Order of Succession – Stabilimentum regni* at Drottningholm from 1693. In the presence of the four estates and a few allegorical figures, Mother Svea carries the regalia to a portrait of Prince Charles surrounded by portraits of his two sisters. Above in the sky the four dead princes' small bodies can be seen. Ellenius, *Karolinska bildidéer*, 52.

[26] According to the Swedish calendar she was born 23 January 1688.

[27] The supporting hand she puts on Charles's head points him out as heir to the throne but also shows her care for him and, more generally, for all her subjects. Sidén, *Den ideala barndomen*, 232.

[28] Spicer, 'The Renaissance Elbow', 86.

[29] Ellenius, *Karolinska bildidéer*, 137.

[30] See for example *Portrait of the King with Turned Head*, early 1698.

[31] Olin, *Det karolinska porträttet*, 192.

[32] Malmborg, 'David von Krafft', 516.

[33] Strömbom, *Svenska kungliga porträtt*, 352.

[34] For example at Salsta and Örbyhus in Uppland, Tidö in Västmanland, and Sövdeborg in Scania. Strömbom, *Svenska kungliga porträtt*, 380 (type KXII:13 e).

[35] The horse lifts its forehand off the ground with lowered hocks so that its body makes about a 45-degree angle with the ground. The levade is the same sort of movement but the horse raises its body to an angle of approximately 30 degrees. Cf. Olin, *Det karolinska porträttet*, 90.

[36] The change of style in dress and hair is discussed in Ericsson, 'Bilden av suveränen', 155-73; cf. Olin, *Det karolinska porträttet*, 115-19; Liljegren, *Karl XII*, 145. See also Olausson, 'Den stora rollen', 187-88. The king would never again wear a wig, something which his sister Ulrika Eleonora does not seem to have fully accepted. When he returned to Sweden after fifteen years, she sent him a wig, 'which he wants to hide in remembrance of the giver but is not happy to be using, because his head is now so long without one that it is difficult to come to terms with such a headdress.' http://www.tacitus.nu/karoliner/kallor/KarlXII/inledning.htm (XXIII).

[37] There remain at least two versions of this

painting, of which the one at Grönsö in Uppland is considered to be the best. Strömbom, *Svenska kungliga porträtt*, 318 (type K XII: 16a).

[38] Georg Philipp Rugendas (1666-1742). Sometime after the king's death the Flemish sculptor Guillielmus de Groff (1676-1742) made a plaster statue inspired by the print (now in the National Museum, Stockholm). The print (p. 353) is one of a series of equestrian portraits of important European personalities, among others the Duke of Marlborough and Prince Eugene of Savoy.

[39] After the victory over Augustus II at Kliszów in July 1702, prints of Charles XII were issued in Paris, which still showed him 'unchanged.' Cf. Schnakenbourg, chapter 11 in this volume. The position of horse and rider is close to a mezzotint of the duke of Schomberg on horseback from around 1689 by Smith, later (1705) replaced by the duke of Marlborough. Johns, 'The British Caesar,' 330.

[40] Strömbom, *Svenska kungliga porträtt*, 357.

[41] Now in the Collection of AS Restor Company, Tallinn. See Holmqvist, 'Johann Heinrich Wedekind,' 56. Cf. Ehasalu, *Rootsiaegne maalikunst Tallinnas*, 312.

[42] Signed on the reverse: 'I.H. Wedekin, Rigae pinxit, habitans Revaliae.'

[43] In 1908 the painting was in the portrait collection in the House of the Black Heads in Riga. Cf. Neumann, *Lexikon baltischer Kunst*, 167. Mistakenly Strömbom writes that it was in the House of the Black Heads in Reval. Strömbom, *Svenska kungliga porträtt*, 357. Since Strömbom had only read about it, he was unaware that it showed the king without a wig and in a soldier's uniform. Its reappearance in the Stockholm Army Museum in 1975 has gone largely unnoticed and its role in the image propaganda has yet to be studied. The only more thorough study is to be found in Holmqvist, 'Johann Heinrich Wedekind,' 56-57. It was shown in the exhibition *Three Stars-Three Crowns* in Riga 2001, but is listed as missing ('destroyed') in Ehasalu 2007, 312. Since 2013 it is part of the Army Museum's permanent exhibition *Krig och fred* (war and peace).

[44] The artistic talents of Axel Sparre (1652-1728) were known also outside the king's inner circle. He was especially appreciated as a painter of miniatures. His brother Konrad Sparre, also an amateur painter, took part in the Swedish expedition to the Orient of 1710-11.

[45] It was also used in *Theatrum Europaeum* and in *Historisch-politisch- und geografische Beschreibung des Königreichs Schweden* (1708). Strömbom, *Svenska kungliga porträtt*, 355. As late as 1707, the Riksdaler that was stamped that year by Arvid Karlsteen, showed him with a wig. It has therefore been called the Wig-Riksdaler

(*Perukriksdalern*). Cf. p. 211.

[46] Strömbom, *Svenska kungliga porträtt*, 359. Adlerfelt says the king saw a portrait of the king of Poland, whom Hatton understood to be King Stanisław Leszczyński, but since he did not become king until 1704, it can have been no other than Augustus II. Adlerfelt, *Leben Karls des zwölften*, 451; cf. Hatton, *Charles XII*, 218.

[47] That it quickly reached France is obvious from a copper print by Bernhard Picart, issued by Crépy, rue St. Jacques 'devant la boëte de la poste,' Paris (see p. 212). Strömbom, *Svenska kungliga porträtt*, 360.

[48] Johan David Swartz (1678-1729), who had studied with David von Krafft, left Stockholm in the autumn of 1702. His first whereabouts thereafter are unknown, but judging from some portraits dated 1705—one of Sofia von der Pfalz, wife of Duke Ernst August von Braunschweig-Lüneburg-Hannover, and three of officers of the king—he must have been in Germany for quite some time before coming to Altranstädt. His improved painting technique as well as his style and colours indicate that he spent time in Paris studying French portrait painting. It is a strange coincidence that Swartz would also paint the very last *ad vivum* portrait of the king, in Skåne in the spring of 1718. The king is depicted against a dark park landscape in the same position as in the Altranstädt portrait but now with aged and hardened facial features, his crown is bald and the hair on the sides has greyed. On the base of a column next to him there is now also a detail from the traditional regent's portrait: the regalia. See Ångström Grandien, Johan David Swartz, *Svenskt biografiskt lexikon*, Stockholm 2015.

[49] The king's field secretary, Nils Reuterholm, wrote this letter, dated 27 July 1707 [Swedish Style], to a friend, the *kammarjunkaren* Jakob Cronstedt in Stockholm. In it, Reuterholm announces the extraordinary news that the king, that very same day, had sat for a portrait. His men had often asked him to do this, but it was only at the request of the king of Poland that he finally had agreed. The painter was a Swede named Swart here ('een svänsk målare som här är benämnd Swart'). Reuterholm's letter was published in *Personhistorisk tidskrift*, 1908, 163.

[50] The letter was written by Major-General Carl Gustaf Creutz. Published in *Karolinska förbundets årsbok*, 1911, 169.

[51] David von Krafft signed several of his copies of the portrait and was therefore long believed to have been the creator of the 'Altranstädt type.' It was not until 1912 that Nils Sjöberg, after having seen the name Swart in Reuterholm's letter, convincingly proved that Swartz was the true inventor. See Sjöberg, 'Några Karl XII-porträtt,'

*Personhistorisk tidskrift*, 1912, 122. The question of who painted what is, however, quite complicated, since Swartz himself copied the paintings from Altranstädt. Some unsigned portraits of Charles XII, showing clear signs of Swartz's hand, are proof that on occasion he also used a drawing from the Altranstädt period of the king in a steel cuirass as a model (Royal Library, Stockholm).

[52] '. . . han är mycket svår att aftaga för målare ty jag har än intet conterfey funnit, som rätt träffar, ibland hundrade iag sedt och hvarmed hela verlden är full, alla boklådor, alla målarbodar och hus förutan andras hus . . . .' A. Alstrin to his uncle, J. Upmarck, in *Historisk tidskrift* 1884, 180.

[53] Kuylenstierna, 'Karl XII:s yttre', 193.

[54] Robert Gardelle (1682-1766) was the most important member of a well-known family of painters in Geneva. The Jesuit Du Cerceau wrote a long poem about the portrait, from which the following is quoted: 'Comme un simple soldat vétu grossierement pour la forme & pour la maniere un habit lui suffit une campagne entiere grand chapeau gands de buffle & pour l'assortiment ceinturon de même parure d'où pend un large coutelas, peu brillant au dehors, peu chargé de dorure mais terrible dans les combats. Enfin cravate à la dragone. C'est tout l'ajustement qu'il souffre en sa personne. Cet air de negligence & de simplicité n'altere point en lui sa Majesté . . .', published in *Poesies Diverses Du Pere Du Cerceau*, 1749.

[55] The brothers also made a small replica on cardboard (13 x 10 cm), with in the bottom left corner the inscription 'Peint par les Frères Gardelle 1708', and on the back 'Charles XII / Roy de Suede / 1708 /par les frères Gardel / Geneuvis.' http://www.bigli.com/artwork/574/robert-gardelle-and-daniel-gardelle/charles-xii-roy-de-suede-1708.aspx.

[56] Hahr, 'Karl XII-porträtten', 588-89. See also Strömbom, *Svenska kungliga porträtt,* 372.

[57] 'iag så när träffat likheten af hans Majestetz Milda ansichte så att alla här å orten samt kånungen sielf funet det wara mycket lijkt.' Quoted from Strömbom, *Svenska kungliga porträtt*, 372.

[58] In the Collections Online, Nationalmuseum, the Gripsholm portrait is still listed as a work by Sparre. http://emp-web-22zalInterface&module=collection&objectId=15793&viewType=detailView.

[59] Seitz, 'Ett porträtt av Karl XII', 33-34.

[60] Sjöblom, 'Historien om ett porträtt', 54. Cf. Olausson, 'Statsporträttet', 76.

[61] Grate, *French Paintings*, 294-96.

[62] Ericson, 'Bilden av suveränen'; Hahr, 'Karl XII-porträtten', 588-89. Cf. Strömbom *Svenska kungliga porträtt*, 372-73. Strömbom must have

based his opinions on photographs taken prior to the painting's restoration since they are basically the same as Hahr's, even though his survey of Swedish royal portraits was published in 1943, more than twenty years later.

[63] Malmborg, *Svensk porträttkonst*, 125-26; Grate, *French Paintings*, 265.

[64] Strömbom mentions the miniature in *Svenska kungliga porträtt*, 373, footnote 1. He had received the information about a miniature at Ham House by Axel Sparre 'väl från Bender' from Charlotte Lewenhaupt, but had not, because of the ongoing war, been able to check it.

[65] According to Nisser, Dahl worked from a sculpted head, but since there are no such known from the king's lifetime, this seems unlikely. Nisser, *Michael Dahl*, 116-17.

[66] Axel Löwen (1686-1772). As early as 1703, in Elbing, at the age of seventeen, Löwen painted a portrait of the king.

[67] It must be pointed out, however, that the mask is probably not a direct cast of his face. In 1917 a comparison of the mask with the king's skull showed that it was slightly too short to fit the king's features, and it has been suggested that it was made in Uddevalla by the French engraver Simon Josse, who happened to be there, having been asked to come to Sweden by Charles XII's minister Georg Heinrich von Görtz, who needed a good engraver for his emergency money. Together with the king's body the the death mask was taken to Karlberg, where several casts were made of it. There exist two versions of the mask. In one, the wounds on the right side of the face are exaggerated, in the other they have a more normal size. For a possible explanation see Stenström, 107-46. Cf. Hatton, Charles XII, 505.

[68] Strömbom, *Svenska kungliga porträtt*, 374. In Löwen's miniature of the king in profile from the same time, the jaw is particularly heavy. Also, this miniature has been judged a near caricature. Cf. Hatton, *Charles XII*, 543-44, footnote 14.

[69] The Hallwyl Collections, Stockholm, hold a por-

trait of the Ystad type attributed to Wedekind. *The Hallwyl Collections*, Nr. 360. Wedekind's portrait series of Charles XII ended posthumously in 1720 with a three-quarter-length portrait in which the king stands pointing towards the Norwegian mountains.

[70] In the Skattkammar Collection, Nr. 611.

[71] Its captain was ennobled Ankarcrona because of this feat and the portrait given to the family by the grateful king. It is still kept at the Ankarcrona family estate Boserup in Scania.

[72] Adlerfelt, *Leben Karls des zwölften*, preface. They would only meet once more, 21 March-2 April 1718 in Kristinehamn.

[73] Strömbom, *Svenska kungliga porträtt*, 376.

[74] 'han skulle komma ihåg honom'; quoted from Lorens Pasch the Younger's memories of his father. See Strömbom, *Lorens Pasch den yngre*, 7.

[75] Adlerfelt, *Leben Karls des zwölften*, preface. According to Krafft himself, the king destroyed the face because he had painted it 'without permission,' something which I interpret to mean that Krafft had not received permission 'to paint it in such a way.'

[76] Strömbom, *Svenska kungliga porträtt*, 377, footnote 1.

[77] *Ibidem*, 378.

[78] The traces of the cuts are still visible. Ericson, 'Bilden av surveränen', 149.

[79] Hatton, *Charles XII*, 6.

[80] The last *ad vivum* portrait of the king was painted by Swartz, a full-length now at Stubbarp in Skåne. The face is close to the Lund type but the background is different, a dark park landscape and a column, with on its base the regalia.

[81] In the crypt Charles X Gustav (1622-60) and his wife Hedvig Eleonora (1636-1715) rest in pewter coffins, the former's designed by Hindrich de La Vallée, the latter's by Nicodemus Tessin the Younger. Charles XI (1655-97) and Ulrika Eleonora the Elder (1656-93) rest in pewter coffins drawn by Tessin the Younger and executed by Carlo Carove

and Burchard Precht. In a corner stand the coffins of Charles XI's sons who died in infancy: Ulrik (d. 1685), Gustaf (d. 1685), Charles Gustaf (d. 1687), and Fredrik (d. 1685). All coffins except Prince Fredrik's are made of gilded pewter; all are made after drawings by Tessin the Younger. Princess Hedvig Sofia (d. 1708) also rests here, as well as Fredrik I (d. 1751) and Ulrika Eleonora the Younger (d. 1741), in sarcophaguses made of green marble from Kolmården drawn by Carl Hårleman.

[82] Gustav Vasa's (d. 1560) and Johan III's (d. 1592) graves are in the cathedral of Uppsala. Charles IX (d. 1609) is buried in the cathedral of Strängnäs, and Erik XIV (d. 1575) in the cathedral of Västerås.

[83] Liljegren, *Karl XII*, 112.

[84] Josephson, *Nicodemus Tessin*, 201.

[85] 'Öfvermåttan lik.' Said by Johan Gabriel Sack, who had met Charles XII as late as in 1717. Sack also owned Rigaud's portrait of the king. *Ansikte mot ansikte*, 215.

[86] Antonsson, 'Franska porträttskulptörer i Sverige under 1700-talet'.

[87] Grate, 'Bildkonsten', 255-56.

[88] *Ansikte mot ansikte*, 215. Cf. Grate, 'Bildkonsten', 255.

[89] See Rodell, *Att gjuta en nation*, 162-05, for the competition and the discussions the idea of the statue caused.

[90] Johan Petter Molin (1814-73). It was cast in two sets at Kungliga Myntet in Kungsholmen by Heroldt. The four mortars that surround the statue, cast in Dresden in 1678, were taken by Charles XII at the recapturing of the fortress Neumünde near Riga from the Saxons, 11 December, 1701. Their reliefs show *The Abduction of Proserpina*.

[91] The pose is based on Johan Niclas Byström's sculpture of Charles XII for Charles XIV's private collection, but may in both cases be traced back to Wedekind's posthumous portrait of Charles with a hand raised and a finger pointing to Norway.

[92] Bengtsson, 'Skulpturen', 285.

## 19 A Literary Charles XII

[1] Bernhard von Beskow to Anders Fryxell, quoted in Fryxell, *Min historias historia*, 104.

[2] There are also brief introductions in Brantly, 'Att söka Sverige i Karl XII:s porträtt', and Oredsson, 'Karl XII och det svenska stormaktsväldets fall'. Literary accounts of the king's death are treated in

Granér, 'Carl XII:s död i svensk diktning'. There is no complete bibliography of literary adaptations of Charles XII, but some of the works are listed in Allen, *Bibliography*.

[3] As an example of how literature has influenced historiography, there are Heidenstam's *Karoliner-*

*na*, a source of inspiration for the so-called New School historians' revaluation of Charles XII in the late nineteenth century, a relationship that some later historians have found 'shocking.' See Zander, *Fornstora dagar*, 121 and the literature cited there.

[4] 'Nu ähr dhen Nordske Hielt, och Swea Rijkz

Hieltinna, | Een dyrbar Prince född, en Ädel Princessinna, | Nu blijr och aff een CARL stadfäst Ehr Konglig Stool | Som framdeels sittia skal widh Swea Rijkes Rool; | I honom skal Ehr dygd, Slijk Hiältom till Exempel, | Ett Ewigt blifwa bygd odödlig Ähros Tempel' (quoted in Ellenius, *Karolinska bildidéer*, 109).

[5] For the texts, see *Smärre dikter av Lejonkulans dramatiker*, 69-86, and Svenska Vitterhetssamfundet's critical editions of Dahlstierna's and Holmström's collected poems.

[6] The poems are in the critical edition of Brenner, *Samlade dikter*, 29-42.

[7] Ekedahl, *Det svenska Israel*, 109-22; for further examples, see Helander, *Neo-Latin Literature in Sweden*, 408-11.

[8] 'Gif Gud dit Hiärta; gif Konungenom din Troo: | Gif Gud din Siäl; och gif din Kung Gods | Lijf och Bloo: | Gif Gud och Kung hwar sitt; Sij så får Fanen inte!' (Dahlstierna, *Samlade dikter*, I, 147).

[9] 'Twå Kungar på en gång til Swerje sig nu nalcka | At med sin nåde-dagg thes ångest-hetta swalcka' (Possieth, *Hosianna, eller Fägnefult glädie-rop*, A2v). See Ekedahl, *Det svenska Israel*, 114; for examples of the millenarian ideas associated with the king, see Lundström, 'Karl XII—Messias', and Ruuth, 'Karl XII i den mystiska separatistiska profetians ljus'.

[10] This was especially the case with the Latin tributes. For an introduction, see Helander, 'Andreas Rydelius', 320-35. Several works have been published in annotated translation, including Andreas Stobaeus, *Narva* (1701), Olof Hermelin, *Ad Carolum XII, Svecorum regem, de continuando adversus feudifragos bello* (1706), and Emanuel Swedenborg, *Festivus applausus in Caroli XII in Pomeraniam suam adventum* (1714). For Charles XII's identification with Alexander the Great as the latter was described by ancient authors, see Sandstedt, 'Karl XII och Alexander-rollen'.

[11] Johannesson, *I polstjärnans tecken*, 297-300; see also Lamm, *Gunno Dahlstierna*, 108-29.

[12] Kruse's political poetry is considered in Bolin, 'Wilhelm Kruse'.

[13] For a comparison of Russian and Swedish war panegyrics, see Ljustrov, *Vojna i kul'tura*; for the chancery's propaganda, see Olsson, *Olof Hermelin*, 287-330, 359-418; Haverling, *Huvuddrag*; and Aili, 'Swedish War Propaganda'.

[14] Westerlund, *Karl XII i svensk litteratur*, 70; for Defoe's characterisation of Charles XII, see Backscheider, *Daniel Defoe*, 366-71.

[15] Voltaire's work as a historian is discussed in Gunnar von Proschwitz's introduction to the critical edition of the biography in *Les œuvres complètes de Voltaire* (see Voltaire, *Histoire de Charles XII*, 78-84).

[16] 'Ainsi périt à l'âge de trente-six et demi Charles XII roi de Suède, après avoir éprouvé ce que la prospérité a de plus grand, et ce que l'adversité a de plus cruel, sans avoir été amolli par l'une, ni ébranlé un moment par l'autre. Presque toutes ses actions, jusqu'à celles de sa vie privée et unie, ont été bien loin au-delà du vraisemblable. C'est peut-être le seul de tous les hommes, et jusqu'ici le seul de tous les rois, qui ait vécu sans faiblesse: il a porté toutes les vertus des héros à un excès où elles sont aussi dangereuses que les vices opposés. . . . Ses grandes qualités, dont une seule eût pu immortaliser un autre prince, ont fait le malheur de son pays . . . homme unique plutôt que grand homme, admirable plutôt qu'à imiter' (Voltaire, *Histoire de Charles XII*, 541-42).

[17] Hildebrand, 'Till Karl XII-uppfattningens historia', I, 355.

[18] Other eighteenth-century writers commented on the Swedish king. Both Alexander Pope and Charles-Louis de Secondat, better known as Montesquieu, made no bones about their opinions: Pope in his *Essay on Man* (1734) rejected the king's belligerence, and Montesquieu in *De l'esprit des loix* (1748) cast doubt on the king's abilities as a strategist. Samuel Johnson took a kinder view in *The Vanity of Human Wishes* (1749), having been seized by what his biographer, James Boswell, described as a poetic rapture in the face of Charles's resolute ambition (see Westerlund, *Karl XII i svensk litteratur*, 132-34).

[19] For the reception of Voltaire's biography in Sweden, see Gunnar von Proschwitz's commentary in Voltaire, *Histoire de Charles XII*, 66-68. One Swedish author who returned several times to Charles XII was Olof Dalin, author of *Sagan om hästen* (1740, A Horse's Tale), a Swedish history in allegorical form in which Charles XII figured under the name Härkuller (Hercules), and *Svenska friheten* (1742, Swedish Freedom), a verse celebration of the king's prowess, though one combined with an explicit repudiation of his politics ('Personen större war hos honom, än Monarken'—'In him, the person was greater than the monarch') (Dalin, *Samlade verk*, 16-18). For Dalin's panegyric for Charles XII, see Granér, 'Karl XII:s död', 45.

[20] For the sources and genesis of Nordberg's biography, see Sandstedt, *Studier rörande Jöran Nordbergs Konung Carl XII:s historia*. Charles's prominence in the propaganda before the war

with Russia is considered in Westerlund, *Karl XII i svensk litteratur*, 97-128.

[21] Westerlund, *Karl XII i svensk litteratur*, 152-60.

[22] For the romantics' heroic ideals, see *ibidem*, 246-69; for more recent perspectives, see Reed, *Meditations*, 1-33; and the essays in Reiling and Rohde, *Das 19. Jahrhundert und seine Helden*.

[23] Westerlund, *Karl XII i svensk litteratur*, 256–62.

[24] Geijer, a professor of history, took a more jaundiced view of Charles XII's reign. In his public lectures he explained that Charles had been an 'illiterate warrior king', that he was so strong in the arm that it turned his head, and that his political aspirations were unrealistic and therefore doomed to end in disaster. At the same time, he was more positive about the king's altruism and drive. The contradictions in his views on the king as a person and on his policies are plain (Hildebrand, 'Till Karl XII-uppfattningens historia', I, 372-78).

[25] 'Kung Carl, den unga hjelte, | han stod i rök och dam. | Han drog sitt svärd från bälte | och bröt i striden fram. | 'Hur Svenska stålet biter, | kom låt oss pröfva på. | Ur vägen, Moscoviter, | friskt mod, I gossar blå! . . . Der slog så stort ett hjerta | uti hans Svenska barm, | i glädje som i smärta, | blott för det rätta varm. | I med- och motgång lika, | sin lyckas öfverman, | han kunde icke vika, | blott falla kunde han' (Tegnér, *Samlade dikter* 54-55). The commentary details all the published versions (including chapbooks) and the secondary publications about the poem.

[26] See Pettersson, *Statens läsebok*, 145.

[27] 'Res upp dig, Tolfte Carl! och se | fullbordadt och odödliggjordt | det storverk, som du började' (Wallin, *Dikter* 2, 39).

[28] Ekedahl, 'Mot en modern mediemonarki', 284-92.

[29] For the celebrations in 1818, see Tegnér, *Samlade dikter* 3, 309-11, and Stenroth, *Sveriges födelse*, 83-92. For a recent account of Karl XIV Johan's plan for monumental statues of Charles X, Charles XI, Charles XII, and Charles XIII, see Widén, *Från kungligt galleri till nationellt museum*, 131-48.

[30] Byron, *Complete Poetical Works*, IV, 175.

[31] See Evdokimova, *Pushkin's Historical Imagination*, 173-208. Pushkin's poem would later provide Tchaikovsky with the material for his opera *Mazeppa* (1884).

[32] For further examples see Allen, *Bibliography*, 92-95.

[33] For Strandberg's juvenilia, see Tarschys, *Talis Qualis*, 153-204, 256-75. It should be noted that Strandberg translated Byron's *Mazeppa* into Swedish in the early 1850s.

[34] 'De svenska män, hvilka med död och fångenskap beseglade sin trohet mot denna verldshistoriska tanke' (Rodell, *Att gjuta en nation*, 141). For the Poltava commemoration in 1862 and the unveiling of the statue of Charles XII in 1868, see *ibidem*, 135-214.

[35] 'Jag blyges ej att bekänna, att jag känner mitt hjerta svälla och mitt öga tåras, när jag midt uti detta rococo-tidehvarf, då alla hof voro skådeplats för den djupaste sedeslöshet, den bottenlösaste falskhet, det löjligaste etikettsväsende och den styfvaste perukstocksmässighet, ser denna höga, svenska gestalt resa sig i all sin storartade enkelhet, ensam med sitt svärd och sin bibel, sin rena sedlighet, sin oskrymtade gudsfruktan' (quoted in Rodell, *Att gjuta en nation*, 158).

[36] Holm, 'Poltava-minnet', 45-47.

[37] Rodell, *Att gjuta en nation*, 188-203. The novel *Den 30 november: skizz från Stockholmslifvet* (Stockholm, 1882), by the pseudonymous Evelyn, describes a lower-middle-class family trying to get tickets to the opening ceremony and the tumult that ensued.

[38] For Charles XII's prominence in the book, see Pettersson, *Statens läsebok*, 129, 155-56.

[39] Klinge, *Idyll och hot*, 268-81.

[40] For Charles XII in the songbooks, see Selander, *Folkrörelsesång*, 168-79. The founding of the temperance society in Uppsala is mentioned by Hildebrand, 'Till Karl XII-uppfattningens historia', II, 387, and Selander, *Folkrörelsesång*, 175.

[41] As late as the 1860s, there was a feeling in conservative circles that the cult of Charles XII was almost revolutionary in tone: 'I dag Carl XII:s staty, i morgon representationsförändring'—'Today a statue of Charles XII, tomorrow a new Parliament,' were the warning words of one senior member of the military (Holm, 'Poltava-minnet', 47).

[42] Rodell, *Att gjuta en nation*, 204-14. According to Sverker Oredsson, the liberal journalists' esteem for the king was questioned by Lars Johan Hierta, S.A. Hedlund, and Rudolf Wall, who abhorred the 'elevation of the king who above all else blighted his country' (Oredsson, 'Karl XII och det svenska stormaktsväldets fall', 282).

[43] See Olsson, *Carl Snoilsky*, 240-44. Snoilsky indirectly accused Charles XII for failing his subjects with his endless wars.

[44] Hildebrand, 'Till Karl XII-uppfattningens historia', II, 31-46.

[45] Linderborg, *Socialdemokraterna skriver historia*, 296-98.

[46] 'Icke blott genom sitt överdåd och sin slutgiltiga fattigdom utan genom nästan varje av sina egenskaper förblir han en urbild både för det svenska lynnets solsidor och för allt vad detta besitter av tragik och brustet geni' (Heidenstam, *Samlade verk* XXIII, 20). For Charles XII as emblematic of Heidenstam's typical Swedish temperament, see Björck, *Heidenstam och sekelskiftets Sverige*, 181-86.

[47] 'Det var vår egen förtegna vilja och lust, som han försvarade mot vår egen tvekan' (Heidenstam, *Samlade verk*, VIII, 229).

[48] Staffan Björk finds that Heidenstam's purpose with his stories was artistic and moral rather than political: 'To call the book chauvinistically Swedish in the nineties' sense is completely misleading. On the contrary, it is striking that the political problem is practically never addressed in *Karolinerna*. . . . The book is no apotheosis of the Swedish Empire, but of what Swedes felt was the glorious manner in which their empire was lost' (Björck, *Heidenstam och sekelskiftets Sverige*, 87).

[49] Ahlund, 'En mental militarisering', 147.

[50] Schoolfield, *Young Rilke*, 362-87.

[51] Landgren, *Mannen från Prag*, 169.

[52] 'Er war zum Schauen aufgewacht: | er schmeichelte der schöne Schlacht um seinen Eigensinn' (Schoolfield, *Young Rilke*, 367). Schoolfield gives the poem in both the original and in English translation.

[53] Torbacke, *Carl Grimberg*, 137-62.

[54] For the production and reception of the film, see Tängerstad, *Fredrik den Store och Karl XII*, 38-104; for Bergman's work on the script, see Werner, *Hjalmar Bergman som filmförfattare*, 129-56.

[55] The term hyper-romantic is used by Oredsson, 'Karl XII och det svenska stormaktsväldets fall', 297. For a more detailed commentary on the work, see Liljegren, 'Om Frans G. Bengtssons Karl XII'. There are clear echoes of Heidenstam's *Karolinerna* in Bengtsson's account of Charles XII's boyish love of adventure.

[56] 'Supiste que vencer o ser vencido | Son caras de un Azar indiferente, | Que no hay otra virtud que ser valiente | Y que el mármol, al fin, será el olvido. | Ardes glacial, más solo que el desierto; |

Nadie llegó a tu alma y ya estás muerto' (Borges, 'A Carlos XII', in *Obras completas*, II, 286). For a brief commentary on the poem, see Ferretti, *Boreale Geltung*, 150-51.

[57] 'Ja; jag var numro femti-åtta, Svält, på Taubes dragoner, och att jag räddade ditt liv ångrar jag nu, ty hade du fått stryka med, vore aldrig Poltava skett och då hade vi njutit sex års fred nu!' (Strindberg, *Samlade verk*, XLVII, 68).

[58] Strindberg, *Samlade verk*, LXVIII, 37). The play's creation, content, and reception is charted in Gunnar Ollén's commentary in Strindberg *Samlade verk*, XLVII, 285-314.

[59] Jacobs, 'Strindberg and the Dramatic Tableau', 71-83.

[60] 'Rövartåg i två gånger nio år, utan annat synligt ändamål än äventyr' (Strindberg, *Samlade verk*, LXVIII, 42). For the ins and outs of the feud, see Meidal, *Från profet till folktribun*, and Nyblom, *Ryktbarhetens ansikte*.

[61] Oredsson, 'Stormaktsdrömmar och stridsiver', 276-91; Zander, *Fornstora dagar*, 271-75.

[62] Wästberg, *Gustaf Adolf Lysholm*, 202-7.

[63] 'Kungen, tänkte Karolina. Kungen var väl där. I säkerhet på sin bår, den som ska skyddas av livgardets drabanter. Runt omkring honom ska de stå vakt och ta de kulor som borde ha träffat honom för längesen. En enda kula nådde sitt mål och den sårade hans fot —gugive den hade träffat som den skulle i stället' (Rydsjö, *Karolinernas kvinnor*, 17).

[64] For Charles XII as a symbol for neo-nazi white supremacists in the late twentieth century, see Lööw, *Nazismen i Sverige*, 386-408. For the fighting between extremist groups and the police in Lund, see Brink Pinto, *Trettionde november*.

[65] For the rock group Ultima Thule, see Lööw, *Nazismen i Sverige*, 184-86.

[66] 'Karl XII ska bli hela Sveriges kung igen', *Dagens Nyheter Kultur*, 19 March 2014.

[67] See Kan, 'Den postsovjetiske Karl XII', 215.

# Index

La Marck, Louis-Pierre Comte de, French diplomat 209

Lambert, Andrew, British historian 117

Lamberty, Guillaume, Hanoverian agent in The Hague 416

Landskrona, Sweden 56, 115

La Vallée, Jean de, Swedish architect 368

La Vie, H. de, French diplomat 318

Le Brun, Charles, French painter 345

Leclerc, Sébastien, French engraver *205*

Leczyca, Poland 290

Lediard, Thomas, biographer of Marlborough 416

Leijoncrona, Christoffer, Swedish envoy in London 172

Leipzig, Saxony 14, **56**, 173-74, 228

Leith, Scotland 155

Lemberg (Lviv, Ukraine) **56**, 79, 102, **104**, 302

Lemke, Johann Philipp, Swedish painter *101*

Lemnos, Greece 252

Lemoyne, Jean-Louis, French sculptor 371

Leopold I, German Emperor 69, 218-19, 223

Lesnaya, Belarus, Battle of (1708) 62, 81, 99, 102, 107, 306

Leszczynski, Stanislaw, King of Poland 16, 19-20, 59-60, 63, 79, 81, 83, 173, 175, 221-25, 227, 230, 244, 249, 282-*85*, 287, 302, 330

Lewenhaupt, Adam Ludwig, Count, Swedish general 62-63, *65*, 81, 99, 107, 108, 240, 306

Libben, Bay of, Rügen 121-22

Liebertwolkwitz, Saxony 228

Liljehök, N.N., Swedish officer 296

Lillieroot, Count see Eosander

Lindegren, Jan, Swedish historian 91

Lindqvist, Herman, Swedish journalist 393

Lindroth, Per, Swedish caricaturist *387*

Lingen 336

Lintelo, Christiaan Carel van, Dutch envoy in Berlin 202

Lithen, John, English engraver 277

Lithuania 16, 94, 99, 112, 281, 326

*Livland*, Swedish man-of-war 115

Livonia, Livland 16-17, 26, 34, 55, 57, 68, 73, 76, 80, 88, 93, **105**, 112, 114, 128, 138, 149, 155, 165, 170, 278, 316, 322, **325**

Löwen, Axel, Swedish officer and miniaturist 365

Londicer, Ernst Wilhelm, Swedish painter 355

London, England 73, 155

Loots, Johannis, Dutch engraver *150*

Louis XIV, King of France 14, 29, 54, 69, 76, 79, 168, 173, 175, 187-88, 190, 205-15, 221-23, 231, 266, 278, 328, 330, 336

Louis XV, King of France 312

Louisa Ulrika, wife of Crown Prince Adolf Fredrik of Sweden 371

Louise Dorothea Sophie of Brandenburg-Prussia, (1st ) wife of Friedrich of Hesse-Kassel 327

Lublin, Poland **56**, 102, **104**, 171, 282

Lubomirski, family, Polish magnates 291

Luchtenburg, Johannes van, Dutch engraver 17

Lübeck 163-64, **324**

Lübeck-Eutin, Bishopric see Eutin-Lübeck

Lüneburg **324** see also Hanover

Lützen, Battle of (1632) 173, 207, 222

Lund, Sweden **62**, **324**, 365-66

Lvív, Lvov see Lemberg

Lybecker, Georg, Friherre, Swedish general 81

Lysholm, Gustaf Adolf, Swedish author 391

# M

Mälaren Lake Valley, Sweden 112

Magnus Ladulås, King of Sweden 368

Mahmud I, Ottoman Sultan 257

Mainz, Elector-Archbishop of 177

Malatitze, Belarus, Battle of (1708) **62**, 102, **104**

Malmö, Sweden 115

Malplaquet, Battle of (1709) 20

Mankell, O.A., Swedish printer *384*

Mányoki, Ádám, Hungarian painter *221*

Mardefeldt, Arvid Axel, Friherre, Swedish general 107

Maria Eleonora, Swedish Queen Dowager 340

Maritime Powers (England, Dutch Republic) 57, 60, 65, 75-80, 83-86, 116, 119-20, 123, 167-70, 173-75, 177, 188, 190, 192, 222, 229, 231, 262, 266, 328, 331-34

Marlborough, Duke of see Churchill, John

Marstrand, Sweden 274

Martin, Pierre-Denis, French painter *52-53*

Mary Stuart, wife of Dutch Stadholder William II 348

Mary Stuart, wife of William III, Dutch Stadholder and King of England 66

Masuria, Poland 61

Matveev, Andrej Artamonovic, Russian diplomat 192, *304-05*

Mavrocordato, Nicolas, dragoman at the Ottoman Court 249, 431

Maximilian II Emmanuel, Elector of Bavaria 223

Mazepa, Ivan, Cossack Hetman 61-63, 81, 100, 307-*08*, 381

Mecklenburg-Güstrow, Duchy of **324**, 327

Mecklenburg-Schwerin, Duchy of 25-26, 28, **56**, **62**, **105**, 120, 181, 191-92, 217, 231, 268, 314, 322, **324**

____, Duke of see Karl Leopold

Mecklenburg-Strelitz, Duchy of **56**, **62**, **105**, **324**, **325**, 327

Mediterranean 199

Mehmed Aga, Ottoman official 250, 252-53, 256

Mehmed Said Efendi, Ottoman official 257

Menshikov, Alexander, Russian general 62-63

Mesmes, Jean-Antoine de, Comte d'Avaux, French diplomat 206

Meybusch, Anton, Swedish medallist *343, 345*

Meyer, Gerhard, Swedish sculptor 371

Meyerfeldt, Count Johan August, Swedish officer 307

Meytens, Martin van, the Elder, Swedish painter *84*

Mignard, Pierre, French painter 345

Minden, Brandenburg-Prussia 325

Minsk, Belarus 61

Mitlushenko, Foma, Cossack officer 309-10

Møn, Island, Denmark 123, 125

Moers, Brandenburg-Prussia 336

Mogilev (Mohilev, Russia) **62**, 99

Mohács, Battle of (1526) 218

Moldavia, Moldova 63

Molesworth, Robert, English diplomat 265

Molin, Johan Peter, Swedish sculptor *370-71*, 382

Moll, Herman, mapmaker 10

Montesquieu see Secondat

Morea 253

Morell, N.N., French general 305

Mortier, Pierre, French engraver *13*

Moscow, Russia 61-62, 99, 154, 303

Mottray, Aubry de la, French author *247*

Müllern, Gustav Henrik von, Swedish official 43, 243, 309

Münster, Bishop of 177

Munthe, Arnold, Swedish historian 72, 84, 113

Muscovy see Russia

Mustafa II, Ottoman Sultan 430

Mytilene, Greece 252

# N

Napoleon, French Emperor 81

Narva, Estonia 16, **56**, **62**, 77, 80, 92, 117, 120, 154-58, 160-63, 303-04, 310-11, **325**

____, Battle of (1700) 16, 57, *61*-62, 102-03, **104**, 107, 113, *204-05*, 207, 300, 355, 379

# Editors & Contributors

**Bulent Ari** (1963) is a member of the Audit Board at the Council of Higher Education in Turkey. A graduate of the Middle East Technical University in Ankara (International Relations), he received his M.A. and Ph.D. from Bilkent University (History Department), also in Ankara, with a thesis on 'The First Dutch Ambassador in Istanbul, Cornelis Haga in 1612' (2003). In 1999 he studied and conducted research at Leiden University's Centre for Non-Western Studies (CNWS). From 2010 until 2014 he was director of the Dolmabahce Palace in Istanbul. In addition to publishing on Ottoman-Dutch historical relations, he specialises in Ottoman naval history, Mediterranean history, and Ottoman-European relations. Ottoman military, naval, and administrative history are also within his scope of research. He recently edited *Anadolu'da Paranın Tarihi* (*History of Money*; Ankara, 2012), and co-edited *Adalet Kitabı* (*The Book of Justice*; Istanbul, 2015) and *Four Centuries of Ottoman-Dutch Relations* (Rotterdam, 2014).

**Gunnar Åselius** (1965) graduated from Stockholm University in 1987 and received his Ph.D. there in 1994. Since 2006 he has been chaired professor of Military History at the National Defence University, Stockholm. His research interests include various aspects of strategy (not least Swedish-Russian relations), military professionalisation, and military culture in a wide chronological frame. His publications include *The 'Russian Menace' to Sweden: The Belief System of a Small Power Security Élite in the Age of Imperialism* (1994), 'La géographie suédoise militaire dans une perspective historique,' *Revue Stratégique* (2003), *The Rise and Fall of the Soviet Navy in the Baltic, 1921-1941* (2005), 'Swedish Strategic Culture since 1945,' *Cooperation and Conflict* (2005:1), 'Schweden und der Krieg, 1500-1814,' in Thomas Kolnberger and Ilja Steffelbauer (eds.), *Krieg in der europäischen Neuzeit* (2010), and 'Command and Control during Sweden's Last War: The Introduction of the Division and the Army Corps in Sweden, 1813-1814,' in Anna Maria Forssberg, Mats Hallenberg, and Jonas Nordin (eds), *Organizing History: Studies in Honour of Jan Glete* (Lund, 2011). He is a member of the Royal Swedish Academy of War Sciences, the Royal Society of Naval Sciences, and the Swedish Society for International Affairs.

**Nils Ekedahl** (1967) is senior lecturer in rhetoric and pro-vice chancellor for education at Södertörn University, Stockholm. He earned his Ph.D. in literature at Uppsala University in 1999 and is specialised in the history of rhetoric and literature in Early Modern Sweden. He has conducted a number of research projects, among them a multidisciplinary project on the formation of the Bernadotte family as a royal dynasty in Sweden and Norway in 1810-60, in cooperation with the Nationalmuseum and The Royal Armoury, Stockholm. His publications include *Det svenska Israel. Myt och retorik i Haquin Spegels predikokonst* (1999) and *En dynasti blir till. Medier, myter och makt kring Karl XIV Johan och familjen Bernadotte* (2010).

**Lars Ericson Wolke** (1957) took his Ph.D. at Stockholm University and is now professor of military history at the National Defence University, Stockholm. He is also assistant professor of military history at the Åbo Academi in Turku, Finland. He has served with the Royal Army Museum (1978-83) and the Military Archives (1983-2000) and is a member of the Royal Swedish Academy for Military Sciences. Between 2005 and 2015 he was a board member of the Commission Internationale d´Histoire Militaire (CIHM) and since 2015 has been a member of CIHM's bibliographical committee. He has published some 30 books and numerous papers, especially on different aspects of the history of the Baltic Sea region, including *Sjöslag och rysshärjningar. Kampen om Östersjön under stora nordiska kriget 1700-1721* (*Seabattles and Russian Ravages: The Struggle about the Baltic Sea during the Great Northern War, 1700-1721*; Stockholm, 2012) and *Kapare och pirater I Nordeuropa under 800 år cirka 1050-1856* (*Privateers and Pirates in Northern Europe during 800 Years, ca 1050 to 1856*; Lund, 2014).

**Linda S. Frey and Marsha L. Frey** (1947) are graduates of the Ohio State University (M.A., 1968; Ph.D., 1971) and currently professors at the University of Montana and Kansas State University, specialising in eighteenth-century international relations and international law. They have in tandem co-written, co-edited, and co-annotated numerous books and articles, including *The History of Diplomatic Immunity* (1999), *The Treaties of the War of the Spanish Succession* (1995), and *'Proven Patriots': The French Diplomatic Corps, 1789-1799* (2011). Grants from the Earhart Foundation, the Newberry Library, the Hagley Museum and Library, the National Endowment for the Humanities, the American Philosophical Society, and the American Council of Learned Societies among others have funded their research. The duo are currently completing a monograph on the culture of French Revolutionary diplomacy and yet another on the French Revolutionary challenge to international law.

**Inga Lena Ångström Grandien** (1952) received her Ph.D. in art history at Stockholm University with a thesis on post-Reformation altarpieces in Sweden (1992). She is associate professor at the University of Uppsala and has been senior lecturer at Stockholm University and Dalarna University. Her recent publications include 'In the Name of God: Religious Works of Art Taken as War Booty by Swedish Troops in the Thirty Years' War,' in *On the Opposite Sides of the Baltic Sea* (Wrocław, 2007), 'The Riddarholmen Church in Stockholm as a Burial Church for Swedish Heroes from the Thirty-Years-War' (2009), http://www.martin-carl-adolf-boeckler-stiftung.de/Heft_24_Angstroem.pdf, 'The Making of a Queen: A Study of the Residences of Johan III of Sweden and Katarina Jagellonica,' in *The Jagiellonian Court* (Leipzig, 2010), 'Nikodemus Tessin the Younger's Plans for a *Castrum Doloris* and a Sarcophagus for Hedvig Sofia,' in *'Princess Hedvig Sofia' and the Great Northern War* (Schloss Gottorf, 2015), and 'An Analysis of Dress in Portraiture of Women at the Swedish Royal Court, 1600-1650,' *Journal of Dress History* (London, 2017). She is currently preparing an article on Nikodemus Tessin the Elder for the Dictionary of Swedish National Biography.

**Alptuğ Güney** (1984) earned his M.A. degree from the University of Munich and is currently a Ph.D. student at the University of Hamburg. He is also a lecturer in Turkish political history at Istanbul Zaim University. His research encompasses the history of political thought, political history, and the history of the Ottoman Empire's foreign relations. Additionally he studies Ottoman military and naval history.

**John B. Hattendorf** (1941), the editor-in-chief of this volume, is Ernest J. King Professor Emeritus of Maritime History at the U.S. Naval War College in Newport, Rhode Island, having held that chair from 1984 to 2016. A serving officer in the United States Navy from 1964 to 1973, he holds degrees in history from Kenyon College (A.B., 1964), Brown University (A.M., 1971), and the University of Oxford (D.Phil., 1979; D.Litt., 2016). In addition to his many contributions to maritime history, he has written a number of books and articles on early eighteenth-century international history, including *England in the War of the Spanish Succession: A Study of the English View and Conduct of Grand Strategy, 1702-1714* (1987), *John Robinson's Account of Sweden, 1688* (*Karolinska förbundets årsbok*, 1996), and 22 biographies of military, naval, and diplomatic figures of the period in *The Oxford Dictionary of National Biography* (Oxford, 2004). He was editor-in-chief of *Marlborough: Soldier and Diplomat* (Rotterdam, 2012) in this series.

**Michael Hochedlinger** (1967) took his Ph.D. from Vienna University. He started his career as head of the Early Modern research department at the National Army Museum in Vienna (1995-99) and has been a senior archivist at the Austrian State Archives since 1999. He has published widely on Early Modern diplomatic and military history. His books include *Austria's Wars of Emergence, 1683-1797: War, State and Society in the Habsburg Monarchy* (2003).

**Rolof van Hövell tot Westerflier** (1940), publisher and associate editor of this volume, earned an L.L.M degree and an M.A. degree from the University of Leiden. He also received a degree in comparative law (M.C.L.) from Columbia University. He has spent the last forty years practising law in the Netherlands Antilles, Rotterdam, and Jakarta. Driven by his lifelong passion for history, he founded Karwansaray Publishers in 2007, a company dedicated to promoting and sharing a multifaceted view of history that crosses cultural and political boundaries. Some of his other productions include three successful magazines (*Ancient Warfare, Medieval Warfare,* and *Ancient History Magazine*) and three earlier volumes in the series *Protagonists of History in International Perspective*: *De Ruyter: Dutch Admiral* (2011*), Marlborough: Soldier and Diplomat* (2012), and *Alba: General and Servant to the Crown* (2013).

**Knud J.V. Jespersen** (1942) is emeritus professor of Early Modern European and Danish history at the University of Southern Denmark, Odense, and royal historiographer to H.M. the Queen of Denmark. He was a visiting fellow at Cambridge University in 1978 and visiting professor at Yale University in 1989. He has published numerous books and articles on European and Scandinavian history in the Early

Modern and Modern periods with special emphasis on military history. He is the author of *A History of Denmark* (London, 2004; second ed., 2011).

**Åsa Karlsson** (1960), associate editor of this volume, is a historian of Early Modern Swedish history. She completed her Ph.D. at Uppsala University in 1994 with the dissertation 'Den jämlike undersåten, Karl XII:s förmögenhetsbeskattning 1713' ('An Equal Subject: Charles XII and the Property Tax of 1713'). She has published work on Charles XII, Queen Hedvig Eleonora (e.g., 'Hedvig Eleonora – kulturmecenat och landsmoder,' [Hedvig Eleonora – Patron of the Arts and Mother of the Swedish Nation], in *Karolinska förbundets årsbok*, 2007) and on network strategies among the political elite of Sweden in 1680-1718. Karlsson has also contributed to several books on the Ottoman art collection put together by the Celsing diplomats in Constantinople in the eighteenth century. Furthermore she has participated in the international project 'When Sweden was ruled from the Ottoman Empire' (*Karl XII och svenskarna i Osmanska riket*, 2015 and *When Sweden was ruled from the Ottoman Empire*, 2016). Since 2002 she has been editor-in-chief of the Dictionary of Swedish National Biography in the Swedish National Archives in Stockholm.

**Pavel A. Krotov** (1961), professor of Russian history at Saint Petersburg State University, specialises in the history of military operations at sea and on land at the time of Peter the Great. He has published monographs on the battles of Gangut (1996, 2013, 2014), Grenhamn (2014), and Poltava (2009, 2014), and on the foundation of Saint Petersburg (2006, 2011), as well as chapters in *History of Native Shipbuilding* (1994), *History of Native Military Repairs of Ships* (2004), and *Documents sur l'expédition de J.-N. De l'Isle à Bérezov en 1740: journal du voyage tenu par T. Königfels et la correspondance de J.-N. De l'Isle* (2008). He has also authored an annotated Russian translation of the *History of the Russian Fleet during the Reign of Peter the Great* by John Deane (1999) and contributed to the publication of the *History of Peter the Great* by F.I. Soymonov (2012) and of *Tales about Peter the Great* by A.A. Nartov (2001). Since 2004 he has been editor-in-chief of the yearbook *Menshikov Memorial Readings* and since 2006 co-editor of the annual publication of *Saint-Petersburg and Northern European Countries*.

**Christer Kuvaja** (1958) is head of research at the Society of Swedish Literature in Finland and associate professor at the Åbo Akademi (Turku). His thesis for his doctoral degree concerned the supply system of the Russian army during the occupation of Finland, 1713-21. He has since then published several articles on the Russian occupation of Finland. He has also written a monograph about the wars in the Baltic region from 1660 to 1721 and another one about the history of Åland Island from 1809 to 1920. In his current research he focuses on bilingual local communities and bilingual persons in Finland from 1721 to about 1850 and has already written a number of articles on this subject.

**Margriet Lacy-Bruijn** (1943), associate and copy editor of this volume, is a native of the Netherlands. She spent most of her adult life in the United States, but recently relocated to her homeland. After studying at the Sorbonne and the University of Strasbourg and after earning degrees in French literature and linguistics at the University of Amsterdam, she completed her Ph.D. in French literature at the University of Kansas in 1972. In addition to her work on the eighteenth-century French novel, she has lectured and published widely on Belle van Zuylen/Isabelle de Charrière. She was professor of French, dean of Humanities and Social Sciences, and associate vice president for instruction at North Dakota State University before holding similar positions at Butler University, where she retired in 2004 and received emeritus status, both as faculty member and as administrator. She has been president and editor-in-chief of the American Association for Netherlandic Studies, served on academic accreditation teams, and edited numerous scholarly volumes.

**Marie Lennersand** (1969), senior archivist and head of the Section for Archives and Collections at Riksarkivet Marieberg in Stockholm, completed her Ph.D. at Uppsala University in 1999 with the thesis 'Rättvisans och allmogens beskyddare. Den absoluta staten, kommissionerna och tjänstemännen, ca 1680-1730' ('Protector of People and Law: The Swedish Absolute State, the Commissions and the Civil Servants, 1680-1730'). She has published on political, social, and military history from the seventeenth to the nineteenth century. In 2012-14 she was part of the 'Gender and Work' research project at the Department of History at Uppsala University and did a study of soldiers and soldier wives in Stockholm from 1680 to

1720. From 2004 to 2015 Lennersand was editor of *Karolinska förbundets årsbok* (*Yearbook of the Swedish Carolingian Society*).

**Gabriela Majewska** (1953) is professor of Early Modern history at the University of Gdańsk. She specialises in the history of Scandinavia, with a particular interest in relations between Sweden and Poland in the Early Modern period. She has published books and articles, including: *Polityka handlowa Szwecji w latach 1720-1809* (*Sweden's Trade Policy in the Years 1720-1809*; Wrocław, 1991), *Szwecja. Kraj - ludzie - rządy w polskiej opinii II połowy XVIII wieku* (*Sweden: The Country, Its People and Government in the Eyes of Poles in the Latter Half of the 18th Century*; Gdańsk, 2004), 'Sweden's Form of Government during the Reign of Gustavus III - in the Eyes of the Journals of Polish Enlightenment,' *Scandinavian Journal of History* (1997), and 'The Swedish Parliamentary System of the Age of Liberty as Seen in the Polish Journals of the Second Half of the 18th Century,' *Historisk Tidskrift* (2000).

**Werner Scheltjens** (1978) is assistant professor at the Chair of Social and Economic History of the University of Leipzig. He studied eastern European languages and cultures at the University of Louvain and received his Ph.D. from the University of Groningen (2009). He specialises in maritime trade and shipping in the Early Modern period and maintains a strong focus on the history of trade through the Danish Sound. He recently published *Dutch Deltas: Emergence, Functions and Structure of the Low Countries' Maritime Transport Sector, ca. 1300-1850* (Leiden and Boston, 2015).

**Eric Schnakenbourg** (1970) is professor of Early Modern history and director of the Centre de Recherche en Histoire Internationale et Atlantique at Nantes University. He is specialised in the history of international relations, more particularly in the relations between France and northern Europe. He is a member of the editorial board of the *Revue d'Histoire Nordique/Nordic Historical Review*. His publications include *La France, le Nord et l'Europe au début du XVIIIe siècle* (Paris, 2008), *La Scandinavie à l'époque moderne (fin XVe-début XIXe siècle)* (Paris, 2010), and *Entre la guerre et la paix: Neutralité et relations internationales, XVII-XVIIIe siècles* (Rennes, 2013). He was editor of *Figures du Nord: Scandinavie, Groenland, Sibérie: perceptions et représentations des espaces septentrionaux du Moyen Age au*

*XVIIIe siècle* (Rennes, 2012), 'Neutralité et culture de la paix en Scandinavie, fin du XVIIe-XVIIIe siècle,' *Revue d'Histoire Nordique* (2012, vol. 14), and 'Le Temps de la Grandeur (Stormaktstiden): l'empire suédois au XVIIe et au début du XVIIIe siècle,' *Revue d'Histoire Nordique* (2015, vol. 18).

**Hamish Scott** (1946) is a Senior Research Fellow of Jesus College, Oxford, and Wardlaw Professor Emeritus of International History at the University of St Andrews. A Fellow of the British Academy and of the Royal Society of Edinburgh, he has published extensively on seventeenth- and eighteenth-century international relations, on enlightened absolutism and on nobility. Among his publications are *The Emergence of the Eastern Powers 1756-75* (Cambridge, 2001) and *The Birth of a Great Power System, 1740-1815* (Harlow, 2007). Most recently he edited *The Oxford Handbook of Early Modern European History, c.1350-1750* (2 vols.; Oxford, 2015). He is currently completing a major study entitled *Forming Aristocracy: The Reconfiguration of Europe's Nobilities, c.1300-1750*.

**Augustus J. Veenendaal, Jr.** (1940), associate editor of this volume, earned his Ph.D. at Radboud University Nijmegen in 1976. He retired in 2005 as senior research historian from the Institute of Netherlands History at The Hague, where he edited the correspondence of Grand Pensionary Anthonie Heinsius: *De Briefwisseling van Anthonie Heinsius 1702-1720* (19 vols., 1976-2001). He has published a catalogue of the Heinsius archives (2001), written many articles on various aspects of the War of the Spanish Succession, edited a collection of articles, and contributed to dictionaries on Heinsius and his contemporaries. He was associate editor of *Marlborough: Soldier and Diplomat* (Rotterdam, 2012) in this series. Besides his work in the early eighteenth century, he has written numerous books and articles on Dutch and American railway history and on international railway finance. From 2001 to 2004 he was seconded to Netherlands Railways to write the history of railways in the Netherlands: *Spoorwegen in Nederland van 1834 tot nu* (Amsterdam, 2014). In 2017 Karwansaray published *Rails to the Front*, which he co-authored with H. Roger Grant.

Templ. S. Mariæ

Templ. S. Nicolai

Templ. S. Francisci

Templ. S. Gertrudis

Templ. S. Ulrica

Templ. S. Francisci

Templ. S. Nicolai